REAL ESTATE
LIMITED PARTNERSHIPS

REAL ESTATE LIMITED PARTNERSHIPS

THEODORE S. LYNN
Webster & Sheffield
New York, New York

HARRY F. GOLDBERG
Blank, Rome, Comisky & McCauley
Philadelphia, Pennsylvania

SECOND EDITION

A WILEY-INTERSCIENCE PUBLICATION

JOHN WILEY & SONS

New York • Chichester • Brisbane • Toronto • Singapore

This publication is designed to provide accurate and authoritative information in regard to the subject matter covered. It is sold with the understanding that the publisher is not engaged in rendering legal, accounting, or other professional service. If legal advice or other expert assistance is required, the services of a competent professional person should be sought.

From a Declaration of Principles jointly adopted by a Committee of the American Bar Association and a Committee of Publishers.

Library of Congress Cataloging in Publication Data:

Lynn, Theodore S
  Real estate limited partnerships.

  (Real estate for professional practitioners, ISSN 0190-1087)
  "A Wiley-Interscience publication."
  Includes bibliographical references and index.
  1.Real estate investment—Law and legislation—United States. 2. Real estate business—United States. 3. Limited Partnership—United States.
  4. Real estate business—Taxation—United States.
  I. Goldberg, Harry F. II. Title. III. Series.

KF1079.L9 1983   346.74′0682   82-15878
ISBN 0-471-09082-4

Printed in the United States of America
10 9 8 7 6 5 4 3 2 1

To

LINDA, SYD, JESSICA and DOUGLAS,
VICKI, HELEN and BEN

SERIES PREFACE

Since the end of World War II, tremendous changes have taken place in the business and residential real estate fields throughout the world. This has been evidenced not only by architectural changes, exemplified by the modern shopping center, but also in the many innovative financing responses that have enabled development of new structures and complexes, such as multiuse buildings. It can be expected that real estate development will speed in new directions at an ever increasing pace to match the oncoming needs of our time. With this perspective, The Real Estate for Professional Practitioners series has been developed in response to professional needs.

As real estate professional activities have become divided into specialties, because of intensive demand for expertise at all stages, so has there developed an increasing need for extensive training and continual education for persons directly involved or dealing in business ventures requiring detailed knowledge of realty procedures.

Perhaps no field of business endeavor is more in need of a series of professional books than real estate. Working in the practical world of business and residential construction and space utilization, or at advanced levels of college training covering these areas, one is constantly aware that too little of existing creative thinking has been transcribed into viable books. Many of the books that have been written do not thoroughly enough encompass both the practical and theoretical aspects of complex subjects. Too often the drive for immediate answers has led to the overlooking of fundamental purposes and technical know-how that might lead to much more favorable results for the persons seeking knowledge.

This series will be made up of books thoroughly and expertly expounding existing procedures in the many fields of real estate, but searching as well for innovative solutions to current and future problems. These books are intended to offer a compendium of each author's wide experience and knowledge to aid the seasoned professional.

The series is addressed to professionals in all walks of realty endeavor. These include business investors and developers, urban affairs specialists, attorneys, accountants, and the many others whose work involves real estate creativity and investment. Just as importantly, the series will present to advanced students in many realty fields the opportunity to review professional thinking that will help to stimulate their own thoughts on modern trends in housing and business construction.

We believe these goals can be achieved by the outstanding group of authors who will create the books in the series.

DAVID CLURMAN

PREFACE

Real estate continues to attract individual, group, and corporate investment notwithstanding the cyclical nature of the industry. Foreign investors are drawn to the United States by our stable economic and political systems and the abundance and relatively low cost of our land. Compared with other forms of investment, real estate provides American investors with long-term security and short-term rewards through tax advantages.

A limited partnership is often the most useful entity for investing in real estate. From the promoter's or builder's viewpoint, selling interests in a limited partnership is an attractive and relatively easy method of raising capital for a planned project. For the investor, an interest in a limited partnership is an opportunity to invest in a property that is perhaps too costly for individual ownership; it is also an opportunity to limit potential liability to the amount of the agreed-on investment and to take advantage of significant income tax benefits.

The "tax shelter" aspect of the investment results from the ability to offset tax deductions generated by the partnership against the investor's income from the investment and possibly against his other income. Although the Tax Reform Act of 1976 curtailed the utility of many tax shelter vehicles, the tax benefits of investing in real estate were left largely intact. This was indeed enhanced by the Economic Recovery Tax Act of 1981, and these benefits are discussed in detail in this Second Edition.

A potential investor should not lose sight of the fact that he is making an investment in an ongoing enterprise, the quality and character of which should be the foremost consideration. Tax benefits may enhance the investment, but the business aspects of the transaction must be analyzed carefully.

This book discusses the legal aspects of a real estate limited partnership and contains a model limited partnership agreement. The state partnership laws (especially the Uniform Limited Partnership Act), the federal tax laws, and the federal and state securities laws are examined in detail. Special emphasis is placed on changes in the tax law effected by the Economic Recovery Tax Act of 1981, and the Tax Equity and Fiscal Responsibility Act of 1982, including the replacement of the useful life method of depreciation with a substantially more favorable method of accelerated cost recovery and the substantial revision of incentives for rehabilitation of older and historic structures. The Second Edition also provides a new in-depth treatment of the deductibility of various expenditures during the construction period and the impact of the Bankruptcy Tax Act of 1980 on real estate limited partnerships. Finally, the Second Edition provides expanded treatment of state securities laws (including specific analysis of New York and California) as they relate to real estate limited partnerships and discusses in detail the new federal private placement rules (Regulation D) adopted by the Securities and Exchange Commission.

The book is aimed primarily at the organization, the structure, and the ongoing operating consequences of such an investment. There is also a chapter on the tax consequences that result when disposing of a partnership interest and when the investment goes bad. The appendixes contain copies of actual documents.

The book has been organized so that the reader need not refer to the note references to enjoy a thorough overview of the area. Although detailed in coverage, this book is not a hornbook for lawyers specializing in real estate limited partnerships. Every possible citation is not included, but there are enough references to keep anyone occupied with background material, if that is desired.

For the prospective investor, general lawyer, accountant, developer, builder, and promoter, this book should serve as a ready reference to the legal structure and workings of the limited partnership entity coupled with an investment in real property.

This is the second edition of this book. The authors wish to thank Dan S. Grossman, Scott P. Spector and G. Michael Stakias for their invaluable assistance with the second edition; Daniel S. Abrams, a coauthor of the first edition; and David Clurman, Richard K. DeScherer, Mark A. Rosenbaum, Daniel F. Wynn, H. Curtiss Martin, Ellen C. Emory, and Margaret M. Stroock.

HARRY F. GOLDBERG
THEODORE S. LYNN

New York, New York
Philadelphia, Pennsylvania

CONTENTS

CHAPTER 4

TAX TREATMENT OF THE PARTNERS   59

CHAPTER 5

DEPRECIATION AND RECAPTURE, REHABS, HISTORIC AND OLDER STRUCTURES   85

CHAPTER 6

INTEREST, TAXES, FEES, "SOFT COSTS," AND CONSTRUCTION PERIOD EXPENDITURES 115

CHAPTER 7

DEATH, DISASTERS, AND DISPOSITIONS OF PARTNERSHIP INTERESTS 141

CHAPTER 8

FEDERAL SECURITIES LAWS AND
REAL ESTATE LIMITED PARTNERSHIPS   177

CHAPTER 11

DISCLOSURE   267

REAL ESTATE
LIMITED PARTNERSHIPS

CHAPTER 1

THE STATE LAWS GOVERNING REALTY LIMITED PARTNERSHIPS

1. GENERAL

Real estate syndications are usually in the form of limited partnerships. One reason for this is that the income and expenses of the enterprise thereby "pass through" to the investors for tax purposes, allowing them to claim allocable deductions on their personal income tax returns. Corporations and business trusts, on the other hand, because they are taxpaying entities, do not offer this benefit. Of course, the property could be held directly by the investor or in a general partnership, but under these arrangements the investor's liability would not be limited to his investment. A second reason for structuring the syndication as a limited partnership, therefore, is that it permits the investor to risk only his investment in the project. Properly constituted, a limited partnership does not subject a passive investor to the debts and liabilities of the enterprise.

This chapter discusses state law limited liability and the other aspects of the state laws of limited partnership. Taxation and securities laws are discussed in subsequent chapters.

1

2. A CREATURE OF STATUTE

There were no limited partnerships under common law,[1] and each state that recognizes limited partnerships has enacted a law setting forth detailed requirements for attaining this classification. Thus, if a passive investor in a partnership is to receive the benefit of limited liability, there must be substantial compliance with the relevant state limited partnership statute.

All states (except Louisiana), including the District of Columbia and the Virgin Islands, enacted, in one form or another, the provisions contained in the 1916 version of the Uniform Limited Partnership Act.[2]

Fifteen states, Arizona, Arkansas, Colorado, Connecticut, Idaho, Iowa, Maryland, Massachusetts, Michigan, Minnesota, Montana, Nebraska, Washington, West Virginia, and Wyoming, have repealed the U.L.P.A. and enacted in lieu thereof versions of the revised Uniform Limited Partnership Act (adopted in 1976 by the National Conference of Commissioners on Uniform State Laws).[3] The extent to which the 1976 Revised U.L.P.A. or variations thereof will be enacted remains to be seen. The Internal Revenue Service recently published a proposed regulation providing that references in the partnership tax classification rules to the U.L.P.A. refer to that Act both as originally promulgated and as revised in 1976.[4] Adoption of the proposed regulation would eliminate an impediment to state enactment of the 1976 Revision.

The purpose of authorizing limited partnerships is to permit a passive investor to join with a general partner in order to make an investment in partnership form without subjecting to risk any capital other than his passive investment.[5] To achieve this, the limited partner must in fact be a passive investor. The general partner, therefore, must have the power and obligation to manage the property and business of the partnership.[6] This relationship is discussed in some detail later in this chapter.

A limited partnership is usually permitted to engage in any business that a general partnership may carry on.[7] However, the Uniform Limited Partnership Act and the 1976 Revision specifically recognize that states may except certain businesses. Thus the applicable state statute must always be consulted. Banking and insurance are the businesses most often prohibited from using the limited partnership format.[8]

3. FORMING THE LIMITED PARTNERSHIP: IN GENERAL

A limited partnership is defined as a partnership formed in compliance with the applicable state law, having as its members at least one general partner and one limited partner.[9] If so, the "limited partners as such shall not be bound by the obligations of the partnership." [10]

To form a limited partnership, two or more persons must sign and swear to a certificate of limited partnership, the function of which is similar to a corporation's certificate of incorporation.[11] Several states permit execution by means of acknowledgment rather than affidavit and allow the limited partners to grant authority to, say, the general partner, to execute the certificate through powers of attorney. This is especially useful when there are many limited partners and when it would be cumbersome to obtain each person's signature on the certificate of limited partnership. New York County (Manhattan) permits the person filing a certificate to produce only one fully executed power of attorney, to file a copy of the power, and to state by affidavit that the power is a specimen of similar powers that were properly executed and given to him by the other limited partners.[12] Alternatively, in practice, it may be possible merely to show all the powers, rather than filing a copy of a power and an affidavit.

As is discussed in this chapter, a certificate of limited partnership must describe the characteristics of the organization, must substantially comply with detailed statutory standards, and must be made available for public and creditor review.

In most states a corporation may serve as general partner, although there may be difficulty in asserting limited liability if the limited partners control the corporate general partner.[13] There are also tax implications in the use of a corporate general partner, which are discussed in Chapter 2.

Unless otherwise provided by the applicable state law, a limited partnership interest can be held by an individual, partnership, corporation, or other association.[14] However, some states may vary the Uniform Act in this respect through operation of their corporation law or otherwise.[15]Further, although infants may be general or limited partners in some states, state law usually limits the extent to which an infant can be held to his contracts, and these limitations might apply to the contract of partnership.[16]

Usually the terms of the voluntary association known as a limited partnership are set forth in an agreement of limited partnership. This is the governing document for the business relationship among the general partners and limited partners. It is often long and rather involved. Appendix 1 contains a model limited partnership agreement for a real estate venture that demonstrates the scope of such documents.

Even in those states that permit a partnership agreement, if it contains all of the provisions required by the statute, to be filed and to serve as the certificate of limited partnership, the parties often wish to keep their detailed business arrangements confidential. Thus they prepare an abbreviated document that is filed as the certificate.[17]

This discussion concerns the legal requirements in forming a limited partnership. Remember, however, that one of the most important functions of the limited partnership agreement is to govern the terms of the business relationship, and the "deal points" should be clearly articulated in the agreement.[18]

4. THE CERTIFICATE OF LIMITED PARTNERSHIP

The numerous details required to be disclosed in the certificate are related to the function of informing potential creditors about the nature of the entity.[19] Since creditors cannot get their debts paid by the limited partners, they are entitled to know about the financial status of the partnership.

Two or more persons must sign and swear to a certificate that states the name and term of the partnership, the character of its business, and the location of the principal place of business.[20] A date certain is usually stated as the ultimate termination date with earlier termination in accordance with events listed in a later dissolution section.[21] The terms of the partnership's properties underlying leases should be considered in selecting the partnership's ultimate termination date so as to avoid adversely affecting the ability to obtain title insurance.

The tendency in drafting corporate articles is to include broad purpose clauses. However, the limited partners may wish to require the general partner to deal only with a specific property, to prohibit reinvestment of sale proceeds, or to otherwise restrict the general partner's business decisions. This may be combined with a limited partner consent provision (but see later discussion about control and limited liability questions). For tax reasons, the business purpose section might contain a statement that the property is to be held for investment and not for resale.

The certificate must also list the name of each partner (general and limited partners being so designated) and each partner's place of residence.

When confidentiality is desired, the use of other partnerships or nominees to hold the limited partnership interests might be considered. As previously noted, confidentiality of some business details may be attained by filing a specially drafted certificate rather than the entire limited partnership agreement,[22] but the essentials described here must be contained in the certificate.

The certificate must also state the amount of cash contributed by each limited partner; must describe any other property (including its agreed value) so contributed; must list any additional contributions which are to be made by each limited partner (including the times and any contingencies); must state any agreements to return contributions (including the times and any contingencies); and must disclose any right of a limited partner to receive property other than cash in return for his contribution.[23] This information is important for potential creditors of the partnership when they assess the risk of dealing with the partnership, and it must be accurate. Although property other than cash may be contributed, services cannot be credited as a limited partner's contribution.[24]

A limited partnership may provide for installment capital contributions (e.g., one third for each of the first three years). (This is a common practice in order to have tax deductions correspond with capital contributions.) If so, the limited partnership agreement should address a failure of a limited partner to make the agreed installment payment. There are security law, tax law, and mechanical problems with installment contributions. Reallocating interests in the event of partial default can be complicated. For the limited partners' protection, the limited partnership agreement might require that the general partner warrant continued good title, no loan default, and so on before an installment payment becomes due.[25]

Since the relative stakes of the different partners and the possibility of changes in membership are of concern to the public, the certificate must also describe the arrangement for profit sharing and for compensation by way of income; must state how and if a limited partner may substitute another person in his place, including any terms and conditions; and must disclose any right of the partners to admit other partners.[26] Additional limited partners are admitted by filing an amendment to the original certificate.[27]

Any priorities among the general partners must be disclosed (including the nature of the priority), as must any right of a remaining general partner to continue the partnership upon the death, retirement, or insanity of another general partner.[28]

It is often wise to have more than one general partner (or at least a standby general partner) and to include a provision continuing the partnership on the death, and so on, of one of the general partners. This may avoid adverse tax consequences and repetition of the formal steps of new formation. Chapter 7 contains the tax analysis, and a suggested provision is included in the model limited partnership agreement of Appendix 1.

The certificate must be filed for record in an office designated by the state statute.[29] In addition, there may be a state requirement of public notice. For example, in New York a copy of the certificate "or a notice containing the substance thereof" must be published immediately after the filing of the certificate every week for six successive weeks in two designated newspapers.[30] Even though six weeks elapse and general partners may forget, proof of publication must also be filed with the same county clerk.

As is discussed later, complete technical compliance with each and every state law requirement is not always necessary. The Uniform Limited Partnership Act states: "A limited partnership is formed if there has been substantial compliance in good faith with the requirements. . . ." [31] Failure to substantially comply in good faith with the statute precludes limited partnership status and may or may not render the association a general partnership.[32]

The certificate must be amended, with all of the appropriate formalities, when: the partnership changes its name or the contribution of any limited partner; a person is substituted as a limited partner; an additional limited partner is admitted; a general partner is admitted; a general partner retires, dies, or becomes insane and the business is continued; the character of the business is changed; there is a false or erroneous statement in the certificate; there is a change of time in partnership dissolution or return of a contribution, or such a time is initially fixed; or the partners wish to make any other change to represent their agreement accurately.[33] The provision of amendment at designated events requires constant attention. "The certificate shall be cancelled when the partnership is dissolved or all limited partners cease to be such." [34]

5. THE GENERAL PARTNER'S RIGHTS, POWERS, AND OBLIGATIONS

One of the aspects of the limited partnership form that must be understood by potential limited partners is that the general partner has almost complete power over the partnership's affairs. Further, unlike directors of corporations, the general partner usually does not have to stand for annual election or even hold annual meetings.

A general partner is subject to all the liabilities of a partner in a general partnership.[35] He has all the rights and powers of such a partner with certain exceptions.

Without the written consent or ratification of the specific act by all of the limited partners, a general partner lacks authority to do any of the following: admit a general partner; confess a judgment against the partnership; do any act in contravention of the certificate; make it impossible to carry on the ordinary business of the partnership; assign or possess partnership property for other than a partnership purpose; or, unless given the right to do so in the certificate, admit a person as a limited partner or continue the business on the death, retirement, or insanity of a general partner.[36]

The general partners of a limited partnership bear a fiduciary relationship to the limited partners and to the partnership.[37] The principles of the law of agency apply to their acts and they can, therefore, bind the enterprise by acts taken within their actual or apparent authority.[38]

Often the partnership agreement should contain language that will assure third parties dealing with the partnership that they need not investigate the authority of the general partner. It should also contain any desired restrictions on the general partner (e.g., limiting his compensation or his right to compete with the partnership). The limited partnership agreement might state that the general partner serves without compensation (except for his interest as a partner) or might articulate additional compensation.

6. THE LIMITED PARTNER'S RIGHTS AND POWERS

Unless otherwise provided in the certificate or agreement, a limited partner has few rights and powers. Therefore, the limited partnership agreement should fully articulate all the terms of the business transaction and of the economic relationship between the general partner, the partnership, and the limited partners, so that the limited partners will have enforceable rights with respect to the business transaction. A limited partner does have the same rights as a general partner to inspect and copy the books of the partnership; to demand true and full information; to obtain "a formal account of partnership affairs whenever circumstances render it just and reasonable . . ."; and to have dissolution by court decree.[39] Limited partners usually are not proper parties in lawsuits by or against the partnership, except to enforce their rights against the partnership or to defend themselves from liability to the partnership.[40]

A limited partner may be permitted to bring a class or derivative action for damages against the general partners for breach of their fiduciary duty or otherwise on behalf of all the limited partners.[41] State law should be consulted as to whether such actions are permitted and if there are any requirements for posting security. In 1968, New York added an amendment to its act which specifically permits a limited partner to bring a derivative action in the right of the limited partnership to procure a judgment in its favor.[42] Delaware has also enacted such a special provision.[43]

A limited partner has the right to receive the profits and compensation stated in the certificate and a limited right to receive back his contribution.[44] These rights can be funded only if partnership assets sufficiently exceed liabilities.[45] Subject to this condition, and to proper certificate amendment or cancellation, a limited partner may demand the return of his contribution upon the consent of all members; upon the dissolution of the partnership; upon a date specified in the certificate; or, in the absence of a specified time for the return of the contribution or for the dissolution of the partnership, after six months notice in writing to all the other members.[46]

If it is not intended to return the limited partners' contributions for some time, the certificate should specify an appropriate date of dissolution; otherwise, the limited partners could demand the return of their contributions six months after notice. Failure to focus on this provision of the law could cause substantial problems.

Unless the certificate provides otherwise, a limited partner has only the right to demand cash in return for his contribution even if he had originally contributed some other form of property.[47]

Some of the most important provisions of a limited partnership agreement are the terms relating to distribution of income and sale proceeds. See the model limited partnership agreement of Appendix 1. Briefly, the limited partnership agreement might articulate the allocation of net income and net loss and distributions in three parts: (a) distributions of cash from operations; (b) distributions of cash from sale, refinancing or other capital transactions; and (c) federal income tax allocations. The business agreement might be that the limited partners will receive 99% of cash flow until recovery of investment and, thereafter, the general partner will receive a larger percentage to give him an incentive for good performance. In addition, or alternatively, the limited partners may receive a guaranteed annual cash flow (cumulative or not) to represent the cost or use of the invested money. If the general partner's affiliate is managing the property, the management fee may or may not be subordinated to such a guaranteed distribution. The general partner may be required to mail distribution checks to the limited partners on a stated periodic basis, say every three months; otherwise the general partner might cause the partnership to retain its cash for long periods.

The limited partner has a right to obtain dissolution or winding up by court decree when he has the right to demand the return of his contribution and either the partnership refuses to return it, or the assets of the partnership are insufficient to satisfy it and the partnership's liabilities to creditors.[48] In addition, a limited partner has the same rights as a partner of a general partnership to obtain dissolution (e.g., in the event of fraud or breach of the partnership agreement by a general partner).[49]

In the absence of agreement, a general partner may be prohibited from competing with the limited partnership but a limited partner may engage in businesses that compete with the partnership.[50] It is wise to specifically state in the partnership agreement what the wishes of the parties are with respect to competition. It is also wise to articulate which general partner expenses will be reimbursed by the partnership.[51] The method of cost sharing might be stated, for example, if the general partner is using the same personnel to manage several partnerships or projects.

The statute authorizes loans and other business transactions between a limited partner and the partnership.[52] Unless he is also a general partner, a limited partner who engages in such transactions may share with general creditors in claim recoveries.

The Uniform Limited Partnership Act also contains provisions governing the situation in which a person is both a general and a limited partner (this is permitted) and granting the limited partners the right to agree to priorities among themselves if, as noted previously, such agreement is stated in the certificate.[53] In the absence of a statement to the contrary in the certificate, all the limited partners must "stand upon equal footing." [54] One who is both a general and a limited partner is subject to unlimited liability, but with respect to any limited partner contribution made by him, he can have the same rights against the other members that any other limited partner has.[55] As discussed later, these rights may include certain priorities over general partners.

A limited partner's interest in the partnership is considered to be personal property.[56] His creditors may thus levy against it,[57] and he may assign it.[58] A limited partner has no property rights in the partnership's property, and a creditor of a limited partner cannot make a successful claim against the partnership property.[59]

A limited partner's interest is assignable, but only an assignee who becomes a substitute limited partner through amendment of the certificate may obtain all the rights of the assignor.[60] If an assignee is not so substituted, he may obtain only the economic rights of the assignor. It is disputed whether this distinction is important to the assignee.[61]

As is discussed in the taxation chapters of this book, the agreement of limited partnership often purports, for tax reasons, to require general partner consent before any assignment of an economic interest can be made or at least before an assignee may become a substituted limited partner.

On the death of a limited partner, his executor or administrator succeeds to all his rights as a limited partner "for the purpose of settling the estate," and his estate is responsible for all his liabilities as a limited partner.[62]

7. DISSOLUTION AND WINDING UP

The retirement, death, or insanity of a general partner dissolves the partnership unless the certificate authorizes the remaining general partners to continue the business, and they do so, or unless 100% of the members consent and there is a continuation.[63] The effect of the 1979 Federal Bankruptcy Act on limited partnership agreements that provide for automatic dissolution based on the bankruptcy of its general partners must be considered.[64]

Therefore, as previously stated, it is wise to provide for these eventualities in the limited partnership agreement. Indeed, the limited partners often wish to prohibit general partner resignation or withdrawal and to obligate a remaining general partner to continue the partnership, if for no other reason than to avoid the adverse tax consequences of partnership dissolution.[65]

Situations in which a limited partner can compel dissolution were considered in the discussion of a limited partner's rights. Any desired variation must be contained in the certificate. Subject to control-limited liability concern, the limited partnership agreement might permit dissolution by the vote of a certain percentage of the limited partners or require dissolution, for example, on the sale of substantially all of the partnership's assets.

An order of preference is provided by statute for settling accounts after dissolution. Priority is first given to the claims of creditors (including limited partners who are creditors without regard to their contributions); then to limited partners (first, for profits, and then for capital); and finally to general partners (first, for other than profits or capital, second, for profits, and third, for capital).[66] The priorities among the general and limited partners can be varied by the agreement (e.g., operating deficit loans by general partners are often granted priority over any distribution to limited partners).[67]

Unless otherwise agreed to, noncreditor limited partners share in the distribution of profits and capital on dissolution among themselves on a basis that is pro rata to each of their contributions and their claims for income.[68]

The limited partnership certificate should be cancelled when the limited partnership is dissolved or the limited partners lose their special status.[69]

8. THE LIMITED PARTNER'S LIABILITIES TO THE PARTNERSHIP

The limited partnership certificate must, as previously stated, declare the amount that each limited partner is to invest. The limited partner remains liable to the partnership for any unpaid portion of this amount.[70] Moreover, he is deemed to hold as trustee for the partnership any money or property wrongfully paid to him on account of his contribution and any property which he agreed, but failed, to contribute to the partnership.[71] However, a failure to contribute the amount specified in the certificate as the limited partner's contribution does not render him liable as a general partner.[72] State decisional law should be consulted as to whether only the partnership can enforce this obligation or whether it can be enforced for the benefit of creditors.[73]

One provision is often overlooked. If a limited partner, receives a return of capital, even though he receives it rightfully, he remains liable to the partnership for a like amount if it ever is needed to discharge partnership liabilities to creditors who extended credit before the limited partner received the return of his capital.[74]

A limited partner's liabilities to the partnership may be waived or compromised by the consent of all the members, but such action cannot adversely affect the claim of a creditor who extended credit before such a waiver or compromise was made.[75]

As was previously stated, on the death of a limited partner, his estate is liable for all his obligations as a limited partner.[76]

9. ACTIONS AND POWERS THAT MIGHT CAUSE LOSS OF LIMITED LIABILITY

Limited liability is one of the most important characteristics of the transaction for the investor who is not a general partner. As stated earlier in this chapter, the limited partner must be a passive investor in order to achieve this result. There is often a conflict between this requirement and business considerations. The limited partners may wish to "have a say" when important business decisions are made, but if they are deemed to manage the business, they can become liable to the claims of creditors.

A limited partner does not become liable as a general partner "unless, in addition to the exercise of his rights and powers as a limited partner, he takes part in the control of the business." [77] That which will be deemed to constitute controlling the partnership business may vary from state to state and is not likely to be settled by case law or interpretative ruling in other than the most specific situations. It may be unclear whether there must be an actual taking part in the control of the business or whether and to what extent the mere existence of certain offending powers can cause general liability.[78] As is discussed later, the choice of law that is applicable to multijurisdictional transactions may also be in question.

The limited partners may wish to be able to remove the general partner, even without cause, by a simply majority vote. Similarly, they might wish to have the power to liquidate the limited partnership, to amend its articles of partnership, or to approve the sale of substantially all, or even any, of the partnership assets. Indeed, some states might insist on variations of so-called shareholder democracy voting rights if a limited partnership syndication is to be sold in those states. Yet the exercise or possibly the existence of such powers may jeopardize the limited liability of the limited partners. A creditor seeking recovery against the limited partner for partnership obligations can be creative in asserting either that the members exercised business control or that the existence of certain powers constitutes the right to control the business.

Because of the confusion, some of the states have added provisions to their adaptations of the Uniform Limited Partnership Act. These additions list certain powers that may be granted the limited partners without fear of causing general liability, such as the right to remove the general partner, to terminate the partnership, to be employed by the partnership or serve as its consultant or attorney, or to continue the business of the partnership if the general partners have been removed.[79]

Great care must be taken in drawing the limited partnership agreement to make sure that the powers granted the limited partners are no greater than those permitted by the applicable limited partnership statute. The discretionary power to discharge a general partner, for example, usually should be avoided unless specifically permitted by the applicable state statute.[80] One possibility would be to provide in the agreement of limited partnership that the ability to exercise possibly offending powers is conditional on obtaining a counsel's opinion or a court decision that exercise of the powers would not create general liability.

Even if the limited partnership agreement is properly drafted, the limited partners cannot in fact control or manage the business of the partnership without risking general liability.[81] The extent to which a limited partner may be involved in the business affairs of the enterprise without risking general liability will depend on the facts in each case, but consultation from time to time has been permitted.[82] In some states, the use of a corporate general partner that is controlled by the limited partners may cause creditor liability concern.[83]

10. MISREPRESENTATIONS THAT MIGHT CAUSE LOSS OF LIMITED LIABILITY

There are other dangers of general liability for a limited partner in addition to excessive powers or actual exercising of control over the partnership business. The reason for imposing liability in these other situations is that creditors should not suffer if they have been led to believe someone would be liable for the partnership's debts, or there are undisclosed restrictions on the payment of partnership debts. Thus, if a limited partner's surname appears in the partnership name, he will be liable as a general partner to relying creditors unless the partnership has been carried on under a name that was the same as the limited partner's name prior to his becoming a partner or the creditors knew that the person was not a general partner when the credit was extended.[84]

By similar reasoning, anyone who executes a certificate knowing it contains a false statement is liable to anyone who suffers loss by reliance on the statement.[85] The same rule applies to one who learns of the false statement subsequent to signing the certificate, "but within a sufficient time before the statement was relied upon" fails to take remedial action.[86]

11. PROCEDURAL DEFECTS THAT MIGHT CAUSE LOSS OF LIMITED LIABILITY

Since a limited partnership is a creature of statute, failure to comply with the filing, amendment, cancellation, or other provisions of the statute may result in the entity being deemed a general partnership.[87] If this happens, the limited partners might become liable for the claims of creditors and judgment holders. Indeed, one of the first things that attorneys for a creditor do when a limited partnership and its general partners become insolvent is to search for an argument that the limited partnership was, in fact, a general partnership.

Absolute technical compliance with the formation provisions is not required; rather, the statute provides that "[a] limited partnership is formed if there has been substantial compliance in good faith" with the technical formation requirements.[88] This concept probably applies to the amendment provision also, but that section does not contain such an explicit statement.[89]

It is not possible to summarize the numerous situations when there may be some good faith nonfatal defect in the procedure, but the purpose served by limited partnerships should be considered in determining the seriousness of any noncompliance. As the act states, it should be construed to effect its general purpose.[90] This purpose, as noted at the beginning of this chapter, is remedial in order to encourage investing by "silent" partners who do not wish to risk more than their capital investment.[91]

We believe that courts should recognize limited liability if in good faith a certificate has been filed with the appropriate state person (and, if required, publication has been made) that reasonably notifies creditors they are dealing with a limited partnership and if there has not been actual damage to the person instituting suit by reason of the technical defect being questioned.[92] Otherwise, creditors would receive a windfall if general liability could be asserted successfully. Thus, for example, we believe general liability should not accrue if the certificate was filed but there was a good faith omission to amend it to show a new substituted limited partner. Similarly, there should be limited liability if a New York certificate has been filed even if partnership business commences before the six-week notice publication has been completed.[93] The mere execution of an agreement of limited partnership without filing the certificate probably would not be considered substantial compliance.[94]

12. RENUNCIATION TO AVOID GENERAL LIABILITY

The Uniform Limited Partnership Act contains a "fail-safe" provision that permits a putative limited partner to avoid general liability under certain circumstances. If someone contributes to the capital of a business erroneously believing that he has become a limited partner, he has the right to renounce "his interest in the profits of the business, or other compensation by way of income" promptly upon learning of the mistake.[95] If he properly renounces, he will not be liable as a general partner or be otherwise bound by the obligations of the person carrying on the business.

The Supreme Court has described this provision as "broad and highly remedial," stating that "[i]t ought to be construed liberally, and with appropriate regard for the legislative purpose to relieve from the strictness of the earlier statutes and decisions." [96]

The statute requires prompt renunciation upon learning of the mistake, but there is no certainty as to the form of renunciation or the definition of "promptly." One case held, with respect to "promptly," that the time began to run when an investor "learned . . . that something was wrong with the organizational setup" of the partnership and that renunciation six months thereafter was not prompt enough.[97] As to the form of renunciation, another case found a proper renunciation in a bill of sale conveying all of an investor's interest in the partnership to the general partners as soon as he learned that creditors were trying to hold him responsible as a general partner.[98]

There may also be a question as the effectiveness of renunciation if profits that have been previously distributed are not returned to the partnership.[99]

13. FOREIGN LIMITED PARTNERSHIPS

The usual single property real estate syndication is formed as a limited partnership in the state where the property exists. There are seldom qualification or choice of laws problems with such a syndication.

A limited partnership formed in one state that engages in activities in another state may present very difficult qualification to do business and choice of laws question.[100] It is customary to require in the partnership agreement that the general partners shall take all the steps necessary to qualify the partnership as a limited partnership in each jurisdiction in which the partnership engages in activities. A model provision to that effect may be found in Appendix 1. Often the title insurance company will require filing the foreign limited partnership certificate in the county where the land is located. Some even suggest publication in those states that require publication.

Will limited liability be recognized by the foreign state? When in doubt, perhaps a new limited partnership should be established in that state with the same general partner and the first limited partnership as the sole limited partner. For example, if the state of formation is conservative with respect to limited partner "control" powers but the state of operations requires limited partner "democracy" powers, new formation might be sensible. The 1976 Revision addresses this problem by calling for registration of a foreign limited partnership with the foreign secretary of state.[101] The legal consequences would then be similar to those of foreign corporation registration.

Failure to comply with at times conflicting applicable state law could result in questioned limited liability, inability to use state courts, and difficulty for those dealing with the partnership.

The State of Louisiana is the only state that has not adopted the Uniform Limited Partnership Act. If activities are to be conducted in Louisiana, a clause asserting limited liability status should be inserted in the limited partnership agreement.[102] This clause is intended to constitute the partnership as a partnership *in commendam,* which is the Louisiana equivalent of a limited partnership.

Limited partnership activities in a foreign nation that does not recognize the limited partnership format may subject the limited partners to general liability for activities in that foreign nation. This is an unsettled area with many unresolved questions, such as whether a domestic court would enforce a foreign judgment against the individual partners.

NOTES

1. 2 ROWLEY ON PARTNERSHIP §53.0 at 550 (Bobbs-Merrill Co., 2d ed., 1960) [hereinafter cited as 2 ROWLEY]; SUGARMAN ON PARTNERSHIP §261 at 334–35 (Alpert Press Inc., 4th ed., 1966) [hereinafter cited as SUGARMAN]; *see Lynn v. Cohen,* 359 F. Supp. 565 (S.D.N.Y. 1973); *Ruzicka v. Rager,* 111 N.E.2d 878 (N.Y. 1953).
2. Hereinafter cited as U.L.P.A. The U.L.P.A. is contained in 6 UNIFORM LAWS ANNOTATED (West Publishing Co., 1969) [hereinafter cited as 6 UNIFORM LAWS]. For New York, *see* N.Y. PARTNERSHIP LAW §§90–119 (38 McKinney's Consolidated Laws of New

York Annotated, West Publishing Co.) [hereinafter cited as 38 McKINNEY'S]. The Uniform Partnership Act [hereinafter cited as U.P.A.] applies to limited as well as general partnerships, except insofar as the statutes relating to limited partnerships are inconsistent therewith. U.P.A. §6(2). The U.P.A. is also contained in 6 UNIFORM LAWS.

3. Hereinafter cited as the 1976 Revision. The 1976 Revision, including the Commissioners' Comments, is set out in Appendix 2 of this book. The 15 states enactment figure is as of August 6, 1982.

4. Prop. Reg. §301. 7701-2(a) (5) published in the Federal Register on October 27, 1980, at 70909. The effect of state law on whether an entity will be classified as a partnership for federal income tax purposes is discussed in Chapter 2. It is the practice of the National Conference of Commissioners on Uniform State Laws to submit an adopted Act to the American Bar Association for approval. Initially, the 1976 Revision was not so presented, because of the uncertainty with respect to the tax status of an entity formed thereunder. However, despite continuing tax questions, the A.B.A. approved the 1976 Revision in 1979.

5. *See* 2 ROWLEY §53.0 at 551; SUGARMAN §262 at 336; *Riviera Congress Associates v. Yassky,* 268 N.Y.S. 2d 854 (App. Div.), *aff'd,* 223 N.E.2d 876 (N.Y. 1966).

6. U.L.P.A. §§7 and 9; *see Durant v. Abendroth,* 97 N.Y. 132, 144 (1884). *Compare* 1976 Revision §§303 and 403.

7. U.L.P.A. §3; *see* 2 ROWLEY §53.3 at 563–64. *Compare* 1976 Revision §106.

8. *See* list of actions in adopting jurisdictions, 6 UNIFORM LAWS 578–79, and the corresponding Cumulative Annual Pocket Part.

9. U.L.P.A. §1. *Compare* 1976 Revision §101(7).

10. U.L.P.A. §1. *Compare* 1976 Revision §303.

11. U.L.P.A. §2. *Compare* 1976 Revision §204.

12. 38 McKINNEY'S §91, 1981-82 Cumulative Annual Pocket Part at 69.

13. *Compare Delaney v. Fidelity Lease Ltd.,* 526 S.W.2d 543 (Tex. 1975) and *Mursor Builders v. Crown Mountain Apt. Assoc.,* 467 F. Supp. 1316 (D.V.I. 1978), with *Frigidaire Sales Corp. v. Union Properties, Inc.,* 544 P.2d 781 (Wash. 1975), *aff'd,* 562 P.2d 244 (1977). *See also Western Camps, Inc. v. Riverway Ranch Enterprises,* 138 Cal. Rptr. 918 (Cal. 1977) (limited liability of a limited partner was not jeopardized when he took an active part in the partnership's affairs as an officer and agent of the corporate general partner). *Compare* 1976 Revision §303.

14. U.P.A. §2; U.L.P.A. §1. *Compare* 1976 Revision §101(11).

15. *See* the action in adopting jurisdictions, 6 UNIFORM LAWS 569–72; SEE ALSO 6 FLETCHER, CYCLOPEDIA CORPORATIONS §2520 (perm. ed. rev. vol. 1979).

16. *See Yates v. Lyon,* 61 N.Y. 344 (1874); 2 ROWLEY §53.2 at 556; SUGARMAN §267 at 341.

17. *See* 2 ROWLEY §53.2 at 554.

18. The Commissioners' Prefatory Note to the 1976 Revision recognizes that the basic document in the limited partnership is the partnership agreement and states that the "certificate of limited partnership is not a constitutive document (except in the sense that it is a statutory prerequisite to creation of the limited partnership), and merely reflects matters as to which the creditors should be put on notice." *See* Appendix 2.

19. The matters required to be set forth in the certificate of a limited partnership formed under the 1976 Revision are similar to those required by the U.L.P.A. *Compare* U.L.P.A. §2 *with* 1976 Revision §201.

20. U.L.P.A. §2(1) (a) (I-III). *Compare* 1976 Revision §201(a)(1)-(3). States usually do not

maintain a central registry of limited partnership names, as they do with respect to corporations. *Compare* 1976 Revision §103, which permits name registration.

21. *See* Appendix 1.

22. Freidberg, "Limited Partnerships: A Non-Tax Analysis," 32 N.Y.U. INST. ON FED. TAX. 1363, 1364 (1974).

23. U.L.P.A. §2(1)(a). *Compare* 1976 Revision §201(a).

24. U.L.P.A. §4; *see* 2 ROWLEY §53.4 at 564–65. *Cf.* §§101(2) and 501 of the 1976 Revision, which permit contributions of services.

25. *See* Appendix 1.

26. U.L.P.A. §2(1)(a). *Compare* 1976 Revision §201(a).

27. U.L.P.A. §8; *see id.* §25 for the formalities of amendment. Under the 1976 Revision §202, the certificate must be amended within 30 days after the admission or withdrawal of a partner.

28. U.L.P.A. §2(1)(a). *Compare* 1976 Revision §201(a)(11).

29. U.L.P.A. §2(1)(b). *Compare* 1976 Revision §201(b).

30. 38 MCKINNEY'S §91(1)(b).

31. U.L.P.A. §(2); *see* 2 ROWLEY §53.2 at 554–55. *Compare* 1976 Revision §201(b).

32. *See and compare Peerless Mills, Inc. v. American Tel. and Tel. Co.*, 527 F.2d 445, 449 n. 1 (2d Cir. 1975); *Filesi v. United States*, 352 F.2d 339 (4th Cir. 1965); *United States v. Coson*, 286 F.2d 453, 461–62 n. 13 (9th Cir. 1961); *Dwinell's Central Neon v. Cosmopolitan Chinook Hotel*, 587 P.2d 191 (Wash. 1978); *Garrett v. Koepke*, 569 S.W.2d 568 (Tex. 1978); *cf. Vulcan Furniture Mfg. Co. v. Vaughn*, 160 So.2d 768 (Fla. 1964).

33. U.L.P.A. §24(2); *see Id.* §25 for the formalities of compliance; 2 ROWLEY §§53.24 and 53.25 at 589–94. *Compare* 1976 Revision §202, which contains a 30-day requirement.

34. U.L.P.A. §24(1). *Compare* 1976 Revision $203.

35. U.L.P.A. §9. The extent of liability of a general partner after removal or resignation may be unsettled in the applicable jurisdiction and a few states have added a procedure to limit continued liability by way of adding language to U.L.P.A. §9. *Compare* 1976 Revision §403.

36. U.L.P.A. §9. *See United States v. Mansion House Center No. Redev. Co.*, 426 F. Supp. 479 (E.D. Mo. 1977) (power of attorney was only for ministerial functions and the general partner was not authorized to choose a replacement general partner). *Compare* 1976 Revision §401, which provides that "additional general partners may be admitted only with the specific written consent of each partner." The Comment calls this "unwaivable." *Cf. Wasserman v. Wasserman*, 386 N.E.2d 783 (Mass. 1979).

37. *See and compare* SUGARMAN §98 at 126; *Hirsch v. Equilateral Associates*, 264 S.E.2d 885 (Ga. 1980); *Bartels v. Algonquin Properties, Ltd.*, 471 F. Supp. 1132 (D.Vt. 1979); *Gundelach v. Gollehon*, 598 P.2d 521 (Colo. 1979); *Miller v. Schweickart*, 405 F. Supp. 366 (S.D.N.Y. 1975); *Bassan v. Investment Exchange Corp.*, 524 P.2d 233 (Wash. 1974); *Boxer v. Husky Oil Co.*, 429 A.2d 995 (Del. 1981); Note, "Procedures and Remedies in Limited Partners' Suits for Breach of the General Partner's Fiduciary Duty," 90 HARV. L. REV. 763 (1977). *See also Newburger, Loeb & Co., Inc. v. Gross*, 563 F.2d 1057 (2d Cir. 1977), *cert. denied*, 434 U.S. 1035 (1978) (transfer of limited partnership assets to a new corporation without the consent of withdrawn limited partners whose capital remained at risk violated New York equivalent of U.L.P.A. §9 and was also a breach of fiduciary duty to the withdrawn partners).

38. U.P.A. §9; *see* 2 ROWLEY §53.9 at 569–70.

39. U.L.P.A. §10; see 2 ROWLEY §53.10 at 570–72. *Compare* §§105, 305, 802 of the 1976 Revision.

40. U.L.P.A. §26; *see Amsler v. American Home Insurance Co.,* 348 So.2d 68 (Fla. 1977) (only general partner could institute a malpractice suit against the partnership's counsel).

41. *See* 1976 Revision Article 10; *Lerman v. Tenney,* 425 F.2d 236 (2d Cir. 1970); *Lichtyger v. Franchard Corp.,* 223 N.E.2d 869 (N.Y. 1966); *Riviera Congress Associates v. Yassky,* 268 N.Y.S.2d 854 (App. Div.), *aff'd,* 233 N.E.2d 876 (N.Y. 1966); *Silver v. Chase Manhattan Bank,* 355 N.Y.S.2d 387 (1974); *Alpert v. Haimes,* 315 N.Y.S.2d 332 (1970); *Bedolla v. Logan and Frazer,* 125 Cal. Rptr. 59 (Cal. 1975); *Smith v. Bader,* 458 F. Supp. 1108 (S.D.N.Y. 1978); *Browning v. Levien,* 262 S.E.2d 355 (N.C. 1980). *See also Kobernick v. Shaw,* 139 Cal. Rptr. 188 (Cal. 1977) (limited partner not only could defend self but could assert a cross-claim based on fraud against the general partner and plaintiff on behalf of himself and his fellow limited partners). *Compare* Hecker, "Limited Partners' Derivative Suits Under the Revised Uniform Limited Partnership Act," 33 VAND L. REV. 343 (1980).

42. 38 MCKINNEY'S §115-a, 1981–1982 Cumulative Annual Pocket Part at 83–84. *See* cases cited in note 41, *supra; see also* §§115-b and 115-c with respect to security for expenses and restrictions to indemnifying general partners for liability in such suits. *See also Wien v. Chelsea Theater Center of Brooklyn,* 397 N.Y.S.2d 865 (N.Y. 1977), *rev'd on other grounds,* 411 N.Y.S.2d 316 (N.Y. 1978) (under New York law, limited partner may bring action on behalf of partnership without establishing that the general partners refusal to initiate suit was improper, that there was a consensus among the partners to bring suit, or that the general partners consented to, or were unable to, bring the action).

43. Delaware has added 6 Delaware Code §1732.

44. U.L.P.A. §§15–17. *Compare* 1976 Revision Article 6.

45. U.L.P.A. §15–17; *compare Allen v. Amber Manor Apartments,* 420 N.E.2d 440 (Ill. 1981)(partner could not retain security interest in partnership contribution) *with Johns v. Jaeb,* 518 S.W.2d 857 (Tex. 1974) (money advanced to partnership was loan rather than contribution).

46. U.L.P.A. §16(1)-(2); *see* 2 ROWLEY §§53.15 and 53.16 at 576–79. *Compare* 1976 Revision §604.

47. U.L.P.A. §16(3). *Compare* 1976 Revision §605.

48. U.L.P.A. §16(4). *Compare* 1976 Revision §606 and Article 8.

49. U.L.P.A. §10; *see* U.P.A. §32; SUGARMAN §272 at 353–54.

50. *See* SUGARMAN §§96, 271 and 272, at 124–25 and 350–54; Note, "Procedures and Remedies in Limited Partners' Suits for Breach of the General Partner's Fiduciary Duty," 90 HARV. L. REV. 763, 764 n.4 (1977).

51. *See* Appendix 1.

52. U.L.P.A. §13. *Compare* 1976 Revision §107. There is debate whether and under what circumstances a limited partner can obtain secured creditor status. *See* Kratovil and Werner, "Fixing up the Old Jalopy: The Modern Limited Partnership Under the ULPA," 50 ST. JOHN'S L. REV. 51, 62–66 (1975); Hecker, "The Revised Uniform Limited Partnership Act: Provisions Affecting the Relationship of the Firm and Its Members to Third Parties," 27 KANSAS L. REV. 1, 9-11 (1979).

53. U.L.P.A. §§12, 14. *Compare* 1976 Revision §404.

54. U.L.P.A. §14.

55. U.L.P.A. §12. *Compare* 1976 Revision §404.

56. U.L.P.A. §18; *see* U.P.A. §26; *Reiter v. Greenberg*, 235 N.E.2d 118 (N.Y. 1968); 2 ROWLEY §53.18 at 582-83. *Compare* 1976 Revision §701.

57. U.L.P.A. §22; *see Bank of Bethesda v. Koch*, 408 A.2d 767 (Md. 1979). *Compare* 1976 Revision §703.

58. U.L.P.A. §19; *see* 2 ROWLEY §53.19 at 583-84. *Compare* 1976 Revision §§702, 704.

59. U.L.P.A. §22; *see* SUGARMAN §283 at 366; *In re Panitz & Co.*, 270 F. Supp. 448 (D. Md 1967), *aff'd*, 385 F.2d 835 (4th Cir. 1967); *Harris v. Murray*, 28 N.Y. 574 (1864); *Bettis v. Leavitt*, 198 S.E.2d 296 (Ga. 1973), *aff'd*, 223 S.E.2d 88 (Ga. 1976); *Maxco Inc. v. Volpe*, 274 S.E.2d 561 (Ga. 1981). *Compare* 1976 Revision §703.

60. U.L.P.A. §19. *Compare* 1976 Revision §704.

61. *Compare* Freidberg, note 22, *supra*, at 1368 *with* SUGARMAN §284 at 367-68.

62. U.L.P.A. §21; *see* 2 ROWLEY §53.21 at 585-86. *Compare* 1976 Revision §705.

63. U.L.P.A. §20; *see* 2 ROWLEY §53.20 at 584-85. *Compare* 1976 Revision Articles 4 and 8. *Cf. Lowe v. Arizona Power and Light Co.*, 427 P.2d 366 (Ariz. 1967). *Compare* 1976 Revision §§402 (which expands the events causing a general partner to cease to be such) and 801(3) (which provides that the partnership may continue if within 90 days all partners agree in writing to continue the business and to the appointment of one or more additional general partners if necessary or desired). *See* Sell, "An Examination of Articles 3, 4 and 9 of the Revised Uniform Limited Partnership Act," 9 ST. MARY'S L.J. 459, 468-469 (1977-78).

64. *See* Section 365(e) (1) (A) of the Federal Bankruptcy Act. Under the apparent terms of this Act, such provisions may not be enforceable during the general partner's bankruptcy proceeding administration. However, they likely will be effective if the applicable state has adopted the 1976 Revision. *See* 1976 Revision Article 4.

65. *See Boylan v. Detrio*, 187 F.2d 28 (5th Cir. 1951).

66. U.L.P.A. §23(1). *Compare* 1976 Revision §804. *See Matter of Dutch Inn of Orlando, Ltd.*, 2 B.R. 268 (Fla. 1980); *Dycus v. Belco Industries, Inc.*, 569 P.2d 553 (Okla. 1977); *Nexsen v. New York Stock Exchange*, 261 N.Y.S.2d 780 (N.Y. 1965); *Kittredge v. Langley*, 169 N.E. 626 (N.Y. 1930); 2 ROWLEY §53.23 at 587-89. *See also Northern Illinois Gas Co. v. Hartnett-Shaw Evanston, Inc.*, 368 N.E.2d 742 (Ill. 1977) (limited partners' claim was in the nature of a creditor claim and had priority over general partner's assignee).

67. U.L.P.A. §23. *Compare* 1976 Revision §804. *See Pierce v. De Rothermann*, 82 N.Y.S.2d 837 (N.Y. 1948); *Application of Gotham Hotel Realty Co.*, 272 N.Y.S.2d 854 (N.Y. 1966); *Lanier v. Bowdoin*, 24 N.E.2d 732 (N.Y. 1939), *rehearing denied*, 25 N.E. 39! (N.Y. 1940). *Compare Dycus v. Belco Industries, Inc.*, 569 P.2d 553 (Okla. 1977) (statute on priority of distribution after dissolution controlled over partnership agreement provision that was deemed to be contrary to law).

68. U.L.P.A. §23(2).

69. U.L.P.A. §24; *see id.* §25 for the formalities of compliance; 2 ROWLEY §§53.24 and 53.25 at 589-94. *Compare* 1976 Revision §203.

70. U.L.P.A. §17(1) (a); *see* 2 ROWLEY §53.17 at 579-82. *Compare* 1976 Revision §502.

71. U.L.P.A. §17(2).

72. *See* 2 ROWLEY §53.17 at 579-82; SUGARMAN §273 at 354.

73. *See and compare Whitley v. Klauber*, 417 N.Y.S.2d 959 (N.Y. 1979), *aff'd*, 435 N.Y.S.2d 568 (1980); *Bell Sound Studios, Inc. v. Enneagram Productions Co.*, 234 N.Y.S.2d 12 (N.Y. 1962); *Donroy, Limited v. United States*, 301 F.2d 200 (9th Cir. 1962).

74.   U.L.P.A. §17(4); *see Whitley v. Klauber,* 435 N.Y.S.2d 568 (1980); *A.T.E. Financial Services, Inc. v. Corson,* 268 A.2d 73 (N.J. 1970); *Kittridge v. Langley,* 169 N.E. 626 (N.Y. 1930); the 1976 Revision provided a one-year statute of limitations for contributions that are returned without violating either the partnership agreement or the 1976 Revision. A six-year statute of limitation applies to contributions wrongfully returned. 1976 Revision §608.

75.   U.L.P.A. §17(3). *Compare* 1976 Revision §502(b).

76.   *See* note 62, *supra.*

77.   U.L.P.A. §7. *Compare* 1976 Revision §303. *See generally* Feld, " 'The 'Control' Test for Limited Partnerships," 82 HARV. L. REV. 1471 (1969); Slater, " 'Control' in The Limited Partnership," 7 JOHN MARSHALL J. OF PRAC. AND PROC. 415 (1974); Augustine, Fass, Lester, and Robinson, "The Liability of Limited Partners Having Certain Statutory Voting Rights Affecting the Basic Structure of the Partnership," 31 THE BUS. LAW. 2087 (1976); O'Neal, "Comments on Recent Developments in Limited Partnership Law," WASH. UNIV. L. QTLY. 669 (1978); 2 ROWLEY §53.7 at 567–69.

78.   *See Gast v. Petsinger,* 323 A.2d 371 (Pa. 1974); *Diversified Properties v. Weil,* 319 F. Supp. 778 (D.D.C. 1970); *cf. Mist Properties, Inc. v. Fitzsimmons Realty Co.,* 228 N.Y.S.2d 406 (N.Y. 1962).

79.   *See* 6 UNIFORM LAWS at 852–86, and the corresponding Cumulative Annual Pocket Part; Feldman, "The Uniform Limited Partnership Act, Revised," 53 CONN. B.J. 204 (1979). The 1976 Revision Article 3, and §303 (b) of that Article, retains the control of business standard but states that a limited partner whose "participation in the control of the business is not substantially the same as the exercise of the powers of the general partner . . ." is liable only to those who have actual knowledge of his participation. Further, the 1976 Revision contains a list of several permissible activities that do not constitute control participation. See Appendix 2. *See also* O'Neal, "Comments on Recent Developments in Limited Partnership Law," WASH. UNIV. L. QTLY. 669 (1978); Hecker, "The Revised Uniform Limited Partnership Act," 27 KANSAS L. Rev. (1978–1979); Pierce, "Limited Partnership Act," 325 S.W.L.J. 1301 (1978–1979).

80.   Freidberg, note 22, *supra,* at 1367; *see also Gast v. Petsinger,* 323 A.2d 371 (Pa. 1974) (partner-consultants were "in control"). *Cf. Weil v. Diversified Properties,* 319 F. Supp. 778 (D.D.C. 1970) and *Stone Mountain Properties Limited v. Heiliner,* 229 S.E.2d 799 (Ga. 1976) (consultation and advice did not result in control). *Compare* 1976 Revision §303.

81.   *See and compare Financial Dynamics, Ltd. v. United States,* 80-2 USTC ¶9585 (M.D. Fla. 1980); *Hirsch v. Dupont,* 396 F. Supp. 1214 (S.D.N.Y. 1975), *aff'd,* 553 F.2d 750 (2d Cir. 1977); *Filesi v. United States,* 352 F.2d 339 (4th Cir. 1965); *Dwinell's Central Neon v. Cosmopolitan Chinook Hotel,* 587 P.2d 191 (Wash. 1978); *Fiske v. Moczik,* 329 So.2d 35 (Fla. 1976); *Grainger v. Antoyan,* 313 P.2d 848 (Cal. 1957); *Silvola v. Rowlett,* 272 P.2d 287 (Colo. 1954); *Rathke v. Griffith,* 218 P.2d 757 (Wash. 1950); *Holzman v. De Escamilla,* 195 P.2d 833 (Cal. 1948).

82.   *See Weil v. Diversified Properties,* 319 F. Supp. 778 (D.D.C. 1970); *Trans-Am Builders, Inc. v. Woods Mill, Ltd.,* 210 S.E.2d 866 (Ga. 1974); *cf.* Feld, note 77, *supra.*

83.   *See* note 13, *supra;* and accompanying text.

84.   U.L.P.A. §5. *Compare* 1976 Revision §§303(d) and 102(2). *See* 2 ROWLEY §53.5 at 565; Note, "The Mississippi Uniform Limited Partnership Act," 45 MISS. L.J. 1037, 1040 (1974).

85.   U.L.P.A. §6(a). *Compare* 1976 Revision §207. *See* 2 *Rowley* §53.6 at 565–67.

86. U.L.P.A. §6(b). Under the 1976 Revision §207(2), only general partners have the obligation to amend because of changed events.

87. U.L.P.A. §§2 and 24. *Compare* 1976 Revision §201.

88. U.L.P.A. §2. *Compare* 1976 Revision §201(b). *See* 2 *Rowley* §53.2 at 554–55 and 561–63.

89. U.L.P.A. §24. *Compare* 1976 Revision §202.

90. U.L.P.A. §28. *Compare* 1976 Revision §1101.

91. *See* 2 ROWLEY §53.28 at 595–96; SUGARMAN §295 at 388–89; *Plasteel Products Corp. v. Helman,* 271 F.2d 354 (1st Cir. 1959); *Stowe v. Merrillees,* 44 P.2d 368 (Cal. 1935).

92. *See* 1976 Revision §303. *Compare Franklin v. Rigg,* 237 S.E.2d 526 (Ga. 1977) (limited liability maintained although certificate of limited partnership was not filed until after contract in issue had been closed, on the theory that the plaintiff had not been damaged because it had dealt initially with a corporation and its president, both of whom became general partners), *and Garrett v. Koepke,* 569 S.W.2d 568 (Tex. 1978) (failure to file certificate did not create general liability when creditors, before dealing with the limited partnership, had the information that would have been provided by a filing) *with Dwinell's Central Neon v. Cosmopolitan Chinook Hotel,* 587 P.2d 191 (Wash. 1978) (failure to file certificate did cause general liability even though plaintiff creditor knew of purported limited partnership status), *and Klein v. Weiss,* 395 A.2d 126 (Md. 1978) (no limited partnership was formed where filed certificate had been fundamentally changed by the general partners without the consent of the limited partners; issue of purported limited partners' liability to creditors was remanded to be determined on general law principles of whether there was a holding out causing estoppel).

93. However, in "an informal and unofficial expression of view," the Attorney General of the State of New York informed the New York County Clerk by letter dated November 13, 1978 that "we conclude that the requirement . . . as to publication, must be complied with for formation of a limited partnership and, consequently, a limited partnership must await completion of publication prior to beginning doing business." The letter does not address itself to the situation where business is commenced before completion of publication and publication is completed thereafter. Is the partnership never to qualify as a limited partnership? We believe that the courts would find "substantial compliance in good faith" at least after completion of the required six successive weeks of publication and, it is to be hoped, after the first publication if followed by five successive publications. Indeed, the courts might find substantial compliance in a good faith factual pattern even if business is commenced before any publication; however, this is a dangerous situation.

94. *See Solomont v. Polk Development Co.,* 71 Cal. Rptr. 832 (1968); *Ruth v. Crane,* 392 F. Supp. 724, 733 (E.D. Pa. 1975); *cf. Brown v. Brown,* 488 P.2d 689 (Ariz. 1971) (estoppel as between purported limited partners); *Tibron Nat. Bank v. Wagner,* 71 Cal. Rptr. 832 (1968); *Garrett v. Koepke,* 569 S.W. 2d 568 (Tex. C.A. 1978) (no liability where creditor had actual notice).

95. U.L.P.A. §11. *Compare* 1976 Revision §304. *See* 2 ROWLEY §53.11 at 573–74; SUGARMAN §277 at 359–60; *Graybar Electric Co. v. Lowe,* 462 P.2d 413 (Ariz. 1969). *See also Voudouris v. Walter E. Heller & Co.,* 560 S.W.2d 202 (Tex. 1977) (giving up of interest as soon as defendant discovered that a limited partnership certificate had never been filed was effective to avoid being subjected to creditor liability). For a general discussion, *see* Banoff, "Can Tax Practitioners Support the Revised U.L.P.A.?" TAXES 97, 109–127 (1982).

96. *Giles v. Vette,* 263 U.S. 553, 563 (1923), *aff'g,* 281 F. 928 (7th Cir. 1922).

97. *Vidricksen v. Grover,* 363 F.2d 372, 373 (9th Cir. 1966).

98. *Rathke v. Griffith,* 218 P.2d 757 (Wash. 1950).

99. *Compare Giles v. Vette,* 263 U.S. 553 (1923); *Gilman Paint & Varnish Co. v. Legum,* 80 A.2d 906 (Md. 1951); *Rathke v. Griffith,* 218 P.2d 757 (Wash. 1950).

100. *See generally* Note, "Foreign Limited Partnerships: A Proposed Amendment to the Uniform Limited Partnership Act," 47 S. CAL. L. REV. 1174 (1974); Kratovil and Werner, note 52, *supra,* at 66–68.

101. 1976 Revision Article 9.

102. See Note, "Partnership *in Commendam:* Tax Consequences and Business Risks," 36 LA. L. REV. 260 (1975).

CHAPTER 2

TAX CONSIDERATIONS IN FORMING THE LIMITED PARTNERSHIP

1. GENERAL

The fundamental reason for selecting the limited partnership as the vehicle for a real estate syndication is that, in general, it is not a taxable entity for federal income tax purposes. Instead, the tax benefits of real estate ownership and operation "pass through" directly to the investors.

If an intended limited partnership is refused partnership tax treatment, it will be taxed as an association (that is, a corporation) and most of the "tax shelter" benefits will be lost. With certain exceptions, a corporation cannot pass its losses through to the investors and is taxed at the entity level on its items of income, gain, and loss.[1] A second tax is imposed on stockholders when the corporation makes a distribution of earnings and profits in the form of money or property.

The definition of a limited partnership that will be classified as a partnership for federal income tax purposes is different in several respects from the state law definition of a limited partnership, discussed in Chapter 1. For federal income tax purposes, a partnership "includes a syndicate, group, pool, joint venture, or other unincorporated organization through or by

23

means of which any business, financial operation, or venture is carried on, and which is not . . . a corporation or a trust or estate." [2] Even if a business entity is a limited partnership under state law and a limited partnership is intended by the parties, it may not be considered a partnership for tax purposes.[3] Similarly, it is possible that, for tax purposes, a partnership may exist even if the parties have no intent to form a partnership, and even if there is no partnership under state law.[4]

To a great extent, whether an entity is a limited partnership for tax purposes is determined independently from the characterization under state law.[5] State law is important, however, in determining whether the entity has certain characteristics and relationships that affect the determination of tax status.[6]

The classification of an organization for tax purposes has long been a subject of controversy.[7] In an attempt at clarification, the Internal Revenue Service issued definitional regulations that set forth factors to be weighed in characterizing an organization.[8] Under a literal application of the regulations, most organizations qualifying as limited partnerships under a state statute corresponding to the Uniform Limited Partnership Act would be characterized as partnerships for tax purposes.[9] The Service nevertheless has at times, and with inconsistent application, interpreted and applied the regulations in a restrictive manner. Two important court decisions that will be discussed later rejected Service positions and applied the regulations to the letter. Regulations that would have made qualification as a partnership much more difficult for most limited partnerships were proposed in 1977 but were almost immediately withdrawn.[10]

This chapter discusses the methods of attempting to assure that an intended partnership will be taxed as a partnership.

2. DEFINITION OF A PARTNERSHIP: THE REGULATIONS

An organization that is a partnership under state law may be taxed as a partnership or as an association (that is, a corporation). The characterization of an organization for federal income tax purposes depends on whether it more closely resembles a partnership or an association. To avoid association status, the entity must not have more than two of four designated corporate characteristics.

The Treasury Regulations set forth six characteristics that are ordinarily found in a pure corporation (although two are disregarded as being common to corporations and partnerships). These "corporate" characteristics are:

1. Associates;
2. An objective to carry on business and divide the gains therefrom;
3. Continuity of life;
4. Centralization of management;
5. Liability for corporate debts limited to corporate property; and
6. Free transferability of interests.[11]

In addition to the major characteristics, the regulations allow consideration of unspecified "other factors" that may be significant in characterizing an organization for tax purposes.[12] The Service, in a 1979 ruling, stated that the following seven items will *not* be considered "other factors" and therefore are not of significance (independent of their bearing on the six major characteristics) in determining the tax classification of limited partnerships: (a) division of partnership interests into units or shares, or sales of such interests in a manner like corporate securities; (b) the managing partner's rights to retain or distribute profits; (c) the limited partners' voting rights as to the removal of the general partner or the sale of substantially all of the partnership's assets; (d) use of certificates of limited partnership ownership; (e) use of corporate formalities or procedures; (f) the limited partners' signing of a partnership agreement; or (g) pooling investments while limiting the liability of some of the participants.[13]

The determination as to classification of an organization is made by taking into account the presence or absence of the six characteristics. Since corporations and limited partnerships both have associates and an objective to carry on business and divide the gains therefrom, however, these characteristics are disregarded and the determination is based on the presence or absence of the remaining four corporate characteristics.[14]

An unincorporated organization will be taxed as an association (corporation) only if it has more corporate characteristics than noncorporate characteristics, that is, if it has at least three of the enumerated characteristics.[15] If an unincorporated entity can establish the absence of at least two of the four characteristics, therefore, it should not be classified as an association taxable as a corporation.

Each of these four characteristics is now discussed.

3. CONTINUITY OF LIFE

Of the corporate characteristics, continuity of life [16] is the easiest to avoid for an entity seeking to be characterized as a limited partnership. Thus the partnership agreement should provide that the entity's life does not continue indefinitely but rather ends, unlike the life of a corporation, on the occurrence of certain events.

The regulations that describe continuity of life rely on the technical concept of dissolution of the organization under local law. Thus continuity of life does not exist if the death, insanity, bankruptcy, retirement, resignation, or expulsion of any partner of a limited partnership causes a dissolution.[17] Further, continuity of life does not exist if the retirement, death, or insanity of a general partner causes a dissolution, even if the remaining general partners or all remaining members may agree to continue the limited partnership.[18]

The regulations further state that, if, under local law, any member has the power to dissolve the organization, continuity of life does not exist.[19] A limited partnership that is subject to a statute corresponding to the Uniform Limited Partnership Act, therefore, lacks continuity of life.[20]

Careful drafting of the limited partnership agreement and certificate could enable the limited partnership to avoid having the corporate characteristic of continuity of life. The documents should state clearly that the limited partnership is dissolved by the death, retirement, insanity, bankruptcy (but remember the Bankruptcy Act of 1979), resignation, or expulsion of a general partner (but not of a limited partner) and that it will be reconstituted and its business continued only on the consent of all remaining general partners or of all remaining members of the partnership. Although it may be consistent with the regulations to provide for prior consent (by a provision for automatic continuation by the remaining general partner or members), such a provision may be dangerous. Consent is more safely obtained on the occurrence of the event that otherwise would cause dissolution.

Most partnerships also contain a fixed date when the partnership will dissolve if it has not been dissolved sooner by events. A fixed date of termination alone, however, would not be sufficient to avoid the continuity of life characteristic.

4. CENTRALIZATION OF MANAGEMENT

It is not nearly so easy to structure a limited partnership to avoid the corporate characteristic of centralization of management. The regulations state that an organization has centralized management "if any person (or any group of persons which does not include all the members) has continuing exclusive authority to make the management decisions necessary to the conduct of the business for which the organization was formed." [21] Such persons, the regulations further state, would resemble, in powers and functions, the directors of a corporation.

Although a limited partnership vests continuing exclusive managerial authority in the general partners, a limited partnership formed pursuant to a statute corresponding to the Uniform Limited Partnership Act does not have centralization of management unless "substantially all the interests" in the limited partnership are owned by the limited partners.[22]

The meaning of "substantially all the interests" in this context is not clear with respect to either the numerical percentage or the definition of "interest" (i.e., capital, profits, or both). The regulations contain two examples in which centralization of management is found to exist in situations where limited partners contributed approximately 94 and 97%, respectively, of total partnership capital.[23] It is understood that the Service may use a rule of thumb that centralization of management does not exist if the general parters have more than 20% of total partnership capital or profits.

It should be noted that in most real estate limited partnerships, especially public syndications, limited partners will generally own, at least in the early years, well in excess of 80% of partnership capital and profits. Therefore, the Service will often assert that the organization has the corporate characteristic of centralization of management.

Even if the general partners have a significant capital interest, the power of the limited partners to remove the general partner may result in a finding of centralized management.[24] Proposed regulations state that such powers produce a facts and circumstances test for centralized management; however, this should not cause centralized management if the power is sufficiently restricted (such as limiting removal power to general partner gross negligence). [25]

As discussed in Chapter 1, limited partners may be found under local law to be liable as general partners if they take part in, or possibly even if they are given the right to take part in, the conduct of the partnership's business.[26] For purposes of tax classification of the limited partnership, such a finding would appear to indicate the absence of centralized management. Nevertheless, it is hoped that this will never be the actual result, since attaining limited liability under local law is of paramount importance to potential investors.

In many limited partnerships, the general partner may neither make a capital contribution nor have an interest in partnership capital. Instead, the general partner is allocated a substantial interest in partnership profits. In such a situation, it can be argued that the limited partners do not own "substantially all" the interests in the partnership. A substantial profits interest of a general partner, therefore, might cause the limited partnership to lack centralized management. It is not wise to rely on such reasoning, however, and if there is any question, the prudent route is to establish clearly the absence of two other corporate characteristics.

5. LIMITED LIABILITY

At this point in our analysis, most real estate limited partnerships can avoid continuity of life, while fewer can avoid centralized management. What about avoiding the corporate characteristic of limited liability? Although most real estate limited partnerships are structured to avoid limited partner liability as a matter of local law, the ultimate question in this area for tax purposes is the identity and substance of the general partner.

The regulations state that "[a]n organization has the corporate characteristic of limited liability if under local law there is no member who is personally liable for the debts of or claims against the organization." [27] Personal liability exists, therefore, if a creditor may seek personal satisfaction against a member to the extent that the organization's assets are insufficient to satisfy the claim. With certain exceptions, described below, personal liability is deemed to exist with respect to each general partner of a limited partnership formed under a statute corresponding to the Uniform Limited Partnership Act.[28] A real estate limited partnership formed under a Uniform Limited Partnership Act statute, therefore, often can avoid the corporate characteristic of limited liability.

The exceptions contained in the regulations are concerned primarily with the financial substance of the general partner (because this is the person who may have personal liability for the partnership's debts). These exceptions appear to differ depending on whether or not the general partner is a corporation.

The regulations state that, in the case of a limited partnership, personal liability does not exist if the general partner has no substantial assets (other than his interest in the partnership) that could be reached by a creditor *and* is merely a dummy acting as an agent of the limited partners.[29] The "dummy" reference is not literally restricted to noncorporate general partners, although the Service may argue that it does not apply to corporate general partners. The regulations further state that if a corporation is a general partner, personal liability exists if the corporation has substantial assets (other than its interest in the partnership) that can be reached by a creditor of the limited partnership.[30]

Thus the regulations could be read as establishing different tests for individuals and corporations. To enable the limited partnership to avoid the corporate characteristic of limited liability, therefore, a literal reading of the regulations leads to the conclusion that an individual general partner need not have substantial assets if he is not a dummy acting as an agent for the limited partners. (Under current ruling policy, however, the Service caveats its private rulings on the lack of limited liability with an assumption that an individual as well as corporate general partner has substantial assets.) On the other hand, the regulations could be read as providing that a corporate general partner, even if not a "dummy," must have substantial assets.[31]

The regulations do not adequately define "substantial assets." Whatever constitutes substantial assets, however, it does not include the general partner's interest in the limited partnership in question. If a limited partnership is involved in large financial transactions, the regulations do indicate that the assets of the general partner(s) may be considered substantial even if the assets are not sufficient to satisfy a substantial portion of the limited partnership's obligations.[32]

Judicial decisions, as in so much of this area, are not very helpful. This is because until the last several years the Service did not audit limited partnerships intensively and brought few situations to the attention of the courts. Obviously, this is no longer the policy.

The Service has attempted to establish standards for determining when a sole corporate general partner will be deemed to have substantial assets. In the absence of articulate regulations or case law, the Service has injected its views in a strange way. It has used the rules defining when it will grant advance rulings in this area.[33] These so-called safe harbor rules, setting forth net worth guidelines for a sole corporate general partner, are discussed on pp. 33–34.

Although there are no corresponding net worth guidelines for individual general partners, the Service seems to be concerned with the assets of human general partners. The better view is that a human general partner (acting alone or with a corporate general partner), who is not a dummy acting as agent for the limited partners, and who has some assets subject to partnership liabilities (i.e., he is not insolvent), qualifies the partnership for the absence of the limited liability characteristic. However, no one wishes to be the test case, and the greater the general partner's net worth, the lower the chance for an adverse decision.

6. FREE TRANSFERABILITY OF INTERESTS

Up to this point in the analysis of the regulations, only the absence of continuity of life can be assured for many real estate limited partnerships. Thus, if the limited partnership is to avoid at least two of the four tests, often there must be an absence of the remaining corporate characteristic of free transferability of interests.

The regulations provide that an organization will have free transferability of interests "if each of its members or those members owning substantially all of the interests in the organization have the power, without the consent of other members, to substitute for themselves in the same organization a person who is not a member of the organization." [34] In addition, the regulations state that a member must be able, without consent of other members, to confer *all* the attributes of his interest on a substitute.[35]

Under the regulations, free transferability of interests will not exist where a limited partner cannot, without the consent of the other members, designate a transferee as a true substitute limited partner, even though he can assign at will his rights to share in partnership profits.[36] In apparent contradiction of its regulations, however, the Service has ruled that, although the general partners of a limited partnership had not consented to a transferee becoming a substituted limited partner as required by the partnership agreement, the transferee was a substituted limited partner for the purpose of reporting a distributable share of partnership income, gain, loss, deduction, and credit.[37] It is unclear whether the Service intends this revenue ruling to apply to the question of partnership tax classification. The conservative draftsman, therefore, might consider prohibiting an assignment of any interest in a limited partnership without the unanimous written consent of the general partners. This may not be enforceable, however, because Uniform Limited Partnership Act Section 19(1) states that "[a] limited partner's interest is assignable." At the least, a partnership agreement that permits profit and loss assignability by limited partners should prohibit a transferee from becoming a substitute limited partner in the absence of general partner consent.[38] If the transferee is already a partner, it is probably unnecessary to require consent.

If more flexibility in terms of transferability of limited partnership interests is required, it might be achieved by the partnership agreement allowing complete transfer after an offer of the interest to other partners.[39] If two of the other three corporate characteristics are present, however, this modified form of free transferability might not be worth the risk.

The Service may not agree that requiring the consent of the general partner before transfer limits free transferability. Rather, the Service may examine whether the standards of consent are meaningful. If it appears that consent usually will be given, the Service probably will take the position that there is free transferability.

7. DEFINITION OF A PARTNERSHIP: *THE LARSON* AND *ZUCKMAN* CASES

The Tax Court and the Court of Claims have considered whether limited partnerships, which were organized under statutes corresponding to the Uniform Limited Partnership Act, constitute associations or partnerships for tax purposes. Both courts decided that, under the definitional regulations discussed previously, such organizations are not taxable as associations.

Two California real estate limited partnerships were considered by the Tax Court in *Larson*.[40] The common corporate general partner had neither substantial assets nor a substantial capital investment in the limited partnerships. Applying the literal language of the regulations, the Tax Court, in a close decision, held that the organizations were partnerships for tax purposes. The court found that the organizations had the characteristics of centralization of management and free transferability of interests, but lacked continuity of life and limited liability. The last finding was reached because, although it did not have substantial assets, the sole corporate general partner was not acting as a mere "dummy" for the limited partners.[41] Each of the four factors was considered equal, and the absence of two factors precluded association qualification. The court indicated that had the factors been applied on a corporate resemblance "continuum," a different conclusion would have been reached, and it appears to invite amendment of the regulations.[42]

It is noteworthy that in an earlier opinion considering the same California limited partnerships, the Tax Court held for association status.[43] This opinion, which was considered incorrect by most tax practitioners, was withdrawn, and the reconsidered opinion discussed previously was issued. The closeness of the latter decision and the earlier decision reaching an opposite result indicate that the Tax Court may not be a favorable forum for litigating partnership status.

The Court of Claims has been strikingly more favorable in finding partnership status. In *Zuckman*, considering a Missouri limited partnership that was almost identical to the organization considered by the Tax Court in *Larson*, the Court of Claims applied the literal language of the regulations and held that the partnership did not meet any of the corporate characteristics.[44] In this case, the sole corporate general partner did not have substantial assets but did have a 61.8% interest in the partnership. The court held that continuity of life does not exist as a matter of law where an organization is formed pursuant to the Uniform Limited Partnership Act; that centralization of management does not exist where the general partner has a substantial interest in the partnership and, therefore, does not act in a representative capacity for the limited partners; that limited liability does not exist where the corporate general partner is not a dummy or where, if the general partner is a dummy, the limited partners have personal liability; and free transferability does not exist where the members could not substitute a transferee without consent and where a transfer by the general partner would dissolve the partnership.

These cases, if generally accepted, indicate that an organization formed pursuant to the Uniform Limited Partnership Act will almost always fail to have continuity of life and limited liability. Lacking two of the four corporate characteristics, the organization probably will be treated as a partnership for tax purposes. As noted earlier, "other factors" evidencing corporate characterization may be considered and may shift the balance toward association status, but neither the Tax Court nor the Court of Claims appears to be disposed to apply such factors. Although the government based its *Larson* appeal on the application of such "other factors," it withdrew the appeal before judicial decision and later listed seven items that will not be considered "other factors." [45]

8. NEW REGULATIONS: PROPOSED AND WITHDRAWN

On January 5, 1977, the Treasury Department proposed new regulations that would have had a devastating influence on real estate limited partnerships.[46] Fortunately, the proposed regulations were withdrawn almost immediately,[47] and the old regulations remain in effect.

The proposed regulations, in substance, would have imposed association status on any organization possessing even two of the corporate characteristics.[48] Since most limited partnerships could avoid continuity of life and probably limited liability, leaving centralization of management and free transferability of interests, many such organizations would have lost their favorable partnership status under the proposed regulations. Even worse, these regulations viewed extensive nonrecourse financing as indicating the presence of the corporate characteristic of limited liability.[49] Applying this interpretation, it would be practically impossible for a real estate limited partnership to avoid limited liability, one of the previously assured "safe" characteristics. Finally, the proposed regulations were intended to be applicable almost immediately to organizations formed after January 5, 1977 and would apply after four years to organizations created on or before that date.

Faced with this prospect, members of the housing industry and the Department of Housing and Urban Development, which depends on private tax shelter financing of government-subsidized low- and moderate-income housing, apparently convinced the Treasury Department to withdraw the proposed regulations.[50] In addition, it would appear that the proposed regulations conflicted with the consistently expressed congressional intent not to eliminate the tax shelter incentive in the housing industry.[51] Congress considered real estate tax shelters and the existing tax regulations when it adopted the Tax Reform Act of 1976, the Revenue Act of 1978, and the Economic Recovery Tax Act of 1981. Presumably, it intends only the changes that were incorporated in those Acts.

The future action of the Treasury Department in this area is uncertain. Change, if any is to be made, should be left to the Congress.

9. REVENUE PROCEDURE 72-13: THE GENERAL PARTNER SAFE HARBOR RULES

The Internal Revenue Service has attempted to discourage tax shelter partnerships by issuing two revenue procedures which limited the circumstances when the Service will issue advance rulings that an organization will not be taxed as an association.[52] Although the refusal to rule is not necessarily a substantive comment, it could have an inhibiting effect, and the principles may be applied informally by agents on Service tax aduits. The Service guidelines are discussed because it is best to comply with them as much as possible. However, few private real estate limited partnerships now seek tax rulings.

In 1972, prompted by voluminous ruling requests in connection with all types of tax shelter limited partnerships, the Internal Revenue Service published Revenue Procedure 72-13.[53] This revenue procedure contains guidelines which must be met by a limited partnership having a sole corporate general partner to obtain an advance ruling that it is taxable as a partnership and not as an association taxable as a corporation. If a limited partnership cannot satisfy these guidelines, it cannot obtain a ruling even if it otherwise does not have any of the four corporate characteristics.

Revenue Procedure 72-13 is complicated and is set out in Appendix 3. In general, the Service will not issue an advance ruling with respect to limited partnership tax status if the limited partners own, individually or in the aggregate, directly or indirectly, more than 20% of the outstanding stock of a sole corporate general partner or any of its affiliates. Further, the sole corporate general partner must have a minimum net worth at all times during the life of the partnership equal to 10% of total contributions to the partnership or, if total contributions are less than $2,500,000, the lesser of 15% of total contributions or $250,000.

The net worth requirements are applied on a cumulative basis for each limited partnership in which the corporation serves as general partner. Thus, if a corporation serves as general partner in two limited partnerships, it must have a net worth equal to the sums of the requirements for each partnership.[54] The current fair market value of corporate assets is used in making the computations. The corporate general partner's interest in the partnership or in any other limited partnership and in notes or accounts receivable from or payable to the partnership are not included in computing its net worth.

A real estate development concern frequently requires a general partner for a limited partnership but does not wish to subject its own assets to general liability. To accomplish this, the developer may form a wholly owned subsidiary corporation to serve as the sole general partner. To provide the subsidiary with sufficient assets to satisfy the net worth requirements, the developers may transfer assets to the subsidiary. The parent often does not wish to commit a significant amount of capital to the subsidiary for the required length of time. One solution might be to have the parent contribute its demand note to the subsidiary in an amount (which would have to be valued and might be less than the face amount) sufficient to satisfy the net worth requirement. If there are corporate law difficulties with respect to contributing a note, the parent might consider whether under state law it could contribute money to the subsidiary, which in turn would purchase a note from the parent for the cash.

It is common to see a provision that the promoter or the real estate developer personally guarantees to maintain the net worth requirements of the corporate general partner. Presumably, the economic realities will determine whether such a guaranty is effective for the purpose being a sought.

Although the Service was attempting to clarify its position, Revenue Procedure 72-13 raises many unanswered questions.

The revenue procedure refers to limited partnerships that have a sole corporate general partner. Presumably, the rules apply even if there are a number of corporate general partners. If there is more than one corporate general partner, the net worth of all corporate general partners is likely to be combined for purposes of the net worth test. The stock ownership test, however, probably will be applied separately to each corporate general partner so that if any of the limited partners, individually or as a group, owns more than 20% of any corporate general partner, the Service may either refuse to rule or consider the "controlled" general partner for purposes of the net worth test.

Perhaps the most important unanswered question is whether the revenue procedure has any bearing on limited partnerships that have a noncorporate general partner either alone or together with a corporate general partner. It is understood that, for ruling purposes, the Service is applying a substantial assets test to individual general partners.

The guidelines of the revenue procedure must be met at all times during the life of the limited partnership. It is not certain what the consequences would be if the guidelines were satisfied initially but were not met at some time during the life of the limited partnership. The Service might take the position that the partnership was incorporated and, when and if the guidelines are satisfied again, liquidated. In such a case, there could be substantial adverse tax consequences.

Limited partnerships often are structured so that the limited partners initially contribute an amount of cash or property to the partnership and undertake an obligation to contribute additional amounts in the future. It would appear that a binding commitment not contingent on the happening of an event should be considered for purposes of computing the corporate general partner's net worth requirement, and that a contingent commitment should not be considered until the occurrence of the event or date on which the contingency is based. It is understood that, nevertheless, the Service takes the position that when cash is to be contributed periodically to a partnership, the net worth requirement is determined only at the time when the contributions are made, whether contingent or not.[55]

The Service has ruled that nonrecourse loans by a general partner and loans by a third party to a limited partnership may, under certain circumstances, be considered contributions to partnership capital.[56] It is possible that the Service would regard such reclassified loans as contributions to partnership capital for purposes of applying the net worth guidelines.

10. REVENUE PROCEDURE 74-17: THE NATURE OF THE GENERAL PARTNER'S INTEREST

To make the real estate limited partnership attractive to potential investors, it is common to allocate most or all of the limited partnership tax benefits to the limited partners. Problems that may arise as a result of such allocations are discussed in Chapter 4.[57] For the purposes of this chapter, the question is: Must any allocation of these items be made to the general partner in order for him or it to be considered a general partner and for the limited partnership to be classified as a partnership for tax purposes?

As with the safe harbor rules, the Service's position with respect to the nature of the general partner's interest was the subject of much speculation and concern. In 1973, the then Commissioner of Internal Revenue stated publicly for the first time that, in the Service's view, a partnership must have a viable general partner with a real interest in partnership affairs. The general partner should have a stake in the venture and share realistically in its success or failure.

The Service's position was stated formally in Revenue Procedure 74-17,[58] which applies to the issuance of advance rulings or determination letters concerning classification of organizations as partnerships. If the rules of this revenue procedure, as well as all other provisions of the Code, regulations, revenue rulings, and other revenue procedures (including Revenue Prcedure 72-13) are satisfied, a favorable ruling generally will be issued; if the rules of the revenue procedure are not met, the Service probably will decline to rule. Although the revenue procedure is not intended to be applied when taxpayers' returns are audited, agents may use the guidelines on an informal basis during audits.

With respect to the nature of the general partner's interest, the revenue procedure provides that the interests of all general partners, in the aggregate, in each material item of partnership income, gain, loss, deduction, or credit must be equal to at least 1% of each such item throughout the term of the partnership, without regard to limited partnership interests the general partners may own.

The 1% test refers to tax items; to satisfy the test, a general partner presumably need not have a corresponding interest in partnership capital and distributions, or make a capital contribution to the partnership. An allocation of tax items without a corresponding interest in partnership capital and distributions, however, might raise other problems, as discussed in Chapter 4.[59]

In addition to the 1% test, which is not difficult to satisfy, the revenue procedure sets out other requirements. The aggregate deductions to be claimed by the partners as their distributive share of partnership losses for the first two years of partnership operations must not exceed the amount of equity capital invested in the limited partnership. Since real estate limited partnerships are exempt from the "at risk rules" [60] and may provide a higher ratio of tax deductions to invested capital than one to one, this requirement has caused many real estate limited partnerships to discard the idea of obtaining a tax ruling.

Finally, the revenue procedure requires that a creditor who makes a nonrecourse loan to the limited partnership must not have or acquire as a result of making the loan any direct or indirect interest in the profits, capital, or property of the limited partnership other than as a secured creditor.

11. SHOULD A PRIVATE LIMITED PARTNERSHIP SEEK A TAX RULING?

Unless required by state security law regulators or other bodies, few private real estate limited partnerships now seek private rulings with respect to federal income tax status. Instead, an opinion of tax counsel usually is obtained.

Avoiding applying for a ruling saves time, avoids expense, and maintains some confidentiality (since private rulings are now mostly a matter of public record). In addition, to obtain a ruling under current guidelines, the business aspects of the transaction must be structured rather unfavorably. This is especially true with respect to the requirement that deductions for the first two years of the limited partnership's existence cannot exceed equity capital.

Further, even if the unreasonable revenue procedure guidelines can be satisfied, current Service rulings may be too "contingent" to be worthwhile. As was discussed earlier, most real estate limited partnerships will not have the corporate characteristic of continuity of life but will have centralized management. With respect to the remaining two characteristics, at least one of which must be absent to have a partnership for tax purposes, the Service apparently conditions its rulings in the following manner: (a) The absence of limited liability is conditioned on the continued maintenance by the general partner of substantial assets that can be reached by creditors; [61] and (b) the absence of free transferability of interests may be conditioned on whether the provision in the partnership agreement requiring general partner consent before transfer is, in fact, a meaningful restriction, that is, on whether the general partner really would refuse to consent under ordinary circumstances. Thus, even if a ruling is obtained, partnership tax status may be left to a fact determination on audit. Such a ruling cannot give much comfort.

NOTES

1. The exceptions include a Subchapter S corporation and a real estate investment trust ("REIT"). For purposes of syndicating an investment in real estate, neither entity may be as advantageous as a limited partnership. However, the recent liberalization of the Subchapter S provisions should be considered. Subchapter S Revision Act of 1982, P.L. 97-354 (1982). Although a Subchapter S corporation is generally limited to 35 stockholders, a new entity may now derive all of its revenues from passive sources, which includes rents from real property. *See* Secs. 1371 *et seq.* Thus, Subchapter S form might be appropriate for a real estate syndication of no more than 35 shareholders if special allocations are not desired, corporate governance is acceptable and deductions of no

more than $1 for each $1 invested are contemplated. An REIT must have at least 100 investors (with other ominous ownership restrictions), almost all taxable income must be distributed rather than reinvested, and operating loss deductions may not be passed through to the investors. *See* Secs. 856 *et seq.*

Unless otherwise indicated, all section references in Chapters 2 to 7 are to sections of the Internal Revenue Code of 1954, as amended through November 30, 1982.

2. Sec. 761(a).

3. Treas. Reg. §301.7701-1(c). *Commissioner v. Tower*, 327 U.S. 280 (1946).

    Unless otherwise indicated, all references to treasury regulations are to the regulations promulgated under the Internal Revenue Code of 1954, as amended through November 30, 1982.

4. *See* Treas. Reg. §301.7701-3(a); *Fowler v. United States*, 78-2 USTC ¶9800 (N.D. Cal. 1978); *Buckley v. United States*, 76-1 USTC ¶9473 (W.D. Tex. 1976); *Francis L. Burns*, 13 B.T.A. 293 (1928).

5. Treas. Reg. §301.7701-1(c); *Hubert M. Luna*, 42 T.C. 1067, 1077 (1964). *See also* Rev. Rul. 77-332, 1977-2 C.B. 484 (non-CPA principals who were not recognized under state law as partners but who had most rights, privileges, and liabilities in common with regular partners were treated as partners for federal income tax purposes); Private Letter Ruling 8046064 (August 21, 1980).

6. Treas. Reg. §301.7701-1(c)

7. *See Morrisey v. Commissioner*, 296 U.S. 344 (1935).

8. Treas. Reg. §301.7701. Promulgated in 1960, these regulations were largely patterned after the Supreme Court's decision in *Morrisey v. Commissioner*, 296 U.S. 344 (1935), which set out various characteristics of an "association." *See generally* Note, "Tax Classification of Limited Partnerships," 90 HARV. L. REV. 745 (1977).

9. *See* Prop. Treas. Reg. §301.7701-2(a) (5), 45 Fed. Reg. 70909A (October 27, 1980) (extending Uniform Limited Partnership Act references to the 1976 Revision). *See, however*, discussion *infra*, this chapter's Section 4. For general discussion of the 1976 Revision and tax questions, *see* Banoff, "Can Tax Practitioners Support the Revised ULPA?," 60 TAXES 97 (1982).

10. Prop. Treas. Reg. §301.7701-1 through §301.7701-3, 42 Fed. Reg. 1038 (Jan. 5, 1977), withdrawn, 42 Fed. Reg. 1489 (Jan. 7, 1977).

11. Treas. Reg. §301.7701-2(a)(1). This regulation states that an association is "an organization whose characteristics require it to be classified for purposes of taxation as a corporation rather than as another type of organization such as a partnership or a trust."

12. *Id.; see Maurice W. Grober*, 31 CCH Tax Ct. Mem. 1179 (1972), *aff'd sub nom. Kahn v. Commissioner*, 499 F.2d 1186 (2d Cir. 1974).

13. Rev. Rul. 79-106, 1979-1 C.B. 448, which is stated to be based on the Tax Court decision in *Philip G. Larson*, 66 T.C. 159 (1976), *acq.* 1979-1 C.B. 1.

14. Treas. Reg. §301.7701-2(a)(2).

15. Treas. Reg. §301.7701-2(a)(3).

16. Treas. Reg. §301.7701-2(b).

17. Treas. Reg. §301-7701-2(b)(1). However, the Service has ruled that this provision has significance only if there exist separate interests that could compel dissolution on the occurrence of these events. Rev. Rul. 77-214, 1977-1 C.B. 408 (two wholly owned subsidiaries that formed a German GmbH as partners were not such separate interests). *Cf. Zuckman v. United States*, 524 F.2d 729 (Ct. Cl. 1975) (usual state law provision about a

partnership dissolution controlled for continuity of life issue, even though partnership agreement provided otherwise).

18. Treas. Reg. §301-7701-2(b)(1); *see Glensder Textile Co.,* 46 B.T.A. 176 (1942) (Acq.).

19. Treas Reg. §301.7701-2(b)(3).

20. *Id. See also* note 9, *supra.* For a period of time there was a "continuity of life" problem with respect to California limited partnerships. This problem was apparently resolved by California legislation. *See* Rev. Rul. 74-320, 1974-2 C.B. 404.

21. Treas. Reg. §301.7701-2(c)(1).

22. Treas. Reg. §301.7701-2(c)(4).

23. Treas. Reg. §301.7701-3(b)(2). *See also* Private Letter Rulings 7737049 (June 17, 1977); 7813117 (December 30, 1977); and 7821139 (February 28, 1978).

24. *See Philip G. Larson,* 66 T.C. 159 (1976), acq. 1979-1 C.B. 1.

25. *See* Prop. Treas. Reg. §301.7701-2(c) (4), 45 Fed. Reg. 70909 (October 27, 1980), which focuses on the 1976 Revision's permission to grant limited partners the right to remove the general partner.

26. *See* pp. 11-12, *supra.*

27. Treas. Reg. §301.7701-2(d)(1). *See* Prop. Treas. Reg. §301.7701-2(a)(2)(3), (4) and (g) example 1, 45 Fed. Reg. 75909 (November 17, 1980) (presumably with respect to limited liability companies.) *and* Announcement 81-14, 1981-5 I.R.B. 65.

28. *Id.*

29. Treas. Reg. §301.7701-2(d)(2).

30. *Id.*

31. *Contra, Philip G. Larson,* 66 T.C. 1959 (1976), discussed *infra* at p. 31.

32. Treas. Reg. §301.7701-2(d)(2).

33. Rev. Proc. 72-13, 1972-1 C.B. 735; Rev. Proc. 74-17, 1974-1 C.B. 438.

34. Treas. Reg. §301.7701-2(e)(1).

35. *Id.*

36. *Id. Compare* Rev. Rul. 77-214, 1977-1 C.B. 408 (there was free transferability when a common corporate parent controlled the two partners, its wholly owned subsidiaries); Private Letter Ruling 7934096 (May 24, 1979) (partnership status upheld under similar circumstances); and *MCA Inc., et al. v. United States,* 80-2 USTC ¶9617 (C.D. Cal. 1980).

37. Rev. Rul. 77-137, 1977-1 C.B. 178.

38. Treas. Reg. §301.7701-3(b)(2)Ex.(1).

39. Treas. Reg. §301.7701-2(e)(2).

40. *Philip G. Larson,* 66 T.C. 159 (1976). *See also Daniel S. Chaffin,* 35 CCH Tax Ct. Mem. 590 (1976). On January 18, 1978, the government withdrew its appeal in *Larson,* thereby permitting the Tax Court's holding to stand. The *Chaffin* appeal was also dismissed. On March 19, 1979, the Service acquiesced to the Larson decision, 1979-1 C.B. 1; *see also Rev. Rul 79-106,* 1979-1 C.B. 448.

41. 66 T.C. at 181-82. This holding is contrary to the inference in the regulations, see discussion on pp. 28-29, *supra,* that a corporate general partner must have substantial assets.

42. 66. T.C. at 185-85.

43. *Philip G. Larson,* 65 T.C. No. 10, withdrawn on November 7, 1975.

44. *Zuckman v. United States,* 524 F.2d 729 (Ct. Cl. 1975). Effective October 1, 1982, the United States Court of Claims was reorganized into the United States Claims Court and the United States Court of Appeals For The Federal Circuit. Federal Court Improvements Act of 1982, P.L. 97-164, 96 Stat. 25 (1982). The Claims Court serves essentially the same function as the former trial division of the United States Court of Claims and the United States Court of Appeals For The Federal Circuit serves as the appellate body for the Claims Court.

45. *See* text discussion accompanying note 13, *supra* (this chapter).

46. 42 Fed. Reg. 1038 (Jan. 5, 1977).

47. 42 Fed. Reg. 1489 (Jan. 7. 1977).

48. Proposed Treas. Reg. §301.7701-2(a)(1) (withdrawn).

49. Proposed Treas. Reg. §301.7701-2(f)(2) (withdrawn).

50. *See* WALL STREET JOURNAL, Jan. 6, 1977 at 16, col. 4; N.Y. TIMES, Jan. 6, 1977 at A-11, col. 3.

51. Real estate investments generally have been excluded from recent legislation curtailing the tax benefits of tax shelter vehicles.

52. In addition to the revenue procedures discussed herein, the Service has issued a checklist of required information to be submitted with requests for rulings concerning partnership classification. The information generally will demonstrate compliance with the revenue procedures discussed in the text. Rev. Proc. 75-16, 1975-1 C.B. 676.

53. 1972-1 C.B. 735.

54. This requirement was involved in Private Letter Ruling 7942053 (July 23, 1979) in which three corporations served as the sole general partners of a partnership, which in turn served as the sole general partner of a second-tier partnership. The corporations were required to meet the requirements of Rev. Proc. 72-13 only as to the first partnership. The first-tier partnership was only required to maintain substantial assets in order for the second tier partnership to qualify as a partnership.

55. Points to Remember No. 6, 26 TAX LAW. 165 (1972).

56. Rev. Rul. 72-350, 1972-2 C.B. 394; Rev. Rul. 72-135, 1972-1 C.B. 200.

57. *See* pp. 70-73, *infra.*

58. 1974-1 C.B. 438 (Rev. Proc. 74-17 is set out in Appendix 4).

59. *See* pp. 70-73, *infra.*

60. The "at risk rules" are discussed at pp. 62-63, *infra.*

61. *See* Private Letter Rulings 8143076 (July 30, 1981) and 8150077 (September 17, 1981).

CHAPTER 3

TAX TREATMENT OF THE PARTNERSHIP

This chapter discusses the federal income tax treatment of a limited partnership. It assumes that proper care has been taken to assure that the entity is classified as a partnership for tax purposes, as discussed in Chapter 2.

1. PARTNERSHIP AS A CONDUIT

The most important point to remember is that a properly constituted partnership is not subject to the payment of federal income taxes; instead, it is treated as a conduit through which the partners realize income, gains, and losses.[1] Thus, the partners must report as income their distributive shares of the partnership's income regardless of whether actual cash distributions have been made to them.[2] Likewise, the partners are required to take into account on their own federal income tax returns their distributive shares of the partnership's deductions and losses.[3]

Although they are not taxpaying entities, partnerships are required to file information income tax returns with the Internal Revenue Service.[4] These returns require the listing of all the partnership's items of income and deduction.[5] The returns do not compute tax liability; they merely inform the Service of the year's results. The information return (Form 1065) is discussed in Section 8 of this chapter.

2. CHARACTERIZATION OF ITEMS OF INCOME, GAIN, LOSS, DEDUCTION, AND CREDIT

Although for tax purposes a partnership generally is viewed as a conduit or record keeper, there are certain instances when a partnership is treated as an entity separate from its partners. The most common example of this is the characterization of items of income, gain, loss, deduction, or credit. The characterization occurs at the entity level and not at the partner level.[6]

The regulations state that "[t]he character in the hands of a partner of any item of income, gain, loss, deduction, or credit . . . shall be determined as if such item were realized directly from the source from which realized by the partnership or incurred in the same manner as incurred by the partnership." [7] The regulations also provide an example: "[A] partner's distributive share of gain from the sale of depreciable property used in the trade or business of the partnership shall be considered as gain from the sale of such depreciable property in the hands of the partner." [8]

The partnership attaches a schedule for each partner to its yearly tax return. This schedule, called a K-1, articulates the partner's share of income and deduction for the year.[9] A copy of the K-1 is sent to the partner for his information.

On each K-1, the partnership reports the partner's distributive share of seven specific classes of income, gain, loss, deduction, and credit.[10] Six of the classes are:

1. Short-term capital gains and losses;
2. Long-term capital gains and losses;
3. Gains and losses on dispositions of certain property used in a trade or business and involuntary conversions;
4. Charitable contributions;
5. Dividends and interest; [11] and
6. Taxes subject to the foreign tax credit.

The seventh specific category is not articulated in the Code. Rather, the Service is authorized to list items that must be specifically reported.[12] For real estate limited partnerships, these include gain or loss recognized on distributions of money or cash,[13] tax preference items (such as accelerated depreciation), investment interest expense,[14] and all items that are subject to a special allocation under the partnership agreement.[15] The Tax Reform Act of 1976 added or amended several items that revised regulations may require to be itemized. These include the additional first-year depreciation allowance,[16] real property construction period interest and taxes,[17] and interest prepaid by a cash basis taxpayer.[18]

The character of the preceding items is important because they may affect the computation of a partner's personal income tax. As is discussed in Chapter 4, each partner is required to report his distributive share of all classes of income, gain, loss, deduction, and credit on his federal income tax return.

There is also an eighth "catchall" class, which consists of the partnership's taxable income or loss exclusive of the items described by the seven specific classes.[19] This eighth class usually constitutes the operating net income of the partnership. The operating net income of the partnership generally is determined in the same manner as the taxable income of an individual.[20] At the partnership level, however, no deductions are allowed for personal exemptions, taxes subject to the foreign tax credit, charitable contributions, net operating losses, certain itemized deductions of individuals, 60% of net long-term capital gains, and capital loss carry-overs.[21] If allowable, these items, or the allocable shares of such items, may be deducted by the individual partners.

The Service has announced that partners must be advised of their share of post-1980 investment in property qualifying for the investment tax credit, accelerated cost recovery deductions for 15-year real property, the purchase date of property acquired before 1981 for which the partnership elects additional first-year depreciation, and other less applicable items.[22]

Since a K-1 is received after the end of each year, the limited partnership agreement might require the general partner to send an estimate of tax results to the limited partners in the fall of the preceding year. This is often useful for tax planning by the investors.

The ability to characterize certain items of income at the partnership level is especially important to limited partners whose dealings in real estate outside the partnership are of sufficient magnitude to constitute them "dealers" for tax purposes. Dealers are persons actively engaged in the business of holding real estate for resale, and generally they cannot report real estate gains as capital gains. If such individuals were to purchase an interest in an apartment building directly, their gain on the sale of the building might be taxed at ordinary rates.[23] If the partnership's activities do not deem it a "dealer," any gain realized as such a sale would be capital gain, and the otherwise "dealer-partner" could realize his distributive share of such gain as capital gain.[24] This result, however, occurs only if the "dealer-partner" holds his partnership interest for investment and not as part of his real property inventory.[25]

If the partnership's activities cause it to be a "dealer" in real estate, however, the reverse could happen. "Nondealer" partners could find themselves realizing ordinary income on the sale of their interests in the partnership or on the partnership's sale of the project.[26] Several large public limited partnerships permit the general partners to buy and sell real properties and to reinvest the proceeds in new properties. "Nondealer" partners may risk "dealer" treatment for such partnerships if the activities of the partnerships are deemed to be the buying and selling of properties in the ordinary course of business.

3. TAX ELECTIONS

Virtually all tax elections affecting the computation of taxable income derived from a partnership must be made by the partnership and cannot be made by the individual partners.[27] If it is desirable that the partnership's property be depreciated using a recovery percentage other than the statutory accelerated rate,[28] the partnership must file the proper election with its information return.[29] Elections for the nonrecognition of gain or loss from the exchange of property held for productive use or investment,[30] from involuntary conversion,[31] from certain sales of low-income housing projects,[32] and for electing not to use the now automatic installment method of reporting income,[33] likewise must be made by the partnership.[34]

The requirement that these elections be made by the partnership is more than a formality. If the partnership fails to make a particular election, the partners must conform to the treatment prescribed in the absence of an election.[35] The partners cannot change the partnership's election or omission to make an election on their individual returns.

We suggest that the partnership agreement specifically require the general partners to make the desired elections.[36] Thus, for example, if the partnership chooses not to depreciate its property by the statutory recovery percentage method, the partnership agreement should so provide. Some partnership elections may be unfavorable to some of the partners. Yet, "[a]ll partnership elections are applicable to all partners equally. . . ."[37] Therefore, a clearly articulated partnership agreement is essential.

Elections made by a partnership apply only to the items of that partnership and not to the partner's other items or interests.[38] It is possible, therefore, to be a partner in two or more partnerships that have made differing elections.

4. ACCOUNTING METHODS

The choice between cash receipts and disbursements and the accrual method of accounting [39] is also made by the partnership.[40] It is not necessary that the partnership use the same method used by its partners. Thus a partner using the cash-basis method of accounting would have to include in his income his proportionate share of partnership items that have been accrued but have not been received by an accrual basis partnership in which he is a partner.

In the past, most real estate syndications used the cash receipts and disbursements method of accounting. Through prudent control over when income items were received and when expense items were paid,[41] partnerships using the cash receipts and disbursements method of accounting could control, to an extent, the timing of the realization of income and the taking of deductions. This method enabled them to attempt, by prepaying, to accelerate the taking of certain deductions, such as interest, into the early taxable years of the partnership. The Service, however, has aggressively challenged many of the attempted deduction accelerations.[42] Finally, the Tax Reform Act of 1976 reduced the benefits of construction period losses and eliminated the ability to accelerate deduction of certain items including, most notably, interest.[43]

Without the ability to accelerate interest and other construction period deductions, the cash receipts and disbursements method may not be more favorable than the accrual method. It may be of some continued benefit when there are substantial fees to be paid. These so-called soft costs often include loan commitment or standby loan fees, rent-up fees, management fees that are in addition to the usual yearly fees, and "guaranteed payments" (discussed in Chapters 4 and 6). Early payment under the cash basis method may accelerate such deductions. However, the Service may question the timing of the deductions or, indeed, their deductibility.[44] If the fees are paid to affiliates of the builder or promoter, the Service may assert that they are disguised capital expenditures that should be amortized or never deducted.

The accrual method of accounting is generally considered to give a more accurate picture of financial operations. In addition, the reporting of income and deductions under the accrual method is less likely to be challenged by the Service. Income and deductions are reported in the year in which the right to receive or duty to pay is fixed, regardless of when actually received or paid.[45] Interest is deducted, therefore, when the liability is incurred, that is, over the term of the loan.[46]

Many real estate limited partnerships may be better advised to elect the accrual method of accounting. Deductions are available before payment under this method (e.g., deduction when interest accrues, or when real estate taxes become due, although payment is not made until the following year). The Service is more likely to accept accrual accounting without objection. Finally, use of the accrual method should enable a real estate partnership to take a properly timed deduction for interest on a net construction loan, even if it can be argued that the interest is never "paid" because it is subtracted from each loan installment by the lender.[47] (If a cash-basis partnership is involved, care should be taken to draw down the gross amount of the loan and to remit, by partnership check, the interest.)

5. SELECTION OF TAXABLE YEAR

Most real estate limited partnerships use a calender year for accounting purposes. As previously discussed, each partner in a partnership must include in his taxable income his allocable share of the partnership's income, gain, loss, deduction, or credit for any taxable year of the partnership ending within or with the taxable year of the partner.[48] The taxable year of a partnership is determined as though the partnership were a separate taxpayer.[49] Since most investors in real estate syndications are individuals who are on a calendar year of accounting for tax purposes, and since it is usually desired that deductions be maximized for those individuals, the partnership usually selects the calendar year as its annual accounting period.

The potential perils of choosing a fiscal year (other than a calendar year) can be seen in the following example. A partnership created on January 1, 1983 adopts a June 30 fiscal year of tax accounting. The partners, who report income on a calendar year basis, would be entitled to report on their 1983 income tax returns their shares of the partnership's deductions and losses only for the period ending June 30, 1983. The partnership's deductions and losses allocable to the period ending after June 30, 1983 and through December 31, 1983 would be reported on the partners' 1984 tax returns. The ability to utilize the partnership's losses and deductions allocable to the last six months of 1983 would be effectively deferred for one year.

A partnership is not, however, free to choose any taxable year. It may adopt a taxable year that is the same as that of all its principal partners[50] (that is, partners having at least a 5% interest in the partnership's profits or capital.[51]) It may adopt a calendar year if all its principal partners do not use the same taxable year.[52] In any other case, a newly formed partnership must secure the prior approval of the Service for the adoption of any taxable year.[53] Technically, when a newly formed limited partnership has no principal partner, which could happen with respect to a large syndication, it is supposed to secure the approval of the Service to adopt any taxable year. In practice, the Service does not object to such a partnership adopting a calendar year.

If the partnership wishes to adopt, or to change to, a fiscal year different from that of all its principal partners, it must apply for approval.[54] The partnership must establish to the satisfaction of the Service that there is a valid business purpose for making the "inconsistent" adoption or change.[55]

Other than a desire to have the tax accounting period coincide with the natural cycle of the partnership's business,[56] there is little guidance as to what constitutes a valid business purpose. The Service has ruled that the ability to report a full year's operations and the convenience of completing income tax returns at a certain time are not valid business purposes.[57]

When requesting approval to adopt or change to a certain fiscal year,[58] the partnership must be prepared to meet the issue of tax avoidance by, or tax deferment for, its partners. It is difficult to sustain that there is no tax avoidance or deferment motive when the partnership has net income and wishes a taxable year ending only a few months after the end of the taxable year of its partners. The Service is more willing to allow a fiscal year ending within three months of the end of the taxable year of its partners and has devised a mechanism that must be adhered to by the partners for minimizing tax deferment in such cases.[59]

6. LAND TRUSTS AND NOMINEE CORPORATIONS

A partnership is chosen as the form for the business entity for the principal purpose of allowing the income and deductions to pass through the partnership to the partners in their individual capacities. For a variety of reasons, such as to avoid usury laws, to eliminate personal liability on mortgage debt, and to insulate against liability for tort claims, the partnership may consider utilizing a land trust or a "nominee corporation" to hold legal title to the project.

If properly structured, a land trust should be treated as a "grantor trust" so that, for tax purposes, the trust's income and deductions will pass through to the partnership as the beneficiary of the trust and will be included in the partnership's income and deductions.[60]

A similar principle applies to the use of a nominee corporation. Use of these corporations, however, entails risk of significant adverse tax consequences. If the corporation is treated as the owner of the property, the income and deductions resulting from the operation of the property must be reported by the corporation and not by the partners. If there is such a determination and the project generates tax losses, which are the backbone of the tax shelter aspect of a real estate limited partnership, the benefit of the loss deductions will be entirely lost to the partners.

Unfortunately, the cases involving nominee corporations do not provide the investor with much reliable information as to when the use of such corporations will not result in adverse tax consequences. Some cases have focused on the issue of whether the nominee corporation's existence should be disregarded for tax purposes and, in general, taxpayers have not had much success.[61] Other cases do not disregard the existence of the corporation but rather focus on whether the nominee corporation is an "agent" for the partnership. As in the "disregard" cases, taxpayers have had little success in these cases as well.[62] In determining whether an "agency" exists, several factors are considered, including whether the corporation operates in the name and for the account of the partnership, whether the corporation binds the partnership by its actions, whether the corporation's business purpose is the carrying on of the duties of an agent, and whether the corporation's relationship with the partnership depends on the fact that it is owned by the partnership.[63]

In view of the great uncertainty in this area it is advisable to avoid use of these entities or at least to obtain a tax ruling.[64]

7. STATE TAX TREATMENT

Not all state taxing authorities follow the Service's definition of what is a partnership: Investors may find themselves in the position of having the partnership taxed as a corporation for state tax purposes and as a partnership for federal tax purposes.

Determining that the partnership will be treated as such for state tax law purposes may not be the end of state tax concerns. Some states impose a tax on unincorporated businesses conducted within the state. It is usually not difficult to understand the state tax picture if the partnership engages in business in only one state. Partnerships engaged in business in several states may have some difficulty. Care should be taken to focus on state and local taxation, as these taxes can no longer be considered to be *de minimis.*

8. THE PARTNERSHIP TAX RETURN

As discussed earlier, partnerships are required to file an information return [65] that is due within 3 1/2 months of the close of the partnership's taxable year.[66] On Form 1065, the partnership states the amounts of partnership items of income, gain, loss, deduction, and credit as well as the name and address of each partner. Form 1065 is an important tool used by the Service to determine which partnerships will be audited. Form 1065, for example, requires disclosure of whether the partnership has utilized non-recourse debt financing, a factor in "abusive" tax shelters as well as in valid real estate limited partnerships. Further, in addition to the items mentioned previously, Form 1065 and its Schedule K-1 require, among other things, disclosure of each partner's percentage of capital, profits, losses, and time devoted to the partnership; whether the partner is a limited partner; and the share of partnership liabilities for which each partner is personally liable. The Schedule K-1 also must state the capital account of each partner, the partner's share of nonrecourse liabilities, and whether each partner's interest in the partnership decreased or terminated during the year.

Form 1065 and Schedule K-1 are reproduced in Appendix 5. The general partner is responsible for causing the partnership to file an adequate Form 1065. Indeed, the Service has asserted that a general partner is an income tax return preparer for purposes of the penalties for negligent or intentional disregard of the rules or understatement of tax liability.[67]

9. AUDITING THE REAL ESTATE LIMITED PARTNERSHIP

a. General The Service has established an active program of auditing real estate limited partnerships, as well as of other types of tax-sheltered partnerships.[68] Indeed, the Service plans to examine 25% of the tax returns of partnerships reporting losses of more than $25,000. Chapters 4 through 7 discuss the many substantive tax questions that may arise; all are subject, of course, to IRS review.

IRS agents will generally focus on so-called soft costs, that is, "front-end" or "start-up" deductions that the Service may assert should not be deducted but rather should be capitalized. These are discussed in Chapter 6. The Service will also audit expenses that perhaps should be deducted over a period of time.

Expenditures that are, in the Service's view, for purposes other than the partnership claims, such as monies paid to the syndicator or to the builder but called other than syndication fees (which are not deductible) or builder's profit (which must be depreciated over a long period of time) will also be carefully audited. Similarly, the Service will concern itself with the true value of assets acquired by the partnership in transactions with related parties to assure that depreciation deductions are not overstated. Another subject of concern is often the receipt of partnership interests for services.[69]

Special allocations among partners, as discussed in Chapter 4, are of great interest to the Service. Whether the partnership is complying with the construction period rules on interest and taxes (discussed in Chapter 6) and whether certain financing expenses are immediately deductible are also areas of concern to the Service.

b. The Service's "Abusive Tax Shelter" Program The Service, in recent years, has been quite concerned about what it perceives to be "abusive tax shelters" that are entered into without true economic motivation or where the substance of the transaction is quite different from the form the parties have attributed to it. Although the "abusive tax shelter" audit program generally is directed at more exotic "investments" (e.g., master recordings, motion pictures), real estate limited partnerships are included in the program also, and the tax returns of such partnerships are subjected to close scrutiny.[70] One of the major concerns of the "abusive" program in relation to real estate limited partnerships is that a partnership may claim greatly inflated values for real estate assets transferred to the partnership by related parties in order to artificially inflate its depreciation deductions.

Even if the real estate limited partnership is deemed to be "abusive," there is a greater possibility than before that the Service will be willing to settle the matter.[71] IRS personnel dealing with tax shelter cases have been directed to identify certain aspects as being susceptible to settlement.[72] The Service modified its previous "no settlement" approach in this area because of the strain that tax shelters are placing on its resources.[73]

c.   Recent Administrative Provisions.   In recent years, Congress has enacted several administrative provisions intended to make the Service more effective in auditing partnerships and imposing deficiencies against partners.

First, there is a civil penalty for the failure of a partnership to file a timely, complete Form 1065.[74] This supplements the criminal penalities for willful failure to file.

The civil penalty is $50 for each month that the return is late or incomplete, or any fraction thereof, not to exceed five months, multiplied by the number of partners in the partnership. Although the penalty is imposed on the partnership, each partner is individually liable to the extent that he would be liable for partnership debts. However, there is a safe harbor where the penalty will not be imposed on partnerships with 10 or fewer individual partners if the partnership is of the kind that historically has not filed partnership returns (e.g., a family business) and if each partner fully reports his share of each partnership item.[75] The penalty also might not be imposed if the partnership can show reasonable cause for the failure to file.[76]

Second, pursuant to the Tax Equity and Fiscal Responsibility Act of 1982 ("TEFRA"), the service generally can now audit a real estate limited partnership at the partnership level.[77] In this connection, TEFRA imposes several complicated procedural audit and other rules. These are set out in the Notes.[78] Unlike the recent past, the Service no longer has to audit each partner. There is currently a large audit backlog because the Service does not have the resources to audit each partner of the many questioned partnerships. The new Service partnership level audit power may prevent future backlogs.

Third, pursuant to TEFRA, the statue of limitations to audit a partnership has been, in effect, extended. The limitations period is now three years from the later of the date that a partnership return was filed or the date the return was due.[79] Previously, the limitations period was based on the partner's personal income tax return. Thus, for the future, if a partnership fails to file a partnership return, the statue of limitations on partnership items remains indefinitely open for the partner. In addition, pursuant to TEFRA a "tax matters" partner must be appointed. This partner must be given the power to extend the audit statute of limitations and to bind all of the partners to that extension.[80] This authority cannot be limited by the other partners. Thus, the Service will no longer have to obtain an extension from each partner. Note that partnerships with ten or fewer natural partners and no special allocation are not subject to the new rules.[81]

The new limitations extension rules are a mixed blessing. The Service no longer needs to obtain extensions from the partners, many of whom cannot be readily found. However, if the partners do not execute individual waivers, the three-year statute of limitations might expire for all of their tax liability except the partnership item. This eliminates the previous concern as to whether a taxpayer can or should file a statute of limitations extension only for the partnership items when the taxpayer is informed by the Service that extension is being requested because of a partnership audit. Tax advisers usually recommended attempting to limit a waiver, if one was to be given, to the possible partnership deficiency. In this regard, TEFRA provides that an individual waiver, unless specifically referenced to partnershp items, will not serve to extend the time to assess a deficiency arising from such items.[82]

Fourth, pursuant to the Economic Recovery Tax Act of 1981 (ERTA) and TEFRA, the interest rate on deficiencies and the penalties for negligent or intentional disregard of income tax rules have been increased.[83] Previously, the interest rate on overpayments and underpayments of taxes was 90% of the prime rate. This has been changed to 100% of the prime rate.[84] The rate will be adjusted semi-annually and interest will be compounded daily. Daily compounding is quite onerous. There has long been penalties of 5% of any deficiency attributable to any extent to the negligent or intentional disregard of income tax rules and 50% of any deficiency attributable to any extent to fraud.[85] ERTA has imposed an additional penalty of 50% of the interest charged on that portion of the deficiency attributable to negligent or intentional disregard of the income tax rules and TEFRA has imposed a like penalty on interest charged on that portion of the deficiency attributable to fraud.[86]

Fifth, ERTA added a penalty to apply in the case of deficiencies caused by overvaluations of assets.[87] The penalty applies where a 50% overvaluation of assets creates a tax deficiency of $1,000 or more. The amount of the penalty is a percentage of the resulting deficiency, which varies from 10%, in cases of valuation exceeding the correct value by more than 50% but less than 100%, to 30%, in cases where the claimed value is over 250% of the correct value. The overvaluation penalty is imposed without regard to the negligence or intent of the taxpayer but may, in the discretion of the Service, be waived or reduced if the taxpayer demonstrates that there is a reasonable basis for the claimed valuation or that the claimed valuation was made in good faith.

TEFRA has provided a number of additional penalties including (i) a penalty which can be imposed on any person who organizes, assists or participates in the sale of any partnership or other interest and who knowingly makes a material false statement about the availability of certain tax benefits or a gross overvaluation statement on a material matter;[88] (ii) a penalty for any person who aids or abets in the preparation of any portion of a tax return, claim or other tax document and who knows that such portion will be used in connection with a material matter under the revenue laws and knows that such portion will result in an understatement of tax liability for another person;[89] and (iii) a penalty for substantial understatements of tax liability which result from a position taken by a taxpayer unless the taxpayer bases his position upon substantial authority or adequately discloses the facts on which it is based (if not arising from an abusive tax shelter) or unless the taxpayer reasonably believes that the position was more likely than not correct (if arising from an abusive tax shelter).[90]

The combination of the foregoing creates a substantial disincentive, as was intended by Congress, for a person to engage in questionable transactions in the hope of avoiding audit. For example, one who engaged in the "audit lottery" in 1982 for his 1981 return by using an overstated asset value is subject to a 10–30% penalty on the overstatement deficiency, an approximate 20% per annual interest charge, a 5% negligence penalty on the entire deficiency, and another negligence penalty of 50% of the interest charge on the overstatement deficiency.

NOTES

1. Sec. 701; Treas. Reg. §1.701-1.
2. Sec. 702(a); Treas. Reg. §1.702-1(a); *George F. Johnson*, 21 T.C. 733 (1954).
3. *Id.* The partners are also subject to the restrictions imposed by Sections 465 and 704(d).
4. Sec. 6031; *see* Form 1065.
5. Treas. Reg. §1.6031-1(a).
6. Sec. 702(b); *United States v. Basye*, 410 U.S. 441 (1973); *Barham v. United States*, 429 F.2d 40 (5th Cir. 1970). There has been considerable controversy with respect to whether

a partnership should be viewed either as an entity, where items of income, gain, loss, etc. are characterized first at the partnership level and then passed through to the individual partners, or as an aggregate, where the character of an item is determined as though realized directly by the partners. The *Basye* decision appears to adopt the view that all items are to be characterized first at the partnership level. The Internal Revenue Service has apparently also taken this position, Rev. Rul. 75-113, 1975-1 C.B. 19, but has indicated that, under certain circumstances, an aggregate approach may be appropriate, Rev. Rul. 75-62, 1975-1 C.B. 188. *See also* Secs. 6221-6232.

7. Treas. Reg. §1.702-1(b)

8. *Id.*

9. Treas. Reg. §1.6031-1(a); *see* Form 1065, Schedule K-1. Schedule K-1 can be found in Appendix 5.

10. The Schedule K-1 is patterned after Sec. 702(a)(1)-(7) and Treas. Reg. §1.702-1(a).

11. Specifically, dividends or interest with respect to which there is an exclusion under Secs. 116 or 128 or a deduction under Part VIII of Subchapter B.

12. Treas. Reg. §1.702-1(a) (8). *See* Rev. Rul. 79-82, 1979-1 C.B. 141. Limited partner distributive shares are no longer net earnings from self-employment for the "social security tax" except for certain guaranteed payments. Sec. 1402 (a) (12). *See* Rev. Rul. 79-53, 1979-1 C.B. 286.

13. *See* Sec. 751(b).

14. Sec. 163(d)(4)(8).

15. *See* Sec. 704(b); discussion on pp. 70–72, *infra.*

16. *See* Sec. 179; discussion on pp. 98–99, *infra.*

17. *See* sec. 189; discussion on pp. 117–120, *infra.*

18. *See* Sec. 461(g); discussion on p. 117, *infra.*

19. Secs. 702(a)(8), 703(a)(1); Treas. Reg. §1.703-1(a)(1).

20. Sec. 703(a); Treas. Reg. §1.703-1(a)(1).

21. Sec. 703(a)(2); Treas. Reg. §1.703-1(a)(2).

22. Announcement 82-9, 1982-3 I.R.B. 48.

23. *See Guy A. Van Heusden,* 44 T.C. 491 (1965), *aff'd,* 369 F.2d 119 (5th Cir. 1966). *But see Scheuber v. Commissioner,* 371 F.2d 996 (7th Cir. 1967).

24. Rev. Rul. 67-188, 1967-1 C.B. 216.

25. *See Corn Products Refining Co. v. Commissioner,* 350 U.S. 46 (1955).

26. *See Morgan A. Stivers,* 32 CCH Tax Ct. Mem. 1139 (1973); *Hyman Podell,* 55 T.C. 429 (1970); Sec. 751(a).

27. Sec. 703(b); Treas. Reg. §1.703-1 (b). There are limited exceptions to the general rule, such as any election under Sec. 57(c) (defining net lease); Secs. 108(b)(5), 108(d)(4) (discharge of indebtedness income); Sec. 617 (certain mining expenditures); Sec. 901 (foreign tax credits); and Treas. Reg. §1.871-10 (nonresident partner election to treat distributive share of partnership real property income on net tax basis).

28. *See* Sec. 168; discussion on pp. 90–94, *infra.*

29. Treas. Reg. §1.703-1(b)(1).

30. Sec. 1031.

31. Sec. 1033. When partnership property is involuntarily converted, the partnership, rather than the individual partners, must replace the converted property. *Estate of Jerome K.*

Goldstein, 35 CCH Tax Ct. Mem. 71 (1976); *Mihran Demirjian,* 54 T.C. 1691 (1970), *aff'd,* 457 F.2d 1 (3d Cir. 1972); *Jordan K. Smith,* 37 CCH Tax Ct. Mem. 1731 (1978). *See McManus v. Commissioner,* 583 F.2d 443 (9th Cir. 1978), *cert. denied,* 440 U.S. 959 (1979); *Alec Rosefsky,* 70 T.C. 909 (1978). *See also* Rev. Rul. 79-82, 79-1 C.B. 141 (a partnership is the qualified electing shareholder that must make Sec. 333 liquidation election).

32. Sec. 1039. Presumably, the replacement qualified housing project would have to be constructed, reconstructed, or acquired by the partnership.

33. Effective October 19, 1980, for dispositions occurring after such date, a partnership will be required to specifically elect out of installment sale treatment under Section 453 where the transaction qualifies in form as an installment sale. Substantial revisions of the installment sale rules were effectuated by the Installment Sales Revision Act of 1980. *See* pp. 146–147, *infra.* Previously, the partnership had to elect installment method reporting. A partnership, unless it elects otherwise, will use the installment method for computing the gain on the sale of real property even if one partner, due to an optional adjustment to the basis of partnership property under Section 743, has a basis in the property greater than that partner's share of the amount realized on the sale. The entire loss should, we believe, be recognized by the partner in the year sustained. *See* Rev. Rul. 79-92, 1979-1 C.B. 180; *John G. Scherf, Jr.,* 20 T.C. 346 (1953). *Compare Albert R. Minchew,* 40 CCH Tax Ct. Mem. 561 (1981).

34. Among other additional elections, the partnership must elect, under Sec. 754, to adjust the basis of partnership property. *See Jones v. United States,* 553 F.2d 667 (Ct. Cl. 1977); Treas. Reg. §1.754-1(b). *Compare* Private Letter Rulings 8007053 (November 3, 1979), and 7804118 (October 27, 1977).

35. *See Estate of Jerome K. Goldstein,* 35 CCH Tax Ct. Mem. 71 (1976); *Boone v. United States,* 374 F. Supp. 115 (D.N.D. 1973).

36. *See* Note, "Procedures and Remedies in Limited Partners' Suits for Breach of the General Partner's Fiduciary Duty," 90 HARV. L. REV. 763 (1977).

37. Treas. Reg. §1.703-1(b)(1).

38. *Id.*

39. Sec. 446. No specific election is required. Instead, the partnership will be required to compute taxable income under the method of accounting the partnership regularly uses to keep its books. Sec. 446(a). The partnership may adopt any permissible method of accounting on its initial income tax return. Treas. Reg. §1.446-1(e)(1).

40. Treas. Reg. §1.703-1(b)(1).

41. Receipts are more difficult to control. Under the doctrine of constructive receipt of income, a cash method taxpayer may be deemed to have received income, even though not actually received, if it is "credited to his account, set apart for him, or otherwise made available so that he may draw upon it at any time. . . ." Treas. Reg. §1.451-2(a). A cash method partnership may not avoid income, therefore, merely by arranging to receive in a later taxable year amounts already due.

42. *See, e.g.,* Rev. Rul. 80-70, 1980-2 C.B. 104; Rev. Rul. 79-229, 1979-2 C.B. 210; Rev. Rul. 75-172, 1975-1 C.B. 145; Rev. Rul. 68-643. 1968-2 C.B. 76; *modified,* Rev. Rul. 69-582, 1969-2 C.B. 29; *see also Edward T. Pratt,* 64 T.C. 203 (1975), *aff'd (on this issue) and rev'd (on another issue),* 550 F.2d 1023 (5th Cir. 1977). In *Martin J. Zaninovich,* 69 T.C. 605 (1978), the Tax Court held that prepaid rent was not immediately deductible even though the prepayment was for a period of less than 12 months. The Ninth Circuit, in reversing the Tax Court, held that where the expenditure creates an asset having a useful life beyond the taxable year of 12 months or less, a full deduction in the year of

payment should be permitted. 616 F.2d 429 (1980). *See also, Blitzer v. United States,* 81-1 U.S.T.C. ¶9262 (Ct. Cl. 1981), *aff'd,* 684 F.2d 874 (Ct. Cl. 1982). *Richard C. Goodwin,* 75 T.C. 424 (1980), *on appeal to 3d. Cir.*

43. Secs. 189, 461(g); *see* pp. 117-120, *infra.*

44. For an extensive treatment of these issues, *see* Chapter 6.

45. Treas. Reg. §1.446-1(c)(1)(ii).

46. *See* Rev. Rul. 68-643, 1968-2 C.B. 76, *modified,* Rev. Rul. 69-582, 1969-2 C.B. 29.

47. *Cf.* Rev. Rul. 74-395, 1974-2 C.B. 45; *Lyndell E. Lay,* 69 T.C. 421 (1977); *John C. Cleaver,* 6 T.C. 452, *aff'd,* 158 F.2d 342 (7th Cir. 1946), *cert. denied,* 330 U.S. 849 (1947). *See also Richard S. Heyman,* 70 T.C. 482 *(1978), aff'd,* 652 F.2d 598 (6th Cir. 1980); *Alan A. Rubnitz,* 67 T.C. 621 (1977); *Kenneth A. Cathcart,* 36 CCH Tax Ct. Mem. 1321 (1977); *John B. Howard,* 36 CCH Tax. Ct. Mem. 1140 (1977); *compare Battlestein v. Commissioner,* 611 F.2d 1033 (5th Cir 1980) and *Donald L. Wilkerson,* 70 T.C. 240 (1978), *rev'd,* 655 F.2d 980 (9th Cir. 1981).

48. Sec. 706(a); Treas. Reg. §1.706-1(a)(1).

49. Sec. 706(b)(1); Treas. Reg. §1.706-1(b)(1)(i).

50. Sec. 706(b)(1); Treas. Reg. §1.706-1(b)(1)(ii). As a corollary, a principal partner may not change to a taxable year that is different from that of the partnership unless he shows a valid business purpose and secures prior approval of the Service. Sec. 706(b)(2); Treas. Reg. §1.706-1(b)(2).

51. Sec. 706(b)(3); Treas. Reg. §1.706-1(b)(3).

52. Treas. Reg. §1.706-1(b)(1)(ii).

53. *Id. See also Oman Construction Co.,* 37 CCH Tax Ct. Mem. 1849 (1978).

54. Sec. 706(b)(1); Treas. Reg. §1.706-1(b)(1)(ii),(iii).

55. Sec. 706(b)(1); Treas. Reg. §1.706-1(b)(4)(iii).

56. Treas. Reg. §1.706-1(b)(4)(iii). The business purpose must be related to the business cycle and must not result in permanent deferral of reporting of income. Rev. Rul. 76-497, 1976-2 C.B. 128.

57. Rev. Rul. 60-182, 1960-1 C.B. 264.

58. To secure approval, the partnership must file Form 1128 with the Service on or before the last date of the month following the close of the taxable year for which approval is sought. Treas. Reg. §1.706-1(b)(4)(ii).

59. Rev. Proc. 72-51, 1972-2 C.B. 832.

60. Sec. 671. *See* Private Letter Ruling 7838080 (June 22, 1978).

61. *See, e.g., Moline Properties, Inc. v. Commissioner,* 319 U.S. 436 (1943); *Ogiony v. Commissioner,* 617 F.2d 14 (2d Cir. 1980), *cert. denied,* 449 U.S. 900 (1980); *Harrison Property Management Co. Inc., v. United States,* 475 F.2d 623 (Ct. Cl. 1973), *cert. denied,* 414 U.S. 1130 (1974); *William B. Strong,* 66 T.C. 12 (1976), *aff'd,* 553 F.2d 94 (2d Cir. 1977); *David F. Bolger,* 59 T.C. 760 (1973). *But see Red Carpet Car Wash, Inc.,* 73 T.C. 676 (1980); *Schlosberg v. United States,* 81-1 U.S.T.C. ¶9272 (E.D. Va. 1981)

62. *See, e.g., National Carbide Corp. v. Commissioner,* 336 U.S. 422 (1949); *Jones v. Commissioner,* 640 F.2d 745 (5th Cir. 1981). *But see Joseph A. Roccaforte,* 77 T.C. 263 (1981).

63. *Joseph A. Roccaforte,* 77 T.C. 263 (1981), citing *National Carbide Corp v. Commissioner,* 336 U.S. 422 (1949).

64. *See, e.g.,* Rev. Rul. 76-26, 1976-1 C.B. 10; Rev. Rul. 75-31, 1975-1 C.B. 10; and Private Letter Ruling 8014106 (January 14, 1980).

65. Sec. 6031; Treas. Reg. §1.6031-1.

66. Sec. 6072; Treas Reg. §1.6031-1(e)(2).

67. Rev. Rul. 81-270, 1981-2 C.B. 250.

68. *See* Internal Revenue Manual-Audit (CCH), Chapter 4200, MT 4236 at pages 7295-51 *et seq.* (October, 1982). *See also* remarks by Jerome Kurtz, Commissioner of Internal Revenue, as reported in 55 TAXES 774 (1977).

69. The Internal Revenue Manual contains a section on the examination of real estate tax shelters. Internal Revenue Manual-Audit (CCH) at 7295-79 (November 6, 1979). This document provides an extensive list of areas to be examined. These are summarized in "Comprehensive Real Estate Tax Shelter Plan Issued by the Service," 52 J. TAX. 115 (1980). *See also* Deductibility of Business Expansion Expenses, Tax Management Memorandum 81-22 (November 2, 1981).

70. *See* "Commissioner's Remarks Focus on Abusive Tax Shelters," 55 J. TAX. 389 (1981). Among the factors that are considered in selecting returns for inclusion in the tax shelter audit program are large net losses, low gross income, large investment tax credits, first or final returns by a partnership, passive investors, and negative capital accounts. Internal Revenue Manual-Audit (CCH) at 7347-31 (October 4, 1982).

71. Internal Revenue Manual-Audit (CCH), Manual Supplement 42G-409 (Rev. 1) at 7429-3 (June 10, 1982).

72. *See* remarks of Roscoe Egger, Commissioner of Internal Revenue as reported in "More Tax Shelter Cases Will Be Settled, Cutting Backlog, Says Service," 56 J. TAX. 53 (1982).

73. *See also* "Tax Shelter Audits Are Hampering Other Exams," 53 J. TAX. 59 (1980).

74. Sec. 6698, for taxable years after 1978.

75. Rev. Proc. 81-11, 1981-1 C.B. 651.

76. *Id.*

77. Secs. 6221-6232.

78. Under TEFRA, proceedings (for example, an audit) to ascertain the proper tax treatment of partnership tax items are to be conducted at the partnership level. Sec. 6221. In general, the Service will, in conducting its proceedings, deal with the "tax matters" partner. However, partners, other than those having less than a 1% interest in a partnership with more than 100 members, are "notice" partners and must be informed of any administrative proceedings pertaining to partnership items and any final adjustments proposed by the Service and are given the right to intervene in such proceedings. Sec. 6223. If the Service and the "tax matters" partner (or any other partner) reach a settlement, the same offer of settlement will be offered to the other partners, who may or may not choose to accept. Sec. 6224. "Notice" partners are not bound by a settlement reached by the "tax matters" partner (or any other partner) and may litigate the issue. Sec. 6224(c)(2). Partners who are not "notice" partners will be bound by the settlement agreement of the "tax matters" partner, unless they elect otherwise. Sec. 6224(c)(3).

    If a settlement is not reached in which all partners join and a final adjustment is made by the Service, the "tax matters" partner may commence an action to contest the final adjustment at the United States Tax Court, United States Claims Court or the United States District Court for the district in which the partnership's principal place of business is located within 90 days of the mailing of the adjustment. Sec. 6226(a). If the "tax matters" partner does not contest during such period, a "notice" partner may do so within 60 days after the period for the "tax matters" partner to commence an action lapses. Sec. 6226(b). If the action is commenced in the Claims Court or the District Court, the partner must deposit with the Service the amount of the tax allegedly owed. Sec. 6226(e).

If the "tax matters" partner does not file a suit, the first action commenced in the Tax Court by a "notice" partner will take priority over all other suits, and all other suits will be dismissed. Sec. 6226(b)(2). If no action is commenced in the Tax Court, the first action filed in the Claims Court or District Court will go forward and subsequent suits will be dismissed. Sec. 6226(b)(3). Each partner is deemed a party to the action and may participate in the action. Sec. 6226(c). The decision of the court is binding upon all the partners. Sec. 6226(f).

Complicated rules are provided for claims for refund with respect to partnership items. Secs. 6227, 6228. Partnerships with ten or fewer natural partners and not having special allocations are, unless they elect otherwise, not subject to these new rules. Sec. 6231(a)(7).

79. Secs. 6229(a), 6501(o). In enacting this provision, Congress has repealed the four-year statute of limitation for public limited partnerships. Sec. 402(c)(5), TEFRA. This provision is discussed in chapter three of the First Edition.

80. Sec. 6229(b).

81. Sec. 6231(a)(1)(B).

82. Sec. 6229(b).

83. Secs. 711, 722, ERTA and Secs. 325, 344, 345, TEFRA.

84. Sec. 6621.

85. Sec. 6653.

86. Sec. 722, ERTA and Sec. 325, TEFRA.

87. Sec. 722, ERTA, adding a new Sec. 6659.

88. Sec. 320, TEFRA, adding a new Sec. 6700. The penalty is the greater of $1000 or 10% of the gross income derived or to be derived by the person from the activity.

89. Sec. 324, TEFRA, adding a new Sec. 6701. The penalty is $1,000.

90. Sec. 323, TEFRA, adding a new Sec. 6661. The penalty is 10% of the amount of any underpayment attributable to the understatement. This penalty is to be applied in coordination with the understatement penalty of Sec. 6659.

CHAPTER 4

TAX TREATMENT
OF THE PARTNERS

Chapter 3 reviewed the tax treatment of the limited partnership at the entity level. This chapter discusses the federal income tax treatment of a limited partnership at the partner level. It assumes that the entity is classified as a partnership for tax purposes, as analyzed in Chapter 2.

1. TAX BASIS OF THE PARTNER'S INTEREST IN THE PARTNERSHIP

a. General. A partner can claim a tax deduction for his share of partnership losses only to the extent of his basis in his partnership interest. Thus, if his basis is $5,000 and his allocable share of partnership losses is $6,000, he may deduct only $5,000 on his personal tax return unless and until his basis increases.

It is also necessary to determine a partner's basis in his partnership interest when computing his gain or loss on the liquidation of the partnership or on the sale or other transfer of his partnership interest. Thus, if a partner has a $20,000 basis in his partnership interest and sells that interest for $30,000, he has a taxable gain of $10,000.

Every partner, both general and limited, has a tax basis for his partnership interest. This tax basis is to be distinguished from a partner's capital account or the partnership's basis in its assets. The effect of nonrecourse

59

debt financing in increasing a partner's basis in a real estate limited partnership, as discussed below, is what permits the so-called "tax shelter" (really tax deferral) effect, and it is an important tax aspect of this form of investment.

Leaving nonrecourse debt financing for later discussion, an investor's basis in his partnership interest is his cost. Whether acquired on formation of the real estate limited partnership or later, the initial basis of an interest acquired from the partnership is the amount of cash the partner transfers to the partnership, the amount of partnership debt for which he becomes personally liable, and the basis in his hands of property he contributes to the partnership.[1] If the partner contributes property that is subject to a liability, the contributing partner's basis in his partnership interest will be reduced by the portion of the liability that is allocable to other members of the partnership.[2] If an investor purchases his interest from a partner, his basis is his acquisition cost.[3] The general basis rules apply to other types of acquisitions, such as by inheritance or gift.[4] The value of services to be contributed to the partnership by a partner is not added to the basis of his partnership interest.[5]

b. When Determined.   A partner is required to determine the tax basis of his partnership interest only when it becomes necessary for other tax computations.[6] For example, it is usually necessary to compute this tax basis at the end of the partnership taxable year in order to determine the extent to which a partner's distributive share of partnership losses may be deducted on his personal income tax return.[7] Only the portion of the partnership loss which is not in excess of his basis is currently deductible.[8] Any excess loss will be deductible in the first succeeding partnership taxable year when the partner's basis exceeds zero.[9] For purposes of determining the limitation on the deduction of losses incurred in the taxable year and of previously disallowed losses, all basis adjustments, except for the current year's loss deduction, must be taken into account.[10]

It is necessary to determine the partner's tax basis in his partnership interest at other times, such as the date of a sale, exchange, or other disposition of the partner's interest or upon liquidation.[11] His tax basis must also be determined when there is a current distribution of money or property from the partnership.[12]

c. Adjustments.   The partner's original tax basis, determined as discussed previously, frequently must be adjusted. These adjustments are in part the result of a basic concept of partnership taxation: Partners are taxed on their distributive shares of partnership gains or losses, regardless of whether money or property is distributed to the partners.[13]

Therefore, a partner's initial tax basis is increased by his distributive shares of partnership taxable and tax-exempt income [14] and decreased (but not below zero) by distributions by the partnership to him of cash and property and by his distributive share of partnership losses and expenditures that are neither deductible nor chargeable to capital account.[15] The preceding rule may not be applicable in unusual circumstances.[16]

Any new contributions by a partner to the partnership increase his tax basis, as does nonrecourse financing. For basis adjustment purposes, noncash distributions are valued at the property's adjusted basis to the partnership immediately before the distribution.[17] Loans by a partner to the partnership, if properly characterized as loans and not deemed to be capital contributions, do not affect the computation of the lending partner's tax basis.[18]

The determination of a partner's tax basis may be illustrated as follows: On September 1, 1982, X contributes $10,000 to the capital of Partnership A. For the year ending December 31, 1982, Partnership A has a net loss of $50,000, of which X's distributive share is $5,000. Partnership A makes no distributions. X is entitled to deduct $5,000 on his personal tax return. His tax basis in Partnership A is then $5,000 ($10,000 initial basis, less $5,000 distributive share of Partnership A tax losses). In 1983, Partnership A makes a cash distribution of $30,000 but, because of accelerated depreciation, has a net loss for tax purposes of $45,000. X's distributive share of Partnership A's distributions and losses is $3,000 and $4,500, respectively. Because distributions are taken into account before losses in computing tax basis, X will not be able to deduct his full distributive share of Partnership A's losses on his personal return:

Tax basis on 12/31/82	$5,000
Less: cash distributions	($3,000)
	$2,000
Less: Partnership losses, but only to the extent basis is not reduced below zero	($2,000)
Tax basis on 12/31/83	$0

Therefore, in 1983, X will be allowed to deduct only $2,000 of his $4,500 distributive share of losses. The remaining $2,500 will be held "in suspense" until he acquires a tax basis sufficient to offset that amount.

2. EFFECT OF NONRECOURSE FINANCING ON TAX BASIS

a.   General.   Investors are attracted to limited partnerships as investment vehicles partly because they afford corporate-type insulation from liabilities of the business. Yet before the Tax Reform Act of 1976, the investor-limited partner in all limited partnerships could share in certain types of liabilities for purposes of determining his tax basis even though he had no personal liability for this debt, thereby often permitting tax deductions greatly in excess of investment. This rule was the subject of criticism and extensive examination by the Service. "Investment" vehicles that offered economic gain much greater than the economic risk incurred solely because of tax deductions were offensive not only to the Service but to the general public.

With respect to most limited partnerships, excluding real estate syndications, the Tax Reform Act of 1976 and the Revenue Act of 1978 effectively eliminated the major advantage of adding nonrecourse liabilities to the tax basis of an interest in a partnership. This was accomplished by limiting the amount of losses that may be claimed by each individual partner to the amount the partner has "at risk" in the venture.[19] However, both the Tax Reform Act of 1976 and the Revenue Act of 1978 contained somewhat differently articulated exceptions with respect to real property, which has preserved tax shelter effect of real estate syndications.[20] Congress recognized that real estate nonrecourse financing was traditional and that it was economically necessary to exclude real estate from the "at risk" rules to encourage construction of homes and offices.

b.   The At Risk Limitations.   The Tax Reform Act of 1976 excluded partnerships "the principal activity of which is investing in real property" [21] from the application of the "at risk" limitation. However, the Revenue Act of 1978 used different wording, excluding from the "at risk" limitation the "holding of real property (other than mineral property)." [22] Some history is useful to understand the current exclusion.

Prior to final passage of the Tax Reform Act of 1976, it was largely understood that traditional real estate limited partnerships would qualify for the exception to the general at risk limitation. For example, the Conference Committee explained that the general at risk provision "will not apply . . . to any partnership the principal activity of which involves real property (other than mineral property.)" [23] This suggested a broad-based exception. However, instead of "involves," the 1976 Act used the term "investing," which was not mentioned in any of the Congressional reports and was not defined by the 1976 Act. Although similar terms are the subject of Code and judicial interpretation,[24] because of uncertainties, many attorneys were unwilling to express opinions as to whether real estate limited partnerships were "investing" in real property as required by the statute.

The change in wording from the 1976 "the principal activity of which is investing in real property" to the 1978 "the holding of real property" was, we believe, intended to clarify that the exclusion encompasses active as well as passive real estate operations and that real property can be held indirectly as well as directly.[25] However, questions may remain as to the proper interpretation and scope of the real property exception to the "at risk" rules.[26]

In addition, the 1978 Act provided that, where a taxpayer combines personal property and services with real property holding, the personal property and services can be treated as part of the activity of holding real property, but only if they are "incidental to making real property available as living accommodations. . ." [27] The legislative history indicates that the operation of motels, hotels, and furnished apartments can thus avoid the "at risk" rules.[28]

If the personal property and services are not "incidental to making real property available as living accommodations," the holding of the real property is treated as a separate activity that is not subject to the "at risk" rules while the other activity is subject to "at risk" (e.g., a nursing home is a holding of real property and a separate providing of health care and meals). The committee reports provide two methods of allocating the income, each of which may cause uncertainty in application and calculation.[29]

In summary, many questions remain as to the proper interpretation and scope of the real estate exception to the "at risk" rules. For example, how should a leasehold interest in real estate be treated? We hope that the Service will provide further interpretative guidance.

The Economic Recovery Tax Act of 1981 extended the "at risk" rules to the investment tax credit.[30] However, it too contains an exemption for the holding of real property.[31]

We will now proceed on the assumption that the "at risk" limitations do not apply to the real estate limited partnerships under consideration.

c. "Nonrecourse" Loans That May Be Added to Basis.   A partner may deduct only his distributive share of partnership losses to the extent of his tax basis.[32] Where none of the partners, general or limited, have any personal liability with respect to a real estate limited partnership obligation, then all partners, including limited partners, are considered as sharing the obligation in the same proportion that they share profits.[33] Limited partners share recourse liabilities in accordance with their loss interest but they share nonrecourse liabilities in accordance with their profits interest (presumably on the theory that out-of-pocket payments on recourse liabilities are losses, but partnership payments of nonrecourse liabilities are a charge against profits). Construction financing is usually recourse financing, while permanent financing is often nonrecourse.

An increase in a partner's share of partnership liabilities is considered a contribution of money to the partnership,[34] and a contribution of money results in an increase in a partner's tax basis.[35] By so increasing his basis, a limited partner in a real estate limited partnership is able to deduct current losses that exceed his actual investment.

The result of nonrecourse financing to a real estate syndication, therefore, is significant: An investor is able to preserve a limitation on his liability to creditors while maximizing the tax benefits and leveraged value of his investment.

A simple example illustrates this point: Assume A, B, and C are each wealthy individuals with high-bracket incomes. Each contributes $10,000 to a real estate limited partnership that qualifies as such for tax purposes. The limited partnership borrows $300,000 from a bank, secured only by its assets (a building to be constructed and land). Assuming A, B, and C share collectively in 95% of the limited partnership's profits (the general partner receives the other 5%), they are each entitled to add $95,000 to the tax basis of their limited partnership interests, giving each an initial basis of $105,000. If, through early year fees, a portion of the construction losses and accelerated methods of depreciation, the partnership generates substantial tax losses in the early years of its existence, the investors can, for a $10,000 out-of-pocket investment, claim tax losses in excess of that amount, which they may use to offset income from other sources. As will be discussed, however, there are restrictions on the claiming of several early year deductions. Further, the Service has been attacking early year deductions. The most potent attack has been its occasional assertion that expenses other than taxes and certain interest, occurring before the certificate of occupancy is issued, should be capitalized rather than immediately deducted. This is discussed in Chapter 6.

At least until the recent revolution in real estate financing, nonrecourse financing has been the rule rather than the exception with respect to permanent mortgage loan financing related to real estate development. The early year tax benefits have made the limited partnership the most popular vehicle for joint venture real estate investment. However, changes in the real estate industry, especially the unwillingness of financial institutions to commit to long-term fixed interest loans in the face of inflation, have had an adverse impact.

As is discussed in Chapter 7, the tax benefits of nonrecourse financing at the outset of a project or partnership are mitigated by the adverse tax consequences upon disposition of the project or of an interest in the partnership.[36] The outstanding amount of a nonrecourse mortgage will usually be considered part of the amount realized on a sale or other disposition of partnership property or of the partnership interest and will cause taxable income, with additional complexity when the nonrecourse liabilities exceed the market value of the property.[37] Under certain circumstances, the ultimate tax liability can be substantially in excess of any cash received. Tax-sheltered investments, therefore, usually result only in tax deferral. If the project is unsuccessful, this can lead to substantial economic loss, although the loss is often mitigated by inflation, that is, by comparing the real value of early year tax savings with the real cost of post-inflation later year tax liability.

d.   "Nonrecourse" Loans That May Not Be Added to Basis.   As with any rule that produces highly desirable tax results, there have been attempts to push the treatment of nonrecourse borrowing beyond its reasonable limits. Reacting predictably, the Service has taken the position that it may disregard what is characterized as nonrecourse debt if it is, in fact, a disguised equity investment.[38] Similarly, the Service may contest the step-up in basis if the nonrecourse debt exceeds the value of the underlying property.[39] Additionally, the nonrecource debt has to be recognized as debt rather than as a contingent liability.[40] Several other variations on the economic reality theme are likely to raise Service objections, such as sham situations where the alleged debt in substance is never intended to be paid and sales with nominal down payments where the property reverts to the seller if the nonrecourse debt is not paid.

Two rulings in the oil and gas area, that may or may not apply to a real estate investment, illustrate the Service's position: The making of a nonrecourse loan by a general partner to an oil and gas limited partnership or to a limited partner in such a partnership was ruled to be a capital contribution; [41] and a nonrecourse loan by an unrelated third party who retained an option to convert the loan to an interest in profits, secured only by unproven oil and gas leases, was ruled to be an equity investment.[42]

A similar detrimental result may occur where the contractor–general partner guarantees all or part of real estate construction or permanent financing. The potential personal liability of the general partner may be deemed to negate the nonrecourse character of the debt, thereby preventing the limited partners from adding any of the liability to their bases. If such guarantees are necessary or desirable, the guaranteed portion of the loan should be evidenced by a separate note. If so, it could be argued that an addition to basis for the true nonrecourse portion of the liability should be allowed.

e.   Service Ruling Policy.   In a further attempt to curtail the use of nonrecourse financing to increase tax deductions, the Service has stated it will not issue a favorable advance ruling with respect to limited partnership status where the projected tax losses of the partnership during the first two years of partnership operations exceed the actual cash or property contributed to capital.[43] As noted previously, this ruling policy does not appear to have any real basis in the law. In addition, the policy appears redundant since the enactment of the "at risk" limitation on excess loss deduction. Nevertheless, the effect of such a policy has been to limit the number of issued tax rulings. If a ruling is required to sell interests in a real estate limited partnership (e.g., a state securities commissioner insists on it), this policy can restrict the structuring of a syndication.

f. "Two-Tier" Partnerships. As previously discussed, it is often desirable to have one limited partnership (the "second-tier partnership") acquire an interest in another limited partnership (the "first-tier partnership") that will construct and operate a real estate project. The first-tier partnership borrows the financing for the project and services the debt. Of the many tax questions, the relevant one here is whether the investors, who are the limited partners of the second-tier partnership, may include in their tax bases any portion of the nonrecourse mortgage to which the property owned by the first-tier partnership is subject.

After a period of uncertainty, the Service ruled that, for purposes of determining the bases of their limited partnership interests in a second-tier partnership, the limited partners could include their allocable shares of the nonrecourse liabilities of the first-tier partnership.[44] However, the use of tier partnerships also requires consideration of the tax effect of recourse debt; conversions of a general partnership interest in one partnership for a limited partnership interest in another; optional basis adjustments to partnership property; and sale or distributions of the first-tier subsidiary's assets.[45]

The tier concept is also important in trying to allocate deductions to partners who are admitted late in the year. This is discussed later in this chapter.

3. TAX CONSEQUENCES OF CONTRIBUTIONS TO A PARTNERSHIP

A partner who contributes property to a partnership realizes no gain or loss on such a contribution.[46] This rule even applies to installment obligations and to property subject to the depreciation recapture rules.[47] There is no distinction between contributions made in the process of formation of the partnership and those made during its term.[48] This rule does not apply, however, to a transaction between a partnership and a partner who is not acting in his capacity as a partner, such as a sale of property by a partner to the partnership.[49] Whether the transfer of property to a partnership is in fact a contribution to the capital of the partnership or a sale will depend on the facts surrounding the transfer and the intent of the parties.[50]

If a partner contributes property to a partnership and the partnership assumes his liabilities in connection with such property, the amount of his decrease in liabilities is treated as a distribution of money to the partner.[51] This rule also applies when a partner contributes property subject to a mortgage.[52] Such a deemed distribution of money to the contributing partner results in a reduction of the partner's tax basis in the partnership and, if it exceeds such tax basis, in a taxable gain.[53]

If one or more partners contribute property to the partnership, it is important to focus on the allocation of depreciation and gain or loss with respect to such property. Without a provision in the partnership agreement dealing specifically with the issue, such items are allocated among the partners as if the property had been purchased by the partnership.[54] Such an allocation may have an unfair result. For example, one partner may contribute cash while the other partner may contribute property of equal value but with a low basis. On the sale of that property, each partner would have to share the capital gain tax, so that the cash investor would in effect pay more for his half share of the partnership.

To remedy this, the partnership agreement may provide for an allocation of such items to take into consideration the difference between the basis of the property to the partnership and its actual value on the date of contribution.[55] Such an allocation may be applicable to all contributed property or to specific items.[56] Under this allocation, the amounts of allocated depreciation, gain, or loss may not exceed a ceiling, the effect of which is to prevent the artificial creation of a loss to the contributing partner and a gain to the other partners.[57]

This is an important concept and should be remembered in any situation where a partner contributes appreciated or depreciated property rather than cash. If the agreement so provides, the appreciation or diminution may be attributed to the contributing partner when the property is sold, or may be used in allocating depreciation with respect to such property to the noncontributing partner.[58]

4. RECEIPT OF PARTNERSHIP INTEREST FOR SERVICES

a. Background.   The promoter of a real estate limited partnership often becomes a general partner without contributing cash or other property to the partnership for his interest. This raises substantial and complex tax problems for the promoter and his advisers and may result in unexpected ordinary income for the general partner.

It was long the belief of many tax advisers that receipt by a service provider of an interest in partnership profits in consideration for services was not a taxable event unless the service provider also received a right to share in capital contributed by other partners or in profits accrued prior to admission to the partnership.[59] It became popular, therefore, to compensate "service partners" with an interest in future partnership profits, which were included in income by the service partner only when his distributive share of partnership profits was realized. Indeed, even the courts appeared to agree with this tax treatment of such an arrangement.[60]

b. Section 83.   Section 83 was added to the Internal Revenue Code by the Tax Reform Act of 1969. It modified the then-existing rules with respect to when the receipt of property would be considered the receipt of taxable income.[61] In general, under Section 83, unless subject to restrictions on transferability and conditions of forfeiture, property received in exchange for services is considered currently taxable ordinary income.[62] Under 1971 (and still) proposed Section 721 regulations, Section 83 applies to the receipt of a capital interest in a partnership in exchange for services.[63] The proposed regulations, however, do not mention the tax treatment of the receipt of a profits interest. Observers continued to assume that a profits interest was not property for the purpose of recognizing income and that receipt of such an interest, whether restricted or not, was not a taxable event.

c. The *Sol Diamond* Case.   Notwithstanding the foregoing, in *Sol Diamond* the receipt of a share of partnership profits for past services with a determinable market value was held to be a receipt of taxable income.[64] This was a substantial departure from what was generally thought to have been a well-established rule. Although it appears troublesome, careful planning can minimize its impact.

Under *Sol Diamond*, a profits interest can be considered property to which Section 83 applies and, therefore, a partner who receives a profits interest that is either freely transferable or nonforfeitable is taxed when he receives his interest.[65]

An election can be made to include in income immediately upon receipt the value of a profits interest, but only if the interest is nontransferable and subject to forfeiture.[66] If the profits interest is subject to forfeiture and is nontransferable when received, it may be wise to consider making this election. The value at the earlier time may be small. If the election is made and there is appreciation in value, upon disposition at least some of the appreciation might be taxable at capital gains rates.[67] This is especially useful for a general partner who hopes to receive a "kicker" or extra lump sum on sale or refinancing of the partnership's property.

If the profits interest is valuable when received and the general partner wishes to avoid immediate taxation, consideration should be given to making the interest nontransferable and subject to a substantial risk of forfeiture upon issuance to him. If so, until his interest either becomes transferable or no longer subject to a substantial risk of forfeiture, the service provider is not treated as a partner.[68] Thus, until that time, actual distributions to the service provider are income in the year paid or accrued rather than partnership distributions. Partnership gains and losses are then taxed to the other partners.

If a service partner is to be taxed upon receipt of his partnership interest, the partnership usually is entitled to receive a corresponding deduction.[69] Another planning technique, therefore, is to attempt to allocate the entire deduction directly to the service partner to offset the effect of including the profits interest in income. As is discussed later in this chapter, however, there is no assurance that such a special allocation will be allowed.[70]

An additional planning technique is to transfer the profits interest to the service partner before the partnership has any value. Unless a variation of the "bargain purchase" rule is asserted, the general partner's interest probably would not be subjected to substantial tax.

We believe that *Sol Diamond,* if it is to have any validity, should be confined to situations where a profits interest is received for past services [71] and where the interest can be valued accurately.

Consideration should also be given to transferring only an interest in profits, and not an interest in the partnership, to the person rendering services. As such, the person might be considered an employee of the partnership and not a partner. Although the employee probably would be required to report the value of the interest in profits as income, he might be permitted to amortize that amount over an appropriate period to offset, at least partially, the reporting of income as the profits are collected.

Finally, the general partner may prefer to contribute property for his interest in order to mitigate or avoid ordinary income danger.

5. THE PARTNER'S INCOME AND LOSS

As mentioned in Chapter 3, in determining his taxable income, each partner must separately take into account his allocable or distributive share of the following partnership items: [72]

1. Short-term capital gains and losses;
2. Long-term capital gains and losses; [73]
3. Gains and losses from sales or exchanges of Section 1231 property; [74]
4. Charitable contributions;
5. Dividends and interest;
6. Taxes subject to the foreign tax credit;
7. Investment interest, income, and expense; and [75]
8. Such other partnership items to the extent provided in the regulations.[76]

In addition, each partner must separately take into account his distributive share of any partnership item that would affect any partner's tax liability differently if that partner did not separately take it into account.[77] An example of such is the partnership's tax preference items.[78] Each partner also must account for his distributive share of partnership taxable income or loss exclusive of the separately stated items.[79] Finally, to determine if any deductions or exclusions allowable to a partner are subject to limitations, the partner must aggregate his separate deductions or exclusions with those that are part of his distributive share of separately stated items.[80]

6. DETERMINATION OF THE PARTNER'S DISTRIBUTIVE SHARE—SPECIAL ALLOCATIONS

A partner's distributive share of each item of income, gain, loss, deduction, or credit generally is determined by the partnership agreement.[81] An oral partnership agreement or an oral modification of a written partnership agreement will be given judicial recognition if it can be proven.[82]

There is an important exception to this general rule. The partnership agreement does not control if a provision of the partnership agreement dealing with a particular item or with "bottom line" profits or losses does not have substantial economic effect.[83] If no such effect exists, or if there is no partnership agreement provision dealing with an item, the partner's distributive share of an item is determined in accordance with the partner's interest in the partnership.[84] Among the factors to be taken into account are the relative interests of the partners in profits, losses, cash flow, and distributions of capital.[85]

Very few areas of partnership tax law have been the subject of as much controversy as the allocation of partnership tax items and of profit and loss generally. As with nonrecourse financing and the determination of tax basis, this has been due in large part to attempts to attain greater and greater tax benefits by forcing legal concepts up to and beyond their reasonable bounds.

Most tax advisers in the real estate limited partnership area will counsel against a "special allocation" of a specific partnership item, such as depreciation or interest. If someone insists on proceeding with a special allocation, he should know that he is involving himself in a high-risk situation, and he should be prepared to have the allocation challenged on audit. Despite all the problems in the area, however, it may be possible to allocate advantageously at least "bottom line" profits and losses.

Before the Tax Reform Act of 1976, special allocations of particular items of partnership income, gain, loss, deduction, or credit were examined by applying six criteria to determine whether the principal purpose of an allocation of a tax item was avoidance or evasion of tax.[86] The determination was to be made in relation to all the surrounding facts and circumstances.[87] Of the circumstances discussed in the regulations, "substantial economic effect" generally was regarded as the most important, especially in the area of real estate limited partnerships. If the allocation of a tax item, such as depreciation, had economic effect other than its tax consequences, it probably would be sustained.[88]

In addition, prior to the 1976 Act there was a line of reasoning that viewed as without problem special allocations of so-called "bottom line" profits and losses rather than specific items. This therory was not without merit. Both Section 704 and the regulations thereunder spoke in terms of "items," rather than losses generally.[89] The theory was also supported in the reasoning of a Tax Court case,[90] although such an allocation remained subject to attack (under a "sham" argument).[91]

The Tax Reform Act of 1976 eliminated the distinction between specific items of income, gain, loss, deduction, or credit and "bottom line" profits and losses. All allocations of such amounts are to be examined under the same standard.[92] The 1976 Act also codified, as the sole criteria, the "substantial economic effect" test of the regulations.[93] Where a special allocation is not recognized, the specially allocated amount must be reallocated in accordance with the partner's "interest in the partnership." [94] Previously, a disallowed special allocation was reallocated according to the general profit and loss sharing provision of the partnership agreement.[95] Now, a partner's interest in the partnership is determined by taking into account all the facts and circumstances,[96] including the partners' interest in profits and losses (if different from that of taxable income and loss), cash flow, and distributions of capital upon liquidation.[97]

For a special allocation to have a substantial economic effect on the partners, it is probably necessary to establish a capital account for each partner and to have the special allocation reflected in the capital accounts.

When the partners ultimately receive cash or property from the partnership, the distribution to them should be in accordance with the balances in their capital accounts. Since the capital accounts would reflect any special allocations, the distributions should reflect the economic effect of the allocations to the partners (e.g., the partner who was allocated greater losses should receive less cash or property on dissolution).[98] In any event, it is important that the partnership agreement articulate the agreement of the parties as to allocations. The Service generally will not issue rulings on the question of substantial economic effect.[99]

As is discussed later, a common form of real estate limited partnership is where the limited partners invest most of the capital, say 95%, and receive a similar percentage of profits, losses and cash flow. However, the 5% general partner is given an incentive by being allocated an additional share after the limited partners have "received their bait (investment) back." In this situation, a special allocation of specific deductions, or, in general, of early losses to the limited partners who bear the economic risk might be sustained, even though there may be a subsequent shift in the allocation.[100]

7. EFFECT OF SHIFTING INTERESTS

As mentioned previously, it is common for real estate limited partnership profit and loss allocations to be shifted after a number of years. For example, the limited partners might be provided 95% of the profits and losses for the first X years and, thereafter, their interest would be reduced to 50% and the general partner's interest increased to 50%. This gives the general partner an incentive to make the partnership successful and usually occurs after the limited partners have received economic benefits that at least equal their investment.[101]

The tax effect of such a so-called "flip-flop" must be considered before agreement is reached. The special allocation question has been reviewed. Further, as discussed, the effect of nonrecourse debt is to increase a partner's basis in his partnership interest.[102] Any decrease of the partner's share of the nonrecourse debt (pursuant to a flip-flop or otherwise) is treated for tax purposes as a distribution of cash.[103] If the partner has sufficient basis, and there is no recapture,[104] the only effect of the flip-flop will be to decrease basis. However, if the partner has insufficient basis, the effect of this "paper" transaction could be a capital gain [105] or, if there is recapture, ordinary income.[106]

Finally, a flip-flop that involves a shift in capital as well as profits might effect a termination of the partnership for tax purposes. As discussed in

Chapter 7, a transfer of 50% or more of the interests in partnership capital and profits in any year may result in a termination of the partnership for tax purposes.[107]

8. RETROACTIVE ALLOCATIONS

An issue closely related to that of the special allocation is the "retroactive allocation." Can a limited partner join the partnership late in the year and be allocated a percentage of partnership profits and losses from the beginning of the partnership's taxable year? Prior to the Tax Reform Act of 1976, this was a common problem for the real estate limited partnership, since investors were more likely to be seeking investments at the end of the year, but the investments were attractive for the most part if the tax deductions for the full year (generally the construction period) were available to them.

However, the 1976 Act effectively eliminated any potential for making retroactive allocations.[108] Under current law, it is now clear that the determination of distributive shares of partnership items of income, gain, loss, deduction, or credit and bottom line profits or losses must reflect the partners' varying interests in the partnership during the taxable year.[109] To prevent narrow application of the statute, the rules regarding determination of a partner's distributive share and the effective amending of a partnership agreement have been cross-referenced to include this new provision.[110]

There is room for tax planning, however.[111] For example, in a cash receipts and disbursements method partnership, an expense may not be deducted until it is actually paid. If the cash method partnership waits, has an interim closing of its books, and pays certain amounts only after entry of a new partner, an argument could be made that the deductible expense was incurred while he was a member of the partnership and thus he should receive his allocable share of the deduction.[112] The statute is unclear with respect to the treatment of such an arrangement, especially if the partnership incurred the liability before, but paid it after, the entry of the new partner. Such an arrangement may fail by analogy to the rules that disallow an anticipatory assignment of income.[113]

Another possible but also risky technique would be to use a two-tiered partnership structure where the taxable years of the first tier operating partnership and of the second tier holding partnership would end on the same date.[114] The taxable income or loss of the second tier partnership would accrue on the last day of the taxable year since that is when its distributive share of income, gain, loss, and so on from the first tier partnership would be determined. Those entering the second tier partnership before that date arguably would be entitled to a full share of the income or loss for that year. Although a creative approach, this arrangement is subject to attack by the Service.[115]

9. GUARANTEED PAYMENTS

Payments made by the partnership to a partner for services or for the use of capital are treated as payments to a third person if these payments are determined without regard to the income of the partnership.[116] These "guaranteed payments" are treated as income to the recipient.[117] Most important, unlike partnership distributions, guaranteed payments are generally deductible by the partnership if they would otherwise qualify as ordinary and necessary business expenses of the partnership.[118]

Many real estate limited partnerships attempt to use guaranteed payments, as opposed to distributions of income, to increase the amount of current deductions to the investors. It is essential to remember, however, that a payment to a partner will be treated as a guaranteed payment only "to the extent" determined without regard to the partnership's income. The regulations take a fairly narrow view on this issue.[119]

If a sole general partner receives $18,000 under a partnership agreement that allocates to him 30% of partnership profits, but not less than $10,000, one might assume that the $18,000 payment would be considered a guaranteed payment "to the extent" of $10,000. The regulations indicate otherwise.[120] Instead, the $10,000 is a deemed partnership distribution to the general partner and 70% of the payment that would have been deductible by the limited partners is not so deductible. If the general partner receives $10,000 for services, plus a percentage of all partnership profits after deducting the payment, the $10,000 may be a deductible guaranteed payment.[121]

The Tax Reform Act of 1976 amended the guaranteed payment provision specifically to prohibit the deduction of so-called capital expenditures, which are not currently deductible. Capital expenditures are incurred to acquire an asset with a useful life extending beyond the taxable year of purchase.[122] The amendment codified case law [123] and is in conformity with the position taken by the Service.[124] In addition, another amendment prevents the partnership from obtaining a deduction of organization and syndication fees by disguising them as guaranteed payments, although organization fees can be amortized over a period of not less than 60 months.[125]

10. PAYMENTS TO A PARTNER NOT ACTING AS SUCH

Many real estate limited partnership agreements provide for the engagement of a partner in a capacity different from that of a partner (e.g., as an accountant or as a managing agent). Payments to such a partner were considered to be currently deductible by the partnership pursuant to specific statutory language.[126]

A Tax Court decision, *Pratt*, dealt a blow to this understanding by holding that such payments were nondeductible partnership distributions.[127] In the case in question, each of two limited partnership agreements provided that the general partners, who were to use their best efforts to manage the partnership, were to receive fees based on a percentage of rentals from the limited partnership's property. Since the fees were not determined without regard to the income of the partnership, the fees to the general partners were held not to be guaranteed payments.[128]

The Internal Revenue Service has recently announced that it will not follow the *Pratt* decision, thereby reversing its prior practice and now favoring taxpayers.[129] The Service states that it will treat a payment for services determined by reference to an item of gross income as a guaranteed payment if, on the basis of all the facts and circumstances, the payment is compensation rather than a share of partnership profits. Relevant facts for making this determination include the reasonableness of the payment and whether the method used in determining the amount of payment would have been used to compensate an unrelated party. The Service also ruled that a payment based on a percentage of gross income that was paid to an investment adviser for the partnership, which was also a general partner of the partnership, was compensation for services rendered in a capacity other than that of partner.[130]

Most payments to general partners who are thought not to be acting in their capacity as partners could be considered nondeductible partnership distributions, because the clauses defining the general partners' powers in partnership agreements are usually very broad. If payments are to be made to the general partners, therefore, care should be taken to determine the amounts without regard to partnership income.

11. CURRENT PARTNERSHIP DISTRIBUTIONS

This section discusses current distributions of cash or property by the partnership to a partner; other partnership distributions, such as upon sale, liquidation, or other disposition of a partner's interest, or upon partnership termination, are discussed in Chapter 7.

It is important to emphasize the distinction between partnership distributions and partnership profits. Profits represent the taxable income of the partnership that is included in the partners' taxable income whether or not distributed. Distributions are actual payments of cash or other property to the partners by the partnership.

The current distribution of the results of partnership operations is usually a nontaxable return of capital.

A distribution of cash is usually nontaxable, except to the extent that it exceeds the partner's tax basis for his partnership interest immediately prior to the distribution.[131] If a cash distribution is in excess of the partner's tax basis, gain is recognized to the extent of the excess and is treated as gain from the sale or exchange of the partnership interest of the distributee partner.[132] The gain, therefore, is generally capital gain subject to the rules regarding "unrealized receivables" and "substantially appreciated inventory items." [133] These rules are discussed in Chapter 7.[134] Current partnership distributions cannot result in losses.[135] As is discussed in Chapter 7, losses are recognized by a distributee partner only in connection with the liquidation of a partner's interest in the partnership.[136] The partner's tax basis for the partnership interest is reduced, but not below zero, by the amount of money distributed to him.[137]

Current or nonliquidating distributions of property other than money are unusual events in real estate syndications. In general, such property distributions do not result in a taxable event for the distributee partner.[138]

The basis of property (other than cash) received by a partner in a current distribution is the partnership's adjusted basis for the property immediately prior to the distribution.[139] This is, however, subject to a limitation.[140] The partner's tax basis for his partnership interest is reduced, but not below zero, by the adjusted basis of the distributed property.[141]

In general, no gain or loss is recognized by a partnership on its distribution of money or other property.[142] Gain or loss may be recognized, however, if the partnership has "unrealized receivables" or "substantially appreciated inventory items," and if it makes a non-pro rata distribution.[143] The basis of undistributed property generally does not change as a result of the distribution of money or other property,[144] although a special election to increase basis may be available to the partnership.[145]

A fairly common event, which may have unforeseen and unfortunate tax consequences, is the distribution that may result from a discharge of partnership obligations.[146] This is most likely to occur when the partnership disposes of its properties in some fashion, or if there is a "flip-flop." [147] As previously discussed, this discharge of indebtedness may cause taxable income even though it is a "paper" transaction and even though no cash is distributed to pay the resulting tax liability.

NOTES

1. Secs. 705(a), 722, 742, 752; Treas. Reg. §§1.722-1, 1.742-1, 1.752-1. *Cf. Rev. Rul. 80-235, 1980-2 C.B. 229 (written personal obligation given by a limited partner as part of his partnership interest purchase price is not included in the basis of his partnership interest until and as payments are made on it).*

2. *Treas. Reg.* §1.722-1. *See also* Secs. 705(a), 722, 733, 752.

3. Secs. 742, 1011 *et seq.;* Treas. Reg. §1.742-1.

4. Sec. 1011 *et seq.*

5. *Long v. United States,* 451 F.Supp. 1009 (W.D.Tex. 1976), *aff'd per curiam,* 575 F.2d 79 (5th Cir. 1978).

6. Treas. Reg. §1.705-1(a) (1).

7. Sec. 704(d); *F. A. Falconer,* 40 T.C. 1011 (1963) (Acq.).

8. *Id.;* Treas. Reg. §1.704-1(d) (1). *See also Harold A. Hobson, Jr.,* 40 CCH Tax Ct. Mem. 223 (1980), *aff'd, unpublished opinion* (5th Cir. 1981).

9. Treas. Reg. §1.704-1(d) (1).

10. *Id.;* Rev. Rul. 66-94, 1966–1 C.B. 166.

11. *See* pp. 144–161, *infra.*

12. *See* pp. 75–76, *infra.*

13. Sec. 702; Treas. Reg. §1.702-1(a).

14. Basis is also increased by items generally not applicable to real estate syndications. *See* Sec. 705(a) (1) (C); Treas. Reg. §1.705-1(a) (2) (i).

15. Secs. 705(a), 733.

16. Basis may be determined by reference to the partner's proportionate share of the adjusted basis of partnership property which would be distributed upon termination of the partnership when "circumstances are such that the partner cannot practically apply the general rule . . ." Sec. 705(b); Treas. Reg. §1.705-1(b); S.Rep. No. 1622, 83rd Cong., 2d Sess. 484 (1954); *cf. Coloman v. Commissioner,* 540 F.2d 427 (9th Cir. 1976).

17. Secs. 732, 733; Treas Reg. 1.732-1. Such value cannot exceed the partner's interest in the partnership reduced by the money distributed to him in the transaction. There are special rules for allocating basis to the distributed properties. Sec. 732(c). The effect of distributions of property other than money on the partner's tax basis will be further discussed. *See* pp. 75–76 and 157–158, *infra.*

18. *See Curtis W. Kingbay,* 46 T.C. 147 (1966).

19. Sec. 465. The Economic Recovery Tax Act of 1981 extended the "at risk" concepts to the investment tax credit. *See* note 30.

20. P.L. 94-455, §213(e)(1976)(adding the last two sentences to Sec. 704(d); H.R. Conf. Rep. No. 94-1515, 94th Cong., 2d. Sess. 423 (1976). Amended by P.L. 95-600 §§201(b)(1), 204(a)(1978) adding Sec. 465(c)(3) and repealing the last two sentences of Sec. 704(d); H.R. Rep. No. 95-1455, 95th Cong., 2d. Sess. 70 (1978).

21. P.L. 94-455, §213(e)(1976) (amended by P.L. 95-600).

22. Sec. 465(c)(3)(D).

23. H.R. Conf. Rep. No. 94-1515, 94th Cong., 2d Sess. 423 (1976).

24. *See e.g.,* Sec. 163(d)(3)(B) ("investment income"); *Alamo Broadcasting Co.,* 15 T.C. 534 (1950); *Charles M. Spindler,* 22 CCH Tax Ct. Mem. 1011 (1963); Treas Reg. §1.1221-1(b); Treas Reg. §1.1231-1(a); *George Rothenberg,* 48 T.C. 369 (1967); *Leland Hazard,* 7 T.C. 372 (1946); *John D. Fackler,* 45 B.T.A. 708 (1941), *aff'd,* 133 F.2d 509 (6th Cir. 1943).

25. *See* Rev. Rul. 77-309, 1977-2 C.B. 216 (two-tier partnership qualified for exclusion even under the 1976 TRA wording).

26. *See e.g.,* Kligman and Brumbaugh, "Soft Spots in the At-Risk Rules," 39 N.Y.U. INST. ON FED. TAX. 24-1, 24-8, 24-13 (1981); Note, " 'At Risk' Rules for Investment Realty Still Unclear," 50 J.Tax. 127 (1979); Shapiro, "1978 Act Favors Real Estate Investments: Analyzing Current Advantages," 50 J.TAX 32 (1979). *Compare* Carlin, "Taxation of Investments in Real Estate Under the New Rules," 36 N.Y.U. INST. ON FED. TAX. 351, 366–372 (1978) (1976 TRA).

27. Sec. 465(c)(3)(D).

28. H.R. Rep. No. 95-1445, 95th Cong., 2d Sess. 70 (1978).

29. *Id.* at 70–71 suggests either allocating to real property income that amount of income "which bears the same ratio to the total amount of income as the real property related deductions bear to total deductions . . ." or, alternatively, using the fair rental value of the property as the amount of income allocable to the real property if the fair rental value of the real property can be clearly established.

30. Sec. 46(c)(8), applicable to property placed in service after February 18, 1981, unless acquired pursuant to a binding contract entered into on or before that date.

31. Sec. 46(c)(8)(A)(1); S.Rep.No. 97-144, 97th Cong., 1st Sess. 66(1981).

32. Sec. 704(d). *See Harold A. Hobson, Jr.,* 40 CCH Tax Ct. Mem. 223 (1980), *aff'd, unpublished opinion* (5th Cir. 1981).

33. Treas. Reg. §1.752-1(e). This rule is based upon the well-known case of *Crane v. Commissioner,* 331 U.S. 1 (1947). *See generally,* Weidman, "Realty Shelters, Nonrecourse Financing, Tax Reform and Profit Purpose," 32 S.W.L.J. 711 (1978); Perry, "Limited Partnerships and Tax Shelters: the *Crane* Rule Goes Public," 27 TAX L. REV. 525 (1972); *Carriage Square, Inc.,* 69 T.C. 119 (1977); *John A. Laney,* 39 CCH Tax Ct. Mem. 491 (1979); *Richard C. Brown,* 40 CCH Tax Ct. Mem. 267 (1980) (nonrecourse loan assumed by partnership became recourse under local law when assumed by general partner).

34. Sec. 752(a); Treas. Reg. §1.752-1(a). *See also Marshall Long,* 71 T.C. 11, *on reconsideration,* 71 T.C. 724 (1979), *aff'd,* 660 F.2d 416 (10th Cir. 1981).

35. Sec. 705(a).

36. *See* pp. 144–161, *infra.*

37. *Crane v. Commissionerr,* 331 U.S. 1 (1947); *Parker v. Delaney,* 186 F.2d 445 (1st Cir. 1950); Rev. Rul. 78-164, 1978-1 C.B. 264, Rev. Rul. 76-111, 1976-1 C.B. 214; Rev. Rul. 74-40, 1974-1 C.B. 159. *Compare Tufts v. Commissioner,* 651 F.2d 1058 (5th Cir. 1981), *revg,* 70 T.C. 756 (1979), *cert. granted,* May 3, 1982. (fair market value is a limitation on the amount realized when nonrecourse liability is discharged). *See Paul B. Brountas,* 73 T.C. 491 (1979), *supplemented at* 74 T.C. 1062 (1980), *rev'd in part* and *aff'd in part,* ———F.2d———(1st Cir. 1982) *and Gibson Products Co.-Kell Blvd. v. United States,*

637 F.2d 1041 (5th Cir. 1981). *See also Millar v. Commissioner,* 577 F.2d 212 (3d Cir. 1978), *cert. denied,* 439 U.S. 1046 (1978); *Estate of Jerrold Delman,* 73 T.C. 14 (1979); Morris, "New Ruling Describes Deed Transfer in Lieu of Foreclosure as 'Sale or Exchange,'" 45 J. TAX 224 (1976).

38. *Joseph W. Hambuechen,* 43 T.C. 90 (1964); *Curtis W. Kingbay,* 46 T.C. 147 (1966).

39. *See and compare Edward B. Hager,* 76 T.C. 759 (1981); *Estate of Franklin v. Commissioner,* 544 F.2d 1045 (9th Cir. 1976); *David L. Narver,* 75 T.C. 53 (1980), *aff'd,* 670 F.2d 855 (9th Cir. 1982); *David F. Bolger,* 59 T.C. 760 (1973). Deductions of interest based on these transactions may also be denied. *See* Chapter 6.

40. *See and compare Manuel D. Mayerson,* 47 T.C. 340 (1966) (Acq.); *Leonard Marcus,* 30 CCH Tax Ct. Mem. 1263 (1971).

41. Rev. Rul. 72-135, 1972-1 C.B. 200.

42. Rev. Rul. 72-350, 1972-2 C.B. 394. *See also, Gibson Products Co.-Kell Blvd. v. United States,* 637 F.2d 1041 (5th Cir. 1981).

43. Rev. Proc. 74-17, 1974-1 C.B. 438, discussed on pp. 35–36, *supra.*

44. Rev. Rul. 77-309, 1977-2 C.B. 216; Private Letter Ruling 7726014 (March 29, 1977); *see* Sapp, "How a Two-Tiered Partnership Arrangement Can Be Used to Minimize Tax Liabilities," 42 J. TAX. 21 (1975). *See also* Rev. Rul. 78-2, 1978-1 C.B. 202 (optional adjustment to basis of assets in two-tier partnership); Rev. Rul. 77-311, 1977-2 C.B. 218 (allocation of losses in two-tier partnership); discussion *infra* at note 114.

45. *See* Hall, "Tier Partnerships—Special Problems," 59 TAXES 813 (1981).

46. Sec. 721; *compare Communications Satellite Corp. v. United States,* 625 F.2d 997 (Ct. Cl. 1980); *Stafford v. United States,* 611 F.2d 990 (5th Cir. 1980). Unlike Sec. 351 transfers to corporations, there is no requirement that the contributing partner be in control of the partnership immediately following the contribution.

47. Secs. 1245(b)(3), 1250(d)(3); Treas. Reg. §§1.453-9(c)(2), 1.721-1(a), 1.1245-4(c)(4) Ex. 2, 1.1250-3(c)(1), 1.1250-3(c)(2)(vi).

48. S. Rep. No. 1622, 83d Cong., 2d Sess. 388 (1954).

49. Sec. 707(a); Treas. Reg. §§1.707-1(a), 1.721-1(a); *see* Rev. Rul. 57-200, 1957-1 C.B. 205. Different rules apply if the transaction is treated as a loan or a lease by the partner to the partnership. *Compare* Sec. 707(a); Treas. Reg. §1.707-1(a); *Edward T. Pratt,* 64 T.C. 203 (1975), *aff'd,* 550 F.2d 1023 (5th Cir. 1977).

50. *See John H. Otey, Jr.,* 70 T.C. 312 (1978), *aff'd,* 634 F.2d 1046 (6th Cir. 1980); *Communications Satellite Corp. v. United States,* 625 F.2d 997 (Ct. Cl. 1980). *Compare* Rev. Ruls. 78-357, 1978-2 C.B. 227 and 78-356, 1978-2 C.B. 226.

51. Treas. Reg. §§1.722-1, 1.752-1(b)(2).

52. Treas. Reg. §1.752-1(c).

53. Secs. 705(a); 731(a).

54. Sec. 704(c)(1); Treas. Reg. §§1.704-1(c)(1), 1.1245-1 (e)(2).

55. Sec. 704(c)(2); Treas. Reg. §1.704-1(c)(2)(i).

56. Treas. Reg. §1.704-1(c)(2)(i).

57. *Id.*

58. Treas. Reg. §1.704-1(c)(2)(i), Exs. 1,2.

59. This belief was based upon Treas. Reg. §1.721-1(b)(1). There are proposed regulations

to replace §1.721-1(b)(1) that reflect the enactment of Section 83 in 1969. *See also Hensel Phelps Construction Co.*, 74 T.C. 939 (1980) (services provided in construction exchanged for 50% partnership interest).

60. *See United States v. Frazell*, 335 F.2d 487 (5th Cir.), *rehearing denied*, 339 F.2d 885 (5th Cir. 1964), *cert. denied*, 380 U.S. 961 (1965), *on remand*, 269 F.Supp. 885 (D.La. 1967); *Herman M. Hale*, 24 CCH Tax Ct. Mem. 1497, 1502 n.3 (1965); *Glenn E. Edgar*, 56 T.C. 717 (1971).

61. The old rules were contained in Treas. Reg. §§1.61-2(d), 1.61-15, 1.421-6.

62. Sec. 83(a).

63. Proposed Treas. Reg. §1.721-1(b)(1). Final Regulations under Section 83 were adopted on July 21, 1978. T.D. 7554 (July 21, 1978).

64. *Sol Diamond*, 56 T.C. 530 (1971), *aff'd*, 492 F.2d 286 (7th Cir. 1974); *accord, F.C. McDougal*, 62 T.C. 720 (1974)(Acq.); *Glenn E. Edgar*, 56 T.C. 717 (1971). *See* Cowan, "Receipt of an Interest in Partnership Profits in Consideration for Services: The *Diamond* Case," 27 TAX L. REV. 161 (1972).

65. Sec. 83(a); Proposed Treas. Reg. §1.721-1(b)(1). *Compare Stafford v. United States*, 611 F.2d 990 (5th Cir. 1980).

66. Sec. 83(b).

67. Treas. Reg. §1.83-1(a). This will occur, of course, only if the partnership interest is a capital asset in the hands of the service partner.

68. Treas. Reg. §§1.83-1(a); 1.83-3(b); 1.83-3(c). If the profits interest is subject to a non-lapse restriction, such as a binding buy-sell or redemption agreement, the value might be significantly reduced. Treas. Reg. §1.83-5(a).

69. Sec. 83(h); Treas. Reg. §1.721-1(b)(2)(i). This would not be the case if the transfer constituted a capital expenditure, such as, for example, if an interest is transferred in exchange for services performed in a syndication. Treas. Reg. §1.83-6(a)(4). If the services were rendered to an existing partner and not the partnership, however, only the partner would be entitled to the deduction. *F.C. McDougal*, 62 T.C. 740 (1974) (Acq.).

70. *See* pp. 70–72, *infra*.

71. *Edward T. Pratt*, 64 T.C. 203 (1975), *aff'd on this issue*, 550 F.2d 1023 (5th Cir. 1977); Private Letter Ruling 7817080 (June 27, 1977) (Ruling 3).

72. Sec. 702(a). The characterization of partnership items of income, gain, loss, deduction and credit is discussed in Chapter 3, pp. 42–44, *supra. See James A. Reed*, 37 CCH Tax Ct. Mem. 301 (1978) (where the partners failed to sign the partnership agreement, the court looked to surrounding circumstances to determine the partner's distributive share of partnership income); *Sellers v. United States*, 617 F.2d 1042 (4th Cir. 1980) (partner's distributive share of partnership losses determined under local law when partners had not agreed as to sharing of losses); *A. O. Champlin*, 36 CCH Tax Ct. Mem. 702 (1977), *aff'd in unpublished opinion* (9th Cir. 1980) (partner was held to terms of the partnership agreement); Rev. Rul. 77-310, 1977-2 C.B. 217 (the distributive share of a partner who increased his interest in a partnership during the year because of additional capital contributions is determined by considering his varying interests during the year); Rev. Rul. 77-137, 1977-1 C.B. 178 (assignee acquiring substantially all of partnership interest is treated as substitute limited partner for income tax purposes). *See also Alberto Vitale*, 72 T.C. 386 (1979) (nonresident alien limited partner taxable on allocable share of income).

73. Gains or losses on dispositions of capital assets qualify for long-term treatment if the assets are held for more than 12 months.

74. Section 1231 property includes certain property used in a trade or business and property which is involuntarily converted. Treas. Reg. §1.1231-1(a).

75. Section 163(d)(4)(B).

76. Sec. 708(a)(7); Treas. Reg. §1.702-1(a)(8)(i). Included in other partnership items are recoveries of bad debts, prior taxes, and delinquency amounts; nonbusiness expenses, income, gain, or loss to the partnership on distributions of property to partners, *see* pp. 75–76 and 157–158, *infra;* and any partnership items subject to a special allocation under the partnership agreement.

77. Treas. Reg. §1.702-1(a)(8)(ii).

78. Treas. Reg. §1.58-2(b). Also included are any items required to be stated separately to qualify any partner for the retirement income credit, Sec. 37, and any items necessary to determine the applicability of the hobby loss provisions, Sec. 183. Treas. Reg. §1.702-1(a)(8)(ii). For a discussion of other items that are required to be separately stated, see Chapter 3.

79. Sec. 702(a)(8); Treas. Reg. §1.702-1(a)(9).

80. Treas. Reg. §1.702(a)(8)(iii).

81. Sec. 704(a); Treas. Reg. §1.704-1(a).

82. *See and compare Raymond W. Schmitz*, 37 CCH Tax Ct. Mem. 1323 (1978) (oral agreement by three partners to make payments of a percentage of gross proceeds to another person on the death of a partner valid under state law; other person was recognized as a partner for tax purposes); *Claire A. Ryza*, 36 CCH Tax Ct. Mem. 269 (1977) (oral partnership agreement to share profits and losses equally was sustained); *Smith v. Commissioner*, 331 F.2d 298 (7th Cir. 1964); *James A. Reed*, 37 CCH Tax Ct. Mem. 301 (1978) (taxpayer had 20% interest in partnership notwithstanding draws in excess of 20%); *A.O. Champlin*, 36 CCH Tax Ct. Mem. 702 (1977) (insufficient evidence to support oral modification), *aff'd in unpublished opinion* (9th Cir. 1980); *Sellers v. United States*, 617 F.2d 1042 (4th Cir. 1980) (oral modification lacked business purpose and was disregarded).

83. Sec. 704(b)(2). *See* S. Rep. No. 94-938, 94th Cong., 2d Sess. 99-100 (1976). Treas. Reg. §§1.704-1(b)(1) and 1.704-1(b)(2) applied this analysis prior to the Tax Reform Act of 1976 to partnership agreement allocations, and possibly to bottom line allocations.

84. Sec. 704(b). *See also John L. Harrell, Jr.,* 37 CCH Tax Ct. Mem. 911 (1978) (where one partner failed to make required capital contribution, the other partner could deduct all of the partnership's losses to the extent of his partnership basis, even though partnership agreement called for equal division of profits and losses).

85. *See* S. Rep. No. 94-938, 94th Cong., 2d Sess. 100 (1976); *Estate of W.F. Williamson*, 29 T.C. 51 (1957) (Acq.); *Sellers v. United States*, 617 F.2d 1042 (4th Cir. 1980).

86. Treas. Reg. §1.704-1(b)(2).

87. *Id.* Included in all facts and circumstances were business purpose for the allocation, substantial economic effect of the allocation, effect on the dollar amount of partners' shares of partnership income or loss independent of tax circumstances, whether related items were similarly allocated, recognition of normal business factors, and the duration of the allocation.

88. For the Tax Court's view of the prior law, which still retains some vitality, *see Stanley C. Orrisch*, 55 T.C. 395 (1970), *aff'd per curiam, unpublished opinion* (9th Cir. 1973); *Leon A. Harris, Jr.,* 61 T.C. 770 (1974); *Robert L. Brock,* 59 T.C. 732 (1973) (Acq.). A discussion of the history and current status may be found in Parker, "Special Allocations in Real Estate Partnerships in Light of the '76 Act;" 12 TAX ADVISER 404 (1981).

89. Prior Sec. 704(b)(2); Treas. Reg. §1.704-1(b)(2).

90. *Jean V. Kresser,* 54 T.C. 1621 (1970).

91. *Id. See also* Tech. Advice Mem. 7707260880A (July 26, 1977).

92. Sec. 704(b); H.R. Conf. Rep. No. 94-1515, 94th Cong., 2d Sess. 422 (1976).

93. *Id.* Treas. Reg. §1.704-1(b)(2).

94. *Id.*

95. Prior Sec. 704(b).

96. Sec. 704(b).

97. S. Rep. No. 94-938, 94th Cong., 2d. Sess. 100 (1976).

98. *See and compare Martin Magaziner,* 37 CCH Tax Ct. Mem. 873 (1978); *Durand A. Holladay,* 72 T.C. 571 (1979), *aff'd,* 649 F.2d 1176 (5th Cir. 1981) (allocation of losses to one partner did not correspond with partners' agreement to share economic profits and bear economic losses); *Joe T. Boynton,* 72 T.C. 1147 (1979), *aff'd,* 649 F.2d 1168 (5th Cir. 1981), *cert. denied,* 102 S. Ct. 1009 (1982); Staff of Joint Committee on Taxation, 94th Cong., 2d. Sess., *General Explanation of the Tax Reform Act of 1976,* at 95 n.6 (1976); Tech. Advice Memo. 8008054 (Nov. 28, 1979); *and* Willis, "Special Allocations of Partnership Profits and Losses," 7 J. REAL ESTATE TAX. 356 (1980) criticizing Tech. Advice Memo. 7707260880A (July 26, 1977). *Cf. Stanley C. Orrisch,* 55 T.C. 395 (1970), *aff'd per curiam, unpublished opinion* (9th Cir. 1973). The taxpayer in *Orrisch* lost the issue of the validity of the special allocation principally because the partnership agreement did not provide a method for allocating losses.

99. Rev. Proc. 80-22, 1980-1 C.B. 654, *superceding* Rev. Procs. 79-14, 1979-1 C.B. 496 and 74-22, 1974-2 C.B. 476.

100. Treas. Reg. §1.704-1(b)(2) Ex. 5; *see S. Rex Lewis,* 65 T.C. 625 (1975).

101. The special allocation of amounts to the equity contributors is discussed in Section 6 in this chapter.

102. *Crane v. Commissioner,* 331 U.S. 1 (1947); Treas. Reg. §1.752-1(e); *see* pp. 62–66, *supra.*

103. Sec. 752(b); *see* pp. 75–76, *infra.*

104. Secs. 751(b), 1245, 1250; *see* p. 144, *infra.*

105. Secs. 731(a), 741; *see* pp. 144–147, *infra.*

106. Secs. 741, 751; *see* p. 144, *infra.*

107. Sec. 708(b)(1)(B); *see* pp. 161–162, *infra.*

108. For treatment of retroactive allocations before the Tax Reform Act of 1976, *see Norman Rodman,* 32 CCH Tax Ct. Mem. 1307 (1973), *rev'd,* 542 F.2d 845 (2nd Cir. 1976); Rev. Rul. 77-119, 1977-1 C.B. 177; *John M. Moore,* 70 T.C. 1024 (1978) (pre-1976 Tax Reform Act retroactive allocation denied; tax avoidance was primary purpose); Rev. Rul. 77-310, 1977-2 C.B. 217 (pre-1976 Tax Reform Act improper method of allocation); *Harry L. Marriott,* 73 T.C. 1129 (1980) (pre-1976 Tax Reform Act provisions in partnership agreement allocated losses on basis of interests at end of year; *Moore* followed); *Williams v. United States,* 80-2 U.S.T.C. 9740 (W.D. Tex. 1980); *Louis R. Gomberg,* 39 CCH Tax Ct. Mem. 1147 (1980) (losses allocated on basis of number of days as partners); Tech. Advice Mem. 7937016 (May 31, 1979) (newly admitted partners).

109. Sec. 706(c)(2)(B); H.R. Conf. Rep. No. 94-1515, 94th Cong., 2d Sess. 421 (1976). The amounts must be allocated either on a daily basis or by dividing the partnership year into two or more segments. *See* H.R. Rep. No.94-658, 94th Cong., 1st Sess. 122-125 (1975); S. Rep. No. 94-938, 94th Cong., 2d Sess. 95-98 (1976); Treas. Reg. 1.706-1(c)(2).

See generally Hess, "Retroactive Allocations Among Contemporaneous Partners—Are They Still Valid?" 58 TAXES 290 (1980).

110. Secs. 704(f), 761(e).

111. *See generally* Cowan, "Retroactive Partnership Allocations: New Restrictions Do Not Bar the Technique," 46 J. TAX. 332 (1977); Fass, "Acceptable Methods of Allocating Losses to Incoming Partners," TAX SHELTERED INVESTMENT LAW REPORT 17 (1981); Heller and Boyd, "Changes of Ownership in a Partnership and How They Affect the Partners' Distributive Shares," 59 TAXES 69 (1981).

112. *See Cecil R. Richardson,* 76 T.C. 512 (1981); *Mahoney v. United States,* Court of Claims, Trial Div., No. 497-77 (Ct. Cl., Nov. 6, 1981); Joseph A. Roccaforte, 77 T.C. 263 (1981). H.R. Rep. No. 94-658, 94th Cong. 1st Sess. 124-25 (1975); S. Rep. No. 94-938, 94th Cong. 2d Sess. 98 (1976).

113. *See Helvering v. Horst,* 311 U.S. 112 (1940); *Rodman v. Commissioner,* 542 F.2d 845, 857 (1976); *John M. Moore,* 70 T.C. 1024 (1978).

114. For discussion of tier partnership problems, *see* Hall, "Tier Partnerships—Special Problems," 59 TAXES 813. *See also* text discussion *supra* at n.44.

115. *See* Rev. Rul. 77-311, 1977-2 C.B. 218. *Compare* Rev. Ruls. 77-309 and 310, 1977-2 C.B. 216 and 217. *See also* IR 1899, 1977 P-H ¶55,987 (then Commissioner Kurtz discusses Rev. Ruls. 77-310 and 77-311 and Tech. Advice Mem. 8017013 (Dec. 18, 1979).

116. Sec. 707(c); Treas. Reg. §1.707-1(c). *See* Rev. Rul. 81-300, 1981-2 C.B. 143; Rev. Rul 81-301, 1981-2 C.B. 144.

117. *Id.;* Secs. 707(c) and 61(a). *See Holman v. Commissioner,* 564 F.2d 283 (9th Cir. 1977) (payments for unrealized receivables to expelled partners were considered ordinary income because they were deemed to be guaranteed payments).

118. Secs. 162(a), 707(c); Treas. Reg. §1.707-1(c).

119. Treas. Reg. §1.707-1(c). *See also Investors Ins. Agency, Inc., 72 T.C. 1027 (1979); John W. Mangham,* 40 CCH Tax Ct. Mem. 788 (1980); *Jack C. Smith,* 40 CCH Tax Ct. Mem. 1025 (1980) (weekly draws were guaranteed payments includable in partners' gross income and not draws against their capital accounts since they were for services rendered). A partner who receives a guaranteed payment under Sec. 707(c) must include the payment in his gross income even where the payments are not deductible by the partnership. Rev. Rul. 80-234, 1980-2 C.B. 203 (finder's fee includable in the partner's gross income in year of receipt even though partnership must capitalize and amortize the expense).

120. Treas. Reg. §1.707-1(c) Ex. 2; *see* Rev. Rul. 69-180, 1969-1 C.B. 183.

121. Treas. Reg. §1.707-1(c) Ex. 1. In all cases, the substance of agreements between the partners and partnership determine whether an amount is a guaranteed payment. *See* Tech. Advice Mem. 7939005 (May 30, 1979) (partner compensated at fixed rate without regard to partnership profit or loss).

122. Secs. 263, 707(c); S. Rep. No. 94-938, 94th Cong. 2d Sess. 92-94 (1976); Proposed Treas. Reg. §1.707-1(c).

123. *Jackson E. Cagle, Jr.,* 63 T.C. 86 (1974), *aff'd,* 539 F.2d 409 (5th Cir. 1976); *Carol W. Hilton,* 74 T.C. 305 (1980), *aff'd,* 671 F.2d 316 (9th Cir. 1982); Rev. Rul. 81-150, 1981-1 C.B. 119.

124. Rev. Rul. 75-214, 1975-1 C.B. 185; Rev. Rul. 80-234, 1980-2 C.B. 203. *See* Internal Revenue Audit Manual, CCH 7297-47 to 7297-48 (June 20, 1979).

125. Sec. 709; Prop. Treas. Regs. §§1.709-1, 1.709-2. *See Sidney Kimmelman,* 72 T.C. 294

(1979) (unsuccessful attempt to characterize the costs of organizing and syndicating a limited partnership as guaranteed payments).

126. Sec. 707(a) provides; "If a partner engaged in a transaction with a partnership other than in his capacity as a member of such partnership, the transaction shall . . . be considered as occurring between the partnership and one who is not a partner."

127. *Edward T. Pratt*, 64 T.C. 203 (1975), *aff'd (on this issue) and rev'd (on another issue)*, 550 F.2d 1023 (5th Cir. 1977). *See* Private Letter Ruling 7813001 (Sept. 30, 1977) (payments treated as distributions of partnership income to the extent they do not exceed partnership net income). *See generally* Cowan, "Compensating the General Partner: The Pratt Case," 56 TAXES 10 (1978).

128. 64 T.C. at 210; *see* Sec. 707(c) and discussion in Section 9 of this chapter. On appeal, it was conceded that interest paid on loans by partners was taxed under Sec. 707(a); *Pratt v. Commissioner*, 550 F.2d 1023 (5th Cir. 1977).

129. Rev. Rul. 81-300, 1981-2 C.B. 143.

130. Rev. Rul. 81-301, 1981-2 C.B. 144.

131. Sec. 731(a)(1); Treas. Reg. §1.731-1(a)(1)(i). This should not be the case if the transaction is treated as a sale. *See Communications Satellite Corp. v. United States*, 625 F.2d 997 (Ct. Cl. 1980) (distributions by partnership not treated as proceeds from sale of partnership interests).

132. Secs. 731(a), 741; Treas. Reg. §1.731-1(a)(3).

133. Secs. 731(c), 751; Treas. Reg. §1.731-1(c).

134. *See* pp. 144–145, *infra.*

135. Sec. 731(a)(2); Treas. Reg. §1.731-1(a)(2).

136. *Id.*

137. Sec. 733(1); Treas. Reg. §1.733-1.

138. *See* Sec. 731(a); Treas. Reg. §1.731-1(a)(1)(i). If the partnership has "unrealized receivables" or "substantially appreciated inventory items," however, there may be a taxable event if the distribution is not pro rata. Secs. 731(c), 751(b); *see* Secs. 1245(b)(3), 1250(d)(3).

139. Sec. 732(a)(1); Treas. Reg. §1.732-1(a).

140. The basis of the distributed property may not exceed the adjusted basis of the distributee partner's interest in the partnership reduced by any cash that may have been distributed in the same transaction. Sec. 732(a)(2); Treas. Reg. §1.732-1(a).

141. Sec. 733(2); Treas. Reg. §1.733-1.

142. Sec. 731(b); Treas. Reg. §1.731(b).

143. Secs. 731(c), 751(b).

144. Sec. 734(a); *see Miller v. Commissioner*, 285 F.2d 843 (10th Cir. 1960).

145. The special election, which may be made only if a partnership election under Section 754 is in effect, allows the partnership to take into account in the basis of undistributed property the gain or loss recognized by, or the increase in basis resulting to, the distributee partner. Sec. 734(b). Such adjustment is allocated under special rules. Sec. 755.

146. Sec. 752(b); Treas. Regs. §§1.752-1(b)(1) and 1.1001-2.

147. *See* p. 72, *supra. See also* Rev. Rul. 80-323, 1980-2 C.B. 124 (transferor of a partnership interest recognizes gain attributable to partnership's nonrecourse liabilities when the limited partnership interest is transferred to a corporation under Sec. 351).

CHAPTER 5

DEPRECIATION AND RECAPTURE, REHABS, HISTORIC AND OLDER STRUCTURES.

1. GENERAL

A major purpose in using the limited partnership format for an investment in real estate is to permit the tax benefits to flow through to the investor. The partnership's depreciation of the cost of its assets generally provides three important benefits to the investor. The first benefit is deferral of tax liability on partnership income, which often permits tax-free cash flow to the partners in early years. This deferral results from deductions for depreciation that offset the income of the partnership. The second benefit is limited conversion of ordinary income into capital gain, subject to recapture income, on the disposition of partnership assets for an amount in excess of the basis of the property. The third benefit is that depreciation, in particular, accelerated depreciation, often permits deductions in excess of the income from the partnership. Such excess deductions may be used to offset income that the partner realizes in other ventures.

Since depreciation is a bookkeeping deduction that does not necessarily reflect an economic cost, it combines with nonrecourse debt to produce the most important tax aspect of a real estate syndication. Real estate syndication investors usually hope that a syndication will have sufficient depreciation to shelter the cash flow from the property so that, subject to the alternative minimum tax,[1] the distribution of cash will not be taxable. They often hope that the syndication will also generate excess deductions to offset income that they have earned in other ventures.

There comes a crossover time when gross income exceeds deductions. Further, because of the need to pay monies to amortize the mortgage loan (a non-deductible payment), tax liability at that time often exceeds cash flow.

On the sale of the property or of the partnership interest, including partnership bankruptcy, there may be tax liability that exceeds the cash return. This is discussed in Chapter 7. As will be reviewed, all or part of the gain on these transactions may be taxable as ordinary income rather than capital gain, because of possible recapture of depreciation.

Substantial changes in the manner in which real estate (and other) depreciation is computed were recently enacted by Congress in the Economic Recovery Tax Act of 1981 ("ERTA") and were somewhat modified in the Tax Equity and Fiscal Responsibility Act of 1982 ("TEFRA"). Unlike the former system of depreciation, which tied the recovery of the cost of depreciable property to its economic useful life ("Useful Life System"), the new system establishes specific and usually shorter recovery periods for different types of business and investment property.

Under ERTA, the amount of the annual deduction, which incorporates certain accelerated methods, is determined by using a table prescribed in the Code or to be prescribed by Regulations. In general, the new accelerated cost recovery depreciation system ("ACRS") is applicable to new and used depreciable business or investment property acquired or placed in service by the taxpayer after December 31, 1980. However, ERTA provides numerous "anti-churning" rules designed to prevent certain acquisitions of depreciable property after 1980 from qualifying under ACRS.

Thus under ERTA the cost of a limited partnership's depreciable real property must be recovered over a legally required period of time (usually 15 years and thus much shorter than the old system's 40 and 45 years for new apartment houses and office buildings) using a limited choice of methods (the best for conventional property approximating the best of the old accelerated methods). Unlike the old system, used property is treated the same as new property, and salvage value is disregarded in computing depreciation.

The new ACRS system applies to "recovery property." Recovery property is tangible property used in a trade or business or held for the production of income that is subject to being depreciated. As will be discussed, exceptions to the definition are provided. This book will use the term depreciable property and recovery property interchangeably.

In addition, ERTA has, among other things, (a) effected new rules for recapture of depreciation, (b) eliminated component method depreciation for ACRS property, and (c) expanded and modified the tax incentives for low-income housing and for rehabilitation of certain historic structures and older buildings. The subsequent sections of this chapter will describe the new depreciation system. Discussion of the old system is contained in Section 5 of this chapter; for a longer discussion, see the first edition of this book.

2. BASIS OF DEPRECIABLE PROPERTY

Depreciation may be taken on "recovery property." As before ACRS, "recovery property" and "depreciable property" mean tangible assets (real and personal) used in a trade or business or held for the production of income if subject to wear and tear, decay, or decline from natural causes or obsolescence.[2] Assets that do not decline in value on a predictable basis or that do not have a determinable useful life, such as land, goodwill, and stock, are not depreciable.

The major component of the depreciation computation is the basis of the property in the hands of the partnership. To be entitled to depreciation deductions, the partnership must establish that it has a basis in the property by demonstrating that the partnership owned the beneficial interest in the property [3] and the amount of such basis.[4]

For a real estate syndication, the depreciable basis of the property generally equals one of the following: (a) the total cost of purchasing or constructing the property, including any liabilities or mortgages incurred in connection with the acquisition or construction,[5] (b) in situations where the property is contributed to the partnership, the adjusted basis of the property in the hands of a contributing partner,[6] or (c) the basis after being "stepped-up" under a special Code section.[7]

Depreciable basis is reduced by: (a) all of the investment tax credit on qualified rehabilitation expenditures [8]; (b) the amount of first year bonus depreciation; and (c) the amount of qualified rehabilitation expenditures for low-income housing that is amortizable over 60 months.[9] Basis is no longer reduced by salvage value.[10]

Where both depreciable and nondepreciable property, such as buildings and land, are purchased for a lump sum, the cost of the properties must be allocated. It is advantageous for the partnership to allocate as much of the cost as is reasonable to the depreciable property. Although the Regulations provide that "the basis for depreciation cannot exceed an amount which bears the same proportion to the lump sum as the value of the depreciable property at the time of acquisition bears to the value of the entire property at that time . . . ," [11] the Service generally allows the allocation assigned in a sales contract that is the result of arm's-length bargaining.

The depreciable basis of purchased property includes the full purchase price, brokerage commissions, cost of title examination, attorneys' fees, and other purchase-related expenses that are not immediately deductible.[12] Where the property is constructed by or for the partnership, the depreciable basis includes all material costs, labor costs, engineering and architectural services, and other construction-related expenses that are not immediately deductible. If the property is constructed by the partnership, the depreciation of equipment owned and used by the partnership during the period of constructing the property is not deductible and must be included as part of the depreciable basis of the property.[13] In either a purchase or construction situation, the partnership may elect on a yearly basis and with respect to each property to add to basis certain taxes and carrying charges that would otherwise be currently deductible.[14] Generally, partnerships prefer to deduct these expenses as soon as possible.

A partner may contribute to the partnership property that previously was not depreciable because it was not used in a trade or business or held for the production of income. If the property is converted to business or income-producing use by the partnership, the property will become depreciable, and the basis for this purpose is the *lower* of the adjusted basis or the fair market value of the property on the date of the conversion.[15]

Where the partnership purchases land on which there is a building, and the partnership intends at the time of purchase to demolish the building, the cost of the land, building, and of demolition is considered the basis of the land and generally is not depreciable.[16] Where there is temporary business use of the building prior to demolition, a portion of the cost of the land and building may be allocated to the building and depreciated.[17] If a building is acquired without an intent to demolish and is subsequently demolished before the expiration of its intended use, the remaining undepreciated basis in the building is not added to the basis of the land, but can be deducted in the taxable year in which the demolition occurs.[18]

Finally, expenditures attributable to improvement or repair of depreciable property are included in the basis of the property if the expenditures increase the value of the property or adapt the property to a new or different use.[19] Amounts paid for incidental repairs and maintenance of a real estate investment are deductible currently, which is usually preferred, and may not be capitalized.[20]

3. THE PERIOD OF DEPRECIATION

As we discussed, depreciation is a bookkeeping deduction that increases deductible losses. If $150,000 is the basis of the depreciable property and it can be deducted over 15 years, the partnership may claim a $10,000 deduction each year for 15 years on a straight line basis. Section 2 of this Chapter discussed basis. This section discusses the period of time over which the depreciation should be claimed.

Prior to the enactment of ACRS, the determination of the period for which depreciation was taken depended on when the property was acquired or placed in service by the partnership and the useful life of the property. Under ACRS, however, the issue of a depreciable property's useful life is irrelevant. Rather, ACRS provides recovery periods for five classes of depreciable property. The periods range from 3 to 15 years.[21] Thus, for property acquired or placed in service by the partnership after December 31, 1980 (and which is not subject to the anti-churning rules described in Section 7 of this chapter), the partnership must recover its basis in the property over the appropriate recovery period. Depreciable property acquired or placed in service by the partnership prior to January 1, 1981 remains subject to the old Useful Life System.[22]

Under ACRS, all eligible *real* property is divided into two recovery classes. Generally, most real property held by a partnership will be included in the 15-year recovery class.[23] That is, the property's basis must be deducted over 15 years. Certain types of real property, however, such as manufactured residential housing and amusement park structures, are grouped in a 10-year recovery class.[24] Further, the partnership may elect to extend the 15-year recovery period to 35 or 45 years.[25]

Under ACRS, depreciable property other than 15-year real property is divided into four recovery classes. These are discussed in the Notes.[26]

If, pursuant to the anti-churning rules described in Section 7 of this chapter, depreciable property acquired or placed in service by the partnership after December 31, 1980 is not ACRS property, the old Useful Life System remains applicable.[27] Under that method, the partnership must depreciate a property over its useful life. Useful life corresponds to the economic life of the property.[28] To determine the useful life of a particular property, the partnership is required to consider the date of construction,

construction materials, physical condition, location and other factors.[29] In addition, "guideline" useful lives may be considered. In 1962, the Service issued "guidelines for depreciation" that contain, with subsequent Service amendments, recommended useful lives for various assets.[30] The guideline useful life is 40 years for apartment buildings and 45 years for office buildings.[31]

Under both ACRS and the Useful Life System, depreciation generally begins when the partnership obtains beneficial ownership of the property.[32] For purchased property, this usually occurs upon delivery of the deed, while for constructed property, this occurs when the building is first "placed in service." [33] Property is first placed in service when it is first available for service and not necessarily when use commences.[34] Depreciation generally ceases when the partnership sells, abandons, or otherwise relinquishes possession of the property, when demolition commences, or when all allowable depreciation deductions have been taken.

4. METHODS OF DEPRECIATION—ACRS

a. General In Section 2 we discussed property basis, and in Section 3 we reviewed the period of time that is appropriate for deducting that basis. In this section, we analyze the available methods of depreciation under ACRS.

Under the old Useful Life System, a partnership was permitted to select one of four methods of depreciation (i.e., straight-line; up to double declining balance; sum of the years-digits; or any other method approved by the Service) depending on the type of depreciable property involved (i.e., personal property, residential real property, nonresidential real property) and whether original use of such property began with the partnership. For property acquired or placed in service prior to January 1, 1981 and for property acquired after December 31, 1980 which is not subject to ACRS as a result of the anti-churning rules, the old Useful Life System remains applicable. The computation of depreciation under the old Useful Life System is discussed in the first edition and in Section 5 of this chapter.

For property acquired or placed in service by the partnership after December 31, 1980, ACRS is generally applicable. Under ACRS, capital costs for recovery property are recovered by using a statutory accelerated method of cost recovery over a predetermined recovery period. The deduction allowable to the partnership in each year of the recovery period is determined by applying a statutory percentage to the unadjusted basis of the recovery (i.e., depreciable) property. This percentage varies according to the particular property's recovery class and the recovery year. In another departure from prior practice, a stated statutory percentage is applicable to a recovery class without regard to whether it is new or used property.

Since ACRS permits either an accelerated system based approximately on the 175% declining balance method switching to the straight-line method or the election from the beginning of the straight-line method, it is useful to describe these methods.

The depreciation deduction under the straight-line method is calculated by dividing 100% by the recovery period of the asset in order to obtain an annual constant percentage rate. This rate is then multiplied by the property's original basis, which remains constant. For example, if the partnership constructs a new apartment house for $5,000,000, the annual straight-line depreciation deduction is likely to be $333,000 a year for 15 years (100% divided by 15-year life = 6.6% × $5,000,000, on a constant basis).

Under the declining balance method, the depreciation rate is a multiple of the straight-line rate that would be applicable to the particular asset and is applied to the basis remaining after reducing it by previously deducted depreciation. Thus, in our example, the first-year deduction under a double (twice) declining balance method would be $666,000, which amount would decline rapidly each year so that depreciation would still be exhausted after 15 years.[35]

Accelerated methods permit greater deductions in earlier years; that is, they "front end" deductions. For example, if the 175% declining balance method is applied, where the depreciation rate is 175%, a partnership may deduct 1¾ as much of the real property's basis in the first year as under the straight-line method. The deduction declines progressively over the recovery period of the property so that after the expiration of some of the recovery period, the straight-line method will be more favorable and a change to this method is incorporated in ACRS.

b. Fifteen-Year Real Property Of most interest to real estate limited partnerships is the depreciation of domestic 15-year real property. (Special, less attractive, rules are provided under ACRS for 15-year real property predominantly used outside of the United States.)[36] Congress has authorized the Treasury to prescribe a schedule of accelerated recovery percentages that will approximate the benefit of using the 175% declining balance method during the initial portion of the recovery period, changing to the straight-line method at a time that maximizes the allowable deduction. In the case of certain low-income housing, the percentage will approximate the 200% declining balance method switching to the straight-line method.[37]

The Treasury has prescribed the following temporary schedule for domestic 15-year recovery real property:

ACRS Cost Recovery Tables for Real Estate

1. All Real Estate (Except Low-Income Housing)

If the Recovery Year Is:	The Applicable Percentage Is: (Use the Column for the Month in the First Year the Property is Placed In Service)											
	1	2	3	4	5	6	7	8	9	10	11	12
1	12	11	10	9	8	7	6	5	4	3	2	1
2	10	10	11	11	11	11	11	11	11	11	11	12
3	9	9	9	9	10	10	10	10	10	10	10	10
4	8	8	8	8	8	8	9	9	9	9	9	9
5	7	7	7	7	7	7	8	8	8	8	8	8
6	6	6	6	6	7	7	7	7	7	7	7	7
7	6	6	6	6	6	6	6	6	6	6	6	6
8	6	6	6	6	6	6	5	6	6	6	6	6
9	6	6	6	6	5	6	5	5	5	6	6	6
10	5	6	5	6	5	5	5	5	5	5	6	5
11	5	5	5	5	5	5	5	5	5	5	5	5
12	5	5	5	5	5	5	5	5	5	5	5	5
13	5	5	5	5	5	5	5	5	5	5	5	5
14	5	5	5	5	5	5	5	5	5	5	5	5
15	5	5	5	5	5	5	5	5	5	5	5	5
16	—	—	1	1	2	2	3	3	4	4	4	3

2. Low-Income Housing

If the Recovery Year Is:	The Applicable Percentage Is: (Use the Column for the Month in the First Year the Property is Placed In Service)											
	1	2	3	4	5	6	7	8	9	10	11	12
1	13	12	11	10	9	8	7	6	4	3	2	1
2	12	12	12	12	12	12	12	13	13	13	13	13
3	10	10	10	10	11	11	11	11	11	11	11	11
4	9	9	9	9	9	9	9	9	10	10	10	10
5	8	8	8	8	8	8	8	8	8	8	8	9
6	7	7	7	7	7	7	7	7	7	7	7	7
7	6	6	6	6	6	6	6	6	6	6	6	6
8	5	5	5	5	5	5	5	5	5	5	6	6
9	5	5	5	5	5	5	5	5	5	5	5	5
10	5	5	5	5	5	5	5	5	5	5	5	5
11	4	5	5	5	5	5	5	5	5	5	5	5
12	4	4	4	5	4	5	5	5	5	5	5	5
13	4	4	4	4	4	4	5	4	5	5	5	5
14	4	4	4	4	4	4	4	4	4	5	4	4
15	4	4	4	4	4	4	4	4	4	4	4	4
16	—	—	1	1	2	2	2	3	3	3	4	4

Generally, the recovery period percentage for 15-year real property will take into account the number of months the property is actually in service during the taxable year.[38]

Instead of the accelerated method, a partnership may elect to use the straight-line method. If so, it may choose a 15-, 35-, or 45-year recovery period.[39] Unlike other recovery classes, in which the election is applicable to all property within the class for the year of election, the partnership can make the election with respect to 15-year real properties on a property by property basis.[40] As in the case of other recovery property, the election is revocable only with the consent of the Service.[41]

c.   Recovery Property Other Than 15-Year Real Property   The statutory accelerated method prescribed under ACRS for recovery property other than 15-year real property approximates the benefit of using the 150% declining balance method for the initial years of the recovery period, changing to the straight-line method at a time that will maximize the allowable deduction.[42]

5. METHOD OF DEPRECIATION—USEFUL LIFE SYSTEM

a.   General   It is useful to briefly describe the old system, which this section does. If property is subject to the Useful Life System (either as a result of the "anti-churning" rules discussed in Section 7 of this chapter or because the property was placed in service before 1981), a partnership may choose various methods of computing depreciation depending on the nature of the property and whether it is new or used. For example, a real estate limited partnership holding residential property usually is permitted to select one of four methods of depreciation: straight-line; up to double declining balance; sum of the years-digits; or any other method approved by the Service.[43]

b.   First User   Under the Useful Life System, most accelerated depreciation methods, such as declining balance and sum of the years-digits, are available only for property of which the partnership is the first user. (That is, the original use of the property must commence with the partnership.) [44] Original use means the first use to which the property is put, whether or not such use corresponds to the use of the property by the partnership.[45] It begins, usually, with the taxpayer who is first entitled to take depreciation deductions with respect to the property.

If property transferred to the partnership after 1980 is not ACRS property as a result of the "anti-churning" rules, and the partnership is permitted to calculate a new depreciation period and method under the Useful Life System, accelerated depreciation may be lost if the partnership is not the first user.[46]

c.   Nonresidential Real Property   Under the Useful Life System, a limited partnership holding office buildings or other nonresidential property for which it is a first user may elect either the straight-line method, a 150% declining balance method, or any other consistent method if the depreciation deductions for the first two thirds of the useful life of the property do not exceed that which would have been permitted if the 150% declining balance method had been elected. Office buildings and other nonresidential real properties may not be depreciated by using sum of the years-digits method of depreciation or by the 200% declining balance depreciation method.[47]

If the limited partnership is not the first user, nonresidential property acquired after July 24, 1969 must be depreciated on a straight-line basis.[48]

d. Residential Real Property Under the Useful Life System, a limited partnership holding residential rental properties of which it is the first user may elect any one of the four accepted depreciation methods, including the most favorable double declining balance method.[49]

Used residential rental property, that is, where the partnership is not the first user, may be depreciated under the Useful Life System at a maximum 125% declining balance rate, but only if the property is acquired after July 24, 1969 and has a remaining useful life of at least 20 years.[50] (There is an exception for expenditures incurred in the rehabilitation of used low-income housing which is discussed in Section 9.) If property cannot qualify for the 125% declining rate, used residential rental property must be depreciated on a straight-line basis.

e. Component Depreciation A popular technique used by taxpayers under the old Useful Life System to maximize depreciation deductions on real property was to depreciate separately the shell and other component parts of the structure. Thus, instead of basing depreciation on one useful life (e.g., 40 years for an apartment building), the partnership used different useful lives for each component of the building (e.g., wiring, plumbing, building structure).[51] Since many components had a shorter useful life than the building structure, use of components reduced the overall useful life and increased the early year depreciation deductions.

Under ACRS, however, component depreciation has been eliminated for those components of a building that are part of the real property (i.e., wiring, plumbing, and lighting).[52] Rather, ACRS requires composite depreciation for the entire structure except for those component costs that are amortized under the special rules for low-income rehabilitation, discussed in Section 9. Under ACRS, the recovery deduction for each component is computed in the same manner as the structure. The recovery period for any component commences either on the date the component is placed in service or on the date that the building is placed in service, whichever is later.[53] For example, if a new component is added to a building at the end of the building's 15-year recovery period, the cost of the component must be recovered over a 15-year period commencing at the time the component is placed in service.

If the components added to a building subject to ACRS constitute a "substantial improvement," the partnership may elect to use a different recovery period or method with respect to the substantial improvement. A "substantial improvement" means that an improvement was made at least three years after the building was placed in service and that over a two-year period the amounts added to the capital account for the building were at least 25% of the adjusted basis of the building (not including depreciation or amortization) as of the first day of that period.[54]

6. DEPRECIATION RECAPTURE

On the sale, exchange, involuntary conversion or other disposition of a real estate limited partnership's depreciable property, including foreclosure of a mortgage on the property, a varying amount of depreciation must be "recaptured" and treated as ordinary income.[55] The effect, therefore, of the depreciation tax benefit is deferral of tax until disposition of the property or partnership interest, rather than permanent tax reduction. The amount of ordinary income resulting from depreciation recapture may not exceed the amount realized on the disposition (which includes the mortgage debt) reduced by the adjusted basis of the property, that is, the gain.[56] In addition, there may be recapture at capital gain rates upon property disposition. (For discussion, see Section 13.)

Under ACRS, for 15-year nonresidential real property, such as office buildings, there is no recapture if the straight-line method is elected. However, if the usual accelerated method is used, there will be complete ordinary income recapture for the gain to the extent of any depreciation that has been claimed previously.[57]

Under ACRS, residential rental property is treated better. Again, there is no recapture if the straight-line method is elected. However, even if the accelerated method is used for 15-year residential rental property, or for certain 15-year real property constructed or acquired under government-assisted programs, recapture for gain is limited, upon disposition, to the extent that the deductions allowed under the accelerated method exceeded the deductions that would have been allowed under the straight-line method.[58] Thus, if the partnership elects to use the optional straight-line method over a 15-year recovery period, no recapture would result upon disposition. In addition, 15-year residential real property or such property constructed or acquired under government-assisted programs (i.e., low-income housing) is permitted the same phaseout of excess depreciation recapture as applicable under the old Useful Life System.[59] Once the residential real property is held for 15 years, no "excess depreciation" recapture can occur since the amount of depreciation claimed under the prescribed statutory accelerated method will not exceed the straight-line amount.

If the partnership uses the prescribed statutory accelerated method to recover costs in a nonresidential building and uses straight-line recovery on a subsequent substantial improvement of the property, the gain on the sale of the entire building will first be treated as ordinary income to the extent of all recovery deductions under the prescribed accelerated method.[60] Thus allocating sales proceeds among portions of the building to attempt to minimize complete recapture may not be fruitful.

Gain on the disposition of depreciated tangible personal property is subject to ordinary income recapture to the extent of the previously claimed depreciation, regardless of whether the partnership has utilized the accelerated statutory percentage or the optional straight-line method.[61]

7. THE ANTI-CHURNING RULES

Significantly greater depreciation deductions may be available under ACRS for property placed in service by a taxpayer after 1980. Thus Congress was concerned that some taxpayers might be tempted to convert pre-ACRS property (i.e., property placed in service prior to 1981) into ACRS property by transfers that did not result in a real change of ownership. To prevent this, ERTA contains numerous provisions under which certain transfers of pre-1981 property will not make such property eligible for ACRS.

ACRS will not apply to depreciable real property acquired by the partnership after 1980 if (a) the partnership or a related person owned the property at any time during 1980, (b) the property is leased to a person who owned the property at any time during 1980 (or a person who is related to such person), or (c) the property is acquired in certain like-kind exchanges, involuntary conversions, repossessions or rollovers of low-income housing to the extent that the partnership takes a basis in the property received that is determined by reference to the property given up.[62] Property acquired in these "churning" transactions is to be depreciated under pre-ACRS rules. For purposes of the anti-churning rules, property will not be considered "owned" before it has been placed in service. Thus property under construction during 1980 generally can be transferred free of the anti-churning rules. A person related to a partnership is a partner owning directly or indirectly more than 10% of the capital or profits in the partnership or another partnership in which the same persons own more than 10% of the capital or profit interests.

The rules applicable to similar transfers of depreciable personal property are presented in the Notes.[63]

Partnership roll-ins to corporate form, contributions by partners to a partnership, and distributions by a partnership to its partners are subject to a variation of the anti-churning rules.[64] Thus, for real (and personal) property placed in service before 1981 and transferred after 1980 in a transaction in which the basis in whole or part is determined by reference to the basis of the property in the hands of the transferor,[65] the transferee will be required to use the same depreciation method and period that the transferor used prior to the transfer. Here, not only is ACRS not available, but the transferee must continue to use the transferor's period and method of depreciation.[66]

The IRS also has been given broad authority to prescribe regulations to deny ACRS treatment to property that is acquired in a transaction in which one of the principal purposes is to avoid the anti-churning rules or the basic rule that ACRS is not applicable to property placed in service by the taxpayer before January 1, 1981.[67]

8. BONUS DEPRECIATION

For years before 1981, a partnership could pass through up to $2,000 of first-year bonus depreciation on the partnership's tangible personal property, allocated pro rata to the partners. Pursuant to ERTA, bonus depreciation has been repealed for taxable years beginning in 1981 and has been replaced with a provision that permits a taxpayer, other than a trust or estate, to treat the cost of certain qualifying property as a currently deductible expense for taxable years beginning after 1981.[68] For taxable years beginning in 1982 and 1983, the dollar limitation on the amount that can be expensed is $5,000; for 1984 and 1985, $7,500; for 1986 and later years, $10,000. As under prior law, the limitation amount is allocated pro rata to the partners who are individually subject to the limitations listed earlier. No bonus allowance was available for 1981.

Under the new law, "qualified property" is property that is acquired by purchase for use in a trade or business and that is eligible for the investment credit (i.e., tangible personal property).[69] "Purchase" does not include acquisitions from certain related persons or acquisitions in which the transferee takes, in whole or in part, a carry-over basis.[70]

Any amount claimed as an expense under this provision is treated as depreciation for purposes of the recapture rules, and upon the property's disposition, it is subject to recapture.[71] To the extent that the partnership elects to utilize this additional first-year allowance, the basis for calculating depreciation is reduced by the amount expensed.[72]

9. REHABILITATION EXPENSES FOR LOW-INCOME HOUSING

Beginning essentially in 1970, an election to amortize qualifying rehabilitation expenditures for low-income housing over 60 months was added to the Code.[73] As a result of the Tax Treatment Extension Act of 1980, 60-month amortization is available for qualifying expenditures paid or incurred by the partnership before January 1, 1984.[74] If a binding contract involving such expenditures is entered into, or rehabilitation has begun, before January 1, 1984, related expenditures qualify for 60-month amortization even if paid or incurred after that date.[75] Recently, Congress in ERTA increased the amount of rehabilitation expenditures that will qualify for 60-month amortization, provided certain additional stringent requirements are met.[76]

In general, the election permits a partnership to depreciate properly qualifying rehabilitation expenditures under the straight-line method using a five-year useful life and no salvage value.[77] It was hoped that this would encourage the upgrading of deteriorated multifamily structures in low-income areas. Unfortunately, because of inadequacies in the corresponding housing legislation and the poor government management of the housing program, there have been many difficulties and foreclosures.

"Rehabilitation expenditures" are expenditures, other than acquisition costs or costs for new construction, that are incurred in connection with the rehabilitation of an existing building with a remaining useful life of at least five years and that are chargeable to the capital account.[78] The building must be used for low-income rental housing.[79] "Low-income rental housing" refers to "any building the dwelling units in which are held for occupancy on a rental basis by families and individuals of low or moderate income . . . ."[80] Eligible income limits are to be determined pursuant to the "Leased Housing Program under Section 8 of the United States Housing Act of 1937."[81]

Prior to ERTA, the maximum amount of rehabilitation expenditures that qualified for 60-month amortization was $20,000 per dwelling unit. In this regard only those expenditures that aggregated more than $3,000 per dwelling unit over a period of two consecutive years qualified for the election.

Under ERTA, the old maximum of $20,000 is maintained but it can be increased to $40,000 if the partnership satisfies certain requirements.[82] To be entitled to use the higher amount, the partnership must conduct the rehabilitation pursuant to a program certified by the Department of Housing and Urban Development (or a state or local agency), a certification of development costs is required, the tenants must occupy the units as their principal residence, the program must provide for sale of the units to tenants demonstrating home ownership responsibility, and certain stringent partnership income tests that limit the investors' economic benefits must be met.[83] The new ceiling applies to rehabilitation expenditures incurred after 1980.

To qualify for 60-month amortization, the partnership must elect this treatment. Thus, it is wise to have a partnership agreement provision that requires the general partner to make this election. Further, the rehabilitation expenditures must be paid or incurred by the partnership. Thus, if the partnership purchases the rehabilitated property after rehabilitation has been completed and the property placed in service, no portion of the cost of purchase may be amortized under the special provision.

The original use of the rehabilitated property must begin with the partnership, that is, the partnership must be the first taxpayer entitled to depreciate the building after it has been rehabilitated.[84] The rehabilitated property is deemed to be placed in service on the date it is "first placed in a condition or state of readiness and availability for a specifically assigned function . . . ." [85]

Thus, even if the tenants have not moved in, if a limited partnership purchases a completed rehabilitation property, there is some danger that the partnership may not be entitled to the special election. Care must be taken. On the positive side, the Regulations provide that the determination of when property is first placed in service is made on a dwelling unit by unit basis.[86]

Qualified rehabilitation expenditures for which the partnership elects 60-month amortization are not part of the property's depreciable basis for purposes of computing depreciation [87] and are subject to recapture by the partnership upon disposition of the property. The recapture amount for property held more than one year is the excess of the amortization claimed over the amount of depreciation that would have been claimed on a straight-line method over 15 years under ACRS. Thus, presumably, there is no recapture for qualifying rehabilitation property held for at least 15 years.[88]

Use of the special election can create very substantial "bookkeeping" losses in the first five years. Real estate limited partnerships that have invested in rehabilitation properties have proven, however, to be very high risk/reward investments. When successful, an investment in a "rehab" partnership can be very rewarding economically. However, the government financing often has the effect of minimizing or even eliminating the possibility of cash flow profit for the investors, and they often lose positive interest after achieving the tax benefits, hoping only to avoid mortgage foreclosure and the resulting tax recapture. Often buildings are not properly maintained and may quickly lose value. The general partner, often the builder, may lose interest after his builder's profit has been earned and any contractual commitments to the limited partners have been satisfied. The government administration of the program has been ponderous and often damaging to its very purpose. Many building abandonments and mortgage foreclosures have been the inevitable consequence.

In recent years, Congress and the Department of Housing and Urban Development ("H.U.D.") have taken cognizance of the problems. Many projects (whether or not devoted to rehabilitation) now involve H.U.D. agreements to pay a rent supplement to private owners of certain housing for lower-income persons. This so-called Section 8 program under Title II of the Housing and Community Development Act of 1974 permits the owner to receive an annually adjusted, federally determined fair market rent, with the tenant paying a stated maximum percentage of his income and the government paying the rest. Certain rent increases can be obtained automatically, based on cost of living standards. This eliminates the often long rent increase delays inherent in other programs.

A properly structured and financed "Section 8" limited partnership can be a sensible investment. However, the new Administration is unenthusiastic about the "Section 8" program and its future is uncertain. There are pending at this writing several proposals that could reduce or even eliminate the economic justification for investment in low-income housing.

Finally, a combination of government aggressiveness in denying early year tax deductions (discussed in Chapter 6) with the lowering of the maximum income tax bracket to 50% has reduced interest in investments with higher tax shelter capacity but lower income and capital gain potential.

10. HISTORIC STRUCTURES AND OLDER STRUCTURES—CREDITS, AMORTIZATION, AND OTHER INCENTIVES

The Code contains incentives to rehabilitate and preserve historic structures and to rehabilitate older commercial buildings. These are discussed here because the tax benefits are often "packaged" in real estate limited partnerships.

Under ERTA, effective after 1981, 60-month amortization of qualified rehabilitation expenditures for certified historic structures was repealed,[89] prohibition of the use of accelerated depreciation methods for property constructed on the site of a demolished or substantially altered certified historic structure was repealed,[90] permission to accelerate depreciation of a substantially rehabilitated certified historic structure in lieu of 60-month amortization was repealed, and the 10% investment tax credit available for expenditures to rehabilitate a building at least 20 years old was substantially amended.[91]

Instead, under ERTA, the 10% credit and the 60-month amortization provision for certified historic rehabilitation expenditures is replaced by a three-tiered investment tax credit (ITC) for qualified rehabilitation expenditures.[92] A qualified rehabilitation expenditure is an amount expended in connection with the rehabilitation of a qualified rehabilitation building that is properly chargeable to capital, is incurred after 1981, and is expended for property with a recovery period of at least 15 years.[93]

The ITC is 15% for structures at least 30 years old, 20% for structures at least 40 years old, and 25% for certified historic structures.[94] Thus no ITC is allowed for rehabilitation of a building less than 30 years old except for certified historic structures on which no age limit is placed.

As under pre-ERTA law, the 15 and 20% credits are limited to nonresidential buildings.[95] The 25% credit for certified historic rehabilitation is available for residential properties used in a trade or business as well as for nonresidential buildings.[96] The ITCs are available only if the partnership elects to use the straight-line method of cost recovery with respect to rehabilitation expenditures.[97]

In order to qualify for the credit there must be substantial rehabilitation of a qualified rehabilitated building.[98] A "qualified rehabilitated building" means a building that was placed in service before rehabilitation commenced, is at least 30 years old or is a certified historic structure, has existed at least 30 years since it was placed in service and the rehabilitation commenced (not applicable to certified historic structures) and retains 75% of the original external walls after rehabilitation.[99] A building has been substantially rehabilitated if the rehabilitation expenditures during the 24-month period ending on the last day of the taxable year exceed the adjusted basis of the property as of the first day of the 24-month period or $5,000, whichever is greater.[100] A 60-month period may be substituted for 24 months if there is a written set of architectural plans and specifications for all phases of the rehabilitation and a reasonable expectation that all phases of the rehabilitation will be completed.[101]

For rehabilitation credits other than the credit for certified historic rehabilitation, the basis of the property must be reduced by the amount of the credit allowed.[102] If there is subsequently a recapture of the credit (i.e., disposition of the property), the resulting increase in tax will increase the basis of the structure immediately before the application of depreciation recapture.[103]

Pursuant to TEFRA, for years subsequent to 1982, depreciable basis is reduced by half of the credit claimed for rehabilitation of certified historic structures.[104] Complicated transitional rules have been provided.[105] If there is subsequently a recapture of the credit, half of the resulting increase in tax will increase the basis of the property immediately before the application of depreciation recapture.[106]

In general, the credit is available for a certified historic structure if approval of the rehabilitation is obtained from the Secretary of the Interior as being consistent with the historic character of the property or the district the property is in.[107]

The credit provisions of ERTA generally apply to expenditures made after 1981 regardless of when the rehabilitation began. Thus if a rehabilitation that qualifies under the new law and prior law was begun before 1982, the old law applies to pre-1982 expenditures and the new law applies to expenditures after 1981. However, a special rule allows a credit, computed under pre-ERTA law, for buildings that are more than 20 but less than 30 years old, if the rehabilitation began before January 1, 1982 and if the rehabilitation qualifies under prior law.[108]

11. REINVESTMENT ROLLOVER

In addition to favorable depreciation and recapture rules that apply to certain government-assisted residential rental property, as discussed previously, investors in such real property may elect to defer tax liability (and possibly to postpone recapture) on any gain realized from the disposition of such property.[109] To be eligible, the investors must reinvest the proceeds in other like-kind housing projects,[110] and they must sell or otherwise dispose of the first project to the tenants living in the project or to an organization formed for their benefit.[111] The proceeds must be reinvested during a period beginning one year before the date of the sale or disposition and ending one year after the end of the first taxable year in which any part of the gain is realized (or a later date if approved upon application to the Service).[112] If the amount realized on the sale or other disposition exceeds the cost of the replacement project, however, the election will not prevent current taxation of the excess amount.[113] In addition, if the disposed-of project is property subject to depreciation recapture, special rules apply, which may limit the current ordinary income recapture.[114]

Note that if the partnership rolls over a project it (or a related person) held at any time during 1980, the acquired project would not be subject to ACRS to the extent that its depreciable basis is determined by reference to the project held during 1980; rather, the rollover property would be subject to the old Useful Life System.[115]

12. "TURN AROUND"

In the normal course of an investment in real property, when an accelerated depreciation method is used, the benefit of the depreciation deductions decreases until it is no longer sufficient to "shelter" income earned by the property.

In the initial years, a real estate limited partnership's investment often results in tax losses that are passed through to the partners. If the property is economically successful, at some point the combination of increasing debt amortization and decreasing depreciation deductions results in increasing taxable income. Accelerated depreciation methods permit smaller and smaller yearly deductions and indeed are usually changed to straight line after a period of time, as incorporated in ACRS. Similarly, the interest part of the "constant" mortgage payment decreases yearly while the non-deductible debt amortization repayment increases. At some point, the deductions can decrease to an extent that the cash distributions from the partnership are no longer sufficient to cover the tax liability generated by the property.

To avoid this, the partners often desire to refinance the debt on the property, in order to increase the deductible portion of otherwise constant mortgage payments, or to dispose of the real property, in order to relieve themselves of the additional taxable income. In either event, the partnership, and hence the partners, may be subject to certain adverse tax consequences. These consequences were discussed in Section 6 of this chapter and will be analyzed in Chapter 7.

13. "CAPITAL GAIN" RECAPTURE

There is another type of recapture. As has been discussed, when a limited partnership purchases property subject to a nonrecourse mortgage, it is permitted to add the amount of the mortgage to the basis of the property (and the partners may add it to the bases of their interests in the limited partnership).[116] This increases the amount of the allowable depreciation deductions and the amount of "tax shelter." In exchange for this benefit, the partnership and the partners must add the amount of the outstanding, unpaid balance of the mortgage to the amount deemed realized on the disposition of the property.[117] If the net cash proceeds from the sale or other disposition (which includes foreclosure) are substantially less than the amount realized for tax reporting purposes, the investor may be forced to use other funds to pay the capital gain tax resulting from the disposition. The risk of "capital gain" recapture is obviously minimized with investments in properties that appreciate in value. This subject is discussed in Chapter 7.

14. SPECIAL RULES REGARDING LEASED PROPERTY

Where the real estate limited partnership owns real property that it leases, special depreciation considerations may apply. For example, where the lessee makes substantial improvements to the property during the term of the lease, the partnership lessor may not depreciate the cost of the improvements since it has no depreciable basis in the property.[118] Where the improvements are in lieu of rent, however, the partnership must report the value as taxable income but may add that amount to the property's depreciable basis.[119] If, at the termination of the lease, the improvements revert to the partnership, the partnership's gross income will not include the increased value of the property [120] but, correspondingly, there will be no increase in the depreciable basis.[121] Other special rules exist with respect to the depreciation of a lessee's improvements made prior to the partnership's purchase of the property,[122] amortization of the value of the favorable leases on the acquired property,[123] depreciation deductions allowable to the lessee,[124] and other issues.

15. SPECIAL ALLOCATION OF DEPRECIATION

As was discussed in Chapter 4, there are numerous problems with special allocations. There have been attempts to specially allocate depreciation.[125] It is not often advisable to attempt a special allocation of depreciation; rather, a special allocation usually should apply to "bottom line" income and losses. Of course, as is discussed in Chapter 4, a special allocation must have substantial economic effect if it is to be recognized for tax purposes.[126]

16. ALTERNATIVE MINIMUM TAX—IMPLICATIONS

A real estate limited partnership may generate substantial deductions (e.g., depreciation, interest) that offset a partner's distributive share of partnership income, and, if greater, reduce other taxable income of a partner. For taxable years beginning before 1983, some of the deductions claimed by a real estate partnership, under certain conditions, resulted in a partner's exposure to the then existing minimum and alternative minimum taxes.[127] Before TEFRA, there was a 15% minimum tax that could be imposed under certain circumstances.[128] This "add-on" minimum tax and the alternative minimum tax provision that was in effect for years beginning before 1983 are discussed in the First Edition.

As a result of TEFRA, effective for taxable years beginning in 1983, the "add-on" minimum tax for individuals has been repealed and a broadened alternative minimum tax is in effect.[129]

The new alternative minimum tax must be paid by a non-corporate taxpayer if it exceeds his regular tax.[130] Thus, two computations must be made: the regular tax and the alternative minimum tax. The taxpayer pays the greater amount.

The alternative minimum tax usually will apply to individuals who have large capital gains substantial "tax preferences," or who exercise incentive stock options and who have relatively little taxable ordinary income; it is intended to insure that every taxpayer pays some tax. The tax rate for the alternative minimum tax is a flat 20% for alternative minimum taxable income above $30,000 for single taxpayers or $40,000 for married taxpayers filing jointly.[131] The alternative minimum taxable income is generally a non-corporate taxpayer's adjusted gross income, *plus* certain items of tax preference, which include (i) the 60% of the excess of net long-term capital gain over net short-term capital loss that is excluded from normal taxable income, (ii) the excess of accelerated depreciation over straight-line depreciation, and (iii) the difference between the exercise price of incentive stock options and the fair market value of the stock on the date of exercise, *less* certain itemized deductions including, (i) charitable contributions, (ii) medical expenses, (iii) interest on principal residences, and (iv) investment interest to the extent of net investment income.[132] Importantly, state and local taxes are not deductible for the purpose of computing the alternative minimun tax.[133]

For purposes of the alternative minimum tax, investors in real estate limited partnerships must be concerned about accelerated depreciation on real property in excess of the amounts that would be allowable under the straight-line method, computed over 15 years under ACRS or the property's useful life under the old system.[134] Although adjusted gross income is generally reduced by accelerated depreciation for regular tax computations, the difference between straight-line depreciation and accelerated depreciation must be added back to adjusted gross income to calculate the alternative minimum tax. Thus, a real estate limited partnership must weigh the normal tax benefits of electing to use accelerated depreciation against the alternative minimum tax detriment and considerations discussed elsewhere in this book such as recapture income upon property sale and other disposition.

NOTES

1. The alternative minimum tax and the recent changes to this provision are discussed in Section 16 of this chapter.

2. H. R. Rep. No. 97-215, 97th Cong., 1st Sess. 206 (1981).

3. *See David L. Narver, Jr.,* 75 T.C. 53 (1980), *aff'd,* 670 F.2d 855 (9th Cir.1982); *Carol W. Hilton,* 74 T.C. 305 (1980), *aff'd,* 671 F.2d 316 (9th Cir.1982), cert.filed, July 27, 1982; *Estate of Charles T. Franklin,* 64 T.C. 752 (1975), *aff'd,* 544 F.2d 1045 (9th Cir. 1976); *David F. Bolger,* 59 T.C. 760 (1973) (Acq.).

4. Secs. 167(g), 168(d).

5. *Crane v. Commissioner,* 331 U.S. 1 (1947); *Manuel D. Mayerson,* 47 T.C. 340 (1966) (Acq.). For a discussion of inclusion of liabilities in basis and the "at risk" provisions in Chapter 4.

6. Sec. 723; Treas. Reg. §1.723-1. *See* Rev. Rul 77-458, 1977-2 C.B. 220 (basis in merger of 10 general partnerships owned by two individuals).

7. For a discussion of the special basis adjustment rules in Secs. 743 and 754, *see* Chapter 7.

8. Sec. 48(q)(1). For years prior to 1983, the credit allowed for qualified expenditures on certified historic structures did not reduce depreciable basis for purposes of computing the ACRS deduction. Pursuant to TEFRA, for years subsequent to 1982, depreciable basis is reduced by half of the claimed credit for certified historic structures.

9. Sec. 168(d)(1)(A)(ii) (adjustment to basis for ACRS property); Treas. Reg. §1.167(k)-1(a).

10. Sec. 168(g)(9). Under the old Useful Life System, salvage value usually reduced depreciable basis. Treas. Reg. §1.167(b)-1 through 4.

11. Treas. Reg. §1.167(a)(5).

12. Real estate transfer taxes and state and local stamp taxes may not be added to cost but must be deducted if the property is used in a trade or business or held for investment. Sec. 164(a); Treas. Reg. §1.164-1(a). Expenses incurred in evaluating a specific property which is not acquired by the partnership may be currently deductible as business losses. Sec. 165; Rev. Rul. 74-104, 1974-1 C.B. 70; *but see John C. Bick,* 37 CCH Tax Ct. Mem. 1591 (1978); Rev. Rul. 77-254, 1977-2 C.B. 63. Depreciable basis does not include organization costs. *See* pp. 129–130, *infra.*

13. Sec. 263(a)(1); *see Blitzer v. United States,* 81-1 USTC ¶9262 (Ct. Cl. 1981), *aff'd,* 684 F.2d 874 (Ct. Cl. 1982). *Commissioner v. Idaho Power Co.,* 418 U.S. 1 (1974); *Betty L. Young,* 36 CCH Tax Ct. Mem. 165 (1977); Rev. Rul. 59-380, 1959-2 C.B. 87.

14. Sec. 266. The election to capitalize may be made with respect to different types of taxes, interest, and other carrying charges, depending on whether the property concerned is real property or personal property. Treas. Reg. §1.266-1(b)(1). The amortization of construction period interest and taxes under Sec. 189 is discussed in Chapter 6.

15. Treas. Reg. §1.167(g)-1.

16. Treas. Reg. §1.165-3(a)(1). The basis of the land is reduced by any net proceeds resulting from the demolition. *Id. See, however,* the discussion in Section 10 of this chapter on the restrictions on deducting demolition costs of certified historic structures.

17. Treas. Reg. §1.165-3(a)(2)(i). The portion is the present value of the right to receive rentals from the building over the period of intended use.

18. Id.; *see William I. Nash,* 60 T.C. 503 (1973) (Acq.). This rule is modified for historic structures, *see* Section 10 of this chapter.

19. Treas. Reg. §§1.1016-2(a), 1.263(a)-1(a), (b).

20. Treas. Reg. §1.162-4.

21. Sec. 168(c).

22. Sec. 168(e)(1). For a discussion of this system, *see* the first edition of this book.

23. Sec. 168(c)(2)(D).

24. Sec. 168(c)(2)(C)(ii).

25. Sec. 168(b)(3).

26. The three-year recovery class includes autos, light-duty trucks, research and experimentation equipment and machinery, and other machinery and equipment that under prior law had an asset depreciation range midpoint life of four years or less. Sec. 168(c)(2)(A). Five-year recovery class property includes all depreciable personal property that isn't included in the 3-, or 15-year recovery classes. Sec. 168(c)(2)(B). Generally, five-year property includes, among other items, heavy-duty trucks, most production line machinery, and most office furniture. The 10-year recovery class consists primarily of short-life public utility property and railroad equipment. Sec. 168(c)(2)(C). Finally, the 15-year recovery class includes long-life public utility property. Sec. 168(c)(2)(E).

27. Sec. 168(e)(4).

28. Treas. Reg. §1.167(a)-1(b); *Massey Motors Inc. v. United States,* 364 U.S. 92 (1960). Where factors indicate a clear and convincing basis for redetermination of the useful life of an asset, such change should be made at the close of the taxable year in which the factors arise. Treas. Reg. §1.167(a)-1(b).

29. *See* Treas. Reg. §1.167(a)-1(b); *Robert C. Honodel,* 76 T.C. 351 (1981), *on appeal to 9th Cir.; University City, Inc.* 38 CCH Tax Ct. Mem. 827 (1979); *Donald R. Huene,* 38 CCH Tax Ct. Mem. 1176 (1979); *Vernon Keith Graves,* 48 T.C. 7 (1967), *aff'd,* 400 F.2d 528 (9th Cir. 1968); *Richard A. Mack,* 35 CCH Tax Ct. Memo. 1628 (1976).

30. Rev. Proc. 62-21, 1962-2 C.B. 418. There are numerous amendments and supplements to this revenue procedure that do not change the original recommended useful life for most real property.

31. *Id.* Another method, the class life asset depreciation range system ("ADR"), may result in useful lives that are substantially shorter than the applicable guideline lives. Sec. 167(m); Treas. Reg. §1.167(a)-11. ADR, however, does not apply to real estate. Accordingly, applicable guideline lives and the facts and circumstances should be considered in the selection of real estate asset useful lives. Pub. L. No.93-625 §5, 88 Stat. 2108(1974); Rev. Proc. 77-10, 1977-1 C.B. 548.

    Since depreciation prior to ACRS represents the expiration of the cost of a property over its useful life, the shorter the useful life, the greater the yearly depreciation deductions will be to the partnership. Thus the partnership should select the shortest useful life that can be defended. Keep in mind, however, that the burden of proving the useful life is on the taxpayer. *Robert C. Hondodel,* 76 T.C. 351 (1981), *on appeal to 9th Cir.*

    The Service has stated that it will not ordinarily issue advance rulings as to the useful lives of assets, depreciation rates, or salvage value. Rev. Proc. 81-10, 1981-1 C.B. 647.

32. Rev. Rul. 69-39, 1969-1 C.B. 59.

33. Treas. Reg. §1.167(a)-10(b).

34. *See* Rev. Rul. 73-518, 1973-2 C.B. 54.

35. The sum of the years-digits method applies a constantly reducing fraction, which is based on numbers assigned to each year of the asset's recovery period, to the asset's basis. Thus, using the example in the text, the first year depreciation deduction would be approximately \$625,000 (15 ÷ 15 + 14 + 13 + . . . × \$5,000,000). In the second year, the fraction would be 14 ÷ 14 + 13 + 12 + . . ., and the basis would remain the same.

36. Sec. 168(f)(2)(B). Such real property is permitted less favorable treatment than domestic real property; essentially 35-year depreciation using the 150% declining balance method and then switching to the straight-line method.

37. Sec. 168(b)(2)(A).

38. Sec. 168(b)(3).

39. Sec. 168(b)(3)(B)(ii).

40. Sec. 168(f)(4)(C).

41. Sec. 168(b)(1)(A); H. R. Rep. No. 97-215, 97th Cong., lst Sess. 207-208 (1981).

The cost recovery tables are based on the half-year convention, which assumes that all recovery property other than real property is placed in service in the middle of a taxable year. H. R. Rep. No. 97-215, 97th Cong., lst Sess. 207-208 (1981).

In addition, the tables assume a taxable year of 12 months. In this regard, ERTA provides that the recovery deduction is reduced in the case of a short taxable year to an amount which bears the same ratio as the number of months in the short year bears to 12. Appropriate adjustments would be made in subsequent years. Sec. 168(f)(5). The Treasury has been authorized to promulgate Regulations that would determine when a tax year begins. Presumably, such Regulations would be similar to present rules under the old Useful Life System, which provide generally that the first taxable year does not begin until the taxpayer is deemed to have commenced business. Treas. Reg. §1.167(a)-11(c)(2)(iv)(c).

Although the rules for recovery property other than 15-year real property generally provide a full year's worth of depreciation on such property whenever acquired or placed in service during the taxable year, if the partnership disposes of such property, the unadjusted basis of the property must be removed from the recovery account as of the first day of the taxable year of disposition. Sec. 168(d)(2)(B). Thus no recovery deduction is allowed for the property in the year of disposition. For purposes of ACRS, disposition includes retirement of the property. Sec. 168(d)(2)(C).

In lieu of the prescribed accelerated method, a partnership may elect to use the straight-line method over the regular recovery period or over an extended recovery period. The following chart summarizes the options available:

Recovery Class	Recovery Period
3-year property	3, 5, or 12 years
5-year property	5, 12, or 15 years
10-year property	10, 25, or 35 years
15-year public utility property	15, 35, or 45 years

If the straight-line method is elected by the partnership for other than 15-year real property for any year, the election covers all property of that class placed in service for that year. Sec. 168(b)(3)(B)(i). The election is revocable only with the consent of the

Service. Sec. 168(f)(4)(C). As with the prescribed statutory accelerated method, the half-year convention applies to the optional straight-line recovery method. Sec. 168(b)(3)(B)(iii).

42. Treas. Reg. §1.167(b)-4(a). In general, a taxpayer may use any consistent method of computing depreciation that does not result in greater depreciation deductions than would otherwise be allowable under the most favorable declining balance method over the first two thirds of the property's useful life. These other methods, such as the sinking fund method or the unit of production method, generally are not favorably applied to real estate investments. *See* Rev. Rul. 79-20, 1979-1 C.B. 137 (computation of earning and profits for corporate partners of partnership using accelerated depreciation).

43. Sec. 167(c),(j)(2). Assets received through partnership mergers may not be depreciated using favorable accelerated methods. Rev. Rul. 77-458, 1977-2 C.B. 220. Property contributed to a partnership and property received in a distribution from a partnership are not eligible for accelerated depreciation as new property. Treas. Reg. §1.167(c)-1(a)(6).

44. Treas. Reg. §1.167(c)-1(a) (2).

45. Treas. Reg. §1.167(a)-10.

46. *Compare* Sec. 168(e)(4)(A), (B) wherein the transferee remains subject to the Useful Life System but is permitted to compute a new method and period under such system; *with* Sec. 168(e)(4)(C) wherein the transferee remains subject to the Useful Life System but must continue using the transferee's method and period of depreciation.

47. Sec. 167(j)(1). Different rules apply to partnership properties that were acquired before July 25, 1969.

48. Sec. 167(j)(4). Different rules apply to partnership properties that were acquired before July 25, 1969.

49. Sec. 167(j)(2)(A). Residential rental properties are buildings that are used to provide living accommodations and from which 80% or more of the yearly gross rental income is from dwelling units. Sec. 167(j)(2)(B). Dwelling units include houses and apartments used for living accommodations, but exclude hotels and the like where more than one half of the units are used on a transient basis. Sec. 167(k)(3)(C). If two or more buildings on a single tract, or contiguous tracts, of land are operated as an integrated unit, they may be treated as a single building. Treas. Reg. §1.167(j)-3(b)(1)(ii).

50. Sec. 167(j)(5). Under ACRS, no distinction is made between new and used property.

51. Where a component's useful life is used, the shell of the depreciable building must have a useful life longer than the recommended guideline life for that type of structure. Rev. Rul. 68-4, 1968-1 C.B. 77, *clarified,* Rev. Rul. 70-383, 1970-2 C.B. 54. *See, generally, Robert C. Honodel,* 76 T.C. 351 (1981), *on appeal to 9th Cir.,* for a discussion of the allocation of various useful lives to components of an apartment complex. Reversing its position taken in Rev. Rul. 66-111, 1966-1 C.B. 46, the Service has ruled that component useful lives may be used by a real estate limited partnership whether it constructs or purchases the property. Rev. Rul. 73-410, 1973-2 C.B. 53, *clarified,* Rev. Rul. 75-55, 1975-1 C.B. 74. For purchased property, an acceptable allocation, such as by appraisal, must be made for each component. *See Merchants National Bank of Topeka v. Commissioner,* 554 F.2d 412 (10th Cir. 1977) and *Louis C. Fieland,* 73 T.C. 743 (1980).

52. Sec. 168(f)(1)(A).

53. *Id.* A special transitional rule has been provided for new components placed in service after 1980 in or on any building placed in service before 1981 and hence under the Useful Life System. ERTA provides that the recovery period and method for the first component placed in service after 1980 will be the same as the recovery period and method that would have been available to the building if it had been placed in service

that year. Sec. 168(f)(1)(B). Thereafter, any subsequent components added to the structure, except for substantial improvements discussed in the text, must use the same period and method elected with respect to the first component. Sec. 168(f)(1)(B).

54. Sec. 168(f)(1)(C).

55. Sec. 1250. Similar recapture rules apply to the disposition of depreciable property other than real property. Sec. 1245. For a real estate syndication this would encompass, among others, component depreciation taken on personal property, elevators, or escalators. Sec. 1245(a)(3). Where a partnership interest is sold or otherwise disposed of, the gain on the disposition may be ordinary income to the extent partnership property includes recapture property. *See* the discussion in Chapter 7, *infra.*

56. Sec. 1250(a)(1)(A). Special rules regarding recapture limitations are applicable to certain transactions, such as like-kind exchanges and disposition of a principal residence. Any gain subject to recapture is attributable first to post-1975 excess depreciation, then to 1970 to 1975 excess depreciation and, if gain remains, to 1964 to 1969 excess depreciation.

For real property not subject to ACRS, all depreciation is recaptured as ordinary income if the real property (residential or nonresidential) is not held for more than 12 months. Sec. 1250(a), (b). With certain exceptions, under the Useful Life System, all post-1975 excess depreciation is recaptured on dispositions of residential or nonresidential property, regardless of the holding period. Sec. 1250(a)(1). Excess depreciation is the amount by which the lower of the aggregate depreciation deductions allowed or allowable exceeds the depreciation that would have been allowed under the straight-line method at the time of disposition. Sec. 1250(b)(1)(3). Other rules apply to pre-1976 years. *See* the first edition.

57. Secs. 1245(a)(5), 1250(d)(11). Real property included in the 10-year recovery class (e.g., mobile homes and amusement park structures) is subject to the same rule.

58. Sec. 1245(a)(2)(E). If held for less than one year, all recovery deductions allowable are subject to recapture.

59. For certain federally assisted residential housing projects (those where a mortgage is insured under Sec. 221(b)(3) or 236 of the National Housing Act of 1967 or where a direct loan is made or insured under Title V of the Housing Act of 1949); for certain low-income rental housing projects (those eligible for subsidies under Section 8 of the United States Housing Act of 1937); for certain similar state- or locally assisted residential programs; and for "rehab" projects discussed in this chapter Section 9 of this chapter, a 1% monthly reduction generally is permitted in the amount of otherwise recapturable post-1975 excess depreciation for each month after the property is held for 100 months or after 100 months from the date "rehab" property was placed in service. Sec. 1250(a)(1)(B), 2(B). For purposes of computing all monthly reductions, the taxpayer's holding period ends when a foreclosure proceeding is instituted. Sec. 1250(d)(10).

60. Sec. 1245(a)(5)(D).

61. Sec. 1245(a)(1), (2)(E).

62. Sec. 168(e)(4)(B)(i)–(iii).

63. ACRS will not apply to depreciable personal property acquired by a partnership after 1980 if (a) the property was owned or used at any time during 1980; by the partnership or a related person; (b) the property is acquired from a person who owned it any time during 1980 and as part of the transaction, the user of such property does not change; (c) the partnership leases the property to a person (or a person related to such person)

who owned or used the property at any time during 1980; or (d) property is acquired in a transaction in which the user of the property does not change and the property is not subject to ACRS in the hands of the person from which the property is so acquired by reason of (b) or (c). Sec. 168(e)(4)(A)(i)–(iv). Thus ACRS will not apply to personal property placed in service before 1981, unless the property is transferred after 1980 in a transaction in which both the owner and the user (if different) change. H. R. Rep. No. 97-215, 97th Cong., 1st Sess. 219 (1981). Unless the user also changes in the same transaction, this general rule cannot be avoided by multiple transfers after 1980.

64. Sec. 168(e)(4)(C).

65. *Id.* For example, to the extent that any gain is recognized by the transferor on a corporate roll-in under Sec. 351, the transferee could utilize ACRS on that portion of its basis in the property which is equal to the gain recognized to the transferor.

66. Sec. 168(e)(4)(C). It would appear that a subsequent transfer of such property in a similar type of transaction would remove the taint.

67. Sec. 168(e)(4)(F).

68. Sec. 179.

69. Sec. 179(d)(2).

70. *Id.*

71. Sec. 1245(a)(2).

72. Sec. 168(d)(1)(A)(ii).

73. Sec. 167(k).

74. Sec. 167(k)(1).

75. Sec. 167(k)(3)(D).

76. Sec. 167(k)(2)(B).

77. Sec. 167(k)(1).

78. Sec. 167(k)(3)(A).

79. *Id.*

80. Sec. 167(k)(3)(B).

81. *Id.*

82. Sec. 167(k)(2)(B).

83. *Id.* The stringent income tests that must be satisfied require that the leasing and sale of the units are pursuant to a program in which the sum of (a) the taxable income from leasing each unit and (b) the amount realized from the sale or disposition of the unit (if sold) normally does not exceed the unadjusted cost of such property over the net tax benefits realized by the taxpayer, consisting of the benefits from depreciation or amortization deductions less the tax incurred from the taxable income on leasing, if any.

84. Treas. Reg. §1.167(k)-(1)(b)(1).

85. *Id.*

86. *Id.*

87. Sec. 168(c)(1)(A)(ii)(I); Treas. Reg. §1.167(k)-1(a)(1).

88. Sec. 1250(b)(4). *See* Sec. 57(a)(2), (12) and Section 16 of this chapter for the tax preference effect of rehabilitation amortization.

89. Sec. 212(d)(1), ERTA. Under that provision, a taxpayer was permitted to elect amortization of certified rehabilitation expenditures over 60 months in lieu of otherwise available depreciation. Sec. 191(d)(1)–(4). Sixty-month amortization was available to taxpayers

who were the first users of the property following the completion of the rehabilitation. Sec. 191(d)(1). A discussion of this provision appears in the First Edition.

90. Sec. 212(d)(1), ERTA. Generally, to discourage the demolition of certified historic structures, a building constructed on a site which on or after June 30, 1976 was occupied by a certified historic structure that was demolished or substantially altered previously could only be depreciated using the straight-line method. Sec. 167(n).

ERTA did not repeal the rule that no deduction is allowed for amounts expended for, or losses incurred as a result of, the demolition of a certified historic structure. Rather such amounts must be added to the basis of the land rather than to the basis of any building constructed on the site. Sec. 280B.

91. Sec. 212(d)(1), ERTA.

92. Secs. 46(a)(2)(F), 48(g).

93. Sec. 48(a)(2). Any rehabilitation expenditure of a lessee of a building will not be a qualified expenditure unless, at the completion of rehabilitation, the remaining term of lease is 15 or more years, without regard to lease renewals.

94. Sec. 46(a)(2)(F).

95. Sec. 48(a)(3).

96. *Id.* The new law provides that a taxpayer who lives in a building that otherwise qualifies for the 25% historic structure credit may claim the investment tax credit on rehabilitation expenditures for all but the taxpayer's unit.

97. Sec. 48(g)(2)(B).

98. Sec. 48(g)(1).

99. Sec. 48(g)(1)(A). Unlike prior law, there is no restriction that rehabilitation occur only once every 30 or 40 years.

100. Sec. 48(g)(1)(C)(i).

101. Sec. 48(g)(1)(C)(ii).

102. Sec. 48(q)(3), added by Sec 205, TEFRA, which repeals Sec. 48(g)(5), effective for taxable years after 1982.

103. Sec. 48(q)(4).

104. Sec. 48(q)(1). This rule is applicable to the regular investment tax credit.

105. Sec. 205(c), TEFRA. Exempted from the new basis adjustment rules are those credits for expenditures claimed after 1982 if: (i) there was a contract to rehabilitate the property entered into after December 31, 1980 and if such contract was binding on July 1, 1982; or (ii) if rehabilitation began between those dates, so long as the building is placed in service prior to 1986.

106. Sec. 48(q)(2).

107. Sec. 48(g)(2)(B)(iv).

108. Sec. 212(3), ERTA.

109. Sec. 1039

110. The reinvestment must be made in a "qualified housing project," which is a project providing rental or cooperative housing for low-income families with respect to which a mortgage is insured under certain sections of the National Housing Act and with respect to which the owner is restricted as to rate of return and rental charges. Sec. 1039(b)(1).

111. The disposition must be approved by the Secretary of Housing and Urban Development. Sec. 1039(b)(2).

112. Sec. 1039(b)(3).

113. Sec. 1039(a).

114. Sec. 1250(d)(8)(A); Treas. Reg. §§1.1039-a(a), 1.1250-3 (h).

115. Sec. 168(e).

116. *See* Chapter 4, pp. 62–65, *supra.*

117. Similarly, the amount of a partner's share of the unpaid balance is added to the amount deemed realized on the disposition of this partnership interest. Sec. 752. *See* Chapter 7, Section 4, *infra.*

118. *Reisinger v. Commissioner,* 144 F.2d 475 (2nd Cir. 1944). The lessee may either depreciate or amortize its costs for permanent improvements made to the lessor's property. Treas. Reg. §1.167(a)-4. The method depends on whether the useful life is equal to, less than, or longer than the term of the lease. A similar rule is provided for ACRS property. Sec. 168(f)(6). *See also* Sec. 178.

119. *See* Sec. 1019; *Your Health Club, Inc.* 4 T.C. 385 (1944) (Acq.).

120. Secs. 109, 1019.

121. Secs. 109, 1019.

122. *See* Rev. Rul. 60-180, 1960-1 C.B. 114; Rev. Rul. 55-89, 1955-1 C.B. 284.

123. *See Commissioner v. Moore,* 207 F.2d 265 (9th Cir. 1953), *cert. denied,* 347 U.S. 942 (1954); *Friend v. Commissioner,* 119 F.2d 959 (7th Cir. 1941).

124. Sec. 178 and Treas. Reg. §1.167(a)-4. Under ACRS, the costs of leasehold improvements are recovered over the lesser of the applicable recovery period or the remaining lease term when the improvement is placed in service.

125. *See, e.g., Stanley C. Orrisch,* 55 T.C. 395 (1970), *aff'd per curiam, unpublished opinion* (9th Cir. 1973). *See also Martin Magaziner,* 37 CCH Tax Ct. Mem. 873 (1978) (special allocation of depreciation was disregarded; no substantial economic effect or business purpose was found). The partnership agreement may provide for special allocations of depreciation (or the gain or loss) with respect to property contributed to the partnership by a partner if the purpose is to account for the difference between the fair market value and the adjusted basis of the property at the time of the contribution. Sec. 704(c)(2); Treas. Reg. §1.704-1(c)(2).

126. Sec. 704(b)(2).

127. Secs. 55, 56 prior to TEFRA.

128. Sec. 56(a) prior to TEFRA.

129. Sec. 201(d)(1)(A)-(E), TEFRA.

130. Secs. 55, 57(a).

131. Sec. 55(a).

132. Sec. 55(b).

133. Sec. 55(c).

134. Sec. 57(a).

CHAPTER 6

INTEREST, TAXES, FEES, "SOFT COSTS," AND CONSTRUCTION PERIOD EXPENDITURES

1. GENERAL

In the preceding chapters, we reviewed the necessity that the partnership be taxed as such and that a partner maintain sufficient basis in his partnership interest so that he can deduct all partnership losses. We then moved to a discussion of how these losses are created, starting in Chapter 5 with the depreciation deduction.

This chapter continues the analysis of appropriate deductions for a real estate limited partnership. Special emphasis is given to the Service attack on deductions that may be claimed during the first few years of a limited partnership.

A real estate limited partnership incurs many costs that cannot immediately be deducted but must be added to the basis of the realty or personalty held by the partnership and depreciated or amortized over that property's useful life. Included in such costs are the costs of construction (which include builder's fees and profits, raw materials, labor utilized in construction), furniture, fixtures, equipment, and architectural, landscape, and design fees associated with the project.[1] Further, while depreciation, and in particular, accelerated depreciation, can yield important deductions in sheltering a partner's income, the depreciation deduction becomes available only when the property is "placed in service." [2]

During the period prior to the property being placed in service (i.e., the construction period) the partnership usually will incur costs that are not associated directly with actual construction. These costs include interest on construction loans, taxes, various financing, service and management fees, and other so-called soft costs.

This chapter discusses whether these expenditures may be deducted in the year paid or accrued; whether they must be capitalized and deducted over the useful life of the project (depreciated) or over some other ascertainable period (amortized); or whether they may never be deducted. Expenditures that may never be deducted must be added to basis and can only be taken into account on disposition of the property (e.g., land cost) or on liquidation of the partnership (e.g., syndication fees).

In general, an expenditure to acquire an asset having a useful life extending beyond the taxable year of the expenditure must be capitalized.[3] Even if the useful life does not extend beyond the expenditure year, to be deductible, the expense must be ordinarily and necessarily incurred in the course of profit-seeking activities.[4] In addition, to be deductible, an expenditure must be reasonable in amount and must be made for the stated purpose.[5] This is especially so when related parties are on both sides of a transaction. (For example, the partnership employs the general partner to manage the partnership's building.)

This chapter will discuss the various statutory and judicial restraints imposed on the amount and timing of deductions for each of the preceding costs. Of course, a partner's basis in his partnership interest also can limit otherwise allowable deductions (as passed through to the partners).[6] The basis limitation and the more restrictive "at risk" rules (which are not generally applicable to investment in real property) are discussed in Chapter 4.

This chapter will also focus on the Service's occasionally asserted position that so-called soft cost expenditures (not including interest or taxes) incurred by a newly formed partnership prior to the completion of the project are nondeductible during the period before the project is finished.[7] The Service assertion may be that the partnership is not in a trade or business until construction is completed and that preconstruction expenditures must be capitalized and depreciated or amortized if an ascertainable useful life can be determined. The chapter begins with a discussion of the interest deduction.

2. INTEREST

a. General   One of the largest deductions available to real estate limited partnerships is derived from interest paid on construction and permanent loans.[8] As a general rule, a deduction is allowed for all interest paid or accrued within a taxable year. Interest is defined as a charge for the use or forbearance of money.[9]

This general rule is subject to a number of modifications and exceptions. First, certain statutory limitations have been imposed on the prepayment of interest by cash-basis taxpayers.[10] Second, there are statutory restrictions on when construction period interest payments can be deducted.[11] Third, the Service has sought to prevent the amortization of prepaid interest over the short construction loan period by asserting that construction and permanent loan financing should be treated as one loan.[12] Fourth, there is question as to whether a cash-basis taxpayer can obtain an interest deduction if he borrows an equivalent sum from the creditor in a transaction closely linked to the payment of interest.[13] Fifth, the statutory limitations on investment indebtedness may be applicable.[14] Each of these is discussed in the following sections.

b. Prepaid Interest   In general, interest that is prepaid by a cash basis taxpayer must be capitalized and may be deducted only to the extent and in the taxable year in which it represents a charge for the use or forbearance of money.[15] Thus interest deductions should be calculated on the basis of the remaining principal balance of the loan over the period that the loan is outstanding. For example, if a real estate limited partnership prepays $100,-000 in interest at the commencement of a 40-year permanent loan, the $100,000 cannot be deducted in the year paid but must be amortized over the life of the loan. This treatment is identical to that of a taxpayer using the accrual method of accounting.[16]

c. Construction Period Interest   Apart from prepaid interest restrictions, there is a statutory restriction on construction period interest.[17] A portion of the construction period interest paid (for other than low-income housing) during a particular taxable year must be capitalized and amortized pursuant to an amortization schedule rather than being immediately deducted.[18] Alternatively, a partnership may elect to add the construction period interest to the depreciable basis of the project and to deduct the amounts over the useful life of the project.[19] The former method generally results in earlier deduction of interest expense.

This construction period restriction also applies to real property tax deductions.

Construction period interest is all interest paid or accrued on indebtedness to acquire, construct, or carry real property to the extent that the interest is attributable, not surprisingly, to the construction period.[20] The construction period is the period between the beginning of construction and the date on which the property is first held for sale or placed in service.[21] Congress did not provide any guidance as to what would constitute the beginning of the construction period.[22] Presumably, commencement of construction requires something more than architectural plans or soil grading. Perhaps driving pilings and diggings of footings would suffice.[23] Interpretive regulations have not been issued.[24]

Interest paid on a mortgage on unimproved land is not subject to the amortization rules since no construction has occurred.[25] In addition, interest paid during the construction period on a project that is not, and cannot be reasonably expected to be, held for business or investment purposes is not subject to these rules.[26] A private home constructed by its owner is an example of such a project.

The capitalization of construction period interest occurs in the year the interest is paid or accrued.[27] A portion of the capitalized interest, however, can be deducted in that year; the balance must be amortized over a period of years.[28] The initial year deduction is the total amount of construction interest paid or accrued and attributable to that year divided by the amortization period that applies to that year. For example, 12½% of the construction period interest paid in 1982 on residential real property was immediately deductible. The amortization of the balance of the capitalized interest begins in the *later* of either the year after payment or accrual, or the year in which the property is ready for sale or placed in service.[29]

The requirement that construction period interest be capitalized and amortized is being phased in at different rates for residential and nonresidential realty.[30] By 1984, the amortization period for both types of real property will be 10 years.[31] Thus, if $1,000 of construction period interest is paid in 1984 by a real estate limited partnership (in which all the partners are individuals) and the project is placed in service in 1987, the partners would be able to deduct an aggregate of $100 of the interest in 1984 and then deduct $100 a year for nine years, commencing in 1987.

With respect to nonresidential real property, the phase-in of amortization of construction period interest commenced in taxable years beginning in 1976. For construction period interest paid or accrued in 1983, 10% of such interest is deductible in that year with the balance amortized over a nine-year period starting in 1984 or when the property is held for sale or placed in service, whichever is later.[32] For residential housing, the phase-in commenced for tax years beginning in 1978 and for certain defined low-income housing, the phase-in was to have commenced for tax years beginning in 1982. However, the construction period interest rules have been repealed with respect to low-income housing.[33] This repeal provides a major incentive for such housing.[34]

The phase-in rules with respect to the periods of time over which the capitalized interest were to be amortized are articulated by the following chart.[35]

Nonresidential Real Property	Residential Real Property	Amortization Period (in years)
1976	—	3 (for 50%)
—	1978	4
1977	1979	5
1978	1980	6
1979	1981	7 } includes first year
1980	1982	8
1981	1983	9
after 1981	after 1983	10

Upon the sale or exchange of real property during the amortization period, a portion of the yearly deduction allowable may be taken in the sale year.[36] For real estate limited partnerships holding depreciable property, the portion of the deduction allowable is determined in accordance with the convention used for depreciation purposes.[37]

It should be noted that the prepayment rules enunciated earlier have not been preempted by the construction period interest rules. Thus, if the partnership prepays interest during the construction period allocable to two or more separate taxable years, the interest must be allocated first to the appropriate taxable period and then amortized in accordance with the rules outlined earlier. For example, if on January 1, 1984 a partnership constructing nonresidential real property prepays $2,000 of interest of which $500 is allocable to the 1984 year, only $500 will be subject to the amortization rules in that year. Thus $50 will be immediately deductible and the balance amortized over a nine-year period. The balance ($1,500) must be deferred and allocated to the appropriate taxable years and, if such years are during the construction period, amortized over the applicable 10 year period.

Assuming that the partnership elects not to capitalize construction period interest by adding it to its depreciable property basis, how is the amount of immediately deductible construction period interest computed for each individual partner? Probably, each partner is allocated his distributive share of the total construction period interest for the taxable year and the computation of the amount that is immediately deductible is made at the partner level.[38] Prior to TEFRA, a corporate partner (not including a Subchapter S corporation) was not subject to the amortization rules and could deduct its entire distributive share of construction period interest.[39] Pursuant to TEFRA, all corporations are subject to the capitalization of construction period interest for nonresidential real property. For residential realty, non-subchapter S corporations are not subject to the capitalization rules. Each partner, then, should maintain his own records as to the gross distributive share of construction period interest allocated to him each year and should compute the amount allowable as an immediate deduction under the amortization tables.

Confusing issues arise as to the impact of a taxable sale or exchange of the property by the partnership before completion of the amortization period at partner level.[40] It would appear that a partner would merely reduce his allocable distributive share of gain or increase his allocable distributive share of loss by the amount of his unamortized construction period interest. In a nontaxable sale or exchange by the partnership, the partners would continue to amortize their allocable construction period interest.[41]

What happens if a partner sells his partnership interest? In the absence of regulations, it would appear that the partner would add the unamortized amount to his basis in his partnership interest in computing capital gain or loss.[42]

d. One Loan or Two? In the effort to prevent amortization of prepaid interest (and service fees relating to project financing) over a short construction loan period, the Service has recently focused on whether the financing of a real estate venture consists of one long-term loan spanning the construction and operating periods, or two loans, one for each period.[43] If there is one long-term loan, interest and fees relating to the construction loan would arguably be deductible over the life of the combined construction period and the long-term financing, often 30 to 40 years.[44]

This issue was initially addressed by the Service in the context of loans insured by the Federal Housing Administration (FHA).[45] FHA transactions generally involve a buy-sell arrangement (commitment) between a construction and permanent holder. Ordinarily, the borrower executes a 30- or 40-year note and mortgage pursuant to which the construction lender finances construction. At the completion of construction and when other conditions of the permanent loan commitment are satisfied, the construction lender may require the permanent lender to purchase the note and mortgage. The stated interest rate and maturity date in the note do not change throughout the transaction. The Service is of the view that only one loan exists and accordingly, any upfront fees characterized as interest (or for services) must be amortized over the entire loan period.[46] Recently, substantial judicial approval of this approach has been expressed.[47]

It has been suggested that such a view is incorrect.[48] Although only a single note may be employed, two lenders are providing money for two specific and different periods. The construction lender may not advance any proceeds until a takeout or permanent lender is properly secured. Moreover, while the construction lender hopes to be paid in full upon completion of the construction project,[49] the permanent lender will be under no obligation to take out the construction debt if there is a breach of performance under the commitment agreement. Oftentimes varying financing fees are paid to construction and permanent lenders to increase the yield on their loans.[50] The better view is that in most cases, two loans exist. Obviously, when planning the transaction, all the formalities of two separate loans should be followed to the extent possible, including using separate notes and actually paying each interest installment as discussed below.

e. Other Restrictions on Cash-Basis Partnerships A cash-basis partnership may not deduct interest until the interest is paid in cash or in a cash equivalent. For this purpose, a note of the partnership is not a cash equivalent.[51] Accordingly, if a taxpayer pays construction period interest with a separate note or has the interest added to the principal of the construction loan note, the interest will not be deemed paid until the taxpayer pays the principal of the loan to the lender.

Similar rules are applicable to interest paid by loan discount. A loan discount occurs when a construction lender doesn't disburse the full amount of the loan. The amount withheld is treated as interest paid. This practice simply increases the principal of the debt by the amount withheld, and courts have treated loan discount as if it were interest paid by note.[52] If a full deduction is desired, there should be full draw down of the loan followed by separate payment of interest. Generally, the construction loan is repaid at the end of the construction period with the proceeds of the permanent or takeout loan. A taxpayer may deduct interest paid with money borrowed from a second lender.[53] Thus, when a cash-basis taxpayer pays off a construction loan with the permanent loan proceeds, the interest should be deemed paid for purposes of the construction period interest amortization rules.

The interplay of the one-loan concept discussed earlier and the cash payment doctrine is significant. Under a successful one-loan argument, the taxpayer might be deemed to pay the construction period interest only as it repays principal over the entire term of the loan. The application of the amortization rules for such interest would result in amortization periods commencing far beyond the completion of construction.

Until recently, the cash payment requirement did not adversely affect most cash-basis taxpayers. Rather than having the borrower issue its note, the lender would disburse the loan proceeds to the borrower which would be deposited in the borrower's account at a separate bank. Thereafter the borrower would pay the interest with its own check. Thus, where the lender disbursed proceeds to the borrower that were commingled with the borrower's funds and the borrower paid the interest with the commingled funds, the interest was deemed paid with cash or its equivalent.[54]

Several recent court decisions, however, have questioned this conclusion.[55] The rationale behind these decisions is that a debtor would not be recognized as having paid interest on a loan if he borrowed an equivalent sum from the creditor in a transaction *closely linked* to the payment of the interest, regardless of the sequence. Moreover, it would not matter whether the borrower had funds of his own upon which he drew for the payment, nor whether he was given unrestricted control of the funds received.

In view of these decisions, the ability of a cash-basis partnership to claim an interest deduction from the use of loan proceeds from a lender to pay interest on another loan to the same lender has become uncertain. If possible, the partnership should utilize the accrual method since interest is deductible when it accrues regardless of when paid. If accrual reporting is not feasible, the loan proceeds should be disbursed to an account maintained at a separate bank and over which the taxpayer has control. Funds should be commingled and left on deposit for several days before payment is made. If possible, the taxpayer should utilize a different source of funds to pay the interest and borrow from the construction lender to pay other expenses.

f. Investment Interest Limitation   A further restriction on the deduction of partnership interest expenditures is imposed at the partner level in respect of the deduction of interest on investment indebtedness. For any given taxable year, a noncorporate taxpayer's deduction for interest on investment related indebtedness is limited to an amount equal to $10,000 plus his net investment income.[56] A partner owning a 50% or more capital interest in a partnership may add to the $10,000 limitation the lesser of $15,000 or the amount of interest on investment indebtedness incurred or continued in connection with the acquisition of the interest in the partnership.[57]

The investment interest limitations are applied at the individual partner level. Each partner is required to take into account his distributive share of the partnership's investment interest and other items of income and expense necessary to determine the limitations under this provision.[58]

The more "investment income" a partner has, the more investment interest he can deduct. What is "investment income?" It includes interest, dividends, rents, royalties, short-term capital gain on dispositions of property held for investment, and recapture ordinary income.[59] It generally does not include long-term capital gains from property held in a trade or business.

Under certain circumstances, interest related to property that is subject to a net lease will be considered investment interest.[60] Interest related to indebtedness incurred or continued in the construction of property used in a trade or business, however, is not treated as investment interest.[61] A limited carry-over to succeeding taxable years of excess investment interest is permitted.[62]

Deduction of interest on investment property is subject to restriction, while deduction of interest on trade or business property may be fully deducted. Thus it is important for a real estate limited partnership to determine whether it owns investment property or property used in a trade or business. If it owns the latter, the restriction on deducting investment interest will not apply to the partners with respect to their income or deductions from the partnership.

It has been held that the ownership and operation of an apartment complex, hotel, or other like property is a trade or business.[63] If these decisions reflect the law, the interest on related indebtedness will not be subject to the investment interest deduction limitation. If a real estate syndication were to own real property subject to a triple net lease, however, the limitation probably would apply.

In many syndications, the promoter or general partner agrees to lend the partnership sufficient monies to pay any net operating losses for a period of time. If the guarantor is financially able to fund the agreement, it could be asserted by the Service that the transaction is, in effect, without risk and therefore an investment rather than a business. Under these circumstances, the limitation on investment interest deductions might be asserted.

3. TAXES

Another major deductible expense is the yearly real property taxes that must be paid to the locality in which the partnership's real property is situated. Deductions for real property taxes generally are allowed in the year such taxes are paid or accrued.[64]

Real property taxes are deductible if they are imposed on interests in real property and are levied for the general public welfare at a like rate against all property in a taxing authority's jurisdiction.[65] Such amounts do not include special assessments, where the benefit inures directly to the property that is taxed.[66]

As with interest deductions, taxpayers using the cash receipts and disbursements method of accounting sometimes consider front-ending deductions by prepaying real property taxes. Despite the general rule that cash-basis taxpayers may deduct expenses when paid, such prepayment probably would meet with little success. In general, the Service has taken the position that real property taxes are considered due on a fixed date which, depending on the jurisdiction, may be the assessment date, lien date, or the date the taxpayer becomes personally liable for the tax.[67] (Election of the accrual method may result in a deduction on such dates, although actual payment may take place at a later time.) Further, the Service has broad discretion to disallow deductions where the effect of such deductions is to materially distort taxable income.[68]

The Tax Reform Act of 1976 treated the deduction of construction period real property taxes in the same manner as deductions for construction period interest. Thus such taxes must be capitalized and may be deducted either over a varying amortization period [69] or over the useful life of the project in the same manner that the cost of the project is depreciated. These provisions are discussed in Section 2 of this chapter.[70]

It should also be noted that where real property is sold, special rules apply to allocate the deduction for real property taxes between the buyer and the seller.[71]

A real estate limited partnership is also entitled to deduct various "payroll taxes" either as taxes or as ordinary and necessary business expenses.[72] For example, federal social security and federal unemployment insurance taxes are deductible as ordinary and necessary business expenses.[73] Partnership contributions to state unemployment or disability funds are deductible as taxes.[74] However, the deductibility of certain of these payroll taxes during the construction period may be in doubt.[75] As discussed in Section 10 of this chapter, the Service may take the position that a newly formed partnership engaged in construction activities is not engaged in a trade or business until the construction project is completed.[76] Accordingly, expenditures dependent on a trade or business requirement would not be deductible during the construction phase.[77] This view has been accepted by the Tax Court but has not been accepted by the Court of Claims.[78] In addition, as discussed in Section 11, payroll taxes deductible as business expenses may be subject to a newly enacted amortization provision dealing with five-year amortization of business start-up costs.[79]

Neither the Service's position nor the new legislation has changed the rule that where a partnership incurs payroll tax liability indirectly through payments to the builder, the amounts are capital expenditures added to the depreciable cost of the project and are recoverable through subsequent depreciation.[80]

4. COSTS ASSOCIATED WITH FINANCING THE PROJECT

A real estate limited partnership incurs a number of expenses, other than stated interest, with regard to financing construction of a real estate project. First, fees may be paid for specific services provided in connection with the particular financing, including brokerage commissions, title searches, and appraisal fees. Second, fees may be paid for standby construction loan guarantees or for commitments to provide takeout financing at the end of the construction term. An example of a commitment fee includes a portion of the amounts paid to the Federal National Mortgage Association or the Government National Mortgage Association to provide the permanent mortgage loan at final endorsement. Third, fees may be paid for a lender's general overhead expenses and may be labeled as loan origination fees or simply as loan fees.

Fees paid for specific services provided in connection with the obtaining of a loan have historically been capitalized and amortized ratably over the life of the loan so secured.[81] In view of the Service's position that a newly formed real estate partnership is not in a trade or business until its construction project is completed, amortization during the construction period of upfront payments for specific services in the procurement of project financing may be challenged. Moreover, to the extent that the service fees are attributable solely to a separate construction loan, it is presently unclear under the Service view how such fees would be treated upon the completion of the project. The Service might argue that the fees should be amortized over the life of the permanent loan, added to the depreciable basis of the project and recovered via depreciation, or never deducted. In this connection, consideration should be given to whether the five-year amortization rules for start-up costs recently enacted by Congress and discussed in Section 11 of this chapter apply to the timing of these deductions.

Until recently, standby and commitment fees to ensure the availibility of loan funds have generally been considered business expenses of a real estate limited partnership.[82] In practice, the timing of the deduction of such fee varies. The most aggressive approach has been to claim deduction in the years paid or incurred. A much less aggressive approach is to capitalize the fee and amortize it over the relevant loan period as though this amount were interest.[83]

In the First Edition, we recommended a middle ground: capitalize the fees and amortize them over the term of the standby or commitment period. This approach was recommended because such fees are paid to guarantee the availability of, or to reserve, funds over a specified commitment period and not for the use or forbearance of money over the term of the loan. Since construction loan funds are received as needed throughout the construction period, standby fees attributable to construction loan funds should be amortized over the life of the construction loan. In addition, since the commitment period ends when the entire amount of the permanent loan is received at the end of the construction period, commitment fees for permanent financing also should be amortized over the life of the construction loan. If a standby loan fee is not amortized, it should be deducted upon expiration of the standby construction period.

Recent developments, however, cast some doubt about the early deduction (or amortization) of loan commitment fees and related charges suggested previously. First, the Service has revoked a prior revenue ruling that treated commitment fees in the nature of standby charges as deductible business expenses.[84] In this regard, the Service's new position is that commitment fees should be treated as the cost of an option. If exercised, it becomes a cost of acquiring the loan and is deducted ratably over the loan term. If not exercised, the Service indicates the taxpayer may be entitled to a loss deduction when the right expires.[85]

Consideration must also be given to the danger that the Service auditor may argue that a newly formed construction partnership is not engaged in a trade or business until the project is completed. If this position is accepted by the courts, amortization of such fees during the construction period would be eliminated. In this regard, the new amortization rules for start-up costs discussed in Section 11 of this chapter may be applicable to these fees. Finally, the unfortunate use of the term "commitment fee" as a substitute for the actual purpose of a payment to a lender (i.e., additional interest or compensation for general or specific services) has in part resulted in seemingly conflicting judicial decisions.[86]

Another area of confusion is the appropriate treatment of "loan fees," "loan origination charges," and "initial service fees" charged by lenders.[87] Historically, the Courts have focused on whether such "general" fees were compensation for specific services rendered in connection with a particular loan (i.e., appraisal fee, architectural fee, title search fees) or compensation for the use or forbearance of money (interest). If all or a portion of the fee was attributable to specific services, that amount was deductible over the life of the loan so secured. If no part of the fee was attributable to specific services, the entire fee would be deemed interest. Thus, to the extent a fee was charged for general overhead of the lender in providing services to the borrower, it was treated as interest.[88]

Recently, however, the Tax Court has not followed this dichotomy, but has examined the fees charged to determine whether they represent compensation for any services, specific or general, provided by the lender.[89] If so, that amount is amortizable over the life of the loan it secures.[90] The balance of the fee would be deemed interest.[91] It should be noted, however, that the Court of Claims in the recently decided *Blitzer* case has treated a similar fee imposed by the lender as interest and has not required any allocation of the fee.[92]

5. "SOFT COSTS": FEES PAID TO AFFILIATES OF THE GENERAL PARTNER OR THE BUILDER

To maximize early year deductions, many partnerships structure the payments due the builder, general partners, and others in the most favorable manner. The builder's profit must be capitalized and added to the depreciable basis of the partnership's property. Partnership distributions to general partners cannot be deducted by the limited partners. To some extent, therefore, payments to builders or affiliates are structured as fees for services rather than builder's profit and payments to general partners are structured as payments for services rather than for acting as general partners.

In the usual real estate limited partnership, fees are paid to affiliates of the general partner or the builder. The fees represent any of several costs connected with constructing or managing a real estate project. Amounts paid for "soft costs," such as rent-up fees, management fees, supervisory fees, service fees, and loan standby or commitment fees traditionally have been claimed as immediate deductions or amortized over a short term. Short-term amortization applies when the services relate to more than a year, such as a rent-up fee where the rent-up period carries over from one accounting year to a second.[93] The ability of the partnership to deduct some or all of these soft costs during the construction period is seriously in doubt. As discussed in Section 10, the Service has argued, with some success, that certain expenditures (not including interest and taxes) of newly formed partnerships incurred prior to the completion of construction may not be deducted, but must be capitalized as the partnership is not in a trade or business until construction is completed.[94] Although this approach was repudiated in a recent case before the Court of Claims, that court indicated that management and supervision fees paid to a general partner (and presumably anyone else) must be allocated to construction cost, financing cost, organization and syndication cost, and general administrative services in order to determine which part of the fee is deductible immediately.[95] Other amounts paid to affiliates, including amounts representing the builder's profit, should be capitalized as part of the cost of construction (i.e., added to the cost basis of the property) and depreciated over the useful life of the building.[96]

Since the characterization of the payment as either a "soft cost" or builder's profit affects the timing of the deduction, care should be taken to properly characterize and substantiate costs that would permit an early deduction.

The Service may also argue that fees paid to general partners, builders, and their affiliates represent current partnership distributions to the general partner or builder's profit and thus are not currently deductible expenses.[97] To sustain a deduction, therefore, any such fees should be reasonable in amount. They should be no greater than the amount that would be charged by unrelated persons in the same community. As an evidentiary matter, it is advisable to obtain letters from unrelated persons stating the amounts they would charge. It is also helpful for unrelated persons to be willing, in fact, to provide the services or commitments and for the partnership to obtain documentation to that effect. Further, to support the bona fides of the arrangement, the partnership should have adequate funds available when such fees are due.

If an affiliate of the general partner or builder will be giving a standby loan commitment, it should have sufficient net worth either to perform the commitment or to secure the guarantee of a person who can perform the commitment. Certain of the more exotic standby commitments often cannot be obtained from unrelated persons, and the deduction of amounts paid to related persons for such commitments may not be sustained.

Covenants not to compete are often obtained by the partnership from the builder in the hope that the payments to the builder for the covenant can be deducted over the short life of the covenant. However, a revenue ruling casts some doubt on this and, at least, requires that the covenant be a valuable bona fide restriction.[98] If the covenant is not recognized, the payments could be considered part of the cost of the property.

The Service has been auditing front-end "soft costs" intensely. Use of these must be considered risky at best, and there appears to be a developing trend by promoters and investors to reduce their use.

A final aspect of partnership taxation should be considered. As discussed in Chapter 4, a partner may engage in a transaction with a partnership in a capacity other than as a partner.[99] In general, deductions for such payments should be allowed if the substance, rather than the form, of the transaction supports such treatment.[100] If the payment is found to be a partnership distribution, however, the deduction will be disallowed.[101] To be deductible, payments to a partner (usually the general partner or its affiliate) should be for services that are not generally provided as an inherent obligation of a general partner.[102]

Even if characterized as a guaranteed payment for services (which are payable to a partner regardless of the income of the partnership), any such payment must clearly be a deductible expense rather than a capital expenditure if a current partnership deduction is desired.[103]

6. MANAGEMENT FEES

Management fees rendered before the property is placed in service and related to the supervision of construction must be capitalized as part of the depreciable basis of the project.[104] Once the project is placed in service, annual or recurring management fees are currently deductible unless the Service can sustain that the amounts are excessive or are disguised payments for something else.[105]

The usual management fee is based on a percentage (e.g., 5%) of gross rent. This percentage payment is usually deductible if it meets the community going rate. If other management fees are added to the annual arrangement and such management is performed by the builder or general partner, or an affiliate, problems similar to those discussed in Section 5 may be encountered.[106]

7. ORGANIZATION AND SYNDICATION FEES

Under prior law, partnerships treated organization and syndication fees paid in connection with establishing the partnership in different ways. Some "aggressive" partnerships claimed an immediate deduction for all such costs, others amortized the costs over a period of years, and still others capitalized but did not amortize the costs.[107]

Beginning in 1977, a new amortization procedure for organization fees became effective.[108] Under the new law, amounts paid or incurred to organize a partnership may be amortized over a period of not less than 60 months, commencing in the month the partnership begins business.[109] Organization fees are defined as expenditures that are incident to the creation of the partnership, chargeable to capital account, and otherwise amortizable over the ascertainable life of a partnership.[110] Legal fees for services incident to the organization of the partnership (e.g., negotiation and preparation of a partnership agreement), accounting fees for establishing a partnership accounting system, and necessary filing fees are examples of organization expenses.[111]

The determination of the date that a partnership begins business (for purposes of the 60-month period) presents a question of fact that must be determined for each case in light of all the circumstances.[112] The mere signing of a partnership agreement is not, under proposed Treasury regulations, sufficient to demonstrate the beginning of business.[113] However, the proposed regulations provide that if the activities of the partnership have advanced to the extent necessary to establish the nature of its business operations, the partnership will be deemed to have begun business. Nevertheless, in view of the Service's position in the soft-cost deduction area that a newly formed partnership is in a trade or business only when construction is completed, it is possible that the Service would interpret its regulation to mean that the 60-month amortization period begins at the end of the construction period. To date, no definitive Service interpretation has been issued.[114] The recommended view, however, is that the partnership should begin its 60-month amortization in the year in which construction activities begin, since it is clear at that time that the partnership activities have advanced to the extent necessary to establish the nature of its business operations.

Syndication expenses are not amortizable over any period but must be capitalized.[115] Syndication expenses are expenses connected with the issuing and marketing of interests in the partnership. Examples of syndication expenses are brokerage fees, registration fees, legal fees of the underwriter or issuer for securities or tax advice pertaining to the adequacy of tax disclosures in the prospectus or placement memorandum, accounting fees for the preparation of representations included in the offering materials, and printing costs.[116]

In general, investment advisory fees are deductible. However, if such a fee is a disguised sales or brokerage commission paid in connection with the acquisition of an investment, the fee must be capitalized.[117]

8. LEGAL AND ACCOUNTING FEES

To the extent that legal or accounting services are attributable to organizing or syndicating the partnership, the discussion of Section 7 will apply. Thus organization-related legal and accounting fees are deductible over at least five years, while syndication-related fees are not deductible.[118] Initial legal and accounting fees may be currently deductible, however, to the extent that they are for ordinary and recurring tax planning services.[119] To support either the current deduction of legal and accounting fees or the five-year amortization, the partnership should request that its lawyers and accountants allocate their fees among ordinary and recurring expenses for tax planning, organization-related fees, and syndication-related fees.

Annual legal or accounting fees usually are deductible in the year that they are paid or incurred.[120]

9. RENT-UP FEES

Real estate limited partnerships often pay rental agents to obtain tenants. These expenditures should generally be either currently deducted or amortized over the rent-up period.[121] To the extent that such fees are paid to a rental agent for services rendered during the construction phase, the Service may argue that such fees are not deductible under the "not in a trade or business" argument. If rent-up fees attributable to the construction period are not deductible during that phase, they would probably be amortizable over the life of the initial lease period. The Service has recently ruled that rent-up fees must be allocated to the leases obtained and amortized over the life of the leases.[122] Of course, as discussed in Section 11, construction period fees may be amortized over a 60-month period under the new business start-up amortization rules.

As discussed previously in this chapter, when such fees are paid to general partners or affiliates and a partnership deduction is desired, the fees should be reasonable in amount and the rent-up activities should not be a required activity of the general partner under the partnership agreement.[123]

10. THE CONSTRUCTION PERIOD EXPENSE ATTACK

The Service has occasionally taken the position that so-called soft cost expenditures (not including interest or taxes) incurred prior to the completion of a project by a newly formed partnership are nondeductible until construction is completed since the partnership is not in a trade or business.[124] When asserted, it is the Service's view that such expenditures must be capitalized and may be amortizable after construction is completed if an ascertainable useful life can be determined. The disallowed deduction presumably would either be allocated to building costs and depreciated over the life of the property or amortized over the appropriate loan period (if the fee is related to project financing).

This position has generally been accepted by the Tax Court and several appellate courts.[125] It has been rejected, however, by the Court of Claims in the recent *Blitzer* case.[126] The Court of Claims has indicated that the "trade or business" requirement under the Internal Revenue Code is relevant only in the threshold inquiry of whether the expenses are of a personal nature or are directed at profit-seeking activity. Since there is no question as to the profit-seeking motive of the partnership, the important inquiry is whether the expenditure is deductible immediately or must be capitalized and appropriately depreciated or amortized.[127] In this regard, "normal recurring expenses" to maintain any business enterprise that are not intended to provide benefits extending beyond the year in question are deductible as ordinary expenses of the partnership whether or not the partnership has completed construction.[128] Normal recurring expenses include deductions for amortization of organization and loan costs, payments of utilities, rent, and salaries and wages of partnership employees (not allocable to construction) with respect to the administrative functions of the partnership.[129]

It should be noted that the opinion of the trial judge in the *Blitzer* case has been affirmed by the entire Court of Claims. In view of this affirmance, it is now understood that the Service has been somewhat more inclined to settle, in a manner favorable to taxpayers, disputes over the deductibility of soft costs prior to the completion of construction. Nevertheless given the Tax Court's treatment on this issue, it is still likely that the Service will continue to pursue its general policy of disallowing deductions for soft costs prior to completion of construction.[130] In addition, consideration must be given to the interplay of the recently enacted start-up cost amortization provision with these judicial developments.[131]

11. 60-MONTH AMORTIZATION OF START-UP EXPENDITURES

A real estate limited partnership may elect to amortize certain "start-up expenditures" over a 60-month or greater period starting with the month in which business begins.[132] An eligible "start-up expenditure" is any amount paid in creating or investigating an active trade or business entered into by the taxpayer that would be currently deductible if paid in connection with the expansion of an existing business in the same field.[133]

A "start-up expenditure" is divided into two types of costs: "investigating costs" and "start-up costs." "Investigating costs" are costs incurred in reviewing a prospective business prior to deciding to acquire or enter the business. These costs include expenses incurred for the analysis or surveys of potential markets, products, labor supply, and transportation facilities.[134]

"Start-up costs" are those expenses incurred subsequent to a decision to establish a particular business and prior to the commencement of that business. Start-up costs include advertising, salaries and wages paid to employees who are being trained, travel and other expenses incurred in lining up prospective distributors or customers, and salaries or fees paid to executives, consultants, and others for similar professional services.[135]

No deduction is allowable under this election unless the expenditure is associated with an active trade or business that is actually commenced or acquired by the taxpayer.[136] Thus the new statute has no effect on the deductibility of investigation expenses that fail to result in the creation or acquisition of a trade or business. The active trade or business requirement also means that expenditures attributable to a mere investment activity are not eligible for amortization. In the case of rental activities, where it is often difficult to determine whether the property is being held for investment or operated as a trade or business, the Senate committee report provides that there must be a "significant furnishing of services incident to the rentals" to constitute an active business. In this regard, the operation of an apartment complex, office building, or shopping center would constitute an active trade or business.[137]

The election excludes from its scope any expenditure for which capitalization is required regardless of the start-up nature of the costs.[138] In this regard, amounts paid for property to be held for sale (i.e., a subdivision) or property that may be depreciated or amortized based on its useful life or under the new ACRS method, including expenses incident to a lease and leasehold improvements, probably are not eligible for 60-month amortization.[139]

We have already discussed the deductibility of certain so-called soft costs of a real estate limited partnership such as financing, commitment, rent-up, and management fees incurred during the construction period. Where the partnership is involved in the construction of an income-producing asset, some of these soft costs incurred during the construction period may have to be capitalized as part of the costs of the constructed asset.[140] Thus the expenses would not be eligible for 60-month amortization. This is illustrated in a recent revenue ruling dealing with the new amortization provision.[141]

There is another aspect of the new amortization provision that may generate controversy. Although the statute was intended to reduce the litigation over the deductibility of start-up costs, the new law fails to clearly answer the question of when a real estate limited partnership's trade or business begins. The statute provides that the 60-month amortization period begins in the month in which the business *begins* and requires the election to amortize to be made in the tax return for the year in which the business *begins*.[142] However, the new law gives little guidance as to when a trade or business is deemed to have begun. In this regard, the Senate committee report states that "[g]enerally, it is anticipated that the definition of when a business begins is to be made in reference to the existing provisions for the amortization of organizational expenditures," and that "[g]enerally, if the activities of the corporation have advanced to the extent necessary to establish the nature of its business operations, it will be deemed to have begun business." [143]

Predictably, the Service has taken a hard line on this issue. In the recent revenue ruling noted above, the Service ruled that the amortization period commences on the date in which a drilling rig under construction is completed and placed in operation.[144] This ruling is consistent with the position taken by the Service and approved in a number of recent cases that a real estate business does not begin until it reaches the income-producing stage (i.e., when construction is completed and the property is placed in service). As discussed in Section 10, this position recently has been rejected by the Court of Claims in *Blitzer.*

It should be remembered that the new provision is not mandatory with respect to start-up expenditures. The statute provides only that eligible start-up expenditures may be treated as deferred expenses. The partnership is free to claim current deductions for all or a portion of the soft costs incurred in the construction period and, if challenged by the Service, to litigate the matter in the Court of Claims [145], which has rejected the Service's restrictive view.

The partnership may wish to make a protective amortization election for the taxable year in which construction ends and actual operations begin and amortize a few incidental start-up expenditures under the election. (For example, what if the Service argues that business began in an earlier year?) Then, if the Service disallows any of the soft-cost deductions claimed during the construction period, the partnership could argue that it still has the option of amortizing these costs over 60 months. Without such an election, if the Service were to successfully challenge the construction period deductions in court, the partnership might be foreclosed from ever taking a deduction for such amounts.

NOTES

1. These are mentioned on pp. 125–129, *supra.*
2. Treas. Reg. §1.167(a)-10(b). The same rule is applicable under the new accelerated cost recovery system. *See* Chapter 5, *infra.*
3. *See* Sec. 263; Treas. Reg. §§1.162-1(b)(2), 1.263(a)-1.
4. Secs. 162, 212; *Blitzer v. United States,* 81-1 U.S.T.C ¶9262 (Ct. Cl. 1981), *aff'd,* 684 F.2d 874 (Ct. Cl. 1982).
5. *See Commissioner v. Lincoln Electric Co.,* 176 F.2d 815, 817-818 (6th Cir. 1949); Treas. Reg. §1.262-7(b)(3).
6. Secs. 705(a), 722, 742, 752.
7. *See,* e.g., Private Letter Rulings 8017007 (Dec. 31, 1979) and 8017008 (Dec. 31, 1979);

Compare Richard C. Goodwin, 75 T.C. 424 (1980), *on appeal to 3rd Cir.; Madison Gas & Electric Co.,* 72 T.C. 521 (1979), *aff'd,* 633 F.2d 512 (7th Cir. 1980); *H. K. Francis,* 36 CCH Tax Ct. Mem. 704 (1977); *Richmond Television Corp. v. United States,* 345 F.2d 901 (4th Cir. 1965), *vacated and remanded on other grounds per curiam,* 382 U.S. 68 (1965), *on remand* 354 F.2d 410 (4th Cir. 1965) *with Blitzer v. United States,* 81-1 U.S.T.C. ¶9262 (Ct. Cl. 1981), *aff'd,* 684 F.2d 874 (Ct.Cl. 1982); *Duffy v. United States,* 81-2 U.S.T.C. ¶9467 (Ct. Cl. 1981); *and Manor Care, Inc. v. United States,* 490 F. Supp. 355 (D. Md. 1980).

8. Sec. 163(a); Treas. Reg. §1.163-1(a); *but see* Sec. 189.

9. *Deputy v. Dupont,* 308 U.S. 488 (1940); *Old Colony R.R Co. v. Commissioner,* 284 U.S. 552 (1940).

10. Sec. 461(g).

11. Sec. 189. Such restrictions are also applicable for real property taxes paid or incurred during the construction period.

12. *See Richard C. Goodwin,* 75 T.C. 424 (1980), *on appeal to 3d Cir.; Lyndell E. Lay,* 69 T.C. 421 (1977); *Blitzer v. United States,* 81-1 U.S.T.C. ¶9262 (Ct. Cl. 1981), *aff'd,* 684 F.2d 874 (Ct. Cl. 1982); Private Letter Rulings 8017007 (Dec. 31, 1979), 8017008 (Dec. 31 1979).

13. *Compare Battlestein v. Commissioner,* 631 F.2d 1182 (5th Cir. 1980), *cert. denied,* 101 S. Ct. 2018 (1981) *and Wilkinson v. Commissioner,* 655 F.2d 980 (9th Cir. 1981), *revg,* 70 T.C. 240 (1978) *with Newton A. Burgess,* 8 T.C. 47 (1947); *G. Douglas Burck,* 63 T.C. (1975), *aff'd,* 553 F.2d 768 (2d Cir. 1976); *and Richard S. Heyman,* 70 T.C. 482 (1978), *aff'd,* 633 F.2d 215 (6th Cir. 1980).

14. Sec. 163(d).

15. Sec. 461(g)(1). For these purposes, interest includes points paid with respect to any indebtedness, excluding those incurred to finance the purchase of a principal residence. Sec. 461(g)(2).

16. *See* Treas. Reg. §1.461-1(a)(2); H. R. Conf. Rep. No. 94-1515, 94th Cong., 2d Sess. 416-17 (1976).

17. Sec. 189; *see* H. R. Conf. Rep. No. 94-1519, 94th Cong., 2d Sess. 408-10 (1976). Prior to TEFRA, Section 189 was not applicable to corporations except electing small business corporations (Subchapter S corporations) and foreign personal holding corporations. Subsequent to 1982 and for construction commencing after that date, all corporations are subject to the rules of Sec. 189 during the construction period of nonresidential realty. Sec. 207, TEFRA.

18. Sec. 189(a).

19. Sec. 266; Treas. Reg. §1.266-1(a).

20. Sec. 189(e)(1).

21. Sec. 189(e)(2).

22. For an extensive discussion of this issue, *see* Cook, "Determining When Construction Period Begins Key to Realty Deductions Under 189," 47 J. Tax. 8 (1977).

23. *See* Treas. Reg. §§1.44-2(a)(1)(i), 1.167(j)-4(a)(2).

24. In a report issued by the Office of Chief Counsel on September 30, 1982, the Service indicated that the issuance of regulations for Section 189 are a high priority item. *See* BNA, *Daily Report for Executives,* No. 208 (October 27, 1982).

25. Sec. 189(c)(1), (2).

26. Sec. 189(d); H.R. Conf. Rep. No. 94-1515, 94th Cong., 2d Sess. 408-09 (1976).

27. Sec. 189(c)(1).

28. *Id.*

29. *Id.*

30. Sec. 189(b).

31. *Id*

32. Sec. 189(f).

33. Sec. 262(c), ERTA

34. See Chapter 5 for general discussion of low-income housing tax incentives.

35. Sec. 189(b). For 1976, 50% was immediately deductible and the chart refers to the remaining 50%.

36. Sec. 189(c)(2)(A).

37. *Id.*

38. Sec. 189(c)(2)(B).

39. Sec. 189(a) prior to TEFRA. New Sec. 189(a) removes the general exclusion for regular corporations and limits the exclusion to residential realty constructed by regular corporations.

40. *See* Sec. 189(c)(2)(B).

41. Sec. 189(c)(2)(C).

42. *See* note 24, *supra.*

43. *See* Rev. Rul. 74-395, 1974-2 C.B. 45; Private Letter Rulings 8017007 (Dec. 31, 1979) and 8017008 (Dec. 31, 1979).

44. *Blitzer v. United States,* 81-1 U.S.T.C. ¶9262 (Ct. Cl. 1981), *aff'd,* 684 F.2d 874 (Ct. Cl. 1982); *Richard C. Goodwin,* 75 T.C. 424 (1980), *on appeal to 3d. Cir.; Lyndell E. Lay,* 69 T.C. 421 (1977).

45. Rev. Rul. 74-395, 1974-2 C.B. 45.

46. *Id.* This "one-loan" approach has recently been applied by the Service in conventional financing arrangements. *See* Private Letter Rulings 8017007 (Dec. 31, 1979) and 8017008 (Dec. 31, 1979). In the rulings, a construction lender entered into a buy-sell with a permanent lender. The borrower was a party to the agreement. Under the agreement, the permanent lender agreed to acquire the construction loan after construction was completed and the property leased. In the Service's view only one loan was created since the tri-party loan arrangement was undertaken to obtain combined construction financing and permanent financing. The Service concluded that the substance of the transaction was a mutually interdependent financing arrangement which, when the permanent mortgagee took over, effected an assignment of the construction period financing.

47. *See, e.g., Blitzer v. United States,* 81-1 U.S.T.C. ¶9262 (Ct. Cl. 1981), aff'd, 684 F.2d 874 (Ct. Cl. 1982); *Richard C. Goodwin,* 75 T.C. 424 (1980), *on appeal to 3d Cir.*

48. *See* Feder, "Financing Real Estate Construction: The IRS Challenge to Construction Period Deductions," 8 J. REAL ESTATE TAX. 3 (1980).

49. *But see Richard C. Goodwin,* 75 T.C. 424 (1980), *on appeal to 3d Cir.*

50. *See Blitzer v. United States,* 81 U.S.T.C. ¶9262 (Ct. Cl. 1981), *aff'd,* 684 F.2d 874 (Ct. Cl. 1982), where an initial service fee charged by the construction lender was treated as interest. *Cf. Richard C. Goodwin,* 75 T.C. 424 (1980), *on appeal to 3d Cir.*

51. *Don E. Williams Co. v. Commissioner,* 429 U.S. 529 (1977); *Battlestein v. Commissioner,* 631 F.2d 1182 (5th Cir. 1980), *cert. denied,* 101 S. Ct. 2018 (1981); *Richard S. Heyman,* 70 T.C. 482 (1978), *aff'd,* 633 F.2d 215 (6th Cir. 1980); *Alan A. Rubnitz,* 67 T.C. 621 (1977).

52. *See, e.g., Richard S. Heyman,* 70 T.C. 482 (1978), *aff'd,* 633 F.2d 215 (6th Cir. 1980); *Alan A. Rubnitz,* 67 T.C. 621 (1977). *See also* Rev. Rul. 80-248, 1980-2 C.B. 164.

53. *See, e.g., Crain v. Commissioner,* 75 F.2d 962 (8th Cir. 1935).

54. *Richard S. Heyman,* 70 T.C. 482 (1978), *aff'd,* 633 F.2d 215; (6th Cir. 1980); *G. Douglas Burck,* 63 T.C. 556 (1975), *aff'd,* 553 F.2d 768 (2d Cir. 1976); *Newton A. Burgess,* 8 T.C. 47 (1947).

55. *Battlestein v. Commissioner,* 631 F.2d 1182 (5th Cir. 1980), *cert. denied,* 101 S. Ct. 2018 (1981); *Wilkerson v. Commissioner,* 655 F.2d 980 (9th Cir. 1981), *rev'g,* 70 T.C. 240 (1978). *Cf. H.C. Franklin,* 77 T.C. 173 (1981).

56. Sec. 163(d)(1). Additional amounts may be deducted on property subject to a net lease. Sec. 163(d)(1)(B).

57. Sec. 163(d)(7).

58. Sec. 163(d)(4)(B).

59. Sec. 163(d)(3)(B). Investment-related expenses other than interest are subtracted from investment income to arrive at net investment income. Sec. 163(d)(3)(C).

60. Sec. 163(d)(4)(A). *See* Rev. Rul. 80-54, 1980-1 C.B. 43 *and* Rev. Rul. 79-136, 1979-1 C.B. 94 for application of the net lease rules.

61. Sec. 163(d)(4)(D).

62. Sec. 163(d)(2).

63. *Edwin R. Curphey,* 73 T.C. 766 (1980); *George Rothenberg,* 48 T.C. 369 (1967); *Leland Hazard,* 7 T.C. 373 (1946); *John D. Fackler,* 45 B.T.A 708 (1941), *aff'd,* 133 F.2d 509 (6th Cir. 1943).

64. Sec. 164(a); Treas. Reg. §§1.164-3(b), 4(a).

65. Treas. Reg. §§1.164-3(b), 4(a).

66. *Id.* Such amounts include "assessments paid for local benefits such as street, sidewalk and other like improvements, imposed because of and measured by some benefit inuring directly to the property against which the assessment is levied. . . ." Treas. Reg. §1.164-4(a).

67. *Messer Oil Corp.,* 28 T.C. 1082 (1957); Rev. Rul. 70-595, 1970-2 C.B. 341, superseding G.C.M. 26069, 1949-2 C.B. 38.

68. *See* Sec. 446(b); Treas. Reg. §1.446-(a)(2); *cf.* Rev. Rul. 71-190, 1971-1 C.B. 70 (prepayment of state income taxes by cash-basis taxpayer was deductible when paid).

69. Sec. 189.

70. *See* pp. 117–120, *supra.*

71. Sec. 164(d); Treas. Reg. §1.164-6.

72. *Shirley W. Keeler,* 70 T.C. 279 (1978); *Joe W. Stout,* 31 T.C. 1199 (1959), *aff'd in part on other issues sub nom., Rogers v. Commissioner,* 281 F.2d 233 (4th Cir. 1960); Rev. Rul. 80-164, 1980-1 C.B. 109; Rev. Rul. 75-156, 1975-1 C.B. 66; Rev. Rul. 75-149, 1975-1 C.B. 64; Rev. Rul. 75-48, 1975-1 C.B. 62.

73. *See* Rev. Rul. 80-164, 1980-1 C.B. 109 and cases cited in note 72, *supra.*

74. *See* Rev. Rul. 81-194, 1981-2 C.B. 54; Rev. Rul. 81-193, 1981-2 C.B. 52; Rev. Rul. 81-192, 1981-2 C.B. 50; Rev. Rul. 81-191, 1981-2 C.B. 49; Rev. Rul. 75-156, 1975-1 C.B. 66; Rev. Rul. 75-149, 1975-1 C.B. 64; Rev. Rul. 75-48, 1975-1 C.B. 62.

75. *See, e.g., Richard C. Goodwin,* 75 T.C. 424 (1980), *on appeal to 3d Cir.*

76. *See, e.g.,* Private Letter Rulings 8017007 (Dec. 31, 1979) and 8017008 (Dec. 31, 1979).

77. *Id.* Under the Service view, FICA and FUTA allocable to the employees of the partnership would be capitalized.

78. *Compare Richard C. Goodwin,* 75 T.C. 424 (1980), *on appeal to 3d Cir. and Madison Gas & Electric Co.,* 72 T.C. 521 (1979), *aff'd, 633 F.2d 512 (7th Cir. 1980) with Blitzer v. United States,* 81-1 U.S.T.C. ¶9262 (Ct. Cl. 1981), *aff'd,* 684 F.2d 874 (Ct.Cl. 1982).

79. Sec. 195.

80. Sec. 263; Treas. Reg. §1.263(a)-1, 2; *see Commissioner v. Idaho Power Co.,* 418 U.S. 1 (1974).

81. *Donald L. Wilkerson,* 70 T.C. 240 (1978), *rev'd (on another issue),* 655 F.2d 980 (9th Cir. 1981); *Lyndell E. Lay,* 69 T.C. 421 (1977); *Longview Hilton Hotel Co.,* 9 T.C. 180 (1947); Rev. Rul. 70-360, 1970-2 C.B. 103.

82. Rev. Rul. 56-136, 1956-1 C.B. 92, *distinguished in* Rev. Rul. 74-395, 1974-2 C.B. 45, and *revoked in* Rev. Rul. 81-160, 1981-1 C.B. 312. However, commitment fees in *Lyndell E. Lay,* 69 T.C. 421 (1977) and the *John N. Baird,* 68 T.C. 115 (1977) were viewed as the costs of securing a loan and were required to be capitalized and amortized over the life of the loan.

83. *See* Rev. Rul. 74-395, 1974-2 C.B. 45. *Cf. Blitzer v. United States,* 81-1 U.S.T.C. ¶9262 (Ct. Cl. 1981), *aff'd,* 684 F.2d 874 (Ct. Cl. 1982).

84. Rev. Rul. 81-160, 1981-1 C.B. 312, *revoking* Rev. Rul. 56-136, 1956-1 C.B. 92. In *Duffy v. United States,* 81-2 U.S.T.C ¶9467 (Ct. Cl. 1981), the Court of Claims permitted the deduction of a loan commitment fee as a business expense, citing the 1956 ruling with approval.

85. *Id. Cf.* Private Letter Ruling 8138092 (June 25, 1981).

86. *Compare Lyndell E. Lay,* 69 T.C. 421 (1977) *and John N. Baird,* 68 T.C. 115 (1977) (commitment fees are costs of securing a loan and must be capitalized over life of the loan) *with Blitzer v. United States,* 81-1 U.S.T.C. ¶9262 (Ct. Cl. 1981), *aff'd,* 684 F.2d 874 (Ct. Cl. 1982) (commitment fee paid to construction lender to reimburse lender's payment of such fee to GNMA constitutes additional interest amortizable over construction and permanent loans) *and H. K. Francis,* 36 CCH Tax Ct. Mem. 704 (1977) (commitment fee paid to construction lender during construction period must be capitalized as cost of construction and recovered through depreciation).

87. If such fees are charged by mortgage brokers, they are generally amortizable over the loan period, *Lyndell E. Lay,* 69 T.C. 421 (1977), but amortization of such fees during the construction period are subject to the Service's pre-opening expense attack.

88. *See Western Credit* Co., 38 T.C. 979 (1962); *Noteman v. Welch,* 108 F.2d 206 (1st Cir. 1939); *Girard Inv. Co. v. Commissioner,* 122 F.2d 843 (3d Cir. 1941). *See also* Rev. Rul. 74-395, 1974-2 C.B. 45.

89. *Richard C. Goodwin,* 75 T.C. 424 (1980), *on appeal to 3d Cir.; Donald L. Wilkerson,* 70 T.C. 240 (1978), *rev'd (on another issue),* 655 F.2d 980 (9th Cir. 1981).

90. *Id.* Application of the Service's position that a newly formed partnership is not in a trade or business until completion of the project may prevent deduction during the construction period of any amortizable amount of the financing services attributable to the construction period.

91. *Richard C. Goodwin,* 75 T.C. 424 (1980), *on appeal to 3d Cir.; Donald L. Wilkerson,* 70 T.C. 240 (1978), *rev'd (on another issue),* 655 F.2d 980 (9th Cir. 1981).

92. *Blitzer v. United States,* 81-1 U.S.T.C. ¶9262 (Ct. Cl. 1981), *aff'd,* 684 F.2D 874 (Ct.Cl. 1982).

93. The Service has recently ruled that rent-up fees must be allocated to the leases obtained and amortized over the lease terms. Rev. Rul. 81-161, 1981-1 C.B. 313. In addition,

commitment fees in the nature of loan standby charges are required to be capitalized and amortized over the life of the loan. Rev. Rul. 81-161, 1981-1 C.B. 313.

94. *See, e.g., Richard C. Goodwin,* 75 T.C. 424 (1980), *on appeal to 3d Cir. See also Estate of W. Burgess Boyd,* 76 T.C. 646 (1981).

95. *Blitzer v. United States,* 81-1 U.S.T.C. ¶9262 (Ct. Cl 1981), *aff'd,* 684 F.2d 874 (Ct. Cl. 1982). *See also Duffy v. United States,* 81-2 U.S.T.C. ¶9467 (Ct. Cl. 1981).

96. Sec. 263(a)(1); *Commissioner v. Idaho Power Co.,* 418 U.S. 1 (1974); *Blitzer v. United States,* 81-1 U.S.T.C. ¶9262 (Ct. Cl. 1981), *aff'd,* 684 F.2d 874 (Ct.Cl. 1982).

97. *Cf.* Sec. 707(c). *See Estate of W. Burgess Boyd,* 76 T.C. 646 (1981).

98. Rev. Rul. 77-403, 1977-2 C.B. 302 (on the facts, covenant had no demonstrable value and the cost must be added to "the cost of the real property rather than the cost of a separate asset").

99. Sec. 707(a); see pp. 74–75, *supra.*

100. Treas. Reg. §1.707-1(a).

101. *See Edward T. Pratt,* 64 T.C. 203 (1975), *aff'd (on this issue) and rev'd (on another issue),* 550 F.2d 1023 (5th Cir. 1977); *Estate of W. Burgess Boyd,* 76 T.C. 646 (1981).

102. *Id.*

103. Secs. 263, 707(c); *Carol W. Hilton,* 74 T.C. 305 (1980), *aff'd,* 671 F.2d 316 (9th Cir. 1982); *Sidney Kimmelman,* 72 T.C. 294 (1979); *Jackson E. Cagle, Jr., 63 T.C. 86 (1976), aff'd,* 539 F.2d 409 (5th Cir. 1976); *George Cheroff,* 40 CCH Tax Ct. Mem. 183 (1980); Rev. Rul. 80-234, 1980-2 C.B. 203. *See* Rev. Rul. 81-150, 1981-1 C.B. 119. (Management fee to managing partner of drilling rig partnership was allocated between cost of drilling rig and administrative partnership services; the portion allocated to drilling rig was capitalized and presumably depreciated over life of rig when placed in service while the portion of fee allocated to administrative services was not deductible prior to rig being placed in service as partnership was not in a trade or business.)

104. Sec. 263; Treas. Reg. §1.263(a)-1, 2; *see also Commissioner v. Idaho Power Co.* 418 U.S. 1 (1974); *Blitzer v. United States,* 81-1 U.S.T.C. ¶9262 (Ct. Cl. 1981), *aff'd,* 684 F.2d 874 (Ct. Cl. 1982); *Estate of W. Burgess Boyd,* 76 T.C. 646 (1981). *See* Rev. Rul. 81-150, 1981-1 C.B. 119, discussed in note 103, *supra.*

105. Treas. Reg. §1.162-1(a).

106. Secs. 707(a), (c); *see, e.g., Sidney Kimmelman,* 72 T.C. 294 (1979); *Edward T. Pratt,* 64 T.C. 203 (1975), *aff'd (on this issue)* and *rev'd (on another issue),* 550 F.2d 1023 (5th Cir. 1977).

107. In 1975, the Service took the position that these costs should be capitalized. Rev. Rul. 75-214, 1975-1 C.B. 185. The Tax Court held that similar payments to the general partner were not deductible by the partnership. *Jackson E. Cagle, Jr.,* 63 T.C. 86 (1974), *aff'd,* 539 F.2d 409 (5th Cir. 1970). *See also Estate of W. Burgess Boyd,* 76 T.C. 646 (1981).

108. Sec. 709(a).

109. Sec. 709(b)(1).

110. Sec. 709(b)(2).

111. Prop. Treas. Reg. §1.709-2(a).

112. Prop. Treas. Reg. §1.709-2(c).

113. *Id.*

114. *Compare* Rev. Rul. 81-150, 1981-1 C.B. 119, where the Service ruled that the 60-month

amortization period begins when a partnership's drilling rig is operational. No amortization was allowed during the construction period.

115. Prop. Treas. Reg. §1.709-1(a).

116. Prop. Treas. Reg. §1.709-2(b). *See* Rev. Rul. 81-153, 1981-1 C.B. 387.

117. *Robert C. Honodel,* 76 T.C. 351 (1981), *on appeal to 9th Cir.*; Rev. Rul. 81-153, 1981-1 C.B. 387; Private Letter Ruling 8108008 (October 31, 1980).

118. Sec. 709. *See* Rev. Rul. 81-153, 1981-1 C.B. 387.

119. The proposed regulations under Section 709 indicate that tax advice pertaining to the adequacy of tax disclosures in the prospectus or placement memorandum is a non-deductible syndication expense.

120. Treas. Reg. §1.162(a); *cf. United States v. Gilmore,* 372 U.S. 39 (1963); *Welch v. Helvering,* 290 U.S. 111 (1933).

121. Sec. 162; Treas. Reg. §1.162-1(a).

122. Rev. Rul. 81-161, 1981-1 C.B. 313.

123. *See Edward T. Pratt,* 64 T.C. 203 (1975) *aff'd (on this issue) and rev'd (on another issue),* 550 F.2d 1023 (5th Cir. 1977).

124. *See* Rev. Rul. 81-151, 1981-1 C.B. 74; Private Letter Rulings 8017007 (Dec. 31, 1979) and 8017008 (December 31, 1979).

125. *Estate of W. Burgess Boyd,* 76 T.C. 646 (1981); *Richard C. Goodwin,* 75 T.C. 424 (1980), *on appeal to 9th. Cir.; Madison Gas & Electric Co.,* 72 T.C. 481 (1978), *aff'd,* 633 F.2d 512 (7th Cir. 1980); *Richmond Television Corp. v. United States,* 345 F.2d 902 (4th Cir. 1965), *vacated and remanded on other grounds per curiam,* 382 U.S. 68 (1965), *on remand,* 354 F.2d 410 (4th Cir. 1965). *But see Manor Care, Inc. v. United States,* 490 F. Supp. 355 (D. Md. 1980) and *Blitzer v. United States,* 81-1 U.S.T.C ¶9262 (Ct. Cl. 1981), *aff'd,* 684 F.2d 874 (Ct. Cl. 1982). *See also Duffy v. United States,* 81-2 U.S.T.C. ¶9467 (Ct. Cl. 1981).

126. *Blitzer v. United States,* 81-1 U.S.T.C. ¶9262 (Ct. Cl. 1981), *aff'd,* 684 F.2d 874 (Ct. Cl. 1982). *See* note 44 in Chapter 2, *supra.*

127. *Id.*

128. *Id.*

129. *Id.*

130. *See* Rev. Rul. 81-151, 1981-1 C.B. 74.

131. Sec. 195.

132. Sec. 195(a). Applies only to post-July 19, 1980 expenditures. *See* S. Rep. No. 96-1036, 96th Cong., 2d Sess. (1980).

133. Sec. 195(b).

134. S. Rep. No. 96-1036, 96th Cong., 2d Sess. (1980).

135. *Id.*

136. *Id.*

137. *Id.*

138. *Id.*

139. *Id.*

140. *See Commissioner v. Idaho Power,* 418 U.S. 1 (1974).

141. Rev. Rul. 81-150, 1981-1 C.B. 119.

142. Secs. 195(a), (c)

143. S. Rep. No. 96-1036, 96th Cong., 2d Sess. (1980).

144. Rev. Rul. 81-150, 1981-1 C.B. 119.

145. *See* note 44 in Chapter 2, *supra.*

CHAPTER 7

DEATH, DISASTERS, AND DISPOSITIONS OF PARTNERSHIP INTERESTS

1. GENERAL

When considering investing in a real estate limited partnership, emphasis is usually placed on the tax-reducing deductions generated in the early years of the investment and on the fact that an investor can usually obtain at the very least a $1 investment at an after-federal, state, and possible local tax cost of substantially less than $1. Further, appreciation in economic value is sought and consideration is given to the economic quality of the project. Perhaps as important, but less likely to be considered at the time of investment, are the tax consequences at the end of the investment.

These tax consequences may be significant. Tax "shelter" usually is attained by "front-ending" partnership deductions when basis is enhanced by nonrecourse financing. The usual effect, however, only is to defer tax liability, not to eliminate it permanently. In some cases the investor may convert income that would otherwise be taxable as ordinary income into capital gain. The law is structured, however, so that many of the prior tax benefits are "recaptured" as ordinary income upon the sale of the partnership's assets, the failure of the partnership, or a partner's transfer of his partnership interest.[1]

There are numerous reasons for getting out of a tax shelter. First, an investor may simply wish to raise cash by selling his investment. Second, after a period of time, a real estate syndication usually "turns around." At that time, the investment, if it is successful, may generate substantial taxable income (since many allocable deductions have been taken in the earlier years) but may provide little cash with which to pay the tax liability (since the cash is used to pay off the nonrecourse debt). At this point, the investor may seek either to shelter this new income, through new tax preferred investments, or to dispose of the investment.

Less voluntary stimuli are also evident. Thus third, an investor may die, at which time his partnership interest or his proportionate share of partnership property is transferred to his successors. Fourth, the investment may become a "leaky tax shelter," or an unsuccessful syndication that causes the partnership's creditors to foreclose on the property or to take a deed in lieu of foreclosure. Such partnership failure is considered to be a taxable event. Fifth, even without such a foreclosure, a partner may choose to abandon his interest in the property or to sell or exchange it. Sixth, the partnership may sell its property and make a new investment or make a current or liquidating distribution of money or property. Finally, a partner may retire from the partnership, at which time the partnership may distribute property to him in liquidation of his interest.

This chapter discusses the tax consequences of partnership interest transfers. Emphasis is placed upon the effect on the disposing partner. Consideration is also given to the effect upon the remaining members of the partnership, and to the consequences of a termination, whether voluntary or not, of the partnership.

Because of the complex nature of the law in this area, the following discussion is extensive. The major principle, however, can be stated simply: The outstanding nonrecourse debt is considered to be realized income when there is a transfer because the partner is relieved of his allocable share of such debt at that time. At the beginning, the nonrecourse debt was assumed to be part of his investment and it permitted him an increased basis and the ability to use his share of the partnership losses as deductions. At the end, to be consistent, the debt is deemed to be received by him, since he is relieved of having to pay it. Further, this taxable income may be, at least in part, ordinary income if the partnership used an accelerated method of depreciation. Thus the usual tax effect of a real estate syndication is to permit extraordinary deductions in the early years that are recaptured on transfer or other disposition. However, a recent Fifth Circuit Court of Appeals case, *Tufts*, represents a minority view that is quite beneficial to taxpayers. The case is on appeal to the United States Supreme Court and is discussed in Section 18 of this chapter. The remainder of the chapter reflects the majority view.

Many partnerships are continued long after there is economic reason because the partners fear the adverse tax consequence of dissolution. Partners with a built-in potential tax recapture problem seek a plan to rid themselves of their difficulty, although usually they cannot find a solution other than paying tax on fictional income. This chapter explores this situation and the alternative methods of disposition.

Section 4 of this chapter begins with the sale of a partnership interest. Before analyzing the types of transfer, however, this chapter discusses the tax treatment of the disposing partner's share of the partnership's income for his last year. It then addresses the so-called "collapsible partnership" provision.

2. A DISPOSING PARTNER'S SHARE OF THE YEAR'S INCOME

The partnership taxable year closes with respect to a partner who sells or otherwise disposes, except by death, his entire partnership interest. [2] The disposing partner must include in his taxable income in the year of disposition his distributive share of partnership items of income, gain, or loss for his partnership year ending with the date of disposition.[3] The partnership does not necessarily have to close its books at that time to determine the distributive share.[4] Instead, the partners may agree to an amount by estimating each partner's pro rata share.[5] If such calculation is reasonable, the partners' agreement will be accepted by the Service.[6]

When a partner dies, the taxable year of the partnership does not close with respect to the deceased partner, unless his death causes a termination of the entire partnership.[7] The decedent's last tax return does not include his distributive share of partnership income for the partial partnership taxable year up to the date of death.[8] Rather, the decedent's estate or successor in interest includes in its taxable income the entire partnership year's distributive share.[9] If the decendent's successor sells or otherwise disposes of the interest, the partnership taxable year will close with respect to the successor with the same resulting tax effects described previously.[10]

Although the partnership's taxable year also does not close with respect to the donor of a partnership interest disposed of by gift,[11] the income, gain, or loss up to the date of the gift is allocated to the donor and included on his return for the taxable year ending with or immediately after the date of the gift.[12] Do not think, however, that the adverse tax consequences of disposition can be avoided by giving the partnership interest away; this is discussed later in this chapter.

3. THE OVERRIDING PRINCIPLE OF "SECTION 751 PROPERTY"

To prevent the conversion of potential ordinary income into capital gain on disposition of a partnership interest or on partnership distribution of assets, the Code contains a Section 751, the so-called "collapsible partnership" provision.[13]

If gain is realized on the sale or exchange by a partner of his partnership interest, the gain is capital gain,[14] except for the amount attributable to the partner's share of "Section 751 property." [15] Gain on transfer of "Section 751 property" is deemed received in exchange for a noncapital asset, resulting in ordinary income for the amount that exceeds the seller's allocable basis.[16]

In addition, if a partner receives a distribution of property from the partnership that in substance changes the partner's allocable share of the partnership's "Section 751 property," the distribution is treated as a sale of such property between the partner and the partnership, and some ordinary income probably results to the party whose allocable share has decreased.[17]

A partnership's "Section 751 property" includes assets that, if sold by the partnership, would give rise to ordinary gain or loss. More specifically, "Section 751 property" is the partnership's "unrealized receivables" [18] and "substantially appreciated inventory." [19]

"Unrealized receivables" include a partnership's right to payment, to the extent not previously included in income, for goods and services (e.g., earned rents that have not been included in income at the time of distribution).[20] Most important for a real estate limited partnership, "unrealized receivables" includes the entire allowable amount of ordinary income recapture of depreciation,[21] computed as if the partnership's property were sold for its fair market value at the time of the disposition of the partnership interest.[22] Each item of recapture property must be analyzed separately and may not be netted against any other.

We will not discuss "substantially appreciated inventory" because single real estate limited partnerships almost always hold their property for investment and therefore generally do not have important inventory items.[23] Multiproject partnerships that have a history of buying and selling properties, or partnerships with "dealer" partners, may risk a Service assertion that they should treat their properties as inventory items.[24]

4. SALE OF A PARTNERSHIP INTEREST

We now discuss the different types of disposition of partnership interests. First is the sale of a partnership interest.

Upon the sale of a partnership interest to a third party or to another member of the partnership,[25] the selling partner will have taxable gain or loss measured by the difference between the amount realized on the sale and his adjusted basis in the partnership interest.[26]

A selling partner is deemed to receive not only the cash or property that is actually transferred to him but also an amount equal to his proportionate share of the partnership liabilities (recourse *and* nonrecourse) of which he is deemed to be relieved.[27] This can be illustrated by the following example: A partner has a one-third interest in a partnership that owns an apartment building subject to a $90,000 nonrecourse loan liability. Upon the sale of the partner's partnership interest for $5,000 in cash, the partner is deemed to realize $35,000 ($5,000 cash plus his one-third share of the $90,000 liability).

Thus the selling partner's tax liability, if the interest is sold at a gain, may substantially exceed the cash actually received in the transaction. If the partnership's property has not sufficiently appreciated in value, the selling partner will not receive enough cash to pay the resulting tax, and the sale may not be an advantageous method of disposing of a partnership interest.

A partnership interest is considered a capital asset, the sale of which produces capital gain or loss.[28] The capital gain or loss will be long-term or short-term depending on whether or not the partner has held his partnership interest for 12 months.[29]

If the partnership owns Section 751 property, however, any amount received by a selling partner that is attributable to his proportionate share of Section 751 property is considered as received in exchange for property other than a capital asset; that is, with regard to that portion of the transaction, ordinary income generally will result.[30] For example, a selling partner may have ordinary income equal to his share of the depreciation recapture income that the partnership would have if it sold its assets.[31]

The next three paragraphs describe in some detail the sale of an interest in a partnership that owns Section 751 property. Those readers desiring only a general explanation of the tax consequences may skip these paragraphs.

The sale of an interest in a partnership that has some Section 751 property is treated as two transactions: the sale of the partner's proportionate share of non-Section 751 property and the sale of his proportionate share of Section 751 property.[32] The total sales price and the partner's basis, therefore, must be allocated between the two types of assets to determine the amount of capital gain or loss and ordinary gain or loss. To determine the total sales price attributable to the partner's interest in Section 751 property, an allocation arrived at in an arm's-length agreement between the selling partner and the buyer generally will be accepted by the Service.[33] In the absence of an arm's-length agreement, an allocation will be made based on relative fair market values.[34] The allocation of basis, however, is more complex. The calculation requires a distinction between the partner's basis in his partnership interest and his proportionate share of the partnership's basis in its assets. Thus a partner's basis in Section 751 property is equal to his proportionate share of the partnership's basis in such property.[35] The partner's basis in non-Section 751 property is equal to the basis in his partnership interest less the amount determined to be applicable to Section 751 property.[36]

The preceding rules are demonstrated in the following example: A owns a one-third interest, his basis in which is $8,500, in partnership ABC. The partnership owns Section 751 property with an adjusted basis of $7,500 and a fair market value of $15,000, and non-Section 751 property with an adjusted basis of $13,500 and a fair market value of $33,000. ABC has no liabilities. A sells his interest for $16,000 (one third of the fair market value of all of the assets of ABC). A has a total gain realized of $7,500 ($16,000–$8,500 basis). Of this total gain, the Section 751 ordinary income is $2,500, determined as follows: The fair market value of A's interest in Section 751 property, $5,000 (1/3 × $15,000), less A's proportionate share of the partnership's basis in Section 751 property, $2,500 (1/3 × $7,500). A's capital gain will be $5,000, determined as follows: The amount received in exchange for non-Section 751 assets, $11,000 ($16,000–$5,000), less A's remaining basis in his partnership interest, $6,000 ($8,500–$2,500).

It is possible that, because the gain on Section 751 property is determined with respect to the partnership's basis in such property and not with respect to the partner's basis in his partnership interest, a partner will have ordinary income under Section 751 even though the remaining transaction results in a capital loss.[37] Thus, in the preceding example, if A's basis were $14,500, he would have had ordinary income, as before, of $2,500 and a capital loss of $1,000, calculated as the amount received in exchange for non-Section 751 property, $11,000 ($16,000–$5,000), less A's remaining basis in his partnership interest, $12,000 ($14,500–$2,500).

Returning to more general matters, we now discuss installment sales. Subject to the partner electing otherwise, a selling partner who receives payments for his partnership interest over more than one year will report any gain on the sale of his partnership interest on the installment basis.[38] Pursuant to the Installment Sales Revision Act of 1980, this is the new rule, and it applies to any disposition occurring after October 19, 1980.[39] The only requirement is that at least one payment must be received after the close of the taxable year in which the sale occurs.[40] (Note that the amount by which any debt which is relieved exceeds the basis is taken into account in determining the amount of gain that must be reported in the year of sale.)[41] Installment sale reporting will enable the partner to "spread out" the tax liability over a number of years. Presumably, if the partnership has Section 751 property, the gain reported on each installment will be fragmented into ordinary income and capital gain components.[42]

Finally, as was discussed earlier, a selling partner is required to recognize his proportionate share of the partnership's income or loss to the date of sale.[43] This proportionate share cannot be converted into capital gain or loss by "selling" this portion of the interest.[44]

5. EXCHANGES OF PARTNERSHIP INTERESTS

Instead of selling his real estate limited partnership interest for cash or other property, a partner may seek to dispose of his investment by exchanging his partnership interest for an interest in another partnership. Although the Service has ruled that the conversion of a general partnership interest to a limited partnership interest in the same partnership is not taxable,[45] it has resisted tax-free exchange treatment for swaps of partnership interests in different partnerships even if swaps of the underlying properties would qualify as a tax-free "like-kind" exchange.

The Tax Court has taken a more liberal view than the Service and has recently reaffirmed its position that an exchange of *general* partnership interests, where each partnership owned and operated rental apartment buildings, qualifies for special tax-free treatment as a "like-kind exchange." [46] Could these cases be extended to imply that *limited* partners may exchange their interests tax-free if the partnership's underlying properties are similar? If so, this might be a way to avoid the built-in recapture tax problems on disposition.

Like-kind exchange treatment for limited partnership interests is subject to many uncertainties. First, the Service "nonacquiesced" to the Tax Court decision involving a general partnership exchange.[47] Second, the Service has ruled that an exchange of general partnership interests does not qualify for nonrecognition.[48] Third, securities are excluded from favorable tax treatment under the like-kind exchange provisions[49] and, arguably, a limited partnership interest, especially in a widely syndicated partnership, is a security.[50] (It certainly is a security for security law purposes, as discussed in Chapter 8.)

Further, the practicalities of a like-kind exchange of limited partnership interests undermine its usefulness. A partner who owns a tax beneficial or tax neutral partnership interest may not wish to exchange it for a partnership interest that carries with it adverse tax consequences. In addition, to meet most successfully the requirements for a like-kind exchange, the exchanging partners should have equal amounts of proportionate partnership liabilities.[51] The effect of these practical considerations may well be that, after the exchange, the exchanging partners will own interests that are similar to those owned before the exchange. Such an exchange may accomplish little. However, a foreign person or someone else in a favorable tax position might be willing to accept an exhausted tax shelter with substantial asset value in exchange for a less valuable partnership interest that provides a better tax position. In addition, an exchange may be beneficial if a Section 754 election can be made to increase basis in partnership property.[52]

If like-kind exchange treatment is available, an exchanging partner generally will have no taxable gain or loss.[53] The partner's basis in his new partnership interest will be "substituted"; that is, it will be the same as his basis in the previous partnership interest.[54] If, however, as a result of the exchange, the partner is relieved of more liabilities than he is deemed to assume with regard to his new partnership interest, the excess amount is likely to be presently taxable.[55] Any gain recognized will be added to the basis of the partnership interest received.[56] If an exchanging partner is deemed to assume greater net liabilities, his basis will be increased without tax liability.

As an alternative to exchanging partnership interests, the partnership may exchange its real property for that of another partnership.[57] Again, in this context the properties must be "like-kind" properties, that is, they must be similar in nature or character.[58] Unimproved real property may be exchanged for improved real property.[59] Care must be excercised to ensure that the nature or quality of the exchanged property is the same under state law. For example, if real property is exchanged for an interest in a joint venture in real property, such interest could be considered personalty, and Section 1031 might not apply.[60]

If the partnership exchanges its property for like-kind property and the property transferred is subject to a mortgage liability, gain probably will be recognized to the extent that this mortgage liability exceeds the liability on the property being received.[61] If the exchange is of certain depreciable property, the gain will be ordinary income to the extent of the depreciation recapture potential.[62] The basis in the property received will be the same as the basis in the property transferred, increased by any gain that is recognized.[63] If greater liabilities are assumed, the partnership's basis in the new property will be increased by the net increase in liabilities.

6. GIFTS OF PARTNERSHIP INTERESTS

a. Charitable Gifts.   A limited partner may consider making a charitable gift of his limited partnership interest to shift adverse tax consequences from himself to a nontaxpaying entity. He may even try to get a charitable contribution deduction for the value of the gift. Although the tax law in this area is unsettled, this sort of gift is likely to result in some current tax liability on the transfer, since the transfer probably will be considered part sale and part gift for tax purposes.

The amount of gain from the deemed part sale probably will be the donor's share of partnership liabilities, reduced by the portion of the donor's basis in his partnership interest that is allocable to the deemed part sale.[64] This would result in tax if there is a gain. The gain will be taxable as capital gain or, to the extent that it represents potential recapture income, ordinary income, although the operation of Section 751 in this area is far from clear.[65]

As will be discussed, there is a stepped-up basis on death to the extent of the value of the tax shelter partnership interest. But if the value is not at least equal to the allocable debt, the same tax consequences are likely to result from a charitable bequest of the partnership interest on death with gain resulting from liabilities exceeding the fair market value of the property at the time of death. The estate probably would qualify for a charitable bequest deduction for estate tax purposes, although it is quite difficult to value a limited partnership tax shelter interest.

Public charities may accept tax deduction exhausted tax shelter interests since the charities generally are exempt from taxation.[66] They are subject, however, to the unrelated business income tax on debt-financed income and may refuse a substantially encumbered tax shelter gift unless it produces net economic benefits for charity.[67]

Despite the part sale adverse tax consequences to the donor, a gift to charity can eliminate the ongoing tax burden of a "turned" tax shelter interest where the annual tax liability is greater than cash flow. Further, under varying theories, if the fair market value of either the partnership interest or the partner's share of partnership assets exceeds the amount of debt, then a portion of the excess should be considered a charitable contribution that is deductible within certain limitations.[68]

b. Private Gifts.   A private gift to a family member can shift the adverse tax consequences of the turned-around limited partnership interest to a person in a lower tax bracket. Prior to making such a gift, however, the partner should consider the practicalities and tax ramifications, since a private gift may present one of the least palatable alternatives: a taxable sale in part (with some ordinary income), a taxable gift in part, and continued negative cash flow suffered by a family member.

As discussed in connection with charitable gifts, a private gift may be considered a taxable sale of the partnership interest to the extent the proportionate share of partnership liabilities exceeds a portion of the partner's basis in his partnership interest.[69] If there is potential recapture income, then, as in all the other "sale" transactions, a portion of any gain will be ordinary income.[70] In addition, if the value of the partnership interest exceeds the partner's proportionate share of partnership liabilities by more than the annual exclusion amount of $10,000 (or $20,000 for a gift by a husband and wife), there will be at least some gift tax liability, except in the case of a gift to the partner's spouse, where there is an unlimited marital gift tax exclusion.[71] Finally, even though the tax consequences of ownership of the partnership interest are successfully transferred to a person in a lower tax bracket, this may not eliminate the problem of inadequate partnership cash flow. Since the donee may have yearly liability but little cash, the investor might consider making future cash gifts to the donee in order to meet the liability.[72]

7. TRANSFER THROUGH A GRANTOR TRUST

It has been suggested that the tax disadvantages of owning and disposing of an exhausted tax shelter investment might be avoided by initially purchasing the interest through a grantor trust, instead of individually.[73] The tax treatment of utilizing a grantor trust, however, is at best questionable and may result in economic disadvantage.

All of the tax attributes, including income, deductions, and credits, of a grantor trust pass through the trust and are taxed to the grantor.[74] A trust is considered a grantor trust when the grantor has retained an interest or a degree of control over the trust that, for tax purposes, negates the substance of the transfer of property to the trust.[75] In the present context, where the grantor would wish to avoid a reversionary interest, the retained power is likely to take the form of an income interest.[76] The "grantor" classification would cease when the interest or control terminated; therefore, the trust would be taxed as a separate entity without any attribution of tax items to the grantor.

Theoretically, a grantor trust arrangement would work as follows: The grantor would set up a trust. He would retain sufficient control to deem the trust to be a grantor trust. (Some gift tax might have to be paid based on the rights retained by the grantor and the value the ultimate beneficiary is to receive. This ultimate beneficiary might be a shell corporation owned by someone else or a family member.) The purchase and retention of a real estate limited partnership interest by the grantor trust [77] would result in the early year partnership losses passing through the partnership to the grantor trust-partner and then through the trust to the grantor. The trust instrument would provide for the termination of the "grantor" classification at about the time the investment turns around and the partnership is generating taxable income but little cash. Any annual income and ultimate disposition income would be taxed directly to the trust or subsequent beneficiary. The grantor, after benefiting from the pass-through of partnership losses, might in this manner avoid the tax disadvantages of disposing of a tax shelter investment.

As a practical matter, such an arrangement would be beneficial only if the tax shelter deductions were the most important aspect of the investment. Once the grantor relinquishes his control, he can no longer benefit from the appreciation of an economically successful property.

As a tax matter, the uncertainty in this area is largely over whether the change in tax character of the trust would be treated as a disposition of the partnership interest by the grantor, with all the resulting disadvantages discussed in this chapter. Further, if the grantor dies while retaining an income interest (or any other substantial interest or control), the value of the trust property may be included in the grantor's taxable estate, although the trust property may not be available to satisfy estate tax liability.[78]

The Service, as might be expected, has ruled that renunciation of grantor trust powers is a taxable event.[79] This ruling involved a situation where a trust had purchased a real estate partnership interest that generated excess losses that were claimed by the grantor, and the renunciation came just before the partnership was to generate income. Whether the courts will adopt the Service's position remains to be seen.

8. INCORPORATING THE PARTNERSHIP INTEREST OR THE PARTNERSHIP PROPERTY

Thought may be given to retaining the investment by transferring it from the high-bracket individual partner to a lower-bracket corporation.[80] Although this method might make more viable retaining the shelter as an investment, the transfer could still be subject to adverse tax consequences.

The Service has taken the position that all incorporation transactions will be treated as if the partnership first transferred its assets and liabilities to the corporation in exchange for its stock, and then distributed the stock to the partners in liquidation of the partnership.[81] This approach would probably be applied to a single partner with regard to his proportionate share of assets and liabilities. On the incorporation of the assets, no gain or loss generally would be recognized. To the extent the corporation assumes liabilities or takes property subject to liabilities that exceed the adjusted basis of the property transferred, however, gain will be recognized.[82] Even if the transaction is viewed as a transfer of a partnership interest, which includes a proportionate share of partnership liabilities, similar tax consequences will result.[83] In addition, under either theory, to the extent that there is ordinary income potential, through either depreciation recapture or Section 751 property, the gain on the transaction would be ordinary income.[84]

Once incorporated, the former partner often would not be able to withdraw cash from the corporation without dividend treatment.[85] Unless the collapsible corporation provisions apply, the former partner should be able to sell his stock in the corporation with capital gains treatment.[86]

A recent development is the use of "swap funds," in which partners in a number of real estate limited partnerships simultaneously contribute their limited partnership interests to a corporation in exchange for its stock, and/ or several limited partnerships contribute their assets in exchange for stock. After the swap, the corporation's shares are often traded publicly, thereby providing the opportunity for liquidity to the former limited partners. These transactions are, to a certain extent, modeled on similar "swap funds" for oil and gas limited partnership interests. However, the Service has recently announced that it has suspended granting tax rulings for these "swap funds."[86a]

The tax effects generally are governed by the same principles as the previously discussed incorporation of a single partnership or the contribution of a partnership interest to a controlled corporation. Thus the transferor will have a tax at the time of the transfer to the extent that his allocable share of transferred liabilities exceeds the depreciated basis in his partnership interest. Thereafter, he will own stock in a corporation that will generally hold and operate a diversified real estate porfolio. As a result, the partner will be able to sell his stock at capital gains rates at the time of his choosing. However, the market will often value the corporation stock at a discount from underlying assets value, and income from the real estate will be subject to double taxation if dividends are declared.

9. FORECLOSURE

Things may become so bad economically that the partners are no longer able to service the debt on partnership property. In this case, the mortgagee may foreclose. The result of foreclosure is often that the investor has taxable gain equal to his proportionate share of the debt that is cancelled.

On foreclosure, the partnership is deemed to have made a sale of the property for the outstanding amount of the mortgage debt.[87] Gain is realized by the partnership and is measured by the difference between the amount of the debt and the basis of the foreclosed property in the hands of the partnership. In general, because of depreciation recapture, much of this gain is taxable as ordinary income. The capital gain and ordinary income flow through to the partners as part of their distributable income shares.[88]

As discussed earlier, the amount of a partner's distributive share is added to the basis in his partnership interest. This addition, however, is quite temporary: Since the foreclosure relieves the partnership of debt, such discharge is treated as a cash distribution [89] that reduces the partner's basis in the partnership.[90] In addition, since basis cannot be reduced below zero, any excess discharged debt will be taxable income. Thus a partner can have taxable income even though he receives no partnership cash distributions.

The net effect of foreclosure, therefore, may be that the partner traded the early tax shelter deductions, which were substantial, for later tax liability and loss of his original investment. This is hardly a promising result unless annual inflation is so high that the early year deductions produce economic value in excess of the value of the inflated dollars that are used to pay the eventual tax liability.

10. DEED OF PROPERTY IN LIEU OF FORECLOSURE

To avoid foreclosure proceedings, the partnership may voluntarily convey the property to the mortgagee. This is likely to result in the same adverse tax consequences as foreclosure, because it will be treated as a sale or exchange of the property by the partnership.[91]

There is older authority indicating that a deed of property in lieu of foreclosure of a nonrecourse debt is not a sale or exchange.[92] It would appear, however, that the better view supports sale or exchange treatment.[93] As before, the partner will have taxable gain generally equal to the amount of his share of discharged debt, and such gain will, in part, be taxable as ordinary income.[94] If not accorded sale or exchange treatment, all of the relieved debt will be taxable as ordinary income.

11. ABANDONING THE PARTNERSHIP INTEREST OR THE PARTNERSHIP PROPERTY

A partner who anticipates significant problems with regard to a formal disposition of his partnership interest or of partnership property may choose simply to "walk away" from his partnership interest. Abandonment, however, will not veil the partner from the tax liability that accompanies getting out of a tax shelter.

An abandonment of an interest in a tax shelter is not distinguishable from a withdrawal from the partnership. The Service has taken the position that a partner's withdrawal results in a deemed cash distribution to the extent of the partner's proportionate share of partnership liabilities.[95] The tax consequences of a deemed cash distribution have been discussed.[96]

Suppose, instead, that the partnership abandons its interest in the debt-encumbered property. As such, any tax consequences will flow through to the partners as an element of their distributable share of partnership income, gain, or loss.[97] If the abandonment is followed by foreclosure, the transaction will be treated as a sale of the property by the partnership for the face amount of the debt, as discussed previously.[98] Sale treatment should also result even if there are no formal foreclosure proceedings,[99] although there is some early, but probably no longer reliable, authority that ordinary gain or loss results from abandonment.[100] As in all other dispositions of the partnership's real property, capital gain is likely to result,[101] except to the extent of depreciation recapture ordinary income.[102]

12. MORTGAGEE IN POSSESSION

A mortgagee may wish to avoid foreclosure and the problems of ownership. For this reason, or for economic considerations, a mortgagee may choose to become a mortgagee in possession when a partnership cannot meet its debt payments. The mortgagee would collect the rents, pay the expenses of the property, and credit any excess cash against the outstanding liability. Since the partnership would continue to own the property and to receive the benefit of the debt amortization credits, the taxable income and deductions, including depreciation, should be accounted for by the partnership and its partners.[103]

Assuming that the partners can pay any yearly tax liability, the mortgagee-in-possession arrangement effectively eliminates the negative cash flow created by debt amortization. In addition, since the partnership remains the owner of the property, no gain-creating disposition has been made, and the adverse tax consequences of getting out of the shelter have been postponed. Further, the partners have retained any investment potential of the property.

It should be noted that a mortgagee probably will require some inducement for deferring foreclosure and agreeing to accept debt payments according to the partnership's cash flows. Thus the partnership may have to make a substantial payment on the principal of the debt at the inception of the mortgagee-in-possession arrangement.

13. REFINANCING THE MORTGAGE

When the partnership cannot meet the principal payments on the debt and foreclosure is approaching, it may seek to refinance the mortgage. Refinancing could reduce the monthly payments and increase the proportion of each payment which constitutes deductible interest. If the principal amount of the debt is increased or at least not reduced, the transaction should have no current tax effect on the partnership or the partners.[104]

As with the mortgagee-in-possession arrangement, the mortgagee may require some inducement for agreeing to a refinancing arrangement. The inducement cost must be weighed against the potential investment value of the project as well as the postponed taxation of a disposition of the partnership interest or property.

14. BANKRUPTCY

Bankruptcy of an economically unsuccessful real estate limited partnership may be voluntary or involuntary. The Bankruptcy Tax Act of 1980 changed prior law by providing that no new taxable entity results from commencement of a bankruptcy case involving a partnership.[105] This rule reverses the Service's prior position that the bankruptcy estate of a partnership was a separate taxable entity from the partnership and that the basis of the partnership property was "carried over" to the bankruptcy estate.[106]

The Bankruptcy Tax Act also changed the rules with respect to the discharge of partnership debt in bankruptcy.[107] Under the Act, income from the discharge of partnership indebtedness is treated as an item of partnership income that is allocated separately to each partner under Section 702(a).[108] The allocation of income to a partner as a result of the discharge of a partnership debt results in the partner's basis in the partnership being increased by the amount of income allocated to him.[109] At the same time, however, the reduction in such a partner's share of partnership liabilities caused by the debt discharge constitutes a deemed distribution resulting in a corresponding reduction of the partner's basis in his partnership interest.[110] Thus there is no net change in the partner's basis in his partnership interest.

In lieu of recognizing his allocable share of income on the discharge of partnership debt, the Act permits a partner to elect to reduce the basis of any depreciable property he owns.[111] His interest in the partnership will be treated as depreciable property to the extent of the partner's proportionate interest in the depreciable property of the partnership,[112] but only if the reduction in the basis of the partner's interest in the partnership is accompanied by a corresponding reduction in the partnership's basis in depreciable property with respect to such partner.[113]

The characterization of income from a deemed cash distribution as ordinary income or capital gain in the bankruptcy context is unsettled. In general, such gain is treated as capital gain, except that ordinary income will result to the extent of partnership recapture potential.[114] It does not appear that the interaction of the bankruptcy deemed cash distribution and collapsible partnership provisions was contemplated.

The rest of this section temporarily leaves tax analysis to discuss the effects of the new Bankruptcy Code on real estate limited partnerships. A new federal Bankruptcy Code was enacted, effective October 1, 1979. It eliminated "acts of bankruptcy" as grounds for granting relief on a bankruptcy petition and substituted two tests in place of the former "acts of bankruptcy" in determining whether to grant the relief requested by an involuntary petition: "(1) the debtor is generally not paying his debts as such debts become due; or (2) within 120 days before the date of the filing of the petition, a custodian, other than a trustee, receiver or agent appointed or authorized to take charge of less than substantially all of the property of the debtor for the purpose of enforcing a lien against such property, was appointed or took possession." [114a]

The Bankruptcy Code renders unenforceable after the commencement of a case under it any provision, with certain limited exceptions, in an executory contract or unexpired lease that permits or provides for the termination or modification of an executory contract or unexpired lease based on (a) the insolvency or financial condition of the debtor at any time before the closing of the bankruptcy proceeding; (b) the commencement of a case under the Bankruptcy Code; or (c) the appointment of or taking possession by a trustee in a case under the Bankruptcy Code or a custodian before the commencement of such a case. [114b]

Provisions in a limited partnership agreement requiring the withdrawal of a general partner from a limited partnership upon his or its bankruptcy may be adversely affected by the Bankruptcy Code. The Uniform Limited Partnership Act does not provide for mandatory withdrawal of a bankrupt general partner. Thus, such provisions may not fall within a Bankruptcy Code exception that permits enforcement where applicable law, apart from the contractual provision itself, excuses the non-debtor party from accepting or rendering performance from or to a trustee or assignee of the contract or lease. [114c] In most states, contracts to provide personal services are not assignable and the party receiving such services cannot usually be compelled to accept personal services from a substitute. Accordingly, it could be argued in such states that the Bankruptcy Code exception does allow contractual provisions providing for the mandatory withdrawal of a bankrupt general partner to operate in a bankruptcy case. [114d]

As an alternative, in order to avoid the uncertainty in this area, it may be desirable to insert a clause in the limited partnership agreement automatically converting the interest of a bankrupt general partner to that of a limited partner upon the bankruptcy of the general partner.

In any event, this question arises only during and after the actual administration of the bankruptcy proceeding. Thus, a clause requiring the withdrawal of a general partner should remain effective at least during the period of insolvency before the petition is filed and also during periods of insolvency in which the debtor may be prohibited from filing a bankruptcy petition.

Under the 1976 Uniform Limited Partnership Act Revision, a provision requiring withdrawal of the general partner on his or its bankruptcy may or may not be valid since the 1976 revision specifically includes "acts of bankruptcy" as one of the events of withdrawal.[114e]

Real estate leases should also be reviewed with the new Bankruptcy Code in mind; contractual provisions terminating or modifying unexpired leases upon the insolvency of a debtor may be unenforceable during administration of the debtor's bankruptcy proceeding.

We now return to tax analysis.

15. LIQUIDATING DISTRIBUTION FROM THE PARTNERSHIP

When a partner decides to divest his real estate limited partnership interest, both the disposing partner and the remaining partners should consider a liquidating distribution from the partnership.

A liquidating distribution increases the remaining partners' proportionate shares in the partnership [115] by using partnership, as opposed to the remaining partners', money or other property.[116] A cash distribution, however, may deplete the partnership's liquid assets or may require the partnership to convert some of its properties to cash.[117] A single-property real estate partnership may have difficulty making a distribution of property, although it might distribute an undivided interest in its real property, that effectively removes the retiring partner from the partnership.[118] The retiring partner, however, would continue as owner of an investment, now a fee interest, that he may have found economically unpromising. In addition, joint ownership may raise difficulties under local real property laws. For these reasons, distributions of property from a real estate partnership are rare and are discussed only briefly in this book.

For tax purposes, a partner's interest is considered liquidated upon the complete termination of the partner's entire interest by means of a single distribution or a series of distributions to the partner from the partnership.[119] Since a retiring partner is considered a partner until the series of distributions is complete, a partnership taxable year will not terminate until the distributions are completed.[120]

The liquidation of a limited partnership interest generally produces complex tax results.[121] Gain usually is recognized only if the retiring partner receives money, including his proportionate share of the partnership liabilities of which he is relieved, and the amount of money exceeds the adjusted basis of his partnership interest.[122] Loss may be recognized [123] if the distribution consists solely of money, unrealized receivables, and inventory items, and if the partner's adjusted basis in his partnership interest exceeds the amount of money received plus his basis in the distributed unrealized receivables and inventory items.[124]

Any gain recognized or a liquidating distribution of money usually will be at least partially taxable as ordinary income to the retiring partner.[125] Thus ordinary income will result from any amount of money received for the retiring partner's proportionate shares of unrealized receivables,[126] such as depreciation recapture, or substantially appreciated inventory,[127] which remain in the partnership. Payments received on account of the partner's share of partnership goodwill, except if provided for in the partnership agreement, will also be taxable as ordinary income.[128] The remaining amount of money distributed, if any, will generate capital gain or loss, depending on the partner's basis in the liquidated interest.[129] The partnership will not recognize gain or loss on the liquidating distribution of money to a partner.[130]

The tax consequences on a liquidating distribution of property are even more complicated. If the partnership has Section 751 property, which includes depreciation recapture property, a distribution of property will result in ordinary income to the partner or the partnership unless all types of property are distributed in proportion to the partner's interest in the partnership.[131] The basis of distributed property in the hands of the distributee partner is limited to the basis in his partnership interest reduced by any money received in liquidation,[132] and such basis must be allocated according to special rules.[133]

On a liquidating distribution of property, the partnership may elect to adjust its basis in remaining partnership property to take into account any gain or loss recognized by the transferee partner and any basis limitations applicable at the transferee partner's level.[134] In certain circumstances where the partner receives a distribution of property within two years of acquiring his partnership interest, he may make an adjustment increasing his basis in the distributed property.[135] It would seem likely that the partnership would realize gain or loss if the liquidating distribution of property constitutes a guaranteed payment.[136]

16. DISPOSITION ON THE DEATH OF A PARTNER

The death of a partner can produce the only effective permanent tax shelter. Tax advisers, nevertheless, are reluctant to recommend death as a tax-planning technique! That death occurs and the tax consequences follow, however, are important considerations with regard to owning property, including an interest in a real estate limited partnership.

On a partner's death, his partnership interest passes to his estate or other successor in interest. This transfer of the partnership interest is not, in itself, a taxable event, and no income tax liability is incurred due to the transfer by the decedent, executor, or successor in interest.[137] At least partial permanent tax shelter may result from the fact that the successor's basis in the partnership interest is "stepped up" to the fair market value of the interest at the date of death,[138] or at the alternate valuation date.[139] On the transfer to the successor, if a special partnership election is in effect,[140] the basis in the partnership assets may be adjusted to reflect the advantageous stepped-up partnership basis.[141] Even some ordinary income property may be adjusted upward without requiring the recapture of any ordinary income.[142] Items of "income in respect of a decedent," [143] which include unrealized receivables and which generally produce ordinary income at the partnership level, however, do not receive a stepped-up basis adjustment on death, and their ordinary income potential is preserved in the successor.[144] The stepped-up basis adjustment on other items, including appreciated inventory, enables the decedent and the successor to escape income taxation on any appreciation occurring before death. Partial permanent tax shelter, therefore, is achieved if the value of the interests is at least equal to the allocable debt.

Indeed, as a result of the Economic Recovery Tax Act of 1981, it is now possible to obtain this partial permanent tax shelter as well as having the decedent's partnership interest excludable in its entirety from estate tax by transferring the partnership interest to a spouse and using the unlimited marital deduction.[145]

In any event "step-up" in basis is likely to be limited to the fair market value of the property at the time of the decedent's death and, further, applies only to decedent-owned interests.[146] What if the decedent owns his partnership interest in joint tenancy with his spouse rather than by himself? Only the portion of the partnership interest owned by the decedent would receive a step-up in basis. As a way of obtaining the full step-up in the partnership interest where the partnership interest is held jointly, a spouse might transfer his or her joint interest in the partnership interest to the decedent immediately before the decedent's death and thus argue that the entire partnership interest passed by the decedent's will to such spouse upon the decedent's death. There would be no gift tax because of the umlimited exclusion for gifts between spouses,[147] and the repeal of the contemplation of death rules.[148] The Service probably will attack such a device.

The final income tax return of a decedent does not include any partnership income earned after the close of the preceding partnership taxable year.[149] Instead, the deceased partner's distributive share is included in the income of the successor.[150] If the interest owned by the successor is sold or liquidated, the taxable year of the partnership closes with respect to the successor, and the distributive share up to that time is included in the income of the successor.[151]

Certain disadvantages may occur from this. For example, if the partnership has substantial income during that year, the benefits of income splitting for a married decedent through a final joint return would be lost.[152] In addition, if the partnership has a net operating loss for that year, no portion of the loss would be included in the partner's final return to offset other current income or to be carried back against the income of prior years.[153]

Methods are available for alleviating these problems. The partnership agreement may designate the spouse as the successor in interest, in which case the distributive share of the partnership income, gain, or loss included by the spouse may be included in a final joint return with the decedent.[154] As an alternative, the deceased partner may provide, by a prior agreement, to sell or exchange the partnership interest on the date of his death.[155] Such a sale would close the taxable year with respect to the decedent on the date of death,[156] and the ratable portion of his distributive share of partnership income, gain, or loss would be included in a final joint return.[157] It could fix the value of the decedent's partnership interest for estate tax purposes.[158] However, it could have adverse tax consequences to the continuing partners if it terminates the partnership.[159]

The successor is in the same position as the former partner in that he may continue to hold the partnership interest as an investment, or he may dispose of the interest through a sale, exchange, or so on. In addition, partnership agreements frequently provide for a liquidation of the partnership interest of a deceased partner.[160] Any such disposition or liquidation will have the tax consequences discussed earlier in the various sections of this chapter.

Liquidating payments that are made for unrealized receivables or goodwill of the partnership, except if payments for goodwill are provided for in the partnership agreement, are considered income in respect of a decedent and are accorded special treatment.[161]

What if the limited partnership interest is worthless, but there is substantial debt? Stepping up of the basis is limited to value. A far-out attempt to achieve complete permanent tax shelter on death would be to arrange to transfer all of the decedent's assets, other than tax shelter interests, outside the probate estate. For example, all of a person's property, except the tax shelters whose value at death are substantially less than the allocable debt, might be held in joint ownership, through grantor trusts or in the form of life annuities. When the person dies, those tax shelter interests that cannot be neutralized by a stepped-up basis would pass to the administrative estate. This estate would have no funds to pay any recapture tax liability. To avoid transferee liability, it has been suggested that the interest be allowed to escheat to the state; transfer to a charity or dummy corporation might also be considered. Whether these would work is questionable.

Alternatively, the decedent's will might provide specifically that the valueless, debt-ridden tax shelter interests not pass by the will but by the state intestacy statute, permitting, hopefully, the heirs to renounce the bequest and the interests to escheat to the state.

Consideration might also be given to bequeathing such tax shelters to corporations controlled by the decedent's heirs or others.[162] Indeed, the will might give a trusted fiduciary the option of transferring limited partnership interests to heirs, trusts, charities, corporations controlled by the decedent's heirs, other corporations, and so on. There is tax danger in every option, but the flexibility might be useful.

Of course, such arrangements are desirable only if the tax shelter investments are economically worthless. In addition, the practical difficulties, procedural hazards, and probable attack by the Service mitigate strongly against the use of these methods.

17. TERMINATION OF A PARTNERSHIP

The termination of a partnership may precipitate considerable tax consequences. Inadvertent technical termination can be disastrous.

The tax consequences occurring on a termination include the possible loss of first-user status with respect to partnership assets and the concomitant loss of accelerated depreciation methods for those properties being depreciated under the old Useful Life System,[163] realization of gain,[164] the closing of the partnership's taxable year,[165] which may result in the inclusion in the remaining partners' income of more than 12 months of partnership income,[166] the cessation of elections made by the partnership,[167] investment credit recapture,[168] realization of gain through disposition of installment obligations,[169] and a termination or partial termination of the partnership's tax-qualified retirement plan.[170]

For tax purposes, a partnership terminates only if either (a) no part of any business, financial operation, or venture of the partnership continues to be carried on by any of its partners in a partnership,[171] or (b) within a 12-month period there is a sale or exchange of 50% or more of the total interest in partnership capital and profits.[172]

The requirement for termination that a partnership cease operations entirely has been strictly construed by the courts.[173] Termination of a partnership, therefore, generally results from the winding up of the partnership business, liquidation of the partnership assets, or withdrawal of all but one of the partners.[174] Where the partnership conducts business through a winding-up period ending on the date of a final cash distribution, termination occurs on the date of the last distribution, which represents the cessation of the partnership business operations.[175]

The termination problems are usually not evident if the business ceases, because the tax effects have occurred on previous sale of the property or other winding-up activities. As noted, however, a partnership also terminates on the sale or exchange of 50% or more of the total interest in partnership capital and profits within a 12-month period.[176]

To avoid a technical termination and its adverse tax consequences, the partnership agreement should give the general partner the right to refuse to consent to any partnership transfer that might cause a termination.

Excluded from characterization as a sale or exchange for this 50% test are the liquidation of a partnership interest, the disposition of a partnership interest by gift, bequest, or inheritance, and the issuance of a partnership interest for the contribution of property to a partnership.[177] In addition, while admission of a new partner is generally not considered a sale or exchange even if capital and profits interests change by 50% or more,[178] a sale or exchange of an interest in partnership capital and profits to another member of the partnership is considered a sale or exchange for these purposes.[179]

Upon merger or consolidation of two or more partnerships, the merged partnership will be terminated only if the members of those former partnerships own aggregate interests that are less than 50% of the capital and profits of the new partnership.[180] If the partners were members of more than one of the merged partnerships, the partnership that is created with the greatest dollar amount of assets will survive, and the other partnerships will terminate.[181] In the case of a partnership division, a partnership terminates unless the members of the resulting partnership owned more than 50% of the interests in the capital and profits of the predecessor partnership.[182]

18. NONRECOURSE DEBT EXCEEDING PROPERTY VALUE

In *Tufts v. Commissioner,*[183] the Fifth Circuit Court of Appeals unexpectedly reversed the decision of the Tax Court and held that the outstanding amount of a nonrecourse mortgage on real estate owned by the partnership is includable in the amount realized upon the sale of the partners' partnership interests *only to the extent* that such mortgage does not exceed the fair market value of the property securing the debt. In reaching its decision, the

Fifth Circuit relied on the famous Footnote 37 of the Supreme Court's old *Crane v. Commissioner*,[184] which implies that there is an exception to the general rule that nonrecourse liabilities are required to be included in the amount realized upon the sale or disposition of property. In addition to relying on Footnote 37, the Fifth Circuit relied on law review articles [185] and stated that it did not understand why when "property does in fact decline in value . . . justice requires the taxpayer to somehow surrender the previous deductions on the gain that he never realized." [186]

Obviously, adoption of the *Tufts* theory would solve most of the problems discussed in this chapter. Although this position is certain to be litigated by the Internal Revenue Service, many taxpayers may rely on its reasoning. Since *Tufts* is in conflict with the Regulations and another Circuit Court decision,[187] the issue will likely be resolved by the Supreme Court which has granted certiorari in *Tufts*. Until the Supreme Court decides the issue or legislation is passed to reverse *Tufts*, taxpayers who dispose of "burned-out" tax shelters or who die without obtaining full "step-up" in basis should consider *Tufts*.

Future judicial developments may sensibly make distinctions between third party nonrecourse loans (i.e., "real" bank loans) and "tax shelter" nonrecourse debt provided by related parties. The *Tufts* reasoning may make sense for the former.

In any event, since the question is based on value, taxpayers with "burned-out" limited partnership investments are advised to obtain appraisals with respect to the fair market value of such interests at the time of disposition.

19. CONCLUSION

As has been discussed, there will usually be adverse tax consequences on disaster or other disposition of partnership interests when a real estate limited partnership has operated for some time and has provided substantial early year tax shelter benefits. The use of money saved in the early years for long periods of time, the cash flow, and, hopefully, the appreciation of the investment may be worth the cost. However, the tax consequences of ending a real estate limited partnership should always be considered at the outset.

NOTES

1. The Internal Revenue Service has added a new chapter to the Internal Revenue Manual to help agents identify transfers of "burned-out" tax shelters. The guidelines identify crossover points at which time the investments have exhausted the tax benefits. The

crossover point for real estate is assumed to be 10–15 years. *See* 6 I.R.S. Practice and Procedures 11-12 (January, 1982) *describing* Manual Transmittal 4236-12.

2. Sec. 706(c)(2)(A); Treas. Reg. §1.706-1(c)(2)(i).

3. Treas. Reg. §1.706-1(c)(2)(ii). The transferee partner must include in his taxable income his distributive share of partnership income, gain, or loss on a pro rata basis as though he had been a partner from the beginning of the partnership's taxable year. *Cf. David A. Foxman*, 41 T.C. 535 (1964), *aff'd*, 352 F.2d 466 (3d Cir. 1965).

4. Treas. Reg. §1.706-1(c)(2)(ii).

5. *Id.*

6. *Id.*

7. Sec. 706(c)(1); Sec. 708(b)(1); Treas. Reg. §1.706-1(c)(3)(i); *Florence K. Applebaum*, 43 CCH Tax Ct. Mem 1420 (1982); *Long v. Commissioner*, 1981-2 U.S.T.C. ¶9668 (10th Cir. 1981).

8. Treas. Reg. §1.706-1(c)(3)(ii); *Estate of Stanley Hesse*, 74 T.C. 1307 (1980).

9. *Id.* This could adversely affect the decedent's successors in interest. *See Estate of Stanley Hesse*, 74 T.C. 1307 (1980); Schuldenfrei and Grushko "Closing a Deceased Partner's Year Can Shift Income From an Estate and Cut Taxes," 55 J. TAX. 150 (1981). Any portion of a distributive share of a successor partner that is attributable to the decedent prior to the date of death is income in respect of a decedent under Section 691. Treas. Reg. §1.706-1(c)(3)(v).

10. Treas. Reg. §1.706-1(c)(3)(i).

11. Treas. Reg. §1.706-1(c)(5).

12. *Id.*; Sec. 704(e)(2) *See also* Sec. 706(c)(2)(B).

13. The motives for the disposition or distribution are irrelevant, which is in contrast to a similar provision concerning "collapsible corporations." *See* Sec. 341; *H. Clinton Pollack, Jr.*, 69 T.C. 142 (1977).

14. Sec. 741; Treas. Reg. §1.741-1(a).

15. Sec. 751(a); Treas. Reg. §1.751-1(a) *See generally* Rev. Rul. 80-323, 1980-2 C.B. 124 (transfer of limited partnership interests to corporation); discussion *infra.* p. 151.

16. The allocation of basis is discussed in Section 4 of this chapter.

17. Sec. 751(b); Treas. Reg. §1.751-1(b). *See* Rev. Rul. 77-412, 1977-2 C.B. 223 (non-pro rata distribution of Sec. 751 property in complete liquidation of two-person partnership). For criticism of this ruling, *see* Seago, "Order of Liquidation May Affect Partners' Tax Liabilities," 48 J. TAX. 308 (1978).

18. Sec. 751(c).

19. Sec. 751(d). *See generally Ralph T. Jensen*, 40 CCH Tax Ct. Mem. 1058 (1980).

20. Sec. 751(c). The rights must have arisen under agreements in effect at the time of sale or distribution, even though enforcement of payment may not be possible until a later date. Treas. Reg. §1.751-1(c)(1)(i); Prop. Treas. Reg. §1.751-1(c)4,5, and 6. *See also* Rev. Rul. 79-51, 1979-1 C.B. 486 (amounts earned under long-term contracts are unrealized receivables); *John W. Ledoux* 77 T.C. 293 (1981) (right to render services and receive ordinary income is unrealized receivable).

"Unrealized receivables" has been liberally interpreted by the courts, such that even remote rights to payment are included. *See United States v. Woolsey*, 326 F.2d 287 (5th Cir. 1963); *Roth v. Commissioner*, 321 F.2d 607 (9th Cir. 1963); *Herman M. Hale*, 24 CCH Tax Ct. Mem. 1497 (1965).

21. Secs. 1245, 1250. Depreciation and recapture of depreciation are discussed in Chapter 5.

22. Sec. 751(c). The fair market value of recapture property can usually be established, to the satisfaction of the IRS, by an arm's-length agreement between the buyer and seller. Treas. Reg. §1.751-1(c)(4)(iii); Prop. Treas. Reg. §1.751-1(c)(4)(x). The partnership's basis in potential recapture income is zero. Treas. Reg. §1.751-1(c)(5).

23. Inventory items include stock in trade, property properly includable in inventory if on hand at the close of the taxable year, unrealized receivables, and property held primarily for sale to customers in the ordinary course of business. Sec. 751(d)(2); Treas. Reg. §1.751-1(d)(2). Numerical tests are provided to determine whether such inventory is substantially appreciated. Sec. 751(d)(1). The determination is made on an aggregate basis. Treas. Reg. §1.751-1(d)(1).

24. Whether real estate is held as inventory has been litigated frequently. For this purpose, the primary intention of the partnership-holder will be determinative, although the courts have looked to such objective factors as acquisition purpose, length of holding period, extent of improvements, use of property, and circumstances of sale. *See Ginsburg v. United States,* 396 F.2d 983 (Ct. Cl. 1968); *Morse v. United States,* 371 F.2d 474 (Ct. Cl. 1967); *Eugene L. Freeland,* 25 CCH Tax Ct. Mem. 1473 (1966), *aff'd,* 393 F.2d 573 (9th Cir.), *cert. denied,* 393 U.S. 845 (1968); *cf. William B. Howell,* 57 T.C. 546 (1972) (*Acq.*).

25. Treas. Reg. §1.741-1(b).

26. Treas. Reg. §1.741-1(a). When feasible, consideration should be given to liquidation of the partnership interest rather than its sale. *See* discussion pp. 157–158, *infra; A.O. Champlin,* 36 CCH Tax Ct. Mem. 802 (1977) (termination of a partner's interest was a liquidation rather than a sale); *Spector v. Commissioner,* 641 F.2d 376 (5th Cir. 1981) (parties' chosen form of transaction is generally binding on them).

27. Treas. Reg. §1.752-1(d). The partner's basis in his partnership interest is determined under Sec. 705. See Chapter 4. *See also* Treas. Reg. §§1.1001-2(b), 1.1001-2(c) Ex. 7. *Compare Tufts v. Commissioner,* 651 F.2d 1058 (5th Cir. 1981), *rev'g,* 70 T.C. 756 (1978), *cert. granted* May 3, 1982 (nonrecourse mortgage amount not included in amount realized on sale if that amount exceeds the fair market value of the asset) and *Paul B. Brountas,* 73 T.C. 491 (1979) (entire amount of nonrecourse debt included); *Estate of Jerrold Delman,* 73 T.C. 15 (1979); *Gibson Products Co. Kell Blvd. v. United States,* 460 F. Supp. 1109 (N.D. Tex. 1978), *aff'd,* 637 F.2d. 1031 (5th Cir. 1981). *See generally* "Notes," 54 J. TAX. 148 (1981).

28. Sec. 741; Treas. Reg. §1.741-1(a). *Cf.* Rev. Rul. 81-38, 1981-1 C.B. 386 (transfer of 50% interest in partnership in Sec. 351 exchange).

29. Sec. 1222.

30. Sec. 741; Treas. Reg. §1.741-1(a).

31. Secs. 751(a),(c). The basis of potential depreciation recapture is zero. Treas. Reg. §1.751-1(c)(5). *See also* Prop. Treas. Reg. §1.751-1(c)(4)(x).

32. Treas. Reg. §§1.741-1(a); 1.751-1(a)(1).

33. Treas. Reg. §1.751-1(a)(2) and (g); Prop. Treas. Reg. §1.751-1(c)(4)(x).

34. *Id.*

35. *See* Treas. Reg. §1.751-1(a)(2), which provides that the basis of Section 751 property will be determined under Section 732. The latter section provides that the selling partner's basis in Section 751 property will be the same as that in the hands of the partnership, as if distributed currently to him, including any specially allowed adjustments under Sec-

tion 732(d). In brief, Section 732(d) allows a partner who acquires his interest by purchase or from a deceased partner to elect to attribute to property distributed to him within two years of the transfer a basis that corresponds to the basis for his partnership interest. This election may not be made if the general partnership election under Section 754 is in effect.

36. Treas. Reg. §§1.741-1(a); 1.751-1(a)(2). *See generally* Rudolph, "Collapsible Partnerships and Optional Basis Adjustments," 28 TAX L. REV. 211 (1973). Treas. Reg. §1.751-1 (a)(3) requires the transferor-partner to file a statement with his tax return setting forth certain information.

37. *See* Treas. Reg. §1.751-1(g)Ex.1. *But see Barnes v. United States,* 253 F. Supp. 116 (S.D. Ill. 1966).

38. Sec. 453. As a result of the Installment Sales Act of 1980, installment method reporting is automatic with respect to sales of real estate and casual sales of personal property occurring after October 19, 1980, unless the taxpayer elects to the contrary. *See* Sec. 453 (d); Emory and Hsorth, "An Analysis of Changes Made by the Installment Sales Revision Act of 1980—Parts I and II," 54 J. TAX 66 and 130 (1981); Liles," Installment Sales Revision Act of 1980," TMM 80-24 (December 1, 1980); Harris, "The Effect of the Installment Sales Revision Act of 1980 on Like-Kind Exchanges—Nonsimultaneous Exchanges Revisited," 59 TAXES 448 (1981). However, installment sale reporting for sales among related parties is subject to special rules. *See* Sec. 453(e). For a discussion of law prior to 1980, *see* Pitts, "The Sale of a Partnership Interest with a Section 453 Election," 58 TAXES 481 (1980).

39. For problems under the prior installment sales rules, *see* the First Edition of this book, p. 112.

40. Sec. 453(b)(1).

41. Temp. Treas. Reg. §15A. 453-1(b)(3).

42. This is because of the "two-sale" concept where the partnership owns Section 751 property. In the absence of an agreement to the contrary, each installment payment is allocated among the assets sold in proportion to the assets' fair market value. It is unclear whether the pro rata treatment differs from the general rule regarding the installment sale of depreciable assets which requires that, to the extent there is depreciation recapture, all installment gain will be ordinary income until the full amount of recapture income has been recognized. *See* Rev. Rul. 75-323, 1975-2 C.B. 346; Treas. Reg. §1.1245-6(d); *see also Dunn Construction Co. v. United States,* 323 F. Supp. 440 (N.D. Ala. 1971).

43. Treas. Reg. §1.706-1(c)(2)(ii); *see* Treas. Reg. §1.741-1(a). This is because the partnership year "terminates" with regard to the selling partner, Sec. 706(c)(2), and may terminate with regard to all the partners, *see* Sec. 708(b)(1) (B), pp. 161-162 *infra.*

44. Treas. Reg. §1.706-1(c)(2)(ii).

45. Private Letter Ruling 7948063 (August 29, 1979).

46. *Peter N. Pappas,* 78 T.C.——— No. 77 (1982); Arthur E. Long, 77 T.C. 1045 (1981). *See* Sec. 1031. *See also Estate of Rollin E. Meyer, Sr.,* 58 T.C. 311 (1972), *aff'd per curiam,* 503 F.2d 556 (9th Cir. 1974); *Miller v. United States,* 63-2 USTC ¶9606 (S.D. Ind. 1963). *Compare Gulfstream Land and Development Corp.,* 71 T.C. 587, (1979). *See also* "Note, The Gulfstream Decision and the Section 1031 Tax Shelter Bail Out Scheme" 66 VA. L. REV. 943 (1980).

47. *Estate* of *Rollin E. Meyer, Sr.,* 58 T.C. 311 (1972), *aff'd per curiam,* 503 F. 2d 556 (9th Cir. 1974) (Nonacq), 1975-1 C.B. 3.

48. Rev. Rul. 78-135, 1978-1 C.B. 256 (referring for support to the parenthetical language of Sec. 1031(a)). For criticism of the Service's reasoning, if not its conclusion, *see* Notes, 49 J. TAX. 63 AND 381 (1978). *Peter N. Pappas,* 78 T.C.———— No. 77 (1982); *Arthur E. Long,* 77 T.C. 1045 (1981). The Tax Court held that the interest was in fact a general partnership interest and thus did not address the issue of applicability of Sec. 1031 to an exchange of limited partnership interests.

49. Sec. 1031(a) excludes the following assets from tax-free exchange treatment: stock in trade, property held primarily for sale, stocks, bonds, notes, choses in action, certificates of trust or beneficial interest, or other securities or evidences of indebtedness or interest. *See also* Treas. Reg. §1.1031(a)-1(a).

50. *See* Blankenship, "After the Meyer Case: An Analysis of Taxfree Partnership Exchanges," 38 J. TAX. 278, 279 (1973); Banoff, "New Opportunities Now Exist for General and Limited Partnership Conversions," 52 J. TAX 130 (1980).

51. *See Arthur E. Long,* 77 T.C. 1045, which discusses the unsuccessful attempt to avoid the recognition of boot in the exchange by incurring liabilities and investing in additional assets immediately prior to the exchange.

52. *See* text on p. 159, *infra. See generally* Whitmire, "Bailing Out of Tax Shelters; Selected Techniques," 30 MAJOR TAX PLANNING 503 (1978).

53. Sec. 1031(a); Treas. Reg. §1.1031(a)-1.

54. Sec. 1031(d); Treas. Reg. §1.1031(d)-1(a).

55. *Arthur E. Long,* 77 T.C. 1045; Sec. 1031(b); Treas. Reg. §1.1031(b)-1(a). In no event will a loss be recognized, Sec. 1031(c); Treas. Reg. §1.1031(c)-1. It is possible that the gain may be ordinary income if the former partnership has Section 751 property and the exchange is viewed as a disposition of such property. Sec. 751 (a).

56. Sec. 1031(d); Treas. Reg. §1.1031(d)-1(b); *Arthur E. Long,* 77 T.C. 1045 (1981).

57. Exchanging partnership property may avoid the securities problem. *See* text at notes 49–50, *supra. See generally Starker v. United States,* 602 F.2d 1341 (9th Cir. 1979); *Biggs v. Commissioner,* 632 F.2d 1171 (5th Cir. 1980); Rev. Rul. 77-297, 1977-2 C.B. 30; Green and Share, "Starker and Beyond: Including the Uncertain Life of the Secured Deferred Exchange," 58 TAXES 724 (1980); Melnick, "Exchanges of Property Under Section 1031—Recent Developments," TMM 80-4 (February 25, 1980); Harris, "The Effect of the Installment Sales Act of 1980 on Like-Kind Exchanges: Nonsimultaneous Exchanges Revisited," 59 TAXES 948 (1981); Kessler and Hirsch, *"Sidestepping the Impact of 'Starker' to Save the Two-Party Tax-Free Exchange,"* 48 J. TAX. 328 (1978).

58. Treas. Reg. §1.1031(a)-1(b). A lease for 30 years or more is considered to be the equivalent of a fee interest in property. Treas. Reg. §1.1031(a)-1(c).

59. Treas. Reg. §1.1031(a)-1(b).

60. *See M.H.S. Co., Inc.,* 35 CCH Tax Ct. Mem. 733 (1976), *aff'd per curiam,* 575 F.2d 1177 (6th Cir. 1978).

61. Sec. 1031(b),(d); Treas. Reg. §1.1031(b)-1(c).

62. Sec. 1245(b)(4); Sec. 1250(d)(4); Treas. Reg. §§1.1245-4(d), 1.1250-3(d)(1).

63. Sec. 1031(d).

64. *Winston F.C. Guest,* 77 T.C. 9 (1981); Rev. Rul. 75-194, 1975-1 C.B. 80; *see Teofilo Evangelista,* 71 T.C. 1057 (1979), *aff'd,* 629 F.2nd 1218 (7th Cir. 1980); *Joseph W. Johnson, Jr.,* 59 T.C. 791 (1973), *aff'd,* 495 F.2d 1079 (6th Cir), *cert. denied,* 419 U.S. 1040 (1974); "Note," 55 J. TAX 182 (1981). *Cf. Magnolia Development Corp.,* 19 CCH Tax Ct.

Mem. 934 (1960); Rev. Rul. 70-626, 1970-2 C.B. 158. The part sale, part gift provisions require that the taxpayer allocate his basis between the sale and gift portions of the transaction. Sec. 1011(b); Treas. Regs. §§1.1001-2(c)Ex.4; 1.1011-2.

65. If the recapture is greater than the gift portion of the transfer, the part sale, part gift rules are not applicable because no deduction is allowable and the donor's basis is not required to be apportioned. Treas. Reg. §1.1011-2(a)(1).

66. Sec. 501(c)(3).

67. *See* Secs. 511, 512, 514. Although charities are taxed on debt-financed income, the indebtedness transferred by gift will generally not produce taxable income to the charity for 10 years following the gift if the encumbrance was placed on the property at least 5 years before the gift. Sec. 514(c)(2). Treas. Reg. §1.514(c)-1(a)Ex.4. Although recently enacted legislation generally permits qualified pension trusts to own debt-financed real estate without being subject to the unrelated business income tax, this provision was not extended to include charities. Sec. 514(c)(9).

68. Sec. 170. The overlap of Section 751 with the charitable contribution deduction provision may result in disallowance of the charitable contribution deduction to the extent of the ordinary income portion of the part gift.

69. *Teofilo Evangelista,* 71 T.C. 1057 (1979), *aff'd,* 629 F.2d 1218 (7th Cir. 1980); *Est. of Aaron Levine,* 72 T.C. 780 (1979), *aff'd,* 634 F.2d 12 (2nd Cir. 1980); *Joseph W. Johnson, Jr.,* 59 T.C. 791 (1973), *aff'd,* 495 F.2d 1079 (6th Cir.), *cert. denied,* 419 U.S. 1040 (1974). *But see Richard H. Turner,* 49 T.C. 356 (1968) (Nonacq.), *aff'd,* 410 F.2d 752 (6th Cir. 1969); Treas. Reg. §1. 1001-2(c)Ex.4.

70. *See* text accompanying notes 13–44.

71. Secs. 2501 *et seq.,* effective with respect to transfers after December 31, 1981. This discussion does not take the unified credit against estate and gift taxes into account. Where there is no reasonable likelihood of a current cash return to the donee from the partnership interest, the gift may not qualify for the annual exclusion. *See Stark v. United States,* 477 F.2d 131 (8th Cir. 1973) (per curiam).

72. Yearly cash gifts in excess of the annual exclusion may cause the former partner to have further gift tax liability.

73. *See* Ginsburg, "The Leaky Tax Shelter," 53 TAXES 719 (1975); Kanter, "Real Estate Tax Shelters," 51 TAXES 770 (1973); Cowan, "Use of Grantor Trusts to Escape a Tax Shelter Without Detrimental Tax Effects," 41 J. TAX. 346 (1974). *See also* Treas. Reg. §1.1001-2 (c)Ex.5. For a general discussion of alternative methods of disposing of tax shelters, *see* Whitmire, "Bailing Out of Tax Shelters: Selected Techniques," 30 MAJOR TAX PLANNING 503 (1978).

74. Sec. 671.

75. *See* Secs. 673–77.

76. Sec. 677; *cf.* WILLIS, PARTNERSHIP TAXATION ¶172.08 (3d ed. 1981).

77. If the investor purchases the partnership interest and later transfers it to an existing trust, rather than having the trust purchase the interest, the investor may have both gift tax liability and, because the investor is relieved of his share of partnership liabilities, taxable gain. *See* Treas. Reg. §1.1001-2(c)Ex.5. *Compare* Rev. Rul. 79-84, 1979-1 C.B. 223 (Service view is that partnership interest contributed to grantor trust is owned by the partner until death and is deemed transferred to the trust, presumably as a taxable event, at death; therefore, the Sec. 754 election to adjust property basis does not occur until death). *See also* Rev. Rul. 77-402, 1977-2 C.B. 222 (discussed, *infra,* note 79).

78. Secs. 2036-38.

79. Rev. Rul. 77-402, 1977-2 C.B. 222. The Service also stated that the result would be the same when the trust ceases to be a grantor trust by reason of the expiration of lapse of the powers, or if grantor trust powers were exercisable by a party other than the grantor and the trust ceased to be a grantor trust, upon release or renunciation of those powers, or expiration or lapse of the powers. *See* Rev. Rul. 79-84, 1979-1 C.B. 223 (similar reasoning on death of the grantor, although the issue was the timing of a Sec. 754 property basis adjustment, as discussed in note 77, *supra*).

80. Transfers of property to controlled corporations generally do not have current income tax effect. Sec. 351. See Rev. Rul 81-38, 1981-1 C.B. 386; Private Letter Ruling 8047105 (August 29, 1980). *Cf.* Rev. Rul. *80-323,* 1980-2 C.B. 1124 (despite Sec. 351 exchange, there was gain to the extent the partner's share of partnership liabilities exceeds his basis.)

81. Rev. Rul. 70-239, 1970-1 C.B. 74. *Compare* Rev. Rul. 77-321, 1977-2 C.B. 98, which involved the opposite transaction (the transfer of assets, pursuant to a Sec. 333 one-month complete corporation liquidation, to a partnership in exchange for a partnership interest, which interest was distributed to the sole shareholder in redemption of his stock in the corporation, was a distribution to the shareholder of the assets in Sec. 333 complete liquidation of the corporation followed by the shareholder's contribution of the assets to the partnership in exchange for the partnership interest; thus the only recognized gain was for any constructively distributed money or post-1953 stock and securities).

82. *See* 357(c); Sec. 752(d); *See Donald A. Jackson,* 42 CCH Tax Ct. Mem 1413 (1982); Rev. Rul. 80-323, 1980-2 C.B. 124. The transfer of high basis assets to the corporation to lessen the excess liabilities probably will not be effective. *See* Sec. 357(b). However, without a tax avoidance motive, the transfer to the corporation of additional unencumbered property might be considered, so that the basis of all the transferred property could equal or exceed the total of the transferred liabilities. *See* Treas. Reg. §1.357-2(a). *See generally,* Whitmire, "Bailing Out of Tax Shelters; Selected Techniques," 30 MAJOR TAX PLANNING 503, 530 (1978).

83. Rev. Rul. 80-323, 1980-2 C.B. 124. *See George W. Wiebusch,* 59 T.C. 777, *aff'd* 487 F.2d 515 (8th Cir. 1973).

84. Secs. 751, 1245(b)(3), 1250(d)(3).

85. Sec. 301.

86. *See* Sec. 341. In general, the collapsible corporation provisions could be avoided by holding the stock for at least three years.

86a. Rev. Proc. 82-56, 1982-41 I.R.B. 17.

87. *See Estate of Jerrold Delman,* 73 T.C. 15 (1979); *R. O'Dell & Sons Co. v. Commissioner,* 169 F.2d 247 (3d Cir. 1948); Handler, "Tax Consequences of Mortgage Foreclosures and Transfers of Real Property to the Mortgagee," 31 TAX L. REV. 193 (1976). *See also* Pratt and Oestreich. "The Voluntary Transfer of Real Estate to Creditors: Is it Treated Like 'Abandonment' or Foreclosure?" 57 TAXES 293 (1979); Cleveland, "Voluntary Conveyances: Sale or Exchanges?" 57 TAXES 287 (1979).

88. Sec. 702(a).

89. Sec. 752(b).

90. Sec. 705(a)(2).

91. *Day's Estate v. Commissioner,* 117 F.2d 208 (7th Cir. 1941); Rev. Rul. 73-36, 1973-1 C.B. 372.

92. *Stokes v. Commissioner,* 124 F.2d 355 (3rd Cir. 1941); *Commonwealth, Inc.,* 36 B.T.A. 850 (1937) (Acq.).

93. Treas. Reg. §1.1001-2 (b); Rev. Rul. 76-111, 1976-1 C.B. 12; *see Crane v. Commissioner,* 331 U.S. 1 (1947); *Parker v. Delaney,* 186 F.2d 445 (1st Cir. 1950); *Eugene L. Freeland,* 74 T.C. 76 (1980); Rev. Rul. 78-164, 1978-1 C.B. 264; Tech. Advice Mem. 7811008 (Dec. 6, 1977); Tech. Advice Mem. 7744006 (July 5, 1977); *Fred H. Lenway & Co.,* 69 T.C. 620 (1978), *aff'd in unpub. opinion,* (9th Cir. 1980); *Gavin S. Millar,* 67 T.C. 656 (1977), *aff'd on this issue,* 557 F.2d 212 (3rd Cir. 1978); *cf.* Rev. Rul. 70-626, 1970-2 C.B. 158.

94. *See* notes 87–90, *supra,* and accompanying text.

95. Rev. Rul. 74-40, 1974-1 C.B. 159.

96. *See* Secs. 731(a), 751, 752(b); text accompanying notes 25–44, *supra.*

97. Sec. 702(a).

98. *See Estate of Jerrold Delman,* 73 T.C. 15 (1979); *R. O'Dell & Sons Co. v. Commissioner,* 169 F.2d 247 (3d Cir. 1948); *see also* pp. 152–153, *supra. See further* Note, "Abandonment of Land Results in Capital Loss," 49 J. Tax. 354 (1978); Pratt and Oestreich, The Voluntary Transfer of Real Estate to Creditors; Is It Treated Like 'Abandonment' or Foreclosure?" 57 Taxes 293 (1979); Cleveland, "Voluntary Conveyances: Sales or Exchanges?" 57 Taxes 287 (1979); *Note,* 54 J. Tax. 223 (1981).

99. Rev. Rul. 74-40, 1974-1 C.B. 159. *See also* Treas. Reg. §1.1001-2 (b); *Eugene L. Freeland,* 74 T.C. 76 (1980); Rev. Rul. 78-164, 1978-1 C.B. 264; Tech. Advice Mem. 7811008 (Dec. 6, 1977); Tech. Advice Mem. 7744006 (July 5, 1977); *Fred H. Lenway & Co.* 69 T.C. 620 (1978), *aff'd in unpub. opinion,* (9th Cir. 1980); *Gavin S. Millar,* 67 T.C. 656 (1977), *aff'd on this issue,* 557 F.2d 212 (3rd Cir. 1978).

100. Polin v. Commissioner, 114 F.2d 174 (3d Cir. 1940); *Commissioner v. Hoffman,* 117 F.2d 987 (2d Cir. 1941). *Cf. Neil J. O'Brien,* 77 T.C. 113 (1981) (loss from abandonment constituted a capital loss).

101. Gain on abandonment would be determined under Section 1231.

102. Secs. 1245, 1250; *Estate of Jerrold Delman,* 73 T.C. 15 (1979).

103. *Penn Athletic Club Bldg.,* 10 T.C. 919 (1948) (Nonacq.), *aff'd,* 176 F.2d 939 (3d Cir. 1949).

104. *Cf.* Rev. Rul. 73-160, 1973-1 C.B. 365 (note holders did not have a taxable event upon exchange of old notes for new longer term obligations).

105. Sec. 1399, added by Bankrupty Tax Act of 1980 Sec. 3(a)(1), effective for bankruptcy cases commencing after March 24, 1981.

106. Rev. Rul. 68-48, 1968-1 C.B. 301. The partnership's holding period for assets was carried over to the bankruptcy estate. Further, the transfer of assets to the estate was not a taxable event. *See Homer A. Martin, Jr.,* 56 T.C. 1294 (1971); *Norris Bloomfield,* 52 T.C. 745 (1969).

107. Sec. 108(d)(6), added by Bankruptcy Tax Act of 1980 Sec. 2(a), generally applicable to transactions occurring after December 31, 1980 (other than transactions occurring in certain proceedings commencing on or before December 31, 1980). For problems under the law prior to the enactment of the Bankruptcy Tax Act of 1980, see the First Edition of this book, p. 120. *See also Stackhouse v. United States,* 441 F.2d 365 (5th Cir. 1971); Rev. Rul. 72-205, 1972-1 C.B. 37; Rev. Rul. 71-301, 1971-2 C.B. 257.

108. Secs. 108(a),(d)(6). The income tax exclusion rules of Sec. 108(a) do not apply at the partnership level. A partnership may not elect to make a basis adjustment under Sec. 703(b)(2). *See generally,* Thompson and Tenney, "Partnership Bankruptcy—The New Entity and Individual Tax Consequences," 35 Tax Law. 89 (1981); Asofsky and Tat-

lock, "Bankruptcy Tax Act Radically Alters Treatment of Bankruptcy and Discharging Debts," 54 J. Tax. 106 (1981); Hirsch, "The Bankruptcy Tax Act of 1980," TMM 81-7 (April 6, 1981). The tax effect on an individual partner depends on his personal financial condition. If a partner is bankrupt or insolvent, there is no income, but his net operating losses and other tax attributes would be reduced. Sec. 108(b)(1). The bankrupt or insolvent partner may elect to first reduce his basis in depreciable assets. Sec. 108(b)(5).

109. Sec. 705.

110. Secs. 733 and 752. *See* S. Rep. No. 1035, 96th Cong., 2d Sess. 21 (1980). These rules are less clear if income from discharge of indebtedness and constructive distributions are allocated in different ratios.

111. Secs. 108(a)(1)(C), (c), (d)(4).

112. Secs. 108(b)(5), (d)(5). This treatment is permitted if an insolvent partner elects to reduce his basis in depreciable property rather than reduce his tax attributes.

113. Sec. 1017(b)(3)(C).

114. Secs. 751, 1245, 1250.

114a. Bankruptcy Code §303(h).

114b. Bankruptcy Code §365(e)(1).

114c. Bankruptcy Code §365(e) 2(A)(1).

114d. *Id.*

114e. *See* Appendix 2, p. 338, *infra.*

115. Of course, the assets of the partnership will be reduced by the amount of the "distribution."

116. The agreement for a liquidating distribution should be entered into at the partnership level. If the remaining partners first agree to purchase the retiring partner's interest and then have the partnership take over their obligation, any payment made by the partnership may be viewed as constructively distributed to the remaining partners. Such constructive distributions could be currently taxable.

117. Sale of partnership property may be a taxable event at the partnership level.

118. The retiring partner and the remaining partnership would probably have to file an election not to be taxed as a partnership because of their co-ownership. Sec. 761(a); Treas. Reg. §1.761-2(b).

119. Sec. 761(d); Treas. Reg. §1.761-1(d); *see* Treas. Reg. §1.736-1(a)(1)(ii). If there is a series of distributions over a period of one or more years, the interest is not considered liquidated until the final distribution. Treas. Reg. §§1.736-1(a)(1)(ii), 1.761-1(d); *cf. Raymond W. Schnitz,* 37 CCH Tax Ct. Mem. 1323 (1978). A distribution in partial liquidation is treated as a current distribution. *Id., see* text on pp.75–76, *supra.*

120. Treas. Regs. §§1.736-1(a)(1)(ii), 1.736-1(a)(6).

121. A liquidation of a partner's interest may resemble a sale of a partner's interest but the tax consequences may differ; thus the parties should carefully structure their transaction. *See generally Spector v. Commissioner,* 641 F.2d. 376 (5th Cir. 1981).

122. Secs. 731(a)(1), 752(b); Treas. Regs. §§1.731-1(a)(1), 1.736-1(b)(6). Since gain generally is recognized only on distributions of money, on a series of distributions the taxable gain may be limited by first distributing money, which reduces basis, and then distributing property, which generally does not produce gain.

123. In contrast, no loss may be recognized on a current distribution of money or property from the partnership. Sec. 731(a)(2); Treas. Reg. §1.731-1(a)(2); *see* text on p. 75, *supra.* *See also H. Clinton Pollack, Jr.,* 69 T.C. 142 (1977) (partner withdrew from the partner-

ship because it did not live up to his hopes of obtaining personal business; court held that the loss was a capital loss from liquidation and not a "Corn Products" ordinary loss).

124. Sec. 731(a)(2); Treas. Reg. §1.731-1(a)(2).

125. *See* Treas. Reg. §1.751-1(g)Ex. 2.

126. Sec. 736(a), (b),(2)(A). Such amounts, if determined with respect to partnership income, will be considered as a distributive share of partnership income, *see* text on pp. 74–75, *supra,* and, if not determined with respect to partnership income, will be considered as a guaranteed payment under Sec. 707(c), *see* text. p. 74, *supra. See also A.O. Champlin,* 36 CCH Tax Ct. Mem. 802 (1977), *aff'd in unpublished opinion* (9th Cir. 1980) (discusses criteria used in deciding whether a liquidation or a sale was effected and decides which part of a liquidation was for the taxpayer's interest in the partnership and which part was a likely deductible guaranteed payment); Treas. Reg. §1.736-1(a)(4). It may be possible to convert a distributive share of partnership income into a guaranteed payment. *See* Private Letter Ruling 7814026 (January 5, 1978). *See also Holman v. Commissioner,* 564 F.2d 283 (9th Cir. 1977); *Elwood R. Milliken,* 72 T.C. 256 (1979), *aff'd in unpublished opinion* (1st Cir. 1980).

127. Secs. 731(c), 736(a), 751(b)(1)(B).

128. Sec. 736(a), (b), (2)(B); Treas. Reg. §1.736-1(b)(3). *See V. Zay Smith,* 37 T.C. 1033, *aff'd,* 313 F.2d 16 (10th Cir. 1962). As discussed in note 126 *supra,* such amounts will be treated as a distributive share or as a guaranteed payment.

129. Secs. 731(a), 741; Treas. Reg. §1.731-1(a)(3).

130. Sec. 731(b); Treas. Reg. §1.731-1(b).

131. Sec. 751(b); Treas. Reg. §1.751-1(g). *See also* Rev. Rul. 77-412, 1977-2 C.B. 223.

132. Sec 732(b); Treas. Reg. §1.732-1(b).

133. Sec. 732(c); Treas. Reg.§1.732-1(c). If the retiring partner's basis in his partnership interest exceeds the partnership basis in distributed unrealized receivables and inventory items, and no other property is distributed, the excess unallocated basis will be a capital loss to the retiring partner. Treas. Reg. §1.732-1(c)(2).

134. Secs. 754, 734(b); Treas. Reg. §1.734-1 Allocations of the increase or decrease in basis are made under Sec. 755. *See also Jones v. United States,* 553 F.2d 667 (Ct. Cl. 1977) (election to adjust basis of partnership property must be filed for the taxable year of the partnership in which the transfer of an interest in the partnership occurs); *Estate of Ernest D. Skaggs,* 75 T.C. 191 (1980), *aff'd,* 672 F.2d 756 (9th Cir. 1982) (no adjustment unless timely election is made).

135. Sec. 732(d). Under certain circumstances, and without regard to the two-year limitation, the Service requires such an election. Sec. 732(d); Treas. Reg. §1.732-1(d)(4).

136. *See* Secs. 61(a)(3) and 707(c). *See also United States v. Davis,* 370 U.S. 65 (1962); Rev. Rul. 75-498, 1975-2 C.B. 29.

137. There is, of course, a federal estate tax and perhaps state estate or inheritance taxes. Sec. 2001.

138. Sec. 1014; Treas. Reg. §1.742-1. For discussion of the carryover basis provisions enacted by the Tax Reform Act of 1976 and later repealed by the Crude Oil Windfall Profit Tax Act of 1980, *see* McGrath and Blattmacher, "Estate Planning for Tax Shelters in View of the Impact of the Carryover Basis Rules," 47 J. Tax. 130 (1977); and pp. 122–124 of the First Edition of this book.

139. Sec. 2032.

140. Sec. 754. The election must be made by the partnership by filing a statement with the

partnership tax return for the taxable year in which the transfer occurs. The election is effective for that taxable year and all subsequent taxable years. Treas. Reg. §1.754-1.

141. Sec. 743(b). The adjustment is with respect only to the transferee's proportionate interest in partnership assets. *Id.;* Treas. Reg. §1.743-1(b). The total adjustment is to be allocated to the various partnership properties under special rules. Sec. 755. *See* Rev. Rul. 78-2, 1978-1 C.B. 202 (optional adjustment to basis is available for both an investment partnership holding an operating real estate partnership interest and the operating partnership on the death of a partner of the investment partnership).

142. Sec. 1245(b)(2); 1250(d)(2); *see* note 145, *infra,* and accompanying text.

143. Sec. 691.

144. Secs. 753; 1014(c). Arguably, Sec. 1245 and Sec. 1250 property, the recapture potential of which is an unrealized receivable, should not be denied a stepped-up basis. *See George Edward Quick Trust,* 54 T.C. 1336 (1970), *aff'd per curiam,* 444 F.2d 90 (8th Cir. 1971). *See also Estate of Ernest D. Skaggs,* 75 T.C. 191 (1980), *aff'd,* 672 F.2d. 756 (9th Cir. 1982); Kalish and Schneider, "Is There Partnership Basis After Death?" 35 Tax Law 143 (1982).

145. Sec. 2056, applicable to estates of decedents dying after December 31, 1981.

146. *But see* discussion at end of this chapter of *Tufts v. Commissioner,* 651 F.2d 1058 (5th Cir. 1981), *reh. en banc. denied, rev'g* 70 T.C. 756 (1978), *cert. granted,* May 3, 1982.

147. Sec. 2523, applicable to gifts made after December 31, 1981.

148. Sec. 2035, applicable with respect to estate of decedents dying after December 31, 1981.

149. Sec. 706(c)(2)(A)(ii); S. Rep. No. 1622, 83d Cong. 2d Sess. 386 (1954). This may not be the case if the partnership is terminated on the partner's death. *See* pp. 161–162 *infra.*

150. Treas. Reg. §1.706-1(c)(3)(ii), (v). Such income is generally income in respect of a decedent. Secs. 691, 753. The value of the right to receive such amounts will be included in the decedent's gross estate for estate tax purposes, *Estate of Robert R. Gannon,* 21 T.C. 1073 (1954), but the estate will receive an income tax deduction for any estate taxes paid with respect thereto, Sec. 691 (c). *See* text accompanying notes 7–10 *supra.*

151. Sec. 706(c)(2)(A)(i). *See* pp. 161–162, *infra.*

152. *See* Sec. 6013.

153. *See* Secs. 172, 702; *Estate of Stanley Hesse,* 74 T.C. 1307 (1980).

154. Treas. Reg. §1.706-1(c)(3)(iii). The decedent must assign his entire interest in partnership capital and profits. Rev. Rul. 68-215, 1968-1 C.B. 312. *See also* Sec. 662; Treas. Reg. §1.706-1(c)(3)(vi)Ex. 3.

155. *See* Treas. Reg. §1.706-1(c)(3)(iv), which indicates that a sale should be clearly distinguished from a liquidation by the partnership of the decedent's partnership interest, and from the passing of the partnership interest by inheritance or other testamentary disposition.

156. Sec. 706(c)(2)(A)(i); Treas. Reg. §1.706-1(c)(3)(iv).

157. Treas. Reg. §1.706-1(c)(3)(vi)Ex. 2.

158. Treas. Reg. §20.2031-2(h). The agreement must be binding during life and at death. *See Estate of Bischoff,* 69 T.C. 32 (1977).

159. Sec. 708(b)(1)(B). *See generally,* Heller and Boyd, "Changes of Ownership in a Partnership and How They Affect the Partners' Distributive Shares," 59 Taxes 639 (1981).

160. These liquidations are often funded, more generally where the partnership is closely held, by life insurance on the decedent's life. The insurance proceeds are not generally included in the decedent's estate. Rev. Rul. 56-397, 1956-2 C.B. 599. However, the

remaining partners may be unable to claim a loss on the subsequent disposition of their partnership interests since the Service may claim that the receipt of the insurance proceeds compensated them for any loss. *See Alson N. Johnson,* 66 T.C. 897 (1976), *aff'd per curiam,* 574 F.2d 189 (4th Cir. 1978).

161. *See* notes 143, 144, 150, *supra.*

162. *See generally,* Whitmire, "Bailing Out of Tax Shelters: Selected Techniques," 30 MAJOR TAX PLANNING 503, 530 (1978).

163. *See* Treas. Reg. §§1.167(c)-1(a); 1.167(b)-0(b). *See also* Rev. Rul. 77-458, 1977-2 C.B. 220.

164. Sec. 731.

165. Sec. 706(c).

166. This will occur if the partnership and the partners have different taxable years. *See generally,* Birkeland and Postlewaite, "The Uncertain Tax Ramifications of a Terminating Disposition of a Partnership Interest—The Constructive Termination of a Partnership," 30 TAX LAWYER 335 (1977).

167. *See* Sec. 703(b); Treas. Reg. §1.703-1(b)(1).

168. *See* Treas. Reg. §1.47-6. The Tax Court has held that the partnership constitutes an entity for the purpose of investment tax credit recapture. *Joseph L. Holloman,* 34 CCH Tax Ct. Mem. 1354 (1975), *aff'd,* 551 F.2d 987 (5th Cir. 1977). *See* Prop. Treas. Reg. §1.48-3 (1980).

169. *See* Sec. 453(d)(1).

170. Private Letter Ruling 8007019 (Nov. 2, 1979); Treas. Reg. §1.401-6(b)(1). *See also* Rev. Rul. 80-129, 1980-1 C.B. 86 with respect to a distribution from a plan upon the termination of the partnership.

171. Sec. 708(b)(1)(A); Treas. Reg. §1.708-1(b)(1); *see David A. Foxman,* 41 T.C. 535 (1964), *aff'd,* 352 F.2d 466 (3d Cir. 1965).

172. Sec. 708(b)(1)(B). *See* Private Letter Ruling 7952057 (Sept. 25, 1979) for discussion of the 50% test.

173. *See David A. Foxman,* 41 T.C. 535 (1964), *aff'd,* 352 F.2d 466 (3d Cir. 1965); *see also Baker Commodities, Inc. v. Commissioner,* 415 F.2d 519 (9th Cir. 1969). *cert. denied,* 397 U.S. 988 (1970); *Ginsburg v. United States,* 396 F.2d 983 (Ct. Cl. 1968); *George D. Ladus,* 35 CCH Tax Ct. Mem. 283 (1976); *John L. Harrell, Jr.,* 37 CCH Tax Ct. Mem. 911 (1978); *Estate of Aaron Levine,* 72 T.C. 780 (1979), *aff'd,* 634 F.2d 12 (2nd Cir. 1980).

174. The death of one member of a two-member partnership does not terminate the partnership if the estate or other successor in interest of the deceased partner continues to share in the profits or losses of the partnership business. Treas. Reg. §1.708-1(b)(1)(i)(a); *Estate of Ernest D. Skaggs,* 75 T.C. 191 (1980), *aff'd,* 672 F.2d. 756 (9th Cir. 1982).

175. Treas. Reg. §1.708-1(b)(1)(i).

176. Sec. 708(b)(1)(B). If the partnership is terminated by the sale or exchange of a partnership interest, the following is deemed to occur: The partnership distributes its assets to the new and remaining partners, and the partners immediately contribute the property to the partnership either for continuation of the business or for dissolution and winding up. Treas. Reg. §1.708-1(b)(1)(iv); *see* Private Letter Ruling 7952057 (Sept. 25, 1979).

177. Treas. Reg. §1.708-1(b)(1)(ii).

178. Rev. Rul. 75-423, 1975-2 C.B. 260. Where the facts indicate a sale, however, the admission of a new partner may result in sale or exchange treatment. Treas. Reg. §1.731-1 (c) (3); *cf. Crenshaw v. United States,* 450 F.2d 472 (5th Cir. 1971), *cert. denied,* 408 U.S. 923

(1972). *Compare* Private Letter Ruling 7948063 (Aug. 29, 1979) (conversion of general partnership to limited partnership does not cause termination).

179. Treas. Reg. §1.708-1(b)(1)(ii). *See* Private Letter Rulings 7902086 (Oct. 16, 1978) and 8028078 (April 18, 1980) involving transfers to controlled corporations.

180. Sec. 708(b)(2)(A); Treas. Reg. §1.708-1(b)(2)(i); *see* Rev. Rul. 68-289, 1968-1 C.B. 314; Private Letter Ruling 8035080 (June 6, 1980).

181. Rev. Rul. 77-458, 1977-2 C.B. 220; Private Letter Ruling 7805028 (Nov. 3, 1977).

182. Sec. 708(b)(2)(B); Treas. Reg. §1.708-1(b)(2)(ii).

183. *Tufts v. Commissioner,* 651 F.2d 1058 (5th Cir. 1981), *reh. en banc. denied, rev'g* 70 T.C. 756 (1978), *cert. granted,* May 3, 1982.

184. *Crane v. Commissioner,* 331 U.S.1 (1947).

185. Bittker, *Tax Shelters, Nonrecourse Debt, and the Crane Case,* 33 TAX L. REV. 277 (1978); Weiss, "The Crane Case Updated," 32 TAX LAWYER 289 (1979); McGuire, "Negative Capital Accounts and the Failing Tax Shelter," 33 J. REAL ESTATE TAX. 439 (1976); Ginsburg, "The Leaky Tax Shelter," 53 TAXES 719 (1975).

186. 651 F.2d 1058, 1061 at n. 4.

187. *See* Treas. Reg. §1.1001-2(b) (1980); *Millar v. Commissioner,* 577 F.2d 212 (3d Cir. 1978), *cert. denied,* 439 U.S. 1046 (1978). *See also Woodsam Associates Inc. v. Commissioner,* 198 F.2d 357 (2d Cir 1952); *Mendham Corp.,* 9 T.C. 320 (1947).

CHAPTER 8

FEDERAL SECURITIES LAWS AND REAL ESTATE LIMITED PARTNERSHIPS

1. GENERAL

Limited partnership interests are considered securities, and thus their issuance, sale, and transfer are subject to federal and state securities laws.

The federal securities laws,[1] which are administered by the Securities and Exchange Commission, apply to all purchases or sales of securities by use of the mails or by means of interstate commerce. In other words, for all practical purposes, these laws apply to all purchases or sales of securities. The laws are designed to protect investors by requiring full and fair disclosure in the offering of securities.

Section 5 of the Securities Act of 1933 ("Securities Act") requires that prior to the sale of any securities, the securities must be registered with the SEC unless there is an exemption from registration. Registration is accomplished, in part, by filing with the SEC a registration statement that includes the information to be furnished investors, thereby giving the SEC an opportunity to review the adequacy of the information on its face and to take appropriate action if the disclosure is considered insufficient.

The Securities Act and the SEC's rules and regulations provide for certain exemptions from the registration provisions where there is no practical need for registration or the public benefits of registration are too remote. For our purposes, the relevant exemptions are the exemption for "private placements" in Section 4(2), the exemption for "intrastate offerings" in Section 3(a)(11), and the exemptions for limited offerings in the SEC's Regulation D.[2] Large-scale public sales of securities (except when done in strict compliance with the exemption for intrastate offerings) would be subject to the registration requirements of the federal Securities Act and involve procedures and considerations that are beyond the scope of this book.

Full disclosure of all material information is required in connection with any sale of securities, whether or not the securities are required to be registered. It is unlawful to misrepresent any material fact or to fail to disclose any material fact.[3]

Failure to comply with the federal securities laws can result in civil or criminal liability or the imposition of administrative sanctions by the SEC. Purchasers of securities sold in violation of the securities laws have the right to sue the sellers for damages or for rescission of the purchases.

This chapter discusses the effect of the Securities Act on the issuance of limited partnership interests and the means of complying with the private placement, intrastate offering, and other exemptions from registration. The laws regulating the sellers of the interests and state regulation will be covered in the following chapters.

2. LIMITED PARTNERSHIP INTERESTS ARE SECURITIES

Neither the Securities Act nor the Securities Exchange Act of 1934 ("Exchange Act") expressly mentions limited partnership interests in their definitions of the term "security." [4] Both statutes, however, include "certificate of interest or participation in any profit-sharing agreement," "investment contract," and any "instrument commonly known as a 'security'" within the definition of "security," and it is under these concepts that limited partnership interests are brought within the scope of the definition of "security" and the requirements of the securities laws. The test in determining whether there is a security within the meaning of these three concepts is whether there is "an investment in a common venture premised on a reasonable expectation of profits to be derived from the entrepreneurial or managerial efforts of others." [5]

An investment is a transaction primarily entered into to obtain profits as opposed to the benefits of use of the item acquired. Thus a purchaser of warehouse receipts for Scotch whisky stored in Scotland, who cannot for all practical purposes take possession of and consume the whisky, is making an investment,[6] while someone who purchases a bottle of liquor to drink is not investing. Limited partnership interests are investments because the limited partner parts with his money with no intention of acquiring something to be used, occupied, consumed, or developed by him. Rather, he is looking to obtain financial returns without involvement in the management of his money or the items acquired therewith.

A common venture involves a sharing of the risks and profits of the investment with others—either other investors or, perhaps, the manager of the investment. In part, the notion of common venture is designed to distinguish traditional agency relationships as well as transactions in which the individual acts solely on his own behalf, whether directly or through agents. In the typical real estate limited partnership, the anticipated economic benefits are received by the general partners as well as by one or more limited partners, which satisfies this test.

Not all investments are securities. The key element in determining whether an investment is a security is whether entrepreneurial or managerial efforts of others, without such efforts by the investor, are to be the source of the return on the investment. If the investor is participating in the management of the investment or if no managerial efforts are involved, then there is no security. Where management is vested in others (e.g., the board of directors of a corporation), there is a security.[7] In the usual limited partnership, the limited partners do not participate in management; in order to obtain limited liability under the applicable version of the Uniform Limited Partnership Act, management is placed in the hands of the general partners. As a result, the element of management by others is present, and the limited partnership interest is a security. On the other hand, the purchase of raw land with the thought of reselling it in the future when property values increase from general economic conditions would be an investment, since there is no intent to use the land, but it would not be a security, since there would be no management of the investment by others.[8]

3. LIMITED OFFERINGS

a. Private Placements   Section 4(2) of the Securities Act exempts "transactions by an issuer not involving any public offering" from the registration requirements of Section 5. This exemption is commonly referred to as the "private offering" or "private placement" exemption. Private placements that are exempt under Section 4(2) are usually contrasted with "public offerings," which are required to be registered with the SEC.

The Supreme Court construed the private placement exemption in the landmark case *S.E.C. v. Ralston Purina Co.*[9] The Supreme Court stated that the exemption must be interpreted in the light of the statutory purpose to "protect investors by promoting full disclosure of information thought necessary to informed investment decisions" and held that the availability of the exemption "should turn on whether the particular class of persons affected need the protection of the Act." The Court further stated that, "An offering to those who are shown to be able to fend for themselves is a transaction 'not involving any public offering,' " and indicated that an offering to executive personnel of the issuer, "who because of their position have access to the same kind of information" that would be made available from registration under the Securities Act, would be an exempt private placement.

In an interpretive release dealing with the private placement exemption, the SEC stated:

> Whether a transaction is one not involving any public offering is essentially a question of fact and necessitates a consideration of all surrounding circumstances, including such factors as the relationship between the offerees and the issuer, the nature, scope, size, type, and manner of the offering.[10]

As a result of the *Ralston Purina* case and the SEC's releases, determination of whether an offering or sale of securities qualifies for the private placement exemption has traditionally revolved about such considerations as the number of offerees and purchasers, their "sophistication," or ability to make investment decisions, their "wealth," or ability to bear the economic risks of the investment, their ability to "fend" for themselves in determining whether to invest, their access to or receipt of information relating to the investment, their intent to acquire the securities for investment, the absence of general solicitation of investors, and restrictions on transfer of the securities by the investors so as to prevent a deferred distribution to the public.

The burden of proof of the availability of the exemption is said to be on the issuer and must be met not only with respect to each purchaser but also with respect to each person to whom the securities are offered.[11]

The difficulty of applying the preceding general factors, the absence of clear guidance in judicial and administrative interpretations, and the existence of unnecessary language in a number of judicial opinions [12] produced uncertainty as to the availability of the private placement exemption. Accordingly, in an effort "to provide more objective standards for determining when offers or sales of securities by an issuer would be deemed to be transactions not involving any public offering," in 1974 the SEC adopted Rule 146 under the Securities Act as one way of complying with the private placement exemption.[13] In 1982 the SEC adopted Regulation D. Rule 506 of Regulation D replaced Rule 146, which was rescinded. Rule 506 provides that an offering made in compliance with its conditions will be deemed not to involve any public offering within the meaning of Section 4(2) of the Securities Act. This rule is not the exclusive means of complying with Section 4(2); an issuer can claim the availability of Section 4(2) outside the rule, even if the issuer has attempted to comply with the rule.

b. Small Offering Exemptions Section 3(b) of the Securities Act permits the SEC to create exemptions for offerings of securities that do not exceed $5,000,000. Rules 504 and 505 of Regulation D were adopted pursuant to this authorization. Regulation D is discussed in the following sections of this book.

The SEC's Regulation A [14] was also adopted under Section 3(b). Regulation A provides an exemption for certain offerings of up to $1,500,000 if specified requirements are met. Generally, to obtain the exemption it is necessary to file with one of the regional offices of the SEC documents that, in effect, constitute a "mini" registration statement and are reviewed at the regional office in much the same manner as a registration statement is reviewed. Accordingly, offerings under Regulation A involve problems similar to offerings registered under Section 5 of the Securities Act and are outside the scope of this book.

4. REGULATION D—GENERAL

Offers and sales of securities that are made in accordance with the conditions of Regulation D [15] are exempt from the registration requirements of Section 5 of the Securities Act. The SEC adopted Regulation D to simplify, and expand the availability of, three predecessor exemptions that were rescinded.

The regulation consists of six rules. Rules 501, 502, and 503 contain definitions and requirements that are applicable to the three exemptions contained in Rules 504, 505, and 506. Rule 501 has the definitions, including definitions of the important concepts of accredited investor and purchaser representative. Rule 502 contains general conditions to be met regarding the integration of offerings, information to be furnished to investors, limitations on the manner of offering securities, and restrictions on the resale of the securities. Rule 503 sets forth instructions for filing notice of the sales of securities under the regulation with the SEC. Rule 504 provides an exemption from registration for offerings of up to $500,000 of securities. Rule 505 is an exemption for offerings that do not exceed $5,000,000. Rule 506 sets forth conditions that will exempt an offering of any size as a private placement under Section 4(2) of the Securities Act. The regulation's requirements for any particular offering are related principally to the amount to be raised and the number and type of investors.

Attempted compliance with Regulation D does not prohibit an issuer from claiming any other exemption that is available.

Anyone involved in making an offering pursuant to the regulation should read it carefully to ensure that he understands and is complying with its provisions.

Although Regulation D represents an evolution from earlier rules of the SEC, it has introduced a number of new concepts that have not been precisely defined. Some guidance is available from the discussion in the SEC's release that announces the adoption of the regulation, and the SEC no-action letters interpreting the predecessor rules are helpful.

The exemptions in Regulation D, as well as the other exemptions discussed in this book, provide exemption only from the registration requirements of the Securities Act. They do not, by themselves, furnish exemption under applicable state securities laws, although many state securities laws have similar exemptions. They also do not furnish any exemption from the full disclosure and antifraud provisions of the securities laws.

The following sections discuss Regulation D, with emphasis on the aspects of the regulation that are relevant to real estate limited partnerships. Later we consider other exemptions.

5. REGULATION D—NATURE OF OFFERINGS

Since all transactions that are part of an offering must meet the applicable requirements of Regulation D for an exemption under the regulation to apply, consideration must be given to what constitutes an offering. The term "offering" is not defined in the regulation. Further, determination of what offers and sales should be treated as comprising a single offering and whether transactions that purport to be separate offerings should be "integrated" and treated as part of one larger offering are questions of fact.

In the case of the sale of interests in a limited partnership owning only one property by a general partner who is not involved in any other limited partnerships, resolution of the question of integration of offerings is fairly easy. In more complex situations, of course, careful analysis will be required.

Although the term "offering" is not defined in Regulation D, the regulation does set forth a limited "safe harbor" provision as to circumstances under which integration is not required. Rule 502(a) provides:

Offers and sales that are made more than six months before the start of a Regulation D offering or are made more than six months after completion of a Regulation D offering will not be considered part of that Regulation D offering, so long as during those six month periods there are no offers or sales of securities by or for the issuer that are of the same or a similar class as those offered or sold under Regulation D, other than those offers or sales of securities under an employee benefit plan as defined in Rule 405 under the Act.

It should be noted that, since all offers and sales in an offering ordinarily would not occur simultaneously, the period covered would normally be greater than 12 months. Other offers and sales during the period of the offering are not excluded by the "safe harbor" provision and, barring unusual circumstances, may be integrated. To qualify under the "safe harbor" provision, it is necessary that there be no offers or sales of similar securities for six months after completion of the offering. Thus careful policing of subsequent transactions is required. If the requirements of the "safe harbor" provision are not met, the offerings are not automatically integrated; rather, the traditional integration factors discussed in Section 26 of this chapter would apply.

6. REGULATION D—MANNER OF OFFERING

Rule 502(c) prohibits the use of any form of general solicitation or general advertising in the offer or sale of securities under the regulation. This limitation applies to all Regulation D offerings other than offerings under Rule 504 (up to $500,000) that are made entirely in, and are registered with, states that require delivery of an offering memorandum or other disclosure document to investors before the sale of the securities.[16] Promotional seminars and meetings are permitted only if the persons attending have not been invited by any general solicitation or general advertising.

Beyond this, the regulation does not define or explain the concepts of general solicitation or general advertising. However, some guidance can be obtained from the practices under, and the interpretations of, Rule 146, which contained a similar limitation.

The offering can be made through a securities broker. The broker would be considered to be acting on behalf of the issuer and would have to comply with Regulation D in selling the securities. Any failure by the broker to meet the requirements of the regulation may be attributed to the issuer.

The key factor in avoiding a general solicitation seems to be the presence of a relationship between the issuer or the broker and the offeree that existed prior to the offering. Using the term "limited solicitation" to include both "(i) the solicitation of persons individually known to the solicitor and (ii) the use of a narrow list such as a list of all accounting partners of major accounting firms of the City of New York," the staff of the SEC concurred in the following positions: [17]

1. A securities broker not engaged either in the making of an offer or in any activity preparatory to a specific offer may engage in a limited solicitation for the purpose of locating qualified offerees for possible subsequent offerings, and this would not preclude reliance on Rule 146 in a subsequent offering to offerees so identified.

2. A broker who is participating in a Rule 146 offering or who anticipates participating in a contemplated offering may at the same time engage in a limited solicitation to identify qualified offerees for possible subsequent offerings, provided the offering in contemplation or progress is not made to any person so identified.

3. If a qualified offeree, although not solicited to so do, suggests that the offering also be made to a previously unidentified person also qualified, the subsequent solicitation of the other person would be permitted.

4. Rule 146(c) does not proscribe the making of an offer through another broker as an intermediary to qualified offerees located by the other broker, assuming the broker intermediary solicits within the confines of Rule 146.

Often issuers and securities brokers ask lawyers, accountants and other intermediaries to introduce them to potential investors. Whether this is permissible appears to hinge on the extent of the use of intermediaries, the relationships among the offeror, the intermediary and the offeree, and what the intermediary is asked to do and in fact does.[18]

The use of institutional advertising by a broker to attract issuers is permissible. However, if individual investors responded to the advertising seeking investments, there would be a question of fact as to whether the restrictions on general advertising had been violated, even though the advertising did not relate to any particular offering being made by the broker.[19]

Absent unusual circumstances, the number of offerees would be immaterial. A preexisting relationship between the issuer or the broker and the persons to whom the securities are offered should be adequate to indicate the absence of general solicitation.[20] A conservative approach would dictate that the persons to whom offers are made and the existence of any such relationships be documented. It may also be sufficient for the issuer and any broker to establish procedures designed to ensure that no general solicitation is made. Under this approach, someone should exercise supervisory oversight with a view to preventing departures from the procedures. Documentation should also be kept as to the persons attending any promotional seminar or meeting and the manner in which they were invited to the meeting.

Under Regulation D there is no limit on the number of permissible offerees, and, unlike Rule 146, there are no qualification requirements for offerees. However, many state securities laws impose requirements as to the qualifications and the number of offerees. Accordingly, if the offering will be made in any of these states, it may be important that the issuer be able to identify all the persons to whom the securities are offered in order to be able to assure itself of compliance with applicable securities laws and so that it can document such compliance. Under these circumstances, the act of offering to sell securities to an investor should be formalized, and procedures should be followed to prevent the making of informal offers. The copies of the offering memorandum should be numbered, and a record should be kept of the persons receiving the copies and whether or not the recipients were offerees. Offers should be made in writing by a separate letter or by notation on the offering memorandum that an offer is being made to an identified person. Other documents distributed to potential investors in connection with the offering should state that they do not constitute offers to sell or solicitations of offers to buy the securities.

7. REGULATION D—ACCREDITED INVESTORS

A key concept, central to Regulation D, is that of accredited investors. If the securities are sold only to accredited investors, it is not necessary to give the investors the information otherwise required by Rule 502(b) in order to obtain an exemption under Regulation D.[21] Accredited investors are not counted in determining the number of purchasers in offerings under Rules 505 and 506, which limit the maximum number of purchasers to 35. Also, accredited investors do not have to meet the sophistication requirement as to knowledge and experience in financial and business matters that is applicable to other investors in a private placement under Rule 506.

Who are accredited investors? Rule 501(a) gives the following definition:

"Accredited investor" shall mean any person who comes within any of the following categories, or who the issuer reasonably believes comes within any of the following categories, at the time of the sale of the securities to that person:

1. Any bank as defined in section 3(a)(2) of the Act whether acting in its individual or fiduciary capacity; insurance company as defined in section 2(13) of

the Act; investment company registered under the Investment Company Act of 1940 or a business development company as defined in section 2(a)(48) of that Act; Small Business Investment Company licensed by the U.S. Small Business Administration under section 301(c) or (d) of the Small Business Investment Act of 1958; employee benefit plan within the meaning of Title I of the Employee Retirement Income Act of 1974, if the investment decision is made by a plan fiduciary, as defined in section 3(21) of such Act, which is either a bank, insurance company, or registered investment adviser, or if the employee benefit plan has total assets in excess of $5,000,000;

2. Any private business development company as defined in section 202(a)(22) of the Investment Advisers Act of 1940;

3. Any organization described in Section 501(c)(3) of the Internal Revenue Code with total assets in excess of $5,000,000;

4. Any director, executive officer, or general partner of the issuer of the securities being offered or sold, or any director, executive officer, or general partner of a general partner of that issuer;

5. Any person who purchases at least $150,000 of the securities being offered, where the purchaser's total purchase price does not exceed 20 percent of the purchaser's net worth at the time of sale, or joint net worth with that person's spouse, for one or any combination of the following: (i) cash, (ii) securities for which market quotations are readily available, (iii) an unconditional obligation to pay cash or securities for which market quotations are readily available which obligation is to be discharged within five years of the sale of the securities to the purchaser, or (iv) the cancellation of any indebtedness owed by the issuer to the purchaser;

6. Any natural person whose individual net worth, or joint net worth with that person's spouse, at the time of his purchase exceeds $1,000,000;

7. Any natural person who had an individual income in excess of $200,000 in each of the two most recent years and who reasonably expects an income in excess of $200,000 in the current year; and

8. Any entity in which all of the equity owners are accredited investors under paragraph (a)(1), (2), (3), (4), (6), or (7) of this §230.501.

As far as real estate limited partnerships are concerned, the important categories are those in the last five paragraphs of the definition.

A general partner of the real estate limited partnership (or an executive officer or director of a corporation, or general partner of a partnership, that serves as general partner of the real estate limited partnership) is an accredited investor. If he purchases a limited partnership interest, he will not be counted for the 35-purchaser test. Of course, he must be a true general partner, not designated as such merely to circumvent the 35-purchaser limitations.[22]

The so-called $150,000 purchaser must invest at least $150,000 within five years of the sale of the limited partnership interests.[23] More than $150,000 may be invested, but the investor's total commitment may not exceed 20% of his net worth.[23a] An investor who is an individual may use the joint net worth of the investor and his or her spouse. If at least $150,000 is not paid on the sale of the interests there must be an unconditional obligation to pay the difference within five years. Presumably conditions that are related to the operations of the partnership, such as a requirement that construction or rental of a building be completed, and are not within the control of the investor, would be considered permissible.[24] If the price of the interests is more than $150,000, only $150,000 need be payable within five years, and the excess may be due later.

The obligation must be to pay cash [25] or securities with readily available market quotations; however, payment does not have to be secured by any collateral.

Also qualifying as an accredited investor is any individual whose net worth exceeds $1,000,000 or whose income for the last two years has exceeded, and for the current year is reasonably expected to exceed, $200,000. The net worth test can be met by the investor's net worth or the combined net worth of the investor and his or her spouse. The income test must be met by the individual investor.

Neither income nor net worth is defined in Regulation D. The release adopting the regulation states that the SEC determined to use a flexible approach regarding income. The release suggests that one way to calculate income would be to increase the investor's adjusted gross income for federal income tax purposes by any deductions for long-term capital gain and depletion, any exclusion for tax exempt interest, and any limited partnership losses allocated to the investor.

We believe that net worth should be treated with equal flexibility, focusing on economic net worth rather than on any artificial accounting conventions. Noteworthy is the fact that, in contrast to the net worth suitability standards imposed by many states, Regulation D does not require the exclusion of an investor's home, home furnishings, and automobiles in determining net worth.

Often a number of investors who by themselves are accredited (other than by reason of Rule 501(a)(5)) will form a partnership or other entity to make investments on their behalf. The entity will be an accredited investor.[25a]

An investor qualifies as an accredited investor if he, in fact, falls into any of the eight specified categories or if the issuer reasonably believes he falls into one of the categories even if it is discovered after the sale that he was not accredited. The required reasonable belief could arise from the issuer's personal knowledge or from information obtained from others. However, more often than not it would be based on information submitted by the investor in response to a questionnaire prepared by the issuer. The questions would relate to the various requirements listed in the definition of accredited investor. This questionnaire could be combined with the one referred to in Section 11 of this chapter for use with private placements under Rule 506.

8. REGULATION D—COUNTING INVESTORS

There is no limitation on the number of permissible investors in offerings under Rule 504. In offerings under Rules 505 and 506, however, the issuer must reasonably believe that there are no more than 35 purchasers of the securities. In determining the number of purchasers, accredited investors are not counted, and certain related investors having the same principal residence (and certain trusts and other entities in which they have more than 50% of the beneficial interest) are counted as only one investor.[26]

A partnership, corporation, or other entity is not counted if it is an accredited investor and counts as a single purchaser if it has not been organized for the specific purpose of acquiring the securities offered. Absent both of these conditions, each beneficial owner of equity interests in the entity counts as a separate purchaser.[27]

A note to Rule 501(e) states that the clients of an investment adviser or securities broker, regardless of the amount of investment discretion granted, will be considered separate purchasers for the 35-purchaser test.

That an investor is excluded in determining the number of purchasers does not relieve the issuer from having to satisfy all the other applicable provisions of Regulation D, including the absence of any general solicitation.

The reasonable belief required of the issuer can be based on representations from the investor in a questionnaire, in his subscription agreement, or otherwise. If the size of any investor's participation is disproportionate to his financial position as indicated in the questionnaire or as known to the partnership or its representatives, or if during the course of the transaction there are indications that others may be sharing in the interest to be acquired by the investor, further inquiry should be made.

In determining the number of purchasers, the doctrine of integration of offerings must be considered. Under this doctrine, the offers and sales in several transactions that purport to be separate offerings are treated as one offering.[28] The doctrine of integration is discussed in Sections 5 and 26 of this chapter.

9. RULE 504—SALES NOT EXCEEDING $500,000

Rule 504 provides an exemption for limited partnerships [29] where the total consideration the partnership receives for the sale of its securities in the offering does not exceed $500,000.[30] This amount is reduced by the price of certain other securities sold during the offering or the 12 months preceding the offering.[31]

To obtain the exemption the partnership must comply with all applicable conditions of Regulation D, which are discussed in earlier and later sections of this chapter. These conditions include limitations on the manner of offering the partnership interests, limitations on resale of the interests by a limited partner, and the partnership's filing of a notice of sale with the SEC. If the entire offering [32] is made only within and in compliance with the laws of states that provide for registration of the interests and require delivery to investors of an offering memorandum or other disclosure document, the restrictions on the manner of offering and on resale of the interests are eliminated.

There are no limitations or conditions as to the number or type of offerees or investors. Also, there is no requirement that any information be furnished to the investors (other than written disclosure of any applicable limitations on resale). However, the securities laws of the states where the offering is made may contain provisions relating to these matters, and sufficient information should be given to comply with the federal and state antifraud rules.

The doctrine of integration of offerings, discussed in Sections 5 and 26 of this chapter, should always be considered, especially in determining whether the $500,000 limitation on sales has been exceeded.

10. RULE 505—SALES NOT EXCEEDING $5,000,000

Compliance with Rule 505 will permit an unregistered offering for the sale of up to $5,000,000 of limited partnership interests.[33] As is the case with Rule 504, this maximum permissible amount may be reduced by the sale of other securities during the offering or the preceding year.[34] The rule is intended to allow sale to a maximum of 35 investors that are not accredited investors.[35] Accordingly, a condition of the availability of the exemption is that the partnership reasonably believe that there are no more than 35 nonaccredited purchasers. This belief, as well as the partnership's belief regarding the status of the other purchasers as accredited investors, ordinarily is based on information in questionnaires and representations obtained from the investors.

There are no other restrictions on the number or type of offerees or investors. However, the partnership has to comply with any limitations imposed by applicable state securities laws.

All the applicable conditions of Rules 501, 502 and 503 must be met.[36] Thus the offering may not be made by any general solicitation or general advertising, and the partnership interests are restricted securities and subject to limitations on resale. The partnership must file a notice of the sale of the interests with the SEC. If partnership interests are sold to any nonaccredited investors, information similar to that required in a prospectus for a public offering registered with the SEC must be furnished to all investors.[37]

Rule 505 contains a special restrictive condition that does not apply to offerings under Rules 504 and 506. Rule 505 is not available if the partnership, any general partner or promoter of the partnership, any person being paid for solicitation of investors, or other specified persons are subject to the disqualifying provisions of Regulation A.[38] These so-called bad boy provisions generally relate to persons who have been subject to administrative or court proceedings for failure to comply with the securities laws or for mail fraud.[39]

As is always the case, consideration should be given to the doctrine of integration of offerings.

Rule 505, like the other exemptions discussed in this chapter, is an exemption only from federal registration of the limited partnership interests; it does not furnish an exemption from the antifraud or civil liability provisions of the federal securities laws or from compliance with applicable state laws.

11. RULE 506—PRIVATE PLACEMENTS

Rule 506 provides that offers and sales by an issuer that satisfy the conditions in Regulation D "shall be deemed to be transactions not involving any public offering within the meaning of Section 4(2) of the Act." Accordingly, such an offering would be an exempt private placement.

There is no restriction on the issuers that may use the rule and no limitation on the amount that may be raised from the sale of the securities.

All of the general conditions specified in Rules 501, 502, and 503, and discussed in other sections of this chapter, are applicable to an offering of limited partnership interests under Rule 506. There can be no general solicitation or general advertising in connection with the offer or sale of the partnership interests. The interests are restricted securities and may not be resold by investors without registration under the Securities Act unless an exemption is available. The partnership must file a notice of sale with the SEC. If any nonaccredited investor purchases any of the securities in the offering, all investors must be given specified types of information. The information required to be furnished in an offering of $5,000,000 or more of partnership interests is more extensive than that necessary for one involving less than that amount. In determining whether these and the other conditions to the exemption have been satisfied, the doctrine of integration of offerings applies.

Rule 506, unlike Rule 146 (which it replaces), imposes no requirements as to the sophistication or wealth of the offerees, and there is no limitation on the number of permissible offerees if no general solicitation or general advertising is used. However, the offering must satisfy any requirements of applicable state securities laws regarding these matters.[40]

As is the case with offerings under Rule 505, a condition of the availability of an exemption under Rule 506 is that the partnership reasonably believe that there are no more than 35 nonaccredited purchasers of the securities.[41] In addition, the partnership must reasonably believe that each nonaccredited investor "has such knowledge and experience in financial and business matters that he is capable of evaluating the merits and risks of the prospective investment." In the language used by securities lawyers, the investor must be "sophisticated." If the partnership does not have this belief, it may not sell the interests to him unless he is assisted by a purchaser representative who the partnership reasonably believes is sophisticated. The requirements that must be met by a purchaser representative are set forth in Rule 501(h) and are discussed in the next section of this chapter.

The standard of knowledge and experience that an investor must possess in order to be sophisticated is not spelled out in the rule beyond his "being capable of evaluating the merits and risks of the prospective investment." The class of permissible investors is not restricted to financial analysts and similar persons. The rule states the requirement in terms of evaluating the prospective investment. Thus sophistication is not an absolute standard. The required degree of sophistication will vary with the complexity of the investment and the knowledge and experience necessary to understand the risks of investing in the securities offered. The level of sophistication will also be related to the amount and type of information furnished to the investor, since the knowledge and experience necessary to understand and evaluate a proposed investment when there has been full and clear written disclosure of all material information is less than that required to ferret out the material facts in the absence of such disclosure.

The fact that an investor consults with his own lawyer or accountant in connection with an offering of real estate limited partnership interests, especially in the case of a tax-oriented investment, does not, of itself, indicate a lack of sophistication since knowledgeable investors frequently consult their professional advisers before investing. Indeed, the investor who does seek such advice is, to a great degree, showing that he is sufficiently sophisticated to recognize risks that should be reviewed by advisers with special expertise. Further, from the partnership's standpoint, it is desirable that investors in a tax-oriented limited partnership obtain advice from their own tax advisers.

In the final analysis, sophistication is a question of fact, which should be determined on the basis of the investor's ability to understand the proposed investment, to weigh the factors involved, and to make an intelligent investment decision.

The belief as to the investor's sophistication or as to his status as an accredited investor can be based on personal acquaintance with the investor or on information obtained from reliable sources or from the investor. Documentation of the grounds for the belief should be prepared and preserved. The documentation should identify the investor and indicate the facts underlying the belief and the source of those facts. Ordinarily the belief is based on, and the documentation consists of, a questionnaire completed by the investor.

The investor's questionnaire could seek information about his personal and educational background, business and employment experience, investment experience including marketable and unmarketable securities and private placements of the type being offered, and the factors that would classify him as an accredited investor. Conclusive statements by the investor indicating that he is sophisticated but without additional information normally would not be sufficient. In connection with the sale of interests in real estate limited partnerships, questions could also be asked about the investor's current and anticipated tax bracket and net worth to obtain information as to whether he meets any suitability standards imposed by state securities laws or by the partnership. Additional questions could seek information as to the investor's state of residence or domicile to determine which state securities laws may apply, as to the investor's understanding that any investment will be illiquid and subject to specified risks, and as to whether the investor intends to acquire the securities for his own account or on behalf of others.

Whether additional inquiry is required for the partnership's belief to be reasonable would depend on the surrounding circumstances, including the information given in the questionnaire and its consistency with other information known about the investor, whether the questionnaire indicates that the investor is clearly or only marginally qualified, and the complexity of the investment.

If the partnership plans to make inquiries to verify the information submitted by the investor in the questionnaire, the questionnaire could ask for the names of references, such as the investor's accountant, lawyer, or banker, and permission to contact them.

Rule 501(a) requires that the partnership's belief as to an investor's qualification as an accredited investor must exist at the time the securities are sold. Thus, if the questionnaire is completed substantially before the sale, it is desirable for the questionnaire to contain an agreement by the investor to advise the partnership of any changes occurring prior to the sale and for the investor's subscription agreement to contain a representation as to the continued accuracy of the information in the questionnaire. Alternatively, the questionnaire should be completed by the investor shortly before the sale is closed.

If the partnership had the required reasonable belief as to an investor's qualifications at the time of sale, the exemption would remain available even if it were discovered after the sale that the investor did not meet the required standards. Further, if the partnership's belief as to the investor's accredited investor status were later determined to be unreasonable, exemption under Rule 506 would still be available if the investor, in fact, met the requirements for being accredited.

12. RULE 506—PURCHASER REPRESENTATIVE

A nonaccredited investor whom the partnership does not consider sophisticated may not purchase the securities unless he has a purchaser representative. The required qualifications of the representative are set forth in Rule 501(h) and include conditions relating to lack of affiliation with the issuer, sophistication, acknowledgment as purchaser representative by the investor, and disclosure of material relationships with the issuer or its affiliates. An investor may have more than one purchaser representative, each of whom must meet the requirements imposed by the rule.

The representative may not be an affiliate, director, officer, or other employee of the issuer or own 10% or more of the equity interest in the issuer except in specified circumstances where the representative is closely related to the purchaser. Employees of a general partner of a limited partnership cannot serve as purchaser representatives for unrelated investors.[42] The issuer may retain and pay the compensation of an investment banker or another person who is available to serve as purchaser representative for investors who are willing to accept the recommended person as their representative. Written disclosure of these arrangements is required.

The purchaser representative (together with the investor and any additional purchaser representatives) must be capable of evaluating the merits and risks of the investment. In this regard, the considerations discussed previously concerning the sophistication of the investor are applicable.

The investor must acknowledge in writing that the representative is his purchaser representative in connection with evaluating the merits and risks of the investment. A separate acknowledgment must be made with respect to each specific prospective investment: blanket acknowledgments for "all private placements" are not sufficient. Prior to this acknowledgment, the purchaser representative must disclose in writing to the investor information as to material relationships between the representative, the issuer, and their respective affiliates as set forth in the rule and any compensation received or to be received as a result of any of these relationships.[43] As pointed out in a note to the rule, these disclosures do not eliminate the representative's obligation to act in the interest of the investor.

As is the case with purchasers of the securities, the issuer must reasonably believe that the purchaser representative satisfies the required conditions. Here too the belief would normally be based on a questionnaire to be completed by the representative. The questionnaire could seek information regarding such matters as the representative's occupation, professional licenses, education, experience in advising investors with respect to similar investments, relationships with the issuer and its affiliates, and disclosure to the investor. It is also sufficient if the representative is, in fact, qualified.

The rule does not specify the services to be performed by the purchaser representative other than to indicate that the representative must act in the interest of the investor. Clearly implied is the representative's duty to assist in evaluating the merits and risks of the investment. Whether the representative must make a recommendation that the investor buy or not buy the securities is not discernible from the rule, and differing views have been expressed by members of the SEC and its staff.[44] We suggest that whether a recommendation must be made will vary from transaction to transaction and will depend on the needs of the investor, the complexity of the transaction, and the reasons for using a purchaser representative. If the investor has the ability to make his own investment decision once his purchaser representative has given him an analysis of the risks, then a recommendation by the representative should not be required. On the other hand, an investor who is completely unsophisticated in business, financial, and investment matters would need a definitive recommendation from his purchaser representative. Also, a purchaser representative who is supplying expertise in only a limited area (e.g., the technical tax aspects of a tax-oriented real estate investment) to an investor who is sophisticated in the other areas involved (e.g., real estate development) should not be required to make a recommendation.

A note to the rule advises purchaser representatives to consider the registration and antifraud provisions relating to brokers and dealers under the Exchange Act and relating to investment advisers under the Investment Advisers Act of 1940.[45] Ordinarily, a purchaser representative whose compensation does not depend on whether the investor purchases the securities offered would not be a broker or dealer.[46]

A purchaser representative who comes within the definition of "investment adviser" in the Investment Advisers Act of 1940 [47] would have to register with the SEC unless exempted from such registration.[48] A person who does not receive compensation for acting as a purchaser representative would not be an investment adviser. A person being compensated for serving as purchaser representative in an isolated instance would presumably not be in the "business" of giving investment advice and thus would not be an investment adviser.[49] Purchaser representatives who intend to act as such for compensation on more than one occasion should carefully review the requirements of the Investment Advisers Act, since the act does not require that giving investment advice must be the investment adviser's principal business.

13. REGULATION D—DISCLOSURE OF INFORMATION

The philosophy underlying the federal securities laws is that investors should have all the information necessary to make informed investment decisions. Thus the antifraud provisions of the securities laws are applicable to all offerings of securities. The Securities Act specifies information to be included in registration statements filed under that act, subject to any changes that may be made by the SEC pursuant to rule or regulation. The SEC has issued registration forms specifying the information to be contained in registration statements filed by various classes of issuers with respect to different types of securities.[50] Consistent with this disclosure philosophy, Regulation D conditions the availability of Rules 505 and 506 for offerings that include nonaccredited investors on the issuer's furnishing of specified information.

There are no specific information requirements for offerings under Rule 504. Rule 504 is intended to be an uncomplicated exemption for use by smaller businesses in small offerings. The SEC has determined to rely on the general antifraud provisions of the securities laws and on regulation by the states to set the standards of disclosure for these offerings.

Specific disclosure conditions have not been imposed for offerings solely to accredited investors under Rules 505 and 506 because these investors are considered to be able to protect their own interests.[51]

Accordingly, if a Regulation D offering is made under Rule 504 or there are only accredited investors in an offering under Rule 505 or 506, Regulation D does not mandate that specific information be furnished. On the other hand, if there are any nonaccredited investors in an offering under Rule 505 or 506, the information requirements in Rule 502(b) must be satisfied.

The required information varies with the size of the offering and the type of issuer. The partnership would normally not be filing the periodic reports required under Section 13 or 15(d) of the Exchange Act for issuers who have had registered public offerings or have publicly traded securities. Thus most real estate limited partnership offerings under Rules 505 and 506 involving nonaccredited investors will have to comply with Rule 502(b)(2) (i), which requires the furnishing of the same kind of information that would be required in the prospectus of an appropriate registration statement form for registration under the Securities Act.[52]

The rule does not explicitly require that the information be in writing, but as a practical matter an offering memorandum similar to the prospectus used in a registered public offering would be prepared and furnished to investors and their purchaser representatives. Rule 502(b) requires that information be furnished only "to the extent material to an understanding of the issuer, its business, and the securities being offered." [52a] This allows the partnership flexibility in determining what to include in the offering memorandum. The memorandum may be tailored to the needs of the investors, and time and effort need not be wasted trying to duplicate the prospectus that would be used in a public offering.

The registration statement forms require the use of audited financial statements.[53] However, there are no issuer financial statements when a limited partnership to be formed has not yet begun construction of a building. Even if financial statements are appropriate, Rule 502(b) permits the use of statements prepared on the basis of federal income tax requirements under certain circumstances.

The exhibits that would be filed with a registration statement need not be included in the offering memorandum if their contents are identified and the exhibits are made available to the purchaser on request.[53a]

The SEC has published guides followed by its staff in reviewing registration statements. The guides include a guide for offerings of interests in real estate limited partnerships. This is the so-called Guide 5, and it is set out in Appendix 9.

The guides represent the policies and practices followed by the SEC's Division of Corporation Finance in reviewing registration statements, but are not official requirements imposed by the SEC.[53b] Thus the information required by the guide is not required to be included in the private placement memorandum in order to comply with Regulation D. However, the substantive aspects of Guide 5 do represent the view of the SEC staff as to desirable disclosure, and should be seriously considered.

At a reasonable time prior to the purchase of the interests by any nonaccredited investor in an offering under Rules 505 or 506, the partnership must furnish the investor with a brief written description of any written information provided by the partnership to any accredited investor. On written request it must furnish this information to the nonaccredited investor.

Prior to the sale, the issuer is required to give the investors the opportunity to ask questions (and receive answers) concerning the offering and to obtain any additional information necessary to verify the information furnished. Thus the offering memorandum should indicate that the issuer will respond to questions and will provide additional information requested by investors or their representatives.[54]

Whether or not disclosure under Rule 502(b) is required, under Rule 502(d) disclosure in writing must be made that the interests have not been registered under the Securities Act and cannot be sold without compliance with the registration provisions of the Securities Act unless an exemption from registration is available. These disclosures could be included in the offering memorandum and/or the investor's subscription agreement, or in separate documents.

It goes without saying that the offering memorandum must be drafted with care, both to give the investor all the information necessary to make an investment decision and to protect the issuer against a subsequent claim by the investor that he did not receive full disclosure of all material facts. As indicated previously, there is an interrelationship between the quality of the disclosure and the degree of sophistication required of an investor or his purchaser representative: the greater the clarity of the memorandum, the less sophistication required to understand it and to evaluate the investment.

Disclosure practices are discussed at greater length in Chapter 11.

14. REGULATION D—LIMITATIONS ON RESALE

To ensure that the limited offering under Regulation D is not expanded into a general public offering by resales or reofferings by the purchasers, Rule 502(d) provides that the securities are restricted securities and cannot be resold by investors without registration under the Securities Act or an exemption from registration. The rule requires (a) that there be reasonable inquiry to determine whether any purchaser is acquiring the securities on behalf of others, (b) that the certificate or other document evidencing the securities be legended to indicate that the securities have not been registered and may not be transferred or sold without compliance with the Securities Act registration requirements or an exemption from registration, and (c) that the restrictions on transfer or sale of the securities be disclosed to the investor in writing prior to the sale of the securities. These conditions would not apply to offerings under Rule 504 that are registered and made solely in states requiring the delivery of a disclosure document.

Typically, the subscription agreement or the partnership agreement to be executed by the investor will contain a representation by the investor that he is acquiring the interest for his own account and not on behalf of others; it will recite the restrictions on transferability and will contain an agreement not to sell the interest without compliance with or exemption from the registration requirements. The restrictions on transferability (under the Securities Act and for tax and other purposes) should also be included in the offering memorandum. Ordinarily, the limited partnership interests will not be represented by separate certificates (as in the case of stock in a corporation).

15. REGULATION D—FILING OF NOTICE OF SALES

Rule 503 requires that issuers file notices of sales made in offerings in reliance on Regulation D with the SEC's principal office in Washington, D.C. The notices would be on Form D, which seeks information as to the issuer and its size and financial status, the offering and the use of the funds raised in the offering, and other matters. Form D is reproduced in Appendix 7; copies of the form can be obtained from the SEC.

An initial notice must be filed or sent by registered or certified mail no later than 15 days after the first sale of the securities. The release in which the SEC adopted Regulation D states that "generally the acceptance of subscription funds into an escrow account pending receipt of minimum subscriptions would trigger the filing requirements." Filing of additional notices may be required.[54a]

Since timely filing of the notice is necessary to obtain an exemption under Regulation D, attention should be given to this at an early stage of the offering.

16. PRIVATE PLACEMENTS NOT UNDER RULE 506

As indicated previously, compliance with Rule 506 is not the only way for an issuer to avail itself of the private placement exemption under Section

4(2) of the Securities Act. In a preliminary note to Regulation D, the SEC stated: "Attempted compliance with any rule does not act as an exclusive election; the issuer can also claim the availability of any other applicable exemption."

This nonexclusivity of Rule 506 is important even to issuers who attempt to comply with the rule. Rule 506 requires that all of its conditions, whether or not material to the particular private placement, must be met for the exemption thereunder to be applicable. Consequently, an issuer that has unknowingly failed to meet one of the rule's conditions would want to be able to claim the availability of the private placement exemption under Section 4(2) other than pursuant to the rule [which we refer to as the "Section 4(2) exemption"] if called on to defend the validity of the offering of its securities. Also, if an issuer during the course of a private placement learns that one of the rule's conditions has not been met, it could seek to utilize the Section 4(2) exemption to complete the offering. In addition, there will be occasions when an issuer determines to use the Section 4(2) exemption because some requirements of Rule 506 that are expensive or burdensome or time-consuming to comply with are not material to the private placement. For example, the relationship of the investors to the issuer may be such that the disclosure documentation required for nonaccredited investors under Rule 506 is unnecessary.

In broad outline, Rule 506 reflects good practices to be followed in making a private placement under the Section 4(2) exemption. However, there are some aspects of the rule that differ from what was generally considered to be the law governing private placements before adoption of the rule. It is to be expected that as time goes on the administrative and judicial interpretations of the Section 4(2) exemption will be influenced by Rule 506, just as they have by Rule 146, although one would hope that all of Rule 506's requirements are not carried over to the Section 4(2) exemption and that emphasis is placed on the Supreme Court's statement in the *Ralston Purina* case that the "focus of inquiry should be on the need of the offerees for the protections afforded by registration." [55] Areas where the rule differs from the Section 4(2) exemption are discussed in the following paragraphs. As a practical matter, we suggest that, where feasible, issuers should attempt to structure and carry out their private placements so as to comply with both Rule 506 and the Section 4(2) exemption.[56]

Under Rule 506, theoretically, there can be an unlimited number of offerees if they are obtained in a proper manner. However, there can be only 35 nonaccredited purchasers of the securities. This is consistent with the statement of the Supreme Court in the *Ralston Purina* case that "there is no warrant for superimposing a quantity limit on private offerings as a matter of statutory interpretation." [57] In private placements made to individuals under the Section 4(2) exemption, issuers have sought to restrict the offering to a limited number of wealthy or sophisticated offerees.[58] It still remains to be seen what effect Rule 506 will have on the Section 4(2) exemption in the light of the rule's elimination of provisions regarding offeree qualification.

A private placement of securities under the Section 4(2) exemption, just as under Rule 506, may not be made by any form of general solicitation or advertising. In general, the method of offering the securities should be designed to ensure that offers are made only to appropriate offerees.

Rule 506 permits a completely unsophisticated investor to purchase securities if he has a purchaser representative. Prior to the adoption of Rule 146 in 1974, the concept of a representative to supply sophistication was not clearly recognized other than in the case of professional investment advisers acting with discretionary investment authority for wealthy investors. In other situations, it was thought that, although the investor could consult lawyers, accountants, and other professional advisers, he had to be sufficiently sophisticated to make his own investment decision. In addition, the investor had to be able to bear the degree of economic risk associated with the particular investment.[59]

Rule 506 has endorsed the position that every investor is not required to have a relationship with the issuer giving him "access" to information about the issuer. If the other conditions of Rule 506 are satisfied, it is sufficient for the issuer to furnish the information to the investors, and if only accredited investors are involved, there is no requirement under Rule 506 to furnish any specific information. Similarly, it would appear that, under the Section 4(2) exemption, investors must have access to information, or the issuer must make such information available.[60] The basic difference is that under the Section 4(2) exemption emphasis can be placed on disclosing what is in fact material to an investor rather than focusing on what would be required in a registration statement under the Securities Act. Nevertheless, the information that would be contained in a registration statement remains a good guide for disclosure in private placements not made pursuant to Rule 506 and, of course, the issuer must give full disclosure of all material information to satisfy the antifraud rules. The information need not be furnished in writing, but, unless the investors are very few in number and highly sophisticated, in the usual private placement of real estate limited partnership interests, written materials would be used.

The requirements of Rule 502(d) as to limitations on disposition of securities acquired in a private placement, which must be complied with if the Rule 506 exemption is to be available, have customarily been followed in Section 4(2) private placements as a matter of good practice. Although these measures are not necessary in order to claim the Section 4(2) exemption, they help ensure that the intended private placement does not become or involve a public offering as a result of reoffers or resales of the securities by the initial purchasers. Thus investors in a Section 4(2) private placement are asked to represent that they are acquiring the securities for investment and not with a view to, or in connection with, any distribution (i.e., reoffering to the public) of the securities. The typical real estate limited partnership does not contemplate that there will be a public trading market for its securities. Accordingly, in many instances there may be a presumption that the investors do not intend to reoffer their securities. Nevertheless, as a matter of practice, issuers should ordinarily follow the procedures outlined previously.[61]

As with Rule 506, the factors relevant to a private placement under the Section 4(2) exemption are interrelated and will vary from offering to offering. Although the Section 4(2) exemption does not require the documentation that accompanies an offering under Rule 506, the burden of proof of the availability of any exemption under Section 4(2) of the Securities Act is said to be on the person claiming the exemption. Accordingly, even under the Section 4(2) exemption, it is desirable that accurate records be maintained to meet the burden of proof of the availability of the exemption.

17. EXEMPTION UNDER SECTION 4(6)

In 1980, the Securities Act was amended by the addition of Section 4(6). This section exempts:

> Transactions involving offers or sales by an issuer solely to one or more accredited investors, if the aggregate offering price of an issue of securities offered in reliance on this paragraph does not exceed the amount allowed under section 3(b) of this title [$5,000,000], if there is no advertising or public solicitation in connection with the transaction by the issuer or anyone acting on the issuer's behalf, and if the issuer files such notice with the Commission as the Commission shall prescribe.

Under the SEC's Rule 215, the definition of an accredited investor for the purposes of Section 4(6) is identical to the definition in Regulation D. As a result, any offering that is exempt under Section 4(6) is also exempt under Rule 505. The converse, however, is not true. Under Section 4(6) the purchaser must in fact be an accredited investor, while under Regulation D it is sufficient if the issuer has a reasonable belief as to the investor's status. Also, Rule 505 offerings may include nonaccredited investors, but only accredited investors are permissible in a Section 4(6) offering. Indeed, Section

4(6) requires that all offerees, as well as purchasers, qualify as accredited investors.

If the offerees and purchasers satisfy the definition of accredited investors, they do not have to meet any special qualifications as to sophistication, and there is no limitation on the number of offerees and purchasers.

Furnishing of information is not required to obtain the exemption; however, as in the case of the other exemptions, there must be compliance with the antifraud rules.

Advertisement and public solicitation are not permitted. Sales commissions may be paid to registered broker–dealers. The securities would be restricted securities and could not be resold by the investor without registration under the Securities Act or exemption from registration.

A report of sales made under the exemption must be filed with the SEC on Form D in the same manner as is required under Regulation D.

Section 4(6) provides an exemption independent from the exemptions adopted by the SEC under Section 3(b) of the Securities Act. Accordingly, sales under Section 4(6) will not reduce the permissible aggregate offering prices for offerings pursuant to Regulation A or Rules 504 and 505 of Regulation D.

The considerations relating to integration of offerings discussed in Section 26 of this chapter apply. Attention to this matter is important because the exemption is available only if offers as well as sales are restricted to accredited investors, and only if the aggregate offering price of the issue does not exceed $5,000,000.

18. INTRASTATE OFFERINGS—GENERAL

Section 3(a)(11) of the Securities Act exempts from the act's registration requirements:

> Any security which is part of an issue offered and sold only to persons resident within a single State or Territory, where the issuer of such security is a person resident and doing business within, or, if a corporation, incorporated by and doing business within, such State or Territory.

Despite the seeming simplicity of this statutory definition of the intrastate offering exemption, the requirements of the exemption are complex and difficult to meet. In many instances, as a result of past interpretations of the exemption, determinations of what securities are "part of an issue" and when a person is "resident" and "doing business within" a state cannot be resolved with the certainty desirable to enable an issuer to rely on the exemption. The mere offer of a security that is determined to be "part of the issue" to an ineligible offeree destroys the exemption with respect to prior and future sales to eligible offerees, even if the ineligible offeree misrepresented his status to the issuer and did not purchase any securities, and regardless of the good faith of the issuer.[62] Consequently, the intrastate offering exemption is of very limited usefulness and should be employed only in situations where the issuer is in a position to be certain of compliance with the exemption.

In an effort to provide more objective standards as to the application of the exemption, the Securities and Exchange Commission adopted Rule 147.[63] However, the rule does not establish exclusive standards for complying with the intrastate offering exemption.

The intrastate offering exemption, whether claimed under Section 3(a)(11) or under Rule 147, is an exemption only from the registration provisions of the federal Securities Act. It does not provide an exemption from the requirements of state securities laws or the antifraud provisions of state and federal securities laws. Persons relying on the rule or on the exemption outside the rule have the burden of establishing compliance with the appropriate requirements for the exemption.

We shall first examine the provisions of Rule 147 and subsequently consider the intrastate offering exemption outside the rule.

19. RULE 147—GENERAL

Paragraph (a) of Rule 147 provides that offers and sales of securities made in accordance with all the terms and conditions of the rule will be deemed to satisfy the exemption in Section 3(a)(11) of the Securities Act. The rule applies only to transactions by the issuer, although the statutory exemption has been interpreted to permit offers and sales by persons controlling the issuer if the statutory exemption would have been available to the issuer at the time of the offering. The rule is nonexclusive, and failure to comply with the rule does not raise any presumption that the statutory exemption is not available.

Since the rule requires that all securities that are part of the same "issue" must be offered and sold in accordance with all the terms and conditions of the rule, it becomes important to determine what offers and sales are included in an issue of securities. This is a question of fact involving the doctrine of integration. Rule 147 has a provision (similar to that in Regulation D) that sets forth circumstances under which certain offers and sales may be excluded from an issue. Paragraph (b)(2) of Rule 147 provides:

> For purposes of this rule only, an issue shall be deemed not to include offers, offers to sell, offers for sale or sales of securities of the issuer pursuant to the

exemptions provided by Section 3 or Section 4(2) of the Act or pursuant to a registration statement filed under the Act, that take place prior to the six month period immediately preceding or after the six month period immediately following any offers, offers for sale or sales pursuant to this rule, provided that, there are during either of said six month periods no offers, offers for sale or sales of securities by or for the issuer of the same or similar class as those offered, offered for sale or sold pursuant to the rule.

If the requirements of Paragraph (b)(2) are not met, the traditional integration factors would apply. The doctrine of integration is discussed at greater length in Section 26 of this chapter. Rule 147 should be carefully read if it is to be relied upon; it is set out in Appendix 8.

20. RULE 147—NATURE OF THE ISSUER

Section 3(a)(11) of the Securities Act requires that the issuer be "a person resident and doing business within" the state in which the offers and sales are made. In paragraph (c) of Rule 147, these concepts are given further definition. Under the rule, an issuer that is a limited partnership is deemed to be a resident of the state under whose laws it is formed. To be "doing business" within that state, the partnership must have its principal office within the state [64] and must meet certain specified tests as to its gross revenues, assets, and use of the proceeds from the sale of the partnership interests.[65]

The rule thus limits the ability of the partnership to own property, or to acquire property with the proceeds of the offering, in more than one state. As a practical matter, the partnership must be organized under the laws of the state where the property is located, the partnership's principal office must be in that state, and, as discussed later, all the investors must reside in that state.

If the limited partnership has not been formed prior to the offering and will not be organized until the closing of the offering, the general partners are considered to be the issuers of preorganization interests in the partnership. Accordingly, in such a case the general partners would have to meet the applicable residency and doing business requirements of the rule.[66] On the other hand, once the limited partnership has been formed, the residence of the general partners is immaterial.[67]

21. RULE 147—OFFEREES AND PURCHASERS

Offers and sales may be made only to persons who, at the time of the offer and sale, are resident within the state under whose laws the partnership is formed. For purposes of determining the residence of offerees and purchasers under the rule, an individual is a resident of the state where his principal residence is located [68] and a corporation, partnership, trust or other form of business organization is a resident of the state where its principal office is located. Temporary residence of an individual in a state (the typical example is that of military personnel) is not sufficient, and if a person purchases securities on behalf of others, the residence of those others must meet the requirements of the rule.[69] An entity organized for the specific purpose of acquiring the securities is a resident of the state only if all the beneficial owners of the entity are residents of the state; however, if the entity is not so organized, the residence of its officers and owners is immaterial.[70]

Determination of the residence of offerees and purchasers is of critical importance, since the position of the SEC is that a single offer to a nonresident destroys the exemption for the entire issue even if the offeree does not purchase the securities and even if the offeree misrepresents his residence. Caution dictates that the facts regarding a potential investor's residence be known and documented, and be confirmed by the investor, before any offer is made to him. A detailed affidavit or questionnaire should be obtained from each prospective offeree setting forth information that will enable the issuer to determine the prospective offeree's residence. In the case of an individual, such information would include the states in which during the past few years he has lived, worked, owned or rented residential real estate, voted or been registered to vote, paid taxes, or been licensed to drive a car. Also included should be a representation from the individual as to the state of his principal residence.[71] Any questionnaire should state that it does not constitute an offer and that offers will only be made to bona fide residents of the state. The investor's status as a qualified purchaser should be reconfirmed at the time of the closing of the offering, for the rule requires that sales as well as offers can be made only to persons meeting the residency requirements.[72]

Unlike Rule 506, Rule 147 does not require that the investors be accredited or sophisticated or that they use purchaser representatives. However, suitability requirements may be imposed by state securities laws. Also unlike Rule 506, under Rule 147 there is no limitation on the number of investors who can purchase securities in the offering.

22. RULE 147—MANNER OF OFFERING

Rule 147 does not impose any specific limitations on the way in which the securities are offered. However, as pointed out previously, it is of vital importance that no offers or sales be made to nonresidents. Consequently, the manner of offering should be structured to avoid the possibility of an inadvertent offer to a nonresident.

Advertisements may be used, provided they are "appropriately limited to indicate that offers to purchase are solicited only from, and sales will be made only to, residents of the particular state involved." [73] Formal procedures as to the making of offers should be adopted, and a potential offeree's residence should be clearly established prior to making any offer to him.

Distribution of offering literature should be carefully controlled and accurate records kept. All offering literature should bear a legend to the effect that offers will be made only to bona fide residents of the applicable state.

The issuer may use a broker or dealer in making the offering. The residence of the broker or dealer would be immaterial as long as the offerees and purchasers meet the requirements of the rule.[74]

23. RULE 147—FURNISHING OF INFORMATION

Other than the disclosures mandated by paragraph (f)(3) of the rule relating to restrictions on resale of the securities, Rule 147 does not require that any information be provided to investors. However, applicable state securities laws probably require the use of an offering memorandum. In any event, in order to comply with the antifraud rules of the federal and state securities laws, the issuer would have to furnish relevant information to the investors. In most respects, the usual offering memorandum would be similar to that furnished in a private placement or registered public offering. Disclosure practices are discussed in Chapter 11.

24. RULE 147—LIMITATIONS OF RESALES; PRECAUTIONS AGAINST INTERSTATE OFFERS AND SALES

The process of distributing an issue of securities is considered to include not only the initial sales by the issuer, but also the initial trading in the securities. For the intrastate offering exemption to apply to a distribution, it is necessary that the entire issue be offered and sold to, and "come to rest" only in the hands of, residents. Resale of the securities to nonresidents by purchasers in the initial offering before the securities "come to rest" in the state would result in the loss of the exemption for the entire issue. Paragraph (e) of Rule 147 gives definition to the concept of "coming to rest" by providing that for nine months after the last sale by the issuer, any resales of the securities must be limited to residents.[75]

To assist in preserving the exemption, paragraph (f) of the rule requires that any certificate for the security bear a legend stating that the security has not been registered under the Securities Act and setting forth the limitations on resale. The issuer must also issue stop transfer instructions to any transfer agent for the securities or note its records as to the resale limitations. Written disclosure of the resale limitations, legending, and stop transfer instructions must be given in connection with any offers or sales. The issuer is also required to obtain a written representation from each purchaser as to his residence.

In the case of offerings of real estate limited partnership interests, immediate transfer of the interests is not contemplated, especially since transfer is usually restricted for tax reasons. (See discussion in Chapters 2 and 7.) Thus the resale limitations of paragraph (e) of Rule 147 should pose no problem. The information as to the resale limitations, legending, and stop transfer instructions would normally be disclosed in the offering memorandum and also in the subscription agreement executed by the investor. The investor's representation as to his residence should be in the subscription agreement as well as in his questionnaire.

25. INTRASTATE OFFERINGS NOT UNDER RULE 147

Rule 147 does not establish exclusive standards for complying with the intrastate offering exemption under Section 3(a)(11) of the Securities Act. Issuers may avail themselves of the intrastate offering exemption other than pursuant to Rule 147 [which we refer to as the "Section 3(a)(11) exemption"] by meeting the standards set forth in relevant administrative and judicial interpretations at the time of the offering. Whether exemption is sought under Rule 147 or Section 3(a)(11), it is important to remember that compliance with the intrastate offering exemption is difficult; thus the exemption should be approached cautiously.

In some respects, Rule 147 differs from prior SEC interpretations of the Section 3(a)(11) exemption. However, in other respects, the rule provides precise criteria that must be met, such as the definitions of "resident" and "doing business." In recent interpretive and no-action letters, the staff of the SEC appears to be using the standards enunciated in Rule 147 in interpreting the Section 3(a)(11) exemption. As a result, the state of the "relevant administrative and judicial interpretations" is unclear, and it would seem that issuers desiring to use the intrastate offering exemption should comply with Rule 147 because of its specificity and because its requirements probably will eventually govern Section 3(a)(11) offerings.[76]

Some of the differences between Rule 147 and the Section 3(a)(11) exemption will now be discussed.[77]

Although the Securities Act and the SEC's releases dealing with the intrastate offering exemption use the term "resident," prior to the adoption of Rule 147, the SEC interpreted that term to mean domicile,[78] which in the case of business organizations was the state where they were organized. Under Rule 147, an individual's residence is in the state where his principal residence is located, and a business organization's residence is where its principal office is located. In its interpretive letters, the staff of the SEC has not distinguished between residence for Rule 147 purposes and residence for the Section 3(a)(11) exemption.[79] However, there has been no definitive statement from the SEC about this possible change of interpretation.

The 80% test with respect to gross revenues, assets, and use of proceeds of the offering, which is set forth in the rule's definition of an issuer's "doing business within" a state, gives mathematical precision to concepts that were used in construing the Section 3(a)(11) exemption.[80] It is not clear whether the 80% test of Rule 147 represents a relaxation or a tightening of the prior standard. In 1961, the SEC required "the performance of substantial operational activities" in the state [81]; in 1974, in the release adopting Rule 147, the SEC stated that "the principal or predominant business must be carried on there." [82] On the other hand, prior to the adoption of Rule 147, it often seemed that the staff of the SEC was using 85% as the test for "doing business." This will seldom be a problem with real estate limited partnerships that hold a single property.

The precautions required by paragraph (f) of Rule 147 usually have been followed in offerings under the Section 3(a)(11) exemption to assure compliance with the exemption. Paragraph (e) of the rule provides that until nine months after the last sale by the issuer, resales by purchasers of the securities may be made only to residents. Before Rule 147, one year was used as the rule of thumb with respect to interstate resales.[83] In promulgating Rule 147, the SEC said that it determined that the nine-month period would be sufficient "for purposes of the rule." Thus it remains uncertain what the test is for purposes of the Section 3(a)(11) exemption.

As we have indicated earlier, use of the intrastate offering exemption involves a high degree of risk because an inadvertent offer or sale to one nonresident destroys the exemption for the entire offering. Thus use of the exemption should be limited to situations where the issuer feels confident of its ability to meet the exemption's requirements. As a result of the present uncertainties regarding aspects of the Section 3(a)(11) exemption, use of Rule 147 ordinarily is to be recommended in cases where the issuer determines to rely on the intrastate offering exemption.

26. INTEGRATION OF OFFERINGS

In determining whether any particular offers or sales are exempt from the registration requirements of the Securities Act of 1933, it is necessary to consider the doctrine of integration. Under this doctrine, what may appear to be a separate offering will not be so considered if it is part of a related series of offerings that constitute one larger offering. The combination or integration of the related offerings may result in one or more of them failing to comply with a claimed exemption from registration if all the offerings, considered as a whole, do not meet the requirements of the exemption. For example, a private placement of securities to nonresidents and a simultaneous widespread intrastate offering of identical securities may be integrated. The integrated offering would not satisfy the intrastate offering exemption because of the sales to nonresidents, and it would not comply with the private placement exemption because of the public nature of the sales to residents.

The doctrine of integration is not limited to any particular types of offerings or exemptions. It can be applied to combine several private placements or otherwise exempt offerings, or to combine an otherwise exempt offering with a registered offering or with an offering under Regulation A. Once it has been decided that the doctrine is applicable, the combined offering must be examined to determine whether the requirements of the Securities Act have been met. Thus application of the doctrine may result in retroactive invalidation of an otherwise proper claim of exemption.

Whether several offerings are to be integrated is a question of fact and depends essentially on whether they are related parts of an overall plan or program. The basic factors to be considered have been set forth by the SEC in its releases [84] and the notes to Rules 502(a) and 147. The factors, any one or more of which may be determinative,[85] are

1. Whether the offerings are part of a single plan of financing.[86]
2. Whether the offerings involve issuance of the same class of securities.[87]
3. Whether the offerings are made at or about the same time.[88]
4. Whether the same type of consideration is to be received.
5. Whether the offerings are made for the same general purpose.[89]

Rule 502(a) of Regulation D and Rule 147 each contain "safe harbor" provisions, which set forth circumstances under which certain offers and sales will not be integrated with an offering under one of those rules. Under these provisions, if during the six-month periods immediately preceding and immediately following an offering under Regulation D or Rule 147 there are no offers or sales of securities by or for the issuer of the same or a similar class, offers and sales prior to or after the respective periods will not be integrated with the offering under the rule.[90] If the "safe harbor" provisions are not met, the traditional integration factors would apply.

Application of the five factors mentioned previously to individual situations may vary, depending on the circumstances. However, some guidance can be inferred from interpretive and no-action letters issued by the staff of the SEC.[91]

1. It has become fairly well established, despite earlier indications to the contrary,[92] that offerings of interests in separate limited partnerships will not be integrated *solely* because there is a common general partner present in each of the partnerships [93] or *solely* because the general partners offer interests in other projects.[94]
2. Offerings that are financially interrelated are more likely to be integrated [95] than financially independent projects.[96]
3. Concurrent offerings by different limited partnerships with the same general partner will not necessarily be integrated.[97]
4. Offerings related to different projects may not involve the "same class of security" and thus may not have to be integrated.[98]

In the final analysis, whether or not several offerings should be integrated is a question of fact that must be determined in the light of all the relevant factors.

27. INSTALLMENT PAYMENTS

Many real estate limited partnership interests are paid for in installments, so that the payments coincide with the partnership's cash requirements or with the availability of tax deductions. In determining the need for registration of the interests or the availability of an exemption from registration, it has generally been considered that the sale takes place at the time the investor becomes contractually committed to purchase the interest if the investor is personally obligated to pay the installments. This is the time the investor makes his "investment decision," since thereafter he has no choice but to make the payments when due. On the other hand, if the investor is not personally liable for the payments and would only suffer a forfeiture or loss of all or part of his partnership interest for failure to pay, an "investment decision" as to whether to invest additional money would arise when each payment is made, and a "sale" would be involved.[99]

Thus the staff of the SEC has taken the position that it would not object to an assessment of limited partners for additional capital contributions without compliance with the registration requirements of the Securities Act, where the partnership agreement specifically authorized the assessment and the limited partners were personally liable.[100] The partnership told the SEC that in connection with the assessement it intended to furnish full disclosure of relevant information to the limited partners. In addition, it should be noted that in issuing no-action letters with respect to private placements that involve installment payment arrangements, the staff of the SEC has not, on its own, questioned the use of installment payments.[101]

The distinction between circumstances in which investors are personally bound and those in which they are not so obligated and must make a new investment decision has also generally been applied in cases interpreting the provisions of the securities laws forbidding fraud in connection with the sale or purchase of securities.[102]

A recent case held that installment payments for limited partnership interests were separate purchases of securities for purposes of the *antifraud* rules because the investors, though contractually committed to make the payments, had legal alternatives due to the continuing management obligations of the general partners. The court indicated that the investors could have, among other things, made the payments, sold their interests, refused to pay based on a claim of breach of the partnership agreement by the general partners, or sought dissolution of the partnership. The court considered that choosing among these alternatives was an "investment decision" and held that payment of each installment was a separate "purchase" of a security.[103] In view of this case, where payments are to be made in installments, general partners should consider obtaining notes from investors to represent the installments and furnishing investors with periodic reports disclosing relevant information, especially if there have been adverse developments.

Additional information regarding installment sales is set forth in note 72 of this chapter and in Section 4 of Chapter 9.

28. INVESTMENT COMPANY ACT

Under the Investment Company Act of 1940,[104] certain issuers engaged in investing in securities are subject to extensive regulation. From the standpoint of real estate limited partnerships, the act is of concern primarily to partnerships that invest the proceeds of the sale of their interests in income-producing securities for an extended period of time pending commitment of the funds to the acquisition of real estate [105] and so-called two-tier partnerships that invest in partnership interests issued by other real estate limited partnerships.[106] However, limited partnerships that sell their partnership interests in private placements would not ordinarily be subject to the Investment Company Act because Section 3(c) (1) of the act excludes from the definition of "investment company," and consequently from the act's coverage, "any issuer whose outstanding securities . . . are beneficially owned by not more than one hundred persons and which is not making and does not presently propose to make a public offering of its securities." [107]

A limited partnership by its very nature normally cannot meet the obligations the Investment Company Act imposes on investment companies.[108] Accordingly, partnerships that are not within the exclusion provided by Section 3(c)(1) of the act and that do not have commitments for use of their funds or are two-tier partnerships must pay attention to meeting the requirements for avoiding characterization as an investment company or for obtaining an exemption from regulation under the act.[109]

NOTES

Releases issued by the SEC are referred to by the designation given by the SEC and the date of the release. The principal SEC releases are reprinted in the Federal Securities Law Reporter (CCH). These notes do not contain specific references to the locations of SEC releases in the Federal Securities Law Reporter (CCH), because the locations can be ascertained by referring to the Release Lists division of that reporter.

The SEC's staff responds by letter to written requests for interpretive advice or for the staff's enforcement position as to proposed transactions. These interpretive ("no-action") letters, which only represent the staff's position and are not precedents binding on the SEC, are cited by the names referenced in the letters and the dates they were made available to the public. If a no-action letter has been published in the Federal Securities Law Reporter (CCH), the location therein is indicated.

1. The principal federal laws with which we will be concerned are the Securities Act of 1933, 15 U.S.C. §§77a–77aa, and the Securities Exchange Act of 1934, 15 U.S.C. §§78a–78jj. These acts will be referred to, respectively, as the "Securities Act" and the "Exchange Act," and citations will be to sections of these acts rather than to the United States Code.

2. 17 C.F.R. §230.501 ff.

3. See Secs. 12(2) and 17 of the Securities Act, Sec. 10(b) of the Exchange Act and Rule 10b-5 under the Exchange Act (17 C.F.R. §240.10b-5).

4. Sec. 2(1) of the Securities Act and Sec. 3(a)(10) of the Exchange Act. However, Rule 3all-1 under the Exchange Act (17 C.F.R. §240.3all-1) defines "equity security" to include limited partnership interests.

5. *United Housing Foundation v. Forman,* 421 U.S. 837 (1975). Absent unusual circumstances, limited partnership interests in real estate limited partnerships would be securities as a matter of law. *Goodman v. Epstein,* 582 F.2d 388 (7th Cir. 1978), cert. denied, 440 U.S. 939 (1979). But *see Frazier v. Manson,* 651 F.2d 1078 (5th Cir. 1981) (general partner owning limited partnership interests). The "profits" sought by the investors could be the tax benefits associated with losses expected to be derived from the partnership's operations. *Sharp v. Coopers & Lybrand,* 457 F. Supp. 879 (E.D. Pa. 1978), affirmed in part, 649 F.2d 175 (3d Cir. 1981). *But see Sunshine Kitchens v. Alanthus Corp.,* 403 F. Supp. 719 (S.D. Fla. 1975).

6. *S.E.C. v. M.A. Lundy Associates,* 362 F.Supp. 226 (D.R.I. 1973).

7. An investment in a general partnership could be a security if the investors were not general partners in the accepted sense and could not participate in the management of the partnership. *Williamson v. Tucker,* 645 F.2d 404 (5th Cir. 1981) The staff of the SEC took the position that interests in a general partnership were not securities where all partners had the power to participate in or to control all management decisions. The partnership agreement provided that the managing partner could be replaced by a majority vote, that unanimous consent of the partners was required to admit new partners, to sell the partnership's property, and to take certain other actions, and that majority consent of the partners was necessary for adoption of construction plans and operating procedures and for taking other specified actions. Wizard Parks, Inc., avail. December 30, 1977, FED. SEC. L. REP. (CCH) ¶81,402. *See also* Brentwood Village Apartments, Ltd., avail. July 21, 1980, FED. SEC. L. REP. (CCH) ¶76,736 (the general partner interests of the general partners of a limited partnership are not securities where the general partners are actively involved in management).

8. *See McGreghar Land Co. v. Meguiar,* 521 F.2d 822 (9th Cir. 1975); *Murphey v. Hillwood Villa Associates,* 411 F.Supp. 287 (S.D.N.Y. 1976); *Hirsch v. du Pont,* 396 F.Supp. 1214 (S.D.N.Y. 1975), *aff'd,* 533 F.2d 750, 758 (2d Cir. 1977); Securities Act Release No. 4877 (August 9, 1967).

9. 346 U.S. 119 (1953).

10. Securities Act Release No. 4552 (November 6, 1962).

11. *Lively v. Hirschfeld,* 440 F.2d 631 (10th Cir. 1971).

12. *See,* e.g., *S.E.C. v. Continental Tobacco Co.,* 463 F.2d 137 (5th Cir. 1972); Hill York Corp. v. American International Franchises, Inc., 448 F.2d 680 (5th Cir. 1971). In *Doran v. Petroleum Management Corp.,* 545 F.2d 893 (5th Cir. 1977), the court explained and limited the impact of much of the troublesome language in these cases.

13. Rule 146 (17 C.F.R. §230.146) was adopted in Securities Act Release No. 5487 (April 23, 1974), effective June 10, 1974. It was amended by Securities Act Releases No. 5585 (May 7, 1975), 5912 (March 3, 1978) and 5975 (September 8, 1978). The rule was rescinded on June 30, 1982.

14. 17 C.F.R. §230.251 ff.

15. Regulation D (17 C.F. R. §230.501 to §230.506) was adopted in Securites Act Release No. 6389 (March 8, 1982), effective April 15, 1982. The regulation is set forth in Appendix 6.

16. See the discussion in Section 9.

17. Arthur M. Bordon, Esq.; Sage Gray Todd & Sims, avail. October 6, 1978.

18. Where the intermediary would only furnish a list of prospective qualified offerees to the issuer or broker and would not have any contact with the prospective offeree, the SEC's staff stated that the solicitation would be of a character and scope different from what

was contemplated by Rule 146 and would not be permissible. Arthur M. Borden, Esquire; Sage Gray Todd & Sims, avail. September 15, 1977, Fed. Sec. L. Rep. (CCH) ¶81,344.

19. ENI Corporation, avail. December 3, 1975; Borden and Ball, avail. October 23, 1974; Damson Oil Corp., avail. July 5, 1974, Fed. Sec. L. Rep. (CCH) ¶79,916. A broker specializing in tax-sheltered investments asked the staff whether he could place a newspaper advertisement seeking "fully structured" real estate limited partnership offerings that he could sell to his customers. The staff stated that the advertisement would constitute the first step in a public offering and would not be permissible under Rule 146. Barry Geller; Econative Corporation, avail. February 27, 1978, Fed. Sec. L. Rep. (CCH) ¶81,539. Tombstone advertisements of completed offerings could constitute solicitation of investors for future offerings. Alma Securities Corp., avail. August 2, 1982.

20. Under Regulation D, a written offer for a current syndication could be mailed to 330 investors in limited partnerships sponsored by the same general partner over the prior three years. At the time of the original investment the investors were sophisticated investors under Rule 146 and met certain financial suitability standards, and the general partner did not know of any changes in any investor's qualifications. Woodtrails–Seattle, Ltd., avail. August 9, 1982.

21. It may be necessary to furnish some information to comply with the antifraud rules. Disclosure requirements and practices are discussed in Section 13 of this chapter and in Chapter 11. Under Rule 502(d)(2), if the offering is not one under Rule 504 (up to $500,000) that is being made solely in, and registered with, states that require delivery of a disclosure document to investors, there must be written disclosure to each investor, whether or not an accredited investor, that the securities have not been registered under the Securities Act and cannot be resold without registration under that act unless an exemption from registration is available.

22. *See* note 7, *supra.* A preliminary note to Regulation D states that the regulation is not available for any transaction that "although in technical compliance with these rules, is part of a plan or scheme to evade the registration provisions of the Act."

23. The release adopting Regulation D states that "in the case of a limited partnership, the sale takes place upon the issuer's acceptance of the subscription agreement or similar commitment by the investor." Winthrop Financial Co., Inc., avail. June 25, 1982, Fed. Sec.L.Rep. (CCH) ¶77,235 (for purposes of Rule 501(a)(5) the time period may be measured from the date the investor's subscription is accepted and the subscription funds are delivered to the issuer by the escrow agent, i.e., from the closing of the sale of the interests).

23a. Lola M. Hale, Esq., avail. August 2, 1982 (nonrecourse obligations need not be counted in determining whether the total purchase price exceeds 20% of the investor's net worth).
Federated Financial Corp., avail. June 14, 1982, Fed. Sec.L.Rep. (CCH) ¶77,236 (the consolidated net worth of a parent savings and loan association may be considered in determining whether its wholly-owned service corporation is an accredited investor; a savings and loan association is not a "bank" as defined for the purposes of Rule 501(a)(1)); Smith Barney, Harris Upham & Co., avail. August 13, 1982 (the aggregate net worth of the general partners of an investment general partnership may be considered in determining the net worth of the partnership where the partnership was not formed for the specific purpose of making the proposed investment).

24. But cf. Gordon Ranch Associates, avail. September 10, 1979, Fed. Sec. L. Rep. (CCH) ¶82,360 (under a similar provision in Rule 146 a limited partner's *contingent* personal liability to pay calls for additional cash capital contributions was not counted).

25. The SEC's interpretations of a similar for "cash" requirement under Rule 146(g)(2)(i)(*d*)

did not appear to be based on a consistent underlying philosophy. It is to be hoped that under Regulation D any unconditional obligation of the investor to furnish cash, whether through a letter of credit or by paying a portion of a loan to the partnership or otherwise, will be sufficient. *See* Hilliard-Lyons Barge Partners, 1979-2, avail. September 21, 1979, Fed. Sec. L. Rep. (CCH) ¶82,359 (it is permissible to allow investors a credit on their notes to the partnership for amounts they pay under their guarantees of the partnership's bank loan and for their share of partnership revenues that are applied against their notes instead of being distributed); PLM, Inc., avail. March 28, 1978, Fed. Sec. L. Rep. (CCH) ¶81,567 (payment funded by recourse loans arranged by the issuer meets the test); Robert S. Sinn Securities, Inc., avail. December 6, 1976, Fed. Sec. L. Rep. (CCH) ¶80,905 (non-recourse note not sufficient).

25a. Thomas Byrne Swartz, Esq., avail. July 12, 1982 (an employee benefit or retirement plan, including a Keogh plan or individual retirement account, is accredited if all the participants are properly accredited); Lawrence B. Rabkin, Esq., avail. August 16, 1982 (a revocable grantor trust is accredited if each grantor is properly accredited).

26. Under Rule 146 nonresident aliens were not counted. Salt Cay Beaches Ltd., avail. October 14, 1974, Fed. Sec. L. Rep. (CCH) ¶79,985. In Securities Act Release No. 6360, November 20, 1981, the SEC proposed to incorporate this no action position as a part of Regulation D. American Real Estate 82-A, avail. August 13, 1982.

27. Kenai Oil & Gas, Inc., avail. April 27, 1979 (an existing partnership seeking voluntary contributions from its existing limited partners to invest in another issuer would not count as a single purchaser where only limited partners making the contribution would share in the investment in that other issuer). A partnership to be organized to invest on a continuing basis in privately placed limited partnership interests would be considered a single purchaser when it makes its first investment if it is not formed for the specific purpose of making that investment. Henry Crown Partnership; Frederick G. Gould, Esq., avail. October 3,1977, Fed. Sec. L. Rep. (CCH) ¶81,372.

28. An investor who purchases interests in two limited partnerships whose offerings are integrated may be regarded as a single purchaser in the integrated offering and his payments to both partnerships may be aggregated to determine whether he has met the $150,000 purchaser test. Henry Exploration Company, avail. November 24, 1978.

29. Rule 504 may be used by issuers that are not partnerships, but it is not available for use by investment companies or by issuers (typically publicly held companies) that are subject to Sections 13 or 15(d) of the Exchange Act, which require the filing of periodic reports with the SEC.

30. Rule 504(b)(2)(i) refers to the "aggregate *offering* price" of the securities. Rule 501(c) defines this term as the "consideration *received*" by the issuer. Thus it is the amount of securities sold, and not the amount offered, that is the determining factor.

31. The $500,000 maximum is reduced by all sales made, during the period indicated, in reliance on any exemption under Section 3(b) of the Securities Act or in violation of the registration requirements of that act. The principal relevant exemptions under Section 3(b) are Rule 504, Rule 505, and Regulation A. Rules 240 and 242, which were re-scinded on June 30, 1982, were also adopted under Section 3(b). Rule 506 was adopted under Section 4(2) of the Securities Act. Thus, absent integration, an offering exempt under Rule 506 does not affect the $500,000 limitation under Rule 504. An offering that was intended to be, but was not, exempt under Rule 506, if not otherwise exempt, violates Section 5(a) of the Securities Act, and sales in that offering would reduce the amount that could be sold under Rule 504. If a transaction under Rule 504 fails to meet the $500,000 limitation, it does not affect the availability of the rule for the earlier transactions considered in determining whether the limitation was exceeded.

32. The release adopting Regulation D makes clear that the entire offering, and not just some of the offers and sales, must be registered with the states in which the offering is made for the restrictions to be eliminated.

33. Rule 505 may be used by any issuer that is not an investment company.

34. *See* note 31, *supra.*

35. The circumstances under which several nonaccredited investors are counted as only one purchaser are discussed in Section 8 of this chapter.

36. These conditions are discussed at greater length elsewhere in this chapter.

37. The notice required to be filed with the SEC contains an undertaking by the partnership to furnish to the SEC on request the information furnished to any nonaccredited investor.

38. A partnership subject to such disqualification could make the offering under another exemption such as Rule 506. On a showing of good cause, the SEC may, in its discretion, waive the disqualification. Rule 505(b)(2)(ii)(C).

39. The disqualifying circumstances are set forth in paragraphs (c) through (f) of Rule 252 of Regulation A, which are as follows:

(c) No exemption under Rules 251 to 264 shall be available for the securities of any issuer if such issuer, any of its predecessors, or any affiliated issuer—

(1) Has filed a registration statement which is the subject of any pending proceeding or examination under section 8 of the act, or is the subject of any refusal order or stop order thereunder within five years prior to the filing of the notification required by Rule 255;

(2) Is subject to any pending proceeding under Rule 261 or any similar rule adopted under section 3(b) of the act, or to an order entered thereunder within five years prior to the filing of such notification;

(3) Has been convicted within five years prior to the filing of such notification of any felony or misdemeanor in connection with the purchase or sale of any security or involving the making of any false filing with the Commission;

(4) Is subject to any order, judgment, or decree of any court of competent jurisdiction temporarily or preliminarily restraining or enjoining, or is subject to any order, judgment, or decree of any court of competent jurisdiction, entered within five years prior to the filing of such notification, permanently restraining or enjoining, such person from engaging in or continuing any conduct or practice in connection with the purchase or sale of any security or involving the making of any false filing with the Commission; or

(5) Is subject to a United States Postal Service false representation order entered under section 3005 of title 39, United States Code, within five years prior to the filing of the notification required by Rule 255; or is subject to a temporary restraining order or preliminary injunction entered under section 3007 of title 39, United States Code, with respect to conduct alleged to have violated section 3005 of title 39, United States Code.

This paragraph (c) of Rule 252 shall not apply to any order, judgment, or decree contemplated by paragraphs (1) through (5) hereunder because of its entry against any affiliated entity before the affiliation with the issuer arose, if the affiliated entity is not in control of the issuer and if the affiliated entity and the issuer are not under the common control of a third party who was in control of the affiliated entity at the time the order, judgment, or decree was entered against it.

(d) No exemption under Rules 251 to 264 shall be available for the securities of any issuer, if any of its directors, officers, general partners, or beneficial owners of ten per-cent or more of any class of its equity securities (beneficial ownership, meaning the power to vote or direct the vote and/or the power to dispose or direct the disposition of such securities), any of its promoters presently connected with it in any capacity, any underwriter of the securities to be offered, or any partner, director or officer of any such underwriter—

(1) Has been convicted within ten years prior to the filing of the notification required by Rule 255 of any felony or misdemeanor in connection with the purchase or sale of any security, involving the making of a false filing with the Commission, or arising out of the conduct of the business of an underwriter, broker, dealer, munici-pal securities dealer, or investment adviser;

(2) Is subject to any order, judgment, or decree of any court of competent jurisdic-tion temporarily or preliminarily enjoining or restraining, or is subject to any order, judgment, or decree of any court of competent jurisdiction, entered within five years prior to the filing of such notification, permanently enjoining or restraining such person from engaging in or continuing any conduct or practice in connection with the purchase or sale of any security or involving the making of a false filing with the Commission, or arising out of the conduct of the business of an underwriter, broker, dealer, municipal securities dealer, or investment adviser;

(3) Is subject to an order of the Commission entered pursuant to section 15(b), or 15B(a) or 15B(c) of the Securities Exchange Act of 1934; or is subject to an order of the Commission entered pursuant to section 203(e) or (f) of the Investment Advisers Act of 1940;

(4) Is suspended or expelled from membership in, or suspended or barred from association with a member of, an exchange registered as a national securities ex-change pursuant to section 6 of the Securities Exchange Act of 1934, an association registered as a national securities association under section 15A of the Securities Exchange Act of 1934, or a Canadian securities exchange or association for any act or omission to act constituting conduct inconsistent with just and equitable principles of trade; or

(5) Is subject to a United States Postal Service false representation order entered under section 3005 of title 39, United States Code, within five years prior to the filing of the notification required by Rule 255; or is subject to a restraining order or preliminary injunction entered under section 3007 of title 39, United States Code, with respect to conduct alleged to have violated section 3005 of title 39, United States Code.

(e) No exemption under Rules 251 to 264 shall be available for the securities of any issuer if any underwriter of such securities was, or was named as, an underwriter of any securities:

(1) Covered by a registration statement which is the subject of any pending pro-ceeding or examination under section 8 of the act, or is the subject of any refusal order or stop order entered thereunder within five years prior to the filing of the notification required by Rule 255; or

(2) Covered by any filing which is subject to any pending proceeding under Rule

261 or any similar rule adopted under section 3(b) of the act, or to an order entered thereunder within five years prior to the filing of such notification.

(f) No exemption under Rules 251 to 264 shall be available for the securities of an issuer which is subject to the requirements of sections 13, 14, 15(d) of the Securities Exchange Act of 1934, unless such issuer has filed all reports required by those sections to be filed during the 12 calendar months preceding the filing of the notification required by Rule 255 (or for such shorter period that the issuer was required to file such reports).

40. Under the rules applicable to securities brokers, if a broker recommends the purchase of a security to a customer, he must have reasonable grounds to believe that the recommendation is suitable based on information furnished by the customer.

41. Rule 501(e) specifies the circumstances under which several nonaccredited investors may be counted as only one purchaser. See the discussion in Section 8 of this chapter.

42. Pension and Investment Associates of America, Inc., avail. November 14, 1977, FED. SEC. L. REP. (CCH) ¶81,405.

43. Fees to be paid by the issuer or its affiliates to investors' advisers who are not purchaser representatives or to finders who refer investors to the issuer should be disclosed. *See* SEC Litigation Release No. 5145 (August 26, 1971). *See also* Securities Act Release No. 5841 (July 5, 1977).

44. 292 SEC. REG. & L. REP. (BNA) at A-8 (March 5, 1975) (Rule 146).

45. The requirements of applicable state security laws should also be considered. *See* discussion, Chapter 10 of this book.

46. Winstead, McGuire, Sechrest, and Trimble, avail. March 25, 1975.

47. 15 U.S.C. §§80b-1 to 80b-21.

48. Section 202(a)(11) of the Investment Advisers Act of 1940 defines the term "investment adviser" as follows: "(11) 'Investment adviser' means any person who, for compensation, engages in the business of advising others, either directly or through publications or writings, as to the value of securities or as to the advisability of investing in, purchasing, or selling securities, or who, for compensation and as part of a regular business, issues or promulgates analyses or reports concerning securities; but does not include . . . (B) any lawyer, accountant, engineer, or teacher whose performance of such services is solely incidental to the practice of his profession . . . [and several others]."

The requirement of registering is set forth in Section 203 of the Investment Advisers Act. Section 203(b) exempts the following investment advisers from the registration requirements: "(1) any investment adviser all of whose clients are residents of the State within which such investment adviser maintains his or its principal office and place of business, and who does not furnish advice or issue analyses or reports with respect to securities listed or admitted to unlisted trading privileges on any national securities exchange; (2) any investment adviser whose only clients are insurance companies; or (3) any investment adviser who during the course of the preceding twelve months has had fewer than fifteen clients and who neither holds himself out generally to the public as an investment adviser nor acts as an investment adviser to any investment company registered under [the Investment Company Act of 1940]."

An investment adviser who is exempt from the registration provisions would still be subject to certain other provisions of the statute, including the antifraud provisions of Section 206.

49. Hydrocarbon Resources, Ltd., avail. February 29, 1975; Epsilon Lambda Electronics Corporation, avail. October 11, 1974. In Winstead, McGuire, Sechrist, & Tremble, avail. February 21, 1975, FED. SEC. L. REP. (CCH) ¶80,131, the staff of the SEC took the

position that inclusion of a law firm on a list of offeree representatives for use by potential investors would constitute engaging in the business of rendering investment advice and that, based on the information presented, the firm's activities as an offeree representative would not be considered solely incidental to its practice of the legal profession. See also Thrailkill & Goodman, P.C., avail. July 16, 1982 and Investment Advisers Act Release No. 770 (August 13, 1981).

50. A registration statement normally consists of a facing sheet (i.e., cover page); the prospectus that is given to investors and that constitutes Part I of the registration statement; Part II, which contains additional information, and various undertakings, signatures, consents of experts, financial statements, and exhibits.

51. Under Rule 146, the "access" of the investor to the required information eliminated the requirement that such information be furnished by the issuer. Under that rule, "access" could exist only by reason of the investor's position with respect to the issuer, and "position" meant an employment or family relationship or economic bargaining power that enabled the investor to obtain information from the issuer in order to evaluate the merits and risks of the prospective investment. Access, as so defined, does not normally exist in the usual private placement of real estate limited partnership interests under Rule 506. The concept of access was not carried forward from Rule 146 to Regulation D.

52. If the sales price of the interests to be offered does not exceed $5,000,000, it is sufficient for the partnership to furnish the information required in Part I of Form S-18, a general registration form for use in certain public offerings of $5,000,000 or less. For offerings in excess of $5,000,000, in the case of real estate limited partnership interests, the registration statement form ordinarily would be Form S-11. Form S-11 is for use by real estate investment trusts and by issuers whose business is primarily acquiring and holding real estate or interests therein for investment. A partnership that intends to make its profits from the purchase and sale of real estate would use Form S-1, a basic form used when no other form is authorized or prescribed.

52a. "Thus, in determining what disclosure is appropriate for an offering in reliance on Regulation D, an issuer should first determine what disclosure would generally be deemed appropriate if the issuer intended to register the proposed offer and sale of securities. Next, the issuer should evaluate that disclosure in terms of its materiality to the investors' understanding of the issuer, its business and the securities being offered." Hopper, Kanouff, Smith & Peryam, avail. October 11, 1982.

53. Financial information as to properties acquired or to be acquired by the partnership may be required in addition to financial information regarding the partnership. Rule 3-14 of Regulation S-X (17 C.F.R. §210.3-14). The financial schedules that would be part of the registration statement but not part of the prospectus need not be furnished.

53a. "Item 601 [of Regulation S-K] requires that the issuer furnish, among other exhibits, an opinion of counsel as to the legality of the securities being issued. Thus, under Rule 502(b)(2)(iii) an issuer in a Regulation D offering should identify the contents of this opinion of counsel and make it available to purchasers upon written request. Item 601 of Regulation S-K also sets forth certain requirements for an opinion of counsel as to tax matters. In a registration statement for a limited partnership, it is generally the case that tax consequences of an investment are material and thus are discussed in the prospectus. . . . If the issuer makes the determination that these tax consequences will be discussed in the Regulation D disclosure document, then Rule 502(b)(2)(iii) requires the issuer to identify and make available to investors the supporting opinion of counsel." Hopper, Kanouff, Smith & Peryam, avail. October 11, 1982.

53b. Securities Act Release No. 6384 (March 3, 1982).

54. The rule requires the issuer to provide additional information only to the extent that it

possesses the information or can acquire it without unreasonable effort or expense.

54a. Filing of a notice is required within 30 days after the last sale of securities. Sometimes offerings are continued after an initial sale of a minimum number of interests. If no additional interests are sold, the "last sale" will have occurred at the time of the initial closing. Thus consideration should be given to filing a notice after the initial closing to cover the possibility that after 30 days have passed the offering may be terminated without any more interests being sold.

55. In Securities Act Release No. 5913 (March 6, 1978), the SEC contrasted the "broad statutory exemption with the narrower criteria of Rule 146," and discussed at length two court decisions involving the availability of the private placement exemption other than pursuant to Rule 146. The cases were *Woolf v. S. D. Cohn & Co.*, 515 F.2d 591 (5th Cir. 1975), rehearing denied, 521 F.2d 225 (5th Cir. 1975), vacated on other grounds, 426 U.S. 944 (1976); and *Doran v. Petroleum Management Corp.*, 545 F.2d 893 (5th Cir. 1977). In each instance, the court made reference to Rule 146 in construing the Section 4(2) exemption. The SEC, in its release, pointed out that in each of the cases the court clearly recognized the nonexclusive nature of Rule 146.

56. A restatement of the status of the Section 4(2) exemption is set forth in "Section 4(2) and Statutory Law," 31 Bus. Law. 485 (1975). See also Schneider, "The Statutory Law of Private Placements," 14 Rev. Sec. Reg. 869 (1981). The Section 4(2) exemption is the subject of Securities Act Release No. 4552 (November 6, 1962). Also relevant is the discussion in Securities Act Release No. 5487 (April 23, 1974), which promulgated Rule 146.

57. 346 U.S. 119, 125 (1953). In Securities Act Release No. 4552 (November 6, 1962), the SEC stated that "it should be emphasized, therefore, that the number of persons to whom the offering is extended is relevant only to the question whether they have the requisite association with and knowledge of the issuer which make the exemption available."

58. The doctrine of integration of offerings discussed in Section 26 of this chapter would be applicable in determining the number of offerees as well as the other requirements of the Section 4(2) exemption.

59. In some instances, a close relationship with the issuer or its principals is considered sufficient to qualify an offeree.

60. *Doran v. Petroleum Management Corp.*, 545 F.2d 893 (5th Cir. 1977); Lawler v. Gilliam, 569 F.2d 1283 (4th Cir. 1978) (buyer did not have access to, and was not furnished with, appropriate information).

61. *See* Securities Act Release No. 5121 (December 30, 1970); Securities Act Release No. 5226 (January 10, 1972). An investor who acquires securities from an issuer intending to "distribute" them would be an "underwriter" as defined in Sec. 2(11) of the Securities Act.

62. Securities Act Release No. 5450 (January 7, 1974); Securities Act Release No. 4434 (December 6, 1961).

63. Rule 147 (17 C.F.R. §230.147) was adopted in Securities Act Release No. 5450 (January 7, 1974), effective March 1, 1974. The text of the rule is set forth in Appendix 8.

64. Alaska Commercial Company, avail. February 9, 1981, Fed. Sec. L. Rep. (CCH) ¶76,820 (out-of-state administrative and expediting office used by 10% of the issuer's employees held to be the issuer's principal office).

65. Constellation Holding Company, avail. July 19, 1978, Fed. Sec. L. Rep. (CCH) ¶81,725 (use of proceeds of an offering to acquire an out-of-state insurance company, which would then become licensed in-state and limit its business to in-state activities, does not meet the "doing business within" test of Rule 147).

66. Securities Act Release No. 5450 (January 7, 1974) ("The rule also provides that an individual who is deemed an issuer, e.g., a promoter issuing preincorporation certificates, will be deemed a resident if his principal residence is in the state or territory."); Helmet Petroleum Corp., avail. August 18, 1975 ("When the partnerships are unformed at the time of offerings, as Helmet's public partnership appears to be, the general partner may be considered the issuer of preformation interests."); JIC Drilling Companies, avail. September 23, 1976, FED. SEC. L. REP. (CCH) ¶80,765; Bernard E. Schneider, Esq./Virtue & Scheck, avail. October 15, 1976; R. Edmund McMullan, avail. October 15, 1976, FED. SEC. L. REP. (CCH) ¶80,799.

67. Landura Corp. of North Carolina, avail. February 6, 1975. A capital contribution to the limited partnership by a nonresident general partner should not affect the exemption; the general partner will manage the partnership and, accordingly, his general partnership interest will not be a "security." Louisiana Motor Inns, avail. June 22, 1972, FED. SEC. L. REP. (CCH) ¶78,902; and *see* Section 2 of this chapter. *But see* Boetel & Co., avail. December 18, 1972, FED. SEC. L. REP. (CCH) ¶78,343, which on analysis of the request for a no-action position seems to be based on the integration of offerings to be made in several states because of their constituting one plan of financing.

68. Palm Resaca Corp., avail. September 24, 1979 (seasonal residence in a mobile home park is not sufficient); Minnesota Cablesystems—Southwest, avail. April 20, 1981, FED. SEC. L. REP. (CCH) ¶76,845 (an offeree's unconsummated intent to move his principal residence is immaterial).

69. A nonresident trustee for resident beneficiaries may acquire securities if the trustee has a purely custodial role and the securities will not be distributed to anyone other than the resident beneficiaries. University Real Estate Partnership V, avail. March 7, 1978, FED. SEC. L. REP. (CCH) ¶81,553 (Keogh plan); Fair Valley Properties No. 2, avail. May 4, 1981, FED. SEC. L. REP. (CCH) ¶77,003 (individual retirement account).

70. North American Investments, avail. March 17, 1980, FED. SEC. L. REP. (CCH) ¶76,366. Cf. Henry Crown Partnership; Frederick G. Gould, Esq., avail. October 3, 1977, FED. SEC. L. REP. (CCH) ¶81,372 (Rule 146), discussed in note 27, *supra.*

71. This would satisfy the requirement of paragraph (f)(1)(iii) of the rule that the issuer obtain such a representation. An individual may have more than one residence. For Rule 147 purposes, it is the individual's principal residence that is important. *See* United Educators, Inc., avail. November 19, 1976.

72. If the investor is to pay for his security in installments, he must be a resident at the time each installment is paid. Opportunities Investment Associates of New London, Connecticut, avail. July 14, 1978, FED. SEC. L. REP. (CCH) ¶81,738; 4 Loss, Securities Regulation 2603 (Supp. 1969).

73. Securities Act Release No. 4434 (December 6, 1961); Palmer & Dodge, avail. September 11, 1975; Quail Corporation, avail. January 11, 1979 (direct mail solicitation may be used if the envelope is marked to restrict forwarding outside the state and the sales literature limits the offering to residents).

74. Securities Act Release No. 4434 (December 6, 1961); Eastern Illinois Telephone Corp., avail. April 14, 1975, FED. SEC. L. REP. (CCH) ¶80,238; Wortman & Mann, Inc., avail. December 26, 1974.

75. The staff of the SEC has expressed the view that the nine-month period does not begin to run until full payment for the securities has been made. Occidental Industries, Ltd., avail. December 20, 1976, FED. SEC. L. REP. (CCH) ¶80,882.

76. But *see* Midwest Management Corp. v. Stephens, FED. SEC. L. REP. (CCH). ¶97,608 (Iowa 1980) ["the [SEC] rulings in which issuers are denied Rule 147 status has less significance in terms of the scope of Section 3(a)(11)"].

77. Prior to the adoption of Rule 147, the basic SEC release dealing with the intrastate offering exemption was Securities Act Release No. 4434 (December 6, 1961). *See also* McCauley, "Intrastate Securities Transactions under the Federal Securities Act." 107 U. PA. L. REV. 937 (1959).

78. Securities Act Release No. 5349 (January 8, 1973).

79. United Educators, Inc., avail. November 19, 1976 ("the teacher is a resident of the State of Massachusetts and . . . Massachusetts is her 'principal residence' for purposes of Rule 147 (d)(2) and Section 3(a)(11) of the Act."); Opportunities Investment Associates of New London, Connecticut, avail. July 14, 1978, FED. SEC. L. REP. (CCH) ¶81,738 (must be a "bona fide resident" for Section 3(a)(11) or Rule 147).

80. *Chapman v. Dunn,* 414 F.2d 153 (6th Cir. 1969); *S.E.C. v. Truckee Showboat, Inc.,* 157 F. Supp. 824 (S.D. Cal. 1957); Grubin, Horth & Lawless, Properties, avail. March 11, 1971 (75% not enough); Parkdale Plaza Shopping Center, Ltd., avail. March 22, 1971; International Housing, Inc., avail. April 30, 1971.

81. Securities Act Release No. 4434 (December 6, 1961).

82. Securities Act Release No. 5450 (January 7, 1974).

83. *See* Brooklyn Manhattan Transit Corp., 1 S.E.C. 147 (1935); Securities Act Release No. 1459 (May 29, 1937).

84. Securities Act Release No. 4434 (December 6, 1961); Securities Act Release No. 4552 (November 6, 1962). *See* Wigder, "Integration," 10 REV. SEC. REG. 933 (1977); "Integration of Partnership Offerings: A Proposal for Identifying a Discrete Offering," 37 Bus. Law. 1591 (1982).

85. It would appear, however, that the first and fifth factors are of greater importance than the others.

86. *S.E.C. v. Murphy,* 626 F.2d 633 (9th Cir. 1980) (each offering was part of an overall plan for financing the promoter's business). In *S.E.C. v. Freeman,* FED. SEC. L. REP. (CCH) ¶96,361 (N.D. Ill. 1978), and Union Home Loans/Union Financial Corporation, avail. July 3, 1978, FED. SEC. L. REP. (CCH) ¶81,726, separate corporate issuers in different states were treated as a single business enterprise with the result that the intrastate offering exemption was not available. Offerings of separate issuers may be considered to be part of a single plan of financing if the issuers' business operations are related. Commercial Credit Co., avail. December 6, 1971, FED. SEC. L. REP. (CCH) ¶78,544; JIC Drilling Co., avail. September 23, 1976, FED. SEC. L. REP. (CCH) ¶80,765; Liberty Loan Corp., avail. December 26, 1974; Amtex Oil & Gas, Inc., avail. April 13, 1978. *See also* SEC Litigation Release No. 7423 (June 1, 1976) and SEC Litigation Release No. 5365 (March 30, 1972).

87. SBT Corp., avail. January 19, 1981.

88. In Securities Act Release No. 5450 (January 7, 1974), which promulgated Rule 147, the SEC stated that "the Commission generally has deemed intrastate offerings to be 'integrated' with those registered or private offerings of the same class of securities made by the issuer at or about the same time."

89. De Lorean Motor Co., avail. September 15, 1977 (private placement of common stock not integrated with registered public offering of common stock).

90. Rule 147 only refers to excluding offers and sales "pursuant to the exemptions provided by Section 3 or Section 4(2) of the Act or pursuant to a registration statement filed under the Act." Thus offers and sales in violation of the Securities Act's registration provisions would not be covered by the safe harbor provisions, and the traditional integration factors would apply. Topeka Chamber Industrial Development Corporation, avail. November 24, 1980, FED. SEC. L. REP. (CCH) ¶76,763.

91. The staff of the SEC no longer issues no-action letters concerning integration. Clover Financial Corporation, avail. April 5, 1979, FED. SEC. L. REP. (CCH) ¶82,091 ("it is our position that counsel, with guidance of Release No. 33-4552, should make a determination as to whether or not particular offerings should be integrated"); Securities Act Release No. 6253 (October 28, 1980).

92. *See* Rifkind & Borton, "SEC Registration of Real Estate Interests: An Overview," 27 BUS. LAW. 649 (1972). In Securities Act Release No. 4552 the SEC had stated: "Thus, in the case of offerings of fractional undivided interests in separate oil or gas properties where the promoters must constantly find new participants for each new venture, it would appear to be appropriate to consider the entire series of offerings to determine the scope of this solicitation."

93. Dogwood Farm, Inc., avail. September 1, 1975 (race horses); Grubb and Ellis Development Co., avail. July 23, 1973 (affiliated general partners); Systech Financial Corp. avail. July 23, 1973 (concurrent offerings); Kassuba Development Corp., avail. May 28, 1973; Calprop Corp., avail. October 1, 1971. *But see* Securities Act Release No. 6389 (March 8, 1982) ("Predecessor and affiliate relationships would be relevant to any consideration of whether prior offerings should be integrated with a proposed offering under Regulation D").

94. Safeguard Mini Storage, avail. October 7, 1974. However, the limited partnership interests in the various partnerships should not be marketed in a manner that indicates that, from the investor's standpoint, the interests are fungible. *See* SEC Litigation Release No. 5365 (March 30, 1972); Exchange Act Release No. 16749 (April 16, 1980); Exchange Act Release No. 17274 (November 6, 1980).

95. *S.E.C. v. Murphy,* 626 F.2d 633 (9th Cir. 1980); Thomas H. Chambers, avail. June 28, 1976, FED. SEC. L. REP. (CCH) ¶80,618; May Petroleum, Inc. avail. August 28, 1974 (co-owner relationship in oil and gas leases).

96. Kaiser Aetna, avail. September 19, 1973 ("separate offerings to separate limited partnerships at different times with respect to separate projects on separate locations would not be integrated provided that the projects offered and sold are not financially interdependent"); National Association of Home Builders, avail. March 23, 1972 ("Separate offerings to limited groups at separate times to finance successive portions of a project, or projects in close proximity, built from time to time as market demand is tested and proven would not be integrated provided the projects are not financially interdependent"); Canon Club Company, avail. June 26, 1978; Vance C. Miller, Jr., avail. March 23, 1979.

In Tele-Tower, Inc., avail. February 27, 1978, FED. SEC. L. REP. (CCH) ¶81,540, a company proposed to form a series of limited partnerships, with common or affiliated general partners, to finance construction of sales promotion booths in shopping centers. Each partnership would own a separate booth in a different shopping center. The staff was of the view that offerings by the partnerships under Rule 146 would not have to be integrated as long as "(1) there is no general pool of offerees from which participants in the various limited partnerships are drawn and (2) each limited partnership is truly separate and distinct and not a part of a single plan of financing for all of the Golden Towers."

97. Stratford Employees' Cattle Program, Ltd., avail. April 8, 1974, FED. SEC. L. REP. (CCH) ¶79,761; Systech Financial Corp., avail. July 23, 1973. Compare De Lorean Motor Co., avail. December 30, 1977.

98. Guardian Oil Co., avail. June 19, 1975.

99. *S.E.C. v. American Founders Life Insurance Co.,* FED. SEC. L. REP. (CCH) ¶90,861 (D. Colo. 1958) (intrastate offering); Stephenson v. Calpine Conifers II, Ltd., 652 F.2d 808 (9th Cir. 1981).

100. Tejon Agricultural Partners, avail. April 12, 1974. Counsel for the partnership was of the opinion that levying the assessment did not involve a new offer or sale of a security, since no new investment decision would be made and the limited partners had no choice as to whether to pay the assessment, and that Rule 136 under the Securities Act (17 C.F.R. §230.136) was inapplicable, since by its terms it applies only to assessable corporate stock and was designed to cure specific abuses not present.

101. *See,* e.g., Cotton Lane 660, Ltd., avail. December 8, 1978 (installment payments over a period of 22 years).

102. *See,* e.g., *Fershtman v. Schectman,* 450 F.2d 1357 (2d Cir. 1971), cert. denied, 405 U.S. 1066 (1972); *Ryan v. J. Walter Thompson Co.,* 453 F.2d 444 (2d Cir. 1971), cert. denied, 406 U.S. 907 (1972); *Radiation Dynamics, Inc. v. Goldmuntz,* 464 F.2d 876 (2d Cir. 1972); *St. Louis Union Trust Co. v. Merrill Lynch, Pierce, Fenner & Smith, Inc.,* 562 F.2d 1040 (8th Cir. 1977), cert. denied, 435 U.S. 925 (1978); *The Toledo Trust Co. v. Nye,* 588 F.2d 202 (6th Cir. 1978); *S.E.C. v. American Founders Life Insurance Co.,* FED. SEC. L. REP. (CCH) ¶90,861 (D. Colo. 1958); *U.S. v. Kormel, Inc.* 230 F.Supp. 275 (D. Nev. 1964); *Ingenito v. Bermec Corp.,* 376 F.Supp. 1154, 1183 (S.D.N.Y. 1974); *Goodman v. Poland,* 395 F.Supp. 660 (D. Md. 1975); *Villada v. Merrill Lynch, Pierce, Fenner & Smith, Inc.,* 460 F.Supp. 1149 (S.D.N.Y. 1978).

103. *Goodman v. Epstein,* 582 F.2d 388 (7th Cir. 1978), cert. denied, 440 U.S. 939 (1979). *See also Ayres v. Merrill Lynch, Pierce, Fenner & Smith, Inc.,* 538 F.2d 532 (3d Cir. 1976), cert. denied, 429 U.S. 1010 (1976) (semble).

104. 15 U.S.C. §§80a-1 to 80a-52.

105. American Realty Fund, avail. April 30, 1972. Rule 3a-2 under the Investment Company Act (17 C.F.R. §270.3a-2) provides relief for certain so-called transient investment companies temporarily investing their funds.

106. Investment Company Act Release No. 8456 (August 9, 1974); cf. Urban Land Investments, Inc., avail. November 4, 1971, FED. SEC. L. REP. (CCH) §78,533.

107. The doctrine of integration is relevant in determining whether the exclusion is applicable. L. Marvin Moorehead, avail. July 4, 1975; William E. Hart, avail. May 6, 1979, FED. SEC. L. REP. (CCH) ¶82,106. "Public offering" in Section 3(c)(1) of the Investment Company Act has the same meaning as under Section 4(2) of the Securities Act, and Rule 506 of Regulation D would be applicable. Securities Act Release No. 6389 (March 8, 1982)(note 33); Duval Management, Inc., avail. June 1, 1982; Continental Bank, avail. September 2, 1982, FED. SEC. L. REP. (CCH) ¶77,248.

108. Brian A. Pecker, avail. October 3, 1974, FED. SEC. L. REP. (CCH) ¶79,997; Alpha-Delta Fund, avail. August 28, 1975, FED. SEC. L. REP. (CCH) ¶80,295.

109. Consideration of these matters is beyond the scope of this book. For additional information, *see* Report of the Real Estate Advisory Committee to the SEC, pp. 50–54 (U.S. Gov't Printing Office, Washington, D.C., 1972); Cohen & Hacker, "Applicability of the Investment Company Act of 1940 to Real Estate Syndications," 36 OHIO ST. L.J. 482 (1975). If the partnership invests in securities, the general partner may be an investment adviser subject to the Investment Advisers Act of 1940, 15 U.S.C. §§80b-1 to 80b-21. *See Abrahamson v. Fleschner,* 568 F.2d 862 (2d Cir. 1977), cert. denied, 436 U.S. 905, 913 (1978); Hydrocarbon Resources Ltd., avail. February 29, 1975; Ruth Levine, avail. December 15, 1976.

CHAPTER 9

REGULATION OF THE SELLERS OF REAL ESTATE LIMITED PARTNERSHIP INTERESTS

1. GENERAL

Persons who are involved in the selling of real estate limited partnership interests may come within the scope of the definitions of "broker" and "dealer" in the Securities Exchange Act of 1934 (the "Exchange Act") and state securities laws. As a result, they may be subject to federal and state regulation. Under the Exchange Act, brokers and dealers must register with the SEC unless they meet the requirements of certain limited exemptions from registration. Most states require the registration of the brokers, dealers, and securities salesmen operating within their jurisdictions. Even if exempt from registering, brokers and dealers may still be subject to regulation, for federal and some state laws contain provisions applicable to unregistered brokers and dealers as well as to registered ones.

Under the Exchange Act, the fact that the securities being sold are exempt from registration under the Securities Act of 1933 (the "Securities Act") is immaterial in determining whether the seller of the securities is a broker or dealer required to register with the SEC, since the intent of the statute is to regulate persons engaged in the securities business.

Federal registration is accomplished by filing an application for registration and additional financial and operational information with the SEC. The registration becomes effective automatically 45 days after filing unless the SEC on request accelerates effectiveness to an earlier date or takes action to delay or prevent effectiveness. Registration under state laws is generally similar.[1]

Once registered, brokers and dealers are subject to substantial federal and state regulation, including net capital, record keeping, and reporting requirements.

Federally registered broker–dealers either join the National Association of Securities Dealers (NASD) or are so-called SECO (SEC only) broker–dealers.[2] In either case, the broker–dealer is subject to extensive rules regulating the conduct of its business and trade practices. Further, its securities personnel and principals must pass examinations as to their knowledge of the securities business and be registered or the subject of a filing with the NASD or the SEC and appropriate state securities commissions.

2. WHO ARE BROKERS AND DEALERS?

As indicated previously, characterization of a seller of securities as a broker or dealer will subject the seller to various forms of regulation, which may include the requirement of registering with the SEC and appropriate state agencies. What are the statutory definitions of the terms "broker" and "dealer" and their application to real estate limited partnerships that sell their securities directly to investors without employing registered broker–dealers to do the selling?

Sections 3(a) (4) and 3 (a) (5) of the Exchange Act define "broker" and "dealer" as follows:

(4) The term "broker" means any person engaged in the business of effecting transactions in securities for the account of others, but does not include a bank.

(5) The term "dealer" means any person engaged in the business of buying and selling securities for his own account, through a broker or otherwise, but does not include a bank, or any person insofar as he buys or sells securities for his own account, either individually or in some fiduciary capacity, but not as a part of a regular business.

These definitions apply to persons whose business involves the purchase or sale of securities, whether or not the securities are registered under the Securities Act or exempt from registration under that act. Thus the fact that a person sells limited partnership interests only in private placements [3] or other limited offerings or intrastate offerings would not of itself result in his not being a broker or dealer.

In selling its real estate limited partnership interests, the partnership may retain independent securities firms or sales personnel to do the selling. It may also seek to sell the interests through its employees, general partners, promoters, or syndicators and their officers, directors, and employees, without the use of or in addition to the use of independent sellers. If firms or persons having no relationship with the partnership other than the sale of its securities are retained to sell the securities, in all likelihood they would be brokers or dealers, either by buying the securities for their own account and reselling to investors or by making sales for the partnership's account on a best efforts basis.[4] It is quite common to see interests in a private real estate limited partnership being sold by an unrelated "sales agent" on a best efforts basis. In almost all such situations, the "sales agent" is a "broker."

What if the partnership and its general partners, promoters, syndicators, and their respective employees, officers, and directors "sell" the limited partnership interests?

If the securities activities of the partnership are limited to selling its own limited partnership interests, the partnership would not be a dealer, since the definition requires that a dealer be in the business of both buying and selling. It should be noted that to be a dealer it is not necessary that the securities be those of another issuer. If the partnership otherwise comes within the definition of dealer, it is a dealer even though the only securities it buys and sells are the limited partnership interests it has issued.[5]

Unlike the definition of "dealer," the definition of "broker" does not require both buying and selling transactions. However, since the partnership would be selling only its own limited partnership interests, it would not be effecting transactions "for the account of others" and would not be a "broker."

Persons related to the partnership who sell on behalf of the partnership normally do not purchase the partnership's securities for their own account and then resell them.[6] Rather, the sellers act on behalf of the partnership. Accordingly, unless the sellers are otherwise engaged in the business of buying and selling securities for their own account, they would not come within the definition of "dealer."

As noted previously, the partnership normally would not be a broker or dealer,[7] and the persons selling the interests for the partnership would not be dealers if their securities activities were restricted to the sale of limited partnership interests for the partnership. Since, as an entity, the partnership can act only through others, such as its general partners and employees, and a corporate general partner can act only through its directors, officers, and employees, our basic question becomes whether persons related to the partnership are "brokers" if they sell partnership interests on behalf of the partnership. In answering this question, the key elements of the definition of "broker" are being "engaged in the business" and effecting securities transactions "for the account of others." Whether the seller is "engaged in business" is primarily related to the recurrence and regularity of his securities dealings. Whether his activities in selling the partnership interests should be deemed to be merely actions by the partnership for its own account is based on the seller's overall relationship to the partnership.

These determinations are questions of fact and will depend on all the facts and circumstances involved in any particular situation. It is not necessary that the seller's only or principal business be the securities business. The presence of a principal-agent (respondeat superior) relationship under the law of agency is not in itself sufficient to ensure that, under the definition of "broker," the seller's acts will be treated as the partnership's acts.[8]

The no-action letters issued by the staff of the SEC indicate that there are seven basic, though somewhat overlapping, conditions which should be met for the seller to avoid characterization as a broker.[9] These are [10]

1. The seller's compensation must not be based directly or indirectly on his success in selling the limited partnership interests.[11]

2. If there is compensation other than partnership distributions, the seller's employer must withhold social security and income taxes from the seller's compensation and must pay any unemployment taxes.

3. The seller must not have had any significant background in the securities business.[12]

4. The seller's employment must have commenced prior to the offering (or be unrelated to selling of the interests) and must continue after the offering.[13]

5. The seller must not have been hired specifically to sell securities.[14]

6. The seller must perform substantial services unrelated to selling the interests and must not devote a significant portion of his time to selling the interests; his sales efforts must be merely incidental to his regular duties.[15]

7. The seller must not have been or intend to be involved in recurring offerings.[16]

The failure to comply with any one of these conditions may result in a determination that the seller is a broker. Although on occasion the staff of the SEC has granted no-action requests where not all the conditions have been met,[17] the trend has been to require compliance with all the conditions.[18]

A person can be a broker even though he does not contact investors but directs his selling efforts at registered broker–dealers. Thus so-called wholesalers who promote an offering with broker–dealers and receive compensation based on sales by the broker–dealers may themselves be brokers.[19] However, there should be no problem if this is done by general partners or their regular officers and employees without additional compensation.[20] If the issuer's personnel supervise the selling activities of broker–dealers, they may be required to register as broker–dealers.[21] Without being "brokers," the issuer's personnel may participate in seminars sponsored by the broker–dealer selling the interests and give information about the partnership and the real estate if the selling efforts are made only by registered representatives of the broker–dealer and the issuer's personnel do not receive compensation based on sales of the interests.[22] If the interests are sold jointly by a registered broker–dealer and an employee of the partnership, the broker–dealer is required to have the sole responsibility for their sale and to supervise all persons participating in the sale of the interests.[23]

3. EXEMPTIONS FROM REGISTRATION

Once it has been determined that a person is a broker or a dealer, it is necessary to consider whether registration with the SEC or any state securities commission is required.

Section 15(a) of the Exchange Act provides, generally, that it is unlawful for an unregistered broker or dealer to do interstate business or use the mails to sell securities unless the SEC provides an exemption.[24]

Most of the exemptions adopted by the SEC are not relevant for persons who sell interests in real estate limited partnerships, and elimination of use of the mails or means of interstate commerce to avoid registration is a practical impossibility. Thus the only viable exemption from registration is for broker–dealers "whose business is exclusively intrastate."

The intrastate exemption from broker–dealer registration is extremely narrow and of very limited application. For the exemption to be available, all the broker–dealer's business must be transacted within the state of his residence.[25] Once the broker–dealer engages in an interstate securities business, he may not thereafter claim the exemption by limiting his activities to intrastate transactions.[26] Both the buying side and the selling side of each transaction must be with residents of the broker–dealer's state, and the broker–dealer may not effect transactions, or otherwise do business, for or with nonresidents, whether they are investors, other broker–dealers, or issuers.[27] The broker–dealer cannot, as agent, represent an out-of-state principal even if the transaction is consummated with a customer in the broker–dealer's own state, and he cannot participate in any transaction executed on a securities exchange wherever located, even in his own state. He cannot advertise in newspapers or other publications distributed outside his state unless the advertisement makes clear that he is doing an exclusively intrastate business and can act only for or with a person within his state in a wholly intrastate transaction.

In determining the residence of the broker–dealer and his customers, the staff of the SEC looks to the standards developed under Section 3(a) (11) of the Securities Act for intrastate offerings of securities and applies the provisions of Rule 147 under the Securities Act. This is discussed in Chapter 8 of this book.

Thus, if an intrastate broker–dealer wishes to sell interests for a limited partnership, the partnership must be a resident of and doing business within the state of the broker–dealer's residence and the customers of the broker–dealer must be residents of that state within the requirements of Rule 147.[28]

It must be remembered that exemption of a broker–dealer from the registration provisions of the Exchange Act does not exempt him from all the requirements and regulations imposed on broker–dealers by that act. For example, the margin requirements of Section 7 and the net capital requirements of Section 15 of the Exchange Act apply to all broker–dealers whether or not registered, while the record-keeping and reporting provisions of Section 17 apply only to registered broker–dealers.

The failure of a broker–dealer to register when required to do so may subject him to administrative or civil action by the SEC, criminal proceedings, and suits for damages or rescission by the purchasers of securities.

4. REGULATION OF INSTALLMENT PAYMENT ARRANGEMENTS

Many real estate limited partnership interests are paid for in installments, usually in order to time the tax deductions and the investments so that at least a $1 deduction will be available in each year that a $1 investment is made.

Sections 7 and 11(d) of the Exchange Act place limitations on the ability of broker–dealers to extend or maintain, or arrange for the extension or maintenance of, credit for customers in connection with securities transactions.[29] These provisions are relevant to the sale of real estate limited partnership interests that are paid for in installments or by notes, because the deferred payment structure is considered to be an extension of credit and the sale by a broker–dealer of such interests is considered to be the arrangement by the broker–dealer for the extension of credit.[30]

Pursuant to Section 7 of the Exchange Act, the Board of Governors of the Federal Reserve System has adopted rules regarding the use of credit and required margin in connection with securities transactions. The board's Regulation T [31] governs credit by broker–dealers and applies to all broker–dealers whether or not they are required to be registered with the SEC. The regulation sets limits on the types of securities on which credit may be given and on the maximum permissible amount of credit.

Since publicly offered real estate limited partnership interests that are registered with the SEC ordinarily would not come within any of the exclusions in this regulation, a broker–dealer may not sell interests having installment payment features in a registered public offering. This prohibition applies to all public offerings of conventional securities such as corporate stock, including offerings made pursuant to Regulation A and exempt intrastate offerings,[32] as well as offerings registered with the SEC.

However, and most importantly for the purposes of this book, broker–dealers are not prevented by Regulation T from selling limited partnership interests that provide for installment payments in exempt private placements.[33] Thus, if the offering of the real estate limited partnership interests qualifies as a private placement (see Chapter 8 of this book), the traditional installment sale arrangement should be permitted. See the model limited partnership agreement contained in Appendix 1.

In addition to Regulation T, Section 11(d) (1) of the Exchange Act prohibits a broker-dealer that engages in business both as a broker and as a dealer [34] from extending or arranging for the extension of credit to its customers on securities that are part of a new issue being distributed by the broker–dealer. This section would prevent persons acting as brokers and dealers, whether or not required to be registered with the SEC, from distributing limited partnership interests that are to be paid for in installments. The statutory prohibition refers to securities that are part of a "distribution" and thus would apply to registered public offerings and public offerings under Regulation A or the intrastate offering exemption of Section 3(a)(11) of the Securities Act. Presumably it does not apply to private placements under Section 4(2) of the Securities Act and other nonpublic limited offerings under Regulation D that do not constitute distributions.[35]

5. NASD REGULATION

Broker–dealers who are members of the National Association of Securities Dealers and their securities personnel are subject to extensive regulation by that association designed, inter alia, to promote just and equitable principles of trade and to protect investors and the public interest.[36]

Section 34 of the NASD's Rules of Fair Practice authorizes its Board of Governors to adopt regulations relating to its members' involvement with direct participation programs, including real estate limited partnerships. The regulations are contained in Appendix F to Section 34 (the "rule").[37]

The rule sets forth extensive requirements that must be met when NASD members participate in a public offering of interests in a direct participation program. The rule would apply whether the offering was registered with the SEC or was made pursuant to Regulation A under the Securities Act or was exempt from registration as an intrastate offering under Section 3(a) (11) of that act.

Most important, the rule would not apply to private placements pursuant to Section 4(2) of the Securities Act, offerings under Rules 505 and 506 of Regulation D, and nonpublic offerings under Rule 504 of Regulation D.

The rule is long and contains many detailed provisions. Although it does not apply to nonpublic offerings, we will discuss its major aspects, because it does apply to intrastate offerings.

Whenever a broker–dealer recommends the purchase of a security to a customer, he must have reasonable grounds to believe that the recommendation is suitable for the customer on the basis of information furnished by the customer. The rule generally imposes higher suitability standards for investment in direct participation programs than for investment in other securities. Under the rule, standards of suitability, typically relating to investors' financial resources and income tax brackets, must be established by the program and be disclosed in the prospectus. The broker–dealer must have reasonable grounds to believe that the investor's financial position will enable him to obtain the expected benefits and that the investor's net worth is appropriate in the light of the risk of loss and the illiquidity of the investment. It is also necessary that the broker–dealer have reasonable grounds to believe that an investment in the program is suitable based on information furnished by the customer as to his investment objectives, other investments, financial situation, and needs, and the broker–dealer must maintain in his files documents showing the basis for the determination of suitability.

The broker–dealer must have reasonable grounds to believe that the prospectus adequately and accurately discloses all the material facts and provides a basis for evaluating the program.

Organization and offering expenses, including selling and related costs, must be fair and reasonable, and, if the broker–dealer or an affiliate is the sponsor of the program, may not exceed 15% of the cash receipts from the offering. Underwriting compensation to an NASD member is limited to a maximum of 10% of the proceeds of the offering plus a maximum of ½ of

1% for reimbursement of bona fide due diligence expenses.[38] The value of the broker–dealer's compensation in connection with the offering must be capable of being definitively determined at the time of the offering; the broker–dealer may not receive compensation of an indeterminate amount. Thus so-called back-end fees, such as an interest in the program's cash flow or proceeds from the sale or refinancing of its property, are prohibited. Accordingly, as a practical matter, compensation is limited to front-end selling commissions and expense allowances.[39] The rule places restrictions on the use of sales incentives for broker–dealers and their personnel. No compensation may be paid to anyone engaged by an investor for investment advice as an inducement to the adviser to recommend investment in the program unless the adviser is a registered broker–dealer.

In addition to the rule, NASD members participating or assisting in a public offering of securities must comply with the Interpretation of the Board of Governors of the NASD as to the Review of Corporate Financing.[40] Under the interpretation, the NASD reviews the underwriting, compensation, and other arrangements in connection with the distribution to ascertain whether they are unfair or unreasonable. If the NASD determines that the arrangements are not fair and reasonable, its members may not be involved in the offering.

The interpretation also provides that NASD members may not participate in an advisory, selling, or other capacity in a nonunderwritten direct public offering by an issuer that hires persons primarily for the purpose of assisting in the distribution. In public offerings where a general partner sells interests directly in addition to sales by NASD members, the NASD will consider whether the general partner is required to register as a broker–dealer and will not permit its members to be involved in the offering if the general partner is not in compliance with the broker–dealer provisions of the Exchange Act. In close cases, the NASD will require a no-action letter from the staff of the SEC as to the issuer's sales activities before allowing its members to participate in the offering.

NOTES

1. The discussion in this chapter will focus on the federal requirements; however, the same considerations would apply generally under the various state laws (*see also* discussion in Chapter 10). Application for registration with the SEC is made on Form BD, which together with supplementary information is accepted by most of the states. Form BD seeks information as to the applicant, its business, and its officers, directors, owners, and

partners and their backgrounds. The procedure for broker–dealer registration with the SEC is contained in the regulations under Section 15(b) of the Exchange Act. Under the Securities Investor Protection Act of 1970, most broker–dealers registered with the SEC are required to join, and pay fees assessed by, the Securities Investor Protection Corporation.

2. If a broker–dealer does not make application to become a member of the NASD within 45 days after the effective date of its SEC registration, within that period it must file Form SECO-5 with the SEC and pay a $500 fee.

3. Wertheim, avail. February 12, 1973, FED. SEC. L. REP. (CCH) ¶79,286.

4. Sanibel Siesta Co., Ltd., avail. April 15, 1973; Energetics, Inc., avail. July 21, 1973; Heming and Hart, avail. November 26, 1979.

5. A partnership could also become a dealer as a result of buying and selling securities for its own portfolio if it engages in this as a business. Cf. Castleman and Co., avail. July 15, 1975, FED. SEC. L. REP. (CCH) ¶80,260.

6. *But see* Hofheimer, Gartlir, Gottlieb, and Gross, avail. November 12, 1972, FED. SEC. L. REP. (CCH) ¶79,098.

7. This is commonly called the "issuer exemption"; however, analytically it is not an exemption, as such, from broker–dealer registration or regulation, but rather is the result of a determination that the definitions do not apply. Many state securities laws do not require both buying and selling to be a dealer, but these laws usually expressly exclude issuers from the definition of "broker–dealer."

8. The absence of a *respondeat superior* relationship would, however, probably be fatal. International Funeral Services of California, Inc., avail. January 1, 1973.

9. Other relevant factors that may be considered include the length of time the offering will be made, the extent of the selling activity, whether sales will be solicited or unsolicited, and whether the seller will register as a broker, dealer, or salesman with any state securities commissions. *See,* e.g., Allied Finance Co., avail. September 28, 1975; ITT Financial Corporation, avail. July 17, 1978, FED. SEC. L. REP. (CCH) ¶81,943 (extended offering period); A&M Financing Company, avail. December 27, 1978, FED. SEC. L. REP. (CCH) ¶81,946 (listing factors that would be considered). Another question is whether a general partner who sells partnership interests becomes an investment adviser subject to the Investment Advisers Act of 1940 as a result of "advising" the limited partners to invest in the partnership. At one time, the staff of the SEC seemed to take the position that under such circumstances the general partner would be an investment adviser. Thomas Beard, avail. May 8, 1975, FED. SEC. L. REP. (CCH) ¶81,141. However, the staff has reconsidered its views and somewhat retreated from this position. Michael Coleman, Lawrence Grenon, avail. July 28, 1976 (based on a representation that the general partners "will not be selling interests in more than one limited partnership at any one time"). If the staff's earlier pronouncement were to be followed, it would lead to the conclusion that every direct sale of securities by an issuer involves an investment adviser, hardly a sensible result.

10. A large number of no-action letters are summarized in 232 SEC. REG. & L. REP. (BNA) at C-1 (December 19, 1973).

11. Professional Lease Management, Inc., avail. August 15, 1974; Louisiana Stud, Ltd., avail. June 10, 1977 (organization fee was deemed to represent compensation for sales). Reimbursement is permissible for out-of-pocket expenses and an allocable portion of salaries. Womprop, Inc., avail. June 15, 1973; Choice Communities, Inc., avail. Decem-

ber 29, 1972, FED. SEC. L. REP. (CCH) ¶79,203; Cola Petroleum, Inc., avail. March 14, 1979.

12. International Funeral Services of California, Inc., avail. January 1, 1973; China Trade Corporation, avail. July 24, 1973, FED. SEC. L. REP. (CCH) ¶81,939 ("none of the Company's employees with any recent experience in the securities industry will participate in the offering").

13. Stratford of Texas, Inc., avail. November 6, 1972, FED. SEC. L. REP. (CCH) ¶79,099.

14. Jammer Cycle Products, Inc., avail. July 26, 1973, FED. SEC. L. REP. (CCH) ¶79,478 (regular officers and directors permitted to sell the securities; however, former registered representatives to be employed solely for distributing the offering may not be used); Maurice S. Holcomb, avail. July 19, 1973.

15. Maurice S. Holcomb, avail. July 19, 1973; VSC, Inc., avail. August 7, 1978, FED. SEC. L. REP. (CCH) ¶81,941; Midland-Guardian Co., avail. December 27, 1978, FED. SEC. L. REP. (CCH) ¶81,947. Some commentators distinguish the treatment of developer-syndicators that are involved in the development, construction, and management of the real estate from the apparently more stringent treatment of professional syndicators that form and sell interests in limited partnerships but do not have a significant role in the real estate aspects of the program. This distinction reflects the requirement that the seller must have significant operational duties unrelated to the selling of the interests. Compare De Matteis Development Corp., avail. October 2, 1971, FED. SEC. L. REP. (CCH) ¶78,415 (employees of developer-general partner could sell the interests) with Boetel and Co., avail. August 20, 1971 (principal business the syndication of real estate properties; broker–dealer registration would be necessary).

16. Inland Realty Investments, Inc., avail. May 20, 1973 (broker–dealer registration necessary due to prior and possible future participation in securities offerings and other factors); Robinson Resources, Inc., avail. July 19, 1973 (registration not required even though the promoter had tentative plans to organize another partnership within two years); Diplomat Cattle Management Corp., avail. December 19, 1973; Carney and Xifaras, avail. September 26, 1975; Equity Management Corp., avail. March 27, 1978 (seven syndications in one year to be sold by employees and shareholders of the corporate general partner; broker–dealer registration required); BLUE SKY L. REP. (CCH) ¶30,560 (Maryland) and ¶48,659 (Pennsylvania). In John B. Ashmun, Thomas B. Grootemaat, avail. July 19, 1973, the staff was unable to conclude that registration was not required where an officer would be involved in one offering per year even though he had never previously engaged in the sale of securities, and determined that another officer who had been involved in prior offerings would have to register before participating in the offering in question. On reconsideration, after it was decided to organize a subsidiary that would be a registered broker–dealer and would assume responsibility for the sales, the staff permitted the two officers to make sales to a limited group of offerees without registration. Wainco 73 Company, avail. August 18, 1973. *See also* John Di-Meno, avail. October 11, 1978, FED. SEC. L. REP. (CCH) ¶81,940 (individual who "on occasions . . . has been involved in finding investors for local business" may be a broker). When Mr. DiMeno represented that he had not previously engaged in any securities offerings and did not intend to engage in any offerings other than as a finder of investors for a specified private placement, the staff agreed that broker–dealer registration was not required. Carl L. Feinstock, avail. April 1, 1979, FED. SEC. L. REP. (CCH) ¶82,067.

17. Landcom, Inc., avail. June 5, 1971, FED. SEC. L. REP. (CCH) ¶78,176 (sales commissions

to be paid to officers who were serving without other compensation); Leisure and Recreation Group, Inc., avail. May 29, 1973 (seller would "benefit substantially" from the sale of the securities); Marisol Corp., avail. August 11, 1973 (sale of condominium securities; bonuses permitted to real estate salesmen selling the units); Rimar Manufacturing, Inc., avail. September 12, 1975 (involvement in intrastate offering in 1969); Hargraves Aerobic Systems, Inc., avail. October 4, 1975 (one person had been employed as a registered representative from 1969 to 1973); Baptist Church Loan Corporation, avail. November 18, 1978, FED. SEC. L. REP. (CCH) ¶81,949 (recurring offerings by regular employees).

18.   In 1977 the SEC proposed the adoption of a new Rule 3a4-1 under the Exchange Act to specify the circumstances under which persons who are associated with an issuer and who participate in the sale of the issuer's securities would not be deemed to be brokers. Exchange Act Release No. 13195 (January 21, 1977).

The proposed rule, which has yet to be adopted or withdrawn, is as follows:

§240.3a4-1. Associated persons of an issuer deemed not to be brokers.

(a)   A person associated with an issuer of securities shall be deemed not to be a broker, as that term is defined in section 3(a) (4) of the Act, solely by reason of his participation in the distribution or sale of securities of such issuer if such person is not subject to a statutory disqualification, as that term is defined in section 3(a) (39) of the Act, and if:

(1)   His participation is confined to transactions in securities:

(i)   Involving offers and sales of securities to a registered broker or dealer, a registered investment company (or separate account), an insurance company, a bank or a trust for which a bank or registered investment adviser is the trustee or is authorized in writing to make investment decisions; or

(ii)   Made through a registered broker or dealer; or

(iii)   Exempted by reason of section 3(a) (7) or 3(a) (9) of the Securities Act of 1933 from the registration provisions of that Act; or

(iv)   In connection with a reclassification, merger or consolidation or transfer of assets within the meaning of Rule 145 under the Securities Act of 1933; or

(2)   He is a bona fide employee of the issuer who:

(i)   Has not participated, within the preceding two years, in the distribution or sale of any securities; and

(ii)   Primarily performs, or is intended primarily to perform at the end of the distribution, substantial duties for, or on behalf of, the issuer otherwise than in connection with transactions in securities; and

(iii)   Is compensated on a basis other than the direct or indirect payment of commissions or other special remuneration based on transactions in securities; or

(3)   He restricts his participation to any one or more of the following:

(i)   The delivery of a prospectus or other communication described in Rule 134 under the Securities Act of 1933;

(ii)   Responding to inquiries concerning the offering of securities; and

(iii)   The ministerial and clerical work of effecting any transaction.

(b)   When used in this section, the term "person associated with an issuer" means any natural person who is a partner, officer, director, or employee of the issuer and who is not an associated person of a registered broker or dealer.

Although the release indicates that the proposed rule would be in the nature of a "safe harbor," it also states: "Only unusual circumstances would be expected to support a conclusion that persons who do not come within the provisions of the proposed rule are not brokers within the meaning of section 3(a) (4)." Although the proposed rule has not been adopted, and may not be adopted or may be substantially modified, it presumably reflected the thinking of the SEC and its staff at the time it was proposed.

19. *See* The Ballard & Cordell Corp., avail. September 30, 1973.

20. Concapco of Georgia, Inc., avail. October 16, 1976; Womprop, Inc., avail. June 15, 1973.

21. Jammer Cycle Products, Inc., avail. July 26, 1973, Fed. Sec. L. Rep. (CCH) ¶79,478.

22. Jones Intercable, Inc., avail. September 24, 1976. This would seem consistent with the requirement of Rule 502(b) of Regulation D that the issuer make information available to prospective investors. Compare UMIC Properties, Inc., avail. September 12, 1977.

23. The Woodmoor Corp., avail. March 5, 1972, Fed. Sec. L. Rep. (CCH) ¶78,653.

24. Section 15(a) of the Exchange Act states: "(1) It shall be unlawful for any broker or dealer which is either a person other than a natural person or a natural person not associated with a broker or dealer which is a person other than a natural person (other than such a broker or dealer whose business is exclusively intrastate and who does not make use of any facility of a national securities exchange) to make use of the mails or any means or instrumentality of interstate commerce to effect any transactions in, or to induce or attempt to induce the purchase or sale of, any security (other than an exempted security or commercial paper, bankers' acceptances, or commercial bills) unless such broker or dealer is registered in accordance with subsection (b) of this section.

    "(2) The Commission, by rule or order, as it deems consistent with the public interest and the protection of investors, may conditionally or unconditionally exempt from paragraph (1) of this subsection any broker or dealer or class of brokers or dealers specified in such rule or order."

    The definition of "interstate commerce" in Section 3(a) (17) of the Exchange Act includes "intrastate use of (A) any facility of a national securities exchange or of a telephone or other interstate means of communication, or (B) any other interstate instrumentality."

25. Boetel & Co., avail. September 29, 1971, Fed. Sec. L. Rep. (CCH) ¶78,343; North Albuquerque Associates, avail. August 18, 1978, Fed. Sec. L. Rep. (CCH) ¶81,958 (exemption available).

26. Winchester Securities Corp., avail. April 30, 1971, Fed. Sec. L. Rep. (CCH) ¶78,119; Jammer Cycle Products, Inc., avail. July 26, 1973, Fed. Sec. L. Rep. (CCH) ¶79,478.

27. Shootin' Iron Realty Co., avail. September 13, 1973 (sales made within the broker-dealer's state to nonresidents are not permissible).

28. Corporate Investment Co., avail. June 22, 1974, Fed. Sec. L. Rep. (CCH) ¶79,953 (exemption not available because the issuer would use approximately one half of the net proceeds of the offering outside the state); Corporate Investment Co., avail. July 17, 1974, Fed. Sec. L. Rep. (CCH) ¶79,954 (exemption available when the issuer agrees to use 80% of the net proceeds within the state); Hargraves Aerobic Systems, Inc., avail. October 4, 1975; Concapco of Georgia, Inc., avail. April 18, 1976; Allied Real Estate Securities, Inc., avail. January 15, 1977, Fed. Sec. L. Rep. (CCH) ¶81,041; John Di-Meno, avail. October 11, 1978, Fed. Sec. L. Rep. (CCH) ¶81,940.

29. Consideration should also be given to the requirements of Rule 15c2-5, 17 C.F.R. §240.15c2-5.

30. Order of the Board of Governors of the Federal Reserve System (March 23, 1972), 12 C.F.R. §220.124, Fed. Sec. L. Rep. (CCH) ¶22, 282; 12 C.F.R. §220.7(a), Fed. Sec. L. Rep. (CCH) ¶22,231; Lake Point Elsinore, Ltd., avail. June 7, 1972, Fed. Sec. L. Rep. (CCH) ¶78,842. The sale of assessable interests may also be deemed to constitute credit arrangements. Financial Service Corp., avail. June 22, 1973; Saul, Ewing, Remick & Saul, avail. October 12, 1973, Fed. Sec. L. Rep. (CCH) ¶79,564.

31. 12 C.F.R. Part 220.

32. Order of the Board of Governors of the Federal Reserve System (November 12, 1975), Fed. Sec. L. Rep. (CCH) ¶80,328.

33. 12 C.F.R. §220.7(a) (2), Fed. Sec. L. Rep. (CCH) ¶22,231. This section of Regulation T refers to "the sale of non-margin securities with installment or other deferred payment provisions if the sale is exempted from the registration requirements of the Securities Act of 1933 under section 4(2) or section 4(6) of the Act." Offerings under Rule 506 are exempt from Regulation T. Securities Act Release No. 6389 (March 8, 1982)(note 33). We understand that the staff of the Federal Reserve Board has advised the staff of the SEC that offerings under Rule 505 are not subject to Regulation T. Offerings of tax shelter programs that are exempt intrastate offerings also are not subject to Regulation T. F.R.B. Staff Op. 5-551, July 27, 1972. The status of offerings under Rule 504 of Regulation D (which are exempt under Section 3(b) of the Securities Act) is uncertain.

34. Premier Corp., avail. August 20, 1973, Fed. Sec. L. Rep. (CCH) ¶79,501.

35. Saul, Ewing, Remick & Saul, avail. October 12, 1973, Fed. Sec. L. Rep. (CCH) ¶79,564; *but see* Great Plains Western Corp., avail. December 9, 1973 (a private placement under the Securities Act may be a "distribution" for purposes of the Exchange Act).

36. Federally registered broker–dealers who are not members of the NASD are subject to similar regulation by the SEC. *See* paragraphs (7), (8), and (9) of Sec. 15(b) of the Exchange Act, the rules thereunder and Exchange Act Release No. 9420 (February 11, 1972).

37. Appendix F was approved on September 16, 1982. NASD Notice to Members 82-50, October 19, 1982.

38. These guidelines are set forth in NASD Notice to Members 82-51, October 19, 1982. Exceeding the guidelines is presumed to be unfair and unreasonable. An NASD member may participate in the distribution of securities of an affiliate only if the requirements of Schedule E to the NASD's bylaws are met; however, a tax-sheltered program that provides flow-through tax benefits would not be an affiliate of the member. NASD Manual ¶1402. SECO broker–dealers are subject to similar restrictions. 17 C.F.R. §240.15b10-9.

39. The NASD is considering a proposed amendment to the rule. The amendment would permit a broker–dealer who reduces his front-end compensation to receive a back-end interest in cash generated by the program after the investors have received distributions equal to their investment. NASD Notice to Members 82–14, March 9, 1982.

40. NASD Manual ¶2151.02. Relevant offering documents and other information are required to be filed with the NASD, and a filing fee must be paid. The manner in which the broker-dealer will comply with Appendix F must be shown in the materials filed pursuant to this requirement.

CHAPTER 10

STATE SECURITIES LAWS
AND REAL ESTATE
LIMITED PARTNERSHIPS

1. STATE SECURITIES LAWS—GENERAL

Offers and sales of interests in real estate limited partnerships must be made in compliance with the securities laws of the states in which the interests are offered and sold. This is in addition to meeting the requirements of the federal securities laws. As indicated in Chapter 8, obtaining an exemption under the Securities Act of 1933 ("Securities Act") for a limited offering or an intrastate offering does not automatically exempt an offering of securities from state securities laws.

Nearly all the states have securities laws applicable to the sale of securities, including limited partnership interests. These laws are commonly referred to as "blue sky" laws, since their aim is to prevent "speculative schemes which have no more basis than so many feet of 'blue sky'." [1]

Typically, the state laws deal with one or more of the following: registration of securities offerings and exemptions from registration, registration of broker–dealers and salesmen, registration of investment advisers, and disclosure and prevention of fraudulent practices. Although there is this common core and although many state laws are modeled on the Uniform Securities Act, there are many variations among the state laws and in the administration of the laws. Accordingly, the law and practice in each state

239

in which an offering is to be made must be carefully considered before commencement of the offering.[2]

In addition to their securities laws, New Jersey and New York have laws relating specifically to real estate syndications which also must be complied with when offerings are made in these states.

As is the case under the federal Securities Act, under state laws an offering of limited partnership interests ordinarily must either be registered with the securities commission or securities administrator of each state in which the offering is made or be exempt from registration. Unlike the SEC, which is empowered only to require full disclosure of the material facts regarding an offering, many state securities administrators by statute have the power to pass on the merits of securities offered in their jurisdictions as well as broad discretionary authority to refuse registration of securities or to deny exemptions, usually on the ground of "unfairness" to investors.

Through exercise of these discretionary powers, the state securities commissions have sought to regulate the types of securities offerings that may be made in their states and to impose substantive requirements relating to the structure of an offering and the rights of investors. In some states, the substantive requirements apply only to registered offerings, while other states mandate them in exempt offerings as well as registered ones.

The precise standards vary from state to state, and sometimes are inconsistent, so that occasionally what one state requires another state forbids or regards with disfavor. Since the requirements affect the structuring of the syndication and the limited partnership, attention must be given to these matters at the early planning stages of any syndication.

Among the areas that securities administrators have sought to regulate in connection with offerings of interests in real estate limited partnerships are the following:

a.   Suitability   Investors may have to meet minimum income, net worth, and tax bracket standards, and there may be minimum amounts that have to be invested by each investor. These requirements are sometimes even imposed on a resale by a limited partner to a new purchaser.

b.   Promoters' Compensation   The sponsors or promoters of a real estate limited partnership may receive compensation from the partnership in various forms, including management fees, real estate or insurance brokerage commissions, profits on sale of property to the partnership, and interests in the partnership. Many states place limitations on the amount of compensation that may be paid to the promoters and may even require that the promoters subordinate some of their interests in the partnership to the investors' interests. Other transactions between the promoters and the partnership may be subject to restrictions.

c. Expenses of the Offering   In some states the expenses of the offering to be paid from the sale of the partnership interests may not exceed a fixed percentage of the proceeds of the offering.

d. Rights of Limited Partners   Some jurisdictions require that the limited partners be granted specific rights, such as voting rights under certain circumstances or rights to inspect partnership records or call meetings of the partners or remove the general partners.

e. Periodic Reports   Many states require that annual or more frequent reports containing specified financial and other information be furnished to investors or filed with the securities commission. Often certified financial statements prepared in accordance with generally accepted accounting principles are required in addition to the tax information that is ordinarily provided to the investors.

f. Blind Pools   Partnerships that have not allocated a substantial portion of their offering proceeds for investment in identified properties (so-called blind pools) may be subject to further regulation in areas such as the experience and qualifications of the promoters, size of the offering and investor suitability. Blind pools may even be totally prohibited in some states.

g. Disclosure   Often there are specific requirements as to the information that must be contained in the offering memorandum or as to the format of the memorandum. Also, some states prohibit or restrict the use of various materials, such as projections, in the offering documents. Sales literature in addition to the offering memorandum is often subject to review or regulation. Full disclosure of all material information is usually mandated by general antifraud provisions in the state securities laws.

As discussed in Chapter 9, most states subject brokers and dealers and other persons engaged in selling securities to extensive regulation.

Failure to comply with applicable state securities laws may result in offeror liability to investors for damages, rescission of the sale of the interest, or administrative, injunctive, or criminal proceedings brought by the state securities commission.

2. STATE REGISTRATION OF SECURITIES

Registration of an offering of securities with a state securities commission generally involves the filing of an application form, an offering memorandum or prospectus, exhibits, and additional information and the payment of a filing fee. In most states the application will be for registration either by "coordination" or by "qualification." Registration by coordination is for offerings that are being registered with the SEC. This simplifies state registration because the materials filed with the SEC will be accepted as satisfying most of the filing requirements of the various states. Registration by qualification is applicable when there is no SEC filing, in which case it is necessary to consider and comply with the specific rules of each state as to the materials to be filed.

Each state has its own form of application for registration.[3] The application usually requires information as to the issuer and its officers, directors, and principal security holders, the amount of securities to be sold in the state, the other states in which the securities are to be registered, and the broker–dealer who will offer the securities in the state. The application usually is signed by either the issuer or a broker–dealer registered in the state. If the issuer is not a local partnership, it normally is required to appoint the state securities administrator or another state official as its agent for service of process in any litigation arising from the offering.[4]

The application and other documents are then reviewed by the securities commission for compliance with its requirements, and typically the commission by telephone or letter advises of its comments and of amendments required if the offering is to be permitted in its state. Additional information as to the offering, the partnership, the promoters, the property to be acquired, and similar matters may be requested. Once comments have been received from all the states in which the initial filing is made, the offering memorandum and other materials are amended and filed for further review and comments.

If registration is refused or onerous conditions are imposed, the application may be withdrawn, usually without prejudice, and the offering may not be made in that state. Many states require that they be notified if the application is withdrawn in, or registration is formally refused by, another state.

While the application is pending, copies of the preliminary prospectus are often distributed to potential investors to obtain indications of interest in investing. Some commissions frown on this practice, especially if registration in the state is to be by qualification; however, most states permit a preliminary prospectus to be distributed if an application for registration by coordination has been filed with the state. In any event, the indications of interest cannot bind the investor, and no money should be received from the investor during this period. The preliminary prospectus normally should have a legend in red on the cover stating that the document is in preliminary form, and is subject to amendment, and that offers by investors to buy the securities cannot be accepted until registration becomes effective.

The applicant will usually request the commissions to declare the registration effective on a specified date. The commissions usually grant the request if the process of review and clearance of the offering by the commissions has been completed. If the offering is registered with the SEC and the state application is for registration by coordination, the state registration automatically becomes effective when the SEC registration is effective, assuming that the offering has otherwise been cleared by the state.

After the registration is effective, the definitive prospectus is distributed and the securities are sold to investors. If, prior to completion of the sale of the securities, there are material changes in the facts relating to the offering, it may be necessary to amend the prospectus and to file these amendments with the securities commissions.

Most states require that copies of the definitive prospectus be filed with the securities commission, and many require that reports of sales or notices of completion of the offering or other information be furnished with respect to offerings in their jurisdictions.

3. EXEMPTIONS FROM STATE REGISTRATION— GENERAL

Various exemptions from the requirement of registering securities are contained in the state securities laws. As far as the sale of interests in real estate limited partnerships is concerned, most of the applicable exemptions revolve about the number of investors.

The conditions for obtaining exemption vary widely. Some exemptions are self-executing, while others require only the filing of a notice or other specified information with the state securities commission. In other instances, the availability of the exemption is within the unrestricted discretion of the securities commission, and substantial information may have to be filed with and approved by the commission; the effect may be that claiming such an exemption amounts to a short form of registration and the offering is subject to similar substantive regulation. Where filings are required, it may be necessary to pay fees, sometimes substantial ones.

The requirements for what may appear to be similar statutory exemptions differ from state to state, and often the regulations of the securities commission impose substantial additional conditions to be met that are not expected in the light of the language of, and may seem inconsistent with, the statute. In other instances, securities administrators have adopted regulations creating exemptions under a general statutory authority to do so. Accordingly, the securities statute, regulations, interpretations, and other published materials must be consulted in seeking an exemption in any particular state.[5] Also, in determining whether an exemption is available for a particular offering, attention must be given to the doctrine of integration of offerings, which is discussed in Chapter 8.

Some of the more common exemptions are discussed in the following sections.

4. EXEMPTIONS FOR LIMITED OFFERINGS

Most states exempt offerings to a limited number of investors, but the similarity stops at this point. The maximum number of permitted investors during a one-year period generally is fixed somewhere between 3 and 50, and the securities commission is often given discretionary authority to increase the number on application. Whether the restriction applies only to purchasers of the securities, or to offerees as well, varies from state to state. In some states the relevant number is the total number of owners of the issuer's securities after completion of the offering. There is also variation among the jurisdictions as to whether all investors are counted or only investors in the state.[6]

Many state exemptions for limited offerings have restrictions on the payment of commissions or other compensation for soliciting sales of the securities, either prohibiting commissions entirely or just forbidding promoters and their affiliates from receiving selling compensation.[7] A prohibition against any commissions would ordinarily, as a practical matter, eliminate the possibility of using a broker–dealer to sell the securities. Other conditions that may be imposed include restrictions on the resale of the securities by investors, limitations on the use of advertising and sales literature, and requirements such as obtaining investment representations from investors, offering investors the right to rescind their purchases for a period of time, using specified legends on the offering memorandum or the partnership agreement, maintaining records, or making periodic reports to the commission and the investors. Some state securities commissions will consider applications for waiver or modification of restrictions (e.g., limitation of the number of purchasers or prohibition of the payment of selling compensation) imposed under their limited offering exemptions.[8]

Some state securities laws do not base their limited offering exemption on a fixed maximum number of investors, but instead exempt nonpublic offerings from registration, either by an expressly stated exemption or by requiring only public offerings to be registered. However, it should not be assumed that an offering which qualifies as a private offering under Section 4(2) of the federal Securities Act or Rule 506 of Regulation D automatically is a nonpublic offering for purposes of state securities laws. There are securities administrators who consider that any offering is "public" unless it is made only to a minimal number of offerees, all of whom must have a previously existing relationship with the issuer or its principals.

One encouraging development is the adoption by a number of state securities commissions of exemptions based on Regulation D. However, compliance with Regulation D may not be sufficient. Additional conditions, such as delivery of an opinion of counsel or the filing of a notice or an application have often been added to the exemption as adopted by the states.[9]

5. OTHER EXEMPTIONS

The securities laws of many states contain an exemption for "any isolated transaction, whether effected through a broker–dealer or not." Usually the securities administrators interpret this exemption to be available only for one or two sales within the state during a one-year period. In determining whether the exemption applies to any particular sale, it is necessary to consider all related transactions that could be considered to be motivated by the same general purpose or to be part of a single plan. Thus the exemption may not be available even for a single sale if several offers are made within the state or if a large number of sales or offers are made by related partnerships. Ordinarily the sale may be made by a properly registered broker–dealer, and it is permissible to pay a sales commission.

Sales to institutional investors, such as banks, investment companies, pension trusts, and profit-sharing trusts, are exempt in most states, and this exemption usually applies whether the institution is acting for itself or in a fiduciary capacity. In addition, some states exempt sales to corporations.

Various other exemptions exist under the state securities laws, and if none of the more common exemptions apply to an offering in any particular state, it is wise to examine its statute and regulations carefully to ascertain whether an unexpected exemption may be available.[10]

6. NORTH AMERICAN SECURITIES ADMINISTRATORS ASSOCIATION STATEMENT OF POLICY

All the states except California are members of the North American Securities Administrators Association. The association has issued a number of "policies" that set forth guidelines for the substantive terms of securities offerings and for disclosure and selling practices. The guidelines are considered by many securities commissions to establish standards that must be met by offerings to be registered in their respective jurisdictions.

The association has adopted a "Statement of Policy Regarding Real Estate Programs" ("Statement of Policy"), which contains recommended standards for real estate limited partnerships.[11] The Statement of Policy consists of numerous detailed requirements that are not necessarily followed by all the members of the association and that may be relaxed in individual instances. However, the standards are followed by a substantial number of states and are illustrative of the type of regulations imposed by other states. Although the Statement of Policy is stated to apply to the registration of securities and to be primarily designed for public syndications, similar considerations may be used by securities administrators in connection with the granting of discretionary exemptions from registration.[12]

The provisions of the Statement of Policy are detailed and complex and are only summarized here.

a. Definitions The Statement of Policy refers to the partnership as a "program," to a limited partner as a "participant," and to the organizer or manager of the program as a "sponsor." It uses "prospectus" as we have been using "private placement memorandum."

b. Sponsors Sponsors and general partners must have at least two years relevant real estate or other experience. Any sponsor or affiliate providing services to the program must have at least four years experience or otherwise demonstrate its qualifications in the field.

The general partners must have an aggregate net worth (exclusive of home, home furnishings, and automobiles, and after evaluation of contingent liabilities) of at least $50,000. The required net worth is increased if the current offering plus offerings sold within the prior year exceeds $1,000,000.

c. Transactions with the Sponsor Typically, the sponsor of a program (or an affiliate) engages in various transactions with the partnership for which it receives consideration. These transactions may include organizing the program, serving as a general partner, locating, developing, constructing, or managing partnership property, selling property to the partnership, and serving as real estate broker or insurance agent. The compensation may be in the form of payment of a fee or the allocation of an interest in the partnership.

The arrangements between the sponsor and the partnership usually are not negotiated at arm's length. They generally involve potential conflicts of interest. Accordingly, the Statement of Policy sets forth standards and restrictions governing these arrangements to help ensure fairness to the participants.

Generally, transactions between the sponsor and the partnership must be at competitive rates and are subject to certain other limitations; must be embodied in written contracts modifiable only by a vote of a majority of the limited partners; and must be fully disclosed in the prospectus. Services other than those specified in the Statement of Policy may be performed only in "extraordinary circumstances fully justified" to the securities commission.

The total consideration of all kinds that may be paid directly or indirectly to the sponsor must be reasonable and must be fully described in the prospectus. If the sponsor receives fees for services to the partnership, it must send the investors quarterly detailed statements regarding the fees and services. Rebates to the sponsor and reciprocal business arrangements that would circumvent the restrictions on dealings with the sponsor are forbidden.

The sponsor may not sell property to the partnership for more than its cost in the absence of a material change that would increase its value. Material changes include the passing of a significant amount of time (not less than two years), obtaining rezoning, and other "extraordinary" events that in fact increase the value of the property.

The sponsor is generally prohibited from providing permanent financing for the program.

A program management fee may be paid to the sponsor or general partner only where the partnership owns unimproved land or government subsidized projects. In each case there are specified limitations on the size of the fee that can be paid.

The partnership may not: (a) make loans to the sponsor; (b) acquire property from a program in which the sponsor has an interest; (c) give the sponsor an exclusive right to sell the partnership's property; or (d) ordinarily, sell or lease property to the sponsor, except leaseback arrangements made at the outset.

The sponsor may not receive a fee or commission in connection with reinvestment or distribution of the proceeds of the sale or refinancing of the partnership's property. However, subject to conditions, a real estate commission may be paid to the sponsor for services actually performed on the sale of property by the partnership. This commission may not exceed the lesser of 3% of the selling price for the property or one half of the standard real estate commission.

Fees and expenses paid by any party for services rendered during the program's organizational or acquisition phase, including organizational and offering expenses and acquisition fees and expenses, are referred to in the Statement of Policy as "front-end fees." The portion of the proceeds of the offering available to pay front-end fees to the sponsor and others is limited by a requirement that a minimum of from 67 to 80% of the participants' capital contributions (the percentage decreases as leverage from mortgages on the property increases) be invested in the program's property. The sponsor or the general partners often receive an interest in the program for little or no cash investment in consideration of their organizing and managing the program. The amount of the interest must be reasonable, and the Statement of Policy provides certain objective standards. Such an interest is presumptively reasonable if it does not exceed either (a) 10% of distributions from cash flow and 15% of distributions of the net proceeds from sale or refinancing of the program's property after the investors have received distributions from the program equal to their capital contributions plus a cumulative annual return of 6% on their capital contributions, or (b) 25% of net proceeds from such a sale or refinancing after the investors have received distributions in the amount previously indicated. If the front-end fees are less than the maximum permitted, for each percentage point of front-end fees not taken, the sponsor may take an additional 1% of the net proceeds from a sale or refinancing.

d.   Participants   Investments in real estate limited partnerships have limited transferability and liquidity and often involve investment risks and tax features oriented toward high tax bracket investors. Therefore, such investments often are not appropriate or suitable for many potential investors.

The Statement of Policy states that

As a general rule, programs structured to give deductible tax losses of 50% or more of the capital contribution of the participant in the year of investment should be sold only to persons in higher income tax brackets considering both state and federal income taxes. Programs which involve more than ordinary investor risk should emphasize suitability standards involving substantial net worth of the investor.

Minimum suitability standards for investors as recommended by the statement include either (a) annual gross income of at least $30,000 and net worth (exclusive of home, furnishings, and automobiles) of at least $30,000 or (b) net worth of at least $75,000. In tax-oriented offerings, higher standards, such as being in the 50% tax bracket, may be necessary, and higher income and net worth standards may be imposed in high-risk offerings. A minimum initial cash investment of $2,500 is also required.

e. Program Structure The Statement of Policy has additional provisions relating to the partnership arrangements and the activities of the partnership.

Installment (or deferred) payments of the price of the investor's limited partnership interest are permissible if the payments coincide with the anticipated cash needs of the partnership. The payments must be represented by a nonnegotiable, recourse note of the investor, which may not contain authorization for the confession of judgment and which the partnership may not sell or assign at a discount. Selling commissions on the deferred payments may be paid only when the payments are made. Assessment of the investors for sums in addition to the purchase price of their limited partnership interests is permissible only to meet taxes and certain other governmental charges. Forfeiture for default in paying an assessment or installment is prohibited, but reasonable penalties may be imposed, including reducing or subordinating the defaulting partner's interest in the partnership or selling his interest.

Limited partners holding more than 10% of the limited partnership interests must have the right to call a meeting of the partnership. To the extent not inconsistent with the state limited partnership act under which the partnership is formed, a majority of the outstanding limited partnership interests (without the necessity for concurrence by the general partner) must have the right to amend the partnership agreement, dissolve the partnership, remove the general partner and elect a new one, and approve or disapprove the sale of all or substantially all the partnership's assets.[13] The investors must be given access to all records of the partnership.

The partnership agreement must provide for a successor general partner if the only general partner is an individual.

The investors must be given annual reports with audited financial statements and information as to the activities of the partnership. If projections were provided to the investors, the annual report must contain a comparison of the actual results with the projected results. Interim reports are also required, as well as the information necessary for the investors to prepare their federal tax returns.

The ability of the sponsor to limit his liability to, or obtain indemnification from, the partnership is restricted:

> Sponsors shall not attempt to pass on to participants the general liability imposed on them by law except that the program agreement may provide that a sponsor shall have no liability whatsoever to the program or to any participant for any loss suffered by the program which arises out of any action or inaction of the sponsor, if the sponsor, in good faith, determined that such course of conduct was in the best interests of the program and such course of conduct did not

constitute negligence of the sponsor. The sponsor may be indemnified by the program against losses sustained in connection with the program, provided the losses were not the result of negligence or misconduct on the part of the sponsors.

Various restrictions exist on the operation of the program. All property acquisitions must be supported by an independent appraisal. The program may not acquire property in exchange for limited partnership interests except for transactions described in the prospectus and completed on effectiveness of the program. Investments by the program in other real estate limited partnerships are prohibited except for investments in governmentally subsidized programs such as under the National Housing Act and certain joint ventures.

Reinvestment of cash flow from operations is not allowed. The proceeds of sale or refinancing may be reinvested if sufficient cash is distributed to the participants to pay income taxes resulting from the sale or refinancing. A program that can reinvest the proceeds of sale or refinancing may be considered one type of "blind pool"; blind pools are discussed in subsequent paragraphs.

The application for registration must contain a favorable ruling from the Internal Revenue Service or an opinion of independent counsel that the partnership will be taxed as a partnership and not as an association for federal tax purposes. Also required is an opinion of independent counsel that the limited partnership interests are duly authorized or created and will be validly issued interests in the partnership and that the liability of the investors will be limited to their investment.

f. Blind Pools   The Statement of Policy defines a nonspecified property program as follows:

> Non-specified Property Program—a program where, at the time a securities registration is ordered effective, less than 75% of the net proceeds from the sale of program interests is allocable to the purchase, construction, or improvement of specific properties, or a program in which the proceeds from any sale or refinancing of properties may be reinvested. Reserves shall be included in the nonspecified 25%.

These programs are commonly called "blind pools," since the investors' money is pooled to acquire unknown properties. These programs are subject to additional requirements because of the inherent risk to investors when the properties have not been identified and will be chosen by the sponsor.

A blind pool must have a minimum of $1,000,000 of proceeds from the offering of its limited partnership interests available for investment in properties. The offering may not extend for more than one year, and any funds not invested within two years after commencement of the offering must be returned pro rata to the investors. Assessment of the investors (for amounts in excess of the purchase price of their interests) and installment payment arrangements are not allowed.

The prospectus must state the types of properties in which the program will invest and the manner of financing acquisitions. There are restrictions on investment in unimproved or non-income-producing property and in junior obligations. The sponsor of a blind pool (or at least one of its principals) must have had five years experience in the real estate business in an executive capacity and two years experience in the management and acquisition of the type of properties to be acquired by the partnership. Quarterly detailed reports of property acquisitions must be sent to all investors.

g. Selling Practices Sellers of the limited partnership interests are required to make every reasonable effort to assure that the interests are suitable investments for the offerees. Subscriptions must be accepted or rejected within 30 days of their receipt, and, if rejected, subscription funds must be returned promptly.

Advertisements of and invitations to seminars or group meetings at which sale of the interests is to be promoted must indicate the purpose of the meeting and set forth certain additional information about the offering. No cash or other valuable gifts may be offered to induce prospective participants to attend. Materials to be used at the meeting must be submitted in advance to the securities commission.

The sponsor is prohibited from directly or indirectly compensating anyone engaged by a potential investor for investment advice as an inducement to the adviser to recommend the purchase of interests in the program.

h. Disclosure The prospectus is required to comply with the SEC's Securities Act Industry Guide 5 (formerly designated Guide 60). Guide 5 is discussed in Chapter 11 of this book and is reproduced in Appendix 9.

i. Sponsor Financial Statements An audited balance sheet of any corporate sponsor as of its fiscal year-end and, if the fiscal year ended more than 135 days before the filing, an unaudited interim balance sheet should be in the prospectus.

Noncorporate sponsors must provide a recent balance sheet to the appropriate securities commissions, which need not be audited but must be sworn to by the sponsor and be subject to a limited review by an independent certified public accountant. This balance sheet does not have to be included in the prospectus. The prospectus should contain either a representation of the amount of any noncorporate sponsor's net worth or a representation that the sponsor meets the net worth requirements contained in the Statement of Policy (as discussed previously, $50,000 subject to certain increases).

j. Forecasts   Forecasts of predicted future results of operations of the partnership are not required, but may be included in the prospectus if the partnership will invest in specified improved property. Blind pools may not use forecasts, and unimproved land programs may use only limited information as to anticipated costs and payments from investors. Any forecasts must meet the detailed standards set forth in the Statement of Policy as to format and information to be included. The possible undesirable tax consequences of an early sale of the partnership's property must be shown.

k.   Other   Other requirements as to the contents of the offering documents are imposed by the Statement of Policy, which should be carefully reviewed when the documents are being prepared.

Disclosure practices are discussed generally in Chapter 11.

7. NEW YORK—GENERAL

New York's blue sky law,[14] commonly called the Martin Act, is contained in Article 23-A of the General Business Law [15] and is administered by the Attorney General and the Department of Law. It does not require the registration of securities in general; its principal thrust is the regulation of brokers, dealers, salesmen, and investment advisers and the prohibition of fraudulent practices. However, as a result of past abuses, real estate syndications and intrastate offerings in reliance on Section 3(a) (11) of the federal Securities Act of 1933 are subject to special regulation and filing requirements.[16]

From the standpoint of a real estate limited partnership, broker–dealer regulation becomes relevant because the New York definition of a "dealer," in addition to the customary provisions, includes "a person, firm, association, or corporation selling or offering for sale from or to the public within or from this state securities issued by it." [17] The New York Attorney General considers that any offering or sale of securities to more than a handful of investors with a close relationship to the seller is an offering or sale "to the public," subjecting the seller to regulation as a dealer. This interpretation of a public offering is more expansive than that used by other securities administrators or in connection with private placements under the federal Securities Act.

As a result, real estate limited partnerships that sell limited partnership interests directly to investors or through registered broker–dealers on a best efforts basis must, unless otherwise exempted, comply with the broker–dealer provisions of the law.[18]

Registration of a real estate limited partnership as a broker–dealer is accomplished by filing an Issuer Statement (N.Y. Form M-11) with the Department of Law. This statement seeks information as to the partnership, its business, its partners and principals, its prior securities activities, any securities salesmen to be employed, and the offering. The statement must be signed by a partner on behalf of the partnership and by all its general partners and principals. Registration is effective when the statement is received in the Department of Law.[19]

If the partnership is not formed under the laws of New York or does not have its principal place of business in New York, the partnership and its general partners and principals must designate the New York Secretary of State as their agent for service of process in proceedings under the Martin Act. The designation must be filed with the Department of State.[20]

In addition, in connection with the broker–dealer registration, a "state notice" setting forth the name and address of the partnership and the names of its general partners, and in connection with the offering, a "further state notice" giving similar information plus the name of the securities to be offered and the name, address, and state of organization of the issuer, must be filed with the Department of State for publication in its New York State Bulletin.

If salesmen other than partners or principals named in the Issuer Statement are to be employed, they must be registered by the filing of Salesman Statements.

The information in the Issuer and Salesman Statements must be updated to reflect changes by the filing of supplemental statements. Registration as a broker–dealer or salesman is effective for four years. If the partnership registers solely to make one particular offering of its securities, consideration should be given to withdrawing the registration when the offering has been completed.[21]

8. NEW YORK REAL ESTATE SYNDICATE ACT

In addition to complying with the broker–dealer provisions where applicable, a real estate limited partnership whose interests are offered in New York will have to meet the requirements of the Real Estate Syndicate Act,[22] which is part of the state blue sky law.

In this regard, "real estate" has been given a broad interpretation. Since registration requirements depend on the type of business, however, it is sometimes desirable to obtain from the Attorney General a threshold determination of whether an entity will be engaging in a real estate securities offering. For example, a large company that participates in many business activities, some of which are clearly unrelated to real estate, may wish to determine the applicability of the Real Estate Syndicate Act when it contemplates financing a real estate project by selling equity interests.

Unless exempt, no "public" offering or sale of real estate limited partnership interests may be made in or from New York until an offering statement (including a prospectus) has been submitted to the Department of Law and the Attorney General has issued a letter stating that the offering has been filed.[23]

To determine whether an offering is "public," the entire offering is examined, including activities engaged in outside New York State. Relevant factors include the number of offerees, the relationship of offerees to each other and to the offeror, the sophistication and wealth of the offerees, the size of units, and the general type and manner of the offering. Use of media, such as newspapers, magazines, or radio, is likely to result in a public offering.[24]

The submission to the Department of Law would consist of a prospectus containing the information required by Section 352-e(1) (b) and the regulations thereunder,[25] appropriate exhibits, Form RS-1 in which the partnership would indicate the location in the prospectus of the required information, and copies of all other proposed offering literature. A fee based on the size of the entire offering (not just the portion to be offered in New York) must be paid.

If the Department of Law considers that there are deficiencies in the materials as submitted, a letter indicating the deficiencies is sent to the partnership, and the partnership would amend the documents to comply with the comments in the letter. Eventually, a letter stating that the offering had been filed would be issued, [26] and the offering could take place.

Some of the more noteworthy provisions regarding real estate syndications are discussed in the following paragraphs; however, the statute and regulations contain detailed requirements and must be consulted in connection with any offering.

Blind pools where less than 65% of the proceeds of the offering are to be used in connection with specific properties identified in the prospectus are subject to special requirements. New York investors must have a net worth of at least $500,000 (exclusive of home, furnishings and automobiles) and must make a minimum investment of $25,000. After 65%[26a] of the proceeds of the offering have been applied to specific properties identified in a supplement to the prospectus, the requirements as to net worth and minimum investment may be reduced.

All funds received from investors (whether in a permitted blind pool or a regular offering) are deemed held in trust until they are actually used as set forth in the prospectus,[27] and the section of the prospectus describing the use of the proceeds of the offering must contain a representation to the effect that: "All proceeds of this offering will be held in trust for the benefit of investors in a special bank account, to be used only for the purposes set forth [in the use of proceeds section]."

The prospectus must include certain audited financial statements as well as a commitment that annual reports with audited financial statements will be submitted to all investors. In addition, annual reports on Form AR-1 with extensive information regarding the partnership and its operations must be filed with the Department of Law, and, when distributions are made to investors, detailed quarterly reports in the format of Form SD-1 must be sent to New York investors, setting forth the source of the distribution and additional information.

Generally, the use of projections in the prospectus or other offering literature is prohibited,[28] but see discussion in Section 9 of this chapter.

Advertising in connection with the offering is subject to regulation, and all advertisements and offering literature must contain specified legends.

9. NEW YORK EXEMPTIONS

The New York statute permits the Attorney General in his discretion on application to exempt certain offerings from the requirements of the Real Estate Syndicate Act, and sellers of specified securities from the broker-dealer registration provisions of the statute.

Where an offering is very limited, the Attorney General, in his discretion, may on request furnish a letter confirming that registration is not required. Such offerings generally are characterized by no more than eight or nine offerees, all of whom are wealthy, sophisticated, and related through business or family. In addition, such a letter may be furnished where an offering is being made almost entirely outside New York if there are only one or two New York offerees who are wealthy and sophisticated and have a preexisting relationship with the partnership or its principals or with the broker-dealer selling the interests. Application for a "no filing required" determination is made by letter and a $75 fee is required. The determination is based solely on the information supplied and does not prevent an investigation or condone a violation of the state laws.

Under Section 352-g, the Attorney General may grant exemptions from the Real Estate Syndicate Act to:

> any offerings of securities (1) made to persons not exceeding forty in number or (2) which securities have been fully registered with the securities and exchange commission of the United States of America or have received an exemption

therefrom for reasons other than said offering is an intrastate offering to residents of the state of New York only.

Under Section 359-f(2) (d), exemption from the broker–dealer registration provisions may be granted to anyone who is a dealer solely by reason of offering: "securities which are to be sold in a limited offering to not more than forty persons, but the attorney-general may grant an exemption for offerings made to more than forty persons when he deems such an exemption within the purposes of this subdivision."

In the case of real estate limited partnerships that come within the definition of a "dealer," the application for exemption under Section 359-f(2) (d) would ordinarily be combined with the application for exemption under the Real Estate Syndicate Act.[29] The application is made in the form of an affidavit or petition complying with Policy Statement 100 (which applies to offerings that are exempt from registration with the SEC under its Regulation D) or with the Instructions for §352-g Exemptions (which covers other applications under Section 352-g).[30]

a. §352-g Exemptions   The application must set forth information as to the partnership, its general partners and principals,[31] the benefits and profits to the promoters, the size and purpose and use of the proceeds of the offering, the property to be acquired, the terms of purchase, and other matters.

If the exemption is sought on the grounds that the offering will be made to 40 or fewer offerees,[32] the proposed offerees must have some existing relationship with the general partners or principals, such as being friends, relatives, or business associates.[33] The names, addresses, and relationships of proposed offerees must be included in the application as well as a description of the type of relationship that will be required of any other offerees. On completion of the offering, an affidavit must be submitted identifying the investors and the offerees who did not invest. Before any money is received from an investor, he must sign a prescribed statement acknowledging that the transaction has not been scrutinized by the Attorney General and making representations as to his investment intent and financial status. A private offering memorandum is not required.[34] However, any offering literature must be submitted to the Department of Law for review, and a memorandum describing the tax aspects of the offering must be furnished to the department.

If the application is under Section 352-g(2) based on an exemption from registration under Section 3(a) of the federal Securities Act, a letter from the SEC or an opinion of counsel as to the availability of such exemption must be provided. Offering literature must be filed in applications under clause (2) of Section 352-g, and, if an exemption from broker–dealer registration is sought pursuant to Section 359-f(2), the grounds therefor should be indicated.

Even though a prospectus will be used under an SEC registration, the Attorney General may request changes in language and format, because issuance of the exemption is discretionary. For that reason, the first draft should be sumbitted at an early stage for review, with letters of comment from the SEC filed as issued, to avoid delays.

b. Policy Statement 100 To coordinate the SEC's Rule 146 with the Martin Act in regard to real estate syndications, in 1975 the Attorney General issued Policy Statement 100. The policy statement provides that the Attorney General will entertain applications for exemption under Section 352-g(2) and Section 359-f(2) (d) on the grounds that the offering will comply with Rule 146.[35] Policy Statement 100 has not been revised to reflect the rescission of Rule 146 and the adoption of Regulation D. However, the Attorney General will entertain applications for exemption under the policy statement based on compliance with Regulation D.

An application under the policy statement would contain information similar to that required for offerings under the §352-g Exemption Instructions, including submission of copies of Form RI-1,[36] as well as letters from the general partners as to their prior real estate syndications and, where applicable, a designation of the New York Secretary of State as agent for service of process. The application should specify whether the offering will be made under Rule 504, 505 or 506. The person executing the application on behalf of the partnership must represent that he is familiar with Regulation D, that he and the partnership intend, and will use their best efforts, to make the offering in accordance with the rule specified in the application, that there will not be more than 35 nonaccredited purchasers of the interests in an offering under Rule 505 or 506, and that the partnership has consulted an identified attorney regarding the appropriate rule and its availability for the offering. If the offering is to be a nonpublic offering under Rule 504 of Regulation D, there are additional requirements. The application must set forth restrictions on the manner of offering the interests and the class of potential investors, so as to prevent a general solicitation of investors. If the investors do not have a preexisting relationship with the partnership or its principals, use of a private placement memorandum will be required. Public offerings under Rule 504 do not qualify under Policy Statement 100.

Within 10 days after the closing of the offering, the partnership must submit to the Attorney General an opinion letter from its counsel addressed to the partnership stating that the offering is exempt from the registration requirements of the federal Securities Act under Section 4(2) or the specified rule. The opinion must state the basis on which it is rendered, but counsel may rely on factual representations made by the partnership and those acting on its behalf. If Regulation D becomes unavailable to the offering for any reason, the offering must cease, and an amended application setting forth the facts must be filed. If the Attorney General does not grant an exemption for the amended application, all funds collected from the investors must be returned to them.

New York investors must sign a statement similar to that required under the §352-g Exemption Instructions before they make any payments.

Policy Statement 100 requires that one copy of the private placement memorandum (or the latest draft) be furnished with the application. The Department of Law's review of the memorandum focuses on disclosure of the profits to be received by the promoters and a few other "fairness" aspects of the offering. The Department of Law requires that meaningful financial suitability standards be imposed for nonaccredited investors. Where the investor is to pay for his partnership interest in installments, his failure to pay an installment may not result in the automatic forfeiture of his partnership interest. In the event of such a default, the interest may be sold under the applicable provisions of Article 9 of the Uniform Commercial Code (dealing with secured transactions and security interests) or other fair and reasonable arrangements may be provided for in the partnership agreement.

After the application has been filed, it is permissible to make "nonfirm" offers. If this is done, a legend similar to the following should be placed on the outside cover page of the private placement memorandum:

> An application for exemption from registration of the units has been submitted to the New York Attorney General, but has not yet been granted. The circulation of this memorandum does not constitute a firm. offering. No firm offering will be made until an exemption is obtained from the Attorney General, and the units may not be sold nor may offers to buy be accepted prior to the time the exemption has been granted.

It is necessary to file any offering literature used in New York within 10 days after it is first used. On request of the Department of Law, copies of the basic documents relating to the offering must be furnished. Within 10 days after closing, a copy of the partnership agreement and the names, addresses, and interests of the investors must be filed. In addition, the Department of Law usually asks for a copy of any tax opinion given by counsel for the partnership.

Projections generally are allowed in Regulation D type offerings if they meet the general requirements of the SEC for inclusion of projections in offering materials.[37] If the projections include a projected sale of the partnership's real estate, the Department of Law will usually require the inclusion of a projection of the consequences of a sale of the property at the price paid for it by the partnership and of a mortgage foreclosure for $1 over the then outstanding balance of the mortgages on the property.

c. General It must be remembered that the exemptions discussed previously are not granted automatically, but are subject to the discretion of the Attorney General. Until an exemption has been granted, the offering is subject to all the provisions of the statute.

In addition, the exemptions are only from certain of the filing requirements of the statute.[38] Other filing and substantive provisions of the statute must be met, as well as the various conditions that must be agreed to and undertaken in the application or offering documents in order to obtain an exemption.[39]

Thus various disclosure requirements are imposed on issuers seeking exemption. The proceeds of the offering must be held in trust for the benefit of investors, just as with offerings that are not exempt.[40] Audited annual financial statements must be provided to the investors,[40a] and source of distribution statements must be furnished as discussed for offerings made without exemption.

10. CALIFORNIA

a. General California's blue sky law, known as the Corporate Securities Law of 1968, is contained in the Corporations Code [41] and is administered by the Department of Corporations and the Commissioner of Corporations. As is typical with such laws, the California statute has provisions dealing with the qualification (i.e., registration) of securities to be offered or sold in the state; exemption from qualification; licensing and regulation of broker–dealers, securities salespersons, and investment advisers; fraudulent and other prohibited practices; and related matters. California is a "fair, just and equitable" state, and the Commissioner is authorized to deny, suspend, or revoke qualifications if he finds the offering or the issuer's plan of business does not meet standards of fairness and honesty.[42]

b. Limited Offering Exemption In 1981 the Corporate Securities Law of 1968 was amended, effective November 1, 1981, to provide a new limited offering exemption. [43] The Commissioner has adopted rules [44] under the exemption and published a release discussing the exemption and the rules.[45] From the standpoint of real estate limited partnerships, the exemption may eliminate the necessity of qualifying their limited partnership interests in many instances. We will now consider the more important provisions of the statute and the rules (which we will refer to collectively as the "exemption"). While the exemption is similar in many respects to the

SEC's Regulation D, there are significant differences. Accordingly, anyone intending to rely on the exemption should read the statute and the rules for a full understanding of their requirements.

The statute provides that securities offered and sold in a transaction meeting each of the specified criteria are exempted from the qualification requirement. The term "transaction" is not defined in the statute, and, thus the issue of integration of offerings (discussed in Section 26 of Chapter 8) becomes relevant. The rules offer a limited safe harbor by excluding from a "transaction" offers and sales that are made more than six months before or after the transaction sought to be covered by the exemption or, under specified circumstances, are made pursuant to a qualification of the securities with the Commissioner. Note that the exemption does not limit the application of any of its requirements solely to California purchasers and offerees. As a result, a real estate limited partnership desiring to rely on the exemption for an offering to be made in several states must tailor the entire offering to comply with the exemption even though the exemption is more restrictive in some aspects than the SEC's Regulation D or the exemptions available in the other states.

Sales of the securities may be made to a maximum of 35 purchasers, including purchasers outside of California. Not counted for purposes of the 35-purchaser test is any investor who purchases at least $150,000 of the securities or who is an individual with a net worth (or joint net worth with his spouse) exceeding $1,000,000 or with income (or joint income with his spouse) for each of the last two years and as anticipated for the current year in excess of $200,000, provided that in each case it can reasonably be assumed that the investor or his professional advisers are able to protect his interests as discussed in the next paragraph or that he can bear the economic risk of his investment.[46] Also excluded are the general partners of the partnership (if they exercise managerial functions), affiliates and promoters of the partnership, institutional investors as defined in the statute and rules, and certain other specified persons. Generally, each beneficial owner of the interests would be counted (or excluded) based on his own qualifications, except that a husband and wife (together with custodians or trustees for their minor children) are counted as one purchaser, as are organizations not specifically formed for the purpose of purchasing the interest and other entities owned entirely by specified persons who would not otherwise be counted.

Each purchaser (whether or not counted for the 35-purchaser test) must either (a) have a preexisting personal or business relationship with "the offeror or any of its partners, officers, directors or controlling persons," or (b) by reason of his or his professional advisers' business or financial experience be capable of being reasonably assumed to have the capacity to protect his own interests in connection with the transaction. The use of the term "offeror" and a reference in the rules to "customers" of a broker–dealer or investment adviser [47] might lead to the inference that a relationship with the partnership or its general partners and promoters is not necessary, and that a relationship with the broker–dealer selling the interests for the partnership could be sufficient. However, the informal position of the Department of Corporations is that "offeror" means "issuer" and, accordingly, that the relationship must be with the partnership or its partners or controlling persons. Ordinarily the relationship must be one that enables a reasonably prudent purchaser to be aware of the character, business acumen, and general financial circumstances of the person with whom he has the relationship.

To qualify as a "professional" adviser, the adviser must be an attorney or certified public accountant or, as a regular part of his business, be customarily relied on by others for investment recommendations or decisions, and must be unaffiliated with, and may not be directly or indirectly compensated by, the partnership or any of its affiliates or selling agents. Qualified advisers would include broker–dealers, licensed investment advisers, banks, and licensed real estate brokers if they have appropriate business or financial experience. As is apparent, the concept of a professional adviser under the exemption is much more restrictive than that of a purchaser representative under Regulation D.

There are no qualification requirements for, or limitations on the number of, offerees. However, the offering may not be made through the public dissemination of offering materials and advertising or similar public solicitation. Distribution of copies of the offering memorandum to persons believed to be interested in purchasing the limited partnership interests or to be qualified purchasers does not constitute public solicitation. Each purchaser must furnish an investment representation that he is purchasing for his own account and not for resale.

The exemption does not mandate the use of a private placement memorandum or require that investors be furnished any particular information, but an offering memorandum would ordinarily be used to comply with the antifraud provisions of the securities laws, including the federal Securities Act, and with the requirements of Regulation D if it is being relied on for exemption under that act. The use of a memorandum would also have a bearing on the ability of an investor or his advisers to protect his interests.

The partnership is required to file a notice (ordinarily on the SEC's Form D) with the Commissioner of Corporations within 30 days after completion of the offering. The form of notice and instructions are covered in Appendix 13 of this book. Failure to file the notice does not affect the availability of the exemption, although it does constitute a violation of the statute and could result in sanctions. If the notice is not filed voluntarily, the Commissioner can demand that it be filed. Under such circumstances, the issuer would have to pay a fee.

c. Qualification If the partnership is unable, or does not desire, to comply with the limited offering exemption and if there is no other applicable exemption available, the partnership will have to qualify the offering with the Commissioner. This would normally be a qualification by permit under Section 25113 of the statute. An application for qualification, consent to service of process, authorization of disclosures by financial institutions of certain financial records relating to the offering, exhibits, and other materials would be filed with the Commissioner, and a filing fee would be paid.[48] The qualification does not become effective until the Commissioner issues a permit after determining that the offering meets the state's fair, just, offering meets the state's fair, just, and equitable standards.

As part of the standards, the Commissioner has adopted guidelines for real estate programs.[49] In many respects, these guidelines are similar to those in the North American Securities Administrators Association's Statement of Policy Regarding Real Estate Programs, discussed in Section 6 of this chapter. If the partnership does not meet the standards required by the Commissioner and cannot change the offering to comply, the Commissioner often will allow the offering to be qualified as a limited offering qualification, a qualification that waives some or all of the requirements and authorizes the offer and sale of the securities in California only to "persons designated therein by name or class." [50] To obtain this type of qualification, the partnership normally must impose significantly higher suitability requirements for California investors (e.g., net worth of $250,000 to $500,000 or more and substantial income) and furnish California investors with written disclosure of the areas where the offering fails to meet the Commissioner's usual standards. A copy of this disclosure document, signed by the investor, must be retained by the partnership. In addition, substantial restrictions on transfer of the partnership interest by the investor would be imposed as required by Rule 260.141.11. A copy of this rule must be given to the investor, who must give the partnership written acknowledgment of receipt thereof,[51] and any certificates representing interests subject to the restrictions must contain a specified legend.

NOTES

1. *Hall v. Geiger-Jones Co.*, 242 U.S. 539, 550 (1917).

2. The state statutes, regulations, and certain other materials are compiled in the Blue Sky Law Reporter (CCH). Thirty-six states have adopted statutes based on the Uniform Securities Act. This act, which was approved by the National Conference of Commissioners on Uniform State Laws in 1956, is set forth in BLUE SKY L. REP. (CCH) ¶5501.

3. For registrations by coordination (SEC filings), most states will accept filings on Form U-1, the Uniform Application to Register Securities. BLUE SKY L. REP. (CCH) ¶5101. Some states accept filings on this form for registration by qualification.

4. Form U-2, Uniform Consent to Service of Process, is accepted by most states for this purpose. BLUE SKY L. REP. (CCH) ¶5111.

5. Some practices and requirements are not published. As a result, communication with the securities commission may be necessary.

6. In some instances, the limited offering exemption may be available only for preorganization subscriptions or in connection with the initial capitalization of the partnership.

7. Some states interpret "selling compensation" broadly and treat any payment of a profit to the sponsor from proceeds of the offering as indirect compensation. See, e.g., *Upton v. Trinidad Petroleum Corp.*, 652 F.2d 424 (5th Cir. 1981) (Alabama); *Schultz v. Rector-Philips-Morse, Inc.*, 552 S.W.2d 4 (Arkansas 1977); *Petroleum Resource Development Corp. v. Oklahoma*, 585 P.2d 346 (Oklahoma 1978).

8. See, e.g., Michigan Administrative Code §451.706.24, BLUE SKY L. REP. (CCH) ¶32,465; 15 Missouri Code of State Regulations §30-54.140, BLUE SKY L. REP. (CCH) ¶35,514.

9. The North American Securities Administrators Association has approved a Uniform Limited Offering Exemption that has been coordinated with the SEC's Regulation D. The exemption provides an exemption from registration for offerings sold in compliance with Sections 501, 502, 503, and 505 of Regulation D and with additional conditions imposed by the exemption. Offerings under Sections 504 and 506 are not covered by the exemption. Thus the exemption would be available only for offerings of $5,000,000 or less that are sold to a maximum of 35 nonaccredited purchasers plus an unlimited number of accredited investors. As approved by NASAA, the exemption reintroduces subjective suitability concepts that Regulation D rejected, requires that persons receiving remuneration in connection with sales of securities be appropriately registered in the state, and contains other restrictive provisions. It remains to be seen whether the states will adopt the exemption in the form approved by the association. Regulation D is set forth in Appendix 6 of this book; the Uniform Limited Offering Exemption is reproduced in BLUE SKY L. REP. (CCH) ¶5294. See Maloney, "Blue Sky Regulation of a Regulation D Offering: A 50 State Survey," 3 Real Est. Sec. J. 57 (1982).

10. Sometimes an exemption is available only to corporate issuers and not to partnerships. Thus it is necessary to review the applicable statutory and regulatory materials with extreme care.

11. BLUE SKY L. REP. (CCH) ¶5361.

12. Where the guidelines in the Statement of Policy conflict with requirements of the Securities and Exchange Commission, the statement will not apply. Statement of Policy §I(A) (3).

13. Consideration should always be given to the possible effect of these matters on the limited liability of the partners. See Chapter 1.

14. The portion of this chapter, regarding New York State laws, has benefited from the personal views of Thomas DiMeo, Principal Attorney, Department of Law, State of New York. We thank Mr. DiMeo.

15. Chapter 20 of the N.Y. Consolidated Laws, Article 23-A.

16. The provisions regarding intrastate offerings are contained in GEN. BUS. L. §359-ff and 13 NYCRR 80.1-80.16. The New York Real Estate Syndicate Act is discussed below.

17. GEN. BUS. L. §359-e(1) (a). Broker–dealer regulation in general is discussed in Chapter 9, and the matters discussed in that chapter should also be considered.

18. Offerings through a registered broker–dealer pursuant to a firm commitment underwriting would not bring the issuer within the definition of a "dealer" nor would private placements to institutional investors. The net capital requrements are not applicable to issuers who are deemed to be dealers solely by reason of issuing their own securities. GEN. BUS. L. §352-k(3).

19. Filing fees are required in connection with the filing of the Issuer Statement and the other documents referred to below.

20. Forms for the designations are available from the Department of Law. The designation must be acknowledged before a notary public by all who sign it, and should be enclosed in a legal backer that has been endorsed with the name of the partnership, the title of the document, and the name and address of the filer. A designation must also be filed in connection with filings and exemption applications under the Real Estate Syndicate Act.

21. This would be accomplished by the filing of a Supplemental Broker–Dealer Statement.

22. GEN. BUS. L. §352-e to §352-j.

23. "Nonfirm" offers (e.g., typical preliminary prospectuses) may be made. GEN. BUS. L. §352-e(1) (a).

24. *See Ledgebrook Corp. v. Lefkowitz*, 77 Misc. 2d 867, 354 N.Y.S. 2d 318 (Sup. Ct. 1974). See discussion in Section 9 of this chapter with respect to "no filing required" letters.

25. The regulations are contained in 13 NYCRR 16.1-16.9. Section 16.4 of the regulations provides for a prefiling procedure, the use of which, though optional, is ordinarily desirable.

26. Issuance of the letter is the equivalent of becoming effective under the blue sky laws of other states. The letter may require that certified copies of the original and amended limited partnership certificates be filed with the Department of Law within 20 days of the closing.

26a. This amount has sometimes been reduced to 50% for large offerings by major syndicators.

27. If the offering or the real estate transaction is abandoned or not consummated, Form RS-3 setting forth the reasons therefor and the disposition of the funds raised must be filed.

28. Limited projections have been permitted in some offerings involving net leases to tenants with substantial credit ratings or government-subsidized public housing. The extent to which such projections may be used has not been published. Accordingly, in such instances the prefiling procedure, *see* note 25, *supra*, should be used.

29. However, two fees would have to be paid, one for each of the exemptions requested. The fee for the application under Sec. 352-g or Policy Statement 100 thereunder would be the same as the fee for a nonexempt filing, ranging from $250 to $10,000, depending on the size of the entire offering, including the portions sold outside New York. The fee for the application under Sec. 359-f(2) (d) is $100, which is equal to the basic fee for filing a Broker–Dealer or Issuer Statement. A separate check for each fee should be submitted.

30. Policy Statement 100 is contained in Appendix 10; *see also* BLUE SKY L. REP. (CCH) ¶42,571. The Instructions for §352-g Exemptions is contained in Appendix 11; *see also* BLUE SKY L. REP. (CCH) ¶42,572. In the unlikely event that exemption is sought only under Sec. 359-f (2) (d), the provisions of the §359-e Issuer Exemption Instruction Sheet, copies of which can be obtained from the Department of Law, would be applicable. Note that exemption under Sec. 359-f(2) (d) does not relieve the partnership of its obligation to file a "further state notice" in connection with an offering of its securities even though the other broker–dealer filings are not required.

31. Each general partner or principal must furnish an executed copy of Form RI-1 giving detailed information as to his business background. If the application is under clause (1) of Sec. 352-g, the general partners must submit letters giving certain information as to all real estate syndications in which they have engaged in the last 10 years which have any New York investors.

32. All offerees, whether or not the offer is to be made in New York, must be counted.

33. It is sufficient if the proposed offerees have other existing relationships, e.g., being clients of a specified attorney or accountant.

34. Although offering literature is not required to obtain the exemption, consideration must be given to the general disclosure and antifraud provisions of the various securities laws.

35. Policy Statement 100 does not establish exclusive procedures; an issuer offering may apply for exemption under Sec. 352-g(1) if there are no more than 40 offerees. The Policy Statement cannot be used for offerings of cooperative, condominium, or home-owners' association interests in real estate.

36. *See* note 31, *supra.*

37. *See* §229.10(b) of the SEC's Regulation S-K and the discussion in Chapter 11.

38. Failure to comply with the requirements of the Martin Act may result in a private cause of action, *see Herzfeld v. Laventhol, Krekstein, Horwath, & Horwath,* 378 F. Supp. 112 (S.D.N.Y. 1974), *modified,* 540 F. 2d 27 (2d Cir. 1976), or an action by the Attorney General for restitution and/or a permanent injunction, *see* GEN. BUS. L. §353 and *People v. Development Services (AJ), Inc.,* BLUE SKY L. REP. (CCH) ¶71,565 (N.Y. Sup. Ct. 1980).

39. Instructions for §352-g Exemptions and Policy Statement 100 contain many such requirements. In addition, a standard statement of "certain special requirements" for offering literature submitted under Section 352-g, which is available from the Department of Law and is reproduced in BLUE SKY L. REP. (CCH) ¶42,571.01, sets forth additional requirements.

40. The undertaking to hold the proceeds in trust must be included in the offering memorandum for an exempt offering, and the exemption application must identify the bank where the proceeds will be deposited in trust.

40a. Unaudited financial statements may be permitted if the partnership agreement requires the partnership to furnish audited statements at the partnership's expense on the request of limited partners owning at least 30% of the limited partnership interests.

41. Cal. Corp. Code §§25000 to 25706. The law is reproduced in BLUE SKY L. REP. (CCH) ¶11,101 et seq.

42. Section 25140.

43. Section 25102(f), which is set forth in Appendix 12 of this book.

44. 10 California Administrative Code, Rules 260.102.12, 260.102.13 and 260.102.14, which are set forth in Appendix 13 of this book.

45. Department of Corporations, Release No. 67-C (October 21, 1981), BLUE SKY L. REP. (CCH) ¶12,558.

46. An investment (including mandatory assessments) that does not exceed 10% of the purchaser's net worth (valuing his principal residence and improvements as set forth in Rule 260.102.13(e)(2)) is presumed to be sufficient.

47. Section (d) of Rule 260.102.12.

48. The procedures for qualification are set forth in 10 California Administrative Code, Rule 260.110 *et seq.,* BLUE SKY L. REP. (CCH) ¶11,821 *et seq.* The Customer Authoriza-

tion of Disclosure of Financial Records form, and other required forms, can be obtained from the Department of Corporations.

49. 10 California Adminstrative Code, Rules 260.140.110.1 *et seq.*, BLUE SKY L. REP. (CCH) ¶11,961 *et seq.*

50. Rule 260.001(e), BLUE SKY L. REP. (CCH) ¶11,742.

51. The disclosure and the acknowledgment customarily take the form of an addendum to the subscription agreement, disclosing the variances in the offering from the California standards and furnishing a copy of Rule 260.141.11.

CHAPTER 11

DISCLOSURE

1. GENERAL

As indicated in the preceding chapters, when an issuer's securities are being sold for its benefit, the various federal and state securities laws impose on the issuer and others participating in the sale an obligation to make available to investors all material information necessary to make an informed investment decision. This obligation exists whether or not the securities are registered or exempt from registration with the SEC or state securities commissions. Typically, the obligation is met by furnishing investors with a prospectus or offering memorandum that describes the offering and the issuer, its management, business, and property.[1]

The extent of the disclosure required of a real estate limited partnership will vary with, among other matters, the type of investment, the nature of the activities to be carried on, the type of real estate to be owned by the partnership, the knowledge and sophistication of the investors, and the regulatory authorities who review the documents.

For example, the offering of a start-up single property construction and holding real estate syndication requires a disclosure very different from that needed for the offering of an ongoing multiproperty venture.

In the case of a public offering registered with the SEC under the Securities Act of 1933 ("Securities Act"), a registration statement, including a prospectus, is filed with the SEC.[2] The SEC has adopted a number of registration forms specifying the information required to be included in registration statements filed by various issuers for offerings of different types of securities. Form S-11 is prescribed for use by issuers whose business is primarily acquiring and holding real estate or interests in real estate for investment and is the form that would be appropriate for most publicly offered real estate limited partnerships.[3] The SEC has published a series of industry guides for the preparation and filing of registration statements under the Securities Act.[4] The guides are not rules of the SEC; they merely represent policies and practices followed by the staff of the SEC in reviewing registration statements for public offerings. Of particular importance for real estate limited partnerships is Guide 5 (formerly designated Guide 60), entitled "Preparation of Registration Statements Relating to Interests in Real Estate Limited Partnerships."[5]

In addition, most state securities commissions have adopted rules setting forth standards for prospectuses used in offerings registered in their jurisdictions.[6] Often these rules provide for disclosures in addition to those mandated for offerings registered with the SEC. Sometimes the rules of one or more states conflict with what the SEC or other states require or permit. When an offering is registered with the SEC, the state commissions sometimes, but not always, will waive compliance with any of their own rules that are inconsistent with the SEC's requirements. In cases of unresolved conflict among the rules of the regulatory authorities, frequently difficult decisions or much ingenuity is necessary.

2. AN APPROACH TO DISCLOSURE

Since failure to make adequate disclosure of all material risks of the investment may result in suits for damages or rescission by investors or in action by the regulatory authorities, the tendency in the drafting of prospectuses has been to emphasize the risks to investors and the negative aspects of the offering, often to the exclusion of information as to the merits of the offering. This reflects the "insurance" function of the prospectus, which, in the extreme, results in the prospectus setting forth every conceivable risk that may be involved in an offering of the type being made. The theory underlying this practice is that an investor should have no grounds for complaint, because a dismal picture has been painted.

The prospectus, however, is intended to serve an information function. From it, investors are supposed to obtain sufficient information to enable them to decide whether or not to purchase the securities offered. Inclusion of excessive, lengthy material about irrelevant negative matters may result in the investor's overlooking important relevant facts. Accordingly, the better view is that the tension between the insurance and information functions should be resolved by a balanced presentation emphasizing the material facts. Irrelevant risk factors should be omitted, and adequate information as to the merits of the offering should be included. This may have an added advantage: The sellers of the partnership interests may not be tempted to induce people to invest by the use of "facts" not in the prospectus.

A generally conservative approach is nevertheless desirable because, in the event of any litigation, the disclosures in the prospectus will be judged in the light of hindsight.

The key to drafting a prospectus is to thoroughly understand the transaction. It is necessary to analyze all aspects of the transaction and to read all relevant documents in order to identify the benefits investors will expect to receive, the mechanism by which these benefits will be generated, and the factors that might prevent or impede the generation of the benefits and their receipt by the investors.[7]

The prospectus should focus on clarity of presentation. Charts, tables, illustrations, maps, and similar devices may be used where appropriate. Typically, during the drafting process additional points will appear and have to be considered, and the prospectus will be revised and redrafted a number of times before a satisfactory result is achieved. The final product should be reviewed as a whole to ascertain whether the overall effect is to clearly and understandably communicate the information. If necessary, additional revisions should be made.

Of course, a prospectus prepared for use in an offering registered with the SEC or the states must meet the standards promulgated by the appropriate agencies in order to obtain registration of the offering. However, merely disclosing the information specifically requested by these agencies may not be sufficient; all material information should be included whether or not specifically called for.[8]

In exempt offerings that are not registered with the SEC or a state securities commission, the standards for registered offerings, especially Form S-11 and Guide 5, provide some guidelines for appropriate disclosure practices. However, since these standards are oriented toward registered public offerings, there are many respects in which they are inapplicable for private placements and other exempt offerings. For example, the undertakings in Section 21 of Guide 5 relate only to offerings registered with the SEC. In addition, because registered public offerings may be made to unsophisticated investors, Form S-11 and Guide 5 of necessity take an extremely conservative approach. In private placements, where the investors are sophisticated or have sophisticated advisers, it is possible to omit or condense information that would otherwise be required in a public offering without adversely affecting an investor's ability to evaluate the investment.[9] Indeed, shortening the prospectus, omitting unnecessary details, and concentrating on the material items may make it easier to evaluate the merits of the offering. Finally, since the original adoption of the guide in March 1976, the Internal Revenue Code has been amended several times in areas relevant to real estate limited partnerships, and thus the guide's suggestions regarding taxes must be modified in certain respects.

Despite these limitations, and inasmuch as they reflect conservative practice, Form S-11 and Guide 5 are helpful starting points and may be of use in connection with the preparation of prospectuses for offerings not registered with the SEC. We will now briefly consider certain of the items covered in Form S-11 and Guide 5.

3. COVER PAGE

In addition to the type of information described in Guide 5 relating to the partnership, the offering, and the risk factors, the cover page of the prospectus normally contains various specific disclaimers required by the SEC or the state securities commissions to the effect that the commissions have not passed on the merits of the securities or the accuracy or adequacy of the prospectus. If the offering has not been registered with any securities commission, a statement to that effect customarily is included. Other legends may include a statement that no information is authorized for use in the sale of the partnership interests which is not contained in the prospectus, a reference to the suitability standards being imposed, and a statement that the prospectus does not constitute an offer in any jurisdiction where the offer would be illegal.

In the case of private placements or intrastate offerings, it is helpful to state on the cover page that no offer is made by the prospectus if the name of an offeree has not been inserted in a specified space, and that no offer shall be deemed to have been made if the identified offeree is not qualified.

Often there are statements that reproduction or redistribution of the prospectus for an exempt offering may not be made without the consent of the general partner and that the recipient of the prospectus agrees to return it to the general partner if the recipient does not invest in the partnership.

4. COMPENSATION OF THE GENERAL PARTNER; CONFLICTS OF INTEREST

The various fees, compensation, interests in the partnership, and other benefits to be received by the general partner, the sponsor, and their affiliates should be summarized. If necessary, cross-references can be made to more detailed disclosures elsewhere in the prospectus.

Contemplated transactions between the partnership and the general partner, the sponsor, or their affiliates must be disclosed. Where these or other transactions may result in conflicts between the interests of the investors and the interests of others involved in the program, the potential conflicts should be discussed. If a method for resolving the conflicts will be adopted, such as the use of independent appraisals where the partnership may acquire property from affiliated parties, this should be set forth in the prospectus.

5. RISK FACTORS

One section of the prospectus should describe the principal risk factors applicable to an investment in the partnership. This section should be brief, and the risk factors need only be summarized, with cross-references to fuller discussion in other parts of the prospectus.

Guide 5 contains examples of the types of risks to be disclosed in the risk factors section. However, this is only illustrative, and in each offering it is necessary to analyze the transaction to ascertain what in fact are the material risks to the investors. Risk factors may be inherent in the tax, real estate, business, partnership structuring, management, financing, and other aspects of the offering, and they may relate generally to offerings of the type being made or arise from the particular offering. In determining the risks to be described, consideration should be given to the principal features on which the success of the investment depends, the factors which could cause the partnership or the limited partner's investment to be unsuccessful, and the aspects in which the transaction may differ from similar investments.

6. SPONSOR'S TRACK RECORD

Guide 5 requests inclusion of a narrative summary and tabular presentations of the previous syndication experience of the sponsor and general partner and their affiliates in both registered and exempt offerings. A lengthy suggested format is set forth in the guide.[10]

With respect to prospectuses for exempt offerings, it is necessary to consider the relevance of the track record of prior performance to the investor, because the extensive disclosure called for in offerings registered with the SEC, which are usually blind pools, may not be necessary or appropriate, especially if the partnership will acquire only one identified property. Judgment must be exercised in the light of the similarity of the current and prior syndications, the extent to which the current syndication's results may depend on the experience of the sponsor, and the extent to which prior syndications experienced adverse conditions or results.

7. DESCRIPTION OF REAL ESTATE

The real estate owned or to be constructed or acquired by the partnership as well as plans for its use, development, or improvement should be described.[11] Form S-11, Guide 5, and Regulation S-K indicate the kinds of information that, depending on the circumstances, should be considered for inclusion.

8. TAXES

The tax consequences of an investment in the partnership are a major concern to the investors, since investments in real estate limited partnerships generally are motivated, at least in part, by anticipated tax benefits. Thus it is not surprising that the longest section of Guide 5 is devoted to disclosures as to the tax aspects of the offering. The discussion of the tax implications of acquiring an interest in the partnership should be tailored to the offering and should not be limited to the matters referred to in the guide. The possibility of changes in the law should be pointed out as well as uncertainties in the interpretation of the law. Customarily, investors are urged to consult their own professional advisers for guidance as to the effect the tax matters may have on them and to rely on their own advisers with respect to the tax aspects of the offering.[12]

9. FINANCIAL STATEMENTS

Many real estate limited partnership offerings involve partnerships that will be formed only after the capital is raised. Further, the partnership will be intended to acquire land and construct and hold a single residential or commercial building. In such instances, no financial statements of the partnership or the property can be obtained.

For existing partnerships, the financial statements to be filed as part of a registration statement on Form S-11 are set forth in Article 3 of Regulation S-X. These include balance sheets as of the end of each of the partnership's last two fiscal years and statements of income, changes in financial position, and partner's equity for the last three fiscal years (or if less than three years, the life of the partnership) plus certain schedules. These financial statements must be audited.[13] If the fiscal year ended more than 134 days prior to filing of the registration statement, and under certain other circumstances, unaudited interim financial statements as of a more recent date are required. A five-year summary of selected financial data is also necessary, as well as a discussion and analysis of the partnership's financial condition and results of operations.[14]

The form and content of financial statements to be filed with the SEC are prescribed in Regulation S-X.[15] The SEC requires that financial statements for limited partnerships be prepared in accordance with generally accepted accounting principles; financial information may be presented on a tax basis in addition to, but not in lieu of, presentation on the basis of generally accepted accounting principles.[16]

Form S-11 does not specifically require financial information as to the sponsor of the program.[16a] Some states may require such financial information. In states that have taken no position on this subject, the extent to which there should be disclosure of financial information regarding the sponsor would depend on the materiality of the information and the amount of the sponsor's financial commitments to the partnership. The form of the disclosure would vary with the circumstances, ranging from a mere representation of the sponsor's net worth to complete financial statements.

10. PROJECTIONS

The status of projections in SEC registered offerings has changed. In the past, the SEC took the position that inclusion of projections in a registration statement was inherently misleading and, therefore, not permissible. The SEC now encourages voluntary disclosure of projections [17] and other items of forward-looking information in filings made with the Commission.[18] To further this goal, the SEC has adopted Rule 175 under the Securities Act. If all the rule's requirements are met, the rule furnishes a safe harbor from liability under the antifraud provisions by interpreting these provisions to require a showing that a projection which turned out to be erroneous was prepared without a reasonable basis and was disclosed other than in good faith. Rule 175 applies only to offerings registered with the SEC (and certain other filings), including registration statements for public offerings by real estate limited partnerships; [19] it does not provide protection for offerings exempt from SEC registration.

In any event, subject to meeting the requirements of the appropriate state securities commissions, prospectuses used in private placements and other limited offerings of real estate limited partnership interests frequently include projections of the expected performance of the partnership. The projections typically consist of statements of projected taxable income and loss, cash flow, and source and use of funds and an analysis of the consequences of the purchase of one unit in the partnership by investors in various tax brackets.[20] Accompanying these statements is a listing of the assumptions on which the projections are based. There may also be a letter from the accountants who prepared or reviewed the projections which, in part, warns that the actual results achieved may vary materially from the projections.

Where appropriate, the use of projections can be extremely helpful in assisting investors to understand the proposed investment. However, since projections may create an unwarranted air of certainty as to the expected results, they must be used with care. The projections should be carefully prepared in good faith by qualified personnel (normally the partnership's accountants), should be based on reasonable, realistic assumptions that are disclosed, and should be accompanied by a clear statement to the effect that they represent a mere prediction of future events based on assumptions which might not occur, may not be relied on as indicating the actual results which will be obtained, and are not a representation that the projected results will be achieved.[21] When the projections are based on assumptions as to the tax treatment of the partnership's operations, it may be useful to ask the partnership's accountants for a letter stating that they expect to prepare the partnership's tax returns in a manner consistent with the projections if the nontax assumptions in the projections occur as anticipated.

NOTES

1. In some instances, the information may be given orally, and in other instances, such as certain private placements, the investor's access to the information may be sufficient. See, generally, the discussion in Section 13 of Chapter 8 of this book.

2. A former SEC commissioner has suggested that there is a need in a number of areas for reconsideration of the federal securities laws and the SEC's activities, including the disclosure philosophy underlying the Securities Act and the SEC's involvement with real estate investments. McCauley, "The Securities Laws—After 40 Years: A Need for Rethinking," 48 NOTRE DAME LAW. 1092 (1973).

3. Form S-11 is also intended for use by real estate investment trusts. Partnerships that will make their profits from buying and selling real estate or from carrying on a business on the property would use Form S-1, a basic form used when no other form is authorized or prescribed. Edward C. Tietig, avail. September 6, 1976, FED. SEC. L. REP. (CCH) ¶80,743 (agricultural business). Form S-18 could be used for offerings up to $5,000,000.

   Much of the information required to be included in registration statements is consolidated in the SEC's Regulation S-K (17 C.F.R. Part 229), and the instructions in the various registration statement forms incorporate by reference the provisions of that regulation. Regulation S-X (17 C.F.R. Part 210) prescribes the requirements for the financial statements to be included in registration statements and for the form and content of the financial statements.

4. Securities Act Release No. 6384 (March 3, 1982).

5. Guide 5 is reproduced in Appendix 9. *See* Clurman & Rose, "Private Offerings of Real Estate," 10 Rev. Sec. Reg. 821 (1977), for a discussion of Guide 5.

6. The Statement of Policy Regarding Real Estate Programs adopted by the North American Securities Adminstrators Association requires that prospectuses meet the requirements of Guide 5. The Statement of Policy is discussed in Chapter 10.

7. In an offering registered under the federal Securities Act, diligence in investigating and verifying the information in the registration statement would constitute a defense against liability under Section 11 of the Securities Act for parties other than the issuer.

8. Rule 408 under the Securities Act, 17 C.F.R. §230.408, provides as follows: "In addition to the information expressly required to be included in a registration statement, there shall be added such further material information, if any, as may be necessary to make the required statements, in the light of the circumstances under which they are made, not misleading."

9. Under Rule 502(b)(2)(i) of Regulation D it is necessary to furnish the same kind of information that would be required to be included in a prospectus in a registration statement filed under the Securities Act; however, such information must be furnished only "to the extent material to an understanding of the issuer, its business, and the securities being offered." It is not mandatory to provide any additional disclosures as required by Guide 5 or otherwise, though such disclosure may be necessary to satisfy the general antifraud provisions of the securities laws. See the discussion in Section 13 of Chapter 8.

10. The disclosure consists of a narrative summary describing the sponsor's experience in the last ten years with all real estate programs and six tables giving data about the sponsor's programs during the last three to five years.

11. *Spatz v. Borenstein*, 513 F. Supp. 571 (N.D. Ill. 1981).

12. Examples of disclosure provisions are contained in "Workbook for Tax Disclosure Provisions (S.E.C. Guide 60)" (American Bar Association, Section of Taxation, Committee on Real Estate Tax Problems, 1980).

13. With respect to financial statements for a limited offering under Regulation D, see Rule 502(b) of that regulation.

14. Items 301 and 303 of Regulation S-K. The requirements for the updating of financial information prior to the registration statement's being declared effective are set forth in Rule 3-12 of Regulation S-X. The financial statements and other information necessary with respect to significant properties acquired or to be acquired by the partnership is specified in Rule 3-14 of Regulation S-X; this would include audited income statements for three years, and, under certain circumstances, a one-year pro forma statement of estimated taxable operating results.

15. *See also* Topic 4-F of SEC Staff Accounting Bulletin No. 40 (January 23, 1981), as amended.

16. Section 405 of SEC Financial Reporting Release No. 1 (April 15, 1982); Exchange Act Release No. 12195 (March 11, 1976). However, Rule 502(b) of Regulation D permits the use of tax basis financial statements in some circumstances.

16a. *But see* Item 21 (h) of Form S-18 which requires audited balance sheets or other financial information as to general partners.

17. Section 229.10 (b) of Regulation S-K.

18. The accounting profession distinguishes a forecast, which is based on management's judgment of the most likely set of conditions and its most likely course of action, from a projection, which is based on assumptions that are not necessarily the most likely. "Guide for a Review of a Financial Forecast" (American Institute of Certified Public Accountants, 1980). We are using the term "projections" to encompass both concepts.

19. Sharon Davis, avail. August 9, 1975 (specified property offering). It is unlikely that projections would be permitted in a blind pool syndication.

20. Sometimes a projection of the tax consequences of a disposition of the real estate at the end of 21 years for $1 over the then outstanding principal balance of the mortgage is also included. The North American Securities Administrators Association's Statement of Policy Regarding Real Estate Programs, which is discussed in Chapter 10, sets forth in detail its approach to the use of projections.

21. *Dolgow v. Anderson,* 53 F.R.D. 664 (E.D.N.Y. 1971), *aff'd per curiam,* 464 F.2d 437 (2d Cir. 1972). *But see Beecher v. Able,* 374 F. Supp. 341 (S.D.N.Y. 1974).

MODEL AGREEMENT OF LIMITED PARTNERSHIP

ABLE ASSOCIATES

AGREEMENT OF LIMITED PARTNERSHIP

[date]

CONTENTS

AGREEMENT OF LIMITED PARTNERSHIP. ABLE ASSOCIATES

AGREEMENT OF LIMITED PARTNERSHIP made as of   1982, by and among ALLAN A. ABLE of New York, New York and ABLE, INC., a Delaware corporation (hereinafter sometimes referred to as the "General Partners"), and the persons signing this Agreement as limited partners (hereinafter sometimes referred to as the "Limited Partners"). The General Partners and the Limited Partners are hereinafter sometimes collectively referred to as the "Partners."

ARTICLE I

FORMATION OF LIMITED PARTNERSHIP

Formation: Certificates.   The Partners hereby form a limited partnership pursuant to the laws of the State of New York. The Partners shall from time to time execute or cause to be executed all such certificates or other documents or cause to be done all such filing, recording, publishing, or other acts as may be necessary or appropriate to comply with the requirements for the formation and the operation of a limited partnership under the laws of the State of New York and all other jurisdictions in which the Partnership may conduct business. Prior to conducting any business in any jurisdiction, the General Partners shall cause the Partnership either to comply with all the requirements for the qualification of the Partnership to conduct business as a limited partnership in such jurisdiction, or to conduct business in such jurisdiction through other partnerships or entities, through the General Partners as the Partnership's agents, or by such other means as the General Partners, upon the advice of counsel, deem appropriate to preserve the Limited Partner's limited liability; *provided, however,* that in the opinion of counsel to the Partnership the conducting of business through any Person other than a partnership would not result in the Partnership being classified for Federal income tax purposes as an association taxable as a corporation and not as a partnership.

ARTICLE II

NAME, PURPOSE, PLACE OF BUSINESS, AND TERM OF PARTNERSHIP

2.1. Name. The name of the Partnership shall be ABLE ASSOCIATES.

2.2. Purpose. The purpose of the Partnership shall be to acquire the Property and develop and construct thereon the Improvements, and generally to own, hold, operate, lease, and maintain the Project.

2.3. Place of Business. The principal place of business of the Partnership shall be at 1 Park Place, New York, New York or such other location as may hereafter be determined by the General Partners on prior notice to each of the Limited Partners.

2.4. Term. The term of the Partnership shall commence as of the date of the filing of the Certificate under the laws of the State of New York and shall continue until December 31, 2010, unless sooner dissolved or terminated as provided in Section 9.2 of this Agreement.

ARTICLE III

DEFINITIONS

As used herein the following terms shall have the following meanings:

(*a*) "Able" shall mean Allan A. Able, a General Partner.

(*b*) "Affiliate" shall mean, with respect to a specified person, a person who, directly or indirectly through one or more intermediaries, controls, or is controlled by or is under common control with, the person specified.

(*c*) "Capital Account Deficit" shall mean the existence of a negative balance in the capital account of a Partner.

(*d*) "Certificate" shall mean the Certificate of Limited Partnership of the Partnership, to be duly filed, published and amended, as herein required, in accordance with the laws of the State of New York.

(*e*) "Code" shall mean the Internal Revenue Code of 1954, as amended.

(*f*) "Construction Loan" shall mean a loan in the maximum principal amount of $3,000,000 with interest at a rate not to exceed 10% per annum on the outstanding principal balance from time to time, made to the Partnership by the Fourth Federal National Bank pursuant to the Construction Loan Commitment, or any substitute for such indebtedness pursuant to the Standby Commitments.

(*g*)   "Construction Loan Commitment" shall mean the commitment dated April 5, 1982 between the Partnership and the Fourth Federal National Bank and any modification thereto as may be agreed to from time to time.

(*h*)   "Event of Bankruptcy" with respect to any Person shall mean (*i*) the entry of a decree or order by a court of competent jurisdiction adjudging such Person a bankrupt or insolvent or approving as properly filed a petition seeking adjustment or composition of or in respect of such Person under any Federal, State, or foreign law relating to bankruptcy or insolvency, or appointing a receiver, liquidator, assignee, trustee, sequestrator (or other similar official) of such Person or of all or a substantial part of the property of such Person, ordering the winding up or liquidation of the affairs of such Person, which decree or order shall remain unstayed and in effect for a period of 30 consecutive days or (*ii*) the institution by such Person of proceedings to be adjudged a bankrupt or insolvent, or the consent by such Person to the institution of bankruptcy or insolvency proceedings against him or it, or the filing by him or it of a petition or answer or consent seeking reorganization or relief under the Federal Bankruptcy Code or any other applicable Federal, State, or foreign law or the consent by such Person to the filing of any such petition or to the appointment of a receiver, liquidator, assignee, trustee, sequestrator (or other similar official) of such Person or of all or a substantial part of the property of such Person, or (*iii*) the Person is generally not paying his or its debts as such debts become due, or that a custodian, other than a trustee, receives, or agent appointed or authorized to take charge of less than substantially all of the Person's property for the purpose of enforcing a lien against such property, was appointed or took possession, or the taking of any corporate or other action by such Person in furtherance of any such action.

(*i*)   "Event of Dissolution" shall mean the withdrawal, retirement, resignation, liquidation, Event of Bankruptcy, death, or incapacity of any Partner.

(*j*)   "Fiscal Year" shall mean the calendar year.

(*k*)   "Improvements" shall mean a 250 unit garden apartment project, together with any social, recreational, or commercial facilities incidental or pertinent thereto.

(*l*)   "Management Agreement" shall mean the agreement between the Partnership and Reliable Management Co., Inc., dated April 15, 1982, providing for management of the Project and subordination and assignment to the Partners of a portion of the fee for such management.

(*m*) "Net Cash Flow" shall mean for each Fiscal Year all cash funds of the Partnership received from operations, less the sum of (*i*) current charges and expenses, (*ii*) debt service payments with respect to the Permanent Loan or any other Partnership Loan or obligation (other than Operating Deficit Loans), (*iii*) expenditures for acquisition of Partnership property and for capital improvements or replacements not financed through capital contributions, borrowings, or reserves previously set aside by the Partnership for such purposes, and (*iv*) payments to reserves for working capital, contingencies, capital improvements, and replacements, paid by the Partnership in such year. Net Cash Flow shall not include Net Cash Proceeds.

(*n*) "Net Cash Proceeds" shall mean the cash proceeds to the Partnership resulting from the refinancing of the Permanent Loan or other loan secured by the Project, or from the sale, exchange, condemnation or similar eminent domain taking, casualty, or other disposition of all or substantially all of the Partnership's property, or from the sale of easements, rights-of-way or similar interests in the Partnership's property or any other similar items which in accordance with generally accepted accounting principles are attributable to capital, after payment of or provision for debts and obligations, repairs and replacements, deduction of all expenses incurred in connection with such cash proceeds and satisfaction of liens pertaining thereto.

(*o*) "Net Profits and Losses" shall mean the profits and losses of the Partnership for Federal income tax purposes for each Fiscal Year determined in accordance with the accounting method followed by the Partnership for such purposes.

(*p*) "Operating Deficit Loans" shall mean non-interest-bearing loans to the Partnership for use in connection with the operation of the Partnership's business as described in Section 6.2 of this Agreement.

(*q*) "Partnership" shall mean the Limited Partnership formed pursuant to this Agreement and the Certificate.

(*r*) "Percentage of Partnership Interest" of a Partner shall mean the particular Partner's percentage of interest in the Partnership, as set forth opposite the Partner's name on Exhibit B hereto.

(*s*) "Permanent Loan" shall mean a loan in the maximum principal amount of $3,000,000, with interest at a rate not to exceed 9¾% per annum and constant annual debt service not to exceed $310,000 per annum, made to the Partnership by the International Insurance Company pursuant to the Permanent Loan Commitment, or any substitute for such indebtedness pursuant to the Standby Commitments.

(*t*) Permanent Loan Commitment" shall mean the commitment dated March 15, 1982 between the Partnership and the International Insurance

Company and any modification thereto as may be agreed to from time to time.

(*u*) "Person" shall mean an individual, trust, estate, partnership, joint venture, association, company, corporation, or other entity.

(*v*) "Project" shall mean the Property and the Improvements.

(*w*) "Property" shall mean the real property located in New York, New York, and more particularly described in Exhibit A hereto.

(*x*) "Representative" shall mean the executor, administrator, guardian, trustee, or other personal representative of a Partner.

(*y*) "Sharing Ratio" shall mean a particular Partner's percentage of interest in any Net Cash Flow, Net Cash Proceeds, or Net Profits and Losses, as set forth opposite the Partner's name on Exhibit B hereto.

(*z*) "Standby Commitments" shall mean the commitments of Able Mortgage and Investment Co., Inc., dated May 1, 1982, to make or arrange for standby construction or permanent mortgage financing for the Partnership in connection with the Project.

(*aa*) "Unit" shall mean the interest in the Partnership of a Limited Partner who has agreed to contributed $40,000 to the capital of the Partnership.

ARTICLE IV

CAPITAL CONTRIBUTIONS, ACCOUNTS, AND WITHDRAWALS

4.1. General Partner Capital Contributions. The General Partners shall contribute to the capital of the Partnership upon execution of the Agreement and the Certificate an aggregate amount of $8,080, as follows:

(*a*) Able   —$4,040; and

(*b*) Able, Inc.—$4,040.

4.2. Limited Partner Capital Contributions

(*a*) Subject to the terms and conditions of this Agreement, the Limited Partners shall contribute in cash to the capital of the Partnership the aggregate amount of $800,000. The capital contribution for each Unit shall be paid (*i*) $10,000 upon execution of this Agreement and the Certificate and admission as a Limited Partner, (*ii*) $15,000 upon the later of (*A*) June 15,

1983 or (*B*) payment to the Partnership of the full amount of the Permanent Loan pursuant to the Permanent Loan Commitment, or the full amount of a substitute loan pursuant to the Standby Commitments, and (*iii*) $15,000 upon the later of (*A*) June 15, 1984 or (*B*) the date on which the Project shall have attained 95% occupancy under written leases the term of each of which is not less than 1 year, as determined by the Partnership's regularly employed certified public accountants. Notwithstanding any other provision in this Agreement to the contrary, if an earlier payment of a capital contribution is not required to be paid by the time a later payment becomes due and payable, such later payment shall be deferred until the earlier payment becomes due and payable and shall be paid simultaneously with such earlier payment.

(*b*)   Each Limited Partner, by his execution of this Agreement, hereby grants and assigns to the Partnership a security interest in his Unit to secure the payment of the amounts to be paid by him pursuant to Section 4.2(*a*). Each Limited Partner agrees that upon the occurrence of any Event of Default (as defined in this Section 4.2(*b*)), the Partnership may, in addition to any other remedies to which it may be entitled, sell the defaulting Limited Partner's Unit at public or private sale, at such price, for cash or on credit, as the General Partners may determine, with the right to the Partnership or any Partner (except the defaulting Limited Partner) to purchase all or any part of such Unit. The net proceeds from any such sale shall be applied to the payment of all obligations to the Partnership of the defaulting Limited Partner and to the reasonable costs of such sale, including attorney's fees and collection costs, and the defaulting Limited Partner shall be liable for any deficiency, or entitled to any surplus, remaining after such application of proceeds.

The occurrence of any of the following events shall constitute an Event of Default hereunder with respect to a Limited Partner to whom such event applies: (*i*) the failure to make payment when due of the cash payable to the Partnership pursuant to Section 4.2(*a*); (*ii*) an Event of Bankruptcy; or (*iii*) the attachment by any creditor of a Limited Partner of any property or credits of such Limited Partner held by the Partnership or in which such Limited Partner has an interest, and such attachment shall not have been discharged within 60 days. Except as provided in Section 4.3(*c*) of this Agreement, each Limited Partner hereby waives presentment, demand for payment or any other notice or demand in connection with any of his obligations to the Partnership.

4.3   Conditions of Limited Partners Capital Contributions

(*a*)   The obligation of each Limited Partner to make the payment described in Section 4.2(*a*)(*i*) is subject to the truth and correctness of the representations and warranties set forth in Article XIV of this Agreement and the receipt by the Limited Partners (at the expense of the General Partners) of an opinion of Messrs. Jones & Jones, counsel for the Partnership, in the form attached hereto as Exhibit C.

(*b*)   The obligation of each Limited Partner to make any payment described in Sections 4.2(*a*)(*ii*) or (*iii*) is subject to the condition that as of the date when such payment is required to be made, (*i*) each of the representations and warranties set forth in subsections (*a*), (*b*), (*c*), and (*h*) of Section 14.1 and Section 14.2 of this Agreement is true and correct; (*ii*) the General Partners or their Affiliates are not in material default with respect to any of their agreements and obligations to the Partnership and the Limited Partners hereunder; and (*iii*) neither the Partnership nor the General Partners or their Affiliates are in material default with respect to any of its or their agreements and obligations in connection with the Partnership's business.

(*c*)   No payment described in Sections 4.2 (*a*)(*ii*) or (*iii*) shall be due until 15 days after the General Partners have given each Limited Partner a written certificate (in the same manner as notice is to be given pursuant to Section 15.2) (*i*) specifying that all conditions applicable to such payment have been fully satisfied and (*ii*) stating the amount due.

4.4.   No Interest on Capital Contributions.   No interest shall be paid by the Partnership on any contribution to Partnership capital.

4.5.   Liability Limited to Capital.   The liability of each Limited Partner shall be limited to the amount of capital contributions which each Limited Partner is required to make in accordance with the provisions of Sections 4.2 and 4.3 of this Agreement, and none of the Limited Partners shall have any further personal liability to contribute money to or in respect of the liabilities or obligations of the Partnership, nor shall the Limited Partners be personally liable for any obligations of the Partnership. If any distribution or distributions shall have been made to the Limited Partners at any time when there shall be any unpaid debts, taxes, liabilities or obligations of the Partnership, and if the Partnership shall not have sufficient assets to pay or meet such debts, taxes, liabilities or obligations, then each Limited Partner, and any successor to such Limited Partner's interest, shall be obligated to repay all or part of any such distributions theretofore made to such Limited Partner or successor. Any repayment of distributions required pursuant to this Section 4.5 shall be made to the Partnership within 30 days after the General Partners shall have delivered to such Limited Partner written notice requesting such repayment, together with a statement of the aggregate amount and the amount chargeable to such Limited Partner to be repaid and an explanation of the necessity for such repayment.

4.6.   Capital Accounts.   A capital account shall be maintained for each Partner and shall be credited with the amounts of his contributions to the capital of the Partnership, and shall be credited or charged, as the case may be, with his distributive share of Net Profits and Losses pursuant to Article VIII of this Agreement and shall be charged with the amounts of any distributions to him pursuant to Article VII of this Agreement. Loans to the Partnership by any Partner shall not be considered contributions to the capital of the Partnership. A Partner shall not be entitled to withdraw any part of his capital account or to receive any distribution from the Partnership, except as provided in this Agreement.

ARTICLE V

DUTIES AND POWERS OF PARTNERS; PARTNERSHIP EXPENSES

5.1.   General Authority and Powers of General Partners.   Subject to the terms and conditions of this Agreement, the General Partners shall have complete authority over and exclusive control and management of the business and affairs of the Partnership and shall devote such time to the Partnership as may be reasonably required for the achievement of its purposes. In connection with such management, the General Partners may employ on behalf of the Partnership any other persons to perform services for the Partnership, including persons employed by, affiliated with, or related to any Partner. Except as expressly provided in this Agreement, the General Partners shall receive no compensation for such services. Without limiting their authority and powers, the General Partners, and each of them, shall have the right, if, as and when they deem necessary or appropriate, on behalf of the Partnership, subject only to the terms and conditions of this Agreement:

(*a*)   to mortgage, sell, convey, assign, lease, transfer, exchange, or otherwise dispose of and encumber the Project and any interests therein;

(*b*)   to borrow money and issue evidences of indebtedness and to secure the same by mortgage, deed of trust, pledge, or other lien or security interest;

(*c*)   to enter into and perform contracts and agreements of any kind necessary or desirable to the development and construction of the Project and in connection with any matters incidental or related thereto;

(*d*)   to take such action and execute such documents as may be required in connection with any mortgage, note, building loan agreement, construction contract, bond, indemnity, security agreement, escrow, or bank letter of credit which may be required in connection with the Construction Loan, the

Permanent Loan, or any substitute for such Loans pursuant to the Standby Commitments;

(*e*) to establish reasonable reserve funds from revenues derived from Partnership operations to provide for future requirements of the Project for maintenance, repair, and replacement;

(*f*) to do all acts which they deem necessary or appropriate for the protection and preservation of the Partnership assets;

(*g*) to carry at the expense of the Partnership such insurance for public liability and other coverage necessary or appropriate to the business of the Partnership in such amounts and of such types as they shall determine from time to time;

(*h*) to make and revoke any election permitted to the Partnership by any taxing authority;

(*i*) to compromise, settle, or submit to arbitration, and to institute, prosecute, and defend any and all actions or claims in favor of or against the Partnership or relating to its business; and

(*j*) generally to possess and exercise any and all of the rights, powers, and privileges of a general partner under the laws of the State of New York.

5.2. No Management by Limited Partners. The Limited Partners shall take no part in, or at any time interfere in any manner with, the management, conduct, or control of the Partnership's business and operations and shall have no right or authority to act for or bind the Partnership in any manner whatsoever.

5.3. Limitations on Authority and Powers of General Partners

(*a*) Notwithstanding any other provision in this Agreement, the General Partners shall not, without the prior written consent of Limited Partners owning at least 66⅔% of the interest in the Partnership of the Limited Partners:

(*i*) enter into an agreement to, or sell, assign, lease, transfer, exchange, or otherwise dispose of or convey all or substantially all of the Project;

(*ii*) except with respect to Operating Deficit Loans, borrow money on behalf of the Partnership at any time prior to December 31, 1987 and, thereafter, in excess of $50,000 outstanding at any time (other than amounts of outstanding Operating Deficit Loans), or mortgage (except in connection with the Construction or Permanent Loans or substitute loans pursuant to the Standby Commitments) all or substantially all of the Partnership's assets;

(*iii*)   refinance, recast, modify, or extend any mortgages which affect any property owned by the Partnership; or

(*iv*)   repay Operating Deficit Loans except as provided in this Agreement.

(*b*)   Notwithstanding any other provision of this Agreement, the General Partners shall not:

(*i*)   alter the primary purpose of the Partnership as set forth in Section 2.2 hereof;

(*ii*)   cause the Partnership to invest in any program, partnership, venture, or real property other than the Project, except as provided in Section 9.2(b) of this Agreement;

(*iii*)   do any act in contravention of this Agreement or which would make it impossible to carry on the business of the Partnership;

(*iv*)   confess a judgment against the Partnership in connection with any threatened or pending legal action;

(*v*)   possess any property or assign the rights of the Partnership in specific property, including the Project, for other than a Partnership purpose;

(*vi*)   admit a person as General Partner except with the consent of the Limited Partners as provided for in this Agreement;

(*vii*)   perform any act which would subject any Limited Partner to liability as a general partner in any jurisdiction;

(*viii*)   amend this Agreement without the consent of each Limited Partner who would be adversely affected by such amendment to: (*A*) convert a Limited Partner into a general partner; (*B*) adversely affect the limited liability of a Limited Partner; (*C*) alter the interests of the Partners in the Net Profits and Losses, Net Cash Flow, or Net Cash Proceeds; or (*D*) adversely affect the status of the Partnership as a partnership for federal income tax purposes; or

(*ix*)   admit any additional Limited Partners.

5.4.   Certain Rights of the Limited Partners.   Subject to the provisions of Section 5.5 of this Agreement, the Limited Partners, in addition to the other rights provided for in this agreement, by vote of Limited Partners owning at least 66⅔% of the interests in the Partnership of the Limited Partners (except with respect to clause (*e*) of this Section 5.4 which requires a vote of 100% of the Limited Partners), shall have the right to:

(*a*)   remove any General Partner for cause in accordance with the provisions of Section 10.2 of this Agreement;

(*b*)   remove any General Partner without cause after December 31, 1987;

(*c*) amend this Agreement; *provided, however,* that no such amendment shall (*i*) affect the vested rights (including, without limitation, the rights to Net Cash Flow, Net Cash Proceeds, and Net Profits and Losses) of any General Partner, or increase any obligation of any General Partner without his or its consent; (*ii*) decrease the vote of the Limited Partners required to exercise the right provided in clause (*e*) of this Section 5.4; or (*iii*) increase the liability of any Limited Partner or alter the amount of Net Cash Flow, Net Cash Proceeds, or Net Profits and Losses distributable or allocable to him hereunder without his prior consent;

(*d*) dissolve the Partnership after December 31, 1995; and

(*e*) continue the business of the Partnership with a substitute General Partner or Partners.

5.5. Restrictions on Limited Partner Rights. The rights of the Limited Partners provided for in subsections (*a*) through (*d*) of Section 5.4 of this Agreement shall each be subject to (*i*) a prior determination by a court of competent jurisdiction, in any action for a declaratory judgment or similar relief brought by or on behalf of the Limited Partners, that neither the grant nor the exercise of the right afforded by such subsections sought to be exercised under the circumstances then in question will be deemed taking part in the control of the business or will otherwise result in the loss of any Limited Partner's limited liability or (*ii*) prior receipt by the Limited Partners of an opinion of counsel of the Limited Partners to the same effect; *provided, however,* that the Limited Partners, by a vote of Limited Partners owning at least 66⅔% of the interests in the Partnership of the Limited Partners, may exercise the right provided in subsection (*a*) of Section 5.4 without obtaining such a determination or such an opinion of counsel.

5.6. Liability of General Partners. Except as to any misrepresentation or the breach of any agreement or covenant contained in this Agreement, none of the General Partners shall be liable, responsible or accountable to the Partnership or to the Limited Partners for any loss in connection with the Partnership's business if such General Partner acts in good faith and is not guilty of willful misconduct or negligence.

5.7. Partnership Expenses. The Partnership shall pay or reimburse the General Partners for all expenses of the Partnership, which expenses may include but are not limited to: (*a*) costs of personnel employed by the Partnership; (*b*) costs of borrowed money, taxes, and assessments on the Property and other taxes applicable to the Partnership; (*c*) costs of obtaining the necessary zoning or use permits, and environmental, engineering, utility and other clearances or permits which may be required in connection with the Partnership's business; (d) legal, audit, accounting, and other fees; (e) fees and expenses paid to independent contractors, mortgage bankers, brokers and servicers, leasing agents, consultants, real estate brokers, insurance brokers, and other agents; (f) expenses in connection with the disposition, replacement, alteration, repair, maintenance, leasing, and operation of the Project; (g) cost of insurance in connection with the business of the Partnership; and (h) expenses or revising, amending, modifying, or terminating the Partnership.

ARTICLE VI

OBLIGATIONS AND AGREEMENTS OF GENERAL PARTNERS

6.1. Transfer of Real Estate. The General Partners agree to cause title to the Property to be transferred to the Partnership at the time of the first payment of the Construction Loan to the Partnership, free and clear of all liens and encumbrances (except as set forth in Section 14.1(a) of this Agreement), at a cost to the Partnership of the lower of $475,000 or the General Partners' cost of the Property.

6.2. Operating Deficit Loans. If, during the period from issuance of permanent certificates of occupany for at least 75% of the apartment units in the Project to December 31, 1987, the Partnership shall require funds for operating costs, expenses or obligations of any nature due and payable during such period, the General Partners hereby jointly and severally agree to make promptly Operating Deficit Loans to the Partnership in amounts required to pay such costs, expenses, and obligations. Operating Deficit Loans shall be repaid to the General Partners only in accordance with Sections 7.1 and 7.2 of this Agreement.

ARTICLE VII

DISTRIBUTIONS

7.1. Net Cash Flow. Net Cash Flow for each Fiscal Year shall be applied and distributed at reasonable intervals during the Fiscal Year, or not later than 90 days after the close of such Fiscal Year, to the Partners, in the following order and manner:

(a) to the payment of an annual distribution of $80,000 to the Limited Partners and $808 to the General Partners; *provided, however,* that if Net

Cash Flow available for distribution pursuant to this Section 7.1(*a*) shall in any year be less than $80,808, then 99% of such lesser amount to the Limited Partners and 1% of such lesser amount to the General Partners;

(*b*) to the payment to the Partners of the Net Cash Flow resulting from subordination and assignment of a portion of the management fee pursuant to the Management Agreement, 99% to the Limited Partners and 1% to the General Partners;

(*c*) to the payment of any outstanding Operating Deficit Loans; *provided, however,* that no payment of Operating Deficit Loans shall be made from Net Cash Flow resulting from subordination and assignment of a portion of the management fee pursuant to the Management Agreement;

(*d*) to the payment to the management agent, without interest, of any unpaid portion of the management fee subordinated and assigned to the Partners pursuant to the Management Agreement; and

(*e*) the balance, 75% to the Limited Partners, 1% to the General Partners, and 24% to the management agent as an incentive management fee pursuant to the Management Agreement.

7.2. Net Cash Proceeds. Net Cash Proceeds shall be distributed in the following order and manner:

(*a*) to the payment of principal and interest owing to any Partner with respect to loans by such Partner to the Partnership, other than Operating Deficit Loans;

(*b*) 99% to the Limited Partners and 1% to the General Partners until the Limited Partners have received an amount equal to the sum of (*i*) the amount of their capital contributions plus (*ii*) an amount equal to 6% per annum, compounded annually, on the amount of their capital contributions, less (*iii*) the aggregate of all previous distributions to the Limited Partners pursuant to Article VII of this Agreement,

(*c*) to the payment of principal owing to the General Partners with respect to Operating Deficit Loans;

(*d*) to the managing agent, without interest, in payment of any unpaid portion of the management fee subordinated and assigned to the Partners pursuant to the Management Agreement; and

(*e*) the balance, 75% to the Limited Partners and 25% to the General Partners.

7.3. Allocation Among Partners. Any distributions to the Limited Partners or the General Partners pursuant to Sections 7.1 or 7.2 of this Agreement shall be allocated among them in accordance with their Sharing Ratios as set forth on Exhibit B hereto.

ARTICLE VIII

PROFITS AND LOSSES

8.1. Net Profits and Losses. Net Profits and Losses, and each item of income, gain, loss, deduction, or credit entering into the computation thereof, shall be allocated 99% to the Limited Partners and 1% to the General Partners; *provided, however,* that the General Partners shall first be allocated (to the extent not previously allocated) Net Profits equal to Net Cash Proceeds received by them pursuant to Section 7.2 in excess of their 1% interest in Net Profits otherwise allocable to the General Partners.

8.2. Allocation Among Partners. Any allocations to the Limited Partners or the General Partners pursuant to Section 8.1 of this Agreement shall be allocated among them in accordance with their Sharing Ratios as set forth on Exhibit B hereto.

ARTICLE IX

TERMINATION AND DISSOLUTION OF THE PARTNERSHIP

9.1. No Termination by Admission or Incapacity of Limited Partners. Neither the admission to the Partnership of any additional Limited Partner, nor the transfer of interest or Event of Dissolution of any Limited Partner, shall result in the termination or dissolution of the Partnership or affect its continuance in any manner whatsoever. If an Event of Dissolution shall occur with respect to any Limited Partner, his Representative shall have the same rights for the purpose of settling his estate or business and shall be subject to the same limitations, conditions, and liabilities as applied to the Limited Partner whose interest he is representing; *provided, however,* that upon the death or incapacity of a Limited Partner, the successor-in-interest to such Limited Partner shall have the right to become a substitute Limited Partner as provided in Section 10.4(*b*) of this Agreement.

9.2. Termination of the Partnership. The Partnership shall be terminated upon the happening of any of the following events, whichever shall first occur:

(*a*)   the removal of (as provided in Sections 5.4 or 10.2 of this Agreement) or Event of Dissolution with respect to, any General Partner, unless upon the occurrence of any of the foregoing the Partnership is continued in accordance with the provisions of Section 9.3 of this Agreement;

(*b*)   the sale, condemnation or other disposition of all or substantially all of the Project, unless all the Partners consent to the election by the Partnership of Section 1033 of the Code;

(*c*)   upon the written agreement of all Partners or, subject to the provisions of Section 5.4, upon the written agreement of the Limited Partners owning at least 66⅔% of the interests in the Partnership of the Limited Partners; or

(*d*)   the expiration of the term provided for in Section 2.4 of this Agreement.

9.3.   Continuation of Partnership Upon Certain Events

(*a*)   Upon the occurrence of any event or events provided in Section 9.2(*a*) of this Agreement with respect to less than all the General Partners, the remaining General Partner shall immediately send notice of such event to the Limited Partners, and such remaining General Partner may then elect, within 30 days after the occurence of such event, to continue the business of the Partnership in accordance with the terms of this Agreement; *provided, however,* that in the opinion of counsel to the Partnership such continuation would not result in the Partnership being classified for Federal income tax purposes as an association taxable as a corporation and not as a partnership. If the remaining General Partner does not so elect, all the Limited Partners may elect, within 30 days after receipt of notice of such event, to reconstitute the Partnership and continue its business in accordance with the terms of this Agreement and with a new General Partner or General Partners selected by the Limited Partners.

(*b*)   Upon the occurrence of any event or events provided in Section 9.2(*a*) of this Agreement with respect to all the General Partners, Limited Partners owning not less than 100% of the Units shall have the right to continue the business of the Partnership in accordance with the terms of this Agreement upon the selection by such Limited Partners within 30 days of such occurrence of a new General Partner and upon such new General Partner executing this Agreement or an amendment hereto and agreeing to be bound by all of the terms and provisions hereof; *provided, however,* that in the opinion of counsel to the Partnership such continuation would not result in the Partnership being classified for Federal income tax purposes as an association taxable as a corporation and not as a partnership.

9.4. Dissolution and Liquidation

(*a*) Upon any termination of the Partnership, and absent any continuation of the Partnership pursuant to Section 9.3, the Partnership shall be dissolved and its affairs shall be wound up as soon as practicable thereafter by the General Partners (or, if there is no General Partner then remaining, by such other person designated by Limited Partners owning not less than 51% of the interests in the Partnership of the Limited Partners). In winding up the affairs of the Partnership, the General Partners or such designated person shall proceed to liquidate the assets of the Partnership in such manner as they shall determine, allowing a reasonable time therefor to enable the General Partners or such designated person to minimize losses attendant upon a liquidation.

(*b*) Upon the termination and dissolution of the Partnership and liquidation of its assets, the proceeds, if any, from such liquidation shall be applied and distributed first to the payment of all debts and liabilities of the Partnership, other than in respect of items described in Section 7.2 of this Agreement, second to the establishment of such reserves which the General Partners shall deem reasonably necessary to provide for contingent and unforeseen liabilities or obligations of the Partnership, other than in respect of items described in Section 7.2 of this Agreement, and third in the manner and order provided in Section 7.2 of this Agreement.

(*c*) The General Partners shall not be personally liable for the repayment of the capital contributions or any advances made by the Limited Partners or any portions thereof. Any such repayments will be made solely from the assets of the Partnership available for such repayment. The General Partners shall not be liable to the Partnership or any Partner to contribute capital to the Partnership on account of a Capital Account Deficit of any Partner; *provided, however,* that the General Partners shall not be relieved of any obligation to pay liabilities of the Partnership to third parties.

ARTICLE X

WITHDRAWAL AND TRANSFER BY PARTNERS

10.1. Voluntary Withdrawal or Assignment by General Partners. No General Partner shall resign or withdraw as a General Partner from the Partnership, or at any time assign, transfer or otherwise dispose of all or any part of his or its Partnership interest, unless all the Limited Partners shall have consented, such General Partner shall have provided an additional or successor General Partner satisfactory to all the Limited Partners and the Partnership shall have received an opinion of its counsel to the effect that such resignation, withdrawal, assignment, or transfer would not subject the Partnership to Federal income taxation as an association taxable as a corporation and not as a partnership, and would not cause a termination of the Partnership for Federal income tax purposes.

10.2. Removal of General Partners.   Subject to the provisions of Section 5.5 of this Agreement, a General Partner may be removed at any time by Limited Partners owning at least 66⅔% of the interests in the Partnership of the Limited Partners if they determine that such General Partner has:

(*a*) violated in any material respect any provision of the Construction or Permanent Loan Commitments, any commitment for any substitute for such Loans provided, pursuant to the Standby Commitments, or any provision of any document related to the Construction or the Permanent Loan or any substitute for such Loans;

(*b*) violated in any material respect any provision of this Agreement or any provision of applicable law; or

(*c*) in conducting his or its affairs or those of the Partnership, jeopardized the status of the Partnership as a partnership for purposes of Federal income taxation in accordance with the then existing provisions of the Code and Treasury Regulations promulgated thereunder or the policies of the Internal Revenue Service.

10.3. Involuntary Withdrawal and Assignment by General Partners.   Upon the occurrence of any of the events provided in Section 9.2(*a*) of this Agreement and the Partnership being continued in accordance with Section 9.3, the General Partner of General Partners to whom such event applied (the ''Retiring General Partner'') shall forthwith cease to have any rights or powers of a General Partner pursuant to this Agreement. The Retiring General Partner or his trustee or legal representative shall offer in writing to sell his interest in the Partnership to the remaining or successor General Partner for the same consideration and on the same terms as contained in a bona fide written offer made by a third-party purchaser, whose name and address must be stated therein, provided that such offer, together with a copy of the third-party offer, shall have been given to the remaining or successor General Partner (*a*) if the Retiring General Partner is not then the sole General Partner of the Partnership, within 30 days after the appointment of the legal representative of the Retiring General Partner, if deceased or incapacitated, but in no event later than 180 days after the death or certified incapacity of such Retiring General Partner, or within 30 days after the occurrence of any other event provided in Section 9.2(*a*) of this Agreement, or (*b*) if the Retiring General Partner is then the sole

General Partner of the Partnership, within 10 days after the occurrence of any event provided in Section 9.2(*a*). If any such offer by a Retiring General Partner to sell his interest in the Partnership is not accepted by the remaining or successor General Partner within 30 days, the Retiring General Partner may sell his interest within the next succeeding 30 days, or within the next succeeding 10 days if the Retiring General Partner is then the sole General Partner, to the designated third party at the price and term stated; *provided, however,* that such designated third party agrees to be substituted as a General Partner and agrees to assume all of the obligations of the Retiring General Partner with respect to the Partnership, and the Partnership receives an opinion of its counsel that such assignment and substitution would not (*i*) result in the Partnership being classified for Federal income tax purposes as an association taxable as a corporation and not as a partnership and (*ii*) cause a termination of the Partnership for Federal income tax purposes. If such sale is not made, or if an offer had not been made to the remaining or successor General Partner as provided above, the Retiring General Partner's interest shall thereupon be transferred to the remaining or successor General Partner without consideration. In no event shall a Retiring General Partner be relieved of any obligation set forth in Section 6.2 of this Agreement.

10.4.   Transfer by Limited Partners

(*a*)   A Limited Partner may at any time sell, transfer, or assign his interest in the Partnership, provided that:

(*i*)   such Limited Partner and the purchaser, transferee, or assignee execute, acknowledge and deliver to the General Partners such instruments of transfer and assignment with respect to such transaction as may be reasonably requested by the General Partners;

(*ii*)   such Limited Partner does not sell, transfer or assign less than his entire interest in the Partnership; and

(*iii*)   such Limited Partner obtains the prior written consent of the General Partners, the granting of which shall be within the sole discretion of the General Partners and may be arbitrarily and capriciously denied.

(*b*) Notwithstanding anything contained in this Agreement to the contrary, no purchaser, transferee or assignee of an interest in the Partnership shall have any right to become a substitute Limited Partner unless the General Partners consent in writing to such substitution. The General Partners shall have sole discretion to arbitrarily and capriciously refuse to grant such consent.

(*c*)   No sale, transfer, assignment or substitution by a Limited Partner, which has otherwise been consented to by the General Partners, shall be effective as against the Partnership until the purchaser, transferee, assignee, or substitute Limited Partner, and all the Partners, execute all such certificates and other documents and perform all such other acts which the General Partners deem necessary or appropriate to constitute such purchaser, transferee, or assignee as such or as a substitute Limited Partner and to preserve the limited liability status of the Limited Partners in the Partnership after the completion of such sale, transfer, assignment, or substitution under the laws of each jurisdiction in which the Partnership is doing business. Each Limited Partner agrees upon request of the General Partners to execute such certificates or other documents and perform such other acts as may be reasonably requested by the General Partners from time to time.

(*d*) Any sale, transfer, or assignment of an interest in the Partnership or substitution of a Limited Partner made in compliance with this Section 10.4 shall be effective as of the first day of the calendar month succeeding the month in which the execution of such instruments, certificates, or other documents and the performance of such other acts by the Partners is completed as provided in subsections (*a*) and (*c*) of this Section 10.4, or in which any required written consent thereto is given by the General Partners pursuant to subsection (*a*) and (*b*) of this Section 10.4, whichever is later.

(*e*) The Net Profits and Losses attributable to an assigned interest in the Partnership shall be allocated among the assignor and assignee of such interest as of the effective date of the assignment thereof, as provided in subsection (*d*) of this Section 10.4.

(*f*) Upon the death or incapacity of a Limited Partner, the successor-in-interest to such Limited Partner shall have the right to become a substitute Limited Partner upon written notice to the Partnership within 90 days after the appointment of such Limited Partner's legal representative, but not later than 180 days after the death or certified incapacity of such Limited Partner, and upon such successor executing this Agreement or an amendment hereto and such other documents as the General Partners may request. If such right is not exercised, the legal representative of the deceased or incapacitated Limited Partner shall have the same rights, subject to the same limitations, as such Limited Partner would have had to assign or transfer his Unit pursuant to this Section 10.4.

(*g*) Notwithstanding anything contained in this Agreement to the contrary, no Unit may be assigned or transferred without an opinion of counsel in form and substance satisfactory to the Partnership that (*i*) registration is not required under the Securities Act of 1933, as amended; (*ii*) such assignment or transfer does not violate any applicable Federal or state securities, real estate syndication, or comparable laws; and (*iii*) such assignment or transfer would not cause a termination of the Partnership for Federal income tax purposes.

ARTICLE XI

RECORDS AND ACCOUNTING

11.1. Books and Records. The books of account, records, and all documents and other writings of the Partnership shall be kept and maintained at the principal office of the Partnership. Each Partner or his designated representative shall, upon reasonable notice to the General Partners, have access to such financial books, records, and documents during reasonable business hours and may inspect and make copies of any of them.

11.2. Accounting Method: Audits and Reports

(a)   The Partnership shall adopt the accrual method of accounting.

(b)   At all times during the continuance of the Partnership the General Partners shall keep or cause to be kept full and true books of account in which shall be entered fully and accurately each transaction of the Partnership. The General Partners shall deliver to the Limited Partners as soon as practicable after the end of each Fiscal Year annual financial statements of the Partnership certified by Smith & Co., Certified Public Accountants, or such other Certified Public Accountants as may be selected by the General Partners, as representing fairly the financial position and results of operations of the Partnership in accordance with generally accepted accounting principles consistently applied. In addition, the General Partners shall deliver to the Limited Partners on or before October 31 of each fiscal year an estimate of the Net Profits and Losses and Net Cash Flow for the year, and shall deliver on or before March 1st of each year so-called "Information Returns" showing the actual Net Profits or Losses allocation thereof to each Partner for the Partnership's preceding Fiscal Year.

11.3. Bank Accounts. The General Partners shall open and maintain on behalf of the Partnership a bank account or accounts with such depositaries as it shall determine, in which all monies received by or on behalf of the Partnership shall be deposited. All withdrawals from such accounts shall be made upon the signature of such person or persons as the General Partners may from time to time designate.

ARTICLE XII

ELECTIONS

Tax Elections. All elections required or permitted to be made by the Partnership under the Code shall be made by the General Partners in the manner as will, in their opinion, be most advantageous to the Partners. Notwithstanding the provisions of this Article XIII, if any Partner transfers all or part of his interest in the Partnership, any basis adjustment attributable to such transfer, whether made under Section 754 of the Code or otherwise, shall be allocated solely to the transferee of such interest.

ARTICLE XIII

POWER OF ATTORNEY

13.1. Description. Upon the execution of this Agreement, each Limited Partner shall execute and acknowledge, in duplicate, and deliver to the General Partners a Power of Attorney, in the form of Exhibit D hereto, constituting and appointing the General Partners, and each of them, his true and lawful attorney in his name and on his behalf to take at any time all such action as provided therein.

13.2. Limitations of Power of Attorney. No document or amendment executed by the General Partners pursuant to this Article XIII shall (*a*) reduce the obligations of the General Partners; (*b*) affect the restrictions regarding the assignability of the interests of the Partners; (*c*) modify the term of the Partnership; (*d*) amend this Article XIII; (*e*) cause the Partnership to be classified for Federal income tax purposes as an association taxable as a corporation and not as a partnership; or (*f*) reduce the rights or enlarge the obligations or liabilities of the Limited Partners. The General Partners shall promptly notify the Limited Partners of any documents or amendments executed by either of them pursuant to this Article XIII.

ARTICLE XIV

REPRESENTATIONS AND WARRANTIES

14.1. Certain Representations and Warranties of the General Partners. The General Partners, jointly and severally, for themselves and for each other represent and warrant to the Partnership and the Limited Partners that on the date hereof and on any date that any payment by the Limited Partners pursuant to Section 4.2(*a*) of this Agreement is due:

(*a*)   the Partnership owns the fee simple interest in the Project, subject to no liens, charges, or encumbrances other than the Construction or Permanent Loan, those set forth in the Policy of Title Insurance issued by First Title Co., dated April 15, 1982, and such liens, charges and encumbrances as have been incurred in connection with the construction of the Project in accordance with the Construction Loan documents, and no such lien, charge, or encumbrance shall prevent the Partnership from carrying out its purpose as set forth herein;

(*b*)   no default, or event which, with the passage of time or the giving of notice or both, would constitute a default, has occurred or is continuing under the Construction or Permanent Loan documents or the construction contract for the Project, and the same are in full force and effect;

(*c*)   the Project is being constructed substantially in accordance with the Construction and Permanent Loan documents, and the construction contract for the Project;

(*d*)   on the date of this Agreement there were no agreements or other documents affecting the Project or the Construction Loan other than the Construction and Permanent Loan documents, the Management Agreement, and the construction contract for the Project;

(*e*)   on the date of this Agreement, the land described in Exhibit A hereto was zoned for the use contemplated by the Partnership; the General Partners have no knowledge of any zoning, building, or use laws, rules, regulations, ordinances or requirements of any Federal, State, or local governmental unit which would inhibit or adversely affect the development of the Project, and all easements, permits, authorizations, and environmental impact statements, if any, required in order to permit construction and operation of the Project as herein contemplated have been and/or will be filed and/or obtained and maintained when and as necessary to comply in all material respects with applicable laws and regulations, and to the extent obtained are in full force and effect;

(*f*)   the Partnership is a validly existing limited partnership in good standing under the laws of the State of New York and has the full legal right, power and authority to enter into and to consummate all transactions contemplated herein to be performed by it and the entering into and consummation of such transactions will not result in a breach or violation of, or a default under, any agreement or other document to which it or any of its affiliates is a party or by which it or any of them or any of its or their properties are bound or any law, administrative regulation, or court decree;

(*g*) Able, Inc. is a validly existing corporation in good standing under the laws of the State of Delaware; the General Partners have the full legal right, power, and authority to enter into this Agreement and to perform their obligations hereunder and the execution and delivery of this Agreement and the consummation of all transactions contemplated herein to be performed by them will not result in a breach or violation of, or a default under, the certificate of incorporation or by-laws of Able, Inc., any agreement or other document to which they, or any of them, are a party or by which they or any of them or their properties are bound or any law, administrative regulation, or court decree;

(*h*) no Event of Bankruptcy has occurred with respect to any of them; and

(*i*) no claim, litigation, governmental investigation or legal proceeding is pending or, to their knowledge and belief, is threatened in any court, commission, administrative body, or other authority which could have a material adverse effect on the Partnership or its properties or the ability of the General Partners to perform any of their obligations contemplated by this Agreement.

14.2. Representation and Warranty of the General Partners Not to Compete. The General Partners, jointly and severally, for themselves and for each other represent and warrant to the Partnership and to each of the Limited Partners that on the date of this Agreement until _____, 1984, the General Partners will not, directly or indirectly, for their own benefit or for the benefit of any Person, give advice to, serve as an employee, director, officer or trustee of, or otherwise participate in the management, operation, business or control of, or have any direct or indirect interest, financial or otherwise, in any Person that competes with the Partnership or engages in real estate activities within a radius of 2 miles from the Property.

ARTICLE XV

MISCELLANEOUS

Section 15.1. Other Activities of the Partners. Except as provided in Section 14.2 of this Agreement, nothing contained herein shall prevent any of the Partners from engaging in or possessing an interest in any real estate activities other than through the Partnership. No Partner shall, by virtue of his interest in this Partnership, have any interest in such other activities of any other Partner.

15.2. Notices. All notices, demands or other communications hereunder shall be in writing and shall be deemed to have been given when the same are (*a*) deposited in the United States mail and sent by certified or registered mail, postage prepaid, return receipt requested, or (*b*) delivered, in each case to the parties at the addresses set forth below or at such other addresses as such parties may designate by written notice to the Partnership:

(*i*)   if to the Partnership or the General Partners, at the principal office of the Partnership; and

(*ii*)   if to the Limited Partners, at the addresses set forth in Exhibit B hereto.

15.3. Further Assurances. The Partners will execute and deliver such further instruments and do such further acts and things as may be required to carry out the intent and purpose of this Agreement.

15.4. Agreement in Counterparts. This Agreement may be executed in counterparts and all so executed shall constitute one agreement binding on all the parties hereto notwithstanding that all the parties hereto are not signatories to the original or to the same counterpart.

15.5. Captions. Captions contained in this Agreement are inserted only as a matter of convenience and in no way define, limit, extend, or describe the scope of this Agreement or the intent of any provisions hereof.

15.6. Construction. None of the provisions of this Agreement shall be for the benefit of or enforceable by any creditor of the Partnership or of any Partner.

15.7. Governing Law: Successors. This Agreement and the rights and obligations of the Partners shall be governed by and construed in accordance with the internal laws of the State of New York without application of the conflict of laws of such state. Except as otherwise expressly provided in this Agreement, all provisions of this Agreement shall be binding upon, inure to the benefit of, and be enforceable by or against, the heirs, successors, legal representatives, and assigns of the parties hereto.

15.8. Survival of Representations, Warranties, and Agreements. All representations, warranties, and agreements herein shall survive until the dissolution and final liquidation of the Partnership, except to the extent that a representation, warranty, or agreement expressly provides otherwise.

15.9.   Amendment.   This Agreement may be modified or amended upon the written agreement of all Partners.

15.10.   Incorporation by Reference.   The Exhibits referred to in this Agreement and attached hereto are hereby incorporated into this Agreement by this reference.

15.11.   Validity of Agreement.   The invalidity of any portion of this Agreement shall not affect the validity of the remainder thereof.

15.12.   Liability of partners.   None of the Partners assumes or shall have personal liability for any payments due under the Permanent Loan.

15.13.   Arbitration.   Any controversy or claim arising out of or resulting from this Agreement, or the breach thereof, shall be settled by arbitration in accordance with the rules and regulations of the American Arbitration Association, and judgment upon the award by the arbitrator may be entered in any court having jurisdiction thereof.

IN WITNESS WHEREOF, the parties hereto have executed and delivered this Agreement as of the day and year first above written.

GENERAL PARTNERS:

_____

Allan A. Able

Able, Inc.

By_____
   President

EXECUTION PAGE

This Execution Page to the Limited Partnership Agreement of Able Associates is to be attached to and made a part of the Limited Partnership Agreement or any counterpart thereof.

Number of Units
Purchased _____

_____
Signature

_____
Residence

_____

_____
    Name of Limited Partner
       [Please Print]

_____
Social Security or Taxpayer Identification Number

EXHIBIT A

DESCRIPTION OF REAL PROPERTY

[insert]

EXHIBIT B

AMOUNTS AND INSTALLMENTS OF PARTNERS' CAPITAL CONTRIBUTIONS

(Subject to the terms of the Agreement of Limited Partnership of Able Associates, dated   , 1977, to which this Exhibit B is attached)

Name and Residence of General Partners	Capital Contribution	Percentage of Partnership Interest	Sharing Ratio
Allan A. Able New York, New York	4,040	0.5%	50%
Able, Inc. Delaware	4,040	0.5%	50%
	$ 8,080	1.0%	100%

Name and Residence of Limited Partners	Initial Installment	Second Installment	Third Installment	Percentage of Partnership Interest	Sharing Ratio
	$200,000	$300,000	$300,000	99%	100%

EXHIBIT C

OPINION OF MESSRS. JONES AND JONES

[insert]

EXHIBIT D

ABLE ASSOCIATES (A LIMITED PARTNERSHIP) POWER OF ATTORNEY

Know all men by these presents, that the undersigned hereby designates and appoints Allan A. Able, and the President, any Vice President and the Secretary of Able, Inc., and each of them, with full power of substitution, the true and lawful attorney for the undersigned, and in the name, place and stead of the undersigned, with the power, from time to time:

(A) to make, execute, swear to, verify, acknowledge, deliver, record and publish:

(1) the Limited Partnership Agreement (the "Agreement") of Able Associates, a limited partnership organized or to be organized under the Uniform Limited Partnership Act of the State of New York (the "Partnership");

(2) any Certificate of Limited Partnership and amendments thereto required or permitted to be made or filed on behalf of the Partnership, and any and all certificates or other instruments necessary to qualify or continue the Partnership as a limited partnership, or partnership wherein limited partners have limited liability, or in connection with the use of the name of the Partnership, in the jurisdictions where the Partnership may be doing business;

(3) such certificates, instruments and documents as may be required or appropriate to reflect:

(a) a change of name or address of the undersigned;

(b) any changes in the Partnership or amendments to the Agreement of any kind as provided in the Agreement; and

(c) any other changes in the Partnership or amendments of the Agreement as may be authorized by the undersigned; and

(4) all statements of interest and holdings on behalf of the undersigned; and

(B) to take any further action, including furnishing verified copies of the Agreement or excerpts therefrom, which any of said attorneys-in-fact shall consider necessary or convenient in connection with any of the foregoing.

The undersigned hereby gives said attorneys-in-fact full power and authority to do and perform each and every act and thing whatsoever requisite and necessary to be done in and about the foregoing as fully as the undersigned might or could do if personally present, and hereby ratifies and confirms all that said attorneys-in-fact shall lawfully do or cause to be done by virtue of this power of attorney.

The power and authority granted herein shall be deemed coupled with an interest and shall survive the death or incapacity of the undersigned, or, if the undersigned is a corporation, partnership, trust or association, the dissolution or termination thereof. This power of attorney shall not be revoked and shall survive the assignment or transfer by the undersigned of all or part of his interest in the Partnership.

The existence of this power of attorney shall not preclude execution of any instrument by the undersigned individually on any matter other than a revocation of this power of attorney. The undersigned shall execute and deliver to Allan A. Able, and Able, Inc., and each successor General Partner of the Partnership within five days after receipt of a request therefor by any General Partner, such designations, power of attorney, and other instruments as such General Partner may deem necessary.

IN WITNESS WHEREOF, this power of attorney has been executed by the undersigned.

_____
Signature
[Please print name under signature]

STATE OF_____)

: ss.:

COUNTY OF_____)

On this _____ day of_____, 1977 before me personally came _____ to me known and known to me to be the individual who executed the foregoing document, who duly sworn acknowledged that he executed the same.

_____
Notary Public

REVISED UNIFORM LIMITED PARTNERSHIP ACT (1976)

UNIFORM LIMITED PARTNERSHIP ACT (1976) *

Drafted by the
NATIONAL CONFERENCE OF COMMISSIONERS
ON UNIFORM STATE LAWS
and by it
Approved and Recommended for Enactment
in All the States

At its
ANNUAL CONFERENCE
MEETING IN ITS EIGHTY-FIFTH YEAR
AT ATLANTA, GEORGIA
JULY 31—AUGUST 6, 1976

* With Prefatory Note and Comments.

PREFATORY NOTE

The Revised Uniform Limited Partnership Act adopted by the National Conference of Commissioners on Uniform State Laws in August, 1976, was intended to modernize the prior uniform law while retaining the special character of limited partnerships as compared with corporations. The draftsman of a limited partnership agreement has a degree of flexibility in defining the relations among the partners that is not available in the corporate form. Moreover, the relationship among partners is consensual, and requires a degree of privity that forces the general partner to seek approval of the partners (sometimes unanimous approval) under circumstances that corporate management would find unthinkable. The limited partnership was not intended to be an alternative in all cases where corporate form is undesirable for tax or other reasons, and the new Act was not intended to make it so. The new Act clarifies many ambiguities and fills interstices in the prior uniform law by adding more detailed language and mechanics. In addition, some important substantive changes and additions have been made.

Article 1 provides a list of all of the definitions used in the Act, integrates the use of limited partnership names with corporate names and provides for an office and agent for service of process in the state of organization. All of these provisions are new. Article 2 collects in one place all provisions dealing with execution and filing of certificates of limited partnership and certificates of amendment and cancellation. Articles 1 and 2 reflect an important change in the statutory scheme: recognition that the basic document in any partnership, including a limited partnership, is the partnership agreement. The certificate of limited partnership is not a constitutive document (except in the sense that it is a statutory prerequisite to creation of the limited partnership), and merely reflects matters as to which creditors should be put on notice.

Article 3 deals with the single most difficult issue facing lawyers who use the limited partnership form of organization: the powers and potential liabilities of limited partners. Section 303 lists a number of activities in which a limited partner may engage without being held to have so participated in the control of the business that he assumes the liability of a general partner. Moreover, it goes on to confine the liability of a limited partner who merely steps over the line of participation in control to persons who actually know of that participation in control. General liability for partnership debts is imposed only on those limited partners who are, in effect, "silent general partners." With that exception, the provisions of the new Act that impose liability on a limited partner who has somehow permitted third parties to be misled to their detriment as to the limited partner's true status confine that liability to those who have actually been misled. The provisions relating to general partners are collected in Article 4.

Article 5, the finance section, makes some important changes from the prior uniform law. The contribution of services and promises to contribute cash, property or services are now explicitly permitted as contributions. And those who fail to perform promised services are required, in the absence of an agreement to the contrary, to pay the value of the services stated in the certificate of limited partnership.

A number of changes from the prior uniform law are made in Article 6, dealing with distributions from and the withdrawal of partners from the partnership. For example, Section 608 creates a statute of limitations on the right of a limited partnership to recover all or part of a contribution that has been returned to a limited partner, whether to satisfy creditors or otherwise.

The assignability of partnership interests is dealt with in considerable detail in Article 7. The provisions relating to dissolution appear in Article 8, which, among other things, imposes a new standard for seeking judicial dissolution of limited partnership.

One of the thorniest questions for those who operate limited partnerships in more than one state has been the status of the partnership in a state other than the state of organization. Neither existing case law nor administrative practice makes it clear whether the limited partners continue to possess their limited liability and which law governs the partnership. Article 9 deals with this problem by providing for registration of foreign limited partnerships and specifying choice-of-law rules.

Finally, Article 10 of the new Act authorizes derivative actions to be brought by limited partners.

SPECIAL COMMITTEE ON UNIFORM LIMITED PARTNERSHIP ACT (1976)

Brockenbrough Lamb, Jr., 1200 Mutual Building, Richmond, VA 23219, *Chairman*

James Falk, The White House, 1600 Pennsylvania Avenue, Washington, D.C. 20500

Howard G. Kulp, Jr., One Centennial Square, East Euclid Avenue, Haddonfield, NJ 08033

Morris W. Macey, 1500 Candler Building, Atlanta, GA 30303

Ben R. Miller, Sr., 3125 McCarroll Drive, Baton Rouge, LA 70809

W. Joseph Shoemaker, 1421 Court Place, Denver, CO 80202

David H. Neiditz, One Lewis Street, Hartford, CN 06103

Thomas H. Needham, 250 Benefit Street, Providence, RI 02903 *Chairman, Division B. Ex Officio*

James M. Bush, 363 North First Avenue, Phoenix, AZ 85003 *President, Ex Officio*

Stephen J. Friedman, 299 Park Avenue, New York, New York 10017 *Reporter*

UNIFORM LIMITED PARTNERSHIP ACT (1976) REVIEW COMMITTEE

Michael P. Sullivan, 300 Roanoke Building, Minneapolis, MN 55402, *Chairman*

John Fox Arnold, 818 Olive Street, St. Louis, MO 63101

Bryce A. Baggett, Suite 600, Fidelity Plaza, Oklahoma City, OK 73102

NATIONAL CONFERENCE OF COMMISSIONERS ON UNIFORM STATE LAWS

645 North Michigan Avenue, Suite 510
Chicago, Illinois 60611

CONTENTS

ARTICLE 1
GENERAL PROVISIONS

ARTICLE 2
FORMATION: CERTIFICATE OF LIMITED PARTNERSHIP

ARTICLE 3
LIMITED PARTNERS

ARTICLE 4
GENERAL PARTNERS

ARTICLE 5
FINANCE

ARTICLE 6
DISTRIBUTIONS AND WITHDRAWAL

ARTICLE 7
ASSIGNMENT OF PARTNERSHIP INTERESTS

ARTICLE 8
DISSOLUTION

ARTICLE 9
FOREIGN LIMITED PARTNERSHIPS

ARTICLE 10
DERIVATIVE ACTIONS

ARTICLE 11
MISCELLANEOUS

UNIFORM LIMITED
PARTNERSHIP ACT (1976)*

ARTICLE 1

GENERAL PROVISIONS

SECTION 101. [**Definitions.**] As used in this Act, unless the context otherwise requires:

(1) "Certificate of limited partnership" means the certificate referred to in Section 201, and the certificate as amended.

(2) "Contribution" means any cash, property, services rendered, or a promissory note or other binding obligation to contribute cash or property or to perform services, which a partner contributes to a limited partnership in his capacity as a partner.

(3) "Event of withdrawal of a general partner" means an event that causes a person to cease to be a general partner as provided in Section 402.

(4) "Foreign limited partnership" means a partnership formed under the laws of any State other than this State and having as partners one or more general partners and one or more limited partners.

(5) "General partner" means a person who has been admitted to a limited partnership as a general partner in accordance with the partnership agreement and named in the certificate of limited partnership as a general partner.

(6) "Limited partner" means a person who has been admitted to a limited partnership as a limited partner in accordance with the partnership agreement and named in the certificate of limited partnership as a limited partner.

(7) "Limited partnership" and "domestic limited partnership" mean a partnership formed by 2 or more persons under the laws of this State and having one or more general partners and one or more limited partners.

(8) "Partner" means a limited or general partner.

(9) "Partnership agreement" means any valid agreement, written or oral,

* [Footnote omitted]

of the partners as to the affairs of a limiteed partnership and the conduct of its business.

(10) "Partnership interest" means a partner's share of the profits and losses of a limited partnership and the right to receive distributions of partnership assets.

(11) "Person" means a natural person, partnership, limited partnership (domestic or foreign), trust, estate, association, or corporation.

(12) "State" means a state, territory, or possession of the United States, the District of Columbia, or the Commonwealth of Puerto Rico.

COMMENT

The definitions in this section clarify a number of uncertainties in existing law and make certain changes.

Contribution: this definition makes it clear that a present contribution of services and a promise to make a future payment of cash, contribution of property or performance of services are permissible forms for a contribution. Accordingly, the present services or promise must be accorded a value in the certificate of limited partnership (Section 201(5)), and, in the case of a promise, that value may determine the liability of a partner who fails to honor his agreement (Section 502). Section 3 of the prior uniform law did not permit a limited partner's contribution to be in the form of services, although that inhibition did not apply to general partners.

Foreign limited partnership: The Act only deals with foreign limited partnerships formed under the laws of another "State" of the United States (see subdivision 12 of Section 101), and any adopting State that desires to deal by statute with the status of entities formed under the laws of foreign countries must make appropriate changes throughout the Act. The exclusion of such entities from the Act was not intended to suggest that their "limited partners" should not be accorded limited liability by the courts of a State adopting the Act. That question would be resolved by the choice-of-law rules of the forum State.

General partner: this definition recognizes the separate functions of the partnership agreement and the certificate of limited partnership. The partnership agreement establishes the basic grant of management power to the persons named as general partners; but because of the passive role played by the limited partners, the separate, formal step of embodying that grant of power in the certificate of limited partnership has been preserved to emphasize its importance.

Limited partner: as in the case of general partners, this definiton provides for admission of limited partners through the partnership agreement and solemnization in the certificate of limited partnership. In addition, the definition makes it clear that being named in the certificate of limited partnership is a prerequisite to limited partner status. Failure to file does not, however, mean that the participant is a general partner or that he has general liability. See Sections 202(e) and 303.

Partnership agreement: the prior uniform law did not refer to the partnership agreement, assuming that all important matters affecting limited partners would be set forth in the certificate of limited partnership. Under modern practice, however, it has been common for the partners to enter into a comprehensive partnership agreement, only part of which was required to be included in the certificate of limited partnership. As reflected in Section 201, the certificate of limited partnership is confined principally to matters respecting the addition and withdrawal of partners and of capital, and other important issues are left to the partnership agreement.

Partnership Interest: This definition is new and is intended to define what it is that is transferred when a partnership interest is assigned.

SECTION 102. [Name.]   The name of each limited partnership as set forth in its certificate of limited partnership:

(1)   shall contain without abbreviation the words "limited partnership";

(2)   may not contain the name of a limited partner unless (i) it is also the name of a general partner or the corporate name of a corporate general partner, or (ii) the business of the limited partnership had been carried on under that name before the admission of that limited partner;

(3)   may not contain any word or phrase indicating or implying that it is organized other than for a purpose stated in its certificate of limited partnership;

(4)   may not be the same as, or deceptively similar to, the name of any corporation or limited partnership organized under the laws of this State or licensed or registered as a foreign corporation or limited partnership in this State; and

(5)   may not contain the following words [here insert prohibited words].

COMMENT

Subdivision (2) of Section 102 has been carried over from Section 5 of the prior uniform law with certain editorial changes. The remainder of Section 102 is new and primarily reflects the intention to integrate the registration of limited partnership names with that of corporate names. Accordingly, Section 201 provides for central, State-wide filing of certificates of limited partnership, and subdivisions (3), (4) and (5) of Section 102 contain standards to be applied by the filing officer in determining whether the certificate should be filed. Subdivision (1) requires that the proper name of a limited partnership contain the words "limited partnership" in full.

SECTION 103. [Reservation of Name.]

(a)   The exclusive right to the use of a name may be reserved by

(1)   any person intending to organize a limited partnership under this Act and to adopt that name;

(2)   any domestic limited partnership or any foreign limited partnership registered in this State which, in either case, intends to adopt that name;

(3)   any foreign limited partnership intending to register in this State and adopt that name; and

(4)   any person intending to organize a foreign limited partnership and intending to have it register in this State and adopt that name.

(b)   The reservation shall be made by filing with the Secretary of State an application, executed by the applicant, to reserve a specified name. If the Secretary of State finds that the name is available for use by a domestic or foreign limited partnership, he shall reserve the name for the exclusive use of the applicant for a period of 120 days. Once having so reserved a name, the same applicant may not again reserve the same name until more than 60 days after the expiration of the last 120-day period for which that applicant reserved that name. The right to the exclusive use of a reserved name may be transferred to any other person by filing in the office of the Secretary of State a notice of the transfer, executed by the applicant for whom the name was reserved and specifying the name and address of the transferee.

COMMENT

Section 103 is new. The prior uniform law did not provide for registration of names.

SECTION 104. [Specified Office and Agent.]   Each limited partnership shall continuously maintain in this State:

(1)   an office, which may but need not be a place of its business in this State, at which shall be kept the records required by Section 105 to be maintained; and

(2)   an agent for service of process on the limited partnership, which agent must be an individual resident of this State, a domestic corporation, or a foreign corporation authorized to do business in this State.

COMMENT

Section 104 is new. It requires that a limited partnership have certain minimum contacts with its State of organization, *i.e.*, an office at which the constitutive documents and basic financial information is kept and an agent for service of process.

SECTION 105. [Records to be Kept.]   Each limited partnership shall keep at the office referred to in Section 104(1) the following: (1) a current list of the full name and last known business address of each partner set forth in alphabetical order, (2) a copy of the certificate of limited partnership and all certificates of amendment thereto, together with executed copies of any powers of attorney pursuant to which any certificate has been executed, (3) copies of the limited partnership's federal, state and local income tax returns and reports, if any, for the 3 most recent years, and (4) copies of any then effective written partnership agreements and of any financial statements of the limited partnership for the 3 most recent years. Those records are subject to inspection and copying at the reasonable request, and at the expense, of any partner during ordinary business hours.

COMMENT

Section 105 is new. In view of the passive nature of the limited partner's position, it has been widely felt that limited partners are entitled to access to certain basic documents, including the certificate of limited partnership and any partnership agreement. In view of the great diversity among limited partnerships, it was thought inappropriate to require a standard form of financial report, and Section 105 does no more than require retention of tax returns and any other financial statements that are prepared. The names and addresses of the partners are made available to the general public.

SECTION 106. [Nature of Business.]   A limited partnership may carry on any business that a partnership without limited partners may carry on except [here designate prohibited activities].

COMMENT

Section 106 is identical to Section 3 of the prior uniform law. Many states require that certain regulated industries, such as banking, may be carried on only by entities organized pursuant to special statutes, and it is contemplated that the prohibited activities would be confined to the matters covered by those statutes.

SECTION 107. [Business Transactions of Partner with Partnership.]   Except as provided in the partnership agreement, a partner may lend money to and transact other business with the limited partnership and, subject to other applicable law, has the same rights and obligations with respect thereto as a person who is not a partner.

COMMENT

Section 107 makes a number of important changes in Section 13 of the prior uniform law. Section 13, in effect, created a special fraudulent conveyance provision applicable to the making of secured loans by limited partners and the repayment by limited partnerships of loans from limited partners. Section 107 leaves that question to a State's general fraudulent conveyance statute. In addition, Section 107 eliminates the prohibition in former Section 13 against a general partner (as opposed to a limited partner) sharing pro rata with general creditors in the case of an unsecured loan.

Of course, other doctrines developed under bankruptcy and insolvency laws may require the subordination of loans by partners under appropriate circumstances.

ARTICLE 2

FORMATION: CERTIFICATE OF LIMITED PARTNERSHIP

SECTION 201. [Certificate of Limited Partnership.]

(a)   In order to form a limited partnership two or more persons must execute a certificate of limited partnership. The certificate shall be filed in the office of the Secretary of State and set forth:

(1)   the name of the limited partnership;

(2)   the general character of its business;

(3)   the address of the office and the name and address of the agent for service of process required to be maintained by Section 104;

(4)   the name and the business address of each partner (specifying separately the general partners and limited partners);

(5)   the amount of cash and a description and statement of the agreed value of the other property or services contributed by each partner and which each partner has agreeed to contribute in the future;

(6)   the times at which or events on the happening of which any additional contributions agreed to be made by each partner are to be made;

(7)   any power of a limited partner to grant the right to become a limited partner to an assignee of any part of his partnership interest, and the terms and conditions of the power;

(8)   if agreed upon, the time at which or the events on the happening of which a partner may terminate his membership in the limited partnership and the amount of, or the method of determining, the distribution to which he may be entitled respecting his partnership interest, and the terms and conditions of the termination and distribution;

(9)   any right of a partner to receive distributions of property, including cash from the limited partnership;

(10)   any right of a partner to receive, or of a general partner to make, distributions to a partner which include a return of all or any part of the partner's contribution;

(11)   any time at which or events upon the happening of which the limited partnership is to be dissolved and its affairs wound up;

(12)   any right of the remaining general partners to continue the business on the happening of an event of withdrawal of a general partner; and

(13)   any other matters the partners determine to include therein.

(b)   A limited partnership is formed at the time of the filing of the certificate of limited partnership in the office of the Secretary of State or at any later time specified in the certificate of limited partnership if, in either case, there has been substantial compliance with the requirements of this section.

COMMENT

The matters required to be set forth in the certificate of limited partnership are not different in kind from those required by Section 2 of the prior uniform law, although certain additions and deletions have been made and the description has been revised to conform with the rest of the Act. In general, the certificate is intended to serve two functions: first, to place creditors on notice of the facts concerning the capital of the partnership and the rules regarding additional contributions to and withdrawals from the partnership; second, to clearly delineate the time at which persons become general partners and limited partners. Subparagraph (b), which is based upon the prior uniform law, has been retained to make it clear that the existence of the limited partnership depends only upon compliance with this section. Its continued existence is not dependent upon compliance with other provisions of this Act.

SECTION 202. [Amendment to Certificate.]

(a)   A certificate of limited partnership is amended by filing a certificate of amendment thereto in the office of the Secretary of State. The certificate shall set forth:

(1)   the name of the limited partnership;

(2)   the date of filing the certificate;
and

(3)   the amendment to the certificate.

(b)   Within 30 days after the happening of any of the following events, an amendment to a certificate of limited partnership reflecting the occurrence of the event or events shall be filed:

(1)   a change in the amount or character of the contribution of any partner, or in any partner's obligation to make a contribution;

(2)   the admission of a new partner;

(3)   the withdrawal of a partner; or

(4)   the continuation of the business under Section 801 after an event of withdrawal of a general partner.

(c)   A general partner who becomes aware that any statement in a certificate of limited partnership was false when made or that any arrangements or other facts described have changed, making the certificate inaccurate in any respect, shall promptly amend the certificate, but an amendment to show a change of address of a limited partner need be filed only once every 12 months.

(d) A certificate of limited partnership may be amended at any time for any other proper purpose the general partners determine.

(e) No person has any liability because an amendment to a certificate of limited partnership has not been filed to reflect the occurrence of any event referred to in subsection (b) of this Section if the amendment is filed within the 30-day period specified in subsection (b).

COMMENT

Section 202 makes substantial changes in Section 24 of the prior uniform law. Paragraph (b) lists the basic events—the addition or withdrawal of partners or capital or capital obligations—that are so central to the function of the certificate of limited partnership that they require prompt amendment. Paragraph (c) makes it clear, as it was not clear under subdivision (2)(g) of former Section 24, that the certificate of limited partnership is intended to be an accurate description of the facts to which it relates at all times and does not speak merely as of the date it is executed. Paragraph (e) provides a "safe harbor" against claims of creditors or others who assert that they have been misled by the failure to amend the certificate of limited partnership to reflect changes in any of the important facts referred to in paragraph (b); if the certificate of limited partnership is amended within 30 days of the occurrence of the event, no creditor or other person can recover for damages sustained during the interim. Additional protection is afforded by the provisions of Section 304.

SECTION 203. [Cancellation of Certificate.] A certificate of limited partnership shall be cancelled upon the dissoluton and the commencement of winding up of the partnership or at any other time there are no limited partners. A certificate of cancellation shall be filed in the office of the Secretary of State and set forth:

(1) the name of the limited partnership;

(2) the date of filing of its certificate of limited partnership;

(3) the reason for filing the certificate of cancellation;

(4) the effective date (which shall be a date certain) of cancellation if it is not to be effective upon the filing of the certificate; and

(5) any other information the general partners filing the certificate determine.

COMMENT

Section 203 changes Section 24 of the prior uniform law by making it clear that the certificate of cancellation should be filed upon the commencement of winding up of the limited partnership. Section 24 provided for cancellation "when the partnership is dissolved."

SECTION 204. [Execution of Certificates.]

(a)   Each certificate required by this Article to be filed in the office of the Secretary of State shall be executed in the following manner:

(1)   an original certificate of limited partnership must be signed by all partners named therein;

(2)   a certificate of amendment must be signed by at least one general partner and by each other partner designated in the certificate as a new partner or whose contribution is described as having been increased; and

(3)   a certificate of cancellation must be signed by all general partners.

(b)   Any person may sign a certificate by an attorney-in-fact, but a power of attorney to sign a certificate relating to the admission, or increased contribution, of a partner must specifically describe the admission or increase.

(c)   The execution of a certificate by a general partner constitutes an affirmation under the penalties of perjury that the facts stated therein are true.

COMMENT

Section 204 collects in one place the formal requirements for the execution of certificates which were set forth in Sections 2 and 25 of the prior uniform law. Those sections required that each certificate be signed by all partners, and there developed an unnecessarily cumbersome practice of having each limited partner sign powers of attorney to authorize the general partners to execute certificates of amendment on their behalf. Section 204 insures that each partner must sign a certificate when he becomes a partner or when the certificates reflect any increase in his obligation to make contributions. Certificates of amendment are required to be signed by only one general partner and all general partners must sign certificates of cancellation. Section 204 prohibits blanket powers of attorney for the execution of certificates in many cases, since those conditions under which a partner is required to sign have been narrowed to circumstances of special importance to that partner. The former requirement that all certificates be sworn has been confined to statements by the general partners, recognizing that the limited partner's role is a limited one.

SECTION 205. [Amendment or Cancellation by Judicial Act.]   If a person required by Section 204 to execute a certificate of amendment or cancellation fails or refuses to do so, any other partner, and any assignee of a partnership interest, who is adversely affected by the failure or refusal, may petition the [here designate the proper court] to direct the amendment or

cancellation. If the court finds that the amendment or cancellation is proper and that any person so designated has failed or refused to execute the certificate, it shall order the Secretary of State to record an appropriate certificate of amendment or cancellation.

COMMENT

Section 205 changes subdivisions (3) and (4) of Section 25 of the prior uniform law by confining the persons who have standing to seek judicial intervention to partners and to those assignees who are adversely affected by the failure or refusal of the appropriate persons to file a certificate of amendment or cancellation.

SECTION 206. [Filing in Office of Secretary of State.]

(a) Two signed copies of the certificate of limited partnership and of any certificates of amendment or cancellation (or of any judicial decree of amendment or cancellation) shall be delivered to the Secretary of State. A person who executes a certificate as an agent or fiduciary need not exhibit evidence of his authority as a prerequisite to filing. Unless the Secretary of State finds that any certificate does not conform to law, upon receipt of all filing fees required by law he shall:

(1) endorse on each duplicate original the word "Filed" and the day, month and year of the filing thereof;

(2) file one duplicate original in his office; and

(3) return the other duplicate original to the person who filed it or his representative.

(b) Upon the filing of a certificate of amendment (or judicial decree of amendment) in the office of the Secretary of State, the certificate of limited partnership shall be amended as set forth therein, and upon the effective date of a certificate of cancellation (or a judicial decree thereof), the certificate of limited partnership is cancelled.

COMMENT

Section 206 is new. In addition to providing mechanics for the central filing system, the second sentence of this section does away with the requirement, formerly imposed by some local filing officers, that persons who have executed certificates under a power of attorney exhibit executed copies of the power of attorney itself. Paragraph (b) changes subdivision (5) of Section 25 of the prior uniform law by providing that certificates of cancellation are effective upon their effective date under Section 203.

SECTION 207.[**Liability for False Statement in Certificate.**] If any certificate of limited partnership or certificate of amendment or cancellation contains a false statement, one who suffers loss by reliance on the statement may recover damages for the loss from:

(1) any person who executes the certificate, or causes another to execute it on his behalf, and knew, and any general partner who knew or should have known, the statement to be false at the time the certificate was executed; and

(2) any general partner who thereafter knows or should have known that any arrangement or other fact described in the certificate has changed, making the statement inaccurate in any respect, within a sufficient time before the statement was relied upon reasonably to have enabled that general partner to cancel or amend the certificate, or to file a petition for its cancellation or amendment under Section 205.

COMMENT

Section 207 changes Section 6 of the prior uniform law by providing explicitly for the liability of persons who sign a certificate as agent under a power of attorney and by confining the obligation to amend a certificate of limited partnership in light of future events to general partners.

SECTION 208. [**Notice.**] The fact that a certificate of limited partnership is on file in the office of the Secretary of State is notice that the partnership is a limited partnership and the persons designated therein as limited partners are limited partners, but it is not notice of any other fact.

COMMENT

Section 208 is new. By stating that the filing of a certificate of limited partnership only results in constructive notice of the limited liability of the limited partners, it obviates the concern that third parties may be held to have notice of special provisions set forth in the certificate. While this section is designed to preserve the limited liability of limited partners, the constructive notice provided is not intended to change any liability of a limited partner which may be created by his action or inaction under the law of estoppel, agency, fraud, or the like.

SECTION 209. [**Delivery of Certificates to Limited Partners.**] Upon the return by the Secretary of State pursuant to Section 206 of a certificate marked "Filed," the general partners shall promptly deliver or mail a copy of the certificate of limited partnership and each certificate to each limited partner unless the partnership agreement provides otherwise.

COMMENT

This section is new.

ARTICLE 3

LIMITED PARTNERS

SECTION 301. [Admission of Additional Limited Partners.]

(a)   After the filing of a limited partnership's original certificate of limited partnership, a person may be admitted as an additional limited partner:

(1)   in the case of a person acquiring a partnership interest directly from the limited partnership, upon compliance with the partnership agreement or, if the partnership agreement does not so provide, upon the written consent of all partners; and

(2)   in the case of an assignee of a partnership interest of a partner who has the power, as provided in section 704, to grant the assignee the right to become a limited partner, upon the exercise of that power and compliance with any conditions limiting the grant or exercise of the power.

(b)   In each case under subsection (a), the person acquiring the partnership interest becomes a limited partner only upon amendment of the certificate of limited partnership reflecting that fact.

COMMENT

Subdivision (1) of Section 301(a) adds to Section 8 of the prior uniform law an explicit recognition of the fact that unanimous consent of all partners is required for admission of new limited partners unless the partnership agreement provides otherwise. Subdivision (2) is derived from Section 19 of the prior uniform law but abandons the former terminology of "substituted limited partner".

SECTION 302. [Voting.]   Subject to Section 303, the partnership agreement may grant to all or a specified group of the limited partners the right to vote (on a per capita or other basis) upon any matter.

COMMENT

Section 302 is new, and must be read together with subdivision (b)(5) of Section 303. Although the prior uniform law did not speak specifically of the voting powers of limited partners, it is not uncommon for partnership agreements to grant such power to limited partners. Section 302 is designed only to make it clear that the partnership agreement may grant such power to limited partners. If such powers are granted to limited partners beyond the "safe harbor" of Section 303 (b)(5), a court may hold that, under the circumstances, the limited partners have participated in "control of the business" within the meaning of Section 303(a). Section 303(c) simply means that the exercise of powers beyond the ambit of Section 303(b) is not *ipso facto* to be taken as taking part in the control of the business.

SECTION 303. [Liability to Third Parties.]

(a)   Except as provided in subsection (d), a limited partner is not liable for the obligations of a limited partnership unless he is also a general partner or, in addition to the exercise of his rights and powers as a limited partner, he takes part in the control of the business. However, if the limited partner's participation in the control of the business is not substantially the same as the exercise of the powers of a general partner, he is liable only to persons who transact business with the limited partnership with actual knowledge of his participation in control.

(b)   A limited partner does not participate in the control of the business within the meaning of subsection (a) solely by doing one or more of the following:

(1)   being a contractor for or an agent or employee of the limited partnership or of a general partner;

(2)   consulting with and advising a general partner with respect to the business of the limited partnership;

(3)   acting as surety for the limited partnership;

(4)   approving or disapproving an amendment to the partnership agreement; or

(5)   voting on one or more of the following matters:

(i)   the dissolution and winding up of the limited partnership;

(ii)   the sale, exchange, lease, mortgage, pledge, or other transfer of all or substantially all the assets of the limited partnership other than in the ordinary course of its business;

(iii)   the incurrence of indebtedness by the limited partnership other than in the ordinary course of its business;

(iv)   a change in the nature of the business; or

(v)   removal of a general partner.

(c)   The enumeration in subsection (b) does not mean that the possession or exercise of any other powers by a limited partner constitutes participation by him in the business of the limited partnership.

(d)   A limited partner who knowingly permits his name to be used in the name of the limited partnership, except under circumstances permitted by Section 102(2)(i), is liable to creditors who extend credit to the limited partnership without actual knowledge that the limited partner is not a general partner.

COMMENT

Section 303 makes several important changes in Section 7 of the prior uniform law. The first sentence of Section 303(a) carries over the basic test from former Section 7—whether the limited partner "takes part in the control of the business"—in order to insure that judicial decisions under the prior uniform law remain applicable to the extent not expressly changed. The second sentence of Section 303(a) reflects a wholly new concept. Because of the difficulty of determining when the "control" line has been overstepped, it was thought unfair to impose general partner's liability on a limited partner except to the extent that a third party had knowledge of his participation in control of the business. On the other hand, in order to avoid permitting a limited partner to exercise all of the powers of a general partner while avoiding any direct dealings with third parties, the "is not substantially the same as" test was introduced. Paragraph (b) is intended to provide a "safe harbor" by enumerating certain activities which a limited partner may carry on for the partnership without being deemed to have taken part in control of the business. Paragraph (d) is derived from Section 5 of the prior uniform law, but adds as a condition to the limited partner's liability the fact that a limited partner must have knowingly permitted his name to be used in the name of the limited partnership.

SECTION 304. [Person Erroneously Believing Himself Limited Partner.]

(a)   Except as provided in subsection (b), a person who makes a contribution to a business enterprise and erroneously but in good faith believes that he has become a limited partner in the enterprise is not a general partner in the enterprise and is not bound by its obligations by reason of making the contribution, receiving distributions from the enterprise, or exercising any rights of a limited partner, if, on ascertaining the mistake, he:

(1)   causes an appropriate certificate of limited partnership or a certificate of amendment to be executed and filed; or

(2)   withdraws from future equity participation in the enterprise.

(b)   A person who makes a contribution of the kind described in subsection (a) is liable as a general partner to any third party who transacts business with the enterprise before an appropriate certificate is filed and, if such enterprise (i) before the person withdraws and an appropriate certificate is filed to show the withdrawal, or (ii) before an appropriate certificate is filed to show his status as a limited partner and, in the case of an amendment, after expiration of the 30-day period for filing an amendment relating to the person as a limited partner under Section 202, but in either case only if the third party actually believed in good faith that the person was a general partner at the time of the transaction.

COMMENT

Section 304 is derived from Section 11 of the prior uniform law. The "good faith" requirement has been added in the first sentence of Section 304(a). The provisions of subdivision (2) of Section 304(a) are intended to clarify an ambiguity in the prior law by providing that a person who chooses to withdraw from the enterprise in order to protect himself from liability is not required to renounce any of his then current interest in the enterprise so long as he has no further participation as an equity participant. Paragraph (b) preserves the liability of the equity participant prior to withdrawal (and after the time for appropriate amendment in the case of a limited partnership) to any third party who has transacted business with the person believing in good faith that he was a general partner.

SECTION 305. [Information.]   Each limited partner has the right to:

(1)   inspect and copy any of the partnership records required to be maintained by Section 105; and

(2)   obtain from the general partners from time to time upon reasonable demand (i) true and full information regarding the state of the business and financial condition of the limited partnership, (ii) promptly after becoming available, a copy of the limited partnership's federal, state, and local income tax returns for each year, and (iii) other information regarding the affairs of the limited partnership as is just and reasonable.

COMMENT

Section 305 changes and restates the rights of limited partners to information about the partnership formerly provided by Section 10 of the prior uniform law.

ARTICLE 4

GENERAL PARTNERS

SECTION 401. [Admission of Additional General Partners.]   After the filing of a limited partnership's original certificate of limited partnership, additional general partners may be admitted only with the specific written consent of each partner.

COMMENT

Section 401 is derived from Section 9(1)(e) of the prior law and carries over the unwaivable requirement that all limited partners must consent to the admission of an additional general partner and that such consent must specifically identify the general partner involved.

SECTION 402. [Events of Withdrawal.] Except as approved by the specific written consent of all partners at the time, a person ceases to be a general partner of a limited partnership upon the happening of any of the following events:

(1)   the general partner withdraws from the limited partnership as provided in Section 602;

(2)   the general partner ceases to be a member of the limited partnership as provided in Section 702;

(3)   the general partner is removed as a general partner in accordance with the partnership agreement;

(4)   unless otherwise provided in the certificate of limited partnership, the general partner (i) makes an assignment for the benefit of creditors; (ii) files a voluntary petition in bankruptcy; (iii) is adjudicated a bankrupt or insolvent; (iv) files a petition or answer seeking for himself any reorganization, arrangement, composition, readjustment, liquidation, dissolution, or similar relief under any statute, law, or regulation; (v) files an answer or other pleading admitting or failing to contest the material allegations of a petition filed against him in any proceeding of this nature; or (vi) seeks, consents to, or acquiesces in the appointment of a trustee, receiver, or liquidator of the general partner or of all or any substantial part of his properties;

(5)   unless otherwise provided in the certificate of limited partnership, [120] days after the commencement of any proceeding against the general partner seeking reorganization, arrangement, composition, readjustment, liquidation, dissolution or similar relief under any statute, law, or regulation, the proceeding has not been dismissed, or if within [90] days after the appointment without his consent or acquiescence of a trustee, receiver, or liquidator of the general partner or of all or any substantial part of his properties, the appointment is not vacated or stayed or within [90] days after the expiration of any such stay, the appointment is not vacated;

(6)   in the case of a general partner who is a natural person

(i)   his death; or

(ii)   the entry by a court of competent jurisdiction adjudicating him incompetent to manage his person or his estate;

(7)   in the case of a general partner who is acting as a general partner by virtue of being a trustee of a trust, the termination of the trust (but not merely the substitution of new trustee);

(8)   in the case of a general partner that is a separate partnership, the dissolution and commencement of winding up of the separate partnership;

(9)   in the case of a general partner that is a corporation, the filing of a

certificate of dissolution, or its equivalent, for the corporation or the revocation of its charter; or

(10) in the case of an estate, the distribution by the fiduciary of the estate's entire interest in the partnership.

COMMENT

Section 402 expands considerably the provisions of Section 20 of the prior uniform law which provided for dissolution in the event of the retirement, death or insanity of a general partner. Subdivisions (1), (2) and (3) recognize that the general partner's agency relationship is terminable at will, although it may result in a breach of the partnership agreement giving rise to an action for damages. Subdivisions (4) and (5) reflect a judgment that unless the limited partners agree otherwise, they ought to have the power to rid themselves of a general partner who is in such dire financial straits that he is the subject of proceedings under the National Bankruptcy Act or a similar provision of law. Subdivisions (6) through (10) simply elaborate on the notion of death in the case of a general partner who is not a natural person. Of course, the addition of the words "and in the partnership agreement" was not intended to suggest that liabilities to third parties could be affected by provisions in the partnership agreement.

SECTION 403. [General Powers and Liabilities.] Except as provided in this Act or in the partnership agreement, a general partner of a limited partnership has the rights and powers and is subject to the restrictions and liabilities of a partner in a partnership without limited partners.

COMMENT

Section 403 is derived from Section 9(1) of the prior uniform law.

SECTION 404. [Contributions by General Partner.] A general partner of a limited partnership may make contributions to the partnership and share in the profits and losses of, and in distributions from, the limited partnership as a general partner. A general partner also may make contributions to and share in profits, losses, and distributions as a limited partner. A person who is both a general partner and a limited partner has the rights and powers, and is subject to the restrictions and liabilities, of a general partner and, except as provided in the partnership agreement, also has the powers, and is subject to the restrictions, of a limited partner to the extent of his participation in the partnership as a limited partner.

COMMENT

Section 404 is derived from Section 12 of the prior uniform law and makes clear that the partnership agreement may provide that a general partner who is also a limited partner may exercise all of the powers of a limited partner.

SECTION 405. [Voting.] The partnership agreement may grant to all or certain identified general partners the right to vote (on a per capita or any other basis), separately or with all or any class of the limited partners, on any matter.

COMMENT

Section 405 is new and is intended to make it clear that the Act does not require that the limited partners have any right to vote on matters as a separate class.

ARTICLE 5

FINANCE

SECTION 501. [Form of Contribution.] The contribution of a partner may be in cash, property, or services rendered, or a promissory note or other obligation to contribute cash or property or to perform services.

COMMENT

As noted in the comment to Section 101, the explicit permission to make contributions of services expands Section 4 of the prior uniform law.

Section 502. [Liability for Contribution.]

(a)   Except as provided in the certificate of limited partnership, a partner is obligated to the limited partnership to perform any promise to contribute cash or property or to perform services, even if he is unable to perform because of death, disability, or any other reason. If a partner does not make the required contribution of property or services, he is obligated at the option of the limited partnership to contribute cash equal to that portion of the value (as stated in the certificate of limited partnership) of the stated contribution that has not been made.

(b)   Unless otherwise provided in the partnership agreement, the obligation of a partner to make a contribution or return money or other property paid or distributed in violation of this Act may be compromised only by consent of all the partners. Notwithstanding the compromise, a creditor of a limited partnership who extends credit, or whose claim arises, after the filing of the certificate of limited partnership or an amendment thereto which, in either case, reflects the obligation, and before the amendment or cancellation thereof to reflect the compromise, may enforce the original obligation.

COMMENT

Although Section 17 (1) of the prior uniform law required a partner to fulfill his promise to make contributions, the addition of contributions in the form of a promise to render services means that a partner who is unable to perform those services because of death or disability as well as because of an intentional default is required to pay the cash value of the services unless the certificate of limited partnership provides otherwise. Subdivision (b) is derived from Section 17(3) of the prior uniform law.

Section 503. [Sharing of Profits and Losses.]   The profits and losses of a limited partnership shall be allocated among the partners, and among classes of partners, in the manner provided in the partnership agreement. If the partnership agreement does not so provide, profits and losses shall be allocated on the basis of the value (as stated in the certificate of limited partnership) of the contributions made by each partner to the extent they have been received by the partnership and have not been returned.

COMMENT

Section 503 is new. The prior uniform law did not provide for the basis on which partners share profits and losses in the absence of agreement.

Section 504. [Sharing of Distributions.]   Distributions of cash or other assets of a limited partnership shall be allocated among the partners, and among classes of partners, in the manner provided in the partnership agreement. If the partnership agreement does not so provide, distributions shall be made on the basis of the value (as stated in the certificate of limited partnership) of the contributions made by each partner to the extent they have been received by the partnership and have not been returned.

COMMENT

Section 504 is new. The prior uniform law did not provide for the basis on which partners share distributions in the absence of agreement. This section also recognizes that partners may choose to share in distributions on a different basis than they share in profits and losses.

ARTICLE 6

DISTRIBUTIONS AND WITHDRAWAL

Section 601. [Interim Distributions.]   Except as provided in this Article, a partner is entitled to receive distributions from a limited partnership before his withdrawal from the limited partnership and before the dissolution and winding up thereof:

(1)   to the extent and at the times or upon the happening of the events specified in the partnership agreement; and

(2)   if any distribution constitutes a return of any part of his contribution under Section 608(b), to the extent and at the times or upon the happening of the events specified in the certificate of limited partnership.

COMMENT

Section 601 is new.

Section 602. [Withdrawal of General Partner.]   A general partner may withdraw from a limited partnership at any time by giving written notice to the other partners, but if the withdrawal violates the partnership agreement, the limited partnership may recover from the withdrawing general partner damages for breach of the partnership agreement and offset the damages against the amount otherwise distributable to him.

COMMENT

Section 602 is new but is generally derived from Section 38 of the Uniform Partnership Law.

SECTION 603. [Withdrawal of Limited Partner.]   A limited partner may withdraw from a limited partnership at the time or upon the happening of events specified in the certificate of limited partnership and in accordance with the partnership agreement. If the certificate does not specify the time or the events upon the happening of which a limited partner may withdraw or a definite time for the dissolution and winding up of the limited partnership, a limited partner may withdraw upon not less than 6 months' prior written notice to each general partner at his address on the books of the limited partnership at its office in this State.

COMMENT

Section 603 is derived from Section 16(c) of the prior uniform law.

SECTION 604. [Distribution upon Withdrawal.]   Except as provided in this Article, upon withdrawal any withdrawing partner is entitled to receive any distribution to which he is entitled under the partnership agreement and, if not otherwise provided in the agreement, he is entitled to receive, within a reasonable time after withdrawal, the fair value of his interest in the limited partnership as of the date of withdrawal, based upon his right to share in distributions from the limited partnership.

COMMENT

Section 604 is new. It fixes the distributive share of a withdrawing partner in the absence of an agreement among the partners.

SECTION 605. [Distribution in Kind.]   Except as provided in the certificate of limited partnership, a partner, regardless of the nature of his contribution, has no right to demand and receive any distribution from a limited partnership in any form other than cash. Except as provided in the partnership agreement, a partner may not be compelled to accept a distribution of any asset in kind from a limited partnership to the extent that the percentage of the asset distributed to him exceeds a percentage of that asset which is equal to the percentage in which he shares in distributions from the limited partnership.

COMMENT

The first sentence of Section 605 is derived from Section 16(3) of the prior uniform law. The second sentence is new, and is intended to protect a limited partner (and the remaining partners) against a distribution in kind of more than his share of particular assets.

SECTION 606. [Right to Distribution.]   At the time a partner becomes entitled to receive a distribution, he has the status of, and is entitled to all remedies available to, a creditor of the limited partnership with respect to the distribution.

COMMENT

Section 606 is new and is intended to make it clear that the right of a partner to receive a distribution, as between the partners, is not subject to the equity risks of the enterprise. On the other hand, since partners entitled to distributions have creditor status, there did not seem to be a need for the extraordinary remedy of Section 16(4)(a) of the prior uniform law, which granted a limited partner the right to seek dissolution of the partnership if he was unsuccessful in demanding the return of his contribution. It is more appropriate for the partner to simply sue as an ordinary creditor and obtain a judgment.

SECTION 607. [Limitations on Distribution.] A partner may not receive a distribution from a limited partnership to the extent that, after giving effect to the distribution, all liabilities of the limited partnership, other than liabilities to partners on account of their partnership interests, exceed the fair value of the partnership assets.

COMMENT

Section 607 is derived from Section 16(1)(a) of the prior uniform law.

SECTION 608. [Liability upon Return of Contribution.]

(a) If a partner has received the return of any part of his contribution without violation of the partnership agreement or this Act, he is liable to the limited partnership for a period of one year thereafter for the amount of the returned contribution, but only to the extent necessary to discharge the limited partnership's liabilities to creditors who extended credit to the limited partnership during the period the contribution was held by the partnership.

(b) If a partner has received the return of any part of his contribution in violation of the partnership agreement or this Act, he is liable to the limited partnership for a period of 6 years thereafter for the amount of the contribution wrongfully returned.

(c) A partner receives a return of his contribution to the extent that a distribution to him reduces his share of the fair value of the net assets of the limited partnership below the value (as set forth in the certificate of limited partnership) of his contribution which has not been distributed to him.

COMMENT

Paragraph (a) is derived from Section 17(4) of the prior uniform law, but the one-year statute of limitations has been added. Paragraph (b) is derived from Section 17(2)(b) of the prior uniform law but, again, a statute of limitations has been added. Paragraph (c) is new. The provisions of former Section 17(2) that referred to the partner holding as "trustee" any money or specific property wrongfully returned to him have been eliminated.

ARTICLE 7

ASSIGNMENT OF PARTNERSHIP INTERESTS

SECTION 701. [Nature of Partnership Interest.]   A partnership interest is personal property.

COMMENT

This section is derived from Section 18 of the prior uniform law.

SECTION 702. [Assignment of Partnership Interest.]   Except as provided in the partnership agreement, a partnership interest is assignable in whole or in part. An assignment of a partnership interest does not dissolve a limited partnership or entitle the assignee to become or to exercise any rights of a partner. An assignment entitles the assignee to receive, to the extent assigned, only the distribution to which the assignor would be entitled. Except as provided in the partnership agreement, a partner ceases to be a partner upon assignment of all his partnership interest.

COMMENT

Section 19(1) of the prior uniform law provided simply that "a limited partner's interest is assignable," raising a question whether *any* limitations on the right of assignment were permitted. While the first sentence of Section 702 recognizes that the power to assign may be restricted in the partnership agreement, there was no intention to affect in any way the usual rules regarding restraints on alienation of personal property. The second and third sentences of Section 702 are derived from Section 19(3) of the prior uniform law. The last sentence is new.

SECTION 703. [Rights of Creditor.]   On application to a court of competent jurisdiction by any judgment creditor of a partner, the court may charge the partnership interest of the partner with payment of the unsatisfied amount of the judgment with interest. To the extent so charged, the judgment creditor has only the rights of an assignee of the partnership interest. This Act does not deprive any partner of the benefit of any exemption laws applicable to his partnership interest.

COMMENT

Section 703 is derived from Section 22 of the prior uniform law but has not carried over some provisions that were thought to be superfluous. For example, references in Section 22(1) to specific remedies have been omitted, as has a prohibition in Section 22(2) against discharge of the lien with partnership property. Ordinary rules governing the remedies available to a creditor and the fiduciary obligations of general partners will determine those matters.

SECTION 704. [Right of Assignee to Become Limited Partner.]

(a)   An assignee of a partnership interest, including an assignee of a general partner, may become a limited partner if and to the extent that (1) the assignor gives the assignee that right in accordance with authority described in the certificate of limited partnership or, (2) all other partners consent.

(b)   An assignee who has become a limited partner has, to the extent assigned, the rights and powers, and is subject to the restrictions and liabilities, of a limited partner under the partnership agreement and this Act. An assignee who becomes a limited partner also is liable for the obligations of his assignor to make and return contributions as provided in Article 6. However, the assignee is not obligated for liabilities unknown to the assignee at the time he became a limited partner and which could not be ascertained from the certificate of limited partnership.

(c)   If an assignee of a partnership interest becomes a limited partner, the assignor is not released from his liability to the limited partnership under Sections 207 and 502.

COMMENT

Section 704 is derived from Section 19 of the prior uniform law, but paragraph (b) defines more narrowly than Section 19 the obligations of the assignor that are automatically assumed by the assignee.

SECTION 705. [Power of Estate of Deceased or Incompetent Partner.]   If a partner who is an individual dies or a court of competent jurisdiction adjudges him to be incompetent to manage his person or his property, the partner's executor, administrator, guardian, conservator, or other legal representative may exercise all the partner's rights for the purpose of settling his estate or administering his property, including any power the partner had to give an assignee the right to become a limited partner. If a partner is a corporation, trust, or other entity and is dissolved or terminated, the powers of that partner may be exercised by its legal representative or successor.

COMMENT

Section 705 is derived from Section 21(1) of the prior uniform law. Former Section 21(2), making a deceased limited partner's estate liable for his liabilities as a limited partner was deleted as superfluous, with no intention of changing the liability of the estate.

ARTICLE 8

DISSOLUTION

SECTION 801. [Nonjudicial Dissolution.] A limited partnership is dissolved and its affairs shall be wound up upon the happening of the first to occur of the following:

(1) at the time or upon the happening of events specified in the certificate of limited partnership;

(2) written consent of all partners;

(3) an event of withdrawal of a general partner unless at the time there is at least one other general partner and the certificate of limited partnership permits the business of the limited partnership to be carried on by the remaining general partner and that partner does so, but the limited partnership is not dissolved and is not required to be wound up by reason of any event of withdrawal, if, within 90 days after the withdrawal, all partners agree in writing to continue the business of the limited partnership and to the appointment of one or more additional general partners if necessary or desired; or

(4) entry of a decree of judicial dissolution under Section 802.

COMMENT

Section 801 merely collects in one place all of the events causing dissolution. Paragraph (3) is derived from Sections 9(1)(g) and 20 of the prior uniform law, but adds the 90-day grace period.

SECTION 802. [Judicial Dissolution.] On application by or for a partner the [here designate the proper court] court may decree dissolution of a limited partnership whenever it is not reasonably practicable to carry on the business in conformity with the partnership agreement.

COMMENT

Section 802 is new.

SECTION 803. [Winding Up.] Except as provided in the partnership agreement, the general partners who have not wrongfully dissolved a limited partnership or, if none, the limited partners, may wind up the limited partnership's affairs; but the [here designate the proper court] court may wind up the limited partnership's affairs upon application of any partner, his legal representative, or assignee.

COMMENT

Section 803 is new and is derived in part from Section 37 of the Uniform General Partnership Law.

SECTION 804. [Distribution of Assets.] Upon the winding up of a limited partnership, the assets shall be distributed as follows:

(1)   to creditors, including partners who are creditors, to the extent permitted by law, in satisfaction of liabilities of the limited partnership other than liabilities for distributions to partners under Section 601 or 604;

(2)   except as provided in the partnership agreement, to partners and former partners in satisfaction of liabilities for distributions under Section 601 or 604; and

(3)   except as provided in the partnership agreement, to partners *first* for the return of their contributions and *secondly* respecting their partnership interests, in the proportions in which the partners share in distributions.

COMMENT

Section 804 revises Section 23 of the prior uniform law by providing that (1) to the extent partners are also creditors, other than in respect of their interests in the partnership, they share with other creditors, (2) once the partnership's obligation to make a distribution accrues, it must be paid before any other distributions of an "equity" nature are made, and (3) general and limited partners rank on the same level except as otherwise provided in the partnership agreement.

ARTICLE 9

FOREIGN LIMITED PARTNERSHIPS

SECTION 901. [Law Governing.] Subject to the Constitution of this State, (1) the laws of the state under which a foreign limited partnership is organized govern its organization and internal affairs and the liability of its limited partners, and (2) a foreign limited partnership may not be denied registration by reason of any difference between those laws and the laws of this State.

COMMENT

Section 901 is new.

SECTION 902. [Registration.] Before transacting business in this State, a foreign limited partnership shall register with the Secretary of State. In order to register, a foreign limited partnership shall submit to the Secretary of State, in duplicate, an application for registration as a foreign limited partnership, signed and sworn to by a general partner and setting forth:

(1) the name of the foreign limited partnership and, if different, the name under which it proposes to register and transact business in this State;

(2) the state and date of its formation;

(3) the general character of the business it proposes to transact in this State;

(4) the name and address of any agent for service of process on the foreign limited partnership whom the foreign limited partnership elects to appoint; the agent must be an individual resident of this State, a domestic corporation, or a foreign corporation having a place of business in, and authorized to do business in, this State;

(5) a statement that the Secretary of State is appointed the agent of the foreign limited partnership for service of process if no agent has been appointed under paragraph (4) or, if appointed, the agent's authority has been revoked or if the agent cannot be found or served with the exercise of reasonable diligence;

(6) the address of the office required to be maintained in the State of its organization by the laws of that State or, if not so required, of the principal office of the foreign limited partnership; and

(7) if the certificate of limited partnership filed in the foreign limited

partnership's state of organization is not required to include the names and business addresses of the partners, a list of the names and addresses.

COMMENT

Section 902 is new. It was thought that requiring a full copy of the certificate of limited partnership and all amendments thereto to be filed in each state in which the partnership does business would impose an unreasonable burden on interstate limited partnerships and that the information on file was sufficient to tell interested persons where they could write to obtain copies of those basic documents.

SECTION 903. [Issuance of Registration.]

(a)   If the Secretary of State finds that an application for registration conforms to law and all requisite fees have been paid, he shall:

(1)   endorse on the application the word "Filed", and the month, day and year of the filing thereof;

(2)   file in his office a duplicate original of the application; and

(3)   issue a certificate of registration to transact business in this State.

(b)   The certificate of registration, together with a duplicate original of the application, shall be returned to the person who filed the application or his representative.

SECTION 904. [Name.]   A foreign limited partnership may not register with the Secretary of State under any name (whether or not it is the name under which it is registered in its state of organization) that includes without abbreviation the words "limited partnership" and that could be registered by a domestic limited partnership.

COMMENT

Section 904 is new.

SECTION 905. [Changes and Amendments.]   If any statement in the application for registration of a foreign limited partnership was false when made or any arrangements or other facts described have changed, making the application inaccurate in any respect, the foreign limited partnership shall promptly file in the office of the Secretary of State a certificate, signed and sworn to by a general partner, correcting such statement.

COMMENT

Section 905 is new.

SECTION 906. [Cancellation of Registration.] A foreign limited partnership may cancel its registration by filing with the Secretary of State a certificate of cancellation signed and sworn to by a general partner. A cancellation does not terminate the authority of the Secretary of State to accept service of process on the foreign limited partnership with respect to [claims for relief] [causes of action] arising out of the transactions of business in this State.

COMMENT

Section 906 is new.

SECTION 907. [Transaction of Business Without Registration.]

(a)   A foreign limited partnership transacting business in this State may not maintain any action, suit, or proceeding in any court of this State until it has registered in this State.

(b)   The failure of a foreign limited partnership to register in this State does not impair the validity of any contract or act of the foreign limited partnership or prevent the foreign limited partnership from defending any action, suit, or proceeding in any court of this State.

(c)   A limited partner of a foreign limited partnership is not liable as a general partner of the foreign limited partnership solely by reason of having transacted business in this State without registration.

(d)   A foreign limited partnership, by transacting business in this State without registration, appoints the Secretary of State as its agent for service of process with respect to [claims for relief] [causes of action] arising out of the transaction of business in this State.

COMMENT

Section 907 is new.

SECTION 908. [Action by (Appropriate Official).] The [appropriate official] may bring an action to restrain a foreign limited partnership from transacting business in this State in violation of this Article.

COMMENT

Section 908 is new.

ARTICLE 10

DERIVATIVE ACTIONS

SECTION 1001. [Right of Action.]   A limited partner may bring an action in the right of a limited partnership to recover a judgment in its favor if general partners with authority to do so have refused to bring the action or if an effort to cause those general partners to bring the action is not likely to succeed.

COMMENT

Section 1001 is new.

SECTION 1002. [Proper Plaintiff.]   In a derivative action, the plaintiff must be a partner at the time of bringing the action and (1) at the time of the transaction of which he complains or (2) his status as a partner had devolved upon him by operation of law or pursuant to the terms of the partnership agreement from a person who was a partner at the time of the transaction.

COMMENT

Section 1002 is new.

SECTION 1003. [Pleading.]   In a derivative action, the complaint shall set forth with particularity the effort of the plaintiff to secure initiation of the action by a general partner or the reasons for not making the effort.

COMMENT

Section 1003 is new.

SECTION 1004. [Expenses.]   If a derivative action is successful, in whole or in part, or if anything is received by the plaintiff as a result of a judgment, compromise or settlement of an action or claim, the court may award the plaintiff reasonable expenses, including reasonable attorney's fees, and shall direct him to remit to the limited partnership the remainder of those proceeds received by him.

COMMENT

Section 1004 is new.

ARTICLE 11

MISCELLANEOUS

SECTION 1101. [Construction and Application.]   This Act shall be so applied and construed to effectuate its general purpose to make uniform the law with respect to the subject of this Act among states enacting it.

SECTION 1102. [Short Title.]   This Act may be cited as the Uniform Limited Partnership Act.

SECTION 1103. [Severability.]   If any provision of this Act or its application to any person or circumstance is held invalid, the invalidity does not affect other provisions or applications of the Act which can be given effect without the invalid provision or application, and to this end the provisions of this Act are severable.

SECTION 1104. [Effective Date, Extended Effective Date and Repeal.]   Except as set forth below, the effective date of this Act is   and the following Acts [list prior limited partnership acts] are hereby repealed:

(1)   The existing provisions for execution and filing of certificates of limited partnerships and amendments thereunder and cancellations thereof continue in effect until [specify time required to create central filing system], the extended effective date, and Sections 102, 103, 104, 105, 201, 202, 203, 204 and 206 are not effective until the extended effective date.

(2)   Section 402, specifying the conditions under which a general partner ceases to be a member of a limited partnership, is not effective until the extended effective date, and the applicable provisions of existing law continue to govern until the extended effective date.

(3)   Sections 501, 502 and 608 apply only to contributions and distributions made after the effective date of this Act.

(4)   Section 704 applies only to assignments made after the effective date of this Act.

(5)   Article 9, dealing with registration of foreign limited partnerships, is not effective until the extended effective date.

SECTION 1105. [Rules for Cases Not Provided for in This Act.]   In any case not provided for in this Act the provisions of the Uniform Partnership Act govern.

REVENUE PROCEDURE 72-13, 1972-1 C.B. 735

26 CFR 601.201: Rulings and determination letters.
(Also Part I Section 7701; 301.7701-3.)

Conditions under which the Revenue Service will issue a ruling concerning classification of an organization as a limited partnership where a corporation is the sole general partner.

REV. PROC. 72-13

SECTION 1. PURPOSE.

The purpose of this Revenue Procedure is to specify the conditions that must be present before the Internal Revenue Service will consider issuing advance rulings concerning classification of organizations as partnerships, for Federal tax purposes under existing regulations (section 301.7701-3 of the Procedure and Administration Regulations), where they are formed as limited partnerships and a corporation is the *sole* general partner. The decision whether the organization may be classified as a partnership under existing regulations will depend on all the facts and circumstances.

SEC. 2. REQUESTS FOR RULINGS.

The Service will consider a request for a ruling on the classification of an organization as a partnership where it is formed as a limited partnership and a corporation is the *sole* general partner under the following conditions:

.01 The limited partners will not own, directly or indirectly, individually or in the aggregate, more than 20 percent of the stock of the corporate general partner or any affiliates as defined in section 1504(a) of the Internal Revenue Code of 1954. For the purpose of determining stock ownership in the corporate general partner or its affiliates the attribution rules set forth in section 318 of the Code are applicable.

.02 If the corporate general partner has an interest in only one limited partnership and the total contributions to that partnership are less than $2,500,000, the net worth of the corporate general partner at all times will be at least 15 percent of such total contributions or $250,000, whichever is the lesser; if the total contributions to that partnership are $2,500,000 or more, the net worth of the corporate general partner at all times will be at least 10 percent of such total contributions. In computing the net worth of the corporate general partner, for this purpose, its interest in the limited partnership and accounts and notes receivable from and payable to the limited partnership will be excluded.

.03 If the corporate general partner has interests in more than one limited partnership, the net worth requirements explained in the preceding paragraph will be applied separately for each limited partnership, and the corporate general partner will have at all times (exclusive of any interest in any limited partnership and notes and accounts receivable from and payable to any limited partnership in which the corporate general partner has any interest), a net worth at least as great as the sum of the amounts required under .02 above for each separate limited partnership.

.04 For purposes of computing the net worth of the corporate general partner in .02 and .03 above, the current fair market value of the corporate assets must be used.

.05 The purchase of a limited partnership interest by a limited partner does not entail either a mandatory or discretionary purchase or option to purchase any type of security of the corporate general partner or its affiliates.

.06 The organization and operation of the limited partnership must be in accordance with the applicable state statute relating to limited partnerships.

SEC. 3. INSTRUCTIONS.

The general procedures of Revenue Procedure 72–3, page 698, relating to the issuance of rulings and determination letters are applicable to requests relating to classification of organizations as limited partnerships.

REVENUE PROCEDURE 74-17, 1974-1 C.B. 438

26 CFR 601.201: Rulings and determination letters.
(Also Part I, Section 7701; 301.7701-3.)

REV. PROC. 74-17[1]

SECTION 1. PURPOSE.

The purpose of this Revenue Procedure is to announce certain conditions under which the Internal Revenue Service will not issue advance rulings or determination letters concerning classification of organizations which raise factual questions as to whether their principal purpose is the reduction of Federal taxes.

---

[1] Also released as Technical Information Release No. 1290, dated May 3, 1974.

SEC. 2. BACKGROUND.

.01   In accordance with Rev. Proc. 72-3, 1972-1 C.B. 698, section 5, the Internal Revenue Service has the discretionary authority to issue rulings and determination letters. There are certain areas where, because of the inherently factual nature of the problem, or for other reasons, the Service will not issue, or ordinarily will not issue, rulings or determination letters. A list of these areas is set forth in Rev. Proc. 72-9, 1972-1 C.B. 719. This list is not all inclusive. Section 3.021 of Rev. Proc. 72-9 indicates that the Service will not rule where the transaction has as its principal purpose the reduction of Federal taxes.

.02   When requested by taxpayers or their authorized representatives, the Individual Income Tax Branch of the Income Tax Division, as part of its functions, issues advance ruling letters on the classification of organizations as partnerships under section 7701 of the Internal Revenue Code of 1954 and section 301.7701-3 of the Procedure and Administration Regulations.

.03   The Individual Income Tax Branch has developed certain operating rules for determining whether a ruling letter will be issued concerning organizations formed as limited partnerships and the conclusions that will be expressed in such ruling letters. Among such operating rules is Rev. Proc. 72-13, 1972-1 C.B. 735, relating to conditions under which the Service will issue a ruling letter on the classification of an organization as a limited partnership where a corporation is the sole general partner.

.04   The operating rules set forth in this Revenue Procedure are being published to make clear the circumstances in which advance rulings will not ordinarily be issued and thus to provide assistance to taxpayers and their representatives in preparing ruling requests, and to assist the Service in issuing advance ruling letters as promptly as practicable. These operating rules do not define, as a matter of law, whether the principal purpose of the organization is the reduction of Federal taxes, nor whether participants in an organization are partners or whether such an organization is a partnership, nor do they define any other terms used in the Internal Revenue Code, Income Tax Regulations, Procedure and Administration Regulations, or Revenue Rulings.

.05   A requested ruling that an organization which is to be formed and operated as a limited partnership is a partnership under section 7701 of the Code will ordinarily be issued if the operating rules set forth in section 3 of this Revenue Procedure are complied with and if all other pertinent provisions of the Internal Revenue Code and regulations thereunder, Revenue Rulings and Revenue Procedures are satisfied.

.06   If the operating rules of section 3 of this Revenue Procedure are not complied with, the Service will ordinarily decline to issue the requested ruling or determination letter.

SEC. 3. OPERATING RULES FOR THIS REVENUE PROCEDURE.

.01   The interests of all of the general partners, taken together, in each material item of partnership income, gain, loss, deduction or credit is equal to at least one percent of each such item at all times during the existence of the partnership. In determining the general partners' interests in such items, limited partnership interests owned by the general partners shall not be taken into account.

.02   The aggregate deductions to be claimed by the partners as their distributive shares of partnership losses for the first two years of operation of the limited partnership will not exceed the amount of equity capital invested in the limited partnership.

.03   A creditor who makes a nonrecourse loan to the limited partnership must not have or acquire, at any time as a result of making the loan, any direct or indirect interest in the profits, capital, or property of the limited partnership other than as a secured creditor.

.04   The rules set forth above must be contained in relevant documents furnished with the request for ruling or, in the absence thereof, by factual representations that such rules will be contained in all relevant documents when they are finalized.

SEC. 4. OTHER INSTRUCTIONS.

The general procedures of Rev. Proc. 72-3, relating to the issuance of rulings and determination letters are applicable to requests relating to classification or organizations formed as limited partnerships, as are the special procedures of Rev. Proc. 72-13, relating to conditions under which the Service will issue a ruling concerning classification of organizations formed as limited partnerships where a corporation is the sole general partner. Also applicable is Rev. Proc. 72-9, which indicates the areas in which the Service will not issue, or ordinarily will not issue, rulings or determination letters. The rules stated above are to be applied only in determining whether ruling and determination letters will be issued and are not intended as substantive rules for the determination of partnership status and are not to be applied as criteria for the audit of taxpayers' returns.

SEC. 5. EFFECTIVE DATE.

The provisions of this Revenue Procedure are effective immediately.

SEC. 6. INQUIRIES.

Inquiries in regard to this Revenue Procedure should refer to its number and should be addressed to the Assistant Commissioner (Technical), Attention: T:I:I, Internal Revenue Service, Washington, D.C. 20224.

FORM 1065 AND SCHEDULE K-1

Form **1065** Department of the Treasury Internal Revenue Service	**U.S. Partnership Return of Income** For calendar year 1981, or fiscal year beginning ...., 1981, and ending ...., 19	OMB No. 1545-0099 **1981**

A Principal business activity (see page 12 of Instructions)	Use IRS label.	Name	D Employer identification no.
B Principal product or service (see page 12 of Instructions)	Other- wise, please print or type.	Number and street	E Date business started
C Business code number (see page 12 of Instructions)		City or town, State, and ZIP code	F Enter total assets from Sched- ule L, line 13, column (D). $

G Check method of accounting: **(1)** ☐ Cash   **(2)** ☐ Accrual   **(3)** ☐ Other (attach explanation)

H Check applicable boxes: **(1)** ☐ Final return **(2)** ☐ Change in address.

IMPORTANT—Fill in all applicable lines and schedules. If you need more space, see page 2 of the Instructions. Enter any items specially allocated to the partners on Schedule K, line 17, and not on the numbered lines on this page or in Schedules A through I.

Income

1a	Gross receipts or sales $ .... **1b** Minus returns and allowances $ .... Balance ▶	1c	
2	Cost of goods sold and/or operations (Schedule A, line 34)	2	
3	Gross profit (subtract line 2 from line 1c)	3	
4	Ordinary income (loss) from other partnerships and fiduciaries (attach statement)	4	
5	Nonqualifying dividends	5	
6	Nonqualifying interest	6	
7	Net income (loss) from rents (Schedule H, line 2)	7	
8	Net income (loss) from royalties (attach schedule)	8	
9	Net farm profit (loss) (attach Schedule F (Form 1040))	9	
10	Net gain (loss) (Form 4797, line 11)	10	
11	Other income (attach schedule)	11	
12	**TOTAL** income (loss) (combine lines 3 through 11)	12	

Deductions

13a	Salaries and wages (other than to partners) $ .... **13b** Minus jobs credit $ .... Balance ▶	13c	
14	Guaranteed payments to partners (see page 4 of Instructions)	14	
15	Rent	15	
16	Interest **(Caution—see page 4 of Instructions)**	16	
17	Taxes	17	
18	Bad debts (see page 5 of Instructions)	18	
19	Repairs	19	
20	Depreciation from Form 4562 (attach Form 4562) $ ...., less depreciation claimed in Schedules A and H and elsewhere on return $ ...., Balance ▶	20	
21	Amortization (attach schedule)	21	
22	Depletion (other than oil and gas, attach schedule—see page 5 of Instructions)	22	
23a	Retirement plans, etc. (see page 5 of Instructions)	23a	
23b	Employee benefit programs (see page 5 of Instructions)	23b	
24	Other deductions (attach schedule)	24	
25	**TOTAL** deductions (add lines 13c through 24)	25	
26	Ordinary income (loss) (subtract line 25 from line 12)	26	

Schedule A—COST OF GOODS SOLD AND/OR OPERATIONS (See Page 6 of Instructions)

27	Inventory at beginning of year (if different from last year's closing inventory, attach explanation) .	27	
28a	Purchases $ .... **28b** Minus cost of items withdrawn for personal use $ .... Balance ▶	28c	
29	Cost of labor	29	
30	Materials and supplies	30	
31	Other costs (attach schedule)	31	
32	Total (add lines 27 through 31)	32	
33	Inventory at end of year	33	
34	Cost of goods sold (subtract line 33 from line 32). Enter here and on line 2, above	34	

Please Sign Here

Under penalties of perjury, I declare that I have examined this return, including accompanying schedules and statements, and to the best of my knowledge and belief it is true, correct, and complete. Declaration of preparer (other than taxpayer) is based on all information of which preparer has any knowledge.

▶ Signature of general partner ▶ Date

Paid Preparer's Use Only	Preparer's signature ▶		Date	Check if self-em- ployed ▶ ☐	Preparer's social security no.
	Firm's name (or yours, if self-employed) ▶ and address			E.I. No. ▶ ZIP code ▶	

For Paperwork Reduction Act Notice, see page 1 of Form 1065 Instructions

Form 1065 (1981)   **Schedule A** *(Continued)*   Page **2**

35 a Check all methods used for valuing closing inventory: *(i)* ☐ Cost | **c** Check if the LIFO method was adopted this tax year for | **Yes** | **No**
(ii) ☐ Lower of cost or market as described in regulations section | any goods. (If checked, attach Form 970) . . . . ☐
1.471–4 (see page 6 of Instructions) *(iii)* ☐ Writedown of "sub- | **d** If you are engaged in manufacturing, did you value your
normal" goods as described in regulations section 1.471–2(c) (see page | inventory using the full absorption method (regulations
6 of Instructions). | section 1.471–11)? . . . .

b Did you use any other method of inventory valuation not | **Yes** | **No** | **e** Was there any substantial change in determining quantities,
described in line 35a? . . . . | cost, or valuations between opening and closing inventory?
If "Yes," specify methods used and attach explanation . . | | | If "Yes," attach explanation.

Schedule D—CAPITAL GAINS AND LOSSES (See Page 6 of Instructions)

Part I   **Short-term Capital Gains and Losses—Assets Held One Year or Less**

a. Kind of property and description (Example, 100 shares of "Z" Co.)	**b.** Date acquired (mo., day, yr.)	**c.** Date sold (mo., day, yr.)	**d.** Gross sales price minus expenses of sale	**e.** Cost or other basis	**f.** Gain (loss) for the year (d minus e)	**g.** Gain (loss) after 6/9/81
1a						

1b Short-term capital gain from installment sales from Form 6252, line 19 or 27 . . . . .

2 Partnership's share of net short-term gain (loss), including specially allocated items, from other partnerships and from fiduciaries . . . .

3 Net short-term gain (loss) from lines 1a, 1b, and 2. Enter here and on Schedule K (Form 1065), line 5 . . . .

Part II   **Long-term Capital Gains and Losses—Assets Held More Than One Year**

4a						

4b Long-term capital gain from installment sales from Form 6252, line 19 or 27 . . . . . .

5 Partnership's share of net long-term gain (loss), including specially allocated items, from other partnerships and from fiduciaries . . . .

6 Capital gain distributions . . . .

7 Net long-term gain (loss) from lines 4a, 4b, 5, and 6. Enter here and on Schedule K (Form 1065), line 6 . . . .

Schedule H—INCOME FROM RENTS (See Page 4 of Instructions) If you need more space, attach schedule.

a. Kind and location of property	**b.** Amount of rent	**c.** Depreciation (explain on Form 4562)	**d.** Repairs (attach schedule)	**e.** Other expenses (attach schedule)

1 Totals . . . .

2 Net income (loss) (subtract total of columns c, d, and e from column b). Enter here and on page 1, line 7 . . .

Schedule I—BAD DEBTS (See Page 5 of Instructions)

a. Year	**b.** Trade notes and accounts receivable outstanding at end of year	**c.** Sales on account	Amount added to reserve		**f.** Amount charged against reserve	**g.** Reserve for bad debts at end of year
			d. Current year's provision	**e.** Recoveries		
1976						
1977						
1978						
1979						
1980						
1981						

Form 1065 (1981)   Page **3**

Schedule K—PARTNERS' SHARES OF INCOME, CREDITS, DEDUCTIONS, ETC. (See Pages 7–11 of Instructions)

	a. Distributive share items		b. Total amount
Income (loss)	1 Ordinary income (loss) (page 1, line 26)	1	
	2 Guaranteed payments	2	
	3a Interest qualifying for exclusion under section 116	3a	
	b Qualifying interest from All-Savers Certificates	3b	
	4 Dividends qualifying for exclusion	4	
	5 Net short-term capital gain (loss) (Schedule D, line 3): a Total for year . . . . . ▶	5a	
	b From sales or exchanges after 6/9/81	5b	
	6 Net long-term capital gain (loss) (Schedule D, line 7): a Total for year . . . . . ▶	6a	
	b From sales or exchanges after 6/9/81	6b	
	7 Net gain (loss) from involuntary conversions due to casualty or theft (Form 4684):		
	a Total for year . . . . ▶	7a	
	b From casualties or thefts after 6/9/81	7b	
	8 Other net gain (loss) under section 1231: a Total for year . . . . ▶	8a	
	b From sales or exchanges after 6/9/81	8b	
	9 Other (attach schedule)	9	
Deductions	10 Charitable contributions (attach list): 50% ...., 30% ...., 20%	10	
	11a Payments for partners to an IRA	11a	
	b Payments for partners to a Keogh Plan (Type of plan ▶..............................) . . .	11b	
	c Payments for partners to Simplified Employee Pension (SEP)	11c	
	12 Other (attach schedule)	12	
Credits	13 Jobs credit	13	
	14 Credit for alcohol used as fuel	14	
	15 Other (attach schedule)	15	
Other	16a Gross farming or fishing income	16a	
	b Net earnings (loss) from self-employment	16b	
	c Other (attach schedule)	16c	
Specially Allocated Items	17a Short-term capital gain (loss) (attach schedule): (1) Total for year . . . . . . ▶	17a(1)	
	(2) From sales or exchanges after 6/9/81	17a(2)	
	b Long-term capital gain (loss) (attach schedule): (1) Total for year . . . . ▶	17b(1)	
	(2) From sales or exchanges after 6/9/81	17b(2)	
	c Ordinary gain (loss) (attach schedule)	17c	
	d Other (attach schedule)	17d	
Tax Preference Items	18a Accelerated depreciation on real property:		
	(1) Low-income rental housing (167(k))	18a(1)	
	(2) Other nonrecovery real property and 15-year real property	18a(2)	
	b Accelerated depreciation on leased property that is personal property or recovery property other than 15-year real property	18b	
	Amortization: c ...., d ...., e ...., f	18c-f	
	g Reserves for losses on bad debts of financial institutions	18g	
	h Depletion (other than oil and gas)	18h	
	i (1) Excess intangible drilling costs from oil, gas, or geothermal wells	18i(1)	
	(2) Net income from oil, gas, or geothermal wells	18i(2)	
Investment Interest	19a Investment interest expense:		
	(1) Indebtedness incurred before 12/17/69	19a(1)	
	(2) Indebtedness incurred after 9/11/75, but after 12/16/69	19a(2)	
	(3) Indebtedness incurred after 9/10/75	19a(3)	
	b Net investment income (loss)	19b	
	c Excess expenses from "net lease property"	19c	
	d Excess of net long-term capital gain over net short-term capital loss from investment property	19d	
Foreign Taxes	20a Type of income		
	b Foreign country or U.S. possession		
	c Total gross income from sources outside the U.S. (attach schedule)	20c	
	d Total applicable deductions and losses (attach schedule)	20d	
	e Total foreign taxes (check one): ☐ Paid ☐ Accrued	20e	
	f Reduction in taxes available for credit (attach schedule)	20f	
	g Other (attach schedule)	20g	

Form 1065 (1981)   Page **4**

Note: Family farm partnerships, family-owned wholesale or retail store partnerships, and co-owners of investment property, see "Filing a Complete Return" on page 11 of the Instructions before completing Schedules L and M.

If the partnership meets **ALL** the requirements shown on page 11 of the Instructions under "Filing a Complete Return," check here . . . . ▶ ☐

Schedule L—BALANCE SHEETS (See Page 11 of Instructions)

ASSETS	Beginning of tax year (A)	(B)	End of tax year (C)	(D)
1 Cash	//////		//////	
2 Trade notes and accounts receivable		//////		//////
a Minus allowance for bad debts				
3 Inventories	//////		//////	
4 Government obligations: a U.S. and instrumentalities . .				
b State, subdivisions of State, etc.				
5 Other current assets (attach schedule) . . .				
6 Mortgage and real estate loans				
7 Other investments (attach schedule)	//////		//////	
8 Buildings and other depreciable assets				//////
a Minus accumulated depreciation		//////		//////
9 Depletable assets				//////
a Minus accumulated depletion		//////		//////
10 Land (net of any amortization)	//////		//////	
11 Intangible assets (amortizable only)				
a Minus accumulated amortization		//////		//////
12 Other assets (attach schedule)	//////		//////	
13 Total assets				
LIABILITIES AND CAPITAL				
14 Accounts payable	//////		//////	
15 Mortgages, notes, and bonds payable in less than 1 year .				
16 Other current liabilities (attach schedule) . . .				
17 All nonrecourse loans (attach schedule) . . .	//////		//////	
18 Mortgages, notes, and bonds payable in 1 year or more . .				
19 Other liabilities (attach schedule)				
20 Partners' capital accounts	//////		//////	
21 Total liabilities and capital				

Schedule M—RECONCILIATION OF PARTNERS' CAPITAL ACCOUNTS (See Page 11 of Instructions)
(Show reconciliation of each partner's capital account on Schedule K–1, item E)

a. Capital account at beginning of year	b. Capital contributed during year	c. Ordinary income (loss) from page 1, line 26	d. Income not included in column c, plus non-taxable income	e. Losses not included in column c, plus unallowable deductions	f. Withdrawals and distributions	g. Capital account at end of year

Schedule N—ADDITIONAL INFORMATION REQUIRED

	Yes	No
1 Is this partnership a limited partnership (see page 2 of Instructions)?	//////	//////
2 Number of partners in this partnership		
3 Is this partnership a partner in another partnership?		
4 Are any partners in this partnership also partnerships?		
5 At any time during the tax year, did the partnership have an interest in or a signature or other authority over a bank account, securities account, or other financial account in a foreign country (see page 11 of Instructions)?		
6 Was the partnership the grantor of, or transferor to, a foreign trust which existed during the current tax year, whether or not the partnership or any partner has any beneficial interest in it? If "Yes," you may have to file Forms 3520, 3520–A, or 926. (See page 11 of Instructions.)		

| SCHEDULE K–1 (Form 1065)
Department of the Treasury
Internal Revenue Service | **Partner's Share of Income, Credits, Deductions, etc.—1981**
For calendar year 1981 or fiscal year
beginning .... , 1981, and ending .... , 19 ....
(Complete for each partner. Instructions for partners attached to Copy C.) | OMB No. 1545–0099
Copy A
(File with Form 1065) |

Partner's identifying number ▶	Partnership's identifying number ▶
Partner's name, address, and ZIP code	Partnership's name, address, and ZIP code

A Is partner a general partner (see page 2 of Instructions)? . . . . ☐ Yes ☐ No

B Partner's share of liabilities (see page 7 of Instructions):
Nonrecourse . . . . $............................
Other . . . . $............................

C Enter partner's percentage of:	(i) Before decrease or termination	(ii) End of year
Profit sharing	...............%	...............%
Loss sharing	...............%	...............%
Ownership of capital	...............%	...............%

D What type of entity is this partner? ▶

E Reconciliation of partner's capital account:

a. Capital account at beginning of year	b. Capital contributed during year	c. Ordinary income (loss) from line 1	d. Income not included in column c, plus nontaxable income	e. Losses not included in column e, plus unallowable deductions	f. Withdrawals and distributions	g. Capital account at end of year

		a. Distributive share item	b. Amount	c. 1040 filers enter the amount in column b on:
Income (loss)	1	Ordinary income (loss)		Sch. E, Part II
	2	Guaranteed payments		Sch. E, Part II
	3a	Interest qualifying for exclusion under section 116		Sch. B, Part I, line 1a
	b	Qualifying interest from All-Savers Certificates		Sch. B, Part I, line 1c
	4	Dividends qualifying for exclusion		Sch. B, Part II, line 3
	5	Net short-term capital gain (loss): a Total for year . . . . . ▶		Sch. D, line 3, col. f. or g.
	b	From sales or exchanges after 6/9/81		See Sch. D, Part IV
	6	Net long-term capital gain (loss): a Total for year . . . . . ▶		Sch. D, line 10, col. f. or g.
	b	From sales or exchanges after 6/9/81		See Sch. D, Part IV
	7	Net gain (loss) from involuntary conversions due to casualty or theft:		
	a	Total for year . . . . ▶		Form 4684, line 20
	b	From casualties or thefts after 6/9/81		Form 4684, line 20
	8	Other net gain (loss) under section 1231:		
	a	Total for year . . . . ▶		Form 4797, line 1
	b	From sales or exchanges after 6/9/81		Form 4797, line 1
	9	Other (attach schedule)		(Enter on applicable lines of your return)
Deductions	10	Charitable contributions: 50% ...., 30% ...., 20%		See instructions for Sch. A
	11a	Payments for partner to an IRA		Form 1040, line 24
	b	Payments for partner to a Keogh Plan (Type of plan ▶............) . .		Form 1040, line 25
	c	Payments for partner to Simplified Employee Pension (SEP)		Form 1040, line 25
	12	Other (attach schedule)		(Enter on applicable lines of your return)
Credits	13	Jobs credit		Form 5884
	14	Credit for alcohol used as fuel		Form 6478
	15	Other (attach schedule)		(Enter on applicable lines of your return)
Other	16a	Gross farming or fishing income		Sch. E, Part IV
	b	Net earnings (loss) from self-employment		Sch. SE, Part I or II
	c	Other (attach schedule)		(Enter on applicable lines of your return)
Specially Allocated Items	17a	Short-term capital gain (loss) (attach schedule):		
		(1) Total for year . . . . ▶		Sch. D, line 3, col. f. or g.
		(2) From sales or exchanges after 6/9/81		See Sch. D, Part IV
	b	Long-term capital gain (loss) (attach schedule):		
		(1) Total for year . . . . ▶		Sch. D, line 10, col. f. or g.
		(2) From sales or exchanges after 6/9/81		See Sch. D, Part IV
	c	Ordinary gain (loss) (attach schedule)		Form 4797, line 9
	d	Other (attach schedule)		Sch. E, Part II

For Paperwork Reduction Act Notice, see page 1 of Form 1065 Instructions.

Tax Preference Items	**18a** Accelerated depreciation on real property:	
	(1) Low-income rental housing (167(k))	Form 4625, line 1(a)(1)
	(2) Other nonrecovery real property and 15-year real property . .	Form 4625, line 1(a)(2)
	b Accelerated depreciation on leased property that is personal property or recovery property other than 15-year real property	Form 4625, line 1(b)
	Amortization: **c** _____ , **d** _____ , **e** _____ , **f** _____	Form 4625, lines 1(c) thru (f)
	g Reserves for losses on bad debts of financial institutions	Form 4625, line 1(g)
	h Depletion (other than oil and gas)	Form 4625, line 1(i)
	i (1) Excess intangible drilling costs from oil, gas, or geothermal wells . . .	See Form 4625 instr.
	(2) Net income from oil, gas, or geothermal wells	
Investment Interest	**19a** Investment interest expense:	
	(1) Indebtedness incurred before 12/17/69	Form 4952, line 1
	(2) Indebtedness incurred before 9/11/75, but after 12/16/69 . .	Form 4952, line 15
	(3) Indebtedness incurred after 9/10/75	Form 4952, line 5
	b Net investment income (loss)	Form 4952, line 2 or 10a
	c Excess expenses from "net lease property"	Form 4952, lines 11 and 19
	d Excess of net long-term capital gain over net short-term capital loss from investment property	Form 4952, line 20
Foreign Taxes	**20a** Type of income	Form 1116, Checkboxes
	b Name of foreign country or U.S. possession	Form 1116, Part I
	c Total gross income from sources outside the U.S. (attach schedule) .	Form 1116, Part I
	d Total applicable deductions and losses (attach schedule)	Form 1116, Part I
	e Total foreign taxes (check one): ☐ Paid ☐ Accrued	Form 1116, Part II
	f Reduction in taxes available for credit (attach schedule)	Form 1116 instr.
	g Other (attach schedule)	Form 1116 instr.
Property Eligible for Investment Credit	**21** Unadjusted basis of new recovery property — **(a)** 3-Year	Form 3468, line 1(a)
	(b) Other	Form 3468, line 1(b)
	Unadjusted basis of used recovery property — **(c)** 3-Year	Form 3468, line 1(c)
	(d) Other.	Form 3468, line 1(d)
	Basis of new nonrecovery investment property — **(e)** 3 or more but less than 5 years . . .	Form 3468, line 3(a)
	(f) 5 or more but less than 7 years . . .	Form 3468, line 3(b)
	(g) 7 or more years	Form 3468, line 3(c)
	Cost of used nonrecovery investment property — **(h)** 3 or more but less than 5 years . . .	Form 3468, line 3(d)
	(i) 5 or more but less than 7 years . . .	Form 3468, line 3(e)
	(j) 7 or more years	Form 3468, line 3(f)
	New commuter highway vehicle	Form 3468, line 5
	Used commuter highway vehicle	Form 3468, line 6
	Qualified rehabilitation expenditures (Enter on Form 3468, line) . .	

		A	B	C	
Property Subject to Recapture of Investment Credit	**22** Properties: **a** Description of property (state whether recovery or nonrecovery property) .	_____	_____	_____	Form 4255, top
	b Original rate . . .	_____	_____	_____	Form 4255, line 1
	c Date placed in service	_____	_____	_____	Form 4255, line 2
	d Cost or other basis .	_____	_____	_____	Form 4255, line 3
	e Class of recovery property or original estimated useful life	_____	_____	_____	Form 4255, line 4
	f Applicable percentage .	_____	_____	_____	Form 4255, line 5
	g Date item ceased to be investment credit property .	_____	_____	_____	Form 4255, line 8
	h Period actually used . .	_____	_____	_____	Form 4255, line 9

Schedule K–1, Copy C
Instructions for the Partner

(References are to the Internal Revenue Code.)

Purpose

The partnership uses Copy C of Schedule K–1 to report to you your share of the partnership's income, credits, and deductions. Please keep it for your records. Do not file it with your income tax return. Copy A has been filed with the IRS.

Although the partnership is not subject to income tax, you, the partner, are liable for income tax on your share of the partnership income, whether or not distributed, and you must include your share on your tax return. Your share of any partnership income, gain, loss, deduction, or credit must also be reported on your return. Please read the **Limitation on Losses** under line 1 to figure how much of your share of any partnership loss is deductible.

General Information

Commodity Futures and Straddle Positions.—For information on how to report gains and losses from regulated futures contracts and straddles, see Form 6781, Gains and Losses From Commodity Futures Contracts and Straddle Positions.

Windfall Profit Tax.—If you are a producer of domestic crude oil, your partnership will inform you of your income tax deduction for the windfall profit tax.

Statute of Limitations.—If you are a partner in a federally registered partnership, see sections 6501 and 6511 for further information.

Errors.—If you believe the partnership has made an error on your Schedule K–1, notify the partnership and ask for a corrected Schedule K–1. Do not change any items on your copy.

International Boycotts.—The partnership must notify you and give you a statement showing that it had operations in a boycotting country, that it participated in or cooperated with an international boycott, and that it filed Form 5713.

You may be required to file Form 5713 if you are a partner in a partnership that has operations in or with:

- a country
- the government of a country
- a national of a country
- a company

that requires participation in, or cooperation with, an international boycott as a condition of doing business. However, if the partnership filed Form 5713, you are not required to file Form 5713 unless the partnership participated in or cooperated with an international boycott.

Further, if the partnership participates in, or cooperates with, an international boycott (as defined in section 999(b)(3)) during the tax year, part of the foreign tax credit will be denied to you. Anyone subject to the reporting requirements of section 999(a), as outlined above, must file Form 5713. The partnership must furnish you a copy of Form 5713 filed by the partnership if there has been participation in or cooperation with an international boycott.

See **Form 5713** for additional information.

Definitions

a. General Partner. A general partner is a member of the organization who is personally liable for the obligations of the partnership.

b. Limited Partner. A limited partner is one whose potential personal liability for partnership debts is limited to the amount of money or other property that the partner contributed or is required to contribute to the partnership.

c. Limited Partnership. A limited partnership is a partnership composed of at least one general partner and one or more limited partners.

d. Nonrecourse Loans. Nonrecourse loans are those liabilities of the partnership for which none of the partners have any personal liability.

Elections.—Generally, the partnership decides how to figure taxable income from its operations. For example, it chooses the accounting method and depreciation methods it will use.

However, certain elections are made by you separately on your income tax return and not by the partnership. These elections are made under section 901 (foreign tax credit), section 617 (deduction and recapture of certain mining exploration expenditures, paid or incurred), section 57(c) (definition of net lease), section 163(d)(6) (limitation on interest on investment indebtedness), and sections 108(b)(5) or 108(d)(4) (income from discharge of indebtedness).

Publications.—For more information on the treatment of partnership income, deductions, and credits, see Publication 541, Tax Information on Partnerships, Publication 535, Business Expenses and Operating Losses, and Publication 550, Investment Income and Expenses.

Specific Instructions

Name, Address, and Identifying Number. Your name, address, and identifying number, as well as the partnership's name, address, and identifying number, should be entered.

Question B. Item (B) should show your share of the partnership's nonrecourse liabilities and other liabilities as of the end of the year. If you terminated your interest in the partnership during the year, item (B) should show the share that existed immediately before the total disposition. (A partner's "other liability" is any partnership liability for which a partner is personally liable.)

Use the total of the two amounts for computing the adjusted basis of your partnership interest. Use the amount shown in "Other" to compute your amount "at risk" if the partnership was engaged in any activity other than real estate (other than mineral property).

If your partnership is engaged in two or more different types of "at risk" activities, or a combination of "at risk" activities and any other activity, the partnership should give you a statement showing your share of nonrecourse liabilities and other liabilities for each activity. However, the partnership should not do this if the activity is covered under section 465(c)(3)(A) and 65% or more of the losses from the activity are allocated to the partners active in the management of the partnership. See **Limitation on Losses** under line 1 for further information.

Lines 1–22

If you are an individual partner, take the amounts shown in column b and enter them on the lines on your tax return as indicated in column c. If you are not an individual partner, report the amounts in column b as instructed on your tax return.

Line 1. The amount shown should reflect your share of ordinary income (loss) from all partnership business operations including "at risk" activities without regard to the "at risk" limitations.

Limitation on Losses.—Generally, you may not claim your share of a partnership loss (including capital loss) that is greater than the adjusted basis of your partnership interest at the end of the partnership's tax year.

However, special "at risk" rules, under section 465, apply if there is a loss from any activity (except the holding of real property, other than mineral property) carried on as a trade or business or for the production of income by the partnership. Generally, your deductible loss from each activity for the tax year is limited to the amount you are "at risk" for the activity at the end of the partnership's tax year.

Generally, you are "at risk" for an activity for the cash and adjusted basis of other property you contributed to the activity and any amounts borrowed for use in the activity for which you are personally liable.

Your "at risk" amount does not include the proceeds from your share of any nonrecourse loan used to finance the activity or the acquisition of property used in the activity. However, you are "at risk" to the extent of the net fair market value of your own property (not used in the activity) which secures borrowed amounts for which you are not liable.

You are not "at risk" for cash, property, or borrowed amounts protected against loss by a guarantee, stop loss agreement, or other similar arrangement.

If your partnership is engaged in an activity described below in a. through e. (but not f.), you are not "at risk" with respect to that activity for amounts borrowed from a person who is related to you under section 267(b), or who has an interest (other than as a creditor) in the activity.

If you have amounts not "at risk" for an activity and share in the loss for that activity, you must figure the allowable loss to report on your tax return.

If the amount you have "at risk" is less than zero, you may be subject to the recapture provisions.

Any loss from a section 465 activity not allowed for this tax year will be treated as a deduction allocable to the activity in the next tax year.

Your interest in the partnership is treated as a single activity if the partnership is engaged in only one activity. If the partnership is engaged in two or more activities, you may be able to treat them as one activity if the activities are one of the following:

a. Films or video tapes

b. Section 1245 property which is leased or held for leasing

c. Farms

d. Oil and gas properties as defined under section 614

e. Geothermal properties as defined under section 614

f. Any other activities except real estate (other than mineral property) which constitute a trade or business carried on by the partnership if 65% or more of the losses for the tax year are allocable to partners who actively participate in the management of the trade or business. You should get a separate statement of income, expenses, deductions, and credits for each activity from the partnership.

If the partnership sells or otherwise disposes of (1) an asset used in the activity to which the "at risk" rules apply or (2) any part of its interest in such an activity (or if you sell or dispose of your interest), you should combine the gain or loss on the sale or disposition with the profit or loss from the activity to determine the net profit or loss from the activity. If this is a net loss, it may be limited because of the "at risk" rules.

Special transitional rules for movies, video tapes, and leasing activities can be found in section 204(c)(2) and (3) of the Tax Reform Act of 1976.

If your partnership is engaged in an activity which is subject to the limitations of section 465(c)(1), you need to determine the amount you are "at risk." To help you do this, the partnership should give you your share of the total pre-1976 loss(es) from a section 465(c)(1) activity (i.e., film or video tapes, section 1245 property leasing, farm, or oil and gas property) for which there existed a corresponding amount of nonrecourse liability at the end of the year in which this loss(es) occurred.

Lines 3 and 4. Recent legislation amended Internal Revenue Code Section 116 and added new section 128.

The change to section 116 adds interest income to the exclusion in that section and doubles the dollar limits for the exclusion. Prior law allowed individual taxpayers to exclude only dividends up to $100 ($200 for stock owned by a husband and wife). The new exclusion allows individual taxpayers to exclude from income up to $200 ($400 on a joint return) of qualifying interest and dividends. The new exclusion is effective for tax years of individuals that begin after December 31, 1980, but before January 1, 1982. **Caution**—If you are a calendar year 1982 partner in a fiscal year 1981–1982 partnership, you may not exclude any of the interest shown on line 3a because your tax year did not begin before January 1, 1982. Also, you may not use the new exclusion under section 116 for any dividend income shown on line 4. See the instructions for your 1982 Form 1040.

New section 128 allows individuals to exclude qualifying interest from All-Savers Certificates. This exclusion is effective for tax years of individuals that end after September 30, 1981. Therefore, if the tax year in which you are reporting the items shown on this Schedule K–1 ended after September 30, 1981, you are eligible for this exclusion. See the instructions for your tax return.

Line 7. The partnership will give you a schedule that shows the loss to enter on Form 4684, line 20, column (B)(f) and column (B)(ii). On line 20, column (A), add the words "From (name of partnership)."

Line 9. Amounts on this line are other items of income, gain, or loss not included on lines 1–8 such as: partnership gains from disposition of farm recapture property (see Form 4797) and other items to which sections 1251 and 1252 apply; recoveries of bad debts, prior taxes, and delinquency amounts (section 111); gains and losses from wagers (section 165(d)); and any income, gain, or loss to the partnership under section 751(b). The partnership should give you a description and the amount of your share for each of these items.

Line 11b. If there is a defined benefit plan, the partnership should give you a statement showing the amount of benefit accrued for the tax year.

Line 12. Amounts on this line are other deductions not included on lines 10–11c such as: other itemized deductions (1040 filers enter on Schedule A); soil and water conservation expenditures (section 175); deduction and recapture of certain mining exploration expenditures paid or incurred (section 617); expenditures for the removal of architectural and transportation barriers to the elderly and handicapped which the partnership has elected to treat as a current expense (section 190); and any interest penalty on early withdrawal of savings. The partnership should give you a description and the amount of your share for each of these items.

Line 13. The amount shown is your share of the jobs credit. See Form 5884 for definitions, special rules, and limitations.

Line 14. Complete Form 6478 and attach it to your return.

Line 15. Amounts on this line are other credits not included on lines 13 and 14, such as: nonconventional source fuel credit; unused credits from cooperatives; and the credit for increasing research activities (enter this credit on Form 6765, Credit for Increasing Research Activities). The partnership should give you a description and the amount of your share for each of these items.

Line 16b. Net earnings from self-employment must be adjusted by the WIN credit, and depletion on oil and gas properties.

If the amount on this line is a loss, enter only the deductible amount on Schedule SE. See Limitations on Losses under line 1.

Line 16c. The partnership should give you a description and amount of your share for each of the following:

a. Taxes paid on undistributed capital gains by a regulated investment company. (1040 filers enter on line 61, and add the words "from 1065.")

b. Number of gallons of the fuels used during the tax year for each type of use identified in Parts I and II of Form 4136 and related instructions.

Partnerships that operate taxicabs must provide you with the number of gallons of gasoline used in the taxicabs and other information as required by Form 4136–T, Computation of Credit or Refund for Federal Tax on Gasoline, Diesel Fuel, and Special Fuels Used in Qualified Taxicabs.

c. Wages paid or incurred by the partnership under a Work Incentive (WIN) Program. The partnership must give you a copy of a schedule showing each WIN program employee's name, social security number, date employment began, and the qualified first-year or second-year WIN program salaries and wages paid or incurred and your allocation for each WIN program employee. For more information on claiming this credit and related wage reduction, see Form 4874.

d. Gross non-farm income which is used by an individual partner to figure self-employment income under the optional method.

e. Your share of gross income from the property, share of production for the tax year, etc., used to figure your depletion deduction for oil and gas wells. The partnership should also allocate to you a proportionate share of the adjusted basis of

each partnership oil or gas property. The allocation is made as specified in section 613A(c)(7)(D).

f. If you are a corporation, (1) any income allocable to you that is "timber preference income" under section 57(e), and (2) your share of construction period interest and taxes for construction begun during the year should be entered. You must add your share of the amortization deduction for these items to your share of partnership income (loss) shown on Schedule K–1, line 1.

Line 17. Any items of income, gain, loss, deduction, or credit subject to a special allocation under the partnership agreement that are different from the allocation of partnership income or loss should be entered here and not on any other line on this form.

Income or gain will be shown as a positive number; losses will be shown with the number in parentheses; a credit will be labeled as "CR."

You must include specially allocated items in determining the limitations on losses discussed under line 1.

Line 19. The partnership should have entered the interest on investment indebtedness and items of investment income and expenses, and gains and losses from the sale or exchange of investment property.

For more information and the special provisions that apply to "out of pocket" expenses and rental income from property subject to a net lease, see section 163(d) and **Publication 550**, Investment Income and Expenses. (Individuals, estates, and trusts, also see Form 4952.)

Note: Generally, if your **TOTAL** investment interest including investment interest **FROM ALL OTHER SOURCES** (including carryovers, etc.) is less than $10,000 ($5,000 if married filing separately), you do not need to get Form 4952. Instead, you may enter the amounts of investment interest directly on Schedule A (Form 1040) and/or Schedule E (Form 1040), whichever is applicable.

Lines 20a–g. Use the information on lines 20a through 20g to figure your foreign tax credit. For more information see:

- Form 1116, Computation of Foreign Tax Credit—Individual, Fiduciary or Nonresident Alien, and the related instructions, or

- Form 1118, Computation of Foreign Tax Credit—Corporations, and the related instructions.

Line 21. Your share of the partnership's investment in qualifying property that is eligible for the investment credit should be entered. You are allowed a tax credit based on your pro rata share of this investment by filing Form 3468, Computation of Investment Credit. (For other information, see Form 3468 and related instructions.)

In addition to the qualifying property reported on line 21, the partnership will give you a separate schedule that shows your share of the partnership's qualified investment in qualified energy property that is eligible for the credit and where to report it.

Line 22. When investment credit property is disposed of or ceases to qualify before the "life-years category" or "recovery period" assigned, you will be notified. You may have to recapture (pay back) the investment credit taken in prior years. Use the information on line 22 to figure your recapture tax on Form 4255.

REGULATION D—RULES GOVERNING THE LIMITED OFFER AND SALE OF SECURITIES WITHOUT REGISTRATION UNDER THE SECURITIES ACT OF 1933 (17 C.F.R. §230.501 to §230.506)

PRELIMINARY NOTES

1. The following rules relate to transactions exempted from the registration requirements of section 5 of the Securities Act of 1933 (the "Act"). Such transactions are not exempt from the antifraud, civil liability, or other provisions of the federal securities laws. Issuers are reminded of their obligation to provide such further material information, if any, as may be necessary to make the information required under this regulation, in light of the circumstances under which it is furnished, not misleading.

2. Nothing in these rules obviates the need to comply with any applicable state law relating to the offer and sale of securities. Regulation D is intended to be a basic element in a uniform system of federal-state limited offering exemptions consistent with the provisions of sections 18 and 19(c)

of the Act. In those states that have adopted Regulation D, or any version of Regulation D, special attention should be directed to the applicable state laws and regulations, including those relating to registration of persons who receive remuneration in connection with the offer and sale of securities, to disqualification of issuers and other persons associated with offerings based on state administrative orders or judgments, and to requirements for filings of notices of sales.

3. Attempted compliance with any rule in Regulation D does not act as an exclusive election; the issuer can also claim the availability of any other applicable exemption. For instance, an issuer's failure to satisfy all the terms and conditions of Rule 506 shall not raise any presumption that the exemption provided by section 4(2) of the Act is not available.

4. These rules are available only to the issuer of the securities and not to any affiliate of that issuer or to any other person for resales of the issuer's securities. The rules provide an exemption only for the transactions in which the securities are offered or sold by the issuer, not for the securities themselves.

5. These rules may be used for business combinations that involve sales by virtue of Rule 145(a) or otherwise.

6. In view of the objectives of these rules and the policies underlying the Act, Regulation D is not available to any issuer for any transaction or chain of transactions that, although in technical compliance with these rules, is part of a plan or scheme to evade the registration provisions of the Act. In such cases, registration under the Act is required.

7. Offers and sales of securities to foreign persons made outside the United States effected in a manner that will result in the securities coming to rest abroad generally need not be registered under the Act. See Release No. 33-4708 (July 9, 1964). This interpretation may be relied on for such offers and sales even if coincident offers and sales are made under Regulation D inside the United States. Thus, for example, persons who are not citizens or residents of the United States would not be counted in the calculation of the number of purchasers. Similarly, proceeds from sales to foreign purchasers would not be included in the aggregate offering price. The provisions of this note, however, do not apply if the issuer elects to rely solely on Regulation D for offers or sales to foreign persons.

RULE 501. DEFINITIONS AND TERMS USED IN REGULATION D

As used in Regulation D, the following terms shall have the meaning indicated:

(a) Accredited Investor "Accredited investor" shall mean any person who comes within any of the following categories, or who the issuer reasonably believes comes within any of the following categories, at the time of the sale of the securities to that person:

(1) Any bank as defined in section 3(a)(2) of the Act whether acting in its individual or fiduciary capacity; insurance company as defined in section 2(13) of the Act; investment company registered under the Investment Company Act of 1940 or a business development company as defined in section 2(a)(48) of that Act; Small Business Investment Company licensed by the U.S. Small Business Administration under section 301 (c) or (d) of the Small Business Investment Act of 1958; employee benefit plan within the meaning of Title I of the Employee Retirement Income Security Act of 1974, if the investment decision is made by a plan fiduciary, as defined in section 3(21) of such Act, which is either a bank, insurance company, or registered investment adviser, or if the employee benefit plan has total assets in excess of $5,000,000;

(2) Any private business development company as defined in section 202(a)(22) of the Investment Advisers Act of 1940;

(3) Any organization described in Section 501(c)(3) of the Internal Revenue Code with total assets in excess of $5,000,000;

(4) Any director, executive officer, or general partner of the issuer of the securities being offered or sold, or any director, executive officer, or general partner of a general partner of that issuer;

(5) Any person who purchases at least $150,000 of the securities being offered, where the purchaser's total purchase price does not exceed 20 percent of the purchaser's net worth at the time of sale, or joint net worth with that person's spouse, for one or any combination of the following: (i) cash, (ii) securities for which market quotations are readily available, (iii) an unconditional obligation to pay cash or securities for which market quotations are readily available which obligation is to be discharged within five years of the sale of the securities to the purchaser, or (iv) the cancellation of any indebtedness owed by the issuer to the purchaser;

(6) Any natural person whose individual net worth, or joint net worth with that person's spouse, at the time of his purchase exceeds $1,000,000;

(7) Any natural person who had an individual income in excess of $200,000 in each of the two most recent years and who reasonably expects an income in excess of $200,000 in the current year; and

(8) Any entity in which all of the equity owners are accredited investors under paragraphs (a) (1), (2), (3), (4), (6), or (7) of this Rule 501.

(b) Affiliate An "affiliate" of, or person "affiliated" with, a specified person shall mean a person that directly, or indirectly through one or more intermediaries, controls or is controlled by, or is under common control with, the person specified.

(c) Aggregate Offering Price   "Aggregate offering price" shall mean the sum of all cash, services, property, notes, cancellation of debt, or other consideration received by an issuer for issuance of its securities. Where securities are being offered for both cash and noncash consideration, the aggregate offering price shall be based on the price at which the securities are offered for cash. If securities are not offered for cash, the aggregate offering price shall be based on the value of the consideration as established by bona fide sales of that consideration made within a reasonable time, or, in the absence of sales, on the fair value as determined by an accepted standard.

(d) Business Combination   "Business combination" shall mean any transaction of the type specified in paragraph (a) of Rule 145 under the Act and any transaction involving the acquisition by one issuer, in exchange for all or a part of its own or its parent's stock, of stock of another issuer if, immediately after the acquisition, the acquiring issuer has control of the other issuer (whether or not it had control before the acquisition).

(e) Calculation of Number of Purchasers   For purposes of calculating the number of purchasers under Rules 505(b) and 506(b) only, the following shall apply:

(1) The following purchasers shall be excluded:

(i) Any relative, spouse or relative of the spouse of a purchaser who has the same principal residence as the purchaser;

(ii) Any trust or estate in which a purchaser and any of the persons related to him as specified in paragraph (e)(1)(i) or (e)(1)(iii) of this Rule 501 collectively have more than 50 percent of the beneficial interest (excluding contingent interests);

(iii) Any corporation or other organization of which a purchaser and any of the persons related to him as specified in paragraph (e)(1)(i) or (e)(1)(ii) of this Rule 501 collectively are beneficial owners of more than 50 percent of the equity securities (excluding directors' qualifying shares) or equity interests; and

(iv) Any accredited investor.

(2) A corporation, partnership or other entity shall be counted as one purchaser. If, however, that entity is organized for the specific purpose of acquiring the securities offered and is not an accredited investor under paragraph (a)(8) of this Rule 501, then each beneficial owner of equity

securities or equity interests in the entity shall count as a separate purchaser for all provisions of Regulation D.

Note. The issuer must satisfy all the other provisions of Regulation D for all purchasers whether or not they are included in calculating the number of purchasers. Clients of an investment adviser or customers of a broker or dealer shall be considered the "purchasers" under Regulation D regardless of the amount of discretion given to the investment adviser or broker or dealer to act on behalf of the client or customer.

(f) Executive Officer "Executive officer" shall mean the president, any vice president in charge of a principal business unit, division or function (such as sales, administration or finance), any other officer who performs a policy making function, or any other person who performs similar policy making functions for the issuer. Executive officers of subsidiaries may be deemed executive officers of the issuer if they perform such policy making functions for the issuer.

(g) Issuer The definition of the term "issuer" in section 2(4) of the Act shall apply, except that in the case of a proceeding under the Federal Bankruptcy Code, the trustee or debtor in possession shall be considered the issuer in an offering under a plan or reorganization, if the securities are to be issued under the plan.

(h) Purchaser Representative "Purchaser representative" shall mean any person who satisfies all of the following conditions or who the issuer reasonably believes satisfies all of the following conditions:

(1) Is not an affiliate, director, officer or other employee of the issuer, or beneficial owner of 10 percent or more of any class of the equity securities or 10 percent or more of the equity interest in the issuer, except where the purchaser is:

(i) A relative of the purchaser representative by blood, marriage or adoption and not more remote than a first cousin;

(ii) A trust or estate in which the purchaser representative and any persons related to him as specified in paragraph (h)(1)(i) or (h)(1)(iii) of this Rule 501 collectively have more than 50 percent of the beneficial interest (excluding contingent interest) or of which the purchaser representative serves as trustee, executor, or in any similar capacity; or

(iii) A corporation or other organization of which the purchaser representative and any persons related to him as specified in paragraph (h)(1)(i) or (h)(1)(ii) of this Rule 501 collectively are the beneficial owners of more than 50 percent of the equity securities (excluding directors' qualifying shares) or equity interests;

(2) Has such knowledge and experience in financial and business matters that he is capable of evaluating, alone, or together with other purchaser representatives of the purchaser, or together with the purchaser, the merits and risks of the prospective investment;

(3) Is acknowledged by the purchaser in writing, during the course of the transaction, to be his purchaser representative in connection with evaluating the merits and risks of the prospective investment; and

(4) Discloses to the purchaser in writing prior to the acknowledgment specified in paragraph (h)(3) of this Rule 501 any material relationship between himself or his affiliates and the issuer or its affiliates that then exists, that is mutually understood to be contemplated, or that has existed at any time during the previous two years, and any compensation received or to be received as a result of such relationship.

Note 1.   A person acting as a purchaser representative should consider the applicability of the registration and antifraud provisions relating to brokers and dealers under the Securities Exchange Act of 1934 ("Exchange Act") and relating to investment advisers under the Investment Advisers Act of 1940.

Note 2.   The acknowledgment required by paragraph (h)(3) and the disclosure required by paragraph (h)(4) of this Rule 501 must be made with specific reference to each prospective investment. Advance blanket acknowledgment, such as for "all securities transactions" or "all private placements," is not sufficient.

Note 3.   Disclosure of any material relationships between the purchaser representative or his affiliates and the issuer or its affiliates does not relieve the purchaser representative of his obligation to act in the interest of the purchaser.

RULE 502. GENERAL CONDITIONS TO BE MET

The following conditions shall be applicable to offers and sales made under Regulation D:

(a) Integration   All sales that are part of the same Regulation D offering must meet all of the terms and conditions of Regulation D. Offers and sales that are made more than six months before the start of a Regulation D offering or are made more than six months after completion of a Regulation D offering will not be considered part of that Regulation D offering, so long as during those six month periods there are no offers or sales of securities by or for the issuer that are of the same or a similar class as those offered or sold under Regulation D, other than those offers or sales of securities under an employee benefit plan as defined in Rule 405 under the Act.

Note. The term "offering" is not defined in the Act or in Regulation D. If the issuer offers or sells securities for which the safe harbor rule in paragraph (a) of this Rule 502 is unavailable, the determination as to whether separate sales of securities are part of the same offering (*i.e.* are considered "integrated") depends on the particular facts and circumstances. Generally, transactions otherwise meeting the requirements of an exemption will not be integrated with simultaneous offerings being made outside the United States effected in a manner that will result in the securities coming to rest abroad. See Release No. 33-4708 (July 9, 1964).

The following factors should be considered in determining whether offers and sales should be integrated for purposes of the exemptions under Regulation D:

(a) Whether the sales are part of a single plan of financing;
(b) Whether the sales involve issuance of the same class of securities;
(c) Whether the sales have been made at or about the same time;
(d) Whether the same type of consideration is received; and
(e) Whether the sales are made for the same general purpose.

See Release No. 33-4552 (November 6, 1962).

(b)   Information Requirements

(1) *When information must be furnished.* (i) If the issuer sells securities either under Rule 504 or only to accredited investors, paragraph (b) of this Rule 502 does not require that specific information be furnished to purchasers.

(ii) If the issuer sells securities under Rules 505 or 506 to any purchaser that is not an accredited investor, the issuer shall furnish the information specified in paragraph (b)(2) of this Rule 502 to all purchasers during the course of the offering and prior to sale.

(2) *Type of information to be furnished.* (i) If the issuer is not subject to the reporting requirements of section 13 or 15(d) of the Exchange Act, the issuer shall furnish the following information, to the extent material to an understanding of the issuer, its business, and the securities being offered:

(A) *Offerings up to $5,000,000.* The same kind of information as would be required in Part I of Form S-18, except that only the financial statements for the issuer's most recent fiscal year must be certified by an independent public or certified accountant. If Form S-18 is not available to an issuer, then the issuer shall furnish the same kind of information as would be required in Part I of a registration statement filed under the Act on the form that the issuer would be entitled to use, except that only the financial statements for the most recent two fiscal years prepared in accordance with generally accepted accounting principles shall be furnished and only the financial statements for the issuer's most recent fiscal year shall be certified by an independent public or certified accountant. If an issuer, other than a limited partnership, cannot obtain audited financial statements without unreasonable effort or expense, then only the issuer's balance sheet, which shall be dated within 120 days of the start of the offering, must be audited. If the issuer is a limited partnership and cannot obtain the required financial statements without unreasonable effort or expense, it may furnish financial statements that have been prepared on the basis of federal income tax requirements and examined and reported on in accordance with generally accepted auditing standards by an independent public or certified accountant.

(B) *Offerings over $5,000,000.* The same kind of information as would be required in Part I of a registration statement filed under the Act on the form that the issuer would be entitled to use. If an issuer, other than a limited partnership, cannot obtain audited financial statements without unreasonable effort or expense, then only the issuer's balance sheet, which shall be dated within 120 days of the start of the offering, must be audited. If the issuer is a limited partnership and cannot obtain the required financial statements without unreasonable effort or expense, it may furnish financial statements that have been prepared on the basis of federal income tax requirements and examined and reported on in accordance with generally accepted auditing standards by an independent public or certified accountant.

(C) If the issuer is a foreign private issuer eligible to use Form 20-F the issuer shall disclose the same kind of information required to be included in a registration statement filed under the Act on the form that the issuer would be entitled to use. The financial statements need be certified only to the extent required by paragraphs (b)(2)(i)(A) or (B) as appropriate.

(ii) If the issuer is subject to the reporting requirements of section 13 or 15(d) of the Exchange Act, the issuer shall furnish the information specified in paragraph (b)(2)(ii)(A) or (b)(2)(ii)(B), and in either event the information specified in paragraph (b)(2)(ii)(C) of this Rule 502:

(A) The issuer's annual report to shareholders for the most recent fiscal year, if such annual report meets the requirements of Rules 14a-3 or 14c-3 under the Exchange Act, the definitive proxy statement filed in connection with that annual report, and, if requested by the purchaser in writing, a copy of the issuer's most recent Form 10-K under the Exchange Act.

(B) The information contained in an annual report on Form 10-K under the Exchange Act or in a registration statement on Form S-1 under the Act or on Form 10 under the Exchange Act, whichever filing is the most recent required to be filed.

(C) The information contained in any reports or documents required to be filed by the issuer under sections 13(a), 14(a), 14(c), and 15(d) of the Exchange Act since the distribution or filing of the report or registration statement specified in paragraph (A) or (B), and a brief description of the securities being offered, the use of the proceeds from the offering, and any material changes in the issuer's affairs that are not disclosed in the documents furnished.

(D) If the issuer is a foreign private issuer eligible to use Form 20-F, the issuer may provide in lieu of the information specified in paragraphs (b)(2)(ii)(A) or (B), the information contained in its most recent filing on Form 20-F or Form F-1.

(iii) Exhibits required to be filed with the Commission as part of a registration statement or report, other than an annual report to shareholders or parts of that report incorporated by reference in a Form 10-K report, need not be furnished to each purchaser if the contents of the exhibits are identified and the exhibits are made available to the purchaser, upon his written request, prior to his purchase.

(iv) At a reasonable time prior to the purchase of securities by any purchaser that is not an accredited investor in a transaction under Rules 505 or 506, the issuer shall furnish the purchaser a brief description in writing of any written information concerning the offering that has been provided by the issuer to any accredited investor. The issuer shall furnish any portion or all of this information to the purchaser, upon his written request, prior to his purchase.

(v) The issuer shall also make available to each purchaser at a reasonable time prior to his purchase of securities in a transaction under Rules 505 or 506 the opportunity to ask questions and receive answers concerning the terms and conditions of the offering and to obtain any additional information which the issuer possesses or can acquire without unreasonable effort or expense that is necessary to verify the accuracy of information furnished under paragraph (b)(2)(i) or (ii) of this Rule 502.

(vi) For business combinations, in addition to information required by paragraph (b)(2) of this Rule 502, the issuer shall provide to each purchaser at the time the plan is submitted to security holders, or, with an exchange, during the course of the transaction and prior to sale, written information about any terms or arrangements of the proposed transaction that are materially different from those for all other security holders.

(c) Limitation on Manner of Offering. Except as provided in Rule 504(b)(1), neither the issuer nor any person acting on its behalf shall offer or sell the securities by any form of general solicitation or general advertising, including, but not limited to, the following:

> (1) Any advertisement, article, notice or other communication published in any newspaper, magazine, or similar media or broadcast over television or radio; and
> (2) Any seminar or meeting whose attendees have been invited by any general solicitation or general advertising.

(d) Limitations on Resale Except as provided in Rule 504(b)(1), securities acquired in a transaction under Regulation D shall have the status of securities acquired in a transaction under section 4(2) of the Act and cannot be resold without registration under the Act or an exemption therefrom. The issuer shall exercise reasonable care to assure that the purchasers of the securities are not underwriters within the meaning of section 2(11) of the Act, which reasonable care shall include, but not be limited to, the following:

> (1) Reasonable inquiry to determine if the purchaser is acquiring the securities for himself or for other persons;
> (2) Written disclosure to each purchaser prior to sale that the securities have not been registered under the Act and, therefore, cannot be resold unless they are registered under the Act or unless an exemption from registration is available; and
> (3) Placement of a legend on the certificate or other document that evidences the securities stating that the securities have not been registered under the Act and setting forth or referring to the restrictions on transferability and sale of the securities.

RULE 503. FILING OF NOTICE OF SALES

(a) The issuer shall file with the Commission five copies of a notice on Form D at the following times:

> (1) No later than 15 days after the first sale of securities in an offering under Regulation D;

(2) Every six months after the first sale of securities in an offering under Regulation D, unless the final notice required by paragraph (a)(3) of this Rule 503 has been filed; and

(3) No later than 30 days after the last sale of securities in an offering under Regulation D.

(b) If the offering is completed within the 15 day period described in paragraph (a)(1) of this Rule 503 and if the notice is filed no later than the end of that period but after the completion of the offering, then only one notice need be filed to comply with paragraphs (a)(1) and (3) of this Rule 503.

(c) One copy of every notice on Form D shall be manually signed by a person duly authorized by the issuer.

(d) If sales are made under Rule 505, the notice shall contain an undertaking by the issuer to furnish to the Commission, upon the written request of its staff, the information furnished by the issuer under Rule 502(b)(2) to any purchaser that is not an accredited investor.

(e) If more than one notice for an offering is required to be filed under paragraph (a) of this Rule 503, notices after the first notice need only report the issuer's name and the information required by Part C and any material change in the facts from those set forth in Parts A and B of the first notice.

(f) A notice on Form D shall be considered filed with the Commission under paragraph (a) of this Rule 503:

(1) As of the date on which it is received at the Commission's principal office in Washington, D.C.; or

(2) As of the date on which the notice is mailed by means of United States registered or certified mail to the Commission's Office of Small Business Policy, Division of Corporation Finance, at the Commission's principal office in Washington, D.C., if the notice is delivered to such office after the date on which it is required to be filed.

RULE 504. EXEMPTION FOR LIMITED OFFERS AND SALES OF SECURITIES NOT EXCEEDING $500,000

(a) Exemption   Offers and sales of securities that satisfy the conditions in paragraph (b) of this Rule 504 by an issuer that is not subject to the reporting requirements of section 13 or 15(d) of the Exchange Act and that is not an investment company shall be exempt from the provisions of section 5 of the Act under section 3(b) of the Act.

(b)   Conditions to Be Met

(1) *General conditions.* To qualify for exemption under this Rule 504 offers and sales must satisfy the terms and conditions of Rules 501 through 503, except that the provisions of Rule 502(c) and (d) shall not apply to offers and sales of securities under this Rule 504 that are made exclusively in one or more states each of which provides for the registration of the securities and requires the delivery of a disclosure document before sale and that are made in accordance with those state provisions.

(2) *Specific condition.*   (i) *Limitation on aggregate offering price.* The aggregate offering price for an offering of securities under this Rule 504, as defined in Rule 501(c), shall not exceed $500,000, less the aggregate offering price for all securities sold within the twelve months before the start of and during the offering of securities under this Rule 504 in reliance on any exemption under section 3(b) of the Act or in violation of section 5(a) of the Act.

Note 1.   The calculation of the aggregate offering price is illustrated as follows:

Example 1.   If an issuer sold $200,000 of its securities on June 1, 1982 under this Rule 504 and an additional $100,000 on September 1, 1982, the issuer would be permitted to sell only $200,000 more under this Rule 504 until June 1, 1983. Until that date the issuer must count both prior sales toward the $500,000 limit. However, if the issuer made its third sale on June 1, 1983, the issuer could then sell $400,000 of its securities because the June 1, 1982 sale would not be within the preceding twelve months.

Example 2.   If an issuer sold $100,000 of its securities on June 1, 1982 under this Rule 504 and an additional $4,500,000 on December 1, 1982 under Rule 505, the issuer could not sell any of its securities under this Rule 504 until December 1, 1983. Until then the issuer must count the December 1, 1982 sale towards the limit of $500,000 within the preceding twelve months.

Note 2.   If a transaction under this Rule 504 fails to meet the limitation on the aggregate offering price, it does not affect the availability of this Rule 504 for the other transactions considered in applying such limitation. For example, if the issuer in *Example 1* made its third sale on May 31, 1983, in the amount of $250,000, this Rule 504 would not be available for that sale, but the exemption for the prior two sales would be unaffected.

RULE 505. EXEMPTION FOR LIMITED OFFERS AND SALES OF SECURITIES NOT EXCEEDING $5,000,000

(a)   Exemption   Offers and sales of securities that satisfy the conditions in paragraph (b) of this Rule 505 by an issuer that is not an investment company shall be exempt from the provisions of section 5 of the Act under section 3(b) of the Act.

(b)   Conditions to Be Met

(1) *General conditions.* To qualify for exemption under this Rule 505, offers and sales must satisfy the terms and conditions of Rules 501 through 503.

(2) *Specific conditions.*   (i) *Limitation on aggregate offering price.* The aggregate offering price for an offering of securities under this Rule 505, as defined in Rule 501(c), shall not exceed $5,000,000, less the aggregate offering price for all securities sold within the twelve months before the start of and during the offering of securities under this Rule 505 in reliance on any exemption under section 3(b) of the Act or in violation of section 5(a) of the Act.

Note.   The calculation of the aggregate offering price is illustrated as follows:

Example 1.   If an issuer sold $2,000,000 of its securities on June 1, 1982 under this Rule 505 and an additional $1,000,000 on September 1, 1982, the issuer would be permitted to sell only $2,000,000 more under this Rule 505 until June 1, 1983. Until that date the issuer must count both prior sales towards the $5,000,000 limit. However, if the issuer made its third sale on June 1, 1983, the issuer could then sell $4,000,000 of its securities because the June 1, 1982 sale would not be within the preceding twelve months.

Example 2.   If an issuer sold $500,000 of its securities on June 1, 1982 under Rule 504 and an additional $4,500,000 on December 1, 1982 under this Rule 505, then the issuer could not sell any of its securities under this Rule 505 until June 1, 1983. At that time it could sell an additional $500,000 of its securities.

(ii) *Limitation on number of purchasers.* The issuer shall reasonably believe that there are no more than 35 purchasers of securities from the issuer in any offering under this Rule 505.

Note.   See Rule 501(e) for the calculation of the number of purchasers and Rule 502(a) for what may or may not constitute an offering under this Rule 505.

(iii) *Disqualifications.* No exemption under this Rule 505 shall be available for the securities of any issuer described in Rule 252(c), (d), (e), or (f) of Regulation A, except that for purposes of this Rule 505 only:

(A) The term "filing of the notification required by Rule 255" as used in Rule 252(c), (d), (e) and (f) shall mean the first sale of securities under this Rule 505;

(B) The term "underwriter" as used in Rule 252(d) and (e) shall mean a person that has been or will be paid directly or indirectly remuneration for solicitation of purchasers in connection with sales of securities under this Rule 505; and

(C) Paragraph (b)(2)(iii) of this Rule 505 shall not apply to any issuer if the Commission determines, upon a showing of good cause, that it is not necessary under the circumstances that the exemption be denied. Any such determination shall be without prejudice to any other action by the Commission in any other proceeding or matter with respect to the issuer or any other person.

RULE 506. EXEMPTION FOR LIMITED OFFERS AND SALES WITHOUT REGARD TO DOLLAR AMOUNT OF OFFERING

(a) Exemption Offers and sales of securities by an issuer that satisfy the conditions in paragraph (b) of this Rule 506 shall be deemed to be transactions not involving any public offering within the meaning of section 4(2) of the Act.

(b) Conditions to Be Met

(1) *General conditions.* To qualify for exemption under this Rule 506, offers and sales must satisfy all the terms and conditions of Rules 501 through 503.

(2) *Specific conditions.* (i) *Limitation on number of purchasers.* The issuer shall reasonably believe that there are no more than 35 purchasers of securities from the issuer in any offering under this Rule 506.

Note. See Rule 501(e) for the calculation of the number of purchasers and Rule 502(a) for what may or may not constitute an offering under this Rule 506.

(ii) *Nature of purchasers.* The issuer shall reasonably believe immediately prior to making any sale that each purchaser who is not an accredited investor either alone or with his purchaser representative(s) has such knowledge and experience in financial and business matters that he is capable of evaluating the merits and risks of the prospective investment.

FORM D—NOTICE OF SALES OF SECURITIES PURSUANT TO REGULATION D OR SECTION 4(6)

FORM D

U. S. SECURITIES AND EXCHANGE COMMISSION
Washington, D. C. 20549

OMB Approval
OMB 3235-0076
Expires December 31, 1984

SEC USE ONLY

NOTICE OF SALES OF SECURITIES

PURSUANT TO REGULATION D OR SECTION 4(6)

SEC USE ONLY

SERIAL

21-   -

Nature of this filing with respect to this offering.

INSTRUCTION: Please check the box(es) corresponding to the exemptive provision applicable to this offering.

Rule 504☐   Rule 505☐   Rule 506☐   Section 4(6)☐

INSTRUCTION: Circle "N" for a new filing or "A" for an amended filing.

ORIGINAL 1 N/A   COMBINED ORIGINAL AND FINAL 2 N/A   SIX-MONTH UPDATE 3 N/A   FINAL 4 N/A

INSTRUCTIONS: The issuer shall file with the Commission five copies of this notice at the following times: (a) no later than 15 days after the first sale of securities in an offering under Regulation D or Section 4(6); (b) every six months after the first sale of securities in an offering under Regulation D or Section 4(6), unless a final notice has been filed; and (c) no later than 30 days after the last sale of securities in an offering under Regulation D or Section 4(6), *except that if the offering is completed within the 15-day period described in "(a)" above, and if the notice is filed no later than the end of that period but after the completion of the offering, then only one notice need be filed*. If more than one notice for an offering is required to be filed, notices after the first notice need only report the issuer's name, information in response to Part C and any material changes from the facts previously reported in Parts A and B. This notice shall be deemed to be filed with the Commission for purposes of the rule as of the date on which the notice is received by the Commission, or if delivered to the Commission after the date on which it is due, as of the date on which it is mailed by means of United States registered or certified mail to the Office of Small Business Policy, Division of Corporation Finance, U.S. Securities and Exchange Commission, Washington, D.C. 20549.

A. Basic Identification of Issuer.

INSTRUCTION: State the address of the issuer's executive offices and, if different, the address at which the issuer's principal business operations are conducted or proposed to be conducted.

NAME		
ADDRESS OF EXECUTIVE OFFICES		
CITY	STATE	ZIP
AREA CODE TELEPHONE NUMBER		
ADDRESS OF PRINCIPAL BUSINESS OPERATIONS		
CITY	STATE	ZIP
AREA CODE TELEPHONE NUMBER		

INSTRUCTION: Please list the full name and address of the following persons: each promoter of the issuer involved in the offering of securities as to which sales pursuant to Regulation D or Section 4(6) are reported on this notice, the issuer's chief executive officer, and each of the issuer's affiliates. Indicate the status of each person named by placing an "X" in the applicable box(es) opposite such person's name. The term "promoter" includes . . .

(a)   Any person who, acting alone or in conjunction with one or more other persons, directly or indirectly takes the initiative in founding and organizing the business or enterprise of an issuer; or
(b)   Any person who, in connection with the founding or organizing of the business or enterprise of an issuer, directly or indirectly receives in consideration of services or property, or both services and property, 10 percent or more of any class of securities of the issuer or 10 percent or more of the proceeds from the sale of any class of securities. However, a person who receives such securities or proceeds either solely as brokerage commissions or solely in consideration of property shall not be deemed a promoter within the meaning of this paragraph if such person does not otherwise take part in founding and organizing the enterprise.

SEC 1972 (3-82)

FORM D

NOTICE OF SALES OF SECURITIES
PURSUANT TO REGULATION D OR SECTION 4(6)

Page 2

CEO	Aff	Pro

NAME

ADDRESS	CITY	STATE	ZIP

CEO	Aff	Pro

NAME

ADDRESS	CITY	STATE	ZIP

1. Has the issuer filed any periodic reports pursuant to Section 13 or 15(d) of the Securities Exchange Act of 1934?

    YES ☐   NO ☐

    If yes, please indicate the file number of the docket in which the periodic reports are filed. ————

2. Please indicate the issuer's IRS employer identification number. If an application for such number is pending, please enter "00-0000000."

3. Please briefly describe the issuer's business.

    ————————————————————

    ————————————————————

    ————————————————————

4. Please indicate the issuer's type of business organization.
    a. corporation   b. partnership   c. business trust   d. other, *please specify* ————————

5. Please indicate the issuer's Standard Industrial Classification (SIC) at the 3 or 4 digit level. If the issuer has more than one SIC, please enter the issuer's primary SIC. If a 3 digit SIC is given, enter "X" in the left-most box.

6. In what year was the issuer incorporated or organized?

7. In what state is the issuer incorporated or organized? Please enter the standard two letter U.S. Postal Service abbreviation. Enter "CN" if the issuer is incorporated or organized in Canada; "FN" if the issuer is incorporated or organized in another foreign jurisdiction.

8. Has the issuer been assigned a CUSIP number for its securities?

    YES ☐   NO ☐

    If yes, please specify the first six (6) digits. If no, please enter "000000."

9. Please check the appropriate box for each exchange or market, if any, where the issuer's securities are traded.

    American Stock Exchange . . . . a. ☐
    New York Stock Exchange . . . . b. ☐
    Other National Securities Exchanges . . . . c. ☐
    Over-the-Counter (including
    National Association of Securities Dealers Automated Quotations System) . . d. ☐
    Other   *Please Specify* . . . . e. ☐

    SEC USE ONLY

    ————————————————————

    ————————————————————

    None. . . . . f. ☐

FORM D

NOTICE OF SALES OF SECURITIES
PURSUANT TO REGULATION D OR SECTION 4(6)

Page 3

B. Statistical Information About the Issuer

INSTRUCTION: Please enter the letter for the appropriate response to each item in Part B in the box
indicated. If the issuer's first fiscal year has not yet ended, furnish the requested
information as of a date, or as to a period ending on a date, no more than 90 days
prior to the first sale of securities in this offering.

1. What were the issuer's gross revenues for its most recently ended fiscal year? ☐

   a. $500,000 or less   b. $500,001 – $1,000,000   c. $1,000,001 – $3,000,000
   d. $3,000,001 – $5,000,000   e. $5,000,001 – $25,000,000   f. $25,000,001 – $100,000,000
   g. Over $100,000,000

2. What were the issuer's total consolidated assets as of the end of its latest fiscal year? ☐

   a. $500,000 or less   b. $500,001 – $1,000,000   c. $1,000,001 – $3,000,000
   d. $3,000,001 – $5,000,000   e. $5,000,001 – $25,000,000   f. $25,000,001 – $100,000,000
   g. Over $100,000,000

3. What was the issuer's net income, or income before partners' compensation, for its most recently ended ☐
   fiscal year?

   a. None or net loss   b. $1 – $50,000   c. $50,001 – $250,000   d. $250,001 – $1,000,000
   e. $1,000,001 – $5,000,000   f. Over $5,000,000

4. What was the issuer's shareholders' or partners' equity at the end of its latest fiscal year? ☐

   a. Negative   b. $1 – $50,000   c. $50,001 – $250,000   d. $250,001 – $1,000,000
   e. $1,000,001 – $3,000,000   f. $3,000,001 – $10,000,000   g. Over $10,000,000

5. How many shareholders or partners did the issuer have at the end of its latest fiscal year? ☐

   a. 0 – 4   b. 5 – 9   c. 10 – 24   d. 25 – 99   e. 100 – 299
   f. 300 – 499   g. 500 or more

6. What percentage of shares outstanding were held by non-affiliated shareholders at the end ☐
   of the issuer's latest fiscal year? [1]

   a. None   b. Less than 5.0%   c. 5.0% – 9.9%   d. 10.0% – 24.9%
   e. 25.0% – 49.9%   f. 50.0% – 74.9%   g. 75.0% or more   h. Not applicable

7. How many shares were outstanding at the end of the issuer's latest fiscal year? ☐

   a. 500,000 or less   b. 500,001 – 1,500,000   c. 1,500,001 – 2,500,000
   d. 2,500,001 – 3,500,000   e. 3,500,001 – 5,000,000   f. Over 5,000,000   g. Not applicable

8. How many full-time equivalent employees did the issuer have at the end of its latest fiscal year? [2] ☐

   a. None   b. 1 – 5   c. 6 – 10   d. 11 – 20   e. 21 – 50   f. 51 – 100
   g. 101 – 500   h. 500 or more

---

[1] *A non-affiliated person is defined to be anyone other than a person that directly or indirectly, through one or
more intermediaries, controls or is controlled by the issuer or is under common control with such person.*

[2] *Full-time equivalent employees is defined to equal the sum of the number of full-time employees plus the
number of part-time employees working 25 or more hours per typical work week.*

FORM D

NOTICE OF SALES OF SECURITIES
PURSUANT TO REGULATION D OR SECTION 4(6)

Page 4

C. Section 3(b) or 4(6) Sales Limit and Other Information About the Offering

INSTRUCTION: If a response to any item is "none" or "zero," please enter zero ("0") in the corresponding space.

1. Type and aggregate offering price of securities intended to be sold pursuant to Regulation D or Section 4(6) in this offering.

   a. Debt . . . . $ _____

   b. Equity . . . . $ _____

   c. Convertible . . . . $ _____

2. Number of accredited and non-accredited investors who have purchased securities in this offering in reliance on Rules 505 or 506 and aggregate dollar amounts of their purchases to date. For sales in reliance on Rule 504 or Section 4(6), please enter the number of persons who have purchased securities and aggregate dollar amounts of their purchases to date on the accredited investor lines.

	Number of Investors (A)	Aggregate Dollar Amount (B)
Accredited investors	_____	$ _____
Non-accredited investors	_____	_____
Total	_____	$ _____

3. If this offering is being made pursuant to Rule 504 or 505, report by exemption and type of security (i.e., debt, equity, convertible) the dollar amount of all Section 3(b) sales of securities (other than sales reported in Item C.2 above) occurring from twelve (12) months prior to the first sale of securities in this offering to date.

	Type (A)	Dollar Amount (B)
Rule 505	_____	$ _____
Regulation A	_____	_____
Rule 504	_____	_____
Total		$ _____

4. Please list the full name and address of each person who has been or will be paid _ iven directly or indirectly any commission or similar remuneration for solicitation of purchasers in connection with sales of securities in this offering pursuant to Regulation D or Section 4(6). If a person to be listed is an associated person of a broker or dealer registered with the Commission and/or with a state or states, then please also list the name of that broker or dealer. If more than five (5) persons to be listed are associated persons of a broker or dealer registered with the Commission and/or a state or states, then the issuer may list the name and address of only such broker or dealer. Please also list, using the standard two-letter Postal Service abbreviation the state or states in which each person, or if an associated broker or dealer is listed, each such broker or dealer, intends to or is offering securities in this offering; if all states, enter "all."

SEC USE ONLY
8 - □□□□□

NAME				
ADDRESS	CITY	STATE	ZIP	
NAME OF ASSOCIATED BROKER OR DEALER				
STATES				

SEC USE ONLY
8 - □□□□□

NAME				
ADDRESS	CITY	STATE	ZIP	
NAME OF ASSOCIATED BROKER OR DEALER				
STATES				

FORM D

NOTICE OF SALES OF SECURITIES
PURSUANT TO REGULATION D OR SECTION 4(6)

Page 5

5. a. Aggregate offering price of securities, from C.1 above $ ☐ _____

   b. Furnish a reasonably itemized statement of all expenses in connection with the issuance and distribution of the securities being offered in this offering. Please exclude any amounts relating solely to the organizational expenses of the issuer. Insofar as practicable, give amounts for the categories listed below. The information may be given as subject to future contingencies. If the expenditure in any category is not known, furnish an estimate and place an "X" in the box to the left of the amount given.

a.	Blue Sky Fees and Expenses	$ ☐ _____
b.	Transfer Agents' Fees	☐ _____
c.	Printing and Engraving Costs	☐ _____
d.	Legal Fees	☐ _____
e.	Accounting Fees	☐ _____
f.	Engineering Fees	☐ _____
g.	Sales Commissions *(including Finders' Fees)*	☐ _____
h.	Other Expenses *(Identify)*	☐ _____
	_____	☐ _____
	_____	☐ _____
	Total	$ ☐ _____

   c. Enter the difference between the aggregate offering price in 5.a. and total costs in 5.b. This difference is the "adjusted gross proceeds to the issuer." $ ☐ _____

6. Indicate below the amount of the adjusted gross proceeds to the issuer *(other than amounts specified in Item 5.b. above)* proposed to be used or used for each of the purposes listed below. If the amount to be used for any purpose is not known, furnish an estimate and place an "X" in the box to the left of the amount given.

		Payments to officers, directors and affiliates (A)	Payments to others (B)
a.	Salaries and fees	$ ☐ _____	$ ☐ _____
b.	Purchase of real estate	☐ _____	☐ _____
c.	Purchase, rental or leasing and installation of machinery and equipment	☐ _____	☐ _____
d.	Construction or leasing of plant building and facilities	☐ _____	☐ _____
e.	Development expense *(product development, research, patent costs, etc.)*	☐ _____	☐ _____
f.	Purchase of raw materials, inventories, supplies, etc.	☐ _____	☐ _____
g.	Selling, advertising, and other sales promotion	☐ _____	☐ _____
h.	Acquisition of other businesses *(including the value of securities involved in this offering which may be used in exchange for the assets or securities of another issuer pursuant to a merger)*	☐ _____	☐ _____
i.	Repayment of loans	☐ _____	☐ _____
	Other – *please specify*		
j.	_____	☐ _____	☐ _____
k.	_____	☐ _____	☐ _____
l.	_____	☐ _____	☐ _____
m.	_____	☐ _____	☐ _____
	Total	$ ☐ _____	$ ☐ _____

FORM D

NOTICE OF SALES OF SECURITIES
PURSUANT TO REGULATION D OR SECTION 4(6)

Page 6

D. Undertaking by issuers filing pursuant to Rule 505.

The undersigned issuer hereby undertakes to furnish to the Securities and Exchange Commission, upon the written request of its staff, the information furnished by the issuer to any non-accredited person pursuant to paragraph (b)(2) of Rule 502.

ISSUER _____

SIGNATURE _____

NAME _____

TITLE _____

E. The issuer has duly caused this notice to be signed on its behalf by the undersigned duly authorized person.

DATE OF NOTICE:

_____

ISSUER _____

SIGNATURE _____

NAME _____

TITLE _____

INSTRUCTION: Print the name and title of the signing representative under his signature. One copy of every notice on Form D shall be manually signed. Any copies not manually signed shall bear typed or printed signatures.

────────── ATTENTION ──────────

Intentional misstatements or omissions of fact constitute Federal Criminal Violations (See 18 U.S.C. 1001).

FORM D Continuation Sheet	NOTICE OF SALES OF SECURITIES PURSUANT TO REGULATION D OR SECTION 4(6)	Page 7
Item of Form *(identify)*	Answer	

FORM D Continuation Sheet	NOTICE OF SALES OF SECURITIES PURSUANT TO REGULATION D OR SECTION 4(6)	Page 8

Item of Form
(identify)   Answer

RULE 147. "PART OF AN ISSUE," "PERSON RESIDENT," AND "DOING BUSINESS WITHIN" FOR PURPOSES OF SECTION 3 (a) (11) (17 C.F.R. § 230.147)

PRELIMINARY NOTES

1. This rule shall not raise any presumption that the exemption provided by section 3(a)(11) of the Act is not available for transactions by an issuer which do not satisfy all of the provisions of the rule.

2. Nothing in this rule obviates the need for compliance with any state law relating to the offer and sale of the securities.

3. Section 5 of the Act requires that all securities offered by the use of the mails or by any means or instruments of transportation or communication in interstate commerce be registered with the Commission. Congress, however, provided certain exemptions in the Act from such registration provisions where there was no practical need for registration or where the benefits of registration were too remote. Among those exemptions is that provided by section 3(a)(11) of the Act for transactions in "any security which is a part of an issue offered and sold only to persons resident within a single State or Territory, where the issuer of such security is a person resident and doing business within * * * such State or Territory." The legislative history of that section suggests that the exemption was intended to apply only to issues genuinely local in character, which in reality represent local financing by local industries, carried out through local investment. Rule 147 is intended to provide more objective standards upon which responsible local businessmen intending to raise capital from local sources may rely in claiming the section 3(a)(11) exemption.

All of the terms and conditions of the rule must be satisfied in order for the rule to be available. These are: (1) that the issuer be a resident of and doing business within the state or territory in which all offers and sales are made; and (ii) that no part of the issue be offered or sold to non-residents within the period of time specified in the rule. For purposes of the rule the definition of "issuer" in section 2(4) of the Act shall apply.

All offers, offers to sell, offers for sale, and sales which are part of the same issue must meet all of the conditions of Rule 147 for the rule to be available. The determination whether offers, offers to sell, offers for sale and sales of securities are part of the same issue (i.e., are deemed to be "integrated") will continue to be a question of fact and will depend on the particular circumstances. See Securities Act of 1933 Release No. 4434 (December 6, 1961). Securities Act Release No. 4434 indicated that in determining whether offers and sales should be regarded as part of the same issue and thus should be integrated any one or more of the following factors may be determinative:

   (i)   Are the offerings part of a single plan of financing;
   (ii) Do the offerings involve issuance of the same class of securities;
   (iii) Are the offerings made at or about the same time;
   (iv) Is the same type of consideration to be received; and
   (v)   Are the offerings made for the same general purpose.

Subparagraph (b)(2) of the rule, however, is designed to provide certainty to the extent feasible by identifying certain types of offers and sales of securities which will be deemed not part of an issue, for purposes of the rule only.

Persons claiming the availability of the rule have the burden of proving that they have satisfied all of its provisions. However, the rule does not establish exclusive standards for complying with the section 3(a)(11) exemption. The exemption would also be available if the issuer satisfied the standards set forth in relevant administrative and judicial interpretations at the time of the offering but the issuer would have the burden of proving the availability of the exemption. Rule 147 relates to transactions exempted from the registration requirements of section 5 of the Act by section 3(a)(11). Neither the rule nor section 3(a)(11) provides an exemption from the registration requirements of section 12(g) of the Securities Exchange Act of 1934, the anti-fraud provisions of the federal securities laws, the civil liability provisions of section 12(2) of the Act or other provisions of the federal securities laws.

Finally, in view of the objectives of the rule and the purposes and policies underlying the Act, the rule shall not be available to any person with respect to any offering which, although in technical compliance with the rule, is part of a plan or scheme by such person to make interstate offers or sales of securities. In such cases registration pursuant to the Act is required.

   4. The rule provides an exemption for offers and sales by the issuer only. It is not available for offers or sales of securities by other persons. Section 3(a)(11) of the Act has been interpreted to permit offers and sales by persons controlling the issuer, if the exemption provided by that section would have been available to the issuer at the time of the offering. See Securities Act Release No. 4434. Controlling persons who want to offer or sell securities pursuant to section 3(a)(11) may continue to do so in accordance with applicable judicial and administrative interpretations.

RULE 147

   (a) *Transactions Covered.* Offers, offers to sell, offers for sale and sales by an issuer of its securities made in accordance with all of the terms and conditions of this rule shall be deemed to be part of an issue offered and sold only to persons resident within a single state or territory where the issuer is a person resident and doing business within such state or territory, within the meaning of section 3(a)(11) of the Act.

   (b) *Part of an Issue.* (1) For purposes of this rule, all securities of the issuer which are part of an issue shall be offered, offered for sale or sold in accordance with all of the terms and conditions of this rule.

(2) For purposes of this rule only, an issue shall be deemed not to include offers, offers to sell, offers for sale or sales of securities of the issuer pursuant to the exemption provided by section 3 or section 4(2) of the Act or pursuant to a registration statement filed under the Act, that take place prior to the six month period immediately preceding or after the six month period immediately following any offers, offers for sale or sales pursuant to this rule, *Provided,* that, there are during either of said six month periods no offers, offers for sale or sales of securities by or for the issuer of the same or similar class as those offered, offered for sale or sold pursuant to the rule.

NOTE: In the event that securities of the same or similar class as those offered pursuant to the rule are offered, offered for sale or sold less than six months prior to or subsequent to any offer, offer for sale or sale pursuant to this rule, see Preliminary Note 3 hereof as to which offers, offers to sell, offers for sale, or sales are part of an issue.

(c) *Nature of the Issuer.* The issuer of the securities shall at the time of any offers and the sales be a person resident and doing business within the state or territory in which all of the offers, offers to sell, offers for sale and sales are made.

(1) The issuer shall be deemed to be a resident of the state or territory in which:

(i) It is incorporated or organized, if a corporation, limited partnership, trust or other form of business organization that is organized under state or territorial law;

(ii) Its principal office is located, if a general partnership or other form of business organization that is not organized under any state or territorial law;

(iii) His principal residence is located, if an individual.

(2) The issuer shall be deemed to be doing business within a state or territory if:

(i) The issuer derived at least 80 percent of its gross revenues and those of its subsidiaries on a consolidated basis

(A) For its most recent fiscal year, if the first offer of any part of the issue is made during the first six months of the issuer's current fiscal year; or

(B) For the first six months of its current fiscal year or during the twelve month fiscal period ending with such six month period, if the first offer of any part of the issue is made during the last six months of the issuer's current fiscal year from the operation of a business or of real property located in or from the rendering of services within such state or territory; provided, however, that this provision does not apply to any issuer which has not had gross revenues in excess of $5,000 from the sale of products or services or other conduct of its business for its most recent twelve month fiscal period;

(ii) The issuer had at the end of its most recent semi-annual fiscal period prior to the first offer of any part of the issue, at least 80 percent of its assets and those of its subsidiaries on a consolidated basis located within such state or territory;

(iii)   The issuer intends to use and uses at least 80 percent of the net proceeds to the issuer from sales made pursuant to this rule in connection with the operation of a business or of real property, the purchase of real property located in, or the rendering of services within such state or territory; and

(iv)   The principal office of the issuer is located within such state or territory.

(d)   *Offerees and Purchasers: Person Resident.* Offers, offers to sell, offers for sale and sales of securities that are part of an issue shall be made only to persons resident within the state or territory of which the issuer is a resident. For purposes of determining the residence of offerees and purchasers:

(1)   A corporation, partnership, trust or other form of business organization shall be deemed to be a resident of a state or territory if, at the time of the offer and sale to it, it has its principal office within such state or territory.

(2)   An individual shall be deemed to be a resident of a state or territory if such individual has, at the time of the offer and sale to him, his principal residence in the state or territory.

(3)   A corporation, partnership, trust or other form of business organization which is organized for the specific purpose of acquiring part of an issue offered pursuant to this rule shall be deemed not to be a resident of a state or territory unless all of the beneficial owners of such organization are residents of such state or territory.

(e)   *Limitation of Resales.* During the period in which securities that are part of an issue are being offered and sold by the issuer, and for a period of nine months from the date of the last sale by the issuer of such securities, all resales of any part of the issue, by any person, shall be made only to persons resident within such state or territory.

NOTES: 1.   In the case of convertible securities resales of either the convertible security, or if it is converted, the underlying security, could be made during the period described in paragraph (e) only to persons resident within such state or territory. For purposes of this rule a conversion in reliance on section 3(a)(9) of the Act does not begin a new period.

2.   Dealers must satisfy the requirements of Rule 15c2–11 under the Securities Exchange Act of 1934 prior to publishing any quotation for a security, or submitting any quotation for publication, in any quotation medium.

(f)   *Precautions Against Interstate Offers and Sales.* (1) The issuer shall, in connection with any securities sold by it pursuant to this rule:

(i)   Place a legend on the certificate or other document evidencing the security stating that the securities have not been registered under the Act and setting forth the limitations on resale contained in paragraph (e);

(ii)   Issue stop transfer instructions to the issuer's transfer agent, if any, with respect to the securities, or, if the issuer transfers its own securities make a notation in the appropriate records of the issuer; and

(iii)   Obtain a written representation from each purchaser as to his residence.

(2)   The issuer shall, in connection with the issuance of new certificates for any of the securities that are part of the same issue that are presented for transfer during the time period specified in paragraph (e), take the steps required by paragraphs (f)(1) (i) and (ii).

(3)   The issuer shall, in connection with any offers, offers to sell, offers for sale or sales by it pursuant to this rule, disclose, in writing, the limitations on resale contained in paragraph (e) and the provisions of paragraphs (f)(1) (i) and (ii) and paragraph (f)(2).

GUIDE 5 OF THE SECURITIES ACT OF 1933 INDUSTRY GUIDES: PREPARATION OF REGISTRATION STATEMENTS RELATING TO INTERESTS IN REAL ESTATE LIMITED PARTNERSHIPS

References to the General Partner and its affiliates, also referred to as sponsors, are intended to include references to the General Partner(s), promoters of the partnership, and all persons that, directly or indirectly, through one or more intermediaries, control or are controlled by, or are under common control with, such General Partner(s) or promoters.

It is suggested that where appropriate, the information in the prospectus be presented in the same order as the following comments. Where the registrant believes that specific comments are not relevant or are otherwise inappropriate, the registrant should bring this to the staff's attention in a letter indicating the reasons therefor.

1. COVER PAGE

A. The disclosure on the cover page should be as succinct and brief as possible.

B. The cover page should set forth, in addition to basic information about the offering, the termination date of the offering, any minimum required purchase and any arrangements to place the funds received in an escrow trust or similar arrangement.

C. The cover page should contain a tabular presentation of the total maximum and minimum interests to be offered:

	Price to Public	Selling Commissions	Proceeds to the Partnership
Per limited partnership interest			
Total minimum			
Total maximum			

D. The cover page also should contain brief identification of the material risks involved in the purchase of the securities with cross-reference to further discussion in the prospectus. The most significant risk factors should be identified where applicable, for example:

i)   Tax aspects
     For example:
          There are material income tax risks associated with the offering.
ii) Use of proceeds
     For example:
          The proceeds of the offering are insufficient to meet the requirements for funds as set forth in the partnership's investment objectives.
iii) Conflicts of interest
     For example:
          The operation of the partnership involves transactions between the partnership and the General Partner or its affiliates which may involve conflicts of interest.

2. SUITABILITY STANDARDS

Standards, if any, to be utilized by the registrant ("suitability standards") in determining the acceptance of subscription agreements should be described immediately following the cover page. Suitability standards should include those established by the registrant, if any, or by any self-regulatory organization or state agency having jurisdiction over the offering of the securities. Registrant should disclose the method(s) it intends to employ to assure adherence to the suitability standards by persons selling the interests and should briefly discuss the factors pertaining to the need for such standards such as lack of liquidity (resale or assignment of securities), importance of the investor's Federal income tax bracket in terms of the tax-benefits to be derived, the long term nature of the investment and possible adverse tax consequences of premature sale of the interests. If suitability standards apply to resale of the interests, this should be discussed.

3. SUMMARY OF THE PARTNERSHIP AND USE OF PROCEEDS

A two-part, concise outline summary relating to the partnership and a tabular summary of use of proceeds should follow the Suitability section of the prospectus. These summaries may replace the Introductory Statement and Use of Proceeds Sections required by the relevant Form if such sections would merely repeat the information in the summaries.

A. Summary of the Partnership The following information should be disclosed in outline form with appropriate cross-references, where applicable:

i) Name, address and telephone number of the General Partner and names of persons making investment decisions for the partnership;

ii) The intended termination date of the partnership;

iii) State, if true, that the General Partner and its affiliates will receive substantial fees and profits in connection with the offering;

iv) If current distributions are an investment objective, state the estimated maximum time from the closing date that the investor might have to wait to receive such distributions;

v) Describe briefly the properties to be purchased. If a material portion of the minimum net proceeds of the offering (allowing for reserves) is not committed to specific properties, so indicate;

vi) Describe the depreciation method to be used;

vii) State the maximum leverage expected to be used by the partnership as a whole and on individual properties, where it may differ;

viii) Include a cross-reference to the Glossary.

B.   Use of Proceeds   The use of proceeds tabular summary will vary according to the partnership but should include, where appropriate, estimates of the public offering expenses (both organizational and sales), the amount available for investment, non-recurring initial investment fees, prepaid items and financing fees, cash down payments, reserves, and acquisition fees including those paid by the seller. Estimated amounts to be paid to the General Partner and its affiliates should be identified. The summary should include both dollar amounts and percentages of the maximum and minimum proceeds of the offering. Inclusion of percentages of the estimated maximum and minimum total assets is optional. An example of a summary of Use of Proceeds is attached as Appendix I, but the summary will vary according to the circumstances.

4. COMPENSATION AND FEES TO THE GENERAL PARTNERS AND AFFILIATES

A. This section should include a summary tabular presentation, itemizing by category and specifying dollar amounts where possible, of all compensation, fees, profits, and other benefits (including reimbursement of out-of-pocket expenses) which the General Partner and its affiliates may earn or receive in connection with the offering or operation of the partnership. If more detailed information is required it should be located in the Summary of Partnership Agreement section with cross-reference to that Summary. The presentation should identify the person, including affiliations with the General Partner, who will receive such compensation, fees, profits or benefits and the services to be performed by such person.

The summary should be organized so as to indicate clearly whether the compensation relates to the offering and organizational stage, the developmental or acquisition stage, the operational stage or the termination and liquidation stage of the partnership. Separate subcaptions are recommended.

The type of compensation, fees, profits or other benefits that should be disclosed includes, but is not limited to, the following: disbursements incident to the purchase and sale of the limited partnership interests, including sales commissions, reimbursements for expenses, and real estate commissions; finder's fees; fees for property acquisitions, marketing or leasing up of properties, financing or refinancing, management of properties, insurance and miscellaneous services; commissions and other fees to be paid upon sale of the partnership's properties; participation by the General Partner in cash flow or profits and losses or capital gains and losses arising out of the operation, refinancing or sale of properties; fees or builder's profits; overhead absorption and/or land write-ups; and all profits on the purchase of investments for the partnership from the General Partner or its affiliates. If the partnership agreement limits the losses the General Partner and its affiliates can sustain, this should be discussed.

B. Maximum aggregate dollar front-end fees to be paid during the first fiscal year of operations should be disclosed based upon the assumption that the partnership's maximum leverage is utilized.

C. Where compensation arrangements are based upon a formula or percentage, the terms of such arrangements should be disclosed and illustrated. The assumptions underlying the dollar figures should be disclosed and the calculations underlying the figures should be submitted to the staff supplementally with the initial filing. Compensation based upon a given return (percentage of contributed investor capital) to investors should disclose whether such return is cumulative or non-cumulative.

D. Where the General Partner or an affiliate receives a disproportionate interest in the partnership in relation to its own contribution, registrants attention is directed to Item 506 of Regulation S-K. A bar chart comparison of the various interests and contributors should be provided.

5. CONFLICTS OF INTEREST

A. This section should include a summary of each type of transaction which may result in a conflict between the interests of the public investors and those of the General Partner and its affiliates, and of the proposed method of dealing with such conflict. The types of conflicts of interest which should be disclosed and discussed, if appropriate, include, but are not limited to:

i) The General Partner is a general partner or an affiliate of the general partner in other investment entities (public and/or private) engaged in making similar investments or otherwise makes or arranges for similar investments.

ii) The General Partner has the authority to invest the partnership's funds in other partnerships in which the General Partner or an affiliate is the general partner or has an interest.

iii) Properties in which the General Partner or its affiliates have an interest are bought from or partnership properties are sold to the General Partner or its affiliates or entities in which they have an interest. Where appraisals are used in connection with any such transaction, it should be made clear that appraisals are only estimates of value and should not be relied on as measures of realizable value. If the appraiser is named as an expert, a consent to the use of his name should be furnished. If specific appraised values are included in the registration statement, the appraiser should be named as an expert, his consent furnished and the appraisals filed as exhibits to the registration statement. If a statement that the purchase price of the property does not exceed its appraised value is included and the appraiser is not named and specific values are not cited, there need not be furnished a consent to use the appraiser's name. In that event, a copy of the appraisal should be submitted supplementally with the registration statement. If any relationship exists between the appraiser and the General Partner or its affiliates this should be stated. If the General Partner intends to buy any properties in which the general partner or any of its affiliates have a material interest, such properties shoul be appropriately described in the prospectus along with the investment objectives of the partnership (see paragraph 10, Investment Objectives and Policies). If it is disclosed in the prospectus that the partnership may purchase properties in which the General Partner or its affiliates have a material interest, but no properties are described, and such properties are thereafter purchased for the partnership, the General Partner will have the heavy burden of demonstrating that it did not intend to purchase such property at the time the registration statement became effective.

iv) The General Partner or its affiliates own or have an interest in properties adjacent to those to be purchased and developed by the partnership.

v) Affiliates of the General Partner who act as underwriters, real estate brokers or managers for the partnership, act in such capacities for other partnerships or entities.

vi) An affiliate of the General Partner places mortgages for the partnership or otherwise acts as a finance broker or as insurance agent or broker receiving commissions for such services.

vii) An affiliate of the General Partner acts (a) as an underwriter for the offering, or (b) as a principal underwriter for the offering thereby creating conflicts in performance of the underwriter's due diligence inquiries under the Securities Act.

viii) The compensation plan for the General Partner may create a conflict between the interests of the General Partner and those of the partnership.

B. An organization chart should be included in this section showing the relationship between the various organizations managed or controlled by the General Partner or its affiliates that will do business with the partnership where the relationships are so complex that a graphic display would assist investors in understanding such relationships.

6. FIDUCIARY RESPONSIBILITY OF THE GENERAL PARTNER

A. A discussion of the fiduciary obligation owed by the General Partner to the Limited Partners should be set forth. The following disclosure is suggested with appropriate modification for the laws of the state of organization:

A General Partner is accountable to a limited partnership as a fiduciary and consequently must exercise good faith and integrity in handling partnership affairs. This is a rapidly developing and changing area of the law and Limited Partners who have questions concerning the duties of the General Partner should consult with their counsel.

B. Where the limited partnership agreement contains an exculpatory provision and/or the right to indemnification, the following disclosure is suggested, as modified to reflect the substance of such provisions:

Exculpation

i) The General Partner may not be liable to the Partnership or Limited Partners for errors in judgment or other acts or omissions not amounting to willful misconduct or gross negligence, since provision has been made in the Agreement of Limited Partnership for exculpation of the General Partner. Therefore, purchasers of the interests have a more limited right of action than they would have absent the limitation in the Partnership Agreement.

Indemnification

ii) The Partnership Agreement provides for indemnification of the General Partner by the Partnership for liabilities he incurs in dealings with third parties on behalf of the partnership. To the extent that the indemnification provisions purport to include indemnification for liabilities arising under the Securities Act of 1933, in the opinion of the Securities and Exchange Commission, such indemnification is contrary to public policy and therefore unenforceable.

Registrant's attention is also directed to Items 510 and 512(i) of Regulation S-K relating to disclosure of indemnification agreements.

7. RISK FACTORS

A. This section should include a carefully organized series of short, concise subcaptioned paragraphs, with cross-references to fuller discussion where appropriate, summarizing the principal risk factors applicable to the offering and to the partnership's particular plan of operations. The risk factors section should be brief.

B. This subsection should summarize each material risk of adverse tax consequences with appropriate cross-references to fuller discussions in the Federal tax section. For example:

i) Where no Internal Revenue Service (IRS) ruling as to partnership tax status has been applied for or obtained, the risk that the IRS may on audit determine that for tax purposes the partnership is an association taxable as a corporation, in which case, investors would be deprived of the tax benefits associated with the offering. As part of this disclosure, it should be stated that a material risk of IRS classification as a corporate association may exist even though registrant relies on an opinion of counsel as to partnership tax status as such opinion is not binding on the IRS. It may also be stated that IRS classification of the partnership as a corporate association would deprive investors of the tax benefits of the offering only if the IRS determination is upheld in court or otherwise becomes final. Any such additional disclosure should explain that contesting an IRS determination may impose representation expenses on investors. (See Federal tax section.)

ii) Where the IRS has advised registrant that it proposes not to rule, or to rule adversely, on any tax issue as to which a ruling was applied for, the risk that investors may lose some or all tax benefits associated with the offering. (See Federal tax section.)

iii) The risk that after some years of partnership operations an investor's tax liabilities may exceed his cash distributions in corresponding years and that to the extent of such excess the payment of such taxes will be out-of-pocket expenses.

iv) Upon a sale or other disposition (*e.g.*, by gift) of a partnership interest or, upon a sale (including a foreclosure sale) or other disposition of partnership property, the risk that an investor's tax liabilities may exceed the cash he receives and that to the extent of such excess the payment of such taxes will be out-of-pocket expenses. The disclosure should indicate to what extent the gain may be taxed as ordinary income, to what extent as capital gain. (See Federal tax section.)

v) The risk that an audit of the partnership's information return may result in an audit of an investor's own tax return. (See Federal tax section.)

C. Risk factors relating to the specific partnership might include, where applicable:

i) Management's lack of relevant experience, or management's lack of success with similar partnerships or other real estate investments;

ii) Where the proceeds of the offering will be insufficient to meet the requirements of the partnership's investment objectives, a discussion of the additional sources of capital for the partnership and of the risk of not being able to satisfy the partnership's objectives as a result of not obtaining additional necessary funds;

iii) Where the partnership has high risk investment objectives, including high leveraging, these should be explained;

iv) The risk that no public market for interests is likely to develop and that holders of interests may not be able to liquidate their investment quickly;

v) Risks associated with contemplated rent stabilization programs, fuel or energy requirements or regulations, and construction in areas that are subject to environmental or other federal, state or local regulations, actual or pending;

vi) Where a material portion of the minimum net proceeds of the offering is not committed to specific properties, disclosure of the particular risk associated with an investment in such an offering. Such disclosure should include the increased uncertainty and risk to investors since they are unable to evaluate the manner in which the proceeds are to be invested and the economic merit merit of the particular real estate projects prior to investment. Also it should be disclosed that there may be a substantial period of time before the proceeds of the offering are invested and therefore a delay to investors in receiving a return on their investment.

D. Risk factors relating to real estate limited partnership offerings in general should be briefly discussed after those relating to the specific partnership. Such risks might include, where applicable: the risks associated with the ownership of real estate, including uncertainty of cash flow to meet fixed and maturing obligations, adverse local market conditions, risks of "leveraging," and uninsured losses.

8. PRIOR PERFORMANCE OF THE GENERAL PARTNER AND AFFILIATES

A narrative summary of the "track record" or prior performance of programs sponsored by the General Partner and its affiliates ("sponsors") containing the information set forth below should be included in the text of the prospectus. Tables following the format of those in Appendix II, relating to historical use of proceeds of prior programs, compensation to the sponsors, operations of prior programs, and acquisitions and sales of properties by prior programs, should be included at the back of the prospectus or in Part II of the registration statement as specified in paragraph B "Prior Performance Tables" hereunder.

Sponsors are urged not to include in the prospectus information about prior performance beyond that required by this Guide except for such further material information as may be necessary to make the required statements, in light of the circumstances under which they are made, not misleading.

Terms Used in the Guide   "Public" programs include all offerings registered under the Securities Act of 1933, all programs required to report under Section 15(d) of the Securities Exchange Act of 1934 ("Exchange Act"), all programs with a class of equity securities registered pursuant to Section 12(g) of the Exchange Act, and all other programs with at least 300 security holders of record that initially raised at least $1 million.

Programs with "similar investment objectives" are those with similar objectives as set forth in the prospectus. Generally, the sponsor has the responsibility to determine which previous programs had "similar investment objectives," taking into consideration the materiality of information about the prior programs in analyzing the registrant's proposed activities.

A sponsor would be considered to have a "public track record" if it has sponsored at least three programs with investment objectives similar to those of the registrant that file reports under Section 13(a) or Section 15(d) of the Exchange Act and at least two public programs with investment objectives similar to those of the registrant that had three years of operations after investment of 90% of the amount available for investment. In addition, at least two of the public offerings for programs with investment objectives similar to those of the registrant must have closed in the previous three years.

A. Narrative Summary

1. The narrative summary in the text of the prospectus should include a description of the sponsor's experience in the last ten years with all other programs, both public and nonpublic, that have invested primarily in real estate, regardless of the investment objectives of the programs. This summary should include at least (a) the number of programs sponsored, (b) the total amount of money raised from investors, (c) the total number of investors, (d) the number of properties purchased and location by region, (e) the aggregate dollar amount of property purchased, (f) the percentage (based on purchase prices rather than on number) of properties that are commercial (broken out by shopping centers, office buildings and others) and residential, (g) the percentage (based on purchase prices) of new, used or construction properties, and (h) the number of properties sold. Aggregate figures should be presented separately for public and nonpublic programs. In addition, the narrative should indicate the approximate percentage of the overall data that represents activities of programs with investment objectives similar to those of the registrant. The summary also should cross-reference the prior performance tables.

2. The narrative summary should include a discussion of those major adverse business developments or conditions experienced by any prior program, either public or nonpublic, that would be material to investors in this program. The narrative summary also should include a cross-reference to further information that may be found in Appendix II as part of Table III.

3. The narrative summary should include a list of all prior public programs sponsored by the General Partner and its affiliates and an undertaking to provide upon request, for no fee, the most recent Form 10-K Annual Report filed with the Commission by any prior public program that has reported to the Commission within the last twenty-four months and to provide, for a reasonable fee, the exhibits to each such Form 10-K.

4. The narrative summary should include a summary of acquisitions of properties by programs in the most recent three years as set forth in Table VI of Appendix II. The summary should include the number of properties purchased, the type, location and method of financing. Reference should be made to the more detailed description of these acquisitions in Part II of the registration statement, and the registrant should undertake to provide the more detailed description from Part II without fee upon request.

B. Prior Performance Tables The information required by the tables set forth in Appendix II should be included in the format shown. Tables should appear at the back of the prospectus except for Table VI, which should appear only in Part II of the registration statement. The instructions to the tables specify the programs and time periods about which information is required.

9. MANAGEMENT

A. If a material portion of the maximum net proceeds (allowing for reserves) is not committed to specific properties, disclosure should be made of the identity of the individuals who will make the investment decisions with appropriate background information including that required by Item 401(f) of Regulation S-K.

B. Any substantial reliance on a nonaffiliate in running the operations of the partnership should be disclosed and any relevant prior experience should be discussed. If material amounts of compensation or fees are to be paid to nonaffiliates, a separate heading should be provided entitled, "Fees and Compensation Arrangements with Nonaffiliates" and a tabular presentation describing such fees should be provided.

C. If there is provision in the partnership agreement or otherwise for a change in the management of the partnership, a description of how such change could be accomplished should be included.

D. The amount of, and reason for, any contingent liabilities of the General Partner and its affiliates with regard to prior programs now in existence should be disclosed. If this information appears in the financial statements it may be incorporated hereunder by reference.

10. INVESTMENT OBJECTIVES AND POLICIES

A. Disclosure should be made of the nature of the property intended to be purchased *(e.g.,* commercial, residential) and the criteria *(e.g.,* method of depreciation, location) to be utilized in evaluating proposed investments.

B. If there is provision in the partnership agreement or otherwise for change in the investment objectives of the partnership, a description of how such change could be made should be included.

C. Generally, where the net proceeds of the offering will be invested in non-specified properties or in properties that do not have any significant operating histories, it is not appropriate to make any statement setting forth a rate of return on the investment.

11. DESCRIPTION OF REAL ESTATE INVESTMENTS

A. Risks associated with specified properties, such as competitive factors, environmental regulation, rent control regulation, fuel or energy requirements and regulation should be noted.

B. If a material portion of the minimum net proceeds (allowing for reasonable reserves) is not committed to specific properties, the issuer should clearly so indicate in the prospectus.

Where a reasonable probability exists that a property will be acquired and the funds to be expended represent a material portion of the net proceeds of the minimum offering, the issuer should describe such property in the registration statement at the time of filing. Where after the registration statement has been filed but prior to its effectiveness a reasonable probability arises that a property will be acquired, a description of such property should be included in a pre-effective amendment to the registration statement. Where a reasonable probability that a property will be acquired arises after the effectiveness of the registration statement and during the distribution period, a 424(c) supplement or post-effective amendment, as appropriate, should be promptly filed. (See Undertaking D.) * Whether

* It has come to the staff's attention that on a number of occasions issuers have identified properties to be purchased and have delayed proceeding with the purchase in order to avoid the necessary disclosure. In the staff's opinion, such practice is not consistent with the obligation of the issuer to disclose material facts relating to the offering.

adequate disclosure of properties to be acquired has been timely made can only be determined by an examination of the facts in each case. This may vary due to different business practices particular to each issuer. Thus, as in all other situations, the burden of making adequate and timely disclosure rests solely with the issuer.

12. FEDERAL TAXES

A. General Instructions This section should summarize under a series of appropriate headings all material Federal income tax aspects of the offering. State tax aspects need usually be summarized only to the extent required by Subsection L, below. Proper citations should be used whenever reference is made to sections of the Internal Revenue Code (the "Code"), the Treasury regulations, decided cases or other sources. An opinion of counsel as to all material tax aspects of the offering should be filed as an exhibit. Such opinion should cite relevant authority for any conclusions expressed. The tax sections of the prospectus should summarize or restate the tax information contained in the opinion.

The function of the tax opinion is to inform investors of the tax consequences they can reasonably expect from an investment in the partnership. If, with respect to an intended tax benefit, counsel are unable to express an opinion that such benefit will be available because of uncertainty in the law or for other reasons, the opinion should so state and also disclose that there is or may be a material tax risk the particular benefit will be disallowed on audit. The tax effect of such disallowance should be explained. Each material risk of disallowance of an intended tax benefit should be disclosed in the tax opinion and under the appropriate heading in the prospectus.

Tax counsel should be aware that their opinion speaks as of the effective date of the registration statement. Such opinion should be updated for any material changes or events occurring subsequent to filing and prior to the effective date. Ruling requests (including amendments) and rulings should also be filed as exhibits with the original filing, or by amendment as soon thereafter as available.

B. Partnership Status This subsection should state whether an IRS ruling has been requested as to the entity's classification as a partnership for Federal income tax purposes. The contents of any ruling, including any conditions therein, should be summarized. Where a ruling or opinion of counsel as to partnership status is conditioned on the maintenance of certain net worth or other standards, there should be disclosure as to how these standards will be maintained in the future. If no IRS ruling as to partnership tax status has been requested or obtained, counsel's opinion as to partnership tax status should be summarized and the risk of IRS classification of the entity as a corporate association, referred to in the Risk Factors section, should be discussed.

C. Taxation of Limited Partners   Insofar as necessary to an understanding of the intended tax benefits and any material risks of their disallowance, this subsection should summarize basic rules of partnership taxation, e.g., that a partnership is not a taxable entity, that a partner will be required to report on his Federal tax return his distributive share of partnership income, gain, loss, deductions or credits, whether or not any actual distribution is made to such partner during his taxable year. The tax treatment of cash distributions to partners should also be explained.

If the partnership agreement provides special allocations among partners of distributive shares of income, gain, loss, deductions or credits, this subsection should set forth an opinion of counsel to the effect that the principal purpose of the allocations is not tax avoidance or evasion under Code Sec. 704(b)(2), and/or a risk disclosure to the effect that the IRS may on audit disallow any special allocation which it determines to have tax avoidance or evasion as its principal purpose. The tax consequences to partners of disallowance of a special allocation should be explained. Where applicable, the tax consequences of retroactive allocations to new partners should be discussed.

D. Basis   This subsection should explain that a partner may deduct his share of partnership losses only to the extent of the adjusted basis of his interest in the partnership. Inclusion of a partner's share of the partnership's nonrecourse debt in the adjusted basis of his partnership interest should be explained. If there is a question as to whether the partnership's nonrecourse debt will enter into bases of the limited partners' interests, that should be disclosed.

Where appropriate, there should be an explanation of the consequences to a limited partner of a reduction in his share of the partnership's nonrecourse debt as may result, for example, from a change in his profit sharing ratio.

E. Depreciation and Recapture   This subsection should explain the method or methods of depreciation to be used by the partnership on its depreciable property as well as the basis for determining useful lives of such property. Any material risks that the IRS may challenge useful lives chosen by the partnership should be disclosed together with an explanation of the possible tax consequences of applying longer useful lives to partnership property. If methods of depreciation available only to a "first-user" are to be utilized, the basis of such "first-user" status should be explained. Depreciation recapture may be explained here with appropriate cross-reference to subsections on Sale or Other Disposition of Partnership Property and Sale or Other Disposition of a Partnership Interest.

F. Deductibility of Prepaid and Other Expenses As to prepaid interest, possible nondeductibility in the year of payment should be discussed. It should be explained that if a partnership takes a large deduction for prepaid interest in its first year of operation, having little or no income in such year, the IRS may determine that the prepayment created a material distortion of income at the partnership level and require that it be allocated over the term of the loan.

As to other material partnership expenses (e.g., interim commitment fees, management fees, permanent mortgage fees, etc.) it should be stated which are deductible, which are nondeductible and as to which deductibility is uncertain. Where applicable, the possible nondeductibility of guaranteed payments under Code Sec. 707(c) should be discussed.

G. Tax Liabilities in Later Years This subsection should discuss the Risk Factors disclosure that after some years of partnership operations an investor's tax liabilities may exceed cash distributions in corresponding years. The tax problems that will arise after partnership property reaches the point when the partnership's nondeductible mortgage amortization payments exceed its depreciation deductions (the crossover point) should be explained.

It should also be explained that where partnership losses offset an investor's earned income taxable at a 50 percent rate, partnership income in later years may be taxed to the investor at a higher rate.

H. Sale or Other Disposition of a Partnership Interest This subsection should begin with a restatement of the Risk Factors disclosure that an investor may be unable to sell his partnership interest as there may be no market for it. The subsection should then discuss the Risk Factors disclosure that taxes payable on a sale of a partnership interest may exceed cash received. The discussion should explain the tax effect on a partner of being relieved from his share of the partnership's nonrecourse liabilities. The discussion should also state to what extent the gain recognized will be taxed as ordinary income, to what extent as capital gain.

Whether or not the partnership plans to make the Sec. 754 election should be disclosed together with an explanation of the possible tax consequences on a transferee Limited Partner should the election not be made.

This subsection should also explain that a gift of an interest in a partnership holding leveraged property may result in Federal income tax (as well as Federal gift tax) liability to the donor. It should be explained that the IRS is likely to consider that a partner who gives away his partnership interest is relieved of his share of the partnership's nonrecourse liabilities and that he may realize a taxable gain on the gift to the extent that his share of such liabilities exceeds his adjusted basis in his partnership interest. It should be stated to what extent the gain will be taxed as ordinary income, to what extent as capital gain.

I. Sale or Other Disposition of Partnership Property   This subsection may use cross-reference to, or be combined with, subsection H in order to avoid repetition.

The subsection should discuss the Risk Factors disclosure that upon a sale (including a foreclosure sale) or other disposition of partnership property an investor's tax liability may exceed cash he would receive. The discussion should explain that the amount received by the partnership on sale (including a foreclosure sale) or other disposition of property will include any nonrecourse indebtedness to which the property was subject. It should be stated to what extent the gain will be taxed as ordinary income, to what extent as capital gain.

If appropriate, the tax treatment of dealer property should be explained. Should the sale of condominium units by the partnership be contemplated, it should be pointed out such units may be treated as dealer property.

J. Section 183   The possible impact of this Code section on investors lacking a profit objective in investing in any tax shelter program which is expected to generate annual net losses for tax purposes for a period of years should be discussed. The discussion should note that the section may apply to the Limited Partners of a partnership notwithstanding any profit objective the partnership itself may be deemed to have.

K. Liquidation or Termination of the Partnership   The tax consequences to a Limited Partner of partnership liquidation or termination should be explained.

L. State, Local and Foreign Taxes   It should be disclosed whether partners will be required to file tax returns and/or be subject to tax in any state or states other than their state of residence, or in any foreign countries. Where applicable, state and foreign tax rates should be noted.

M. Tax Returns and Tax Information   It should be disclosed what kind of tax information will be supplied to Limited Partners and when, and whether the same kind of information will also be supplied to assignees who are not substitute limited partners.

It should be explained that the information return filed by the partnership may be audited and that such audit may result in adjustments or proposed adjustments. Any adjustment of the partnership information return would normally result in adjustments or proposed adjustments of a partner's own return. Any audit of a partner's return could result in adjustments of nonpartnership as well as partnership income and losses.

N. Other Headings Where applicable the tax section should also discuss the limitation on deductions of investment interest, the minimum tax on tax preference income, the impact of tax preference items on the maximum tax on earned income, and any other tax information deemed material in the particular offering.

13. GLOSSARY

If terms are used in the prospectus that are technical in nature or are susceptible to varying methods of computation, e.g., acquisition fees, book value, capital contribution, cash flow, cash available for distribution, construction fees, cost of property, development fee, net worth, organization and offering expenses, profit, partnership management fee and property management fee, definitions should be provided. For purposes of uniformity, it is suggested that these definitions conform to those that appear in the Statement of Policy Regarding Real Estate Programs of the North American Securities Administrators Association, or that any variations, and the economic effect thereof, be disclosed.

14. SUMMARY OF PARTNERSHIP AGREEMENT

A brief summary of the material provisions of the Limited Partnership Agreement should be included.

15. REPORTS TO LIMITED PARTNERS

The registrant should identify all reports and other documents that will be furnished to Limited Partners as required by the partnership's Limited Partnership Agreement and the undertakings to the registration statement. In particular, registrant should disclose: (1) whether the financial information contained in such reports will be prepared on an accrual basis in accordance with generally accepted accounting principles, with a reconciliation with respect to information furnished to limited partners for income tax purposes: (2) whether independent certified public accountants will audit the financial statements to be included in the annual report; (3) whether the annual report will be provided to limited partners within 90 days following the close of the partnership's fiscal year: (4) that a detailed statement of any transactions with the General Partner or its affiliates, and of fees, commissions, compensation and other benefits paid, or accrued to the General Partner or its affiliates for the fiscal year completed, showing the amount paid or accrued to each recipient and the services performed, will be furnished to each limited partner at least on an annual basis pursuant to the registrant's undertaking; (5) that the information specified by Form 10-Q (if such report is required to be filed with the Commission) will be furnished to limited partners within 45 days after the close of each quarterly fiscal period pursuant to the registrant's undertaking; and (6) if the registrant has applied for, but not received an IRS ruling as to the tax status at the time of effectiveness of the registration statement, that the registrant will promptly notify each limited partner, in writing, pursuant to its undertaking of the receipt of the ruling or of an adverse ruling or refusal to rule by the IRS.

16. THE OFFERING—DESCRIPTION OF THE UNITS

In addition to the disclosure required by the relevant items of Form S-1 or S-11, disclosure should be made of all restrictions on transfer of the interests, including those in the Partnership Agreement, those imposed by state suitability standards or blue sky laws, and those resulting from the tax laws.

17. REDEMPTION, REPURCHASE AND RIGHT OF PRESENTMENT AGREEMENTS

There should be a discussion of any provisions in the partnership agreement that allow the General Partner or its affiliates to redeem or repurchase the offered security or that allow the investor to seek redemption or repurchase. The conditions or formulae used, *e.g.*, purchase price less capital returns, should also be disclosed. Registrant should be careful to appropriately describe the investor's right—whether it be redemption, repurchase, or merely a right of presentment. The discussion should include the following factors:

(1) That appraisals are simply estimates of value and may not necessarily correspond to realizable value;

(2) The order in which redemption requests will be honored (post mark or other objective standard);

(3) Whether the General Partner and its affiliates will defer their redemption requests until requests for redemption by the Limited Partner public investors have been met;

(4) The source and amount of funds (together with any legal or practical limitations) available for this purpose;

(5) The circumstances under which a later request will be honored, while an earlier request is still pending;

(6) Tax consequences related to redemption;

(7) The period of time during which a redemption request may be pending prior to its being granted or rejected;

(8) Whether there is to be allocation of funds among partners requesting redemption in circumstances where redemption requests exceed funds available for this purpose. If so, state and briefly describe the allocation process;

(9) Whether Limited Partners must hold an interest in the partnership for a specified period prior to making a redemption request; and

(10) A detailed statement of the procedure that must be followed in order to redeem or seek repurchase of the interest, including the forms that must be presented, and whether signature guarantees will be required.

18. CAPITALIZATION

Disclosure should be made in accordance with Form S-1 or S-11, as appropriate.

19. PLAN OF DISTRIBUTION

A. If there is an understanding or arrangement, whether written or oral, between the registrant and any broker or dealer, relating to the distribution of the interests, which is intended to be finalized after effectiveness of the registration statement, such understanding or arrangement should be disclosed.

B. If, after the registration statement becomes effective, the registrant enters into any selling arrangement which calls for the payment of more than the usual and customary compensation, a sticker supplement (Rule 424(c)) describing such arrangement should be filed.

C. If the registant intends to pay referral or similar fees to any professional or other persons in connection with the distribution of the interests, this fact should be disclosed.

D. If the General Partner or its affiliates intend to purchase interests, and such interests will be included in satisfying the minimum offering requirements, it should be disclosed whether such interests are intended to be resold, and if so, the period of time these interests will be held prior to being resold. Depending on the circumstances, such interests may be considered to be unsold allotments under Section 4(3) of the Act. (See Securities Act Release 4150.)

20. SUMMARY OF PROMOTIONAL AND SALES MATERIAL

A. The sales material should present a balanced discussion of both risk and reward. The contents of the sales material or sales meetings or seminars should be consistent with the representations in the prospectus.

B. A section which identifies all written sales material proposed to be transmitted to prospective investors orally or in writing should be included. The sales material should be appropriately identified by title and character and should be separately categorized either as the registrant's material or that of another person. If material provided by the latter is to be used, state the name of the author and publication and the date of prior publication, if any, identify any persons who are quoted without being identified, and, except in the case of a public official document or statement, state whether or not the consent of the author and publication have been obtained for the use of the material as sales materials. Sales materials include memoranda, summary descriptions, graphics, supplemental exhibits, media advertising, charts and pictures relating to the offering of the security and proposed to be transmitted to prospective investors.

C. If any other material is to be used subsequent to the effective date, a "sticker" supplement (424(c) prospectus) should be filed to describe any such sales material.

D. Any sales material that is intended to be furnished to investors orally or in writing, other than that which is used for internal purposes of the registrant, and including all material described in paragraph B above, should be submitted to the staff supplementally, prior to its use. For purposes of this paragraph only, sales material includes all marketing memoranda that are sent by the General Partner or its affiliates to broker/dealers or other sales personnel and may include material labeled "for broker/dealer use only." Staff comments, if any, will be promptly communicated to the registrant. Registrant should check with the staff before using sale material that has been submittd to the staff.

E. Wherever public sales meetings or seminars are to be employed to discuss the offering, individually or in conjunction with other tax sheltered offerings, the staff should be provided, as supplemental information, copies of any written scripts or outlines which are prepared for use in such meetings a reasonable time prior to their use.

F. Reference in sales material or at such sales meetings or seminars to Federal income tax treatment of the partnership and its investors should refer to either a ruling of the IRS or an opinion of counsel. Counsel should be named, his acknowledgement furnished supplementally with respect to such use, and any qualification contained in counsel's opinion should be referred to in such material by cross-referencing to the prospectus. Where the program has not sought a ruling as to the tax status (partnership) from the IRS and is relying on an opinion of counsel, it should be indicated that an opinion of counsel is not binding on the IRS.

21. UNDERTAKINGS

A. The following undertaking should be included in the registration statement if the securities to be registered are to be offered in a continuous offering over an extended period of time:

The registrant undertakes (a) to file any prospectuses required by Section 10(a)(3) as post-effective amendments to the registration statement, (b) that for the purpose of determining any liability under the Act each such post-effective amendment may be deemed to be a new registration statement relating to the securities offered therein and the offering of such securities at that time may be deemed to be the initial bona fide offering thereof, (c) that all post-effective amendments will comply with the applicable forms, rules and regulations of the Commission in effect at the time such post-effective amendments are filed, and (d) to remove from registration by means of a post-effective amendment any of the securites being registered which remain at the termination of the offering.

B. The following undertaking should be included in every registration statement:

The registrant undertakes to send to each limited partner at least on an annual basis a detailed statement of any transactions with the General Partner or its affiliates, and of fees, commissions, compensation and other benefits paid, or accrued to the General Partner or its affiliates for the fiscal year completed, showing the amount paid or accrued to each recipient and the services performed.

C. The following undertaking should be included in every registration statement:

The registrant undertakes to provide to the limited partners the financial statements required by Form 10-K for the first full fiscal year of opertions of the partnership.

D. The following undertakings relating to investment of the proceeds of an offering in which a material portion of the maximum net proceeds (allowing for reasonable reserves) is not committed (i.e., subject to a binding purchase agreement) to specific properties should be included in the registration statement:

The registrant undertakes to file a sticker supplement pursuant to Rule 424(c) under the Act during the distribution period describing each property not identified in the prospectus at such time as there arises a reasonable probability that such property will be acquired and to consolidate all such stickers into a post-effective amendment filed at least once every three months, with the information contained in such amendment provided simultaneously to the existing Limited Partners. Each sticker supplement should disclose all compensation and fees received by the General Partner(s) and its affiliates in connection with any such acquisition. The post-effective amendment shall include audited financial statements meeting the requirements of Rule 3-14 of Regulation S-X only for properties acquired during the distribution period.

The registrant also undertakes to file, after the end of the distribution period, a current report on Form 8-K containing the financial statements and any additional information required by Rule 3-14 of Regulation S-X, to reflect each commitment (i.e., the signing of a binding purchase agreement) made after the end of the distribution period involving the use of 10% or more (on a cumulative basis) of the net proceeds of the offering and to provide the information contained in such report to the Limitd Partners at least once each quarter after the distribution period of the offering has ended.

Note. Offers and sales of the interests may continue after the filing of a post-effective amendment containing information previously disclosed in sticker supplements to the prospectus, as long as the information disclosed in a current sticker supplement accompanying the prospectus is as complete as the information contained in the most recently filed post-effective amendment.

E. If the registrant has applied for a ruling from the IRS as to tax status, and has not received it at the time of effectiveness:

The registrant undertakes to promptly notify each limited partner, in writing, of the receipt of the ruling or of an adverse ruling or refusal to rule by the IRS, and undertakes to file with the Commission a Form 8-K describing such event.

APPENDIX I. EXAMPLE OF SUMMARY OF THE USE
OF PROCEEDS SECTION

Estimated Application of Proceeds of This Offering

	Minimum Dollar Amount	Percent	Maximum Dollar Amount	Percent
Gross offering proceeds	$	100.00%	$	100.00%
Public offering expenses:				
Underwriting discount and commissions paid to affiliate				
Organizational expenses (1)				
Amount available for investment	$	%	$	%
Prepaid terms and fees related to purchase of property (2)				
Cash down payment (equity)				
Acquisition fees (real estate commissions) (3)				
Working capital reserve				
Proceeds invested				
Public offering expenses				
Total application of proceeds	$	%	$	100.00%

The Corporate General Partner and its affiliates may receive a maximum of $ (%) if the minimum dollar amount is sold and $ (%) if the maximum dollar amount is sold from the sellers of the properties as Real Estate Commissions on purchases of properties. Real estate commissions are normally paid by the seller of a property rather than the buyer. However, the price of a property will generally be adjusted upward to take into account this obligation of the seller so that in effect the Partnership, as purchaser, will bear all or a portion of the commission in the purchase price of the property. The partnership also expects to pay commissions in connection with the sale of properties which will reduce the net proceeds to the Partnership of any such sales.

   (1) Includes a $ non-recurring organization fee to be received by the Corporate General Partner and legal, accounting, printing and other expenses of this offering. To the extent, if any, that expenses of the offering exceed $ per interest, the excess will be paid by   .
   (2) Includes prepaid interest, points, loan commitment fees and legal and

other costs of acquisition. The percentage of such items to be capitalized is . . . .%.

(3) "Real Estate Commission" is defined as the total of all fees and commissions paid by any person to any person, including the Corporate General Partner or affiliates in connection with the selection, purchase, construction or development of any property by the Partnership, whether designated as real estate commission, acquisition fees, finders fees, selection fees, development fees, construction fees, non-recurring management fees, consulting fees or any other similar fees or commissions howsoever designated and howsoever treated for tax or accounting purposes. (See "Compensation to Management." Page   .)

APPENDIX II. PRIOR PERFORMANCE TABLES

Instructions to Appendix II   1. The prior performance tables should be preceded by a narrative introduction that cross-references the narrative summary in the text, explains the significance of the track record and the tables, explains where additional information (Part II of the registration statement or Form 10-K Annual Reports for prior programs) can be obtained on request and includes a glossary of terms used in the tables.

This introduction also should include a discussion of the factors the sponsor considered in determining which previous programs had "similar investment objectives" to those of the registrant.

2. Each of the tables should be introduced by a brief narrative explaining the objective of the table and what it covers so that the investor will be able to understand the significance of the information presented. There also should be set forth with or in each table any further material information that may be necessary to make the required tabular data, in light of the circumstances under which it is presented, not misleading.

Table I. Experience in Raising and Investing Funds (on a percentage basis)
Instructions: 1. Include information only for programs the offering of which closed in the most recent three years.

2. Sponsors with a "public track record" should include information relating only to public programs with investment objectives similar to those of the registrant.

3. If the sponsor does not have a "public track record," information must be given for each prior program, public or nonpublic, with investment objectives similar to those of the registrant. If the sponsor has not sponsored at least five such programs, then information must be given for each prior program, public or nonpublic, even if the investment objectives for those

programs are not similar to those of the registrant. In that case, nonpublic programs with investment objectives that are not similar to those of the registrant should be grouped together according to investment objective and information about those programs presented on an aggregate basis by year. If so presented, the number of programs that have been aggregated should be disclosed. The sponsor also should indicate by note if the investment objectives of any program are not similar to those of the registrant and should briefly describe those investment objectives.

	Program X	Program Y
Dollar amount offered		
Dollar amount raised (100%)		
Less offering expenses:		
Selling commissions and discounts retained by affiliates		
Organizational expenses		
Other (explain)		
Reserves		
Percent available for investment		
Acquisition costs:		
Prepaid items and fees related to purchase of property		
Cash down payment		
Acquisition fees		
Other (explain)		
Total acquisition cost		
Percent leverage (mortgage financing divided by total acquisition cost)		
Date offering began		
Length of offering (in months)		
Months to invest 90% of amount available for investment (measured from beginning of offering)		

Table II. Compensation to Sponsor

Instructions: 1. Include in a separate column for each program aggregate payments made to the sponsor only by real estate programs the offering of which closed in the most recent three years. Include in another separate column aggregate payments to the sponsor in the most recent three years from all other programs and indicate the number of programs involved.

2. Sponsors with a "public track record" should include information relating only to public programs with investment objectives similar to those of the registrant.

3. If the sponsor does not have a "public track record," information must be given for each prior program, public or nonpublic, with investment objectives similar to those of the registrant. If the sponsor has not sponsored at least five such programs, then information must be given for each prior program, public or nonpublic, even if the investment objectives for those programs are not similar to those of the registrant. In that case, nonpublic programs with investment objectives that are not similar to those of the registrant should be grouped together according to investment objective and information about those programs presented on an aggregate basis by year. If so presented, the number of programs that have been aggregated should be disclosed. The sponsor also should indicate by note if the investment objectives of any program are not similar to those of the registrant and should briefly describe those investment objectives.

4. The table should include any real estate commissions and other fees paid to the sponsor in connection with the acquisition or disposition of any properties by the program by entities other than the program itself.

Type of Compensation	Program X	Program Y	Other Programs
Date offering commenced			
Dollar amount raised			
Amount paid to sponsor from proceeds of offering:			
Underwriting fees			
Acquisition fees			
Real estate commissions			
Advisory fees			
Other (identify and quantify)			
Other			
Dollar amount of cash generated from operations before deducting payments to sponsor			
Amount paid to sponsor from operations:			
Property management fees			
Partnership management fees			
Reimbursements			
Leasing commissions			
Other (identify and quantify)			
Dollar amount of property sales and refinancing before deducting payments to sponsor			
Cash			
Notes			
Amount paid to sponsor from property sales and refinancing:			
Real estate commissions			
Incentive fees*			
Other (identify and quantify)			

* Explain subordinated commissions in a note.

Table III. Operating Results of Prior Programs
Instructions:

1. Include information only for programs the offerings of which closed in the most recent five years. Financial data for each program should be presented separately for each year.

2. Sponsors with a "public track record" should include information relating only to public programs with investment objectives similar to those of the registrant.

3. If the sponsor does not have a "public track record," information must be given for each program, public or nonpublic, with investment objectives similar to those of the registrant. If the sponsor has not sponsored at least five such programs, then information must be given for each prior program, public or nonpublic, even if the investment objectives for those programs are not similar to those of the registrant. In that case, nonpublic programs with investment objectives that are not similar to those of the registrant should be grouped together according to investment objective and information about those programs presented on an aggregate basis by year. If so presented, the number of programs that have been aggregated should be disclosed. The sponsor also should indicate by note if the investment objectives of any program are not similar to those of the registrant and should briefly describe those investment objectives.

4. Information should be presented on the basis of generally accepted accounting principles ("GAAP") where indicated. However, where information about nonpublic programs is required to be included, such information may be presented on a tax basis if the program's books have not been kept on a GAAP basis. If there are any significant differences in operating results between accounting on a tax and GAAP basis, they should be explained. This explanation should provide the reader with any additional information about the particular programs presented that may be necessary to make the information contained in the Table not materially misleading in light of the circumstances under which the information is given.

	Program X		
	Year 1	Year 2	Year 3
Gross revenues			
Profit on sale of properties			
Less: Operating Expenses			
Interest expense			
Depreciation			
Net income—GAAP basis			
Taxable Income			
From operations			
From gain on sale			
Cash generated from operations *			
Cash generated from sales			
Cash generated from refinancing			
Cash generated from operations, sales and refinancing			
Less: Cash distributions to investors			
From operating cash flow			
From sales and refinancing			
From other			
Cash generated (deficiency) after cash distributions			
Less: Special items (not including sales and refinancing) (identify and quantify)			
Cash generated (deficiency) after cash distributions and special items			
Tax and Distribution Data Per $1000 Invested			
Federal Income Tax Results:			
Ordinary income (loss)			
From operations			
From recapture			
Capital gain (loss)			
Cash Distributions to Investors			

	Program X		
	Year 1	Year 2	Year 3
Source (on GAAP basis)			
Investment income			
Return of capital			
Source (on cash basis)			
Sales			
Refinancing			
Operations			
Other			
Amount (in percentage terms) remaining invested in program properties at the end of the last year reported in the Table (original total acquisition cost of properties retained divided by original total acquisition cost of all properties in program).			

* Indicate in a note what amount is from sources other than operations, such as guaranteed rents or interest.

Table IV. Results of Completed Programs
Instructions:

1. Include programs that have completed operations (no longer hold properties) in the most recent five years, even if they still hold notes.

2. Sponsors with a "public track record" should include information relating only to public programs with investment objectives similar to those of the registrant.

3. If the sponsor does not have a "public track record," information must be given for each prior program, public or nonpublic, with investment objectives similar to those of the registrant. If the sponsor has not sponsored at least five such programs, then information must be given for each prior program, public or nonpublic, even if the investment objectives for those programs are not similar to those of the registrant. In that case, nonpublic programs with investment objectives that are not similar to those of the registrant should be grouped together according to investment objective and information about those programs presented on an aggregate basis by

year. If so presented, the number of programs that have been aggregated should be disclosed. The sponsor also should indicate by note if the investment objectives of any program are not similar to those of the registrant and should briefly describe those investment objectives.

Program name
  Dollar amount raised
  Number of properties purchased
  Date of closing of offering
  Date of first sale of property
  Date of final sale of property
Tax and distribution data per $1000 investment through . . .
  Federal income tax results:
    Ordinary income (loss)
      From operations
      From recapture
    Capital gain (loss) *
    Deferred gain †
      Capital
      Ordinary
Cash distributions to investors
  Source (on GAAP basis)
    Investment income
    Return of capital
  Source (on cash basis)
    Sales
    Refinancing
    Operations
    Other
Receivable on net purchase money financing ††

* Note 60% capital gain exclusion.
† Explain in a note deferred capital gain.
†† Explain in a note the terms of notes taken back and annual payments, and the fact that the amounts presented are face amounts and do not represent discounted current value.

Table V. Sales or Disposals of Properties

Instructions:

1. Include all sales or disposals of property by programs with similar investment objectives within the most recent three years.

2. Sponsors with a "public track record" should only include information relating to public programs. If the sponsor does not have a "public track record," then information should be given about sales or disposals of properties by public and nonpublic programs. Where properties held by nonpublic programs are included, information should be on a GAAP basis where feasible without undue effort or expense.

Property	Date Acquired	Date of Sale [1]	Selling Price, Net of Closing Costs and GAAP Adjustments					Cost of Properties Including Closing and Soft Costs			Excess (Deficiency) of Property Operating Cash Receipts over Cash Expenditures [6]
			Cash received net of closing costs	Mortgage balance at time of sale	Purchase money mortgage taken back by program [2]	Adjustments resulting from application of GAAP [3]	Total [4]	Original mortgage financing	Total acquisition cost, capital improvement, closing and soft costs [5]	Total	

[1] Note if sales of properties are to related parties.

[2] Indicate in a note that the amounts shown are face amounts and do not represent discounted current value. In addition, describe the terms of purchase money mortgages taken by the partnership, including the interest rate, any balloon payment requirements and other special provisions. Also, describe those sales made with a leaseback or any other guarantees which require continued seller involvement.

[3] Include an explanation of any GAAP adjustments.

[4] Note the allocation of the taxable gain between ordinary and capital, and identify those sales that are being reported for tax purposes on the installment basis.

[5] Identify real estate commissions carried but not taken. Indicate that the amounts shown do not include prorata share of original offering costs.

[6] Do not include amounts otherwise included under "Selling Price, Net of Closing Costs and GAAP Adjustments" or "Cost of Properties including Closing and Soft Costs." Costs incurred in the administration of the partnership not related to the operation of properties need not be included if so indicated in a note to the Table.

Table VI. Acquisitions of Properties by Programs
Instructions:

1. Include the following table only in Part II of the registration statement.

2. Include all properties acquired by any prior programs with similar investment objectives in the most recent three years.

3. Sponsors with a "public track record" should only include information relating to public programs. If the sponsor does not have a "public track record," then information should be given about properties acquired by public and nonpublic programs.

Program X

    Name, location, type of property
    Gross leasable space (sq. ft.) or number
       of units and total square feet of units
    Date of purchase
    Mortgage financing at date of purchase
    Cash down payment
    Contract purchase price
      plus acquisition fee
    Other cash expenditures expensed
    Other cash expenditures capitalized
    Total acquisition cost

POLICY STATEMENT 100 [STATE OF NEW YORK, DEPARTMENT OF LAW]

[Policy Statement 100 has not been revised to reflect the rescission of Rule 146 and the adoption of Regulation D. However, the Attorney General will entertain applications for exemption under the policy statement based on compliance with Regulation D. See the discussion in Section 9 of Chapter 10.]

EXEMPTION APPLICATION UNDER SECTIONS 352-g(2) AND 359-f(2) OF THE GENERAL BUSINESS LAW FOR REAL ESTATE SYNDICATION OFFERINGS MADE PURSUANT TO RULE 146 UNDER THE FEDERAL SECURITIES ACT OF 1933

To coordinate SEC Rule 146 with Article 23-A of the General Business Law in regard to real estate syndication offerings, the Attorney General will entertain applications for exemption from the provisions of §352-e pursuant to Clause (2) of §352-g of the General Business Law, on the grounds that the securities to be offered will be exempt from registration with the Securities and Exchange Commission through compliance with Rule 146. This procedure is not exclusive and an issuer making a Rule 146 offering may still apply for exemption under Clause (1) of §352-g, if the offering will be "made to persons not exceeding forty in number." by following the Instructions for §352-g Exemptions issued by this Bureau.

Policy Statement 100 can not be used for offerings of cooperative, condominium or homeowners' association interests in real estate.

An issuer applying for this Policy Statement 100 exemption must wait until it is granted before commencing the firm offering. To seek such exemption an issuer (or someone acting on behalf of an unformed issuer) should submit an application (affidavit or petition) in duplicate, verified by a principal officer, general partner, trustee or other principal having knowledge of the facts contained therein, setting forth in full the following information:

1. The name, address, and legal nature (corporation, trust, limited partnership, etc.) of the issuer entity (the "applicant").

2. The name, residence address and affiliation of the individual affiant, his business or profession, and his business address.

3. The names and residence addresses of all principal officers, directors, general partners, trustees, principal shareholders (effectively controlling 10% or more) and other principals (including founders, syndicators, sponsors and promoters), together with a statement that there are no other principals or controlling persons of the issuer, and that attached to and made part of the application are forms RI-1 for each general partner, trustee, and other principal including officers, directors, and principal shareholders of a corporate general partner (or copies of executed forms already submitted).

4. To the best of affiant's knowledge after reasonable investigation, whether or not any principal officer, director, trustee, general partner or other principal ever was adjudged a bankrupt, made an assignment for benefit of creditors, or was an officer, director or principal of any entity reorganized in bankruptcy, adjudged a bankrupt or which made an assignment for benefit of creditors. (If so, specify details.)

5. To the best of affiant's knowledge after reasonable investigation, whether or not any principal officer, director, trustee, general partner or other principal was ever convicted of any crime excluding minor traffic violations, or the subject of any injunction, cease and desist order, suspension or restraining order, revocation of a license to practice a trade, occupation or profession, or denial of an application to renew same, stipulation or consent to desist from any act or practice, or any other disciplinary action by any court or administrative agency, or whether any such action or proceeding is presently pending. (If so, specify details.)

6. A statement that the application is made pursuant to §§352-g(2) and 359-f, subd. 2(d) on the grounds that the offering and sale of the particular securities will be, through compliance with Rule 146, exempt from registration with the Securities and Exchange Commission as a non-public offering within §4(2) of the Securities Act of 1933.

7. The affiant, on behalf of the issuer applicant, must acknowledge that he is familiar with, and represent that he and the applicant in good faith intend to make the offering in accordance with, all of the conditions and limitations of Rule 146 and will use their best efforts to do so.

8. A representation that the applicant has consulted an attorney regarding the conditions and limitations of SEC Rule 146 and its availability to this specific offering, stating the name and address of the attorney consulted.

9.   An undertaking that if SEC Rule 146 subsequently becomes unavailable to the offering for any reason whatsoever, such as through the failure to comply with all of its conditions and limitations: (i) all offers and sales of the securities will immediately cease; (ii) all monies collected prior to cessation of the offering will be retained in trust for the benefit of investors; (iii) an amendment to this application setting forth in detail the facts regarding the unavailability of Rule 146 will be submitted to the Department of Law for its consideration; and (iv) if exemption is not granted to the amended application, all monies collected will be returned to the investors, unless otherwise provided by the Attorney General. (The issuance of exemptions hereunder shall not preclude investigation and prosecution by the Attorney General of fraudulent practices committed by any applicant under the guise of compliance with Rule 146.)

10.   An undertaking to comply with the requirements of Regulation 16.9 regarding Source of Distributions Statements, and an acknowledgement that the applicant is familiar with said regulation.

11.   The total dollar amount of the offering, including any optional units and any shares underlying warrants, the number of units to be offered and the minimum dollar amount of the interest that will be offered to any one person.

12.   The purposes of the offering (e.g.—to purchase the fee or leasehold of described property at a stated address). Specify with as much detail as is reasonably possible the breakdown of how the proceeds of the offering will be used.

13.   An undertaking that the proceeds of the offering will be received and held in trust for the benefit of these investors, and will be retained in trust after closing to be used only for the purposes set forth in paragraph 12 above. State the name and location of the bank(s) where the proceeds will be deposited in trust.

14.   An undertaking that upon a written request by the Department of Law, one true copy of each basic document that is material to this investment, including purchase contracts or options, financing commitments, construction contracts, limited partnership agreements and certificates, subscription forms, leases, mortgages and deeds, will be furnished to the Department of Law within two weeks of the receipt of said written request.

15.   (a) An undertaking that beginning after the closing of the offering, all investors will be provided annually with financial statements, including a balance sheet and the related statements of income and retained earnings and changes in financial position, accompanied by a report of an independent public accountant stating that an audit of such financial statements has been made in accordance with generally accepted auditing standards, stating the opinion of the accountant in respect of the financial statements and the accounting princi-

ples and practices reflected therein and as to the consistency of the application of the accounting principles, and identifying any matters to which the accountant takes exception and stating, to the extent practicable, the effect of each such exception on such financial statements. (If the records are kept on a cash basis and that accountant can opine that the financial statements fairly present the financial position, the changes therein and the results of operations on a cash basis consistently applied, then the financial statements can be on a cash basis).

(b) An undertaking that any private offering memorandum or prospectus used in connection with this offering will set forth the above undertaking to provide annual certified financial statements and, if a private offering memorandum containing the above undertaking is not used, that the statement which paragraph 17 below requires each investor to sign, will contain the above undertaking to provide audited financial statements.

16. An undertaking that the books and records of the issuer will be maintained at its principal place of business and will be available upon reasonable notice, for inspection by investors at reasonable hours during the business day.

17. An undertaking that all purchasers who are offered these securities within or from the State of New York, will be required to sign and submit the following statement BEFORE ANY MONIES ARE RECEIVED FROM THEM:

"I understand that this offering of interests in _____ has not been reviewed by the Attorney General of the State of New York because of the offeror's representations that this is intended to be a non-public offering pursuant to SEC Rule 146 and that if all of the conditions and limitations of Rule 146 are not complied with, the offering will be resubmitted to the Attorney General for amended exemption. I understand that any offering literature used in connection with this offering has not been pre-filed with the Attorney General and has not been reviewed by the Attorney General. This interest is being purchased for my own account for investment, and not for distribution or resale to others. I agree that I will not sell or otherwise transfer these securities unless they are registered under the Federal Securities Act of 1933 or unless an exemption from such registration is available. I represent that I have adequate means of providing for my current needs and possible personal contingencies, and that I have no need for liquidity of this investment.

It is understood that all documents, records and books pertaining to this investment have been made available for inspection by my attorney and/or my accountant and/or my offeree representative and myself, and that the books and records of the issuer will be available upon reasonable notice, for inspection by investors at reasonable hours at its principal place of business." (If a private offering memorandum or prospectus containing the financial statements undertaking in the above 15(a) is not used, add that undertaking to this letter.)

18. An undertaking that any private offering memorandum or prospectus used in connection with this offering will contain

(a) the following legend on its cover page:

THIS PRIVATE OFFERING MEMORANDUM HAS NOT BEEN RE-VIEWED BY THE ATTORNEY GENERAL PRIOR TO ITS ISSUANCE AND USE. THE ATTORNEY GENERAL OF THE STATE OF NEW YORK HAS NOT PASSED ON OR ENDORSED THE MERITS OF THIS OFFERING. ANY REPRESENTATION TO THE CONTRARY IS UN-LAWFUL.

(b) the trust fund undertaking in the above paragraph 13; and

(c) The following representation: This private offering memorandum does not contain an untrue statement of a material fact or omit to state a material fact necessary to make the statements made, in light of the circumstances under which they are made, not misleading. It contains a fair summary of the material terms of documents purported to be summarized herein.

19. An undertaking that 5 copies of any prospectus or other offering litera-ture and all amendments thereto used in connection with the offering shall be filed with the Department of Law within 10 days after the time such material is first used to offer these securities to any person within or from the State of New York. One copy of the prospectus, private offering memorandum or latest draft thereof must be submitted as an exhibit with the application.

20. An undertaking that within 10 days after closing of this offering the applicant will submit to the Attorney General a copy of a letter from its coun-sel, addressed to the issuer, containing an opinion of counsel that the offering is exempt from the registration requirements of the Securities Act of 1933 under §4(2) thereof, which opinion shall state the basis on which it is rendered.

21. An undertaking that upon the completion of the offering the issuer will file with the Department of Law a duplicate original or photostatic copy of the executed Partnership Agreement, Certificate of Incorporation, or Venture Agreement, and, if the names and addresses of all participants in the offering and the extent of their participation is not contained therein, a supplemental af-fidavit containing such information.

22. As supplemental information, submit a letter signed by each general partner and other principal listed in paragraph 3., including officers, directors and principal shareholders of corporate general partners, listing all real estate syndications the person has taken part in during the last 10 years which have any New York residents as investors and stating whether or not filings were made pursuant to §352-e and §359-e or exemptions were obtained pursuant to §352-g and §359-f(2) as to each such syndication having New York resident investors.

23. A statement that no previous application or filing under §§352-e, 352-g, 359-e or 359-f of the General Business Law has been made by the applicant or any affiliate regarding the property involved in this application. List all exceptions.

24. A concluding statement reading: "WHEREFORE, it is respectfully requested that the offering for sale of the securities of (*the issuer*) be exempted under §§352-g(2) and 359-f, subd. 2(d) from the filing provisions of §§352-e and 359-e subds. 2,3,4,5, and 6 of the General Business Law."

25. The application must be sworn to or verified by the affiant.

26. Out-of-state issuers must file a Designation of the Secretary of State as Agent for Service of Process. State in the application or covering letter whether such has been or is being filed.

FEES

Separate checks must be submitted for the fee imposed for the Section 352-g exemption and the fee imposed for the Section 359-f exemption. The fee for the Section 352-g exemption is one-tenth of one percent of the amount of the offering of securities, however the minimum fee is $250 and the maximum fee is $10,000. This fee is based on the aggregate offering amount *without* apportionment for the amount to be offered within New York. The fee for the Section 359-f(2) exemption is $100, by separate check. Both checks should be made out to the State of New York, Department of Law. These fees will not be refunded, once the exemptions are granted.

No fee is required to amend an application for exemption previously granted, unless the total dollar amount of securites is increased.

SUBMISSION

Applications with supporting documents and fees should be sent to: Bureau of Real Estate Financing, Department of Law, State of New York, 2 World Trade Center, New York, NY 10047. Attention: Syndication Division.
Caveat:

The exemption granted pursuant to Section 359-f(2) from the provisions of Section 359-e, does not exempt the issuer, the underwriter or any broker-dealer from subdivision 8 of Section 359-e. Therefore a Further State Notice form must be filed with the Department of State in Albany, New York.

If exemption is *not* sought under §359-f. subd. 2 from the provisions of §359-e. attention is directed to the issuer's dealer registration requirements under Section 359-e of the General Business Law. This ordinarily requires a Broker-Dealer Statement filed with the Department of Law (with fee paid by separate check), and a separate filing of a State Notice and Further State Notice (and for out-of-state issuers, a Designation of the Secretary of State as Agent) sent to the Department of State. Albany, New York.

INSTRUCTIONS FOR §352-g EXEMPTIONS (Real Estate Syndications) (STATE OF NEW YORK, DEPARTMENT OF LAW)

Submit an application (affidavit or petition) in duplicate, verified by an officer, general partner, trustee or other principal having requisite knowledge, setting forth in full the following information:

1. The name, address, and legal nature (corporation, trust, limited partnership, etc.) of the issuer entity (the "applicant").

2. The name, residence address and affiliation of the individual affiant, his business or profession, and his business address.

3. The names and residence addresses of all officers, directors, general partners, trustees, principal shareholders and other principals, together with a statement that there are no other principals or controlling persons, and that attached to and made part of the application are forms RI-1 for each general partner, trustee, officer, director and principal (or copies of executed forms already submitted).

4. Whether or not any officer, director, trustee, general partner or other principal ever was adjudged a bankrupt, made an assignment for benefit of creditors, or was an officer, director or principal of any entity reorganized in bankruptcy, adjudged a bankrupt or which made an assignment for benefit of creditors. (If so, specify details.)

5.   Whether or not any officer, director, trustee, general partner or other principal was ever convicted of any crime, or the subject of any injunction, cease and desist order, suspension or restraining order, revocation of a license to practice a trade, occupation or profession, or denial of an application to renew same, stipulation or consent to desist from any act or practice, or any other disciplinary action by any court or administrative agency. (If so, specify details.)

6.   An undertaking to comply with the requirements of Regulation 16.9 regarding Source of Distributions Statements, and an acknowledgement that the applicant is familiar with the said regulation.

7.   The total dollar amount of the offering, including any optional units and any shares underlying warrants and the number of units to be offered.

8.   The purpose of the offering (e.g.—to purchase the fee or leasehold of described property at a stated address). Specify with as much detail as is reasonably possible the breakdown of how the proceeds of the offering will be used.

9.   An undertaking that in compliance with §352-h of the General Business Law, the proceeds of the offering will be received and held in trust for the benefit of these investors to be used only for purposes set forth in paragraph 8, above, and the names and branch addresses of the banks where proceeds will be deposited in trust.

10.   The terms of purchase of property to be acquired with the proceeds— total purchase price, cash requirements, mortgages and terms thereof, profits and benefits to the promoters, pertinent details, and whether or not property was acquired at arm's length. In an underwritten offering, also set forth the total compensation (direct and indirect) of all underwriters. (Any prospectus may be referred to by stating that full and complete response appears in specified sections.)

11.   A representation and undertaking that all investors will be provided with annual financial statements including a written balance sheet and statement of profit and loss which shall be prepared by an independent public accountant and contain an express opinion by such accountant that such statements fairly present the financial position and results of operations of the issuer.

12.   A statement that this application is in lieu of any previous application, if this affidavit supersedes a previous one.

Additional Items if the Application Is Made under Section 352-g Clause (1)

13.   A statement that the purpose of the application is for an exemption pursuant to §§352-g(1) and 359-f, subd. 2(d) on the grounds that the offering will be made to a limited number of persons as provided thereunder.

14. A statement that the offering is, in fact, to be made by personal contact to only (number of persons) of the personal friends, relatives and business associates of the affiant and other general partners or principals of the issuer (according to the facts) except as otherwise noted and as set forth at length therein. A statement of the minimum dollar amount of the interest that will be offered to any one person.

15. The names, addresses, and relationships, and length thereof, to the promoters of each person to be solicited or asked to participate.

16. An undertaking that on the completion of the offering the affiant will furnish a supplemental affidavit containing the following:

a. A list of the names and addresses of the participants in the offering and the extent of their participation;

b. An additional list of persons to whom the offering was made, but who did not participate;

c. A duplicate original or photostatic copy of the executed Partnership Agreement, Certificate of Incorporation, or venture agreement.

17. (A) A statement that no prospectus, offering literature or private offering memorandum has been prepared or will be used; or

(B) A statement that annexed as an Exhibit and made part of the Application is a true copy of the definitive Private Placement Memorandum or other offering literature that will be used by the issuer in connection with the offering.

18. A statement that if any (any other) prospectus, private offering memorandum, "broker's set-up" or other offering literature, or any advertisement or advertising material whatsoever, is to be used or is hereinafter prepared, the same will be submitted to the Department of Law for review prior to any use, as well as any subsequent changes or amendments respecting same.

19. A representation that the books and records of the issuer will be maintained at its principal place of business and will be available upon reasonable notice, for inspection by shareholders or limited partners at reasonable hours during the business day.

20. A representation that all investors will have signed the following statement BEFORE ANY MONIES ARE RECEIVED FROM THEM:

"I understand that I am purchasing this interest in _____ without being furnished any offering literature or prospectus (other than a Private Placement Memorandum dated _____) and that this transaction has not been scrutinized by the Attorney General of the State of New York as a full registration because of the offeror's representations of the small number of persons solicited and the private aspects of the offering. This interest is being purchased for my own account and not for the interest of any other and not for resale to others. I represent that I have adequate means of providing for my current needs and possible personal contingencies, and that I have no need for liquidity of this investment. I further warrant that my personal net worth is in excess of $_____ (specify amount).

21. As supplemental information, provide: (a) a memorandum setting forth the tax aspects of the proposed transaction (or state the pages in the attached offering memorandum where the tax aspects and risks are discussed); and (b) a letter signed by each general partner and other principal listed in paragraph 3, including sponsors and officers, directors and principal shareholders of corporate general partners, listing all real estate syndications the person has taken part in during the last 10 years which have any New York residents as investors and stating whether or not filings were made pursuant to §352-e and §359-e or exemptions were obtained pursuant to §352-g and §359-f(2) as to each such syndication having New York resident investors.

22. A concluding statement reading: "WHEREFORE, it is respectfully requested that the offering for sale of the securities of (the issuer) be exempted under §§352-g(1) and 359-f. subd. 2(d) from the filing provisions of §§352-e and 359-e. subds. 2, 3, 4, 5 and 6 of the General Business Law."

Additional Items if the Application Is Made under Section 352-g Clause (2)

23. A statement that the purpose of the application is for exemption pursuant to Section 352-g(2) on the grounds that the securities to be offered have been fully registered with the S.E.C. [Where the application is based upon an exemption under Section 3(a) of the Securities Act of 1933, the grounds are that the securities to be offered have been exempted pursuant to a specified subdivision of Section 3(a), 15 USC 77c (a). A letter from the S.E.C. or an opinion of counsel should be appended as an Exhibit. For a non-profit or charitable organization the I.R.S. exemption letters should also be appended.]

24. If exemption of the issuer from the provisions of §359-e, is sought pursuant to §359-f, subd. 2, a statement of the facts upon which the exemption is sought and of the particular paragraph of §359-f, subd. 2 under which it is sought.

25. A statement that attached as an Exhibit to the Application and made a part thereof is the definitive final prospectus or such other offering literature in the form as made effective by the S.E.C. (or in conformity therewith under Rule 424) actually to be used by the applicant in connection with the offering in the State of New York and elsewhere.

26. An undertaking by the issuer to submit to the Department of Law all

amendments to such definitive prospectus and all other offering literature employed by the issuer in the State of New York.

27.   A concluding statement reading: "WHEREFORE, it is respectfully requested that the offering for sale of the securities of (the issuer) be exempted under §§352-g(2) from the filing provisions of §352-e of the General Business Law." [If exemption of the issuer from the provisions of §359-e, is sought pursuant to §359-f, subd. 2, add: and under §359-f, subd. 2 from the provisions of §359-e, subds. 2, 3, 4, 5 and 6 of the General Business Law.]

FEES

The fee for the Section 352-g exemption is one-tenth of one percent of the amount of the offering of securities, however, the minimum fee is $250 and the maximum fee is $10,000. This fee is based on the aggregate offering amount *without* apportionment for the amount to be offered within New York.

If exemption is also sought pursuant to §359-f, subd. 2 from §359-e, a *separate* check for $100 must be submitted.

All checks are payable to the Department of Law, State of New York.

No fee is required to amend an application for exemption previously granted, unless the total dollar mount of securities is increased.

SUBMISSION

Applications with supporting documents and fees should be sent to: Bureau of Real Estate Financing, Department of Law, State of New York, Two World Trade Center, New York, New York 10047. *Attention:* Syndication Division.

Caveat:

The application must be sworn to or verified by the affiant.

Out-of-state issuers must file a Designation of the Secretary of State as Agent for Service of Process. State in the application or covering letter whether a Designation has been or is being filed.

The exemption granted pursuant to Section 359-f(2) from the provisions of Section 359-e, does not exempt the issuer, the underwriter or any broker-dealer from subdivision 8 of Section 359-e. Therefore a Further State Notice form must be filed with the Department of State in Albany, New York.

If exemption is *not* sought under Section 359-f, subdivision 2 from the provisions of Section 359-e, attention is directed to the issuer's dealer registration requirements under Section 359-e of the General Business Law. This ordinarily requires a Broker-Dealer Statement filed with the Department of Law (with fee paid by separate check), and a separate filling of a State Notice and Further State Notice (and for out-of-state issuers, a Designation of the Secretary of State as Agent) sent to the Department of State, Albany, N.Y.

SECTION 25102 (f) OF THE CALIFORNIA CORPORATE SECURITIES LAW OF 1968

Sec. 25102   The following transactions are exempted from the provisions of Section 25110:

(f) Any offer or sale of any security in a transaction (other than an offer or sale to a pension or profit-sharing trust of the issuer) which meets each of the following criteria:

(1) Sales of the security are not made to more than 35 persons, including persons not in this state.

(2) All purchasers either have a preexisting personal or business relationship with the offeror or any of its partners, officers, directors or controlling persons, or by reason of their business or financial experience or the business or financial experience of their professional advisors who are unaffiliated with and who are not compensated by the issuer or any affiliate or selling agent of the issuer, directly or indirectly, could be reasonably assumed to have the capacity to protect their own interests in connection with the transaction.

(3) Each purchaser represents that the purchaser is purchasing for the purchaser's own account (or a trust account if the purchaser is a trustee) and not with a view to or for sale in connection with any distribution of the security.

(4) The offer and sale of the security is not accomplished by the publication of any advertisement. The number of purchasers referred to above is exclusive of any described in subdivision (i), any officer, director or affiliate of the issuer and any other purchaser who the commissioner designates by rule. For purposes of this section, a husband and wife (together with any custodian or trustee acting for the account of their minor children) are counted as one person and a partnership, corporation or other organization which was not specifically formed for the purpose of purchasing the security offered in reliance upon this exemption, is counted as one person. The commissioner may by rule require the issuer to file a notice of transactions under this subdivision; provided, however, that the failure to file the notice or the failure to file the notice within the time specified by the rule of the commissioner shall not affect the availability of this exemption. An issuer who fails to file the notice as provided by rule of the commissioner shall, within 15 business days after demand by the commissioner, file the notice and pay to the commissioner a fee equal to the fee payable had the transaction been qualified under Section 25110.

CALIFORNIA RULES FOR LIMITED OFFERING EXEMPTION

RULE 260.102.12. INTERPRETATIONS.
RULE 260.102.13. EXCLUDED PURCHASERS.
RULE 260.102.14. NOTICE OF TRANSACTION.

[10 CALIFORNIA ADMINISTRATIVE CODE,
RULES 260.102.12, 260.102.13 AND
260.102.14]

Rule 260.102.12. Limited Offering Exemption—Interpretations (a) The provisions of this section apply to the provisions of Section 25102(f) of the Code.

(b) Integration. The term "transaction" does not include (1) any offer or sale of a security made more than 6 months prior to or after the offers and sales which constitute the transaction under the exemption, (2) any offer or sale of a security pursuant to a qualification under Section 25110 or 25120 which became effective after the filing of the notice of the transaction pursuant to Rule 260.102.14, or (3) any offer or sale of a security pursuant to a qualification or amended qualification under Section 25110 or 25120, if the application, or the application as amended as the case may be, discloses the transaction under the exemption, whether past, current or proposed. This subsection does not create any presumption that offers and sales not excluded from the transaction by its provisions are to be integrated for the purposes of the exemption and that determination shall be made without reference to this subsection.

(c) Purchaser. The term "purchaser" means a person who acquires the beneficial ownership of the security, whether individually or in joint ownership, in the transaction under the exemption. Each person who takes in joint ownership with another is to be counted as one except as otherwise provided in Section 25102(f).

(d) Relationship. The term "preexisting personal or business relationship" includes any relationship consisting of personal or business contacts of a nature and duration such as would enable a reasonably prudent purchaser to be aware of the character, business acumen and general business and financial circumstances of the person with whom such relationship exists. A relationship of employer-employee, or as a security holder of the issuer, or as a customer of a broker-dealer, investment adviser or other person, does not necessarily involve contacts of a nature which are sufficient to establish a "preexisting personal or business relationship" within the meaning of Section 25102(f). This subsection does not create any presumption that relationships not falling within its terms are not within the statutory language, and the determination of whether or not such a relationship is within the statutory language shall be made without reference to this subsection.

(e) Partners. The term "partners" in Section 25102(f)(2) means general partners.

(f) Controlling Person. The term "controlling person of the offeror" includes but is not limited to a person who, in connection with transactions within one year of the formation of the issuer, is a "promoter" of the issuer. "Promoter" means a person who, acting alone or in conjunction with one or more other persons, takes the initiative in founding and organizing the business or enterprise of an issuer.

(g) Professional Advisor. The term "professional advisor" means a person who as a regular part of such person's business, is customarily relied upon by others for investment recommendations or decisions, and who is customarily compensated for such services, either specifically or by way of compensation for related professional services, and attorneys and certified public accountants.

(1) The foregoing includes but is not limited to persons licensed or registered as broker-dealers, agents, investment advisers, banks and savings and loan associations. The foregoing also includes licensed real estate brokers with respect to those securities referred to in Section 25206 of the Code.

(2) A person is not the professional advisor of a purchaser unless designated as such by the purchaser.

(h) Unaffiliated. The relationships which will render a person not "unaffiliated" include (1) a present or intended relationship of employment, either as an employee, employer, independent contractor or principal, (2) any relationship within the definition of the term "affiliate" or as an officer or director of an affiliate and (3) the beneficial ownership by the professional advisor of securities of the issuer or its affiliates or selling agent, except that the ownership of 1% or less of such securities shall not render a professional advisor not unaffiliated.

(i) Affiliate. "Affiliate" of the issuer means a person controlling, controlled by or under common control with, the issuer. A person controls another person within the meaning of this subsection through the possession, direct or indirect, of the power to direct or cause the direction of the management, policies or actions of such other person.

(j) Publication of Advertising. Section 25102(f)(4) of the Code is to be interpreted so as to facilitate the circulation of disclosure materials to offerees and purchasers, so long as such materials are not disseminated to the public (see Sections 25002 and 25014 of the Code). Private placement memoranda, offering circulars and similar disclosure documents are not "disseminated to the public" for the purposes of Section 25102(f) of the Code if the issuer limits such circulation (1) to persons reasonably believed to be interested in purchasing the securities or (2) to persons whom the issuer believes may meet the qualifications required of purchasers pursuant to such section and the rules thereunder. The preceding sentence does not create any presumption that a dissemination of materials otherwise than as described therein is a "publication of advertising," and the determination of that question shall be made without reference to that sentence.

(k) Institutional investors. The reference in Section 25102(f) of the Code to purchasers described in Section 25102(i) includes those persons designated in Rule 260.102.10.

(l) For purposes of Section 25102(f), when a person is both an "affiliate of the issuer" or a purchaser excluded by Rule 260.102.13 and a partnership, corporation or other organization which was specifically formed for the purpose of purchasing the security offered in reliance upon the exemption, each beneficial holder of its securities shall be counted or excluded from the count in accordance with the provisions of Section 25102(f).

Rule 260.102.13.   Limited Offering Exemption—Excluded Purchasers For the purposes of Section 25102(f) of the Code, the following purchasers are excluded from the count of purchasers for purposes of Subparagraph (1) of that subdivision, except as provided in Subsection (1) of Rule 260.102.12:

(a) The trustee of an issuer which is a trust and the general partner of an issuer which is a partnership, who exercise managerial functions with respect to such entities, and any officer, director or general partner of a general partner of an issuer which is a partnership.

(b) Any person who occupies a position with the issuer, or with a general partner of an issuer which is a partnership, with duties and authority substantially similar to those of an executive officer of a corporation.

(c) (1) Any relative, spouse or relative of the spouse of a purchaser who has the same principal residence as the purchaser; (2) any trust or estate in which a purchaser and any of the persons related to such purchaser as specified in Clause (1) or Clause (3) collectively have more than 50% of the beneficial interest (excluding contingent interests); and (3) any corporation or other organization of which a purchaser and any of the persons related to such purchaser as specified in Clause (1) or Clause (2) collectively are beneficial owners of more than 50% of the equity securities (excluding director's qualifying shares) or equity interests. "Relative" means a person related by blood, marriage or adoption.

(d) Any individual who is a "promoter" of the issuer, as defined in Subsection (f) of Section 260.102.12.

(e) Any person who purchases $150,000 or more of the securities offered in the transaction, provided each such purchaser meets either of the following:

(1) Such person, or such person's professional advisor, may be reasonably assumed to have the capacity to protect such person's own interests in connection with the transaction, as provided in Section 25102(f)(2).

(2) Such person can reasonably be assumed to be able to bear the economic risk of such person's investment in the transaction. An investment (including mandatory assessments) not exceeding 10% of such person's net worth shall be presumed to meet the provisions of this Subsection (2). For the purpose of determining a person's net worth, the principal residence owned by an individual shall be valued either at (A) cost, including the cost of improvements, net of current encumbrances upon the property or (B) the appraised value of the property as determined upon a written appraisal used by an institutional lender making a loan to the individual secured by the property, including the cost of subsequent improvements, net of current encumbrances upon the property. For the purposes of this provision, "institutional lender" means a bank, savings and loan company, industrial loan company, credit union or personal property broker or a company whose principal business is as a lender upon loans secured by real property and which has such loans receivable in the amount of $2,000,000 or more.

(f) A small business investment company licensed by the U.S. Small Business Administration under Section 301(c) or (d) of the Small Business Investment Company Act of 1958, a business development company as defined in Section 2(b)(48) of the Investment Company Act of 1940, and a private business development company as defined in Section 202(a) (22) of the Investment Advisors Act of 1940.

(g) An individual whose net worth, or whose joint net worth with such individual's spouse, at the time of purchase exceeds $1,000,000, or an individual whose income, or whose joint income with such individual's spouse, exceeded $200,000 in each of the two most recent years and who reasonably expects an income in excess of $200,000 in the current year, provided in either case that such purchaser meets the provisions of either Subsection (1) or (2) of Subsection (e). For the purposes of this subsection, the terms "income" and "net worth" shall be interpreted in a manner consistent with the interpretation of those terms as used in Subsections (6) and (7) of Rule 230.501(a) under the Securities Act of 1933 (17 CFR Part 230), subject to the valuation of the principal residence owned by the individual as provided in Subsection (e).

(h) Any entity in which all of the equity owners are persons specified in Section 25102(i) of the Code; Rule 260.102.10; or Subsections (a), (b), (c), (d), (f) and (g) of this rule; or who are "officers, directors or affiliates of the issuer" as that term issued is used in Section 25102(f) of the Code.

Rule 260.102.14.   Limited Offering Exemption—Notice of Transaction

(a) An issuer who conducts a transaction under Section 25102(f) of the Code shall file a notice with the Commissioner as follows:

(1) If in connection with the transaction the issuer is filing a notice with the Securities and Exchange Commission pursuant to Section 4(6) of the Securities Act of 1933 or Regulation D (Rule 230.503), the notice shall be in the form pursuant to, and shall contain the information required by, those provisions on completion of the offering; or

(2) If the issuer is not subject to Subsection (1) and if the gross proceeds of the transaction exceed $25,000 and the notice is required by Subsection (b) to be filed on or before June 30, 1983, the notice shall be in the form prescribed by Subsection (d) and in accordance with the instructions in Subsection (c); or

(3) If the issuer is not subject to Subsection (1) and if the gross proceeds of the transaction are $25,000 or less or if the notice is required to be filed after June 30, 1983, the notice shall be in the form and contain the information specified in Subsection (e).

(b) A notice required by this section shall be filed with the Commissioner within 30 calendar days after the completion of the transaction or, if the issuer has failed to file a notice, within 15 business days after demand by the Commissioner. For the purposes of this section, a transaction is completed when the issuer has obtained all of the contractual commitments to purchase the securities which it intends to obtain in connection with the transaction, or when it terminates the offering, whichever first occurs. No notice is required if none of the securities offered are purchased.

(c) Instructions. The following instructions apply to the form specified in Subsection (d).

COMMISSIONER OF CORPORATIONS
STATE OF CALIFORNIA

[Form 25102(f)-A]

Notice of Transactions Pursuant to Corporation Code Section 25102(f)

INSTRUCTIONS

General Instructions

1. This Notice is designed to supply information on transactions conducted under the Section 25102(f) exemption from the qualification requirements of Section 25110 of the Corporate Securities Law of 1968 and under the Rule 260.103 exemption from the qualification requirements of Section 25120 of that law. The information called for by the form is not designed necessarily to indicate whether or not the transaction complies with the requirements for those exemptions. The instructions are designed to simplify your task in completing the Notice and they should be followed exactly. If you have questions regarding these instructions, contact any office of the Department of Corporations or telephone (916) 322-3554.

2. *When to File Notice.* The Notice (Form 25102(f)-B) must be filed with, or mailed to, the Commissioner within 30 calendar days after the completion of the transaction or, if the Issuer has failed to file a notice, within 15 business days after demand by the Commissioner. A transaction is completed for this purpose when the Issuer has obtained all of the contractual commitments to purchase the securities which it intends to obtain in connection with the transaction, or when it terminates the offering. No notice is required if none of the securities offered are purchased.

3. *When to File an Amended Notice.* An amended notice is required only when there is a significant change (as defined below) in the information provided in the following items:

> PART I–Item I
>
> PART II–Amend this part only if (a) a "seller" is added or
>   (b) all "sellers" are deleted.
>
> PART III–Item A, B or C ⟩
>   ⟩ Amend any of these items which
> PART IV–Item A, B or C ⟩ increase or decrease by 10%
>   ⟩ or more from the data
> PART V–Item A or B   ⟩ provided.
>
> PART VI–Amend if there is any change in the type of security which is specified pursuant to Instruction (19).

An amended notice may also be filed whenever the issuer wishes to change any of the information contained in the prior notice. However, an amended notice may not be used when a new notice would be required.

An amended notice must be filed within 30 days after a change occurs which requires the filing of an amended notice in accordance with the above, unless the change causes the Issuer to seek new purchasers, in which event the amended notice must be filed within 30 days after obtaining the contractual commitments of the new purchasers, or when the Issuer terminates the offering, with or without obtaining new purchasers.

4. *Content of Amended Notice.* Only the following portions of an amended notice are required to be completed: (a) the heading; (b) Part I, Items A and B, (c) the changed item(s) and (d) Part VI.

5. *Where to File.* A Notice or Amended Notice may be filed in any office of the Department. If filed by mail, address it to:

Commissioner of Corporations
1025 P Street, Room 205
Sacramento, CA 95814

Instructions

The numbers in parentheses below correspond to those numbers as they appear in the Notice (Form 25102(f)-B).

The Heading: Check the appropriate box in Item A and in Item B and insert the date.

(1) *Name.* Give the Issuer's legal name.

(2) *Address.* Give the street address, and the mailing address if different, of the Issuer's major business office or location.

(3) *Type of entity.* Use that one of the following terms which best identifies the Issuer.

Corporation	Limited partnership	Trust
Nonprofit corporation	General partnership	Association
Cooperative	Joint venture	Individual

(4) *Years in business.* Give the number of years the Issuer has been in business, directly or through predecessors.

(5) *Location of business.* If 50% or more of the Issuer's facilities, employees and operations (including those of subsidiary companies) are located in a single state, insert the name of that state. Otherwise, use that one of the following terms which best describes the location of the Issuer's business: Regional, National, International.

(6) *Total assets.* State the Issuer's total net assets immediately prior to the transaction. While the term "total net assets" is used here with reference to a balance sheet presentation in accordance with GAAP, the Issuer may use any source for the information it considers reasonably reliable. The figure should be stated in thousands of dollars.

(7) *Holder of equity securities.* The figure given should be those immediately prior to and after the noticed transaction, and should be stated with reference to the records of the Issuer or its transfer agent. It should be accurate within 5%. "Equity security" means those securities which are asterisked in Item (19) below.

(8) *Federal registration.* If the Issuer has a current registration under the Securities Exchange Act of 1934 or the Investment Company Act of 1940, check the appropriate box or insert the section number under which registration is made. If not so registered, insert "none."

(9) *The seller.* Complete this part only if outstanding securities of the Issuer are being sold in an "issuer transaction" (see Corp. Code Section 25011 and Rule 260.011). In a transaction in which securities of the Issuer are issued in exchange for outstanding securities of the Issuer, the holders of the outstanding securities are not "sellers" for the purposes of this part.

(10) *Underwriter.* The term "underwriter" is defined in Corp. Code Section 25022.

(11) *Number of counted purchasers.* The purchasers should be counted in accordance with the provisions of Section 25102(f).

(12) *Counted purchasers who are California residents.* This question is to be answered based on the information available to the Issuer as to the residence of the beneficial purchasers of the securities (Rule 260.102.12(c)).

(13) *Professional advisors.* State the number of purchasers who were qualified by the Issuer based on the qualifications of the purchaser's professional advisor (see Rule 260.102.12(g)).

(14) *The not counted purchasers.* In determining compliance with the 35 purchaser limitation of Section 25102(f)(1), Section 25102(f) provides that such number is exclusive of any described in Rule 260.102.13, Section 25102(i) (including Rule 260.102.10) and officers, directors and affiliates of the Issuer. (See Rule 260.102.12(i).) In making the count for this item, use purchasers of record rather than beneficial purchasers.

(15) *Gross proceeds and selling expenses.* "Gross proceeds" should be equal to the total consideration paid by all purchasers for the securities. "Commissions" mean underwriting and brokerage discounts and commissions.

(16) *Use of proceeds.* State the use to be made of the net proceeds of the offering received by the Issuer. If the transaction is under Rule 260.103, use this space to briefly describe the transaction (e.g., merger, change of rights, acquisition).

(17) *Filing under Securities Act of 1933.* If the transaction was registered under the 1933 Act, insert "registered." If conducted pursuant to an exemption from registration under that act which requires a filing with the Securities and Exchange Commission, indicate the number of the rule pursuant to which such filing was made. If no such filing was made, insert "none."

(18) *Type of security.* Set forth the name or title of each class and type of security sold in the transaction.

PART VII

See Instruction 3 in Part VII as to who may sign the notice. If the person the Department is to contact in the event of questions concerning the transaction or the notice is different than the signer, insert the contact person's name, telephone number and correspondence address in the spaces provided. Otherwise, provide this information with respect to the signer.

(d) Form of Notice. The following form is to be used for transactions covered by Subsection (a)(2).

[Form 25102(f)-B]
COMMISSIONER OF CORPORATIONS
STATE OF CALIFORNIA
NOTICE OF TRANSACTION PURSUANT TO CORP. CODE
SECTION 25102(f)
GROSS PROCEEDS EXCEEDING $25,000

[This form required only for notices required to be filed before 6/30/83.]

NOTE: The numbers in parentheses below refer to the instructions in Form 25102(f)-A. The various items in this form are not self-explanatory and the instructions must be used to properly complete this form.

A. Check one: ( ) ORIGINAL NOTICE
    ( ) AMENDMENT TO NOTICE DATED _____

B. Check one: FILING UNDER: ( ) Rule 260.102.14
    ( ) Rule 260.103

C. _____
  DATE

PART I. THE ISSUER

A. Name (1) _____

B. Address (2) _____

C. Type of entity (3) _____

D. Year organized _____ E. Years in business (4) _____

F. Location of business (5) _____

G. Total assets prior to the transaction, in thousands (6) $ _____

H. Number of holders of Issuer's equity securities, prior to transaction (7) _____

I. Number of holders of Issuer's equity securities, after transaction (7) _____

J. Federal registration (8): ( ) 12(b) ( ) 12(g) ( ) 1940 Act ( ) 15(d) Other _____

PART II. THE SELLER (9)

A. Number of selling security holders _____

B. Is any selling security holder acting as an underwriter? (10)
    ( ) Yes ( ) No

PART III. THE COUNTED PURCHASERS

A. Number of counted purchasers (11) _____

B. Number of counted purchasers who are California residents (12) _____

C. Number of counted purchasers using professional
   advisors (13) _____

PART IV. THE NOT COUNTED PURCHASERS (14)
A. Number of purchasers not required to be counted: _____

PART V. THE TRANSACTION
A. Gross proceeds of transaction (15) $_____
B. Commissions paid (15)   ( ) Yes ( ) No
C. Use of proceeds (16)   _____
D. Filing under Securities Act of 1933 (17)   _____

PART VI. TITLE OF CLASS OR TYPE OF SECURITIES SOLD (18)

_____

_____

_____

PART VII. EXECUTION

1. DO NOT ATTEMPT TO COMPLETE THIS FORM WITHOUT REF-
   ERENCE TO THE INSTRUCTIONS (FORM 25102(f)-A)

2. Material changes in the information supplied in this notice may require
   you to file an amended notice, as indicated in the General Instructions in
   Form 25102(f)-A.

3. This notice should be signed on behalf of the Issuer by the Issuer, if the
   Issuer is an individual, or by an authorized officer, director, general
   partner or trustee of the Issuer (or a person occupying a position with the
   Issuer of equivalent responsibility) or by the authorized attorney of the
   Issuer.

Signature _____   Contact person _____
Name of signer _____   Telephone number (___)_____
          type or print
Title of signer _____   Correspondence address _____
Telephone number (___)_____
                                              _____
   (e) Form of Notice. The following form is to be used for transactions
covered by Subsection (a)(3).

[Form 25102(f)-C]
COMMISSIONER OF CORPORATIONS
STATE OF CALIFORNIA
NOTICE OF TRANSACTION PURSUANT TO
CORPORATIONS CODE SECTION 25102(f)

A. Check one: ( ) ORIGINAL NOTICE
              ( ) AMENDMENT TO NOTICE FILED _____

B. Check one: Transaction under ( ) Section 25102(f) ( ) Rule 260.103.

1. Name of Issuer

_____

2. Address of Issuer

_____
      Street   City   State   Zip

3. Area code and telephone number: _____

4. Issuer's state (or other jurisdiction) of incorporation or organization:

_____

5. Issuer's date of organization:

_____

6. Title of class or classes of securities sold in transaction:

_____

_____

7. Aggregate dollar amount of sales in the transaction: $ _____

Note: Check the following box if the consideration
was wholly or partly other than cash.   ( )

8. Date of notice _____   _____
                         Issuer

                  _____

                  Authorized signature

                  _____

                  Printed name of signatory

INDEX

465